344·046 J ®

D0512962

Europa Law Publishing, Groningen 2012

European Environmental Law

After Lisbon

Prof. Jan H. Jans & Prof. Hans H.B. Vedder

Fourth edition

Europa Law Publishing is a publishing company
specializing in European Union law, international trade
law, public international law, environmental law and
comparative national law.
For further information please contact Europa Law
Publishing via email: info@europalawpublishing.com
or visit our website at: www.europalawpublishing.com.

Typeset in Scala and Scala Sans, Graphic design by
G2K Designers, Groningen/Amsterdam

NUR 828
ISBN 9789089521057 (hardback)
ISBN 9789089521064 (paperback)

Acknowledgments

Many people contributed to this fourth edition of *European Environmental Law*, to all of whom we owe a debt of gratitude. In the first place, our colleagues at the Department of Administrative Law and Public Administration and the Department of European Law of the University of Groningen. They let us work on this book while, perhaps, they considered that more pressing university commitments should have taken priority instead.

We thank in particular also those persons who have commented in the many book reviews on the third edition. We do hope that that their invaluable remarks are reflected in this edition.

The book has been brought up to date to present new legislation, case law and literature as it stood on 1 September 2011. New developments after that date have only incidentally been taken into account.

As always, the authors will be pleased to receive any comments or suggestions readers may care to make.

Jan Jans, Hans Vedder
Groningen/Appingedam, September 2011

Abbreviations

AB	Administratiefrechtelijke Beslissingen
ACP	African, Caribbean and Pacific (states which are party to the Lomé Convention)
ACEA	Association des constructeurs européens d'automobile
ALARA	As low as reasonable achievable
BAT(NEC)	Best available technology (not entailling excessive costs)
CAP	Common Agricultural Policy
CCS	Carbon Capture Storage
CDM	Clean Development Mechanism
CEN	Comité Européen de Normalisation
CENELEC	Comité Européen de Normalisation Electrotechnique
CER	Certified Emissions Reduction
CITES	Convention on International Trade in Endangered Species of Wild Flora and Fauna
C.M.L.R.	Common Market Law Reports
CMLRev.	Common Market Law Review
COM	Communication of the European Commission
CO2	Carbon dioxide
DSD	Duales System Deutschland
DöV	Die öffentliche Verwaltung
DVBl.	Deutsches Verwaltungsblatt
EEAP	Energy Efficiency Action Plan
EIA	Environmental Impact Assessment
EINECS	European Inventory of Existing Chemical Substances
EAGGF	European Agricultural Guidance and Guarantee Fund
EAEC	European Atomic Energy Community (Euratom)
EEA	European Economic Area
ECA	European Chemicals Agency
ECJ	European Court of Justice
E(E)C	European (Economic) Community
ECR	European Court Reports
ECU	European Currency Unit
EEAP	Energy Efficiency Action Plan
EELR	European Environmental Law Review
EEELR	European Energy and Environmental Law Review
EFTA	European Free Trade Association
ECHR	Reports of Judgments and Decisions of the European Court of Human Rights
EFSA	European Food Safety Authority
EIA	Environmental Impact Assessment
ELR	European Law Review
ELV	End of Life Vehicles
EMAS	European eco-management and audit scheme
Env. L.R.	Environmental Law Reports
EP	European Parliament

EPER	European Pollutant Emission Register
EPL	European Public Law
ERDF	European Regional Development Fund
ERU	Emissions Reduction Unit
ESD	Effort Sharing Decision
ESF	European Social Fund
ET(S)	Emissions Trading (Scheme)
ETP	Eastern Tropical Pacific Ocean
EU	European Union
EUEB	European Union Eco-labeling Board
EuR	Europarecht
EWC	European Waste Catalogue
FAO	Food and Agriculture Organization
FEU	Treaty on the Functioning of the European Union
GATT	General Agreement on Tarrifs and Trade
GDB	Genossenschaft Deutscher Brunnen
GDP	Gross domestic product
GHS	Globally Harmonised System of Classification and Labelling of Chemicals
GLP	Good laboratory practice
GMM	Genetically modified micro-organism
GMO	Genetically modified organism
IBA	Inventory of Important Bird Areas in the European Community
ICRP	International Commission on Radiological Protection
IE	Industrial Emissions
IFCO	International Fruit Container Organization
ILM	International Legal Materials
ILO	International Labour Organization
IMO	International Maritime Organization
IMPEL	Network for the Implementation and Enforcement of Environmental Law
IPP	Integrated product policy
IPPC	Integrated Prevention and Pollution Control
IRLR	Industrial Relations Law Reports
ISO	International Standards Organisation
JEL	Journal of Environmental Law
JI	Joint Implementation
JWT	Journal of World Trade Law
LCA	Life cycle analysis
LIEI	Legal Issues of European/Economic Integration
LIFE	Financial Instrument for the Environment
LMO	Living modified organism
MARPOL	Convention on Maritime Pollution
MEP	Member of European Parliament

M&R	Tijdschrift voor Milieu en Recht
MR	Milieurechtspraak
MRL	Maximum Residue Levels
NAP	National allocation plan
NJ	Nederlandse Jurisprudentie
NJB	Nederlands Juristenblad
NVwZ	Neue Zeitschrift für Verwaltungsrecht
N.y.r.	Not yet reported
OECD	Organisation for Economic Co-operation and Development
OJ	Official Journal
OLAF	Office européen de lutte anti-fraude
PIC	Prior Informed Consent
PPM	Production and Processing Methods
PRTR	Pollutant Release and Transfer Register
REACH	Registration, Evaluation, Authorisation and Restriction of Chemicals
REALaw	Review of European Administrative Law
RECIEL	Review of European Community and International Environmental Law
RES	Renewable Energy Sources
ROHS	Restriction of certain hazardous substances
SAC	Special Area of Conservation
SCI	Site of Community Importance
SEA	Single European Act
SEA	Strategic Environmental Assessment
SEW	Sociaal-Economische Wetgeving
SME	Small and Medium-sized Enterprise
SOLAS	International Convention for the Safety of Life at Sea
SPA	Special Protection Area
TA	Technische Anleitung
TEU	Treaty on European Union
TFEU	Treaty on the Functioning of the European Union
TiO2	Titanium dioxide
TREM	Trade Related Environmental Measure
UNCLOS	United Nations Convention on the Law of the Sea
UNEP	United Nations Environment Programme
UNFCCC	United Nations Framework Convention on Climate Change
VAT	Value Added Tax
VOTOB	Vereniging van Onafhankelijke Tankopslag Bedrijven
WEEE	Waste Electrical and Electronic Equipment
WHO	World Health Organization
WTO	World Trade Organization
YEEL	Yearbook of European Environmental Law
YEL	Yearbook of European Law

CHAPTER I

Development and Principles

1 The Development of European Environmental Law

The first phase

The development of European environmental law can be
separated into a number of phases. The first phase began with the entry into
force of the original version of the EEC Treaty on 1 January 1958 and continued
up to 1972. This was the period during which the European institutions paid no
specific attention to the development of an environment policy. Only incidentally were decisions taken which, in retrospect, could perhaps be regarded as
environmental measures. For example, in 1967, Directive 67/548[1] relating to the
classification, packaging and labelling of dangerous preparations, and, in 1970,
Directive 70/157, relating to the permissible sound level and the exhaust system
of motor vehicles.[2] Although these were primarily measures taken with a view to
the attainment of the common market, environmental considerations undoubtedly played a part.

The second phase

In fact, the true starting signal for the development of a European environment policy was only given in 1972 when, at a European Council Summit meeting, it was declared that economic expansion, which is not an end in itself, must
as a priority help to attenuate the disparities in living conditions. It was thought
that it must result in an improved quality as well as an improved standard of life.
Also, special attention should be paid to non-material values and wealth and to
the protection of the environment so that progress could serve mankind. The
European Council stressed the value of a European environment policy.[3] Therefore, they requested that the European institutions draw up an action program
with a precise schedule before 31 July 1973. This Declaration marked the beginning of the second phase, which lasted until the entry into force of the Single
European Act on 1 July 1987. In the Declaration of the Council of the European
Communities and of the representatives of the Governments of the Member
States meeting in the Council of 22 November 1973 on the programme of action
of the European Communities on the environment, we read:

'Whereas in particular, in accordance with Article 2 of the Treaty, the task of the
European Economic Community is to promote throughout the Community a
harmonious development of economic activities and a continuous and balanced
expansion, which cannot be imagined in the absence of an effective campaign to
combat pollution and nuisance or of an improvement in the quality of life and the
protection of the environment.'

---

[1]   OJ 1967 L 196/1.

[2]   OJ 1971 L 42/16.

[3]   Bulletin EC 1972, No. 10.

Although the term 'environmental protection' was not as such found in the objectives enumerated in Articles 2 and 3 of the EEC Treaty in those days, this Declaration did in effect mean that, by an extensive interpretation of concepts like 'harmonious development of economic activities' and 'a continuous and balanced expansion', which were expressly included in Article 2 EEC, environmental protection could become the subject of European decision-making. Henceforth, economic development was to be regarded not only in quantitative terms, but also qualitatively. Despite the Declaration, the extent of the competence of the EEC to effect a comprehensive environment policy remained a matter of controversy. Nevertheless, numerous directives and regulations have been adopted on almost every conceivable aspect of environment policy since 1971. One feature of this second phase was that policy which was specifically presented as European environment policy was developed on the basis of a treaty having no specific environmental competences.

In this second phase, decision-making in respect of European environment policy was based primarily on Articles 100 and 235 EEC (now Articles 115 and 352 TFEU). Examples of environmental measures dating from this period that were based exclusively on Article 100 EEC were:
- Directive 85/210 concerning the lead content of petrol;[4]
- Directive 73/404 relating to detergents;[5]
- Directive 78/1015 on the permissible sound level and exhaust system of motor cycles.[6]

Article 100 EEC could be used where differences in national environmental legislation had a detrimental effect on the common market. This practice was confirmed by the Court of Justice in Case 92/79, in a judgment in which the validity of Directive 75/716 relating to the maximum sulphur content of liquid fuels was raised.[7] In the words of the Court:

'It is by no means ruled out that provisions on the environment may be based upon Article 100 of the Treaty. Provisions which are made necessary by considerations relating to the environment and health may be a burden upon undertakings to which they apply and if there is no harmonization of national provisions on the matter, competition may be appreciably distorted.'

Most of the environmental legislation dating from the period before the Single European Act (1987) was based on both Article 100 and Article 235 EEC. Important examples include:
- Directive 76/464 on pollution caused by certain dangerous substances discharged into the aquatic environment of the Community;[8]

---

4   OJ 1985 L 96/25.
5   OJ 1973 L 347/51.
6   OJ 1978 L 349/21.
7   Case 92/79 *Commission* v. *Italy* [1980] ECR 1115.
8   OJ 1976 L 129/23.

- Directive 84/360 on the combating of air pollution from industrial plants;[9]
- Directive 82/501 on the major-accident hazards of certain industrial plants[10] and
- Directive 78/319 on toxic and dangerous waste.[11]

In practice, it was apparent that in the field of environmental protection there was a clear need for an additional legal basis besides the 'old' Article 100 EEC. After all, the objectives of Article 100 EEC, namely the abolishing of measures affecting the functioning of the common market, placed constraints on the use that could be made of that article as a legal basis for environment policy. On the principle that the powers extend only to what has been conferred by the Treaty, Article 100 EEC could not be employed where other or more far-reaching environmental measures had to be taken than were merely necessary for the proper functioning of the common market. Moreover, the 'old' Article 3(h) EC provided that the approximation of laws was only possible 'to the extent required for the proper functioning of the common market.'

To remedy this lacuna, the Council would generally invoke Article 235 EEC. This provision could be used 'if action by the Community should prove necessary to attain, in the course of the operation of the common market, one of the objectives of the Community and this Treaty has not provided the necessary powers'. It has already been noted that, by extensive interpretation of Article 2 EC, environmental protection was already considered an objective of the EC. This was confirmed by the Court of Justice in 1985 in the *ADBHU* case.[12]

> This case concerned the validity of a directive on the disposal of waste oils. It was contended that provisions imposing a system of permits on undertakings which disposed of waste oils and a system of zones within which such undertakings had to operate were incompatible with the principle of the free movement of goods. The directive in question was based on both Article 100 and Article 235 EEC. This joint legal basis was justified in the preamble to the directive as follows. On the one hand, it was pointed out that any disparity between the provisions on the disposal of waste oils in the various Member States could create unequal conditions of competition, thus necessitating the use of Article 100 EEC as the legal basis for approximation. On the other hand, the Council felt it necessary to accompany this approximation of laws by wider regulations so that one of the aims of the Union, protection of the environment, could be achieved. For this purpose, it invoked Article 235 EEC (now Article 352 TFEU) as an additional legal basis. The Court held as follows: 'In the first place it should be observed that the principle of freedom of trade is not to be viewed in absolute terms but is subject to certain

---

9   OJ 1984 L 188/20.

10 OJ 1982 L 230/1.

11 OJ 1978 L 84/43.

12 Case 240/83 *ADBHU* [1985] ECR 531.

limits justified by the objectives of general interest pursued by the Community provided that the rights in question are not substantively impaired. There is no reason to conclude that the directive has exceeded those limits. The directive must be seen in the perspective of environmental protection, which is one of the Community's essential objectives.'

The Court continued:

'It follows from the foregoing that the measures prescribed by the directive do not create barriers to intra-Community trade, and that in so far as such measures, in particular the requirement that permits must be obtained in advance, have a restrictive effect on the freedom of trade and of competition, they must nevertheless neither be discriminatory nor go beyond the inevitable restrictions which are justified by the pursuit of *the objective of environmental protection*, which is in the general interest. That being so, Articles 5 and 6 cannot be regarded as incompatible with the fundamental principles of Community law mentioned above.'[13]

The significance of this judgment was that the Court had for the first time recognised 'environmental protection' as one of the Community's essential objectives.[14] This meant that Article 235 EEC could be used not only as a supplementary legal basis to Article 100 EEC, but could *itself* form the legal basis for European environment policy. An example of a directive based solely on Article 235 EEC is the Wild Birds Directive.[15] Nevertheless, only a few measures have been based solely on Article 235 EEC, for example, Directive 82/884 on a limit value for lead in the air[16] and Recommendation 81/972 concerning the re-use of paper and the use of recycled paper.[17]

The third phase
The third phase in the development of a European environment policy commenced on 1 July 1987, the date on which the changes to the EEC Treaty brought about by the Single European Act came into force, and continued until the date the Treaty on European Union ('Maastricht') entered into force. Although the case law of the Court of Justice had specifically dealt with environmental protection before then, this phase was notable because, for the first time, the objectives of the environment policy were enshrined in the Treaty. The inclusion in the Treaty of provisions designed specifically to protect the environment,

---

[13] Emphasis added by the authors.

[14] This has been confirmed in other case law: Case 302/86 *Commission* v. *Denmark* [1988] ECR 4607, para. 8; Case C-213/96 *Outokumpu* [1998] ECR I-1777, para. 32 and Case C-176/03 *Commission* v. *Council* [2005] ECR I-7879.

[15] Directive 79/409 on the conservation of wild birds, OJ 1979 L 103/1. See for the codified version Directive 2009/147 OJ 2009 L 20/7.

[16] OJ 1982 L 378/15.

[17] OJ 1981 L 355/56.

for example Articles 130r, 130s, 130t, 100a(3) and 100a(4) EEC,[18] confirmed the Community's task in developing a European environment policy. The Treaty incorporated specific powers aimed at the protection of the environment.

In view of these express environmental powers, it was not surprising that the 'old' Article 235 EEC was in that period hardly ever invoked as a legal basis for environmental measures. The explicit environmental provisions of the Treaty made this unnecessary. Only in exceptional cases, such as Directive 93/76 to limit carbon dioxide emissions by improving energy efficiency,[19] there was a need to base environmental measures on this 'catch all' provision.

The fourth phase

The fourth phase of European environmental law started with the entry into force on 1 November 1993 of the Treaty on European Union. In other words, the post-Maastricht phase. For the first time, the term 'environment' was actually referred to in the key Articles 2 and 3 of the EC Treaty, which set out the objectives and activities of the Community. Article 2 referred to 'the promotion, throughout the Community, of a harmonious and balanced development of economic activities, sustainable and non-inflationary growth respecting the environment', while Article 3(k) stated that one of the activities for attaining this was 'a policy in the sphere of the environment'.[20]

The formulation 'sustainable growth' in Article 2 EC was criticised as being a departure from the more usual formulation 'sustainable development'.[21] From the point of view of environmental protection, the concept of 'sustainable growth' seemed marginally weaker than that of 'sustainable development'. Be that as it may, the incorporation of an environmental objective was certainly of great political significance.

The fourth phase is also distinct in that, for the first time, decisions under the Title on the Environment could be taken by a qualified majority. A further striking change as a result of 'Maastricht' was the status given to the action programmes on the environment. The increased competences of the European Parliament in the adoption of these programmes should also be noted. These programmes could be adopted under what is known as the co-decision procedure, which meant the European Parliament could exercise a veto.

The fifth phase

The fifth phase is the post-Amsterdam and post-Nice phase. The Treaty of Amsterdam (1997) introduced a number of interesting changes to the legal

---

[18] Now Articles 191, 192, 193, 114(3) and 114(4) TFEU.

[19] OJ 1993 L 237/28. Now repealed by Directive 2006/32 on energy end-use efficiency and energy services; OJ 2006 L 114/64.

[20] Acknowledged by the Court in Case C-213/96 *Outokumpu* [1998] ECR I-1801, para. 32.

[21] A reference to 'sustainable growth' in European secondary legislation can be found in the preamble of Directive 94/62 on packaging and packaging waste, OJ 1994 L 365/10: 'the reduction of waste is essential for the sustainable growth specifically called for by the Treaty on European Union'.

framework of European environmental policy. In the first place, the constitutional status of 'environmental protection' was clarified. The text of Article 2 EC improved considerably. It stated that the Community shall have as its task promoting a harmonious, balanced and sustainable development of economic activities. This formulation was much more in line with internationally accepted practice in the environmental policy area.[22]

Sustainable development means the improvement of the standard of living and welfare of the relevant populations within the limits of the capacity of the ecosystems, by maintaining natural assets and their biological diversity for the benefit of present and future generations. In other words: to meet the needs of the present generation without compromising those of future generations.[23]

> The sustainable development strategy launched in 2001 by the Göteborg European Council summit has been reviewed recently.[24] The current strategy underlines that in recent years the EU has mainstreamed sustainable development into a broad range of its policies. In particular, the EU has taken the lead in the fight against climate change and the promotion of a low-carbon economy. At the same time, unsustainable trends persist in many areas and the efforts need to be intensified.
>
> The European Council in December 2009 confirmed that sustainable development remains a fundamental objective of the European Union and that a number of unsustainable trends require urgent action. Significant additional efforts are needed to curb and adapt to climate change, to decrease high energy consumption in the transport sector and to reverse the current loss of biodiversity and natural resources. The shift to a safe and sustainable low-carbon and low-input economy will require a stronger focus in the future.[25]

Being perhaps more a guideline to policy action than a normative-legal concept, the political importance of the concept 'sustainable development' cannot be underestimated. Of course, the text was not entirely satisfactory, because

---

[22] See for a reference to the concept of 'sustainable development' in secondary legislation, Article 12 of Directive 2008/50 on ambient air quality and cleaner air for Europe, OJ 2008 L 152/1 and Directive 2009/128 establishing a framework for Community action to achieve the sustainable use of pesticides, OJ 2009 L 309/71.

[23] Presidency Conclusions European Council at Göteborg, 15 and 16 June 2001, point 19. At this summit the European Council declared sustainable development to be 'a fundamental objective under the Treaties.' Cf. also the 'classic' definition from the Brundtland report: 'Sustainable development is development that meets the needs of the present without compromising the ability of future generations to meet their own needs'; World Commission on Environment and Development, *Our Common Future* (Oxford 1987), at 8. See for a more in-depth treatment of the issue of sustainable development and European law, Lee (2005), chapter 2.

[24] Commission's Communication, Mainstreaming sustainable development into EU policies: 2009 Review of the European Union Strategy for Sustainable Development, COM (2009) 400 final.

[25] European Council Conclusions 10 and 11 December 2009, EUCO 6/09.

there was still a link in Article 2 EC between the use of the terms 'sustainable development' and 'economic activities' and because there was a slightly different formulation in Article 2 of the Treaty on European Union.[26] Nevertheless, it must be said that as a whole the text really improved.

As far as the constitutional status of environmental protection is concerned, there was however a second improvement. The Amsterdam Treaty not only spoke of sustainable development, in Article 2 EC, it also introduced as a task to promote 'a high level of protection and improvement of the quality of the environment'. This 'high level of protection principle' will be dealt with more extensively in section 3.2 of this chapter. It is generally understood that within the objectives laid down in the Treaties, there is no hierarchy.[27]

A third improvement concerned the legal status of the so-called 'integration principle' (Article 6 EC; now Article 11 TFEU). This principle, according to which environmental protection requirements had be integrated into the definition and implementation of other Community policies, was promoted to a 'General Principle' of EC law. The legal consequences are discussed in section 2 of this chapter.

With respect to the possibilities of derogation, after harmonisation, from internal market related measures by virtue of environmental protection requirements, it cannot be denied that the text introduced by the Amsterdam Treaty ('old' Article 95(4) to (6) EC; now Article 114(5) to (6) TFEU) was an improvement as well, not only from a substantive, but also from a procedural point of view. The procedure will be discussed in detail in Chapter 3, section 6.

The provisions of the environmental paragraph, now Articles 191-193 TFEU, were not changed by the Amsterdam Treaty in their material, their substantive meaning. Slight changes in the text of Article 175 EC (now Article 192 TFEU) however have been made by the Treaty of Nice (2001). A major change brought about by the Amsterdam Treaty however concerned the decision-making procedures. The co-decision procedure became the standard decision-making procedure for environmental legislation. Although co-decision did not automatically lead to more environmentally friendly legislation, this change was important. It has been a long way from decision-making by unanimity under the old Articles 100 and 235 EEC to majority voting and a strong role for the European Parliament under an explicit environment paragraph in the Treaty.

The sixth phase[28]

The so-called 'Lisbon Treaty' introduced the next and current phase.[29] The Treaty of Lisbon had important effects for the structure of the European Union. The European Community and the EC Treaty have disappeared and are replaced with the European Union. The EC Treaty is replaced and is now entitled the

---

[26] 'a balanced and sustainable development'.

[27] Cf. Bär & Kraemer (1998) at 316 and Case C-20/01 *Commission* v. *Germany* [2003] ECR I-3609, para. 47.

[28] This section builds upon Vedder (2010).

[29] OJ 2007, C 306.

Treaty on the Functioning of the European Union.[30] The Treaty on European Union (TEU) has the same legal value as the Treaty on the Functioning of the European Union (TFEU). The Treaty of Lisbon also integrated Police and Judicial Cooperation in Criminal Matters (Title VI of the old EU Treaty) into 'mainstream' Union law. So what else has changed by the Lisbon Treaty as far as it concerns environmental protection?

To start with the more political side of the matter, the preamble to the TEU maintains the reference to sustainable development in the same, not entirely satisfactory manner, as the old EU Treaty did.[31]

> We refer to the 8th recital of the preamble to the old and the 9th recital of the new EU Treaty: 'DETERMINED to promote economic and social progress for their peoples, *taking into account the principle of sustainable development* and within the context of the accomplishment of the internal market and of reinforced cohesion and *environmental protection*, and to implement policies ensuring that advances in economic integration are accompanied by parallel progress in other fields'. [emphasis added by the authors]

Given that sustainable development already involves taking into account other factors in economic development, taking sustainability into account hardly amounts to an unequivocal commitment to environmental protection as such or even to sustainability. On the upside of things, the objectives of the Union have been extended to incorporate what are now the objectives of the old EC Treaty. This means that Article 3 TEU now includes a third paragraph that basically reiterates the Union's commitment to sustainable development and a high level of protection and improvement of the quality of the environment. Interestingly, the old Article 2 EC Treaty referred to the sustainable development of economic activities,[32] whereas Article 3 TEU now states that the European Union 'shall work for the sustainable development of Europe'. This makes sustainable development an ever more cross-cutting or horizontal objective that is not just confined to economic development but may also relate to technological development. The objectives of the Union have also been updated to include the agenda for relations between the European Union and the world.[33] According to this agenda the European Union shall 'contribute to [...] the sustainable development of the earth, [...] free and fair trade'. The latter is particularly important in view of the important role that developing countries may play in achieving sustainable development. The international agenda for the European Union contains another reference to sustainable development in the Title containing General Provisions on the Union's External Action. According to Article 21 TEU, this

---

[30] See for the Consolidated versions of the Treaty on European Union and the Treaty on the Functioning of the European Union, OJ 2010 C 83.

[31] See above.

[32] The reference in Art. 2, first indent, EU also appears to be confined to economic development.

[33] Art. 2(5) TEU.

action shall 'foster the sustainable economic, social and environmental development of developing countries, with the primary aim of eradicating poverty; [and]
help develop international measures to preserve and improve the quality of the
environment and the sustainable management of global natural resources, in
order to ensure sustainable development'.[34] These objectives shall guide external action in general but also the common foreign and security policy of the
European Union. This is reinforced by the inclusion of an integration clause in
Article 21(3) TEU. The conclusion must be that environmental protection and
sustainable development continue to occupy a prominent place in the objectives
of the European Union.

As far as the integration principle is concerned, the Treaty of Lisbon presents
an interesting surprise in that it now contains *three* environmental integration
principles. This excludes the numerous references to sustainable development, which basically entail an integration exercise as well, and the integration principle in the EU Fundamental Rights Charter. The first environmental
integration principle is to be found in Article 11 TFEU. This provision is a literal
transposition of the old Article 6 EC Treaty. This is compounded by Article 13
TFEU which contains a second and specialised integration principle for animal
welfare. Finally, Article 194(2) TFEU envisages another specialised environmental integration principle for the Union's energy policy. Whereas in the current
situation the environmental integration principle can be distinguished from
all other integration principles because of its unique position in the general
principles Title, the Treaty of Lisbon has changed this because more integration
principles have been promoted to the status of 'provisions having general application'. In Articles 7-13 TFEU we now find a general integration principle, a sex
equality integration principle, an employment and social integration principle, a
non-discrimination integration principle and a consumer protection integration
principle alongside the environmental and animal welfare integration principle.
In a way this demotes the environmental integration principle to 'just another
integration principle'.[35] This leads for instance to the question of a possible
hierarchy between these principles. The special status of *the* integration principle (the old Article 6 EC, now Article 11 TEU) has certainly diminished. The
increased equality of integration principles is confirmed by Article 7 TFEU. This
provision can be called a super-integration clause in that it requires the Union to
ensure consistency between all its policies and activities. The conclusion must
therefore be that there is no hierarchy between the various integration principles
mentioned in Title II TFEU.

With respect to the Environment Title, The Environment Title it has already
been said that the old Articles 174-176 EC Treaty have basically been copy-pasted

---

[34] Art. 21(2)(d) and (f) TEU.

[35] See on this special status Dhondt (2003). Cf. on this prolifiration of integration principles also Jans
      (2010).

to become Articles 191-193 TFEU. A purely cosmetic change concerns the inclusion of climate change as an example of a regional or worldwide environmental problem that falls within the ambit of EU environmental policy. Of course, the European Union has a well-developed climate change policy and moreover plays an active role in the international climate change arena. It is therefore submitted that the Treaty of Lisbon did not go beyond confirming an existing reality.[36] At most, the inclusion of climate change can be seen as a political signal on the part of the European Union.

An interesting innovation is the introduction of a Title on Union energy policy (Title XXI). Again, this Title probably contains little more than a codification of the *status quo*. Before the entry into force of the Treaty of Lisbon energy law was implemented on the basis of the provisions on the internal market, the competition provisions and environmental protection. The new Article 194 TFEU reiterates the connection with the internal market as well as the environmental protection component of European energy policy.[37]

As far as competences are concerned the Treaty of Lisbon again contains some innovations that will not directly affect environmental policy. There may, however, be a number of more indirect effects on environmental policy-making. As part of an answer to the anxiety in some Member States concerning the emergence of a 'European Super state', three categories of competences are introduced in the EU Treaty and TFEU. These are the exclusive (Article 3 TFEU) and shared competence (Article 4 TFEU) and areas where the EU may only support, coordinate or supplement the actions of the Member States (Article 6 TFEU) excluding harmonisation (Article 2(5) TFEU).

The Treaty of Lisbon confirms that the European Union has an *exclusive* competence for the conservation of marine biological resources under the common fisheries policy.[38] Similarly, the already existing thoughts about environmental competence as a *shared* competence find their way back in the TFEU.[39] An interesting innovation is the explicit shared competence for the European Union in the energy area.[40] Up to the entry into force of the Treaty of Lisbon European energy law has developed on the basis of the internal market, competition and environment provisions.

One institutional innovation that may very well have an impact on environmental policy is the citizens' initiative.[41] According to this provision no less than one million citizens of the European Union who are from a significant number of Member States may invite the Commission to come up with a proposal. As

---

[36] Cf. Benson & Jordan (2008) at 284. This is also evidenced by the leadership position the EU sees for itself with the Energy and Climate Package.

[37] Cf. also Chapter 2, section 7.1.

[38] Art. 3(1)(d) TFEU; cf. Joined Cases 3, 4 and 6/76 *Kramer* [1976] ECR 1279. See also Markus (2009) and Markowski (2010).

[39] Art. 4(2)(e) TFEU.

[40] Art. 4(2)(i) TFEU.

[41] Art. 11(4) TEU.

the wording already makes clear, this initiative is only an invitation. Even if the Commission follows up on the invitation, it is still for the Council and the European Parliament to turn a proposal into legislation. Whether this is likely to happen depends on whether or not there is a competence for the European Union to act and the decision-making procedures laid down for the exercise of that competence.

2 General Principles of Union Law in Relation to Environmental Protection

The principle of conferred powers
        Why is it necessary to concern ourselves with the legal basis of European environment policy? Does it have any practical significance, apart from satisfying academic curiosity? The answer has to be: yes, it does! Establishing the legal basis of a proposed European measure on the environment is important for at least three reasons. In the first place because the institutions do not have the unlimited competences of the national legislators to take whatever measures they please. The institutions' powers extend only to what has been expressly conferred by treaty. As provided in Article 13(2) TEU: 'Each institution shall act within the limits of the powers conferred on it in the Treaties, and in conformity with the procedures, conditions and objectives set out in them.' In European law, acting without competence results in invalid measures.

        Deciding the proper legal basis of a European environmental measure is thus in the first place important in order to determine the extent of the competence in the matter in question, and thus the validity of measures taken on the basis of this competence.[42]

        In the second place, deciding the legal basis is relevant for the decision-making procedure to be followed when adopting a particular environmental measure. In Chapter 2, we shall see that European law provides for various decision-making procedures in respect of environmental measures. The role played by the various participants in the decision-making process (European Commission, European Parliament and Council), and thus their means of influencing the environment policy, is different under each of these procedures. It is clear from the Court's case law that the choice of the correct legal basis depends on the 'main object' of the measure.[43] If the centre of gravity of a measure harmonising, for example, environmental product standards is the internal market, Article 114 TFEU is the appropriate legal basis. If the centre of gravity is protection of the environment, decision-making under Article 192 TFEU is appropriate.[44]

        In the third place, the choice of legal basis affects the extent to which Member States are entitled to adopt more stringent environmental mea-

---

[42] Cf. Joined Cases C-14/06 and C-295/06 *Parliament and Denmark v. Commission* [2008] ECR I-1649.

[43] Case C-155/91 *Commission v. Council* [1993] ECR I-939; Case C-187/93 *EP v. Council* [1994] ECR I-2857.

[44] See on this more in detail Chapter 2, section 4.

sures than the European standards agreed upon. This important point will be discussed in detail in Chapter 3, sections 5 and 6.

The subsidiarity principle

The second paragraph of Article 5 TEU refers to the principle of subsidiarity in general terms:

> 'Under the principle of subsidiarity, in areas which do not fall within its exclusive competence, the Union shall act only if and in so far as the objectives of the proposed action cannot be sufficiently achieved by the Member States, either at central level or at regional and local level, but can rather, by reason of the scale or effects of the proposed action, be better achieved at Union level.'[45]

The principle thus contains both a negative criterion (not sufficiently achieved by the Member States) and a positive one (better achieved by the Union) by which to judge European acts. European action must meet both criteria to be justified. Any (proposed) legislation must be justified with regard to the principle. Legislation to date in general provides justification in this respect.[46] However, the references in the preamble of European environmental measures do have a somewhat 'standard' and therefore obligatory character.

> See for instance the reference to the subsidiarity principle in Directive 2004/101 establishing a scheme for greenhouse gas emission allowance trading, in respect of the Kyoto Protocol's project mechanisms. Point 19 of the preamble reads: 'Since the objective of the proposed action, namely the establishment of a link between the Kyoto project-based mechanisms and the Community scheme, cannot be sufficiently achieved by the Member States acting individually, and can therefore by reason of the scale and effects of this action be better achieved at Community level, the Community may adopt measures, in accordance with the principle of subsidiarity [...]. In accordance with the principle of proportionality [...] this Directive does not go beyond what is necessary in order to achieve that objective.'
>
> Or take the preamble (point 15) of Directive 2005/35 on ship-source pollution and on the introduction of penalties for infringements: 'Since the objectives of this Directive, namely the incorporation of the international ship-source pollution standards into Community law and the establishment of penalties – criminal or administrative – for violation of them in order to ensure a high level of safety and environmental protection in maritime transport, cannot be sufficiently achieved by the Member States and can therefore be better achieved at Community level, the Community may adopt measures, in accordance with the principle of subsidiarity

---

[45] Cf. on the emergence of this principle and its consequences for environmental law, Lenaerts (1993). Cf. also Protocol No 1 on the Role of National Parliaments in the European Union, OJ 2010 C 83/203 and Protocol No 2 on the application of the principles of subsidiarity and proportionality, OJ 2010 C 83/206.

[46] OJ 2004 L 338/18.

[...]. In accordance with the principle of proportionality [...] this Directive does not go beyond what is necessary in order to achieve those objectives.'[47]

As far as the likely implications of the subsidiarity principle for environmental law are concerned, the following should be noted. In the first place, action is justified where the issue under consideration has transnational aspects, which cannot be satisfactorily regulated by action by Member States.[48] This means that European action to prevent cross-border environmental effects satisfies the subsidiarity principle. In view of the territorial limitations of many national powers, unilateral action by Member States is clearly going to be less effective than concerted action where the source of pollution is situated abroad. This would, for example, apply to action to restrict all kinds of transfrontier environmental pollution of a regional (water and air pollution) or global (depletion of the ozone layer, greenhouse effect resulting from CO2 emissions, maintenance of biodiversity) nature[49] or to the protection of wild fauna and flora.[50]

As early as 1987 the Court held in Case 247/85 that the Wild Birds Directive is based on the assumption that the protection of wild birds is 'typically a transfrontier environment problem entailing common responsibilities for the Member States'.[51] The Habitats Directive[52] also stipulates that it is necessary to take measures at European level to conserve threatened habitats and species, as these form part of the Community's natural heritage and the threats to them are often of a transboundary nature. A further example is provided by Directive 91/676 on pollution caused by nitrates from agricultural sources.[53] Its preamble states that action at European level is necessary because pollution of water due to nitrates in one Member State can influence waters in other Member States. Other examples of directives in which the preamble refers to possible transfrontier effects are Regulation 1005/2009 on substances that deplete the ozone layer[54] and Directive 2008/1 concerning integrated pollution prevention and control.[55] One of the argu-

---

[47] OJ 2005 L 255/11.

[48] See also Lee (2005) at 10.

[49] See for instance Directive 2001/81 on national emission ceilings for certain atmospheric pollutants, OJ 2001 L 309/22, point 13 of the preamble. It was stated that in accordance with the subsidiarity principle 'limitation of emissions of acidifying and eutrophying pollutants and ozone precursors, cannot be sufficiently achieved by the Member States because of the transboundary nature of the pollution'.

[50] Cf. however Lee (2005) at 12, who makes a distinction between physical spillovers (transnational pollution) and 'psychic' spillovers (protection of the EU's common heritage).

[51] Case 247/85 *Commission v. Belgium* [1987] ECR 3029.

[52] Directive 92/43 on the conservation of natural habitats, OJ 1992 L 206/7.

[53] OJ 1991 L 375/1.

[54] OJ 2009 L 286/1.

[55] OJ 2008 L 24/8.

ments supporting the conclusion of the Convention on the protection of the Alps was the cross-border nature of the ecological problems of the Alpine area.[56]

In the *Umweltanwalt von Kärnten* Case the Court ruled that a project cannot 'escape' from an environmental impact assessment under the EIA Directive just because the project is transboundary in nature and part of it is located in the territory of another Member State.[57]

In general, therefore, action by the EU on transfrontier environmental matters would seem to pass the test of subsidiarity.

Another important element of the application of the subsidiarity principle is whether action by Member States alone or lack of European action would conflict with the requirements of the treaties, such as the need to correct distortion of competition or avoid restrictions on trade or strengthen economic and social cohesion.[58] As far as the environment is concerned, this could apply in the following situation, for instance. A purely national, product-oriented environmental policy could easily result in restrictions on the import and export of goods, which might harm the environment. Harmonisation of environmental product standards at a European level can ensure that effective environmental policy need not be at the expense of the operation and functioning of the internal market. As the scope of protection pursued by environmental product standards have immediate effects on trade, it is clear that these measures comply with the subsidiarity principle.[59]

More problematic from a subsidiarity point of view is its role in respect of emission and environmental quality standards.[60] On the one hand, it can be said that European standard setting tends to even out competitive differences and avoids 'a race to the bottom'.[61] On the other hand, it deprives Member States of the opportunity of maintaining 'healthy' policy competition. A reasonable balance could be attained here if European environmental rules were mainly cast in the mould of minimum harmonisation. This would allow the provision of a minimum level of protection throughout the EU, without depriving the Member States of the power to adopt more stringent standards for their own territory. Policy competition would then only be possible with regard to a level of environmental protection that is higher than the European minimum standard.

A third guideline for application of the subsidiarity principle is whether action at European level would produce clear benefits by reason of its scale or effects compared with action at the level of the Member States. Here, too, it

---

[56] OJ 1996 L 61/32, concluded by Council Decision 96/191, OJ 1996 L 61/31.

[57] Case C-205/08 *Umweltanwalt von Kärnten* [2009] ECR I-11525.

[58] Cf. Lee (2005) at 11.

[59] Cf. Case C-377/98 *Netherlands* v. *EP and Council* [2000] ECR I-6229. The case concerned an application for annulment of Directive 98/44 on the legal protection of biotechnological inventions; OJ 1998 L 213/13. Cf. also point 23 of the preamble of Directive 2011/65 on the restriction of the use of certain hazardous substances in electrical and electronic equipment OJ 2011 L 174/88.

[60] Cf. also Faure (1998) and Revesz (2000).

[61] Cf. Revesz (2000), Scott (2000) at 56, Lee (2005) at 11.

could be said that the objective of attaining a certain minimum level of protection throughout the EU can only be achieved effectively by European legislation. The objectives set out in Article 191 TFEU imply this.

An examination of European environmental legislation in the light of the above guidelines would reveal that probably not one environmental directive or regulation would fail to pass the test. It should however be noted that the importance of the subsidiarity principle is above all political. The few judgments of the Court of Justice on the subject hardly give the impression that it would be quick to annul a Union environmental measure for non-compliance with the principle of subsidiarity.[62]

The principle of proportionality

The fourth paragraph of Article 5 TEU continues: 'Under the principle of proportionality, the content and form of Union action shall not exceed what is necessary to achieve the objectives of the Treaties.[63] The following guidelines seem pertinent. All charges, both for the Union and for the national governments must be kept to a minimum and be proportionate to the proposed objective. The European legislature must choose measures, which leave the greatest degree of freedom for national decisions, and the national legal system should be respected. As much use as possible should be made of minimum standards, whereby Member States are free to lay down stricter national standards. Use of the directive is to be preferred above use of the regulation, and the framework directive is to be preferred above detailed measures. Non-binding instruments such as recommendations should be used wherever possible, as well as voluntary codes of conduct.[64]

> Examples of such voluntary codes can already be found in various environmental acts. Article 4 of Directive 91/676 on pollution caused by nitrates[65] provides that the Member States must establish codes of good agricultural practice, to be implemented by farmers on a voluntary basis. The purpose of these codes is to reduce the pollution of water caused by nitrates from agricultural sources. Another example is Regulation 66/2010 on the EU Ecolabel.[66] This regulation, which regulates an EU Ecolabel award scheme, operates on a wholly voluntary basis. Where a product meets the applicable environmental criteria, the ecolabel may be used. What is remarkable here is that the various interest groups (industry,

---

[62] Cf. e.g. Joined Cases C-154/04 and C-155/04 *Alliance for Natural Health and Others* [2005] ECR I-6451; Case C-491/01 *British American Tobacco (Investments) and Imperial Tobacco* [2002] ECR I-11453 and Case C-377/98 *Netherlands* v. *EP and Council* [2000] ECR I-6229. Cf. also more recent outside environmental law Case C-58/08 *Vodafone and others*, Judgment of 8 June 2010.

[63] Cf. in general on proportionality Jans et al. (2007), Chapter V, section 4.

[64] See Council Resolution on the drafting, implementation and enforcement of Community environmental law; OJ 1997 C 321/1. Cf. Winter (1996) and Verschuuren (2000).

[65] OJ 1991 L 375/1.

[66] OJ 2010 L 27/1.

retailers, environmental organisations etc.) must be consulted for the purpose of defining the criteria that should apply. In the same vein is the Eco-audit Regulation 1221/2009 (EMAS).[67] The eco-management and audit scheme is a management tool for companies and other organisations to evaluate, report and improve their environmental performance. Participation is completely voluntary.

A similar development is the growing interest in the use of voluntary environmental agreements.[68] Environmental agreements between public institutions and industry are increasingly used to implement environmental policies. A first example at the EU level was the 1998 agreement between the Commission and the European car industry (ACEA).[69] A more recent example concerns environmentally friendly plastic.[70] Agreements can also be used, under certain conditions, to implement provisions of environmental directives.[71]

The EU's environment policy can also be said to comply with the guidelines in terms of its use of the directive. From the start it has been customary to use the directive for action in the field of the environment. Regulations have been used in only a few cases, above all in those sectors where a more uniform regime is indeed necessary, for example, to implement international agreements or to regulate international trade. Examples are Regulations 338/97 on the protection of species of wild fauna and flora by regulating trade therein,[72] 348/81 on imports of whales and other cetacean products[73] and 1013/2006 on shipments of waste.[74] These all regulate the trade in certain goods or products between Member States and with third countries. A more or less uniform regulation is required at the external frontier of the EU in order to avoid deflections of trade. In these cases, a regulation is a more appropriate instrument than a directive, because of its direct applicability. However, regulations are used not only to regulate international trade. They are also used when it is necessary to grant certain rights directly to manufacturers, importers or even particular companies, or to impose obligations on them.[75] The element of uniformity and identical application of rules throughout the EU was also the primary reason to opt to

---

[67] OJ 2009 L 342/1.

[68] See the Commission's Communication, Environmental Agreements at Community Level, COM (2002) 412 final. Cf. Lee (2005) at 231-237.

[69] See Commission Recommendation of 5 February 1999 on the reduction of CO2 emissions from passenger cars; OJ 1999 L 40/49.

[70] Commission press release IP/05/170, 14 February 2005.

[71] Commission Recommendation 96/733 concerning environmental agreements implementing Community directives, OJ 1996 L 333/59 and Council Resolution on environmental agreements, OJ 1997 C 321/6. See for a more detailed discussion Chapter 4, section 3.4.

[72] Regulation 338/97, OJ 1997 L 61/1.

[73] OJ 1981 L 39/1.

[74] OJ 2006 L 190/1.

[75] Cf. Regulation 1907/2006 concerning the Registration, Evaluation, Authorisation and Restriction of Chemicals (REACH), OJ 2006 L 396/1.

use this instrument for the measures on the EU Ecolabel and eco-management and audit schemes.[76]

As far as the preference for minimum harmonisation expressed in the guidelines is concerned, minimum standards have regularly been utilised in European environmental law. The principle is even stated in so many words in the Treaty itself, in Article 193 TFEU.[77] In the vast majority of European environmental legislation, for example, the measures to combat water and air pollution, rules are laid down for the fixing of emission limit values, without going as far as complete harmonisation. There is in general no need for complete harmonisation. It should be noted also that the phenomenon of framework legislation can already be found in European environmental law, for example, in the Water Framework Directive,[78] and the Waste Framework Directive.[79]

The case law of the Court shows that the Court is in principle willing to review European environmental measures, as well as the national measures implementing them,[80] in the light of the proportionality principle. However, it will respect the 'wide discretion' available to the European institutions and the political choices and complex assessments to be made. In general, the legality of EU environmental measures can be affected only if the measure is 'manifestly inappropriate'.[81]

In the *Standley* case, the Court considered the Nitrates Directive.[82] It was argued that this directive gave rise to disproportionate obligations on the part of farmers, so that it offended against the principle of proportionality. The Court was not impressed. After a careful study of the Nitrates Directive, it came to the conclusion:

---

[76] Regulations 66/2010, OJ 2010 L 27/1 and 1221/2009, OJ 2009 L 342/1.

[77] See on this more in detail Chapter 3, section 5.

[78] Directive 2000/60 establishing a framework for the Community action in the field of water policy; OJ 2000 L 327.

[79] Directive 2008/98, OJ 2008 L 312/3.

[80] Cf. e.g. Case C-76/08 *Commission* v. *Malta* [2009] ECR I-8213, concerning the Wild Birds Directive and Case C-2/10 *Azienda Agro-Zootecnica Franchini*, Judgment of 21 July 2011, with respect to the proportionality principle of Article 13 of Directive 2009/28 on the promotion of the use of energy from renewable sources.

[81] Cf. Joined Cases C-154/04 and C-155/04 *Alliance for Natural Health and Others* [2005] ECR I-6451, para. 52; Case C-77/09 *Gowan Comércio Internacional e Serviços*, Judgment of 22 December 2010 and Case C-221/09 *AJD Tuna Ltd*, Judgment of 11 March 2011. Cf. on the proportionality principle also Chapter 6, section 4.5.

[82] Case C-293/97 *Standley* [1999] ECR I-2603. Cf. also Case C-102/97 *Commission* v. *Germany* [1999] ECR I-5051, para. 42. The same approach can also be found in the Court's judgment in Case C-6/99 *Association Greenpeace France* v. *Ministère de l'Agriculture et de la Pêche* [2000] ECR I-1651, on the precautionary principle; See below section 3.2 of this chapter.

> 'that the Directive contains flexible provisions enabling the Member States to observe the principle of proportionality in the application of the measures which they adopt. It is for the national courts to ensure that that principle is observed.' In general the Court, in its assessment of the proportionality of a Union measure, will apply the so-called 'manifestly inappropriate' test: 'the legality of a measure adopted [...] can be affected only if the measure is manifestly inappropriate having regard to the objective which the competent institution is seeking to pursue'.[83]

The conclusion in *Standley* that the flexible provisions of the directive enables the Member States to observe the principle of proportionality will be applicable to most, if not all, European environmental legislation.

> With respect to the National Emission Ceilings Directive the Court of Justice ruled 'that the wide flexibility accorded to the Member States by the NEC Directive prevents limits from being placed upon them in the development of the programmes and their thus being obliged to adopt or to refrain from adopting specific measures or initiatives for reasons extraneous to assessments of a strategic nature which take account globally of the factual circumstances and the various competing public and private interests.[84] The imposition of any requirements to that effect would run counter to the intention of the European Union legislature, whose aim in particular is to allow the Member States to strike a certain balance between the various interests involved. Furthermore, that would result in excessive constraints being placed on the Member States and would, accordingly, be contrary to the principle of proportionality'.

Flexible provisions in a Union environmental measure may not be 'abused' by the Member States, as this could run counter to the objectives of the measure and would violate the proportionality principle. However, national legislation of Member States exercising their right under Article 193 TFEU taking more stringent protective measures, cannot be reviewed in the light of the proportionality principle, although, according to the Court of Justice, they still exercise powers governed by Union law.[85]

---

[83] Case 331/88 *Fedesa* [1990] ECR I-4023. Cf. also Case C-189/01 *Jippes* [2001] ECR I-5689, para. 83 and Case C-27/00 *Omega Air a.o.* [2002] ECR I-2569, para. 72. In the latter case, concerning threshold levels for noise produced by airplanes, the Court did not find that the Council committed a manifest error of assessment even if alternative measures could have been taken which would have been economically less damaging. Cf. also, with respect to the Waste Oils Directive, Case C-15/03 *Commission* v. *Austria* [2005] ECR I-837, para. 38 in particular and Case C-92/03 *Commission* v. *Portugal* [2005] ECR I-867 and with respect to the Waste Framework Directive Case C-254/08 *Futura Immobiliare srl Hotel Futura* [2009] ECR I-6995.

[84] Case C-165/09 to C-167/09 *Stichting Natuur en Milieu and others*, Judgment of 26 May 2011, paras. 88-89.

[85] Case C-6/03 *Deponiezweckverband Eiterköpfe* [2005] ECR I-2753, para. 31. See on this judgment also Chapter 3, section 5.

Equal treatment

Arguably one of the most fundamental general principles of Union law is the principle of equal treatment.[86] This general principle of equal treatment requires that comparable situations must not be treated differently and different situations must not be treated in the same way unless such treatment is objectively justified. The case law of the Court of Justice shows that the answer to what is objectively justified, full account of the environmental principles of the Treaty must be given. This principle played an important role in a number of judgments of which the *Arcelor* case is probably the most important one.[87]

> Arcelor Atlantique et Lorraine and some other companies are undertakings in the steel sector. The argued that the steel industry is in a comparable situation as the chemical and non-ferrous metal (plastics and aluminium) industry, and that by excluding the plastics and aluminium sectors from the scope of Directive 2003/87, the Union legislature breached the principle of equal with respect to the steel sector. The Court found indeed that the steel, chemical and non-ferrous metal sectors are, for the purposes of examining the validity of Directive 2003/87 from the point of view of the principle of equal treatment, in a comparable position while being treated differently. However, this difference was justified. According to the Court of Justice, a difference in treatment is justified if it is based on an objective and reasonable criterion, that is, if the difference relates to a legally permitted aim pursued by the legislation in question, and it is proportionate to the aim pursued by the treatment. The Court accepted the novelty of the allowance trading scheme established by the directive, its complexity both political and economic. The Court also argued that the Union legislature can lawfully make use of 'a step-by-step approach' and may review the measures adopted, also in view of including other sectors of industry under the allowance trading scheme. The Court acknowledged that the Union legislature has a broad discretion where its action involves political, economic and social choices and where it is called on to undertake complex assessments and evaluations. Finally, the Court concluded that the Union legislature did not infringe the principle of equal treatment by treating comparable situations differently when it excluded the chemical and non-ferrous metal sectors from the scope of Directive 2003/87.[88]

---

[86] Cf. also Article 18 TFEU.

[87] Cf. e.g. Case C-127/07 *Arcelor Atlantique and Lorraine and others* [2008] ECR I-9895. See also Case C-221/09 *AJD Tuna Ltd*, Judgment of 11 March 2011, where the Court accepted 'the long-term viability of the fisheries sector through sustainable exploitation of living aquatic resources based on the precautionary approach' as legitimate grounds for a differential treatment and Case C-2/10 *Azienda Agro-Zootecnica Franchini*, Judgment of 21 July 2011, where the Court ruled that, in the context of the Habitats and Wild Birds Directives a difference in treatment between projects for the construction of wind turbines and projects relating to other industrial activities proposed for sites forming part of the Natura 2000 network may be justified on the basis of objective differences between those two kinds of projects.

[88] Cf. on comparable situations, emission trading and the concept of selectivity with respect to state aid Case C-279/08 P *Commission v. Netherlands*, Judgment of 8 September 2011. See also Chapter 7, section 7.2.

Although the Euratom Treaty does not contain any explicit provision which corresponds to Article 18 TFEU the Court pointed out that the principle of prohibition of any discrimination on grounds of nationality is a general principle which is also applicable under the Euratom Treaty.[89]

> Like the law in many other countries Austrian law provides that the owner of a building may prevent nuisance to neighbouring property if it exceeds the usual level and affects the normal use of the building. However, if the operator of the installation is in possession of the required authorisation, the owner can only request compensation for damage incurred. Problem is that Austrian law does not take into account authorisations from another member state. So the question rose whether the Austrian Supreme Court (*Oberster Gerichtshof*) could grant an injunction to close a nuclear power plant located in the Czech Republic without taking into account the operating authorisation issued by the Czech authorities? The Court of Justice ruled that if the Czech authorisation is not being taken into account, this would be discriminatory, which cannot be 'justified on grounds of protecting life, public health, the environment or property rights.'

The integration principle

One of the most important principles of EU law of relevance for environmental protection is the integration principle stated in Article 11 TFEU:

> 'Environmental protection requirements must be integrated into the definition and implementation of the Union's policies and activities, in particular with a view to promoting sustainable development.'

The importance of the integration principle is reaffirmed in the Sixth Environment Action Programme, which stipulates that 'integration of environmental concerns into other policies must be deepened' in order to move towards sustainable development.[90] This refers to what is known as external integration, in other words, the integration of environmental objectives in other policy sectors. The principle was introduced into the Treaty by the Single European Act. There it was provided that 'Environmental protection requirements shall be a component of the Community's other policies.' It is notable that the current version of the Treaty is worded more forcefully and refers explicitly to implementation of the Union's policies. Moreover, the general formulation makes it clear that the operation of the integration principle extends to the entire Treaties. Rather important is the clause 'in particular with a view to promoting sustainable development.' This has given the concept of 'sustainable development' some

---

[89] Case C-115/08 ČEZ, Judgment of 27 October 2009.

[90] Decision 1600/2002 laying down the Sixth Community Environment Action Programme, OJ 2002 L 242. Cf. also Communication from the Commission, A partnership for integration: a strategy for integrating the environment into EU policies, COM (1998) 333 and Commission working document, Integrating environmental considerations into other policy areas – a stocktaking of the Cardiff process, COM (2004) 394.

legal 'weight' and therefore cannot be seen as merely stating a policy objective to be achieved.[91]

The first question which presents itself is what precisely has to be integrated. The Treaty refers to 'environmental protection requirements'. What should this be taken to mean? Certainly, it would seem to include the environment policy objectives of Article 191(1) TFEU. It also seems likely that it includes the principles referred to in Article 191(2) TFEU, such as the precautionary principle and the principle that preventive action should be taken. And finally integration of the environment policy aspects referred to in Article 191(3) TFEU should not a priori be excluded, though it is true that the Treaty does not state that these aspects have to be integrated, but only that they should be taken into account. This wide interpretation of the integration principle in effect leads to a general obligation on the European institutions to reach an integrated and balanced assessment of all the relevant environmental aspects when adopting other policy.

The next problem concerns the question of whether the integration principle implies that the Unions's environment policy has been given some measure of priority over other European policy areas. Probably, it has not, at least if by priority it is meant that, in the event of a conflict with other policy areas, environment policy has a certain added value from a legal point of view.[92] The text of the Treaty does not support such a conclusion. The integration principle is designed to ensure that protection of the environment is at least taken into consideration, even when commercial policy is involved or when other decisions are being taken and have to be worked out in detail, for example in the fields of agriculture, fisheries,[93] transport,[94] energy,[95] development aid,[96] trade and external relations,[97] internal market[98] and competition policy, regional policy, etc.[99] Also, the existence nowadays of multiple integration principles, does not support the idea of a priority for environmental policy.[100] Therefore, the manner in which potential conflicts between protection of the environment and, for example, the functioning of the internal market should be resolved cannot be inferred from the integration principle as such. Such conflicts should be resolved against

---

[91] Cf. Bär & Kraemer (1998) at 316-318.

[92] See for a discussion of this issue Bär & Kraemer (1998) at 318-319.

[93] Case C-221/09 AJD Tuna Ltd, Judgment of 11 March 2011.

[94] Mahmoudi (2005).

[95] Dhondt (2005).

[96] Williams (2005).

[97] See Marín Durán & Morgera (2006).

[98] Cf. for instance with respect to the freedom to provide services the Services Directive, Directive 2006/123 on services in the internal market (OJ 2006 L 376/36), which states in its preamble at point 7: 'This Directive also takes into account other general interest objectives, including the protection of the environment'.

[99] Cf. Dhondt (2003) and Vedder (2003).

[100] See above, section 1 of this chapter.

the background of the body of case law established by the Court of Justice in respect of the principles of equal treatment[101] and of proportionality. If European legislation for the protection of the environment, which the Court has already designated as one of the essential objectives in the *ADBHU* case, results in restrictions of trade, this is regarded as permissible as long as the measures are not discriminatory and do not entail restrictions that go beyond what is strictly necessary for the protection of the environment.[102] The principle of proportionality may also prove a useful guide in relation to other areas of policy in which conflicts flowing from the integration principle are involved.

At the same time, it should be noted that when interpreting Article 39 TFEU, in the context of the common agricultural policy, the Court also has to weigh various objectives against each other. The institutions of the Union have wide discretionary powers when harmonising policy in relation to the various objectives contained in Article 39 TFEU (increasing productivity, ensuring a fair standard of living for the agricultural community, stabilising markets, assuring the stability of supplies and ensuring supplies reach consumers at reasonable prices). One or more of these objectives may (temporarily) be given priority, as long as the policy does not become so focused on a single objective that the attainment of other objectives is made impossible. This approach could also be employed in respect of the environment. It would then be arguable that, if a given objective could adequately be achieved in a variety of ways, the integration principle would entail a choice for the least environmentally harmful.

Now that the question of the priority has been addressed, the problem of the legal enforceability of the integration principle looms large. The following comments are called for. The Court's judgments clearly show that the contention that the integration principle is of no value whatsoever is not correct. For example, the principle fulfils an important function in the choice of the proper legal basis of environmental measures and has been used by the Court to justify 'environmental' legislation under legal bases other than Article 192 TFEU.

> In the *Chernobyl I* case, the issue was whether Regulation 3955/87 on the conditions governing imports of agricultural products originating in third countries following the accident at the Chernobyl power station was rightly based on Article 113 (now Article 207 TFEU) rather than Article 130s (now Article 192 TFEU).[103] The Court held that the 'the principle whereby all Community measures must satisfy the requirements of environmental protection, implies that a Community measure

---

[101] Cf. Case C-127/07 *Arcelor Atlantique and Lorraine and others* [2008] ECR I-9895. See also our remarks on this judgment in section 2 of this chapter.

[102] Case 240/83 *ADBHU* [1985] ECR 531.

[103] Case C-62/88 *EP* v. *Council* [1990] ECR I-1527. In the *TiO2* case (Case C-300/89 *Commission* v. *Council* [1991] ECR I-2867), the Court confirmed this, stating: 'That principle implies that a Community measure cannot be covered by Article 130s [now Article 192 TFEU] merely because it also pursues objectives of environmental protection.'

cannot be part of Community action on environmental matters merely because it takes account of those requirements.' In the *TiO2* case,[104] the Court confirmed this.

A second legal consequence of the integration principle, closely connected with the above, is the following. The principle broadens the objectives of the other powers laid down in the Treaty and thus limits the role of the specific powers doctrine in environmental policy.

> The *Chernobyl I* case and the *TiO2* case demonstrate that environmental objectives can be pursued in the context of the common commercial policy and its internal market policy. The principle has been used also in the interpretation of directives in the area of public procurement, leading to the conclusion that this does not exclude the possibility of using environmental criteria in identifying the economically most advantageous tender.[105] Without the integration principle, it is debatable to what extent environmental objectives, for example in connection with the approximation of laws for the attainment of the internal market, could be taken into account by the Council.

It was not without reason that most European environmental measures in the period prior to the Single European Act were based on a combination of the old Articles 100 and 235 EEC Treaty. The powers of approximation were limited in Article 3(h) EEC 'to the extent required for the proper functioning of the common market'. And because the requirements of a properly functioning common market were not always and automatically synonymous with the requirements of environmental protection, it was necessary to invoke the additional legal basis supplied by Article 235 EEC. The integration principle makes such artificial devices unnecessary. Not only does it extend the objectives of the internal market policy and the common commercial policy, but environmental objectives can also be taken into account in other policy areas without the attributed powers doctrine interfering.

> Thus in *Pinaud Wieger*, the Court held that the achievement of freedom to provide services in the transport sector can only be attained in an orderly fashion in the context of a common transport policy 'which takes into consideration the economic, social and ecological problems'.[106] And with respect to competition

---

[104] Case C-300/89 *Commission v. Council* [1991] ECR I-2867.

[105] Case C-513/99 *Concordia Bus Finland* [2002] ECR I-7213, para. 57 and Case C-448/01 *EVN and Wienstrom* [2003] ECR I-14527. See also Directive 2004/18, OJ 2004 L 134/114 with explicit references tot the integration principle and environmental protection requirements. Or even the Decision of the European Central Bank 2011/397 on the environmental and health and safety accreditation procedures for the production of euro banknotes OJ 2011 L 176/52!

[106] Case C-17/90 *Pinaud Wieger* [1991] ECR I-5253. See also Case C-195/90 *Commission v. Germany* [1992] ECR I-3141.

law, we argue that the impact on the environment must be taken into account in assessing whether agreements between undertakings violate Article 101 TFEU and is relevant to the European Commission's when deciding whether or not to approve state aid under Article 107(3) TFEU.[107] Here, too, the environmental consequences can now be taken into account.[108]

Another aspect which is important when evaluating the legal status of the integration principle is whether the legitimacy of actions of the Council and European Commission can be reviewed by the Court in the light of the principle. Can the validity of a directive or regulation, for example in the field of transport or agriculture, be questioned on the grounds that the decision has infringed the environmental objectives of the Treaty? In other words, the question as to the legal enforceability of the integration principle is in fact a question as to the legal significance of the objectives, principles and other aspects referred to in Article 191(1), (2) and (3) TFEU. It has already been noted that the present version of the principle has been formulated more forcefully than under the Single European Act. In principle, the review of European measures in the light of the environmental objectives should therefore be regarded as possible.

Indeed, in its judgment in the *Chernobyl I* case, the Court speaks in just such strong terms ('must satisfy the requirements of environmental protection'). In the *Betatti* case, in which the lawfulness of Ozone Regulation 3093/94 was disputed, the Court was also prepared to examine the compatibility of a measure with the environmental objectives and principles of the Treaty.[109] It observed that Article 191 TFEU 'sets a series of objectives, principles and criteria which the Community legislature must respect in implementing [Community environmental] policy.' However, it should be borne in mind that the institutions have wide discretionary powers as to how they shape the Union's environment policy, and will have to balance the relative importance of the environmental objectives and other Union objectives as they proceed. The Court expressed this in the following terms: 'However, in view of the need to strike a balance between certain of the objectives and principles mentioned in Article 130r [now Article 191 TFEU] and of the complexity of the implementation of those criteria, review by the Court must necessarily be limited to the question whether the Council, by adopting the Regulation, committed a manifest error of appraisal regarding the conditions for the application of Article 130r of the Treaty.'

The conclusion that can be drawn from these judgments seems to be that only in very exceptional cases will a measure be susceptible to annulment (or being declared invalid) because certain environmental objectives seem not to have

---

[107] Cf. the 2008 Guidelines on Environmental Aid, OJ 2008 C 82/1 containing a clear reference to the integration principle. See also Chapter 7 extensively.

[108] Cf. Chapter 7, section 7.3.

[109] Case C-341/95 *Gianni Bettati* [1998] ECR I-4355.

been taken sufficiently into account.[110] Another factor which will probably also have to be taken into account is that the degree to which measures are open to judicial review may differ depending on whether the objectives of Article 191(1) TFEU, the principles of Article 191(2) TFEU or the policy aspects of Article 191(3) TFEU are involved. As far as the latter are concerned, the Treaty states that the Union shall 'take account of' these aspects, which is not the same as observing them. Besides this, Article 191(2) TFEU that the Union shall 'aim' at a high level of protection. The conclusion must surely be that the application of the integration principle is amenable to judicial review, but that the extent of that review is limited and may differ from one case to the next.

Perhaps more important than the possibility of relying on the principle before the Court of Justice is the following legal consequence. In our opinion, secondary European legislation can – and indeed must – be interpreted in the light of the environmental objectives of the Treaty, even outside the environmental field.

> For example it has emerged as an important factor in justifying the application of the precautionary principle, in particular in relation to the protection of public health.[111] In *Association Greenpeace France* v. *Ministère de l'Agriculture et de la Pêche* the Court assessed if the precautionary principle was taken into account in Directive 90/220 on the deliberate release into the environment of genetically modified organisms.[112] Another example can be found in the *ARCO Chemie Nederland* case.[113] In that case, the Court of Justice ruled that the concept of 'waste', in view of the prevention and precautionary principle, cannot be interpreted restrictive. This is, as it were, a special form of the generally accepted method of interpreting European law so as to be compatible with the Treaty.[114] Furthermore, one could argue that the Treaty itself, for instance the provisions on the free movement of goods, has to be interpreted in the light of the environmental objectives and principles mentioned in Article 191 TFEU.[115] In Chapter 6, we will see that the principle has been key in justifying recourse to the mandatory requirement relating to environmental protection to justify a directly discriminatory barrier to trade.[116]

---

[110] See also the *Standley* case discussed above in the context of the proportionality principle; Case C-293/97 *Standley* [1999] ECR I-2603.

[111] See Joined Cases T-74, 76, 83, 85, 132, 137, 141/00 *Artegodan GmbH a.o.* v. *Commission* [2002] ECR II-4945, para. 183.

[112] Case C-6/99 *Association Greenpeace France* v. *Ministère de l'Agriculture et de la Pêche* [2000] ECR I-1651. The legal basis of the directive was Article 100a EEC. See now Directive 2001/18, OJ 2001 L 106/1.

[113] Joined Cases C-418/97 and C-419/97 *ARCO Chemie Nederland* [2000] ECR I-4475. See also Case C-270/03 *Commission* v. *Italy* [2005] ECR I-5233, para. 12. Case C-1/03 *Van de Walle a.o.* [2004] ECR I-7613, para. 45.

[114] Case 172/82 *Inter-Huiles* [1983] ECR 555.

[115] See for instance Case C-209/98 *Sydhavnens Sten & Grus* [2000] ECR I-3743, para. 48.

[116] Case C-379/98 *PreussenElektra* [2001] ECR I-2099.

A final question that should be discussed in connection with this principle is that of the possible consequences for Member States. In principle, in view of the fact that the text of the Treaty expressly refers to 'Union's policies and activities', the integration principle should have no direct legal consequences for the Member States. Of course, there will be indirect effects, in the sense that the Council and the European Commission will observe the principle in their legal acts, which are often addressed to the Member States. As these are often integrated regulations and directives, the Member States will also be required to observe a certain degree of integration. Also one could argue that where Member State exercise some discretion under a EU policy the integration duty might apply directly to them.

On the other hand, the Member States are not bound by the environmental objectives and principles of the Treaty as in areas that have not been harmonised, other than by the general obligation of sincere cooperation contained in Article 4(3) TEU.[117] They are only bound by the environmental principles of the Treaty when they do implement Union law.[118]

> In the *ERG II* case, regarding Italian legislation on environmental liability the Court ruled: 'Since Article 174 EC [now Article 191 TFEU], which establishes the 'polluter pays' principle, is directed at action at Community level, that provision cannot be relied on as such by individuals in order to exclude the application of national legislation – such as that at issue in the main proceedings – in an area covered by environmental policy *for which there is no Community legislation adopted on the basis of Article 175 EC* [now Article 192 TFEU; emphasis added by the authors] that specifically covers the situation in question.'[119]
>
> In the *Peralta* case, the lawfulness of Italian environmental legislation was disputed, *inter alia* because of alleged incompatibility with Article 130r EC (now Article 191 TFEU).[120] The Court rejected this claim and observed that this provision is confined to defining the general objectives of the European legislature in the matter of the environment. Responsibility for deciding what action is to be taken is conferred on the Council by Article 175 EC (now Article 192 TFEU). Moreover, Article 193 TFEU states that the protective measures adopted pursuant to Article 192 TFEU are not to prevent any Member State from maintaining or introducing

---

[117] Cf. Krämer (2007) at 6. This lack of direct applicability prompted the Avosetta group of European environmental lawyers to suggest adding the following provision in the Treaties: 'Subject to imperative reasons of overriding public interests significantly impairing the environment or human health shall be prohibited.' See for more details: http://www.avosetta.org (last visited 7 October 2011).

[118] Cf. the cases discussed above in the context of the proportionality principle; Case C-293/97 *Standley* [1999] ECR I-2603 and Case C-165/09 to C-167/09 *Stichting Natuur en Milieu and others*, Judgment of 26 May 2011.

[119] Joined Cases C-379/08 and C-380/08 *ERG and others* [2010] ECR I-2007 (*ERG II*), para. 39. Emphasis added by the authors. Cf. also Case C-378/08 *ERG and others* [2010] ECR I-1919 (*ERG I*).

[120] Case C-379/92 *Peralta* [1994] ECR I-3453.

more stringent protective measures compatible with the Treaty. Article 191 TFEU therefore could not preclude the disputed Italian legislation.

The scarce national case law on the subject also points in the same direction. In *Duddridge*, the English High Court held that the precautionary principle did not as such impose obligations on Member States.[121]

The integration principle is also reflected in the Charter of Fundamental Rights of the European Union.[122] Article 37 of the Charter contains a text similar, but not identical, to Article 11 TFEU:

'A high level of environmental protection and the improvement of the quality of the environment must be integrated into the policies of the Union and ensured in accordance with the principle of sustainable development.'

A difference is, for instance, that Article 37 Charter only refers to EU 'policies' and not to EU 'activities'. Furthermore, Article 11 TFEU refers more broadly to 'environmental protection requirements', whilst the Charter requires only 'a high level of environmental protection and the improvement of the quality of the environment' to be integrated. According to Article 6(1) TEU, the provisions of the Charter 'shall have the same legal value as the Treaties'.[123]

Fundamental rights and the environment

According to Article 6(3) TEU, fundamental rights, as guaranteed by the European Convention for the Protection of Human Rights and Fundamental Freedoms and as they result from the constitutional traditions common to the Member States, shall constitute general principles of the Union's law. It is well known that this provision is a codification of the case law of the Court of Justice.[124]

The *Rubach* case showed the relevance of the ECHR for Union environmental law.[125] This case involved the duty to prohibit illegal trade in the context of Regulation 338/97 on the protection of species of wild fauna and flora by regulating trade therein. Although Member States enjoy a wide discretion, they are bound to respect the provisions of the European Convention for the Protection of Human Rights and Fundamental Freedoms.

---

[121] High Court, Queen's Bench Division (Smith L.J. & Farquharson L.J.) 3 October 1994, *R. v. Secretary of State for Trade & Industry*, ex parte *Duddridge & others* [1995] 3 C.M.L.R. 231. See also the judgment of the Dutch Den Haag District Court in the *Waterpakt* case, 24 November 1999 *Waterpakt* [2000] *MR* 1, which ruled in the same manner.

[122] OJ 2010 C 83/389.

[123] See on the Charter also our remarks below.

[124] Case 29/69 *Stauder* [1969] ECR 419.

[125] Case C-344/08 *Rubach* [2009] ECR I-7033.

According to Article 6(2) TEU the Union shall accede to the European Convention for the Protection of Human Rights and Fundamental Freedoms.

Although this is not the place to give a treatment of the case law of the European Court of Human Rights relevant to the protection of the environment, environmental issues nowadays do play a more important role than ever before.

> The following *Öneryildiz* case is just to illustrate the importance of this case law.[126] Öneryıldız is a Turkish national who, along with twelve members of his family, was living in a shantytown of Hekimbaşı Ümraniye near Istanbul. This town was nothing more than a collection of slums built on land surrounding a rubbish tip which had been used jointly by four district councils since the 1970s and was under the authority and responsibility of the main City Council of Istanbul. An expert report drawn up on 7 May 1991 at the request of the Üsküdar District Court drew the authorities' attention to the fact that no measure had been taken with regard to the tip in question to prevent a possible explosion of the methane gas being given off by the decomposing refuse. On 28 April 1993, a methane gas explosion occurred on the waste-collection site and the refuse erupting from the pile of waste buried eleven houses situated below it, including the one belonging to Öneryıldız, who lost nine members of his family. Criminal and administrative investigations were carried out into the case, following which the mayors of Ümraniye and Istanbul were brought before the courts. On 4 April 1996, the mayors in question were both convicted of 'negligence in the exercise of their duties' and sentenced to a fine of 160,000 Turkish liras (TRL) and the minimum three-month prison sentence provided for in Article 230 of the Criminal Code, which was, moreover, commuted to a fine. The court ordered a stay of execution of those fines.
>
> Subsequently, the applicant lodged, on his own behalf and on the behalf of his three surviving children, an action for damages in the Istanbul Administrative Court against the authorities whom he deemed liable for the death of his relatives and the destruction of his property. In a judgment of 30 November 1995, the authorities were ordered to pay the applicant and his children TRL 100,000,000 in non-pecuniary damages and TRL 10,000,000 in pecuniary damages (the equivalent at the material time of approximately 2,077 and 208 euros respectively), the latter amount being limited to the destruction of household goods. The applicant complained, under Article 2 (right to life) of the ECHR, that the accident had occurred as a result of negligence on the part of the relevant authorities. He also complained of the deficiencies in the administrative and criminal proceedings instituted subsequently under Article 6 § 1 (right to a fair hearing within a reasonable time) and of Article 13 (right to an effective remedy). The Court held that there had been a violation of Article 2 (right to life) on account of the death of the applicant's relatives and the ineffectiveness of the judicial machinery; that there had been a violation of Article 1 of Protocol No. 1 (protection of property); and that there was no need to examine the applicant's other complaints.

---

[126] ECHR 18 June 2002 *Öneryildiz v. Turkey* – 48939/99 [2002] ECHR 496.

From the case law of the European Court of Human Rights, it is clear that in particular Article 2 (protection of life), Articles 6 and 13 (access to court), Article 8 (privacy), Article 10 (freedom of expression) and Article 1 Protocol 1 (property) can be of some importance for the protection of the environment.[127]

Broadly speaking European environmental legislation probably meets the minimum requirements of the European Convention, with one possible exception[128] and that concerns the limited remedies available to third parties desiring to challenge measures taken by the EU institutions affecting the environment. The arguments of the Court of Justice to the effect that these limited remedies do not violate Articles 6 and 13, in particular, of the European Convention are not very convincing.[129]

In this section, some reference is also necessary to the Charter of Fundamental Rights of the European Union.[130] We already mentioned Article 37 of the Charter containing a text similar to Article 11 TFEU. Although the Charter was, before the entry into force of the Lisbon Treaty, as such not legally binding, the Court of Justice seemed to be willing to acknowledge some sort of legal effect of the Charter, in particular where a directive makes a reference to the Charter.[131] However, this has changed by the Lisbon Treaty. Now the Charter has, according to Article 6(1) EU 'the same legal value as the Treaties.' The provisions of the Charter are binding upon to the Union institutions, bodies, offices and agencies, but upon the Member States only 'when they are implementing Union law'.[132]

> Nowadays, in environmental directives we find a default reference to the Charter. For instance in the preamble of Directive 2003/87 establishing a scheme for greenhouse gas emission allowance trading we read at point 27: 'This Directive respects the fundamental rights and observes the principles recognised in particular by the Charter of Fundamental Rights of the European Union.'[133]

---

[127] Cf. Daniel García San José, *Environmental protection and the European Convention on Human Rights* Council of Europe Publishing 2005. See for a recent example *Dubetska and others* v. *Ukraine*, Application No. 55723/00, Judgment of 10 February 2011.

[128] Cf. in a more general sense European Court of Human Rights 30 June 2005 *Bosphorus Airways* v. *Ireland* 45036/98 [2005] ECHR 440. The Court found that the protection of fundamental rights by Union law can be considered 'equivalent' to that of the Convention system. Also in more recent case law the European Court of Human Rights took EU environmental law into account: cf. ECHR 28 September 2010 *Mangouras* v. *Spain*, Application No. 12050/04.

[129] See on this extensively Chapter 5, section 5.2.

[130] OJ 2000 C 346/1.

[131] Case C-540/03 *EP* v. *Council* [2006] ECR I-5769, para. 38 and Case T-377/00 *Philip Morris International* v. *Commission* [2003] ECR II-1, para. 122.

[132] Article 51(1) Charter.

[133] OJ 2003 L 275/32. See for another example Directive 2005/35 on ship-source pollution and on the introduction of penalties for infringements, OJ 2005 L 255/11. Point 16 of the preamble reads: 'This Directive fully respects the Charter of fundamental rights of the European Union; any person suspected of having

3 Article 191 TFEU

3.1 The Objectives of European Environment Policy

The environmental objectives to be pursued by the EU are formulated in the first paragraph of Article 191 TFEU.[134] They are:
· preserving, protecting and improving the quality of the environment;
· protecting human health;
· prudent and rational utilisation of natural resources;
· promoting measures at international level to deal with regional or worldwide environmental problems, and in particular combating climate change.

Preserving, protecting and improving the quality of the environment
The first objective formulated in Article 191 TFEU is fairly general and indeterminate. The term environment is given no further definition in the Treaty itself.[135] On the one hand, this is an advantage in that the objective is sufficiently flexible to be adapted to new developments and new needs for protection.[136] On the other hand, it is impossible to determine with absolute certainty from the Treaty itself what might be understood by a European environment policy. The following problems of interpretation present themselves in connection with the scope of these environmental objectives.

Having regard to, *inter alia,* the Habitats Directive, it seems quite clear that this objective also include protection of nature and landscape values. The first consideration of the preamble to this directive states that the preservation, protection and improvement of the quality of the environment, 'including the conservation of natural habitats and of wild fauna and flora, are an essential objective of general interest pursued by the Community'. In view of Article 13 TFEU one could even argue that 'animal welfare' seems to be covered by this objective.[137]

The Zoo Directive illustrates that the care and accommodation of animals in zoos is within the scope of application of Article 191 TFEU, albeit that animal welfare

---

committed an infringement must be guaranteed a fair and impartial hearing and the penalties must be proportional'.

[134] Although Article 191 TFEU defines the objectives to be pursued in the context of environmental policy, Article 192 TFEU constitutes the legal basis on which Community measures are adopted; Case C-284/95 *Safety Hi-Tech* [1998] ECR I-4301, para. 43.

[135] Cf. also the European Council's Declaration on the environmental imperative of 15 June 1990, Bulletin EC 1990 No. 6, at 16-20.

[136] Cf. Krämer (2007) at 2 who refers to an all-embracing concept.

[137] Cf. Directive 1999/22 relating to the keeping of wild animals in zoos, OJ 1999 L 94/24. See however Directive 2010/63 on the protection of animals used for scientific purposes OJ 2010 L 276/33 which is based on Article 114 TFEU. Cf. also Regulation 1007/2009 on trade in seal products OJ 2009 L 286/36.

cannot be regarded a 'general principle of Community law'.[138] In general, however, animal welfare will find its regulatory basis in the Treaty provision on the Common Agricultural Policy (CAP); the Articles 39 *et seq.* TFEU.[139] It is also possible that certain aspects of animal welfare are integrated in secondary legislation. For instance, Article 4 (1)(b)(iii) of the Pesticide Directive 91/414 stipulates that a plant protection product is not authorised unless 'it does not cause unnecessary suffering and pain to vertebrates to be controlled'.[140]

Not only measures which result *directly* in the improvement of the environment fall under this objective, but also those which *result* in the improvement of the environment in a more indirect fashion fall within its scope.

In the preamble to Directive 2003/4 on public access to environmental information, it is stated that 'increased public access to environmental information and the dissemination of such information contribute to a greater awareness of environmental matters, a free exchange of views, more effective participation by the public in environmental decision-making *and, eventually, to a better environment*.[141] More generally, it is arguable that decision-making in respect of the non-substantive or procedural aspects of environmental legislation, such as issues of legal protection, authorisation procedures and even measures concerning the administrative organisation of the environment sector, is also within its compass.

With respect to the REACH Regulation the Court ruled that the registration obligation imposed on manufacturers and importers serves to improve information for the public down the supply chain as to the risks and that, consequently, such registration must be regarded as a means of enhancing the objective of protecting human health and the environment.[142]

A political 'hot potato', prior to the entry into force of the Lisbon Treaty, concerned the question to what extent, if any, Article 192 TFEU could be used as legal basis to harmonise national criminal law.

Based on the so-called 'Second Pillar' of the 'old' EU Treaty, the Council adopted Framework Decision 2003/80 on the protection of the environment through criminal law.[143] In essence, this framework decision laid down a number of environmen-

---

[138] Case C-189/01 *Jippes a.o.* [2001] ECR I-5689, paras. 71-79. See in general on animal welfare: the Amsterdam Treaty Protocol on protection and welfare of animals, OJ 1997 C 340/110. Cf. Krämer (2007) at 2-3.

[139] For instance Directive 1999/74 laying down minimum standards for the protection of laying hens, OJ 1999 L 203/53 and Regulation 882/2004 on official controls performed to ensure the verification of compliance with feed and food law, animal health and animal welfare rules, OJ 2004 L 165/1. See on CAP also Chapter 2, section 7.2.

[140] Cf. Case T-229/04 *Sweden v. Commission* [2007] ECR II-2437.

[141] OJ 2003 L 41/26, emphasis added by the authors. Cf. Lee (2005) at 69-73.

[142] Case C-558/07 *S.P.C.M.* [2009] ECR I-5789, paras. 41, *et seq.*

[143] OJ 2003 L 29/55.

tal offences, in respect of which the Member States were required to introduce criminal penalties. The Commission challenged the Council's choice of the legal basis for the decision. It submitted that the purpose and content of the latter are within the scope of the Articles 174 to 176 of the old EC Treaty (now Articles 191 to 193 TFEU). The Court of Justice acknowledged that the framework decision did indeed entail partial harmonisation of the criminal laws of the Member States and that as a general rule, neither criminal law nor the rules of criminal procedure fall within the scope of the Articles 174 to 176 of the old EC Treaty. However, the Court followed by noting that this 'does not prevent the Community legislature, when the application of effective, proportionate and dissuasive criminal penalties by the competent national authorities is an *essential measure* for combating serious environmental offences, from taking measures which relate to the criminal law of the Member States which it considers *necessary* in order to ensure that the rules which it lays down on environmental protection are fully effective.' [emphasis added] The framework decision had as its main purpose the protection of the environment (and not harmonising criminal law as such) and therefore could have been properly adopted on the basis of Article 175 EC (now Article 192 TFEU).

This judgment was confirmed in Case C-440/05 *Commission* v. *Council*.[144] In that case the Commission was seeking annulment of Council Framework Decision 2005/667 to strengthen the criminal-law framework for the enforcement of the law against ship-source pollution.[145] However, the Court made it in that case perfectly clear that 'the determination of the type and level of the criminal penalties to be applied does not fall within the Community's sphere of competence'.

In sum: whenever criminal penalties are essential for combating serious offences against the environment Article 192 TFEU provides for the correct legal basis to require Member States to introduce such penalties,[146] but it does not provide a legal basis to determine the *type* and *level* of criminal penalties. This would require legislative measures under Article 82 *et seq.* TFEU.

In the pre-Maastricht period, the territorial limitation of the environmental objectives was a matter for discussion. In other words, can the the European legislature act not so much to protect its own environment, but to preserve the environment outside the EU, to address global and regional environmental problems, or even the environment of other states? Since 'Maastricht' this problem of interpretation has largely been resolved now the fourth objective of Article 191 TFEU explicitly includes 'promoting measures at international level to deal with regional or worldwide environmental problems.' And the Lisbon Treaty added 'and in particular combating climate change'. This objective will be discussed in slightly more detail below.

---

[144] Case C-440/05 *Commission* v. *Council* [2007] ECR I-9097.

[145] OJ 2005 L 255/164.

[146] Cf. now Directive 2008/99 on the protection of the environment through criminal law, OJ 2008 L 328/28 and Directive 2009/123 amending Directive 2005/35 ship-source pollution and on the introduction of penalties, OJ 2009 L 280/52. See on these directives Chapter 4, section 5 in particular.

An entirely different matter is the question whether the EU is entitled
to concern itself with *local* and *regional* environmental problems. Would, for
instance, the Union legislature has a competence to maximise the allowed noise
level caused by local bars and nightclubs? As Article 191 TFEU does not contain
any such restriction, this must be regarded as a possibility.[147] Of course, the
principle of subsidiarity would have to be taken into consideration here, which
might require restraint in this respect. Article 2(3) of the Habitats Directive is
relevant in this context. Protective measures taken pursuant to this directive
must explicitly take account of 'regional and local characteristics.'

The last problem of interpretation that must be discussed concerns the
formulation 'preserving, protecting and improving'. This is also broadly and
flexibly worded. It affords possibilities to take environmental measures of a
preservative, curative, repressive, precautionary and active nature. There is no
question of a restriction to a certain type of measure.

> A reference to 'preserving, protecting and improving the quality of the environ-
> ment' can, for example, be found in the preamble to Regulation 1367/2006 on the
> application of the provisions of the Aarhus Convention on Access to Information,
> Public Participation in Decision-making and Access to Justice in Environmental
> Matters to Community institutions and bodies and Directive 2006/7 concerning
> the management of bathing water quality.[148]

Protecting human health

The most important question of interpretation in respect of this objective
is whether 'protecting *human* health' is a wider concept than protecting *public*
health. The answer must be that it is. Protection of public health indicates measures required to protect the *collective* health interests of people in a given society. However, the wording of Article 191 TFEU makes action possible even when
it is not so much a collective interest that is at stake as the interest of certain
individuals or groups in society. Of course, the principle of subsidiarity must be
taken into account in such cases.

However, it should be noted that the distinction between the various
concepts of 'health' has become somewhat blurred, both in the practice of the
Union legislature as well as in the judgments of the Court of Justice.

> A rather standard reference to protect human health can be found, for example,
> in Directive 2001/18 on the deliberate release into the environment of genetically

---

[147] Cf. however Case C-309/96 *Annibaldi* [1997] ECR I-7493 where the Court ruled that as the law stands at
present, regional legislation, which establishes a nature and archaeological park in order to protect and
enhance the value of the environment and the cultural heritage of the area concerned, applies to a situation which does not fall within the scope of Community law. The case concerned the authorities' refusal
to grant Annibaldi permission to plant an orchard of 3 hectares within the perimeter of a regional park.

[148] OJ 2006 L 264/13 and OJ 2006 L 64/37.

modified organisms.[149] According to Article 1 of the Directive its objective is 'to protect human health and the environment'. A similar reference can be found in Article 1 of the new Bathing Water Directive.[150] References to *public* health' can be found in many Union environmental measures, for instance in Article 12 of Directive 2009/128 establishing a framework for Community action to achieve the sustainable use of pesticides.[151] Finally, a reference to *personal* health' can be found in point 2 of the preamble of Directive 2003/35 providing for public participation in respect of the drawing up of certain plans and programmes relating to the environment.[152]

The blurring of the distinction between the concepts 'human health' and 'public health' is also manifest in the judgments of the Court of Justice, for example, in the *Fumicot* case, where the applicability of Article 36 TFEU to measures restricting the importation of plant protection products was at issue.[153] This provision does in fact talk of the protection of health and life of humans, animals or plants, and not of 'public health'. However, in its judgment, the Court equates the two concepts: 'In that respect, it is not disputed that the national rules in question are intended to protect public health and that they therefore come within the exception provided for in Article 36.'

A second problem of interpretation concerns the fact that the article only refers to *human* health. Does this therefore mean that the protection of animal health and flora and fauna must be regarded as lying outside the scope of the objective? On the other hand, it has been shown above that the protection of flora and fauna and animal welfare may be included within the first objective mentioned in Article 191 TFEU. The restriction of the second objective to the protection of human health does not therefore seem essential.

Prudent and rational utilisation of natural resources

It is understood that according to international law, states have the sovereign right to exploit their own resources pursuant to their own environmental and developmental policies.[154] It is also understood that to achieve sustainable development states should reduce and eliminate unsustainable patterns of production and consumption.[155] In the Sixth Environment Action Programme, a prudent use of natural resources has been acknowledged as a condition for sustainable development.[156] However, what precisely should be understood by

---

[149] OJ 2001 L 106/1. See for another reference to *human* health' point 2 of Directive 2011/65 on the restriction of the use of certain hazardous substances in electrical and electronic equipment OJ 2011 L 174/88.

[150] Directive 2006/7 concerning the management of bathing water quality OJ 2006 L 64/37.

[151] OJ 2009 L 309/71.

[152] OJ 2003 L 156/17.

[153] Case 272/80 *Frans-Nederlandse Maatschappij voor Biologische Producten* [1981] ECR 3277.

[154] Cf. Principle 2 of the so-called Rio Declaration on Environment and Development.

[155] Principle 9 of the Rio Declaration.

[156] Decision 1600/2002, OJ 2002 L 242/1.

'natural resources' is not entirely clear.[157] From an international law point of view, Principle 2 of the Declaration of the United Nations Conference on the Human Environment (the Stockholm Declaration)[158] may offer some assistance. Here natural resources are taken to mean: 'natural resources of the earth including the air, water, land, flora and fauna and especially representative samples of natural ecosystems [...]'. The following natural resources can assumed to be included: wood, minerals, water, oil, gas and chemical substances. The following policy items might give some indication as to what might fall under the management of natural resources: nature conservation, soil protection, waste disposal (encouraging re-use), policy on urban areas, coastal areas and mountainous areas, disaster policy, water management, an environmentally friendly agricultural policy and energy-saving.[159] On the basis of the above, it can be concluded that this objective also has a wide scope.

> References to this objective can be found in e.g. Directive 2010/75 /on industrial emissions[160] (integrated pollution prevention and control), Directive 91/676 on nitrates[161] (protection of living resources), in Regulation 106/2008 on a Community energy-efficiency labelling programme for office equipment[162] (rational use of energy), Directive 1999/94 relating to the availability of consumer information on fuel economy and CO_2 emissions in respect of the marketing of new passenger cars[163] and the Water Framework Directive (surface waters and groundwater).[164]

According to Article 192(2)(c) TFEU Union 'measures significantly affecting a Member State's choice between different energy sources and the general structure of its energy supply' are still to be decided by the Council acting unanimously.[165]

Regional or worldwide environmental problems

At the time of the Single European Act, the question to what extent the environmental objectives were limited in a territorial sense was a matter of discussion. In the present version of the Treaty, it has at any rate become clear that Article 191 TFEU does in principle allow room for extraterritorial environmental

---

[157] Cf. the Communication from the Commission, Thematic Strategy on the sustainable use of natural resources, COM (2005) 670 final.

[158] *ILM* 1972, at 1416.

[159] Cf. Krämer (2007) at 14.

[160] OJ 2010 L 334/17.

[161] OJ 1991 L 375/1.

[162] OJ 2008 L 39/1.

[163] OJ 1999 L 12/16.

[164] Directive 2000/60 establishing a framework for Community action in the field of water policy, OJ 2000 L 327/1. Cf. also Directive 2006/7 concerning the management of bathing water quality OJ 2006 L 64/37.

[165] See more on this provision in Chapter 2, section 1.

objectives. By the inclusion of 'promoting measures at international level to deal with regional or worldwide environmental problems, and in particular combating climate change', existing practice has been confirmed.[166]

An important part of European environment policy is not concerned primarily with protecting the EU's own environment, but the environment outside the EU. The Sixth Environment Action Programme stresses the need for a positive and constructive role of the European Union in the protection of the global environment.[167] The carrying capacity of the global environment is even regarded as one of the Union's objectives to be pursued at the international level. The following legislative measures are examples of its concern and responsibility for the environment outside the EU:

- Regulation 3254/91 prohibiting the introduction of pelts;[168]
- Regulation 348/81 concerning the protection of whales;[169]
- Directive 89/370 concerning the importation of skins of seal pups;[170]
- the measures in Regulation 1013/2006 on shipments of waste;[171]
- Regulation 338/97 on the protection of species of wild fauna and flora by regulating trade therein.[172]

However, even some directives that are primarily designed to protect the EU environment contain references to 'the global environment' or the environment of 'third countries'.

For example, the overall objective of Directive 99/31 on the landfill of waste refers to measures to prevent negative effects on the environment, 'and on the global environment, including the greenhouse effect'.[173] Another example is provided by Article 1 of Directive 94/62 on packaging and packaging waste.[174] The directive specifically aims to protect the environment of all Member States as well as of third countries.

In addition, the Union is a party to several multilateral conventions which have an extraterritorial objective, such as the 1985 Vienna Convention for the

---

[166] Cf. Krämer (2007) at 3.

[167] Decision 1600/2002 laying down the Sixth Community Environment Action Programme, OJ 2002 L 242/1.

[168] OJ 1991 L 308/1.

[169] OJ 1981 L 39/1.

[170] OJ 1989 L 163/37.

[171] OJ 2006 L 190/1.

[172] Regulation 338/97, OJ L 61/1.

[173] Article 1 of Directive 1999/31, OJ 1999 L 182/1. Other measures aimed at reducing emissions causing global warming include, e.g., Directive 2003/87 establishing a scheme for greenhouse gas emission allowance trading within the Community, OJ 2003 L 275/32.

[174] See, for example, Directive 94/62 on packaging and packaging waste, OJ 1994 L 365/10. The directive aims to protect the environment of all Member States *as well as of third countries* (Art. 1).

protection of the ozone layer and the 1987 Montreal Protocol, the 1989 Basel Convention on the control of transboundary movements of waste, the 1992 Framework Convention on Climate Change and subsequent Protocols[175] and the 1992 Convention on Biological Diversity.[176] All implementing measures of the Union are of course also directed to the global or extra-territorial objectives of the agreements.

Although there is ample practice of European legislative measures aiming to protect the environment outside the EU, the phrase 'regional or worldwide environmental problems' is still unclear in several respects. For example, is it intended to exclude unilateral measures? A large part of the EU's present extraterritorial environment policy has in fact been created by means of such measures. Nor is it clear whether, by referring only to 'regional or worldwide' problems, action to protect the environment of only one or a few third states is excluded. Take, for example, a prohibition on imports of tropical hardwood that has not been sustainably produced. It is highly debatable whether this would amount to a regional or worldwide environmental problem. In general, this kind of case will involve specific consequences for the environment in one state or a number of states.

For the time being, there is a lot to be said in favour of not interpreting Article 191 TFEU too narrowly. Nor should unilateral environmental measures or environmental measures directed at protecting the environment in only one state or a few states *a priori* be excluded, even though the problem of the international law constraints of such measures is at its most pronounced in this very case. Article 191 TFEU leaves room to seek to attain extraterritorial protective objectives, though this power should be interpreted in accordance with principles of public international law. Support for this view can be found both in Article 191 TFEU and in the case law of the Court of Justice.

With respect to the Treaty, we may also point to Article 52 TEU, which provides that the Treaties apply to the states named in the article. According to general principles of international law, this means that the Treaties in any event bind the parties with respect to the entire territory over which they are sovereign, unless the Treaties allow exceptions or apply special rules (e.g. Article 355 TFEU). As Article 52 TEU does not contain any reference to the territory of the Member States, it cannot be regarded as limiting the territorial scope of the Treaties to territory which falls under the sovereignty (or full jurisdiction) of the Member States. The scope of the Treaties and other European law may indeed extend beyond that territory, to the extent international law allows the Member States to exercise a limited functional jurisdiction.

> Directive 2001/81 on national emission ceilings for certain atmospheric pollut-ant provides a rare example of an environmental measure explicitly expanding

---

[175] OJ 1994 L 33/13.
[176] OJ 1993 L 309/1.

39

its scope beyond the 'territory' of the Member States.[177] Article 2 states: 'This Directive covers emissions in the territory of the Member States *and their exclusive economic zones* from all sources of the pollutants referred to in Article 4 which arise as a result of human activities.'[178] With respect to the Habitats Directive, we may also refer to case law applying that directive to the Continental Shelf.[179]

Examples outside the environmental sector are the competence of Member States in respect of the Continental Shelf, the fishery zones and any exclusive economic zones. Being able to exercise such powers outside the direct territory of the EU Member States is conditional on the subject matter of the functional jurisdiction falling within the material sphere of operation of the relevant Treaty provisions, and on the provisions themselves not containing any restriction limiting the territorial sphere of operation to the territory of the Member States. This view finds support in the case law of the Court, and particularly in the *Kramer* case.[180] One of the matters at issue was to what extent the authority of the Union extended to fishing on the high seas. After the Court had established that the European legislature had internal competence to adopt measures for the conservation of the biological resources of the seas, it continued 'it follows [...] from the very nature of things that the rule-making authority of the Community *ratione materiae* also extends – in so far as the Member States have similar authority under public international law – to fishing on the high seas.' This judgment was confirmed by the Court in the *Drift-Net* case, in which a prohibition on the use for fishing of drift-nets longer than 2.5 km was held to be valid.[181] The validity of the measure was disputed on the grounds that the Union was not competent to take measures to preserve fish populations in the open sea. The Court dismissed this line of reasoning here, too.

A translation of the judgments in the *Kramer* and *Drift-Net* cases in terms of environmental law leads to the following conclusion. In so far as the Member States are competent under international law to protect the environment outside their own territories, the Union must also be regarded as being competent to take such measures, at least to the extent the subject matter of the measure falls within the scope of application of Article 191 TFEU. Action to protect the environment extraterritorially cannot therefore be regarded as being confined to international agreements or to those sectors where regional or global problems are at issue. The fourth indent of Article 191(1) TFEU should not be interpreted restrictively. In view of the transboundary nature of the environment,

---

[177] OJ 2001 L 309/22.

[178] Emphasis added.

[179] English High Court, Queen's Bench Division (Maurice Kay J) 5 November 1999 *Regina* v. *Secretary of State for Trade and Industry*, ex parte *Greenpeace* [2000] Env. L.R. 221 which ruled, relying *inter alia* on the *Kramer* case that the Habitats Directive is also applicable outside the territorial waters of the UK. Cf. also Case C-6/04 *Commission* v. *UK* [2005] ECR I-9017, para. 119.

[180] Joined Cases 3, 4 and 6/76 *Kramer* [1976] ECR 1279.

[181] Case C-405/92 *Etablissements Armand Mondiet* v. *Société Armement Islais* [1993] ECR I-6133.

this follows – to quote the *Kramer* judgment – 'from the very nature of things'. However, it should be remembered that extraterritorial environmental powers must be exercised in accordance with international law, including the provisions of the WTO.[182] In exercising its extraterritorial powers in respect of the environment, the Union has to act with regard to international law constraints. As has been stated, any interpretation of Article 191 TFEU, which would bring the Union into conflict with its obligations under international law, must be rejected.

3.2   The Principles of European Environmental Policy

Article 191(2) TFEU sets out the principles on which European environment policy is based.[183] Union policy on the environment 'shall aim' at a high level of protection taking into account the diversity of situations in the various regions of the Union. And it 'shall be based' on:
- the precautionary principle;
- the principle that preventive action should be taken (the prevention principle);
- the principle that environmental damage should as a priority be rectified at source (the source principle) and
- the principle that the polluter should pay (the polluter pays principle).

European environmental legislation will have to translate these principles into concrete obligations for the Member States. It will then be possible to interpret the Union measures in the light of these principles. In this chapter, section 2, we have discussed in the context of the integration principle the question to what extent these principles are legally enforceable. We concluded that only in exceptional cases would a measure be susceptible to annulment because the environmental principles of Article 191(2) TFEU were not sufficiently taken into account.

High level of protection

Article 191(2) TFEU provides that a European environment policy shall aim at a high level of protection taking into account the diversity of situations in the various regions of the Union. This high level of protection principle is one of the most important substantive principles of European environment policy. It is stated at various places in the Treaties. It was the Treaty of Amsterdam which ensured that the principle was included in the general objectives of the EC Trea-

---

[182] See in a general sense the Court's judgment in Case C-286/90 *Anklagemindigheden v. Poulsen and Diva Navigation* [1992] ECR I-6019 and more recently Case C-308/06 *Intertanko and others* [2008] ECR I-4057, para.51. Cf. Wiers (2002) and Montini (2005) with respect to the WTO.

[183] Cf. in general De Sadeleer (2005) and on the way national courts apply the European environmental principles Macrory (2004).

ty.[184] Under Article 2 EC, it was a task to promote 'a high level of protection and improvement of the quality of the environment'. Nevertheless, it should be quite clear that a high level of protection is not the same thing as the *highest* possible level of protection.[185] Furthermore, the case law of the Court of Justice shows that the high level of protection principle does not preclude the Union legislature, exercising its discretion under this provision, to achieve a degree of balance between, on the one hand, environmental protection and, on the other hand, legitimate economic interests.[186]

This 'high level of protection' principle can also be found in the 'internal market' provision Article 114(3) TFEU which now reads as follows:

> 'The Commission, in its proposals envisaged in paragraph 1 concerning health, safety, environmental protection and consumer protection, will take as a base a high level of protection, taking account in particular of any new development based on scientific facts. Within their respective powers, the European Parliament and the Council will also seek to achieve this objective.'[187]

That the enforceability of the principle is limited, is apparent from the text of Article 191(2) TFEU. European policy 'shall aim' at a high level of protection.'[188] The text of Article 114(3) TFEU points in the same direction. This provision requires the Commission to 'take' a high level of protection as a base for its proposal, however, the 'seek to achieve' obligation upon the Union legislature still makes it doubtful indeed whether this principle is subject to intense review in a court of law to challenge the legality of the measures adopted by it. Krämer however argues that where a Commission proposal is not based on high level of environmental protection, the European Parliament has right of action against the Commission under Article 263 TFEU. We fail to see however how a proposal of the Commission can be regarded as an 'act' in the meaning of Article 263 TFEU.[189]

> An explicit reference to this principle can, for instance, be found in Directive 2008/1 concerning integrated pollution prevention and control, the so-called

---

[184] Although its origin lies in the 'old' Article 100a(3) EEC, included in the Treaty by the Single European Act.

[185] Cf. Case C-284/95 *Safety Hi-Tech Srl* v. *S. & T. Srl* [1998] ECR I-4301, para. 49: 'whilst it is undisputed that Article 130r(2) of the Treaty requires Community policy in environmental matters to aim for a high level of protection, such a level of protection, to be compatible with that provision, does not necessarily have to be the highest that is technically possible.'

[186] Case C-343/09 *Afton Chemical*, Judgment of 8 July 2010, para. 64.

[187] See also Chapter 2, section 3.

[188] The standard of review to be applied is, once again, the 'manifestly inappropriate' test; see Case C-343/09 *Afton Chemical*, Judgment of 8 July 2010.

[189] Krämer (2007) at 13.

IPPC Directive.[190] Its aim is to achieve integrated prevention and control of pollution 'in order to achieve a high level of protection of the environment taken as a whole.' Other examples of legislation containing such references in their preambles include Regulation 1013/2006 on shipments of waste and Directive 2002/49 relating to the assessment and management of environmental noise.[191] Also the, current, Sixth Community Environment Action Programme contains various references to this principle.[192]

The precautionary principle[193]

Since 'Maastricht' the Treaty has stated that Union policy on the environment shall be based on the precautionary principle. This principle has its roots in what is described in German environmental law as the *Vorsorgeprinzip*.[194] This means that, if there is a strong suspicion that a certain activity may have environmentally harmful consequences, it is better to act before it is too late rather than wait until full scientific evidence is available which incontrovertibly shows the causal connection.[195] In other words, the principle of precaution may therefore justify action to prevent damage in some cases even though the causal link cannot be clearly established on the basis of available scientific evidence.[196] Its objective is to avoid potential risks.[197] Or as some authors have put it: *in dubio pro natura*.[198] Another implication of the precautionary principle, at least according to the European Commission, is that the Union has the right to establish the level of protection of the environment, human, animal and plant health, that it deems appropriate.[199]

According to the Commission guidelines the precautionary principle is all about 'risk-management', which does not mean that all risks must be reduced to zero. Judging what is an acceptable level of risk for society is a political responsibility. Where action is deemed necessary, measures based on the precautionary principle should be proportional to the chosen level of protection, non-discriminatory in their application, consistent with similar measures already taken,

---

[190] OJ 2008 L 24/18.

[191] OJ 2006 L 190/1 and OJ 2002 L 189/12.

[192] Decision 1600/2002 laying down the Sixth Community Environment Action Programme, OJ 2002 L 242/1.

[193] Cf. in general, Trouwborst (2006), De Sadeleer (2006) and Lee (2005) at 97 *et seq.*

[194] Cf. Marr & Schwemer (2003).

[195] Cf. also Principle 15 of the Rio Declaration: 'In order to protect the environment, the precautionary approach shall be widely applied by States according to their capabilities. Where there are threats of serious or irreversible damage, lack of full scientific certainty shall not be used as a reason for postponing cost-effective measures to prevent environmental degradation.'

[196] The Communication of the Commission, Single Market and the Environment, COM (99) 263. Cf. Heyvaert (2006).

[197] Case T-229/04 *Sweden* v. *Commission* [2007] ECR II-2437, para. 161.

[198] Backes & Verschuuren (1998) at 43.

[199] COM (2000) 1, containing Commission guidelines on how to apply the precautionary principle.

based on an examination of the potential benefits and costs of action or lack of action and subject to review in the light of new scientific data.

In the meantime, the precautionary principle has been applied by the Court of Justice in its case law.[200] Where there is scientific uncertainty as to the existence or extent of risks to human health, the *institutions* may take protective measures without having to wait until the reality and seriousness of those risks become fully apparent.[201] A correct application of the precautionary principle presupposes, according to the Court of Justice, identification of the potentially negative consequences for health of the proposed use of the substance at issue, secondly, a comprehensive assessment of the risk to health based on the most reliable scientific data available and the most recent results of international research.[202] In *Gowan* the Court concluded:

> 'Where it proves to be impossible to determine with certainty the existence or extent of the alleged risk because of the insufficiency, inconclusiveness or imprecision of the results of studies conducted, but the likelihood of real harm to public health persists should the risk materialise, the precautionary principle justifies the adoption of restrictive measures, provided they are non-discriminatory and objective.'

This case law shows the consequences of the precautionary principle also for the interpretation of the first sentence of Article 191(3) TFEU, which provides that in preparing its policy on the environment, the Union shall take account of 'available scientific and technical data'. In the 'old' days, this could easily have been used by the Union as a ground for not acting until there was absolute proof of the causes of certain undesirable environmental effects. Such an interpretation would now be at odds with the precautionary principle.

With respect to the Member States, the Court also acknowledged the importance of the precautionary principle in applying so-called 'safeguard clauses' in directives.[203]

---

[200] Cf. for instance, with respect of non-compliance by France of GMO Directive 2001/18, Case C-121/07 *Commission* v. *France* [2008] ECR I-9159, para. 74, calling the precautionary principle a 'fundamental principle' of environmental protection.

[201] Cf. Case C-157/96 *National Farmers' Union a.o.* [1998] ECR I-2211, para. 63 and Case C-180/96 *UK* v. *Commission* [1998] ECR I-2265, para. 99. Cf. also Joined Cases T-125/96 *Boehringer* [1999] ECR II-3427 and Case C-236/01 *Monsanto Agricoltura Italia and Others* [2003] ECR I-8105.

[202] Case C-333/08 *Commission* v. *France* [2010] ECR I-757, para. 92; Case C-343/09 *Afton Chemical*, Judgment of 8 July 2010 and Case C-77/09 *Gowan Comércio Internacional e Serviços*, Judgment of 22 December 2010.

[203] See on safeguard clauses this chapter, section 3.2.

With respect to the safeguard clause of Article 12(1) of Regulation 258/97,[204] the Court of Justice ruled that:[205]

'protective measures may be taken pursuant to Article 12 of Regulation No 258/97 interpreted in the light of the precautionary principle even if it proves impossible to carry out as full a risk assessment as possible in the particular circumstances of a given case because of the inadequate nature of the available scientific data [...].

Such measures presuppose, in particular, that the risk assessment available to the national authorities provides specific evidence which, without precluding scientific uncertainty, makes it possible reasonably to conclude on the basis of the most reliable scientific evidence available and the most recent results of international research that the implementation of those measures is necessary in order to avoid novel foods which pose potential risks to human health being offered on the market.'

Indeed, the inadequate nature of available scientific data does not preclude a Member State or the EU institutions from taking protective measures. However, the Court of Justice is not giving a *carte blanche* either in the sense that the burden of proof is reversed unreservedly.[206] Nor will mere hypothetical risks suffice for taking action.[207] Protective measures can be adopted only if a risk assessment has first carried out which is as complete as possible given the particular circumstances of the individual case, from which it is apparent that, in the light of the precautionary principle, the implementation of such measures is necessary in order to ensure that there is no danger for the human health and the environment.

The case law on the precautionary principle is also relevant with respect to the application of Article 114(5) TFEU. This provision requires 'new scientific evidence' in order to accept Member States' introducing environmental legislation derogating from internal market measures. Article 114 TFEU should be

---

[204] Which reads: 'Where a Member State, as a result of new information or a reassessment of existing information, has detailed grounds for considering that the use of a food or a food ingredient complying with this regulation endangers human health or the environment, that Member State may either temporarily restrict or suspend the trade in and use of the food or food ingredient in question in its territory. It shall immediately inform the other Member States and the Commission thereof, giving the grounds for its decision.'

[205] Case C-236/01 *Monsanto* [2003] ECR I-8105.

[206] See, for instance, Case C-314/99 *Netherlands v. Commission* [2002] ECR I-5521, where the Court annulled Section 3 of the Annex to Commission Directive 1999/51 (tin, PCP and cadmium). The Commission acknowledged in that case that it did not possess sufficiently reliable scientific information for the measures taken.

[207] Case T-229/04 *Sweden v. Commission* [2007] ECR II-2437, para. 161. This case concerned the annulment of Commission Directive 2003/112 to include paraquat as an active substance ex Article 5 of the Pesticide Directive 91/414. Cf. also Case C-77/09 *Gowan Comércio Internacional e Serviços*, Judgment of 22 December 2010.

interpreted in the light of the precautionary principle.[208] Of course, this does not mean that the precautionary principle implies that the conditions for application of that provision do not have to be met at all.[209] Finally, it is the authors' opinion that the Member States' powers under Article 36 TFEU and the 'rule of reason' must be interpreted in the same manner.[210]

A clear example of the precautionary principle in secondary law could be found in the Directives 90/219 and 2001/18 on genetically modified micro-organisms.[211] It is stated that whereas the precise nature and scale of risks associated with genetically modified micro-organisms are not yet fully known, the risk involved must be assessed case by case. And that the Member States are required, in accordance with the precautionary principle, to ensure that all appropriate measures are taken to avoid adverse effects on human health and the environment which might arise from the deliberate release or the placing on the market of GMOs.

Another example can be found in Annex IV of Directive 2008/1 (the IPPC Directive).[212] Annex IV contains considerations to be taken into account when determining best available techniques 'bearing in mind the likely costs and benefits of a measure and the principles of precaution and prevention'. One of the considerations is formulated as 'the need to prevent or reduce to a minimum the overall impact of the emissions on the environment and the risks to it'. With respect to definition of 'waste', it is also clear that this concept has to be interpreted in the light of the precautionary principle.[213]

With respect to the Habitats Directive, Article 6(3) must be mentioned. According to the first sentence of it, any plan or project not directly connected with or necessary to the management of the site but likely to have a significant effect thereon, either individually or in combination with other plans or projects, is to be subject to appropriate assessment of its implications for the site in view of the site's conservation objectives. The Court of Justice has held that the requirement for an appropriate assessment of the implications of a plan or project is thus conditional on its being likely to have a significant effect on the site. In the light, in particular, of the precautionary principle, such a risk exists if it cannot be excluded

---

[208] Cf. Commission Decision 1999/832, OJ 1999 L 329/25 (*Dutch creosote*). See also Chapter 3, section 6.

[209] Joined Cases T-366/03 and T-235/04 *Land Oberösterreich and Austria* v. *Commission* [2005] ECR II-4005, para. 71.

[210] See Chapter 6, sections 4.3 and 4.4.

[211] OJ 1990 L 117/1 and OJ 2001/106/1. See also Article 1 of Regulation 1946/2003 on transboundary movements of genetically modified organisms, OJ 2003 L 287/1. Cf. also Case C-6/99 *Association Greenpeace France* v. *Ministère de l'Agriculture et de la Pêche* [2000] ECR I-1651, paras. 40-47. Cf. in general on GMO and the precautionary principle Weiner (2010).

[212] OJ 2008 L 24/18. See on this directive Chapter 8, section 5.

[213] E.g. Case C-9/00 *Palin Granit and Vehmassalon kansanterveystyön kuntayhtymän hallitus* [2002] ECR I-3533, paras. 22 and 23. See also Chapter 8, section 17.1.

on the basis of objective information that the plan or project will have a significant effect on the site concerned.[214]

The prevention principle

European policy on the environment shall be based on the fundamental[215] principle that preventive action should be taken. The principle of preventive action was included in the Treaty by the Single European Act. Put simply, prevention is better than cure. The prevention principle allows action to be taken to protect the environment at an early stage. It is no longer primarily a question of repairing damage after it has occurred. Instead the principle calls for measures to be taken to prevent damage occurring at all.

> This is demonstrated by Directive 94/62 on packaging and packaging waste.[216] The directive makes it quite clear that the best means of preventing the creation of packaging waste is to reduce the overall volume of packaging. Article 9 of the directive requires Member States to ensure that packaging may be placed on the market only if it complies with all essential requirements defined by the directive. The prevention principle must not be confused with the precautionary principle, which is in essence more far-reaching (see above).[217]
>
> Another example is Directive 2011/65 on the restriction of the use of certain hazardous substances in electrical and electronic equipment.[218] Prevention is defined, *inter alia*, as measures that reduce the content of harmful substances in materials and products.
>
> Pollution prevention is of course also the key word in the IPPC Directive.[219]
>
> Finally, we can mention Regulation 842/2006 on certain fluorinated greenhouse gases which contains various references to the prevention and minimisation of emissions of fluorinated greenhouse gases.[220]

The Third Environmental Action Programme focused strongly on the prevention principle.[221] Prevention rather than cure was the central theme of this

---

[214] Case C-6/04 *Commission* v. *UK* [2005] ECR I-9017, para. 54. Cf. also Case C-127/02 *Landelijke Vereniging tot Behoud van de Waddenzee* [2004] ECR I-7405, para. 58. The Court ruled 'that the authorisation criterion laid down in the second sentence of Article 6(3) of the Habitats Directive integrates the precautionary principle'.

[215] See Case C-121/07 *Commission* v. *France* [2008] ECR I-9159, para. 74, calling the prevention principle a 'fundamental principle' of environmental protection.

[216] OJ 1994 L 365/10.

[217] See for another example in the waste sector the report of the Commission on the Thematic Strategy on the Prevention and Recycling of Waste, COM(2011) 13 final.

[218] OJ 2011 L 174/88.

[219] Directive 2008/1 concerning integrated pollution prevention and control, OJ 2008 L 24/8.

[220] OJ 2006 L 161/1.

[221] OJ 1983 C 46/1.

programme. According to the programme the following conditions must, *inter alia*, be met, if the prevention principle is to have full effect:

- · the requisite knowledge and information must be improved and made readily available to decision-makers and all interested parties, including the public;[222]
- · it is necessary to formulate and introduce procedures for judgment which will ensure that the appropriate facts are considered early in the decision-making processes relating to any activity likely to affect the environment significantly. The Environmental Impact Assessment (EIA) Directive should be noted in this connection.[223] The preamble to the EIA Directive, referring to the first three Environmental Action Programmes, states 'that the best environment policy consists in preventing the creation of pollution or nuisances at source, rather than subsequently trying to counteract their effects'. For the same reason, account should be taken of the consequences of planning and decision-making processes for the environment at as early a stage as possible. Environmental impact assessment is an excellent example of an instrument in which the principle of prevention plays a vital role;
- · the implementation of adopted measures must be monitored to ensure their correct application and their adaptation if circumstances or new knowledge should so require. Relevant in this respect are provisions in directives concerning the adaptation of technical standards to technical and scientific progress.[224]

The Court of Justice has used the prevention principle frequently to interpret the concept of 'waste' of the Waste Framework Directive.[225]

The source principle

European policy on the environment shall be based on the principle that environmental damage should as a priority be rectified at its source. According to the source principle, damage to the environment should preferably not be prevented by using end-of-pipe technology. This principle also implies a preference for emission standards rather than environmental quality standards, especially to deal with water and air pollution. Environmental directives requiring the Member States to reduce the emissions is not dependent on the general environmental situation of the region in which the emissions occur.[226]

---

[222] See, for example, Directive 2003/4 on public access to environmental information, OJ 2003 L 41/26.

[223] Directive 85/337, OJ 1985 L 175/40.

[224] For example, Article 13 of the Sewage Sludge Directive 86/278, OJ 1986 L 181/6.

[225] Cf. e.g. Joined Cases C-418/97 and C-419/97 *ARCO Chemie Nederland* [2000] ECR I-4475, paras. 39-40 and Joined Cases C-175/98 and C-177/98 *Lirussi and Bizzaro* [1999] ECR I-6881.

[226] Cf. Case C-364/03 *Commission* v. *Greece* [2005] ECR I-6159, para. 34 with respect to emissions of sulphur dioxide and nitrogen oxide under Directive 84/360.

References to this principle can be found, for instance, in Union water pollution legislation.[227]

Other references to the source principle can be found in Directive 2002/96 on waste electrical and electronic equipment[228] (WEEE Directive) and in the EIA Directive 85/337.

The principle was given an unexpected dimension in the *Walloon Waste* case, where the Court of Justice applied it in determining to what extent Walloon measures restricting imports of foreign waste were discriminatory.[229] The Court held that the principle means that every region, municipality or other local authority must take those measures which are necessary to ensure the reception, processing and removal of its own waste. The waste must be disposed of as close as possible to the place of production in order to limit its transport as far as possible. Consequently, the Court held that, in view of the differences between the waste produced at various locations and the connection with the place of its production, the Walloon restrictions could not be considered discriminatory. In this case, the source principle was thus equated with what is known as the 'proximity principle' in waste law.[230]

In the waste case *Sydhavnens Sten & Grus*, the Court seems to be willing to apply the source principle in a more direct manner.[231] In that case, the Court ruled that the source principle could not serve to justify restrictions on exports of waste, particularly in the case of waste destined for recovery. *A fortiori*, the Court of Justice continued, the source principle cannot be used to justify restrictions where environmentally non-hazardous waste is involved.

The polluter pays principle

Action is based on the principle that the polluter should pay. This principle was one of the cornerstones of a European environment policy even before it was incorporated into the Treaty. It was referred to as a principle of Union environment policy in the First Action Programme on the Environment.[232] In simple terms: this is the principle that the costs of measures to deal with pollution should be borne by the polluter who causes[233] the pollution.

The polluter pays principle is set out in a Communication from the European Commission to the Council in 1975 regarding cost allocation and action by public authorities on environmental matters.[234] It states that 'natural or legal

---

[227] Directive 2008/105 on environmental quality standards in the field of water policy, OJ 2008 L 348/84 and Directive 2008/56 OJ 2008 L 164/19. See also Chapter 8, section 11.

[228] OJ 2002 L 37/24.

[229] Case C-2/90 *Commission* v. *Belgium* [1992] ECR I-4431.

[230] See Chapter 8, section 17.1. See also Case C-422/92 *Commission* v. *Germany* [1995] ECR I-1097.

[231] Case C-209/98 *Sydhavnens Sten & Grus* [2000] ECR I-3743, para. 48. See also Chapter 6, section 4.3.

[232] OJ 1973 C 112/1. Cf. on the 'early days' of the polluter pays principle in EU law: Vandekerckhove (1994).

[233] Cf. on causation and the polluter pays principle, Mossoux (2010).

[234] OJ 1975 L 194/1.

persons governed by public or private law who are responsible for pollution must pay the costs of such measures as are necessary to eliminate that pollution or to reduce it'. The 1975 communication is still the guiding principle for policy in that respect. The communication is not as such binding. The Council has however recommended that Member States conform to the principles contained in the communication. Both the communication and the recommendation were prompted by the consideration that the costs connected with the protection of the environment against pollution should be allocated according to the same principles throughout the EU.

This is, on the one hand, to avoid distortions of competition affecting trade, which would be incompatible with the proper functioning of the internal market, and on the other, to further the aims set out in the First Action Programme on the environment. This programme is based on the principle that charging polluters the costs of action to combat the pollution they cause will encourage them to reduce that pollution and endeavour to find less polluting products or technologies. This would enable a more rational use to be made of scarce environmental resources. Apart from the use of charges, the principle can also be implemented by imposing environmental standards. Companies, which are required to observe environmental standards, will have to make various investments in their production process if they are to comply with the statutory standards. Setting standards in this way also helps ensure the polluter bears the cost of pollution.

The EU must therefore ensure, especially by laying down standards, environmental charges or creating a system of environmental liability,[235] that persons who are responsible for pollution in fact bear the cost. In other words, environmental protection should not in principle depend on policies which rely on grants of aid and place the burden of combating pollution on society. On the other hand, the polluter pays principle also requires that a European measure must avoid putting burdens on persons and undertakings for the elimination of pollution to which they have not contributed or allocate costs to certain holders of waste which are manifestly disproportionate to the volumes or nature of the waste that they are liable to produce.[236]

The polluter pays principle is of particular relevance with respect to the Guidelines on state aid for environmental protection.[237] According to the Commission, the costs associated with protecting the environment should be internalised by firms just like other production costs. Aid control and environ-

---

[235] Cf. Directive 2004/35 on environmental liability with regard to the prevention and remedying of environmental damage, OJ 2004 L 143/56. Article 1 reads: 'The purpose of this Directive is to establish a framework of environmental liability based on the 'polluter-pays' principle, to prevent and remedy environmental damage.'

[236] Case C-293/97 *Standley* [1999] ECR I-2603; Case C-188/07 *Commune de Mesquer* [2008] ECR I-4501; Case C-254/08 *Futura Immobiliare srl Hotel Futura* [2009] ECR I-6995 and Case C-172/08 *Pontina Ambiente* [2010] ECR I-1175. Cf. on the polluter pays principle in the case law of the Court, Bleeker (2009).

[237] OJ 2008 C 82/1. See Chapter 7, section 7.3.

mental policy must, in the Commission's view, also support one another in ensuring stricter application of the polluter pays principle.[238]

> Several references to the polluter pays principle can be found in EU secondary legislation. Article 14 of the Waste Framework Directive 2008/98[239] states that, in accordance with the polluter-pays principle, the costs of waste management shall be borne by the original waste producer or by the current or previous waste holders.
>
> Interesting is also the case law of the Court of Justice pertaining to the, now repealed, Waste Oils Directive.[240] Article 14 provided that indemnities may be granted to collection and/or disposal undertakings for services rendered. And that these indemnities may be financed by a charge imposed on products, which after use are transformed into waste oils, or on waste oils. Article 15 of the directive required that the financing of indemnities had to be in accordance with the polluter pays principle. According to the Court of Justice in the *ADBHU* case, provisions like these do not conflict with the Treaty rules on state aid.[241]
>
> Outside environmental law, in view of the integration principle, a reference can be found in Directive 2006/38 on the charging of heavy goods vehicles for the use of certain infrastructures.[242] A fairer system of charging for the use of road infrastructure, for instance through the variation of tolls to take account of the environmental performance of vehicles, was felt necessary by the European legislature in order to encourage sustainable transport in the EU.

Safeguard clauses

Article 191(2) TFEU also provides that harmonisation measures answering environmental protection requirements shall include, where appropriate, a safeguard clause allowing Member States to take provisional measures; for non-economic environmental reasons, subject to a Union inspection procedure.

This clause is clearly of a different order from the above principles. It is debatable whether its place in the Treaty, next to the true principles, is well chosen.

> In practice, there are many examples where this kind of safeguard clause is actually embodied in the legislative act in question. For example, Article 32 of the Biocides Directive states: 'Where a Member State has valid reasons to consider that a biocidal product which it has authorised, registered or is bound to authorise or

---

[238] See, for example, the Commission Decision in the *Cartiere del Garda* case, OJ 1993 L 273/51, where the Commission directly examined a national aid measure in the light of the polluter pays principle. In that case the Commission concluded that the proposed aid 'does not meet the polluter pays principle'. For a discussion of this case see Chapter 7, section 7.1.

[239] OJ 2008 L 312/3. Cf. on the polluter pays principle and the Waste Framework Directive, e.g., Case C-188/07 *Commune de Mesquer* [2008] ECR I-4501. See for a comment on this case De Sadeleer (2009).

[240] OJ 1975 L 194/31.

[241] Case 240/83 *ADBHU* [1985] ECR 531. See also XXIVth Competition Report, point 388.

[242] OJ 2006 L 157/8.

register pursuant to Articles 3 or 4, constitutes an unacceptable risk to human or animal health or the environment, it may provisionally restrict or prohibit the use or sale of that product on its territory. It shall immediately inform the Commission and the other Member States of such action and give reasons for its decision. A decision shall be taken on the matter within 90 days'.[243]

Similar safeguard provisions can be found particularly in those environmental directives where there is a strong link with the functioning of the internal market. It is the authors' opinion that these safeguard clauses must be interpreted in line with the precautionary principle.[244]

3.3 The Policy Aspects to be Taken into Account

According to Article 191(3) TFEU the Union shall, in preparing its policy on the environment, take account of:
· available scientific and technical data;
· environmental conditions in the various regions of the Union;
· the potential benefits and costs of action or lack of action;
· the economic and social development of the Union as a whole and the balanced development of its regions.

By comparison with the formulation of, for instance, the integration principle in Article 11 TFEU ('must be integrated'), the language of this paragraph ('take account of') is much less forceful. Account shall be taken of the policy aspects referred to in it. The Treaty does not therefore prescribe observance of these criteria in all cases. It is true that inclusion of these policy aspects does not imply that the environmental objectives of Article 191(1) TFEU are in a legal sense subordinate to them. However, in practice, Member States will no doubt seize on them to delay environmental policies that do not suit them.

Available scientific and technical data
It is said that the function of this criterion under the Single European Act was to ensure the Union would only act when sufficient scientific data was available to prove that a given activity or product – for example, CFCs in aerosols – would have a harmful effect on the environment – in this case depletion of the ozone layer. As has already been shown in the discussion of the precautionary principle, a different interpretation would now seem more appropriate.[245]

---

[243] Directive 98/8, OJ 1998 L 123/1.

[244] See this chapter, section 3.

[245] See this chapter, section 3.2. See for an example of connecting the precautionary principle with this policy aspect: Annex II of Directive 2001/18 on the deliberate release into the environment of genetically modified organisms (OJ 2001 L 106/1). According to this annex the environmental risk assessment to be carried out prior to a release of GMOs should be carried out 'in accordance with the precautionary principle' 'in a scientifically sound and transparent manner based on available scientific and technical data'.

Indeed, all kinds of provisional, indicative and tentative scientific data may now be sufficient to require protective measures and action by the Union.

> References to 'available scientific and technical data' can, *inter alia*, be found in the Bathing Water Directive and in the Water Framework Directive.[246] The Nitrates Directive, for instance, requires in Article 5 that the action programmes be established in respect of so-called 'vulnerable zones'. The action programmes shall take into account 'available scientific and technical data, mainly with reference to respective nitrogen contributions originating from agricultural and other sources'.[247]
>
> The case law of the Court shows that EU measures based on inadequate scientific and technical data can result in an annulment.[248]

Environmental conditions in the various regions

Application of this criterion entails a differentiated environmental policy based on the quality of the environment in a given region.

> A good example can be found in the Nitrates Directive. The action programmes to be established in respect of vulnerable zones have to take into account 'environmental conditions in the relevant regions of the Member State concerned'. With respect to recovery of costs for water services the Water Framework Directive requires (Article 9) 'have regard to the social, environmental and economic effects of the recovery as well as the geographic and climatic conditions of the region or regions affected'.

This criterion may also give rise to the assumption that there is a preference for environmental quality objectives rather than emission limits. After all, the quality of the receiving environment would then determine the extent of emission of pollutants. However, from the point of view of the source principle, there is a preference for emission standards rather than environmental quality standards. It is up to the European legislature to consider in more depth the relative merits of these different aspects.

On the other hand, the criterion could also be applied differently. Additional protective measures might well be called for precisely in order to conserve those areas in which the environmental quality is high.

---

[246] Directive 2006/7 concerning the management of bathing water quality, OJ 2006 L 64/37 and Directive 2000/60 establishing a framework for Community action in the field of water policy, OJ 2000 L 327/1.

[247] Directive 91/676 concerning the protection of waters against pollution caused by nitrates from agricultural sources, OJ 1991 L 375/1.

[248] E.g. Case C-3/00 *Denmark v. Commission* [2003] ECR I-2643.

See, for example, the 'old' air quality directives of the 1980s.[249] These directives enable Member States to lay down more stringent air quality standards than those set out in the directives, for zones, which in the view of the Member State, require special protection from an environmental point of view. This approach has been followed in Article 9 of Directive 96/62 on ambient air quality assessment and management, according to which Member States shall draw up a list of zones and agglomerations in which the levels of pollutants are below the limit values.[250] They are required to maintain the levels of pollutants in these zones and agglomerations below the limit values and shall endeavour to preserve the best ambient air quality, compatible with sustainable development.

Potential benefits and costs

This criterion requires that the potential costs and benefits of action be assessed. Besides producing benefits for the environment, environmental action by the Union entails costs for Member States, in the sense of legislation, administrative organisation, enforcement, etc., and for private actors, such as industrial plants which cause pollution, and manufacturers and importers of goods and products which are harmful to the environment. Viewed in this way, the criterion could be seen as prompting application of the principle of proportionality, and thus adding little to what has already been provided in Article 5(4) TEU.

It is the authors' opinion that the concept of 'best *available* technology/techniques' is clearly related to this criterion.

An 'early' example of this can be found in Article 4 of Directive 84/360 on the combating of air pollution from industrial plants.[251] An authorisation may only be issued when the competent authority is satisfied that 'all appropriate preventive measures against air pollution have been taken, including application of the best available technology, provided that the application of such measures does not entail excessive costs'. The Industrial Emissions Directive also provides an example of this in its definition of the term 'best available techniques': '"available techniques" means those developed on a scale which allows implementation in the relevant industrial sector, under economically and technically viable conditions, taking into consideration the costs and advantages, whether or not the techniques are used or produced inside the Member State in question, as long as they are reasonably accessible to the operator'.[252]

---

[249] See for instance Article 4(2) of Directive 85/203 on air quality standards for nitrogen dioxide (OJ 1985 L 87/1): 'In zones which the Member State concerned considers should be afforded special environmental protection, it may fix values which are generally lower than the guide values in Annex II'.

[250] OJ 1996 L 296/55.

[251] OJ 1984 L 188/20, now repealed.

[252] Article 3(10)(b) of Directive 2010/75, OJ 2010 L 334/17. See on this directive, section 6 of Chapter 8. Reference to this definition can also be found in other environmental directives. E.g. Directive 2006/66 on batteries and accumulators and waste batteries and accumulators, OJ 2006 L 266/1, preamble point 17.

A final example might be Euratom Directive 96/29 laying down basic safety standards for the protection of the health of workers and the general public against the dangers arising from ionizing radiation.[253] One of its basic general principles is the so-called 'justification principle' according to which practices resulting in exposure to ionizing radiation are justified by their economic, social or other benefits in relation to the health detriment they may cause.

Further references to 'potential benefits and costs' can be found in the preamble of the Water Framework Directive and in the Council Resolution the drafting, implementation and enforcement of Community environmental law.[254]

Economic and social development of the Community as a whole and the balanced development of its regions

In fact this aspect is an elaboration of the more general principle contained in Article 27 TFEU. Differentiated environmental policies may be adopted, whether or not on a temporary basis, depending on the economic and social development of certain regions. This opens – it goes without saying, in addition to the possibilities provided by the Treaty in the context of 'enhanced cooperation' under Article 20 TEU and Article 326 TFEU *et seq.* – the possibility of a multi-speed environmental policy.

An example of such a multi-speed policy was given by Directive 88/609 on the limitation of emissions of certain pollutants into the air from large combustion plants.[255] Article 5 provided that Spain was temporarily entitled to apply less stringent emission standards than those normally laid down by the directive. This was explained in the preamble to the directive by pointing out that Spain considered it needed a particularly high amount of new generating capacity to allow for its energy and industrial growth.

Another example can be found in Directive 94/62 on packaging and packaging waste.[256] Article 6(7) provides that Greece, Ireland and Portugal may, because of their specific situations, namely respectively the large number of small islands, the presence of rural and mountain areas and the current low level of packaging consumption, decide to:

a) attain, no later than 30 June 2001, lower targets than those fixed in paragraphs 1(a) and (c), but shall at least attain 25% for recovery or incineration at waste incineration plants with energy recovery; b) postpone at the same time the attainment of the targets in paragraphs 1(a) and c) to a later deadline which shall not, however, be later than 31 December 2005; c) postpone the attainment of the targets referred to in paragraphs 1(b), (d) and (e) until a date of their own choice which shall not be later than 31 December 2011.

---

[253] OJ 1996 L 159/1.

[254] Directive 2000/60 establishing a framework for Community action in the field of water policy, OJ 2000 L 327/1; Resolution of 7 October 1997, OJ 1997 C 321.

[255] OJ 1988 L 336/1. The directive is repealed from 27 November 2002 by Directive 2001/80 on the limitation of emissions of certain pollutants into the air from large combustion plants, OJ 2001 L 309/1.

[256] As amended by Directive 2004/12 on packaging and packaging waste, OJ 2004 L 47/26.

A further reference to this criterion can be found in the preamble of the Water Framework Directive.[257]

Apart from giving certain Member States the power to derogate from European standards, the element of economic and social development can also be translated in terms of financial support by the Union for those Member States, which find it difficult to meet the standards required by a directive.

An example of this is the Habitats Directive 92/43.[258] Article 8 provides for a system of co-financing where measures to protect priority natural habitats and priority species would result in excessive financial burdens for some Member States.

Another example is provided by Article 192(5) TFEU. If an environmental measure is adopted based on Article 192(1) TFEU, which involves disproportionately high costs for the public authorities of a Member State, such measure shall lay down appropriate provisions in the form of temporary derogations and/or financial support from the Community's Cohesion Fund (Article 177 TFEU).[259]

---

[257] Directive 2000/60 establishing a framework for Community action in the field of water policy, OJ 2000 L 327/1.

[258] OJ 1992 L 206/7.

[259] For a more detailed discussion of the phenomenon of the Union's environmental aid, see Chapter 7, section 7.4.

CHAPTER 2

Legal Basis

1 Article 192 TFEU (Environment)

Above it was stated that the Treaty of Lisbon had important effects for the structure of the European Union. It has succeeded in less complex decision-making in the context of the Title on the Environment. The standard procedure is now, according to Article 192(1) TFEU, the 'ordinary legislative procedure', as regulated in Article 289 TFEU:

> 'The European Parliament and the Council, acting in accordance with the ordinary legislative procedure and after consulting the Economic and Social Committee and the Committee of the Regions, shall decide what action is to be taken by the Union in order to achieve the objectives referred to in Article 191.'

Under this procedure, the European Parliament is twice consulted on the measure proposed and has the ultimate power to prevent the adoption of a measure. Although the participation of the European Parliament does not automatically lead to more environmentally friendly legislation, the fact that they are now a genuine co-legislator must nevertheless be welcomed. We have come a long way from decision-making by unanimity to majority voting. Also important is that, already since the Treaty of Amsterdam, there is no longer a difference in the procedure between internal market legislation and purely environmental legislation. This means that time consuming inter-institutional battles fought before the Court of Justice concerning the choice of legal basis are less likely.[1]

The second paragraph of Article 192 TFEU states that by way of derogation from this procedure, and without prejudice to the provisions of Article 114 TFEU, the Council acting unanimously in accordance with a *special* legislative procedure and after consulting the European Parliament, the Economic and Social Committee and the Committee of the Regions, shall adopt:

a) provisions primarily of a fiscal nature;
b) measures affecting:
- · town and country planning,
- · quantitative management of water resources or affecting, directly or indirectly, the availability of those resources,
- · land use, with the exception of waste management;
c) measures significantly affecting a Member State's choice between different energy sources and the general structure of its energy supply.

Although Article 192(2) TFEU is hardly used in practice, its interpretation generates considerable problems. These include the following.

---

[1]   Like for instance in Case C-300/89 *Commission* v. *Council* [1991] ECR I-2867; Case C-70/88 *EP* v. *Council* [1991] ECR I-4529 and Case C-155/91 *Commission* v. *Council* [1993] ECR I-939.

Provisions primarily of a fiscal nature

In the first place, it should be noted that the Treaty does not provide for a definition of the term 'fiscal nature'. Arguably, this term should be interpreted in the same vein as the term 'fiscal provisions' in Article 114(2) TFEU.[2] The Court of Justice ruled in Case C-338/01 that fiscal provisions 'cover not only all areas of taxation, without drawing any distinction between the types of duties or taxes concerned, but also all aspects of taxation, whether material rules or procedural rules'.[3] The present formulation of Article 192(2) TFEU could be interpreted in such a way that measures which concern the harmonisation of national taxes, but which ultimately aim to attain environmental objectives, could only be taken unanimously. However the addition *primarily* – arguably the term can be regarded purely as a contrast with *incidentally* – leads to another interpretation. This implies that unanimity is not required to adopt an environmental measure, which only incidentally touches upon tax harmonisation. When an environmental measure has only incidental fiscal effects, the primary decision-making rule contained in Article 192(1) TFEU applies. In other words, Article 192(2) TFEU does not intend to exclude any measure of tax harmonisation from the application of Article 192(1) TFEU.[4]

It is also not clear how Article 192(2) TFEU accords with Article 113 TFEU, which regulates the Council's power of harmonisation in respect of turnover taxes, excise duties and other forms of indirect taxation. Apparently Article 192(2) TFEU does not apply without prejudice to the provisions of Article 113 TFEU. For that to have been the case, Article 113 TFEU would have had to have been specifically excluded in the same way as it has been done with respect to Article 114 TFEU. This would mean that environmental measures primarily of a fiscal nature relating to the harmonisation of turnover taxes, excise duties and other forms of indirect taxation would have to be based on Article 192(2) TFEU and not on Article 113 TFEU. The specific rule of Article 192(2) TFEU would then have to be regarded as taking precedence over the general rule contained in Article 113 TFEU.[5] Measures primarily of a fiscal nature with only incidental effects on environmental protection should have Article 113 TFEU as its legal basis.[6] However, this is all of relative practical importance as the decision-making procedure provided for in Article 192(2) TFEU is no different from that in Article 113 TFEU.[7] Both require unanim-

---

[2] Article 114(2) TFEU states that Article 114(1) TFEU shall not apply to 'fiscal provisions'.

[3] Case C-338/01 *Commission* v. *Council* [2004] ECR I-4829, para. 63.

[4] Applying, by analogy, the rule to be derived from Case C-36/98 *Spain* v. *Council* [2001] ECR I-779, para. 50.

[5] The Court has consistently held that, where there is a specific legal basis, this should form the basis of the measure to be adopted; Case C-271/94 *Parliament* v. *Council* [1996] ECR I-1689.

[6] Cf. Directive 2003/96 restructuring the Community framework for the taxation of energy products and electricity, OJ 2003 L 283/51.

[7] Except for the fact that under Article 113 TFEU the Council is not required to consult the Committee of the Regions.

ity. However, an important difference remains the legal consequences Article 193 TFEU attaches to decisions adopted pursuant to Article 192 TFEU.[8]

Measures affecting town and country planning, land use and quantitative management of water resources

.The exceptions referred to in the second sentence of Article 192(2) TFEU are also problematic. Measures 'affecting'[9] town and country planning are also excepted from the ordinary legislative procedure. However, is there then any power at all to pursue an independent town and country planning policy under the title on the environment? This does not follow from the objectives of Article 191(1) TFEU. Nor will a comprehensive competence in the field of town and country planning be found elsewhere in the Treaty. However, if such a power does not fall within the scope of Article 191 TFEU, there is no need to except it. The current text of the Treaty which speaks of 'affecting' rather then 'concerning' makes clear that the mere fact that a measure which has consequences for the physical layout of the territory of a Member State does not mean that it should be taken unanimously. Otherwise, that would mean that any area-related environmental policy would have to be adopted unanimously, whether within the framework of the protection of flora and fauna (Wild Birds and Habitats Directives), water quality policy (designation of fishing and swimming areas) or the combating of air pollution (zoning in connection with air quality policy). And what about measures in connection with environmental impact assessment? The Court held that this provision covers measures which, just like those based on Article 192(1) TFEU, are intended to attain the objectives referred to in Article 191 TFEU, 'but which regulate the use of the territory of the Member States, such as measures relating to regional, urban or rural management plans or the planning of various projects concerning the infrastructure of a Member State'.[10] Once again we have to conclude that, Article 192(2) TFEU does not intend to exclude any measure on town and country planning from the application of Article 192(1) TFEU.[11]

The same can be said with respect to the rule of unanimous decision-making in respect of measure affecting land use. Directive 96/82 on the control of major-accident hazards involving dangerous substances, the 'Seveso II' Directive provides an example.[12] According to Article 12 of the directive Member States are required to ensure that the objectives of preventing major accidents and limiting the consequences of such accidents are taken into account in their land-use policies. They shall pursue those objectives through controls on:

---

[8] See Chapter 3, section 5.

[9] And not just 'concerning' like in the pre-Nice text of the provision!

[10] Case C-36/98 *Spain* v. *Council* [2001] ECR I-779, para. 51.

[11] Applying, by analogy, the rule to be derived from Case C-36/98 *Spain* v. *Council* [2001] ECR I-779, para. 50.

[12] OJ 1997 L 10/13.

· the siting of new establishments;
· modifications to existing establishments;
· new developments such as transport links.

Member States are also required to ensure that their land-use policies take account of the need to maintain appropriate distances between establishments covered by the directive and residential areas, areas of public use and areas of particular natural sensitivity or interest. Although the effects on land use are clear, the directive was correctly adopted using the standard procedure and not the procedure of Article 192(2) TFEU.

An exception (to the exception of measures affecting land use) is made to the requirement of unanimity for waste management. In these cases the ordinary legislative procedure mentioned in Article 192(1) TFEU applies again. This means that Directive 99/31 on the landfill of waste (or indeed any other measures designed to protect the soil against environmental hazards caused by waste) in *any* event fall within the scope of application of Article 192(1) TFEU. Directive 99/31 is therefore correctly based on Article 175(1) EC (now Article 192(1) TFEU).[13]

The post-Nice text of Article 192(2) TFEU makes clear that only the regulation of the *quantitative* aspects of management of water resources is subject to unanimity voting. In the pre-Nice text, the various language versions caused some confusion.[14] For instance, the Dutch text of the Treaty spoke of '*kwantitatief*'. The Dutch text implied that only measures concerning the *quantity* of water are covered by the exception. However, the English text referred simply to 'management of water resources', the French to '*la gestion des ressources hydrauliques*' and the German to '*der Bewirtschaftung der Wasserressourcen*', in other words without the addition of 'quantitative'. The current text has remedied this.

Measures significantly affecting a Member State's choice between different energy sources

Thirdly, Article 192(2) TFEU excludes 'measures significantly affecting a Member State's choice between different energy sources and the general structure of its energy supply' from the ordinary legislative procedure of Article 192(1) TFEU. The paragraph is particular problematic in respect of the interpretation of the term 'significantly affecting'. First of all, the difference between 'measures affecting' (under b) and '*significantly* affecting' are obvious. The threshold 'significantly affecting' is clearly much higher than 'affecting'.

---

[13] OJ 1999 L 182/1.

[14] Cf. Case C-36/98 *Spain v. Council* [2001] ECR I-779.

Take for example the European Commission's proposal on the CO_2 tax.[15] Does such a tax significantly affect the choice between various sources of energy or not? Or is it a measure primarily of a fiscal nature? Or is it one involving the harmonisation of indirect taxes (Article 113 TFEU)? Or does this proposal primarily fall whithin the scope of the specific provisons on energy (Article 194 TFEU). The Commission is presenting its proposal as a revision of the Energy Taxation Directive 2003/96.[16]

Another example is given by Directive 2001/80 on the limitation of emissions of certain pollutants into the air from large combustion plants.[17] This directive sets emission limit values for combustion plants designed for production of energy. The requirements of this directive (and its predecessor Directive 88/609) are so stringent that those Member States in which brown coal is used for power production face serious difficulties. The question which arises here is whether this directive 'significantly affects' a Member State's choice between the various sources of energy or not? Probably not as the directive was based on Article 175(1) EC (now Article 192(1) TFEU).

The same can be argued about the measures to comply with the United Nations Framework Convention on Climate Change and subsequent Protocols. All implementing measures have Article 175(1) EC (now Article 192(1) TFEU) as their legal basis.

In any event, Directive 2006/32 on energy end-use efficiency and energy services was correctly based on Article 175(1) EC (now Article 192(1) TFEU).[18] The purpose of this directive is to enhance the cost-effective improvement of energy end-use efficiency in the Member States by *inter alia* providing the necessary indicative targets as well as mechanisms, incentives and institutional, financial and legal frameworks to remove existing market barriers and imperfections that impede the efficient end use of energy.

These questions demonstrate that the interpretation of this category of measures, to which the requirement of unanimity ought to apply, will, at least in theory, give rise to the necessary problems.

The 'passerelle'

The second subparagraph of Article 192(2) TFEU states:

The Council, acting unanimously on a proposal from the Commission and after consulting the European Parliament, the Economic and Social Committee and the

---

[15] Commission Communication, Smarter energy taxation for the EU: proposal for a revision of the Energy Taxation Directive, COM (2011) 168 final.

[16] See on this directive also section 7.4 of this chapter and Chapter 7, section 7.3.

[17] OJ 2001 L 309/1. Directive 2001/80 is repealed with effect from 1 January 2016 and is replaced by the regulatory framework of Directive 2010/75 on industrial emissions (integrated pollution prevention and control), OJ 2010 L 334/17.

[18] OJ 2006 L 114/64.

Committee of the Regions, may make the ordinary legislative procedure applicable to the matters referred to in the first subparagraph.

This provision enables the Council unanimously to decide that another decision-making procedure applies. This *passerelle* is certainly a welcome improvement for the position of the European Parliament in that it allows for making the ordinary decision legislative procedure applicable whereas the old *passerelle* (Article 175(2), last paragraph, EC) only allowed for a switch to qualified majority voting in the Council without any improvement of the Parliament's involvement. In view of the relatively 'green character' of the European Parliament, this could have a positive effect if and when it is applied.[19]

General action programmes

According to Article 192(3) TFEU the ordinary legislative procedure also applies to the adoption of what the Treaty calls 'general action programmes setting out priority objectives to be attained'.[20]

It may be assumed that action programmes on the environment, which are adopted under the this procedure, may cover the whole environmental spectrum. However, it would seem that only priority objectives can be set in these action programmes and that they cannot give rise to direct legal consequences for the Member States. This interpretation is supported by the second subparagraph of Article 192(3) TFEU. Measures which are necessary for the implementation of these programmes must be based on paragraph 1 or 2 of Article 192 TFEU, depending on the subject matter. Obligations for Member States could then only be imposed by adopting the necessary measures of implementation (directives and regulations).

2 Articles 191-192 TFEU and External Relations

The Union is a participant in international legal affairs. Within that framework, the Union may conclude environmental treaties, operate in international organisations which concern themselves with the environment and is otherwise actively involved with third countries in respect of environmental issues.[21] In its relations with third countries, the Union is of course required to respect its obligations under international law.[22]

---

[19] See Wilkinson (2008) 81.

[20] Cf. the current Sixth Community Environment Action Programme, Decision 1600/2002, OJ 2002 L 242.

[21] Cf. in general Montini (2009).

[22] Case C-308/06 *Intertanko and others* [2008] ECR I-4057; Case C-286/90 *Anklagemindigheden* v. *Poulsen and Diva Navigation* [1992] ECR I-6019 and Case C-341/95 *Gianni Bettati* [1998] ECR I-4355. See also Chapter 5, section 2.1.

Implied powers

Even before the entry into force of the Single European Act and the confer-ring of explicit external competence in what is now Article 191(4) TFEU, the Union had concluded environmental agreements with third countries. It derived this competence from a construction (*implied powers* doctrine), which has been developed by the Court of Justice, whereby internal competence can also be used in respect of external policy. The Court has determined that external competence can follow from internal competence in two cases. Firstly, where the Union has already implemented internal measures on the basis of that internal competence.[23]

> An application of the principle formulated in the case in respect of external environmental policy can be seen in Council Decision 81/462 on the conclusion of the Convention on Long-Range Transboundary Air Pollution.[24] This decision was based on Article 235 EEC (now Article 352 TFEU). In the preamble, the Council states that the European Community will participate in the implementation of the Convention 'by exercising its competence as resulting from the existing common rules as well as those acquired as a result of future acts adopted by the Council'. The competence, at least according to the Council, thus flows from the internal competence to lay down rules to prevent air pollution, in so far as this competence is or will in the future be exercised by means of internal legislation.

Alternatively, where the Union has not yet implemented internal rules, if the exercise of external powers is *necessary* to attain its objectives.[25]

> The declaration made in the Convention on Climate Change[26] is relevant in this context. The commitment set out in Article 4(2) of that convention to limit emissions of anthropogenic carbon dioxide will 'be fulfilled in the Community as a whole through action by the Community and its Member States, within the respective competence of each.' At the time the convention was concluded, there were no measures in force implementing the commitment. There was only a Commission proposal to introduce a tax on carbon dioxide emissions.[27] In other words, there was no internal legislation on which the competence to implement Article 4(2) could have been based. The conclusion must therefore be that the Council based its competence on Article 175(1) EC (now Article 192(1) TFEU), even though there was no internal legislation in place at the time. Thus the Court's conclusions in the *Kramer* case and Opinion 1/76 have implicitly been applied.

---

[23] Case 22/70 *ERTA* [1971] ECR 273.

[24] OJ 1981 L 171/11.

[25] Joined Cases 3, 4 and 6/76 *Kramer* [1976] ECR 1279 and Opinion 1/76 *Laying-up fund* [1977] ECR 754.
Cf. also Case C-459/03 *Commission v. Ireland* [2006] ECR I-4635 (*MOX* case).

[26] OJ 1994 L 33/13.

[27] OJ 1992 C 196/92.

Explicit competences

Nowadays there is hardly any need to rely on the doctrine of *implied powers* to establish a competence in the area of external environmental relations, as we have now an explicit provision in the Treaty: Article 191(4) TFEU. The Union can enter into agreements in the area of environmental protection even if the specific matters covered by those agreements are not yet, or are only very partially, the subject of internal rules at European level.[28] Article 191(4), first subparagraph TFEU reads as follows:

> 'Within their respective spheres of competence, the Union and the Member States shall cooperate with third countries and with the competent international organisations. The arrangements for Union cooperation may be the subject of agreements between the Union and the third parties concerned.'

The material scope of the Union's external competence is determined in the same way as its internal competence, by the objectives contained in Article 191(1) TFEU and the principles referred to in Article 191(2) TFEU. In that sense, there are no additional legal difficulties involved in determining the material external competence in the field of the environment. Of course, for the Union to be able to conclude a treaty, it is not sufficient for it to be competent under Union law. The other parties to the treaty must also make accession possible. A treaty on the environment will generally include a clause stating that accession is open not only to states, but also to 'regional economic integration organizations'.[29]

> Most recent important multilateral environmental conventions provide for the possibility of accession by the Union. The main exception to this rule remains the 1973 Washington Convention on International Trade in Endangered Species of Wild Fauna and Flora (CITES).[30] Accession by the Union has still not been made possible. The Union therefore applies the provisions of the Convention unilaterally by means of Regulation 338/97.[31]

Conventions that were concluded on the basis of the Title on the Environment in the Treaty include the following:
- the 1985 Vienna Convention for the Protection of the Ozone Layer and the 1987 Montreal Protocol on Substances that Deplete the Ozone Layer;[32]
- the 1989 Basel Convention on the Control of Transboundary Movements of Hazardous Wastes and Their Disposal;[33]

---

[28] Case C-459/03 *Commission* v. *Ireland* [2006] ECR I-4635 (*MOX* case), para. 94 in particular.

[29] See, for example, Article 33 of the 1992 Rio de Janeiro Convention on Biological Diversity, OJ 1993 L 309/1.

[30] OJ 1982 L 384/7.

[31] OJ 1997 L 61/1.

[32] OJ 1988 L 297/10 and OJ 1988 L 297/21, concluded by Council Decision 88/540, OJ 1988 L 297/8.

[33] OJ 1993 L 39/3, concluded by Council Decision 93/98, OJ 1993 L 39/1.

- the 1992 Rio de Janeiro Framework Convention on Climate Change;[34]
- the 1992 Rio de Janeiro Convention on Biological Diversity;[35]
- the 1991 Espoo Convention on Environmental Impact Assessment in a Transboundary Context;[36]
- the 1992 Helsinki Convention on the Transboundary Effects of Industrial Accidents;[37]
- the 1992 Helsinki Convention on the Protection and Use of Transboundary Watercourses International Lakes;[38]
- the United Nations Convention on the Law of the Sea (UNCLOS);[39]
- the 1998 Aarhus Convention on access to information, public participation in decision-making and access to justice in environmental matters.[40]

Division of powers

The competences of the EU on environmental protection must be regarded, also in the words of the Article 4(2) TFEU, as a 'shared competence'.[41] A shared competence implies that the Union and the Member States may legislate and adopt legally binding acts in that area. However, the Member States shall exercise their competence only to the extent that the Union has not exercised, or has decided to cease exercising, its competence.[42] In view of this, some attention should be paid to the second subparagraph of Article 191(4) TFEU. It reads:

---

[34] OJ 1994 L 33/13, concluded by Council Decision 94/69, OJ 1994 L 33/11. See also the subsequent Kyoto Protocol, OJ 2002 L 130/1.

[35] OJ 1993 L 309/3, concluded by Council Decision 93/626, OJ 1993 L 309/1. Cf. also the Cartagena protocol on biosafety to the convention on biological diversity, OJ 2002 L 201/50.

[36] Bull. EC 1/2-1991. Signed on 26 February 1991. Ratified on 26 June 1997.

[37] OJ 1998 L 326/6, concluded by Council Decision 96/685, OJ 1998 L 326/1.

[38] OJ 1995 L 186/44, concluded by Council Decision 95/308, OJ 1995 L 186/42.

[39] 16 years after it was signed, the EC became a party to UNCLOS. The Convention contains several provisions on the protection of the environment, in particular Articles 145 to 147 and Part II (Articles 192 to 237). Decision 98/392 concerning the conclusion by the EC of the United Nations Convention of 10 December 1982 on the Law of the Sea and the Agreement of 28 July 1994 relating to the implementation of Part XI thereof, OJ 1998 L 179. The decision is based on the combined articles 37, 133 and 175(1) EC (now Articles 43, 207, 192(1) TFEU).

[40] OJ 2005 L 124/4, concluded by Council Decision 2005/370, OJ 2005 L 124/1.

[41] Cf. Article 4(2) under e) TFEU lists 'environment' as such a shared competence. Cf. also Protocol No 25 on the Exercise of Shared Competences and Declaration No 18 in Relation to the Delimitation of Competences. Cf. for case law Case C-114/01 *AvestaPolarit Chrome* [2003] ECR I-8725, para. 56, and Case C-459/03 *Commission v. Ireland* [2006] ECR I-4635 (*MOX* case), para. 92, with respect to the external competences of the Union in regard to the protection of the (marine) environment. See also Lee (2005) at 10. Cf. in general on the multi-level aspects of environmental administration in the EU, Winter (2005).

[42] See also Chapter 3, sections 2 and 3 in particular.

'The previous subparagraph shall be without prejudice to Member States' competence to negotiate in international bodies and to conclude international agreements.'

This provision has been inserted by the Single European Act and has caused
confusion since then. This formulation is open to the risk that it can be interpreted in such a way that Member States might still be able to negotiate international conventions on the environment, even though the Union had already
adopted internal legislation. Such an interpretation is contrary to the case law
of the Court of Justice and in particular to its judgment in the *ERTA* case.[43]
However, a Declaration was added in the Final Act of the Single European Act
to the effect that this paragraph does not affect the principles resulting from the
judgment handed down by the Court of Justice in the *ERTA* case.

This was no doubt intended to remove any doubt that the fact that the
Treaty currently gives the Union express competence to conclude treaties on
the environment does not therefore necessarily imply that it is exclusive. But
having said that, it is reasonable to ask when does a competence to conclude an
environmental treaty become exclusive? First of all it should be said that, like
common commercial policy measures, measures with regard to the conservation of marine biological resources are also within the exclusive competence of
the Union.[44] In the Declaration concerning the competence of the Union with
respect to matters governed by UNCLOS,[45] it was pointed out that:

'its Member States have transferred competence to it with regard to the conservation and management of sea fishing resources. Hence in this field it is for the
Community to adopt the relevant rules and regulations (which are enforced by the
Member States) and, within its competence, to enter into external undertakings
with third States or competent international organisations.'

However, this process of transferring competence to the Union is not always
entirely clear. After all, 'the scope and the exercise of such Community [read:
Union] competence are, by their nature, subject to continuous development'.[46]
In the *ERTA* case, the Court held that the Union's implied external authority is
exclusive where competence in internal matters has been transferred from the
Member States to the Union.[47] Whether or not the Union's external competence
is exclusive thus depends on the extent of the measures the European institutions have taken internally or externally. If the Union has laid down internal

---

[43] Case 22/70 *ERTA* [1971] ECR 273.

[44] Cf. Article 3(1) under d) and e) TFEU.

[45] Declaration concerning the competence of the EC with respect to matters governed by UNCLOS, OJ
1998 L 179/3.

[46] Declaration concerning the competence of the EC with respect to matters governed by UNCLOS, OJ
1998 L 179/3.

[47] Case 22/70 *ERTA* [1971] ECR 273.

rules, the Member States no longer have the right, acting outside the framework of those common rules, to undertake obligations which would affect those rules. Again quoting the Declaration concerning the competence of the EC with respect to matters governed by UNCLOS:

> 'with regard to the provisions on maritime transport, safety of shipping and the prevention of marine pollution [...] the Community has exclusive competence only to the extent that such provisions of the Convention or legal instruments adopted in implementation thereof affect common rules established by the Community.'

Particularly in the case of total harmonisation, there will be a transfer of internal competence resulting in exclusive external competence.[48] The Member States will no longer have any competence of their own. Any treaty concluded by the Member States will affect the internal rules implementing total harmonisation.

However, a large part of European environment policy consists not of total harmonisation but of minimum standards, whereby Member States are expressly permitted to take more stringent environmental measures than provided for in the acts in question.[49] It is arguable that, to the extent that European law leaves the Member States competent to adopt more stringent environmental standards than the European standards, there can hardly be any question of wholly exclusive external Union competence in respect of the environment. As far as the adoption in an international context of such environmental minimum standards is concerned, there can be no question of exclusive competence.

> Suppose a convention was under consideration which would lay down more stringent emission standards to prevent air pollution (discharges of no more than 2 mg of the hazardous substance) than those contained in an internal directive (no more than 5 mg). The fact that a Member State agreed to the more stringent standard in an international context would in no way prevent compliance with the European standard. Compliance with the more stringent international standard would necessarily imply compliance with the European standard in this respect. Nor would it be problematic if the convention were to lay down a less stringent standard (discharges of no more than 5 mg) than the European standard (no more than 2 mg). As long as it is clear that the standards laid down in the convention must also be regarded as minimum standards, Member States would be able to continue to apply the more stringent European standard.

The mere fact that the European environmental standard may come under pressure as a result of the less stringent international standard is not sufficient

---

[48] See Opinion 1/94 *WTO* [1994] ECR I-5267, in particular para. 96. See also Opinion 2/91 [1993] ECR I-1061 (*ILO-convention no. 170*).

[49] See, for example Article 193 TFEU, which will be discussed in detail in Chapter 3, section 5.

to make it a matter for exclusive Union competence. The Court confirmed this view in Opinion 2/91.[50] Only if the convention on the environment were to prevent the more stringent European environmental standard being applied would there be a problem. However, in that case, there would be no question of minimum harmonisation. Conclusion of such a convention, in fact intended to amend internal legislation on the environment, would seem an exclusive matter for the Union.

Thus, in the case of minimum harmonisation, there can be no question of exclusive external Union competence. In that case competence resides in the Union and the Member States jointly, and conclusion of such a convention on the environment should be effected in the form of a mixed agreement, in other words, one to which both the Union and the Member States are party. An illustration of this can be found in the Declaration concerning the competence of the Union with respect to matters governed by UNCLOS,[51] which states:

> 'When Community rules exist but are not affected, in particular in cases of Community provisions establishing only minimum standards, the Member States have competence, without prejudice to the competence of the Community to act in this field.'[52]

Mixed agreements

Thus, and in view of the remarks just made, in the case of external environmental relations, there is, generally speaking, no question of exclusive external Union competence. In that case, competence is found with both the Union and the Member States and the conclusion of such a convention on the environment should be effected in the form of a *mixed agreement*, in other words, one to which both the Union and the Member States are party.

It is clear from the case law of the Court of Justice that when a convention falls partly within the competence of the Member States and partly within that of the Union, it can only be implemented – according to the 'principle of sincere cooperation' mentioned in Article 4(3) TEU – by means of a 'close association between the institutions' of the Union and the Member States 'both in the process of negotiation and conclusion and in the fulfilment of the obligations entered into'.[53]

> The relevance of this principle – also known as the principle of Union loyalty' – became once more clear in the *Stockholm Convention on Persistent Organic Pollutants* case.[54] In that case the Court of Justice ruled that Sweden, by unilaterally proposing that a substance, perfluoroctane sulfonate, was to be added to Annex

---

[50] Opinion 2/91 [1993] ECR I-1061 (*ILO-convention no. 170*).

[51] OJ 1998 L 179/3-134.

[52] Emphasis added by the authors.

[53] Opinion 2/91 [1993] ECR I-1061 (*ILO-convention no. 170*).

[54] Case C-246/07 *Commission v. Sweden* [2010] ECR I-3317.

A to the Stockholm Convention on Persistent Organic Pollutants, failed to fulfil its obligations under the 'principle of sincere cooperation'. The Court of Justice, while acknowledging that the subject matter of the Convention did not fall whithin the exclusive competence of the Union, ruled that *in casu* Sweden incorrectly dissociated itself from a concerted common EU strategy.

The practice of concluding treaties in the field of the environment shows indeed that the Member States have been parties to virtually all the conventions on the environment concluded by the Union.

The conclusion of mixed agreements requires that certain matters must be regulated as regards the relationship between the Union and its Member States on the one hand, and the other parties to the convention on the other. Thus multilateral conventions in particular generally contain a provision on the exercise of voting rights under the treaty.

For example, Article 31(2) of the Convention on Biological Diversity[55] provides that regional economic integration organisations, in matters within their competence, shall exercise their right to vote with a number of votes equal to the number of their member states which are parties to the convention. However, the Union may not exercise its right to vote if the Member States exercise theirs, and vice versa. Similar provisions can be found in other conventions on the environment.[56]

Another problem with regard to mixed environmental agreements concerns the extent to which the Union and its Member States are bound by them vis-à-vis the other contracting parties. After all, mixed agreements are concluded because neither the Union nor the Member States has exclusive competence. To what extent does this internal division of powers affect the legal position of the other parties? Is the Union only bound as far as third countries are concerned in respect of those provisions which fall within its competence? To overcome these problems, most recent multilateral treaties on the environment contain specific provisions on the matter.

Again, the Convention on Biological Diversity provides an example. Article 34(2) of the convention provides that, if the Union becomes a party to the convention without any of the Member States being a party, it shall be bound by all the obligations under the convention. If one or more of the Member States should be a party to the convention, the Union and its Member States must decide on their respective responsibilities under the convention. To that end they must declare the extent of their competence to the other parties to the convention (Article 34(3)). Similar provisions can be found in other conventions on the environment.[57]

---

[55] OJ 1993 L 309/1.

[56] See, for example, Article 24(2) of the Basel Convention, OJ 1993 L 39/23.

[57] See, for example, Articles 22(2) and (3) of the Basel Convention, OJ 1993 L 39/23.

However, in most cases, closer study of such declarations only reveals the contours of the internal delineation of competence. Thus the Declaration by the Union regarding the extent of its competence in the context of the Convention on Biological Diversity reads:[58]

'In accordance with the relevant provisions of the Treaty establishing the European Economic Community, the Community alongside its Member States has competence to take actions aiming at the protection of the environment.

In relation to the matters covered by the Convention, the Community has adopted several legal instruments, both as part of its environment policy and in the framework of other sectoral policies, the most relevant of which are listed below: [...]'

Following which twelve directives and regulations are mentioned, including the Directive on Wild Birds[59] and the Habitats Directive.[60] It cannot be inferred from this Declaration how the precise division of competence between the Union and its Member States, with specific reference to the individual provisions of the convention, is regulated. Nor are the similar declarations in most other multilateral environmental conventions models of clarity and precision.[61]

The advantage to the Union and its Member States is that they are still able to operate with some degree of flexibility. The disadvantage of such an imprecise declaration to the other parties is, however, that it is not always clear which party they can call to account for performance of the obligations under the Convention.

A good example of the confusion caused by these imprecise declarations is provided by the *Slovak Bears* case.[62] A Slovak NGO (LZV) requested that the Slovak ministry for the environment inform it of any administrative decision-making procedures which might potentially affect the protection of nature and the environment, or which concerned granting derogations to the protection of certain species or areas. On the 21st of April 2008 the Ministry took a decision granting a hunting association's application for permission to derogate from the protective conditions accorded to brown bears. In the course of that procedure it notified the Ministry that it wished to participate, seeking recognition of its status

---

[58] OJ 1993 L 309/1.

[59] OJ 1979 L 103/1, later amended.

[60] OJ 1992 L 206/7.

[61] Cf. with respect to UNCLOS, Case C-459/03 *Commission* v. *Ireland* [2006] ECR I-4635 (*MOX* case), para. 105 *et seq.* where the Court of Justice ruled that within the specific context of that Convention the Declaration of Community competence confirms that a transfer of areas of shared competence, in particular in regard to the prevention of marine pollution, took place within the framework of the Convention, subject only to the *existence* of Union rules. Cf. on this case also Lavranos (2009).

[62] Case C-240/09 *Lesoochranárske zoskupenie VLK*, Judgment of 8 March 2011 (*Slovak Bears*). See critically on that judgment Jans (2011).

as a 'party' to the administrative proceedings under the provisions of Article 14 of the Slovakian Administrative Procedure Code. In particular, LZV asserted that the proceedings in question directly affected its rights and legally protected interests arising from the Aarhus Convention. It also considered that convention to have direct effect. The Ministry however, argued that LZV did not have the status of 'party' but of 'participant' or 'interested party'. This status precludes NGOs from directly initiating proceedings themselves to review the legality of decisions, also according to the Bratislava Regional Court. In appeal the Slovak Supreme Court referred preliminary questions on the interpretation of the Aarhus Convention to the Court of Justice. In particular, it wanted to know whether Article 9(3) of the Aarhus Convention is directly effective within the meaning of settled case law of the Court of Justice.

With respect to the Aarhus Convention, the Council declared:

> '[...] that the legal instruments in force do not cover fully the implementation of the obligations resulting from Article 9(3) of the Convention as they relate to administrative and judicial procedures to challenge acts and omissions by private persons and public authorities other than the institutions of the European Community as covered by Article 2(2)(d) of the Convention, and that, consequently, its Member States are responsible for the performance of these obligations at the time of approval of the Convention by the European Community and will remain so unless and until the Community, in the exercise of its powers under the EC Treaty, adopts provisions of Community law covering the implementation of those obligations.'

In view of this declaration one might have expected the Court of Justice to have abstained – in line with the opinion of Advocate General Sharpston – from giving a ruling on the possible direct effect in EU law of Article 9(3) Aarhus Convention. Basically the question is, whether the Court of Justice itself or the competent court of a Member State is best-placed to determine whether Article 9(3) of the Aarhus Convention has direct effect or not? The general rule on this has been laid down by the Court in *Merck Genéricos*.[63] In essence the Court held in that judgment, that the jurisdiction to ascribe direct effect to a provision of a mixed agreement depends on whether that provision is found in a sphere in which the EU had legislated. If so, EU law would apply; if not, the legal order of a Member State was neither required nor forbidden to accord to individuals the right to rely directly on the rule in question. The Court, however, took another view and decided 'that Article 9(3) of the Aarhus Convention does not have direct effect in EU law'.[64]

In order to reach this conclusion, the Court started its reasoning by pointing out that the dispute concerns the grant of derogations to the system of protection

---

[63] Case C-431/05 *Merck Genéricos Produtos Farmacêuticos* [2007] ECR I-7001.

[64] Cf. also Chapter 5, sections 5.1 and 5.2.

for brown bears, a species mentioned in Annex IV(a) to the Habitats Directive. It follows, according to the Court, that the dispute falls within the scope of Union law and that the dispute 'relates to a field covered in large measure' by an Union directive.

This inevitably means that Article 9(3) of the Aarhus Convention would almost always fall within the scope of EU law. The interpretation of the Court of Justice makes the declaration of competence to the Aarhus Convention more or less obsolete and useless.

3 Article 114 TFEU (Internal Market)

Article 114 TFEU provides that the Council, acting in accordance with the ordinary legislative procedure, shall adopt the measures for the approximation of national legislation 'which have as their objective the establishment and functioning of the internal market.' It will be clear that many measures which can be characterised as environmental measures may also have a significant impact on the establishment of the internal market. This is recognised in the Treaty. The provisions of Article 114(3) TFEU, by which the Commission, in its proposals on, *inter alia*, environmental protection, will take as a base a high level of protection, indicates that at any rate certain environmental measures fall within the scope of Article 114 TFEU. The Court also held that whenever the conditions for recourse to Article 114 TFEU as a legal basis are fulfilled, the European legislature cannot be prevented from relying on that legal basis on the ground that 'public health protection' or 'consumer protection' are decisive factors in the choices to be made.[65] It is the authors' opinion that, in view of Article 114(3) TFEU, the same can be said with respect to 'environmental protection'.

Thus it could be said that the harmonisation of the conditions under which certain environmentally harmful products are placed on the market is important for attaining the free movement of goods. After all, as long as the environmental product standard rules continue to differ in the various Member States, there can be no question of the free movement of environmentally hazardous goods. Harmonisation of the conditions under which such products are allowed to be placed on the market and/or used will thus often fall within the scope of Article 114 TFEU.[66] However, many other environmental measures may also relate

---

[65] Cf. on 'public health protection' Case C-491/01 *British American Tobacco (Investments) and Imperial Tobacco* [2002] ECR I-11453 and Joined Cases C-154/04 and C-155/04 *Alliance for Natural Health and Others* [2005] ECR I-6451. And on 'consumer protection' Case C-58/08 *Vodafone and others*, Judgment of 8 June 2010, para. 36.

[66] But not always as is shown by the *Chernobyl II* case; Case C-70/88 *EP* v. *Council* [1991] ECR I-4529. Regulation 3954/87 laid down maximum permitted levels of radioactive contamination of foodstuffs and feeding-stuffs. Products with too high a level of contamination may not be placed on the market.

to the functioning of the internal market. In general one could say that any national rule concerning production conditions has an effect on competition and may therefore be subject to decision-making under Article 114 TFEU. This has been acknowledged by the Court of Justice. In the *TiO2* case concerning emission limit values, the Court of Justice, referring to its judgment in Case 92/79[67] observed:

> 'Action intended to approximate national rules concerning production conditions in a given industrial sector with the aim of eliminating distortions of competition in that sector is conducive to the attainment of the internal market and thus falls within the scope of Article 100a, a provision which is particularly appropriate to the attainment of the internal market.' The Court held that the content of Directive 89/428 on the reduction of pollution caused by waste from the titanium dioxide industry[68] fell within the scope of Article 100a EEC. The directive contained rules prohibiting or requiring the reduction of the discharge of waste and lays down timetables for the implementation of the various provisions. An unusual feature of this case was of course that the directive applied to a specific industry. The Court referred to this in its judgment.

The question which accordingly arises is to what extent environmental measures which have a more diffuse effect on the competitive position of companies could in principle fall within the scope of this article. In its judgment in the *Waste Framework Directive* case the Court acknowledged that the obligation contained in Article 4 of that directive – under which Member States were required to take the necessary measures to ensure that waste is recovered or disposed of without endangering human health and without harming the environment – can have a *certain* harmonising effect.[69] However, the mere fact that the internal market is *concerned* was insufficient to cause Article 114 TFEU to apply. It therefore seems that this case can be used to show that a measure does not fall within the scope of Article 114 TFEU, if the effect of attaining market integration is only incidental.

It is reasonable to conclude that the scope of Article 114 TFEU is in principle more than sufficient to serve as a basis for measures approximating national laws on environmental product standards and for environmental measures which regulate conditions of production and remove appreciable distortions of

---

The Court held that the regulation was designed to protect the general public and that as a result the regulation falls outside the scope of Article 100a (now Article 95).

[67] Case 92/79 *Commission* v. *Italy* [1980] ECR 1115, discussed in Chapter 1, section 1.

[68] OJ 1989 L 201/56.

[69] Case C-155/91 *Commission* v. *Council* [1993] ECR I-939. The Court's approach in the *Waste Framework Directive* case has been confirmed in Case C-187/93 *EP* v. *Council* [1994] ECR I-2857. See also, outside environmental law, Case C-376/98 *Germany* v. *EP and Council* [2000] ECR I-2247, para. 108, where the Court of Justice ruled that, in order to trigger a competence under Article 114 TFEU, the distortion must be 'appreciable'.

competition in a particular industry. In those cases it could be argued that the primary objective of the measure is related to 'the establishment or functioning of the internal market'. For more general environmental measures, which rather than having a *specific* effect on the competitive position of companies have a more *diffuse* effect, it can be concluded from the case law that when the effects are of an incidental nature, the measure falls outside the scope of Article 114 TFEU and should therefore be based on Article 192 TFEU. Examples of environmental measures the Council has based on Article 114 TFEU and its 'predecessors' the 'old' Article 95 EC and Article 100a EEC are:

- Directive 2001/18 on the deliberate release into the environment of genetically modified organisms;[70]
- the 'old' and 'new' Batteries Directive;[71]
- Directive 92/112 on procedures for harmonizing the programmes for the reduction and eventual elimination of pollution caused by waste from the titanium dioxide industry;[72]
- Directive 94/62 on packaging and packaging waste;[73]
- the Biocides Directive;[74]
- Directive 2006/40 relating to emissions from air conditioning systems in motor vehicles;[75]
- Regulation 1907/2006 on the Registration, Evaluation and Authorisation of Chemicals (REACH)[76] and
- Directive 2009/125 establishing a framework for the setting of ecodesign requirements for energy-related products.[77]

These are indeed measures in which the preamble states that European action is needed on the one hand because the laws in force in the Member States may constitute a barrier to trade or result in unfair conditions of competition and on the other because measures are necessary from the point of view of protecting the environment.

---

[70] OJ 2001 L 106/1.

[71] Directive 91/157, OJ 1991 L 78/38, repealed by Directive 2006/66, OJ 2006 L 266/1.

[72] OJ 1992 L 409/11.

[73] OJ 1994 L 365/10.

[74] Directive 98/8, OJ 1998 L 123/1.

[75] OJ 2006 L 161/12.

[76] OJ 2006 L 396/1; See on this regulation Chapter 8, section 15.1.

[77] OJ 2009 L 285/10.

4   Article 192 or Article 114 TFEU?

It is settled case law that the choice of the legal basis for a European measure must be based on objective factors which are amenable to judicial review and include in particular the aim and content of the measure.[78] In other words, the European legislature is not free to choose a legal basis as he sees fit. With respect to the use of Article 192 or Article 114 TFEU (or any other legal basis),[79] it is important to look for the 'centre of gravity' of the measure. Or in the words of the Court of Justice:

> 'If examination of a Community measure reveals that it pursues a twofold purpose or that it has a twofold component and if one of those is identifiable as the main or predominant purpose or component, whereas the other is merely incidental, the act must be based on a single legal basis, namely that required by the main or predominant purpose or component'.[80]

The fact that a measure pursues an environmental objective does not necessarily imply that Article 192 TFEU is the correct legal basis.[81] The main rule is: a single legal basis, either Article 192 TFEU or Article 114 TFEU. And indeed, it is clear from the practice of the past few years that environmental directives and regulations are based either on Article 192 or Article 114 TFEU. Exceptionally, if on the other hand it is established that the act simultaneously pursues a number of objectives or has several components that are 'indissociably linked', without one being secondary and indirect in relation to the other, such an act will have to be founded on both legal bases, the Court followed in Case C-178/03. This is provided that the procedures laid down for each legal basis are not incompatible with each other and the use of two legal bases does not undermine the rights of the Parliament.[82] Where different decision-making procedures are combined, their modalities must also be combined. In practice this means that the 'more

---

[78] Case 45/86 *Commission* v. *Council* [1987] ECR 1493, para. 11; Case C-300/89 *Commission* v. *Council (TiO2)* [1991] ECR I-2867, para. 10; Case C-268/94 *Portugal* v. *Council* [1996] ECR I-6177, para. 22; Case C-176/03 *Commission* v. *Council* [2005] ECR I-7879, para. 45 and Case C-411/06 *Commission* v. *Parliament and Council* [2009] ECR I-7585, para. 46.

[79] Cf. with respect to the claim of the Commission that Regulation 1013/2006 on shipments of waste should have had a dual legal basis (environment and common commercial policy): Case C-411/06 *Commission* v. *Parliament and Council* [2009] ECR I-7585. The Court dismissed the action.

[80] Case C-178/03 *Commission* v. *EP and Council* [2006] ECR I-107, para. 42. And more recent Case C-411/06 *Commission* v. *Parliament and Council* [2009] ECR I-7585, paras. 46-47.

[81] E.g. Case C-377/98 *Netherlands* v. *EP and Council* [2000] ECR I-6229. The case concerned an application for annulment of Directive 98/44 on the legal protection of biotechnological inventions; OJ 1998 L 213/13.

[82] Case C-178/03 *Commission* v. *EP and Council* [2006] ECR I-107, para 59. But see already Case C-300/89 *Commission* v. *Council (TiO2)* [1991] ECR I-2867.

demanding' of the procedures must be adhered to plus any additional requirements of the less demanding procedure.

> Todays practice shows a few examples of environmental measures which have
> a dual legal basis. Take for instance Regulation 842/2006 on certain fluorinated
> greenhouse gases.[83] According to the EU legislature, it is the primary objective
> of the regulation to reduce the emissions of the fluorinated greenhouse gases
> covered by the Kyoto Protocol and thus to protect the environment and that there-
> fore the legal base should be Article 192(1) TFEU. Nevertheless, the legislature
> felt it appropriate to take measures on the basis of Article 114 TFEU to harmonise
> requirements on the use of fluorinated greenhouse gases and the marketing and
> labeling of products and equipment containing fluorinated greenhouse gases.
>   Other examples of a combined 192/114 legal basis include Directive 2006/66 on
> batteries and accumulators and waste batteries and accumulators and Directive
> 2009/28 on the promotion of the use of energy from renewable sources.[84]

These examples demonstrate that the combination of the decision-making
procedures of Article 114 TFEU and Article 192(1) TFEU is clearly possible. Both
provide for use of the ordinary legislative procedure. However, when combined,
the Committee of the Regions must be consulted. Furthermore, the measure in
question must address the problem of more stringent national measures. As far
as the measure is based upon Article 192 TFEU, Article 193 TFEU is applicable.
As far as provisions are based upon Article 114 TFEU and Member States want
to derogate from them by taking more stricter environmental standards, the
procedure and the conditions of Article 114(4-6) TFEU have to be followed.[85]

> An elegant solution to the problems caused by the differences between the two
> can be found, e.g. in Article 14 of Regulation 842/2006. This example makes
> it quite clear than the differences between Article 193 TFEU and Article 114(4-
> 6) TFEU do not make the decision-making procedures of Article 192 TFEU and
> Article 114 TFEU incompatible. Article 14 reads: 'Without prejudice to Article 9(3),
> Member States may maintain or introduce more stringent protective measures in
> accordance with the procedures laid down in Article 95 of the Treaty [now Article
> 114 TFEU], in relation to Articles 7, 8 and 9 of this Regulation, or Article 176 of the
> Treaty [now Article 193 TFEU] in relation to other Articles of this Regulation.'

Whether the decision-making procedure of Article 114 TFEU can be combined
with Article 192(2) TFEU seems questionable. In fact this would mean that the

---

[83] OJ 2006 L 161/1. See for another example Directive 2006/66 on batteries and accumulators and waste
batteries and accumulators, OJ 2006 L 266/1.

[84] OJ 2006 L 266/1 and OJ 2009 L 140/16, respectively.

[85] Cf. on Articles 193 TFEU and 114(4-6) TFEU and their differences, Chapter 3, sections 5 and 6 in
particular.

Council would have to act unanimously during the ordinary legislative procedure. That would make the *ordinary* legislative procedure a *special* one!

With respect to the combination of the decision-making procedures of Article 207 TFEU and Article 192(1) TFEU the Court ruled in Case C-178/03 that they are not incompatible.[86]

5   Article 207 TFEU (Common Commercial Policy)

Where environmental product standards are applied to direct imports from third countries, the question arises as to how this is compatible with the Union's competence in respect of the common commercial policy, as conferred by Article 207 TFEU. This question is relevant in at least two respects:

· the decision-making procedure for measures implementing the common commercial policy is different from the procedures in respect of Union environment policy and
· the Union's powers in respect of the common commercial policy are in principle *exclusive,* meaning that national measures are, in principle *ultra vires.*[87]

An important question, therefore, is to what extent an external environment policy – if it also affects trade with third countries – must be regarded as common commercial policy within the meaning of Article 207 TFEU. For years there has been a conflict between the institutions, in particular the Council and the European Commission, as to the extent of the Union's competence in respect of the common commercial policy. The Commission prefers to take a more *objective* and *instrumental* approach to the interpretation of the article. This implies that all the common commercial policy measures listed (not exhaustively) in Article 207 TFEU, whether unilateral or by international agreement, as well as all related measures, fall within the competence of the Union, irrespective of the purpose for which the measures are applied. According to the Commission, measures regulating international trade often pursue a wide range of different objectives, but this does not mean that they must be adopted on the basis of the various Treaty provisions relating to those objectives. Thus, in the environmental sector, the Commission has regarded measures implementing a system of import and export licences in the trade in endangered species of wild fauna and flora and a system of notification on the import of certain dangerous chemicals as common commercial policy measures.[88]

---

[86]   Case C-178/03 *Commission* v. *EP and Council* [2006] ECR I-107, paras. 58-59.

[87]   Cf. Article 3(1) under e) TFEU. Cf. also Case C-173/05 *Commission* v. *Italy* [2007] ECR I-4917, where the Court declared that an environmental tax levied on Algerian methane gas violates a.o. Article 207 TFEU.

[88]   See, for example, the proposal of the Commission to implement the CITES Convention, OJ 1980 C 243/16 and the proposal of the Commission for the Whales Regulation, OJ 1980 C 121/5.

In contrast with the *instrumental* doctrine pursued by the European Commission is the more *subjective* approach taken by the Council, looking to the content of a measure to identify its objectives. In this view, it is the objectives of an intended measure that are paramount. If these are not common commercial policy objectives, but are rather prompted by considerations of development policy or environmental protection, they cannot be based on Article 207 TFEU. Normal common commercial policy measures, for instance containing a system of import and export licences, were based on Article 192 TFEU or on Article 352 TFEU, where the purpose of the measure was the protection of species of wild fauna and flora or the environment.[89] Only in exceptional cases has it based measures on the common commercial policy provision in the Treaty, for example Regulation 3254/91 prohibiting the use of certain kinds of traps,[90] which it based both on Article 207 TFEU and on Article 192 TFEU. However, the preamble to the regulation offers no clue as to why Article 207 TFEU was used in this case.

The Court of Justice handed down a number of important judgments concerning the borderline between environmental protection and common commercial policy. The first case to be discussed is the *Chernobyl I* case.[91]

> This case concerned uniform rules on the conditions under which agricultural products from third countries, which could be radioactively contaminated, could be imported into the EU. In its judgment, the Court held that such a measure comes under the exclusive common commercial policy competence of the Union and not within the sphere of operation of the environmental Title of the Treaty. The preamble to the regulation stated that 'the Community must continue to ensure that agricultural products and processed agricultural products intended for human consumption and likely to be contaminated are introduced into the Community only according to common arrangements' and that those 'common arrangements should safeguard the health of consumers, maintain, without having unduly adverse effects on trade between the Community and third countries, the unified nature of the market and prevent deflections of trade'. According to the Court the regulation established uniform rules regarding the conditions under which agricultural products likely to be contaminated may be imported into the Community from non-member countries: 'It follows that, according to its objectives and its content, as they appear from the very terms of the regulation, the regulation is intended to regulate trade between the Community and non-member countries; accordingly it comes within the common commercial policy within the meaning of Article 113 [now Article 207 TFEU] of the EEC Treaty.'

---

[89] See for instance the CITES-Regulation 3626/82, OJ 1982 L 384/1 (and its successor Regulation 338/97, OJ 1997 L 61/1) and Regulation 304/2003 concerning the export and import of dangerous chemicals, OJ 2003 L 63/1.

[90] OJ 1991 L 308/1.

[91] Case C-62/88 *EP* v. *Council* [1990] ECR I-1527.

This judgment makes it clear that common commercial policy measures which at the same time pursue environmental objectives may fall within the sphere of operation of Article 207 TFEU. If a measure, according to its objective and its content, is intended to regulate trade with countries outside the Union, it is a common commercial policy measure, even if it includes provisions concerning environmental protection. However, it will have to be determined in each individual case whether a measure, according to its objective and its content, is intended to regulate trade between the Union and third countries.

The second case to be discussed is the Court's judgment in de *Cartagena Protocol* case.[92] In the context of the Convention on Biological Diversity, the parties to that convention negotiated a protocol on biosafety, specifically focusing on transboundary movement, of any living modified organism (LMO) resulting from modern biotechnology that may have adverse effect on the conservation and sustainable use of biological diversity, setting out for consideration, in particular, appropriate procedure for advance informed agreement (the so-called Cartagena Protocol). The European Commission and the Council had different views on the correct legal basis to conclude the protocol. While the Commission's proposal was based on Articles 207 TFEU and 192(4) TFEU, the Council argued that the protocol should be concluded on the basis of Article 192(1) TFEU alone. On request of the Commission, the Court gave an Opinion pursuant to Article 218(11) TFEU and ruled that a single use of Article 192(1) TFEU is the appropriate legal basis for conclusion of the Protocol on behalf of the Union.

> The key question in this case was, whether the protocol constitutes an agreement principally concerning environmental protection which is liable to have incidental effects on trade in LMOs, or whether, conversely, it is principally an agreement concerning international trade policy which incidentally takes account of certain environmental requirements. After a close examination of the Cartagena Protocol the Court concluded that 'the Protocol is, in the light of its context, its aim and its content, an instrument intended essentially to improve biosafety and not to promote, facilitate or govern trade.'

The importance of Opinion 2/00 is in particular that, with respect to the delimitation of powers between common commercial policy and environmental protection, the Court for the first time applied the *centre of gravity* doctrine, discussed already in section 4 of this chapter. In this case the Commission argued that the fact that provisions governing international trade in certain products pursue objectives which are not primarily commercial cannot have the effect of excluding the Union's exclusive competence and justifying recourse to, in the case of environmental objectives, Article 192 TFEU. By applying the *centre of gravity* doctrine, the Court showed that this interpretation can no longer be maintained.[93]

---

[92] Opinion 2/00 [2001] ECR I-9713.

[93] Cf. for a similar approach of the Court of Justice applying the centre of gravity doctrine and referring to its Opinion 2/00, Case C-411/06 *Commission* v. *Parliament and Council* [2009] ECR I-7585. The Court

The third case we would like to mention is the *Energy Star Agreement* case.[94] In 1992 the United States Environmental Protection Agency (the EPA) set up a voluntary labeling programme for office equipment, called the Energy Star Program. The programme, which enjoyed a high level of manufacturer participation, encouraged the vast majority of manufacturers to introduce energy-saving features and raised consumer awareness of the energy losses of office equipment in stand-by mode. After observing that the Energy Star requirements were becoming the standard worldwide, the European Commission decided that, rather than developing a separate labelling programme for energy-efficient office equipment in the EU, the better course was to introduce the Energy Star Program there. On 1 July 1999 the Commission submitted to the Council, for the purpose of concluding an agreement with the United States (the Energy Star Agreement), a proposal for a decision based on Article 207 TFEU. On 14 May 2001 the Council, by Decision 2001/469, approved the Energy Star Agreement on the basis of Article 192(1) TFEU. Accordingly, it was signed in Washington on 19 December 2000. The Commission, however, was of the opinion that Decision 2001/469 should have been adopted on the basis of Article 207 TFEU, on the ground that the Energy Star Agreement seeks to facilitate trade and brought an action for annulment under Article 263 TFEU. The Court concluded that 'the Energy Star Agreement simultaneously pursues a commercial-policy objective and an environmental-protection objective.' However, the commercial-policy objective pursued by the agreement had to be regarded as predominant, so that the decision approving the agreement should have been based on Article 207 TFEU:

'It is true that in the long term, depending on how manufacturers and consumers in fact behave, the programme should have a positive environmental effect as a result of the reduction in energy consumption which it should achieve. However, that is merely an indirect and distant effect, in contrast to the effect on trade in office equipment which is direct and immediate.'[95]

It seems that the *direct* and *immediate* effects on trade were decisive for the Court to rule that the Energy Star Agreement fell within the scope of Article 207 TFEU. This case also makes clear that, although the ultimate goal of the Energy Star logo is to persuade producers to manufacture (and consumers to buy) products with a reduced energy consumption, this does not mean that Agreement concerning the use of such a logo makes the agreement an environmental agreement.

Finally, the *Rotterdam Convention* case on the Prior Informed Consent (PIC) Procedure for certain hazardous chemicals and pesticides in international trade

---

dismissed the claim of the Commission that Regulation 1013/2006 on shipments of waste should have had a dual legal basis (environment and common commercial policy) in stead of Article 192 TFEU alone.

[94] Case C-281/01 *Commission* v. *Council* [2002] ECR I-12049. See also Chapter 8, section 8.1.

[95] Paras. 40 and 41 of the judgment.

should be mentioned.[96] According to Article 1 of the Rotterdam Convention, its objective is 'to promote shared responsibility and cooperative efforts among Parties in the international trade of certain hazardous chemicals in order to protect human health and the environment from potential harm and to contribute to their environmentally sound use'. Article 5 of the Convention established a procedure for the exchange of information concerning actions taken by the parties in order to ban or severely restrict the use of a chemical product on their territory, while Article 12 of the Convention imposed on the same parties an obligation to send an export notification to the importing party where a banned or severely restricted chemical is exported from their territory and which also calls on the latter party formally to acknowledge receipt of that notification. Those provisions are intended, in essence, to ensure that no party, in particular a developing country, is confronted with imports of hazardous chemicals without first having had an opportunity to take the requisite precautions to protect human health and the environment. The proposal of the Commission to approve the convention was based on Article 207 TFEU, but the Council took its decision exclusively on Article 192 TFEU. The Court found that the decision approving that Convention should have been based on the combined legal bases of Articles 207 and 192(1) TFEU. The Court held that it cannot be denied that the protection of human health and the environment was the most important concern in the mind of the signatories of the Convention. However, that alone does not justify Article 192 TFEU as a single legal basis, as the Court found that the commercial component of the Convention is not 'purely incidental':

> 'A reading of the provisions of the Convention and, more particularly, of its articles concerning the PIC procedure, prompts the conclusion that the Convention also contains rules governing trade in hazardous chemicals and having *direct* and *immediate* effects on such trade' [emphasis added]. [...] 'it must therefore be concluded that the Convention includes, both as regards the aims pursued and its contents, two indissociably linked components, neither of which can be regarded as secondary or indirect as compared with the other, one falling within the scope of the common commercial policy and the other within that of protection of human health and the environment. In accordance with the case-law cited in paragraph 36 of the present judgment, the decision approving that Convention on behalf of the Community should therefore have been based on the two corresponding legal bases, namely, in this case, Articles 133 EC and 175(1) EC [now Articles 207 and 192(1) TFEU] [...].'

---

[96] Case C-94/03 *Commission* v. *Council* [2006] ECR I-1. See also Chapter 8, section 13.4. Cf. also on dual grounds, with respect to CITES, Case C-370/07 *Commission* v. *Council* [2009] ECR I-8917.

6 'Comitology', Delegated Acts and Implementing Measures

As in most national systems, the legislature can delegate implementing powers to the executive. Of course, the Commission's implementing powers are governed by the principle of conferred powers and that may act only within the limits of the powers conferred upon them by the Treaties.[97] When Council and Parliament adopt a new environmental measure in most cases the measure itself only provide the broader framework. But more detailed measures, for example lists of substances or products still need to be defined. The Commission is often empowered to implement EU legislation with the assistance of committees composed of representatives from the Member States, in accordance with a procedure known as 'comitology'.[98] In practice this meant that, each legislative instrument specified the scope of the implementing powers conferred on the Commission by the Council. Relations between the Commission and the committees were based on models set out in a Council Decision, the so-called Comitology Decision.[99] In general a directive or a regulation contained a reference to the applicable procedure to be followed.[100] This system was criticised for its lack of transparency and democratic oversight.

The Lisbon Treaty changed this to a certain extent by making a distinction between *delegated* and *implementing* powers. According to Article 290(1) TFEU a legislative act may *delegate* to the Commission the power to adopt non-legislative acts of general application to supplement or amend certain non-essential elements of the legislative act. The objectives, content, scope and duration of the delegation of power shall be explicitly defined in the legislative acts. The essential elements of an area shall be reserved for the legislative act and accordingly shall not be the subject of a delegation of power. The adjective 'delegated' is to be inserted in the title of delegated acts.

On the other hand Article 291 TFEU states that Member States shall adopt all measures of national law necessary to *implement* legally binding Union acts. However, where uniform conditions for implementing legally binding Union acts are needed, those acts shall confer implementing powers on the Commis-

---

[97] Joined Cases C-14/06 and C-295/06 *Parliament and Denmark* v. *Commission* [2008] ECR I-1649, concerning an action for annulment of Commission Decision 2005/717 amending the Annex to Directive 2002/95 on the restriction of the use of certain hazardous substances in electrical and electronic equipment.

[98] See for a more in-depth treatment of the issue Lee (2005) at 85 *et seq.*

[99] Regulation 182/2011 laying down the rules and general principles concerning mechanisms for control by Member States of the Commission's exercise of implementing powers, OJ 2011 L 55/13. This regulation repeals the procedure of Council Decision 1999/468. Cf. Case C-378/00 *Commission* v. *EP and Council* [2003] ECR I-937, in respect to the implementation of the Financial Instrument for the Environment (LIFE) and Case C-122/04 *Commission* v. *EP and Council* [2006] ECR I-2001, in respect to the implementation of the Forest Focus programme.

[100] E.g. Article 9 of Directive 2006/118 on the protection of groundwater against pollution and deterioration, OJ 2006 L 372/19.

sion. Paragraph 3 of Article 291 TFEU makes clear that the implementing measures of the Commission are still under 'comitology' control, via regulation 182/2011, by the Member States.

Although it is not always easy to make a clear distinction between between *delegated* and *implementing* measures, the 'delegated act' is defined in terms of its scope and consequences – as a general measure that supplements or amends non-essential elements – whereas the 'implementing act' is determined by its rationale – the need for uniform conditions for implementation. In the system introduced by Article 291 TFEU (implementing acts) the Commission does not exercise any real normative competence; its power is purely executive.

> As an example we take Directive 2010/75 on industrial emissions (integrated pollution prevention and control).[101] According to Article 76 of the Directive the Commission can exercise its *delegated* powers with respect to, a.o., the emission monitoring provisions in Annex V. This delegation of power, however, may be revoked at any time by the European Parliament or by the Council (Article 77). European Parliament or the Council can exercise some *ex post* control as they may object to a delegated act whithin a period of 2 months. If either the European Parliament or the Council objects to the delegated act it shall not enter into force. On the other hand, according to Article 41 of the Directive, *implementing* rules shall be established concerning, e.g., the determination of the start-up and shut-down periods referred to in point 27 of Article 3 and in point 1 of Part 4 of Annex V of the directive. These implementing measures are to be exercised under 'comitology' (Article 75 of the directive).

These differences might be the potential for future institutional disagreement over the classification of acts, as delegated or implementing and over the choice to use one or another category to be determined by the legislator in a legislative act.

7   Other Incidental Legal Bases

7.1   Article 194 TFEU (Energy)

As we already mentioned in Chapter 1 an interesting innovation brought by the Treaty of Lisbon is the introduction of a Title on Union energy policy (Title XXI). Again, this Title probably contains little more than a codification of the *status quo*. Before the entry into force of the Treaty of Lisbon energy law was implemented on the basis of the provisions on the internal market, the competition provisions and the provisions on environmental protection. The new Article 194 TFEU reiterates the connection with the internal market as well as the environmental protection component of European energy policy. Con-

---

[101] OJ 2010 L 334/17.

cerning the latter the third indent of Article 194(1) TFEU states that EU energy policy shall aim, *inter alia*, to 'promote energy efficiency and energy saving and the development of new and renewable forms of energy'.[102] The Energy Title contains a legal basis in the form of Article 194(2) TFEU. Interestingly, the Energy Title allows only for an EU energy policy 'in the context of the establishment and functioning of the internal market and with regard for the need to preserve and improve the environment'. This places EU energy policy clearly in an environmental perspective. At the same time it entails a significant restriction of the scope of this Title in that such policy appears to be constrained to the internal market. This market entails free movement of goods[103] and undistorted conditions of competition.[104] This may allow only for a European energy policy insofar as the internal market in energy is concerned.

> See for example Directive 2010/30 on the indication by labelling and standard product information of the consumption of energy and other resources by energy-related products.[105] This directive is a recast of Directive 92/75 on the indication by labelling and standard product information of the consumption of energy and other resources by household appliances. Remarkable is that Directive 92/75 had the 'old' Article 100a EEC as its legal basis (internal market). This seems to imply that derogating from the new recast directive, by taking more stringent measures by the Member States, is no longer possible.[106]

An *external* energy environment policy will probably have to be conducted on the basis of Article 192 TFEU as it is outside the scope of the internal market. The inclusion of climate change as a regional or worldwide environmental problem that may be addressed in the European Union's environmental policy confirms this.

7.2   Article 39 TFEU (Common Agricultural Policy)

Under Article 39 TFEU the objectives of the common agricultural policy (CAP) are: to increase agricultural productivity; to ensure a fair standard of living for the agricultural community; to stabilise markets; to assure the availability of supplies; and to ensure that supplies reach consumers at reasonable prices. In view of the integration principle, it is still strange that the text of Article 39 TFEU does not contain any reference whatsoever to the envi-

---

[102] In Case C-2/10 *Azienda Agro-Zootecnica Franchini*, Judgment of 21 July 2011, para. 55, the Court ruled that the objective of developing new and renewable forms of energy does not imply that this objective should take precedence over the environmental protection objectives pursued by the Habitats and Wild Birds Directives.

[103] Art. 26(2) TFEU.

[104] Cf. Lisbon Treaty Protocol No 27 on the Internal Market and Competition.

[105] OJ 2010 L 153/1.

[106] See also Chapter 3, section 6.

ronmental objectives or to sustainable development, even though it is generally acknowledged that the CAP can be a major source of environmental damage.[107] Furthermore, there are strong links between agriculture and biodiversity, genetic resources, genetically modified organisms, climate change, soil protection, pesticides, forestry, nitrates and water pollution. Environmental considerations have played a role in some measures which have been adopted, even if only in part, within the context of the common agricultural policy.[108] Important measures which have been taken in this context concern:

- Directive 1107/2009 concerning the placing of plant protection products on the market;[109]
- Regulation 834/2007 on organic production and labelling of organic products.[110]

Similarly, at the international level, the Union is a party to the Agreement on the International Dolphin Conservation Programme.[111]

As far as the relationship between the provisions on CAP and the environment paragraph in the Treaty is concerned, the *Hormones* case is of particular interest.[112] In that judgment the Court of Justice stated that:

'Article 43 of the Treaty [now TFEU] is the appropriate legal basis for any legislation concerning the production and marketing of agricultural products listed in Annex II to the Treaty which contributes to the achievement of one or more of the objectives of the common agricultural policy set out in Article 39 of the Treaty [now TFEU]. There is no need to have recourse to Article 100 [now Article 115 TFEU] of the Treaty where such legislation involves the harmonisation of provisions of national law in that field.'

In this connection, one could argue that the Union powers in respect of the common agricultural policy and the common transport policy are indivisible and include everything necessary for the management of these sectors: the attainment of free movement, price intervention measures, external relations, as well as flanking measures, such as elements of social policy relating specifically to these sectors. It seemed that the provisions on CAP (and the same holds for the provisions on transport policy) have priority over all provisions conferring competence in so far as the measures in question concern agricultural products or transport services, and are designed to attain the specific objectives of these

---

[107] Cf. Strategy for integrating the environmental dimension into the CAP, adopted at European Council in Helsinki (December 1999).

[108] See for a detailed study of the application of the integration principle in CAP, Dhondt (2003).

[109] OJ 2009 L 309/1.

[110] OJ 2007 L 189/1.

[111] Decision 1999/337 on the signature by the EC of the Agreement on the International Dolphin Conservation Programme, OJ 1999 L 132.

[112] Case 68/86 *UK v. Council* [1988] ECR 855.

sectoral policies. In these cases there is neither room nor need for an additional legal basis in either Article 114 or Article 192 TFEU.

As far as the relationship between Article 43 and Article 192 TFEU is concerned, in the *Drift-Net* case[113] the Court of Justice stated that Regulation 345/92,[114] which prohibited the use of drift-nets, was rightly based on Article 43 (now TFEU) since its principal objective was the protection of marine resources. The integration principle implies that a European measure cannot be part of Union action on environmental matters merely because it takes account of environmental requirements.

However, the theory of the 'indivisibility' of the CAP may require rethinking in view of the Court's judgment in Case C-164/97.[115] The case concerned an action brought by the European Parliament for the annulment, first, of Regulation 307/97 on the protection of the Community's forests against atmospheric pollution and, second, Regulation 308/97 on protection of the Community's forests against fire.[116] The regulations, whose purpose was to extend for a further five years the duration of Union schemes to increase the protection of forests against, respectively, atmospheric pollution and fire, were adopted on the basis of Article 43 TFEU. The Parliament maintained that they were adopted on an inappropriate legal basis, so that its prerogatives in respect of the procedure involving its participation in the drafting of legislation were undermined. In its view both regulations should have been based on Article 192 TFEU. The Court ruled that:

'Although the measures referred to in the regulations may have certain positive repercussions on the functioning of agriculture, those indirect consequences are incidental to the primary aim of the Community schemes for the protection of forests, which are intended to ensure that the natural heritage represented by forest ecosystems is conserved and turned to account, and does not merely consider their utility to agriculture. Measures to defend the forest environment against the risks of destruction and degradation associated with fires and atmospheric pollution inherently form part of the environmental action for which Community competence is founded on Article 130s [now Article 192 TFEU] of the Treaty.'

The Court added:

'With more particular reference to the common agricultural policy and the Community environmental policy, there is nothing in the case-law to indicate that, in principle, one should take precedence over the other. It makes clear that

---

[113] Case C-405/92 *Etablissements Armand Mondiet* v. *Société Armement Islais* [1993] ECR I-6133.

[114] OJ 1992 L 42/15.

[115] Joined Cases C-164/97 and C-165/97 *EP* v. *Council* [1999] ECR I-1139.

[116] OJ 1997 L 51/9 and OJ 1997 L 51/11.

a Community measure cannot be part of Community action on environmental matters merely because it takes account of requirements of protection referred to in Article 130r(2) of the EC Treaty' [now Article 191(2) TFEU].

This seems to indicate that the Court has dissociated itself from the doctrine of the indivisibility of the CAP. Indeed, the *Huber* case, indicates that the 'centre of gravity' doctrine is also applicable with respect to delimit the agricultural competences from those under the environment paragraph.[117] The case involved the correct legal basis of Regulation 2078/92 on agricultural production methods compatible with the requirements of the protection of the environment and the maintenance of the countryside.[118] The regulation had as its legal basis Articles 42 and 43 TFEU. The Court ruled that it was clear from the regulation that the main purpose was to regulate the production of agricultural products. Promoting more environmentally friendly forms of production was considered by the Court as 'certainly a genuine objective, but an ancillary one, of the common agricultural policy'. The judgment in *Huber* seems to suggest that the Court will accept Article 192 TFEU as legal basis for those agri-environmental measures which do as their main purpose the protection of the environment.

7.3   The Provisions on the Common Transport Policy

The second sector in which the Treaty refers to a common policy is transport. In the same way as with agriculture, environmental considerations play a part in transport policy.[119] Council measures on transport, based at least partly on Articles 70-80 EC (now Articles 90-100 TFEU), and where environmental considerations figure are:

· Regulation 216/2008 on common rules in the field of civil aviation and establishing a European Aviation Safety Agency;[120]
· Directive 92/6 on the installation and use of speed limitation devices for certain categories of motor vehicles within the Community;[121]
· Directive 89/629 on the limitation of noise emissions from subsonic aircraft;[122]
· Directive 2005/35 on ship-source pollution and on the introduction of penalties for infringements.[123]

To a certain extent environment-related transport measures will be established on other Treaty provisions, in particular Article 114 TFEU. Measures harmonis-

---

[117] Case C-336/00 *Huber* [2002] ECR I-7699.

[118] OJ 1992 L 215/85.

[119] Cf. Dhondt (2003) and Rodi (2006).

[120] OJ 2008 L 79/1.

[121] OJ 1992 L 57/27.

[122] OJ 1989 L 363/27, later amended.

[123] OJ 2005 L 255/11.

ing motor vehicle emissions (Directives 98/69[124]) or environmental fuel quality specifications for petrol and diesel (Directive 98/70[125]) have their legal basis in Article 95 EC (now Article 114 TFEU).

7.4 Harmonisation of Indirect Taxes

These days a great deal is said about making more frequent use of market-oriented instruments for the pursuit of environmental policy. Financial instruments should be used to attain certain environmental objectives. One of the means at the disposal of the Member States is indirect taxation. As will be seen in Chapter 6, section 3, where Article 110 TFEU is discussed, Member States may use environmental criteria to justify tax differentiation. Put briefly, the Treaty allows the possibility of taxing products that cause more environmental pollution more than those that cause less. However, it will be clear that, if Member States introduce varying differentiations based on environmental considerations, this will have a negative impact on the operation of the internal market. Thus Article 113 TFEU offers the Council a legal basis on which to adopt provisions for the harmonisation of legislation concerning turnover taxes, excise duties and other forms of indirect taxation. The more popular the national authorities find the use of financial instruments to protect the environment, the more frequently the Council will be required to use its powers under Article 113 TFEU.[126] It should be noted that Article 113 TFEU does not provide a basis for a truly European environmental tax in the sense of an environmental tax introduced by the Union and for the Union. The only basis for such a tax is found in Article 192(2) TFEU, and would, in any case, require an extensive interpretation of the provision.

Up to now Article 113 TFEU has played only a modest role in the field of the environment. In the context of completion of the internal market, important steps have been made in harmonising the rates of VAT and customs duties. Directive 2006/112 sets out narrow margins within which the Member States may set their VAT rates.[127] Differential taxation on environmental grounds is virtually ruled out as far as VAT is concerned. It is true that the harmonised VAT rates are minimum rates, but any increase must apply to all products. In other words, goods that have been sustainably produced may not be taxed at a lower rate than those that have not.

---

[124] OJ 1998 L 350/1. See as from 1 January 2013: Regulation 715/2007 on type approval of motor vehicles with respect to emissions from light passenger and commercial vehicles (Euro 5 and Euro 6) and on access to vehicle repair and maintenance information, OJ 2007 L 171/1.

[125] OJ 1998 L 350/58.

[126] See in general Commission Communication, Tax policy in the European Union – Priorities for the years ahead, COM (2001) 260 final, OJ 2001 C 284/6.

[127] OJ 2006 L 347/1.

Directive 2008/118 concerning the general arrangements for excise duty[128] leaves more latitude for a differential system of environmental charges. It explicitly permits Member States to impose taxes on products other than those covered by the directive. However, Article 1(3) requires that these taxes should not give rise to border-crossing formalities in trade between Member States. This requirement may well prove a serious obstacle to practical implementation. The 'border', traditionally the place where imports are subjected to the national tax systems, here ceases to perform this function.[129] Other means will have to be found in national tax laws to actually impose taxes on goods, including imports.

Other influences on national environment policy can be found in Directive 2003/96 on taxation of energy products and electricity (the Energy Taxation Directive).[130] This directive extended the existing European system of minimum rates, which under a previous directive was confined to mineral oils, to coal, natural gas and electricity. Under this directive, the levels of taxation applied by the Member States may not be lower than the minimum rates set in the directive. According to Article 14 of the directive, exempt from taxation are *inter alia* energy products and electricity used to produce electricity and electricity used to maintain the ability to produce electricity. However, Member States may, for reasons of environmental policy, subject these products to taxation. And under Article 15 of the directive Member States may apply total or partial exemptions or reductions in the level of taxation to, *inter alia*, energy products used under fiscal control in the field of pilot projects for the technological development of more environmentally-friendly products or in relation to fuels from renewable sources; biofuels;[131] forms of energy which are of solar, wind, tidal or geothermal origin, or from biomass or waste. Finally, Article 19 of the directive allows for further exemptions or reductions 'for specific policy considerations'. These further reductions or exemptions need to be approved, on a proposal of the Commission, by a unanimous decision of the Council.[132] In its decisions the Council should ensure, in accordance with the integration principle, that its decisions are in line with the environmental policy of the Union.[133]

> The United Kingdom applied for a derogation allowing them to continue to apply an exemption from their climate change levy (CCL) for low-value solid fuel. According to the Council, a tax exemption would support the use of low-value solid fuel

---

[128] OJ 2008 L 9/12.

[129] See for instance Case C-313/05 *Brzeziński* [2007] ECR I-519, paras. 42-53, with respect to certain requirements relating to Polish excise duties on second-hand vehicles.

[130] Directive 92/81 was repealed by Council Directive 2003/96 restructuring the Community framework for the taxation of energy products and electricity, OJ 2003 L 283/51.

[131] Cf. Case C-201/08 *Plantanol* [2009] ECR I-8343.

[132] To the extent that an approved exemption/reduction constitutes State aid, the normal rules apply and it should be notified to the Commission in accordance with the rules on State aid.

[133] Decision 2005/153, OJ 2005 L 51/17. Cf. also Decision 2002/550 authorising the United Kingdom to apply a differentiated rate of excise duty to fuels containing biodiesel, OJ 2002 L 180/20.

for energy production instead of landfilling it. While energy use is preferable to landfilling from an environmental policy point of view, the polluter-pays principle would lead to the application of a lower rate of tax to such low-value solid fuel. The Council therefore decided that a complete exemption could be acceptable as a temporary measure only and should therefore be time-limited.

In 2011 the Commission tabled a proposal for a major revision of the Energy Taxation Directive.[134] According to the Commission is the current Energy Taxation Directive unsustainable and sets the wrong incentives. The current minimum rates based on the volume of energy products consumed do not reflect the energy content or the CO_2 emissions of the energy products, leading to inefficient energy use and distortions in the internal market. They also create incentives that are contradictory to the EU energy and climate change goals. Key of the proposal is the introduction of a CO_2-related taxation, based on the CO_2 emissions of the energy product, fixed at a level of 20 euro per tonne CO_2.

In view of its existing international obligations as well as the maintaining of the competitive position of European companies, Article 14 of Directive 2003/96 continues to exempt from taxation energy products supplied for air and sea navigation and sea navigation.[135]

7.5 Nuclear Energy and Basic Safety Standards

The most significant environmentally relevant legal bases outside the Treaty on the Functioning of the European Union are to be found in the Euratom Treaty. Chapter 3 of Title II of that Treaty in particular deserves mention here. Articles 30 to 39 require that basic standards be laid down for the protection of the health of workers and the general public against the dangers arising from ionizing radiation.[136] According to Article 30 the expression 'basic standards' means:

· maximum permissible doses compatible with adequate safety;
· maximum permissible levels of exposure and contamination;
· the fundamental principles governing the health surveillance of workers.

---

[134] Commission Communication, Smarter energy taxation for the EU: proposal for a revision of the Energy Taxation Directive, COM (2011) 168 final.

[135] National law implementing this provision cannot be regarded Sate aid in the meaning of Article 197 TFEU; Case T-351/02 *Deutsche Bahn AG* v. *Commission* [2006] ECR II-1047. Cf. also Case C-346/97 *Braathens Sverige AB* [1999] ECR I-3419, where the Court ruled, under Directive 92/81, that as this directive provided for a mandatory exemption for all public air navigation, a Member State is not allowed to levy another indirect tax on that use as it would render the exemption entirely ineffective.

[136] See Directive 96/29 laying down basic safety standards for the protection of the health of workers and the general public against the dangers arising from ionizing radiation, OJ 1996 L 159/1 and Commission Communication concerning the implementation of Council Directive 96/29/Euratom, OJ L 133/3. See further Chapter 8, section 18.1. The 'basic standards' referred to in Article 30 *et seq.* of the Euratom Treaty must be regarded as minimum standards, according to Case C-376/90 *Commission* v. *Belgium* [1992] ECR I-6153. See on this case Chapter 3, section 4.

The Union legislature has based various decisions on Articles 31 and 32 Euratom for the purpose of attaining these objectives.[137] These decisions relate to radiation from permanent plants, radioactive products, cross-border transport of radioactive waste and products contaminated with radiation. The case law shows that if the Union's measures, according to their objectives and their content, are designed to protect the general public and workers against the dangers of radioactivity, they will fall within the scope of application of Article 31 Euratom.

> In the *Chernobyl I* case, the European Parliament tried to restrict the scope of Article 31 Euratom to measures concerning protection against primary radiation, in other words, radiation released directly from a nuclear plant or resulting from the handling of fissile materials.[138] In the view of the European Parliament, Article 31 Euratom did not relate to so-called secondary radiation, that is, radiation emanating from contaminated products and other incidental consequences of primary radiation. The Court rejected this restricted interpretation: 'There is no support in the relevant legislation for that restrictive interpretation which cannot therefore be accepted. The indications are rather that the purpose of the articles referred to is to ensure the consistent and effective protection of the health of the general public against the dangers arising from ionizing radiations, whatever their source and whatever the categories of persons exposed to such radiations.'

The only real restriction on the scope of application of the article is to be found in its objectives. Advocate General Van Gerven properly concluded that Article 31 Euratom cannot be used as a legal basis for the adoption of measures relating to the establishment and functioning of the internal market. Thus the question arises as to what extent measures of the Council, based exclusively on Article 31 Euratom, may contain provisions which limit the freedom of Member States to enact more stringent measures than those actually provided for in the measures in question.[139]

Although current legal practice assumes that Articles 31 and 32 Euratom have a wide sphere of application, there is some uncertainty as to what kind of measure does fall within their scope and what does not, especially in relation to the sphere of application of the Treaty on the Functioning of the European Union.

> In the *Chernobyl II* case, the European Parliament petitioned the Court for the annulment of Regulation 3954/87 laying down maximum permitted levels of radioactive contamination of foodstuffs and feedingstuffs following a nuclear accident or other case of radiological emergency.[140] This regulation is based on Article 31 Euratom. The European Parliament contested that, in view of its effects on the

---

[137] See Chapter 8, section 18.

[138] Case C-70/88 *EP v. Council* [1991] ECR I-4529.

[139] This will be discussed in more detail in Chapter 3, section 4.

[140] Case C-70/88 *EP v. Council* [1991] ECR I-4529. See also Chapter 8, section 18.2.

internal market, it should have been based on Article 100a EEC (now Article 114 TFEU). Relevant to this problem of demarcation is Article 106a Euratom, which provides that the provisions of the Treaty on European Union and of the Treaty on the Functioning of the European Union 'shall not derogate' from the provisions of those of the Euratom Treaty. This provision therefore implies that if Article 31 Euratom provides an adequate legal basis for a given measure, Article 114 TFEU cannot apply, even if it could be shown that Article 114 TFEU would in principle be appropriate.

The Court noted that, according to the preamble, the aim of the regulation was to provide for the establishment of basic standards for the protection of the health of the general public and workers. As far as its content is concerned, the regulation lays down maximum permitted levels of radioactive contamination of foodstuffs and feedingstuffs. If these levels are exceeded, the product may not be placed on the market. However, this does not justify the conclusion that the regulation is also a harmonisation measure within the meaning of Article 114 TFEU. The Court stated that the prohibition of marketing is only one condition for the effectiveness of the application of the maximum permitted levels. The regulation therefore has only an *incidental* effect of harmonising the conditions for the free movement of goods within the EU, inasmuch as, by means of the adoption of uniform protective measures, it avoids the need for trade in foodstuffs and feedingstuffs which have undergone radioactive contamination to be made the subject of unilateral national measures.

Another problem is to what extent a distinction should be made, as far as it concerns the question of Union competences, between the protection of the health of the general public and the safety of *sources* of ionising radiation.

With respect to the conclusion by the Union of the Convention on Nuclear Safety, the Council argued that no article of the Euratom Treaty bestowed on the Union the competence to regulate the opening and operation of nuclear facilities. That competence was retained by the Member States. The Union has competence only as regards protection of the general public. The Court ruled however 'it is not appropriate, in order to define the EC's [now Union's] competences, to draw an artificial distinction between the protection of the health of the general public and the safety of sources of ionising radiation'.[141]

---

[141] Case C-29/99 *Commission v. Council* [2002] ECR I-11221, para. 82.

CHAPTER 3

Harmonisation

1 General Remarks

The dual objective of many European environmental measures has been referred to more than once in the previous chapters. On the one hand, it is aimed at attaining European environmental objectives, but on the other it can be aimed at integration and the establishment and proper functioning of the internal market.[1] This dual objective is also very relevant as regards the degree of freedom Member States enjoy to pursue national policies in fields in which Union legislation already exists. To what extent may the Member States, following harmonisation, adopt additional or even more stringent environmental standards than the European standards. Are they entitled to adopt less stringent standards? And, if so, under what conditions? These questions will be addressed in this chapter.

The instrument most frequently used in the harmonisation of national environmental provisions is the directive. A directive shall be binding, as to the result to be achieved, upon each Member State to which it is addressed, though it is left to the national authorities to choose form and methods (Article 288 TFEU). Directives, including environmental directives, thus impose on Member States an obligation to achieve a particular result. This they have to implement and incorporate into national law within the time set by the directive. An important feature is that the national legislature has in principle to act within the limits set by the directive. Thus, once national environmental laws have been harmonised, the extent to which the Member States are still free to pursue policies of their own depends primarily on the content of the directive. It is therefore important to examine the various methods of harmonisation more closely, at least in so far as they are relevant to environmental policy. This means examining the mechanisms of total harmonisation on the one hand, and minimum harmonisation on the other.

In addition the question will be addressed as to what extent Member States are free to pursue additional national environmental policies outside the system of harmonisation legislation or to derogate from EU environmental measures. Articles 114(4) and 193 TFEU in particular will be discussed.

2 The Scope of Harmonisation

It has been pointed out in Chapter 2 that in the area of environmental protection competences are 'shared' between the EU and the Member States. Until national laws have been harmonised, Member States are completely free to pursue any environmental policy of their own, under the condition that it complies with the relevant provisions of the Treaty, such as *inter alia* the

---

[1] Cf. in particular Case C-64/09 *Commission* v. *France* [2010] ECR I-3283, were the Court of Justice refers to 'the smooth functioning of the internal market' and avoiding 'distortions of competition' being objectives of Directive 2000/53 on end-of-life vehicles. See on this directive Chapter 8, para. 17.3.

provisions on the free movement of goods. However, once a matter has been regulated by an environmental directive, the Member States competencies are first of all dependent on the content of the directive concerned. One of the consequences of exhaustive harmonisation is that Member States may no longer have recourse to the provisions of Article 36 TFEU or the 'rule of reason',[2] for example to justify environmental measures restricting imports or exports. In other words: recourse to Article 36 TFEU or the rule of reason is not possible where European directives provide for harmonisation of the measures necessary to achieve the specific objective which would be furthered by reliance upon Article 36 TFEU or the rule of reason.[3]

Harmonisation and the scope of the European measures

However, it must be noted that the legal consequences of harmonisation only come into play if the directive was actually intended to regulate the matter in question. Anything outside the scope of the directive remains within the competence of the Member States. Outside the scope of the directive their competence is, once again, limited only by primary Union law. This means that if a matter falls outside the scope of a harmonisation measure, it is irrelevant whether Article 114(4-6) TFEU or Article 193 TFEU are applicable.[4] Where there is no European standard, there can be no question of 'more stringent' national environmental rules. There can thus be no question of a requirement, under Article 114(4-6) TFEU or Article 193 TFEU, to notify national legislation, which is outside the scope of a harmonisation directive.

What is crucial is whether a directive applies in a given field. However, it is not always easy to determine whether a national environmental standard is or is not within the scope of a directive. If a national standard falls within the sphere of application of a directive, then the European legislative framework in principle given by that directive or regulation is said to be 'exhaustive'.

Thus the Court of Justice observed in the *Compassion in World Farming* case that with respect to the directive laying down minimum standards for the protection of calves 'the Community legislature laid down exhaustively common minimum standards'.[5] As a result it was impossible to rely on Article 36 TFEU to justify the British legislation in question. After all, the European legislative framework for that

---

2   See Chapter 6, sections 4.3 and 4.4.

3   See Case C-473/98 *Kemikalieninspektionen* v. *Toolex Alpha AB* [2000] ECR I-5681, para. 25 and Case C-324/99 *DaimlerChrysler* [2001] ECR I-9897, paras. 41-43. In the latter case the Court ruled that the so-called 'Basel Regulation' (Regulation 259/93) regulated shipments of waste in a harmonised manner and that accordingly, any national measure relating to shipments of waste must be assessed in the light of the provisions of the regulation and not of Articles 34-36 TFEU.

4   Cf. Case C-127/97 *Burstein* [1998] ECR I-6005. See on Articles 114(4-6) and 193 TFEU, sections 5 and 6 of this chapter.

5   Case C-1/96 *Compassion in World Farming* [1998] ECR I-1251. See now Directive 2008/119, OJ 2008 L 10/7.

national policy was given by the directive. This approach was also clearly stated by the Court of Justice in the *Red Grouse* case.[6] The Dutch Supreme Court referred to the Court of Justice for a preliminary ruling a question on the interpretation of what are now Articles 34 and 35 TFEU. That question arose in criminal proceedings instituted against a trader in foodstuffs, Gourmetterie Van den Burg. The Supreme Court questioned the compatibility of Article 7 of the Dutch *Vogelwet*, containing a prohibition on the marketing of red grouse on the domestic market, with Article 36 TFEU: 'With regard to Article 36 the Court has consistently held that a directive providing for full harmonisation of national legislation deprives a Member State of recourse to that article.' The Court held that, in view of the fact that the Wild Birds Directive 'has [...] regulated exhaustively the Member States' powers with regard to the conservation of wild birds', compatibility with Article 36 was not at issue. The Court then proceeded to consider whether the prohibition contained in Article 7 of the *Vogelwet* was in conformity with the directive.

On the other hand the *Radlberger* case illustrates that as regards the reuse of packaging, Article 5 of Directive 94/62 on packaging and packaging waste does no more than allow the Member States to encourage, in conformity with the Treaty, systems for the reuse of packaging that can be reused in an environmentally sound manner. In view of the fact that the directive did not exhaustively harmonised this, the Court went on to discuss the German rules on deposit and return obligations for non-reusable packaging on the basis of the Treaty provisions relating to the free movement of goods.[7]

Finally, in *Nordiska Dental*, the Court of Justice ruled that Article 4(1) of the Medical Devices Directive 93/42 precluded Swedish legislation under which the commercial exportation of dental amalgams containing mercury is prohibited on grounds relating to protection of the environment and of health.[8]

It is not always easy to say what falls within and what falls outside the scope of a directive. The first thing that has to be determined is the personal, territorial, temporal and substantive scope of the directive.

A good example can be found in comparing the 'old' Batteries Directive 91/157 with the Batteries Directive 2006/66.[9] The 'old' directive provided for harmonisation of national laws in respect of levels of mercury contained by batteries and accumulators, which are placed on the market. However, it applied only to batteries and accumulators expressly listed in Appendix I of the directive. Those which are not on the list were therefore excluded from the scope of application of the directive. Member States were thus entirely free to determine the mercury content of such batteries and accumulators, though of course subject to the provisions of Articles 34 to 36 TFEU. The substantive scope of new directive however is much

---

6 Case C-169/89 *Gourmetterie v.d. Burg* [1990] ECR I-2143.

7 Case C-309/02 *Radlberger Getränkegesellschaft and S. Spitz* [2004] ECR I-11763.

8 Case C-288/08 *Nordiska Dental* [2009] ECR I-11031.

9 Directive 91/157, OJ 1991 L 78/38, repealed by Directive 2006/66, OJ 2006 L 266/1.

broader. Article 2 of it states that the directive 'shall apply to all types of batteries and accumulators, regardless of their shape, volume, weight, material composition or use.'

With respect to the temporal scope of a Union directive the *ERG I* case must be mentioned.[10] The Court confirmed that the Environmental Liability Directive 2004/35 is not applicable to damage caused before the expiry of the deadline for implementation of the directive and that subsequently such damage is governed by national law.

Other examples, which show that it is not always an easy matter in practice to determine the extent to which an environmental directive has regulated a particular subject matter, are provided by the following *Improsol* cases.

Th *Improsol* case concerned the extent to which Dutch plant protection legislation was compatible *inter alia* with Directive 79/117 prohibiting the placing on the market and use of plant-protection products containing certain active substances.[11] Because the substances contained by the product Improsol were not prohibited by the directive, the importer concluded that this implied that Improsol had to be allowed under the directive. The Court held otherwise: 'However, the prohibition imposed by Directive 79/117/EEC of marketing and using plant-protection products containing certain active substances applies only, by virtue of Article 3 thereof, to the substances listed in the annex. Directive 79/117/EEC does not therefore pursue complete harmonization of national rules concerning the marketing and use of plant-protection products.' And went on to discuss the compatibility of the Dutch legislation with Article 36 TFEU.[12]

Also interesting in this respect is the *Toolex* case.[13] In that case the Court ruled that the directive relating to the classification, packaging and labelling of dangerous substances covers a very clearly defined field, namely the notification, classification, packaging and labelling of dangerous substances. As regards the use of such substances, the classification directive merely requires that their packaging bear safety recommendations designed to inform the general public of the particular care that should be taken when handling the substance in question. Therefore, it does not harmonise the conditions under which dangerous substances may be marketed or used, which are the very matters that fall within the purview of national legislation.

---

[10] Case C-378/08 *ERG and others* [2010] ECR I-1919 (*ERG I*).

[11] Case 125/88 *Nijman* [1989] ECR 3533. In the same vein Case 94/83 *Albert Heijn* [1984] ECR 3263 and Joined Cases C-54/94 and C-74/94 *Stanghellini and Cacchiarelli* [1995] ECR I-391.

[12] A broadly similar case, but then in the waste sector, was the *Balsamo* case. See Case 380/87 *Balsamo* [1989] ECR 2491.

[13] Case C-473/98 *Kemikalieninspektionen* v. *Toolex Alpha AB* [2000] ECR I-5681. See also Regulation 1272/2008, OJ 2008 L 353/1.

The last case we want to mention in this respect is the *Burstein* case.[14] There the question was raised whether the limit values established by Directive 76/769[15] relating to restrictions on the marketing and use of certain dangerous substances and preparations were applicable only to PCP, its salts and esters and to preparations produced from those substances, or also to products treated with those substances or preparations. The Court decided that they were not, so that was a matter the Member States were free to regulate.

Apart from the necessity of determining the substantive scope of application of a directive, it is in the second place important to examine its objectives. If European rules do exist, but do not relate to environmental requirements, the directive will not affect the competence of Member States to take additional protective measures. As the Court held in the *Holdijk* case, European law will not in principle prevent a Member State from introducing or maintaining national rules if these are designed to achieve different aims from the European rules.[16]

But even if a directive is intended to achieve environmental objectives, it is not always clear whether Member States are prevented from acting at all. It may be, or it may be not, that the directive harmonises different aspects of the matter in question from those that are regulated by the national laws.

An example of this is provided by the decision of the UK House of Lords in the *London Lorries* case.[17] The case concerned a London Council byelaw which prohibited lorries from driving through certain London boroughs during the night. The purpose of the byelaw was to reduce the noise nuisance caused by the lorries. The problem was that there were two directives governing the permitted noise levels of lorries. One related to the requirements on the braking systems of lorries,[18] and the other to the maximum permissible sound levels of exhaust systems.[19] Both directives contained a free movement clause, to the effect that if vehicles met the requirements of the directive, Member states were no longer entitled to take restrictive measures: 'No Member State may, on grounds relating to the permissible sound level and the exhaust system, refuse of prohibit the sale, registration, entry into service or use of any vehicle in which the sound level and the exhaust system satisfy the requirements of Annex I.' That one of the aims of the directives was to prevent noise nuisance seems evident. Nevertheless, the House of Lords held that there was no question of infringement of the directives, as they were not intended to regulate local traffic and the consequent noise nuisance. The direc-

---

[14] Case C-127/97 *Burstein* [1998] ECR I-6005.

[15] This directive is repealed by the REACH Regulation 1907/2006, OJ 2006 L 396/1. See on REACH, chapter 8, section 15.1.

[16] Joined Cases 141-143/81 *Holdijk* [1982] ECR 1299.

[17] House of Lords 24 July 1991 *Regina* v. *London Boroughs Transport Committee; ex parte Freight Transport Association Ltd. a.o.* [1992] 1 C.M.L.R. 5.

[18] Directive 71/320, the Brakes Directive, OJ 1971 L 202/37, later amended.

[19] Directive 70/157, the Sound Level Directive, OJ 1970 L 42/16, amended many times since then.

tives did not therefore prohibit local authorities from taking certain measures to prevent noise nuisance at a local level. The House of Lords' judgment was not uncontroversial at the time, and it has been pointed out that the matter should perhaps have been referred to the Court for a preliminary ruling.[20]

In *Nordiska Dental* the Court ruled that the Medical Devices Directive 93/42 – a so-called 'New Approach' Directive – does not only protect of health *stricto sensu* but also the safety of persons. A Swedish environment inspired ban of commercial export of dental amalgams containing mercury was not considered falling outside the scope of the directive and therefore not allowed.[21]

Of course, the opposite may also apply. An environmental directive will not prevent Member States from regulating other, non-environmental, aspects. This is generally clear from the formulation of a so-called 'free movement' or 'market access' clause.[22]

> For example, Article 18 of Directive 99/45 provides that 'Member States may not prohibit, restrict or impede the placing on the market of preparations because of their classification, packaging, labelling or safety data sheets if such preparations comply with the provisions laid down in this Directive'.[23] Or take as an example Article 6 of the Batteries Directive 2006/66: 'Member States shall not, *on the grounds dealt with in this Directive*, impede, prohibit, or restrict the placing on the market in their territory of batteries and accumulators that meet the requirements of this Directive.' [emphasis added]

These formulations indicate that the legal consequences of harmonisation do not extend beyond the objectives of the directive in question.

> A clear example in the case law of the Court of Justice can be found in the *Geharo* case.[24] The case concerned criminal proceedings brought before the Dutch Supreme Court against Geharo for having stocked toys with a cadmium content greater than the maximum content permitted under Dutch law (Article 2(1) of the Decree relating to cadmium). This Decree aimed at implementing Directive 76/769 as amended, *inter alia*, by Directive 91/338 relating to restrictions on the marketing and use of certain dangerous substances and preparations.[25] Geharo argued that it complied with the so-called Safety of Toys Directive 88/378 which

---

[20] Cf. the *London Lorries* case with Commission Decision 98/523, OJ 1998 L 1998 L 233/25. The case concerned Swedish noise-related restrictions affecting access to Karlstadt airport.

[21] Case C-288/08 *Nordiska Dental* [2009] ECR I-11031. Cf. on this judgment critically L. Krämer in *Journal for European Environmental & Planning Law* [2010] 124-128.

[22] See, more extensively, this chapter, section 4. See also Regulation 1272/2008, OJ 2008 L 353/1.

[23] OJ 1999 L 200/1.

[24] Case C-9/04 *Geharo* [2005] ECR I-8525.

[25] OJ 1991 L 186/59.

contains also specific standards concerning cadmium.[26] The Court had a close look at both directives. Although both directives contained rules on cadmium, the objectives of the directives differ. According to the Court, Directive 88/378 seeks to protect the user of a toy against the risks connected with the chemical properties of the product at the time of use, whereas Directive 91/338 is part of a policy which seeks to protect the general population against the dispersion of cadmium into the environment. The Court concluded: 'Having regard to the different content and the different objectives of those standards, the application to toys covered by Directive 88/378 of a limit in the amount of cadmium, such as that laid down by Directive 91/338, is not incompatible with the application to the same toys of the limit in bioavailability laid down by Directive 88/378'. Therefore, Geharo had to comply with the Dutch Decree relating to cadmium.

It has already been shown above several times that if a given subject matter falls outside the scope of a directive, the Member States are still competent to take the necessary national measures. It must however be stressed that the sole fact that a particular matter is not specifically addressed by a directive does not imply that it therefore falls outside the directive's scope of application. There might have been what could be called 'implied harmonisation'.

An example of just such a form of implied harmonisation is provided by the Inter-Huiles case.[27] This case concerned the extent to which a Member State could employ policy instruments other than those provided for in the directive in question. The validity of French restrictions on the export of waste oils was disputed. The French Government maintained that the disputed legislation satisfied an economic requirement, since only the collection of all waste oils would be sufficient to ensure the profitability of undertakings approved for the disposal of waste oils and, therefore, the achievement of the aims of the directive. However, the Court held: 'That argument cannot be accepted. Articles 13 and 14 of the directive provide that, by way of compensation for the obligations imposed on the undertakings for the implementation of Article 5, Member States may, without placing restrictions on exports, grant to such undertakings "indemnities" financed in accordance with the principle of "polluter pays".'

As the directive provided for financial instruments with which the objectives of the Waste Oils Directive[28] could be achieved, the French export prohibitions could not be accepted. Nevertheless, this does not justify the conclusion that application of different instruments from those envisaged by a directive is never possible. This will depend on the objectives, content and system of the directive.

---

[26] OJ 1988 L 187/1.

[27] Case 172/82 Inter-Huiles [1983] ECR 555.

[28] OJ 1975 L 194/31, later amended.

The above shows that it is very important to determine precisely what a direc-tive is intended to harmonise. There can only be harmonisation to the extent a particular subject matter actually does fall within the scope of the direc-tive. When deciding whether or not this is the case, it is important to examine what products are covered by the directive, to what extent the directive is also intended to harmonise environmental objectives, what these environmental objectives are, and what instruments are applied in the directive.

Once it has been established that a directive (exhaustively) regulates a matter, it can be determined what *degree* or intensity of harmonisation the Union measure provides for, for example minimum harmonisation or total harmonisation. It is important to note that exhaustive regulation is not the same thing as total harmonisation. It is easy to confuse this distinction, particularly as the Court on occasion refers to 'exhaustive harmonisation' as 'full harmonisa-tion'[29] and 'total harmonisation' as 'comprehensive',[30] 'complete'[31] or 'exhaustive harmonisation'.[32] There is perhaps some consolation in the thought that it is not the Court's task to write textbooks!

We will discuss matters regarding the intensity of harmonisation in the following sections of this chapter.

3 Total Harmonisation

General remarks
Harmonisation is said to be *full* or *total* when a directive is intended to provide for a more or less uniform European standard in a particu-lar field, from which it is no longer possible to derogate. In principle this kind of directive excludes both more stringent and less stringent national rules. Of course, such a directive may itself provide exhaustively for derogation.

An example where total harmonisation was at issue is the *VAG Sverige AB* case.[33] Swedish legislation required that vehicles meet Swedish exhaust emission require-ments before they could be registered. However, the directive provided for total harmonisation of the rules on exhaust emissions and noise.[34] The Court ruled that a Member State may refuse to register a vehicle with a valid EU type-approval certificate only if it finds that the vehicle is a serious risk to road safety. In this case the Swedish refusal to register was linked to considerations of protection of the

---

[29] Cf. Case C-169/89 *Gourmetterie v.d. Burg* [1990] ECR I-2143.

[30] Cf. Case C-2/90 *Commission* v. *Belgium* [1992] ECR I-4431 on Directive 84/631.

[31] Case C-422/92 *Commission* v. *Germany* [1992] ECR I-1097, once again on Directive 84/631! Cf. also Case C-318/98 *Fornasar* [2000] ECR I-4785, para. 46 and Case C-82/09 *Dimos Agiou Nikolaou* [2010] ECR I-3649, para. 24.

[32] Case 278/85 *Commission* v. *Denmark* [1987] ECR 4069.

[33] Case C-329/95 *VAG Sverige AB* [1997] ECR I-2675.

[34] See now on these rule the Framework Directive 2007/46, OJ 2007 L 263/1.

environment. As a result the Court held the Swedish legislation to be in breach of the directive.

Total harmonisation is found above all in those fields of environmental policy where there is a definite relationship with the free movement of goods. In particular, the Council makes use of total harmonisation in legislation to harmonise product standards, as it is the only way to ensure the free movement of the goods in question. This means that total harmonisation is encountered particularly frequently in environmental measures based on Article 114 TFEU.

Derogation precluded

Total harmonisation precludes any derogation other than that allowed by the directive itself. This applies both to derogation allowing less stringent national requirements and to derogation providing for more stringent national requirements. Directives which are intended to implement total harmonisation can often, but not always, be recognised by the inclusion of a 'free movement clause'. This is a clause which provides that if a given (environmentally harmful) product or substance meets the requirements laid down by the directive, it may not be refused access to the internal market.

> See, for example, once again Article 6 of Directive 2006/66 on batteries and accumulators and waste batteries and accumulators:[35] 'Member States shall not, on the grounds dealt with in this Directive, impede, prohibit, or restrict the placing on the market in their territory of batteries and accumulators that meet the requirements of this Directive.'

The justification for such a provision is that directives which harmonise product standards are designed not only to protect the environment, but also to achieve a properly functioning internal market. As long as the national rules on batteries and accumulators have not been harmonised, there is the danger of disparities between the various national systems. A given battery may be allowed in one country, but not in another. However, if – as is the case in Directive 2006/66 – conditions have been laid down under which batteries to which the directive applies may be marketed (thus implementing the directive's environmental objectives), the inclusion of a free movement clause will prevent Member States imposing their own stricter requirements. The *quid pro quo* of such a clause is of course that products that do not meet the requirements of the directive are not placed on the market or are withdrawn from it.[36]

---

[35] OJ 2006 L 66/1.

[36] E.g. Article 6(2) of Directive 2006/66: 'Member States shall take the necessary measures to ensure that batteries or accumulators that do not meet the requirements of this Directive are not placed on the market or are withdrawn from it.'

Another example is provided by the *Ratti* case.[37] In its consideration of Italian requirements in respect of solvents, which differed from those contained in the relevant directive, the Court held: 'The combined effect of Articles 3 to 8 of Directive No 73/173 is that only solvents which "comply with the provisions of this directive and the annex thereto" may be placed on the market and that Member States are not entitled to maintain, parallel with the rules laid down by the said directive for imports, different rules for the domestic market. Thus it is a consequence of the system introduced by Directive No 73/173 that a Member State may not introduce into its national legislation conditions which are more restrictive than those laid down in the directive in question, or which are even more detailed or in any event different, as regards the classification, packaging and labelling of solvents and that this prohibition on the imposition of restrictions not provided for applies both to the direct marketing of the products on the home market and to imported products.'

The judgment of the Court in Case 278/85, dealing with Denmark's failure to fulfil its obligations under one of the directives on dangerous substances, will serve to illustrate the contention that total harmonisation imposes constraints on the freedom of Member States to pursue policies of their own.[38]

The case involved Directive 79/831, the sixth amendment to Directive 67/548, which contained rules for the marketing of 'new' substances as well as rules on 'old' substances, in other words, substances which had been placed on the market before the directive entered into force (on 18 September 1981).[39] The core of the directive was the requirement in Article 6 that notification be given of 'new substances'. Any manufacturer or importer into the EU was required to submit a notification to the competent national authority at the latest 45 days before the substance was placed on the market. This notification had to include, *inter alia*, a technical dossier supplying the information necessary for evaluating the foreseeable risks for man and the environment. As regards 'old' substances, however, the directive required the Commission to draw up an inventory of such substances, on the basis in particular of information provided by the Member States. According to the directive the obligation to notify did not apply to old substances until six months after the publication of the inventory and, six months after publication of the inventory, to substances which appear in that inventory. However, the relevant Danish legislation contained the provision that a chemical substance should be regarded as new if it had not been placed on the market or imported into Denmark as a chemical substance or constituent of a chemical product before 1 October 1980. The Commission complained that, in adopting that provision, the Danish Government departed from the directive by fixing a date prior to 18 September 1981 and by thus imposing an obligation to notify even substances

---

[37] Case 148/78 *Ratti* [1979] ECR 1629.

[38] Case 278/85 *Commission* v. *Denmark* [1987] ECR 4069.

[39] See Chapter 8, section 15.2.

placed on the market before 18 September 1981. Thus the compulsory notification would have applied to a wider group of substances and products than provided for by the directive. In its judgment the Court noted that the directive was designed to attain two objectives: the protection of the population and the environment and the elimination of obstacles to trade in dangerous substances. It went on to point out that the date provided for in the directive (18 September 1981) was meant to be the date from which both objectives, in particular the measures concerning the obligation to notify new substances, were to take effect. It follows, held the Court, that the European legislature had laid down exhaustive rules on this point and that it had not left the Member States any scope to introduce earlier or later dates in their rules adopted to implement the directive.

Total harmonisation is not only employed in the field of environmental *product* standards. For example, Directive 84/631[40] on the transfrontier shipment of hazardous waste contained a complete regulation of the way in which Member States were entitled to intervene in respect of the import and export of dangerous substances. It provided for an extensive system of notification and objections, which meant that national authorities have the option of raising objections and therefore prohibiting a particular transfer of dangerous waste (as opposed to transfers of such waste in general) in order to overcome problems relating to the protection of human health and the environment. The Court regarded this detailed regulation as a comprehensive system, whereby the system did not imply that the Member States had the power to prohibit transfers of waste generally.[41] What was remarkable was that the directive did not contain similar measures in respect of waste that was not regarded as hazardous. It would therefore, in principle, have been quite possible to introduce a general, more global restriction on imports of non-hazardous waste. This seems contradictory, but in fact it is not. Once national laws have been harmonised, there is no need for additional national regulations to protect the environment, as this aim has been achieved at European level, provided at least that the directive is not intended to implement minimum harmonisation. If there has been no harmonisation, Member States will still feel the need to adopt measures to protect the environment until the European institutions have taken legislative action in that respect.

Another example can be found in Directive 94/62 on packaging and packaging waste.[42] Article 6 of the directive requires Member States to attain targets pertaining to the recovery and recycling of packaging waste. No later than five years from the date by which the directive must be implemented in national law, between 50% as a minimum and 65% as a maximum by weight of the packag-

---

[40] Now replaced by Regulation 1013/2006 on shipments of waste, OJ 2006 L 190/1.

[41] Case C-2/90 *Commission* v. *Belgium* [1992] ECR I-4431. Cf. also the *Dusseldorp* case where the Court ruled, with respect to Regulation 259/93, that the principles of self-sufficiency and proximity cannot be applied to waste for recovery, Case C-203/96 *Dusseldorp* [1998] ECR I-4075.

[42] OJ 1994 L 365/10.

ing waste must be recovered. Within this general target, and with the same time limit, between 25% as a minimum and 45% as a maximum by weight of the totality of packaging materials contained in packaging waste must be recycled with a minimum of 15% by weight for each packaging material. Member States are only permitted to go beyond these targets if they meet the conditions and comply with the procedure set out in Article 6(6) of the directive.[43]

4 Minimum Harmonisation

General remarks

As far as European environmental law is concerned, minimum harmonisation can be defined as a form of European legislation which leaves Member States competent to adopt more stringent environmental standards than the European ones. It is often used in fields in which differences in national standards affect the functioning of the internal market less than do differences in product standards. This applies, for example, to measures to protect the quality of water and air, flora, fauna, and to measures in respect of waste, protection against radiation, etc. In this sense, European emission standards and quality standards can all be regarded as minimum standards. There is less need for absolute uniformity in these areas. Differences in emission and quality standards do not detract from the free movement of goods. They can however affect conditions of the competitive position of businesses. Some degree of harmonisation is therefore necessary, if only to prevent Member States using flawed environmental legislation as an instrument of industrial policy. It is not strictly necessary to place constraints on the Member States' competence to take more stringent measures, though it cannot be entirely ruled out. Market forces will probably ensure that national legislatures do not get too much out of line with those in other Member States, as this would be to the detriment of their own industries. This is another example of the difference between stricter emission standards and quality objectives on the one hand and stricter product standards on the other. As more stringent national product standards are likely above all to affect foreign manufacturers and products, it is not surprising that minimum harmonisation is used much less frequently as a means of regulation in this area.

Environmental directives which implement minimum harmonisation could always be easily recognised by their 'minimum harmonisation clause'. They regularly contained a provision similar to the following: 'Member States may, at any time, fix values more stringent than those laid down in this Directive.'[44] Such provisions were especially frequent in environmental directives setting European quality standards for air and water. Environmental quality standards

---

[43] This procedure is to a certain extent similar to the Article 114(4) TFEU procedure. See section 6 below.

[44] E.g. Article 5 of Directive 85/203 on air quality standards for nitrogen dioxide, OJ 1985 L 87/1, later amended.

are standards laid down with legally binding force which prescribe the levels of pollution or nuisance that may not be exceeded in a given environment or part of an environment. Similar provisions are also to be found where emission standards are harmonised: these are standards which set the levels of pollutants or nuisances not to be exceeded in emissions from plants.[45] Member States may require compliance with emission limit values and time limits for implementation which are more stringent than those set out in the directive itself. Court of Justice case law seems to require that the consequences of such additional requirements are consistent with the objective pursued by the directive.[46] These examples demonstrate that a large part of European law implements a form of minimum harmonisation, whereby minimum standards are adopted which Member States are required at the very least to meet (except where they apply special safeguard clauses). In other words, a minimum level is set in the legislation on environmental protection.

However, even where a directive contains such a minimum harmonisation clause, close attention must be paid to the context within which the directive was adopted. This was demonstrated by the Court of Justice in the *Red Grouse* case.[47]

> In this case the Dutch Government invoked a provision of the Wild Birds Directive,[48] which provided that Member States were allowed to adopt stricter measures to protect birds than those provided for under the directive (Article 14). The directive provided *inter alia* that red grouse could be hunted within the Member State in which they occurred (the UK). After interpreting the directive, the Court reached the conclusion that only the United Kingdom was competent to adopt stricter measures to protect the bird in question, and that other Member States were not: 'It follows from the foregoing that Article 14 of the directive does not empower a Member State to afford a given species which is neither migratory nor endangered stricter protection, by means of a prohibition on importation and marketing, than that provided for by the legislation of the Member State on whose territory the bird in question occurs, where such legislation is in conformity with the provisions of Directive 79/409.'

A good example of minimum harmonisation combined with a form of total harmonisation was provided by Article 16 of Directive 80/778 relating to the quality of water intended for human consumption.[49] Member States were allowed to lay down more stringent provisions than those provided for in the

---

[45] See, for example, Article 4 of Directive 2001/80 on the limitation of emissions of certain pollutants into the air from large combustion plants, OJ 2001 L 309/1.

[46] Cf. Case C-232/97 *Nederhoff* [1999] ECR I-6385, para. 58. See also Case C-6/03 *Deponiezweckverband Eiterköpfe* [2005] ECR I-2753. In section 5 of this chapter we will deal more extensively with Case C-6/03.

[47] Case C-169/89 *Gourmetterie v.d. Burg* [1990] ECR I-2143.

[48] OJ 1979 L 103/1, later amended.

[49] OJ 1980 L 229/11, now repealed and replaced by Directive 98/23, OJ 1998 L 330/23.

directive, but were not allowed to prohibit or impede the marketing of foodstuffs on grounds relating to the quality of the water used where the quality of such water meets the requirements of the directive.

Today, it is less likely for environmental directives to contain a minimum harmonisation clause. Indeed, it is not unknown for such a clause to be removed from an 'old' environmental directive when it is amended.[50] This is because the principle that European protective measures lay down a minimum standard which can be enhanced by the Member States has now been incorporated into Article 193 TFEU.[51]

Minimum standards and the Euratom Treaty

The 'basic standards' referred to in Article 30 *et seq.* of the Euratom Treaty must also be regarded as minimum standards. The Court has held thus in Case C-376/90.[52]

In that case the Commission brought an action for a declaration that, by failing to take the steps necessary to implement Article 10(2) of Directive 80/836 on health protection against the dangers of ionizing radiation,[53] Belgium had failed to fulfil its obligations under the directive. The Commission considered that Article 10(2) did not authorize Member States to fix different dose limits from those laid down in that provision, even if they were stricter. The Belgian Government argued that the dose limits laid down in the directive represented the minimum level of protection that Member States were obliged to ensure and that they were free to set stricter limits if they considered it desirable to do so. The Commission relied *inter alia* on Article 2(b) of the Euratom Treaty, which provides that 'uniform safety standards' must be established. This would seem to indicate that Member States were not entitled to set stricter national standards. The Court rejected this argument. The standards laid down in the directive were based on the recommendations of the International Commission on Radiological Protection (ICRP), according to which the dose limits represented the dose levels whose consequences for the health of persons regularly exposed to ionizing radiation were at the limit of what was tolerable and that the choice of dose limits necessarily included assessments which might vary according to the companies concerned. There was no indication in the directive that the European legislature had adopted a different

---

[50] See for instance Directive 97/11 amending Directive 85/337 on the assessment of the effects of certain public and private projects on the environment, OJ 1997 L 73/5, which deleted the minimum harmonisation clause in Article 13 of Directive 85/337.

[51] See below, section 5. However, they still occur: see e.g. Article 9 of Directive 2006/11 (OJ 2006 L 64/52) on pollution caused by certain dangerous substances discharged into the aquatic environment of the Community and Article 1 of Directive 2010/31 on the energy performance of buildings, OJ 2010 L 153/13.

[52] Case C-376/90 *Commission v. Belgium* [1992] ECR I-6153.

[53] OJ 1980 L 246/1, later amended. Now replaced by Directive 96/29, OJ 1996 L 159/1. See on this directive Chapter 8, section 18.1.

position from that of the ICRP in relation to dose limits, and that it did not leave Member States any discretion to provide for a higher standard of protection than that laid down in the directive.

The conclusion that can be drawn from this judgment in respect of the legal status of the present dose limits contained in the directive must therefore be that this is a case of minimum harmonisation. Member States are thus entitled to set stricter standards than those laid down in the directive.

Minimum harmonisation and Article 114 TFEU

Whenever the European legislature takes a measure under Article 114 TFEU, for instance laying down environmental product standards, one must assume that such a measure is intended to eliminate obstacles to trade resulting from the existence of divergent national rules in the field directly affecting the establishment and functioning of the internal market.

With respect to Directive 76/769 relating to restrictions on the marketing and use of certain dangerous substances and preparations, the Court ruled that it 'thus follows from its legal basis as well as from its recitals that Directive 76/769 aims to eliminate obstacles to trade within the internal market in the substances'.[54] And with respect to the submission, i.e. from the Dutch Government, that this directive merely brings about minimum harmonisation and therefore permits the Member States to lay down additional conditions, the Court answered:

'the objective of Directive 76/769 would not be attainable if the Member States were free to widen the obligations provided for therein. The provisions of that directive have exhaustive character and the retention or adoption by the Member States of measures other than those laid down by the directive is incompatible with its objective [...]'.

From this judgment we can learn that minimum harmonisation is not the default *habitus* of an 'Article 114' directive. Because such a directive is primarily aimed at removing obstacles to trade and the internal market, most of these directives will contain total harmonisation. However, this triggers the question whether environmental measures which are based on Article 114 TFEU can implement minimum standards at all. Or is this *legally* impossible, in view of the functioning of the internal market? According to Advocate General Geelhoed, the objective of the unity and functioning of the internal market does not accord with the view that an 'Article 114 directive' only provides for minimum harmonisation.[55] The Court's view on this issue does not seem crystal clear.

---

[54] Case C-281/03 *Cindu Chemicals* [2005] ECR I-8069.

[55] Cf. his Opinion concerning the Product Liability Directive in Case C-52/00 *Commission* v. *France* and Case C-183/00 *González Sánchez* v. *Medicina Asturiana SA* [2001] ECR I-3827 en I-3901, para. 50.

Its rulings on the Product Liability Directive are open for different interpretation and therefore some confusion.[56] This could also explain why the Commission, in its proposal for the Batteries Directive 2006/66, opted for the combined legal basis of Articles 192 and 114 TFEU.[57] According to the Commission, these two articles of the Treaty set different conditions as regards the right of Member States to maintain or introduce more stringent protective measures. As a consequence, the Commission felt necessary to specify the legal basis for each part of the proposal. Article 114 TFEU should be the appropriate legal basis to harmonise the laws of the Member States as regards product requirements (like a mercury ban and labelling requirements). This legal basis was felt appropriate by the Commission 'since the disparities between the laws of the Member States on product requirements could create barriers to trade and distort competition in the Community and thus have a direct impact on the establishment and functioning of the internal market.' On the other hand, the Commission found it more appropriate that harmonisation measures to prevent or reduce the generation of spent batteries and accumulators and to prevent or reduce the negative environmental impacts of the metals used in them, are based on Article 175 EC (now Article 192 TFEU): '[T]hese measures, which aim to provide a high level of environmental protection, should not prevent Member States from adopting more stringent measures on their national territory.' Arguably, the Commission was under the impression that Article 95 EC (now Article 114 TFEU) could not be used to serve as a legal basis for the minimum harmonisation of environmental product standards. However, it is the authors' opinion that it is not the legal basis as such which determines whether or not minimum harmonisation is being implemented, but the content of the measure in question. In sum, in the event that product standards were harmonised on the basis of Article 114 TFEU, there is no reason to rule out minimum harmonisation altogether.

It is clear however that when the European legislature harmonises environmental product standards by way of minimum harmonisation, this should be accompanied with a market access clause.[58]

A good example can be found in Directive 94/62 on packaging and packaging waste.[59] On the one hand Article 11 requires Member States to ensure that the sum of concentration levels of lead, cadmium, mercury and hexavalent chromium present in packaging or packaging components shall not exceed certain levels, the use of 'shall not exceed' indicating minimum harmonisation. On the other hand Article 18 provides that Member States shall not impede the placing on the market

---

[56] Case C-52/00 *Commission v. France* and Case C-183/00 *González Sánchez v. Medicina Asturiana SA* [2001] ECR I-3827 and I-3901.

[57] COM (2003) 723, at point 9.

[58] See Case C-376/98 *Germany and EP v. Council* [2000] ECR I-8419.

[59] OJ 1994 L 365/10.

of their territory of packaging which satisfies the provisions of this directive, thus precluding the application of more stringent standards to imported products.

In any case, it is clear from the example of the TiO2 Directive,[60] which was based on Article 100a (now Article 114 TFEU), that the measures this directive contains to control *emissions* must specifically be seen as a form of minimum harmonisation, whereby Member States are permitted to require stricter standards. One of the recitals in the preamble to the directive deals expressly with this. Minimum harmonisation and Article 114 TFEU need not therefore be regarded as mutually exclusive.

5   Article 193 TFEU

The practice of minimum harmonisation as a means of attaining environmental objectives has now been enshrined in Article 193 TFEU:

'The protective measures adopted pursuant to Article 192 shall not prevent any Member State from maintaining or introducing more stringent protective measures. Such measures must be compatible with the Treaties. They shall be notified to the Commission.'

In the previous section of this chapter we have mentioned that sometimes 'Article 193-like' clauses can be found in secondary Union legislation as well. It seems that the Court of Justice treats both types of clauses in a similar way.[61]

Although there is no hard empirical data on the use of Article 193 TFEU by the Member State, the impression is that Member States hardly make any use of their powers.[62] Therefore, the impact of Article 193 TFEU on national law making should not be overestimated. One of the reasons for this could be that, in view of the express text of the article, it relates only to more stringent national measures adopted pursuant to Article 192 TFEU. Case law of the Court of Justice requires that the consequences of taking more stringent measures are consistent with the objective pursued by the directive.[63] In the *Deponiezweckverband* case the Court ruled that Article 193 TFEU makes provision for and authorises the minimum requirements laid down by a Union measure to be exceeded 'to the extent that a measure of domestic law pursues the same objectives as' the European measure. We assume that by this the Court means to say not only that when national legislation pursues other objectives than those of the directive,

---

[60] Directive 92/112, OJ 1992 L 409/11.

[61] Case C-2/10 *Azienda Agro-Zootecnica Franchini*, Judgment of 21 July 2011, para. 50.

[62] Cf. Pàgh (2005) and Jans & Squintani (2009).

[63] Cf. Case C-232/97 *Nederhoff* [1999] ECR I-6385, para. 58. Cf. Case C-6/03 *Deponiezweckverband Eiterköpfe* [2005] ECR I-2753, para. 58, Joined Cases C-379/08 and C-380/08 *ERG and others* [2010] ECR I-2007 (*ERG II*) and Case C-2/10 *Azienda Agro-Zootecnica Franchini*, Judgment of 21 July 2011.

this legislation cannot be considered to be a more far-reaching measure of protection, but also that such legislation is not allowed. In any event, Article 193 TFEU does not confer competence on Member States to adopt *less* stringent protective measures.[64] Nor can Article 193 TFEU be used to adopt protective measures in connection with Union environmental legislation which has not been adopted pursuant to Article 192 TFEU, but pursuant to other provisions of the Treaty like Articles 114, 207 or 43 TFEU.

What are 'more stringent' measures?

The question is whether it is at all necessary to rely on Article 193 TFEU (and thus to have to report the more stringent measures to the European Commission) if the European measure itself leaves room, implicitly or explicitly, for more stringent national measures. The Court clarified the issue in the *Deponiezweckverband* case.[65]

> *Deponiezweckverband Eiterköpfe* concerned the compatibility with European law of German legislation on waste. The Deponienzweckverband is an association of administrative districts, for the purpose of waste disposal, in the region of Koblenz, and operates the central landfill site Eiterköpfe. This association sought a permit from the *Land* Rheinland-Pfalz to fill, after 31 May 2005, two landfill cells site with waste that had been treated by mechanical processes only. The *Land* Rheinland-Pfalz argued that the *Verordnung über die umweltverträgliche Ablagerung von Siedlungsabfällen* (Regulation on the environmentally sound deposit of municipal waste) does not allow this. This regulation was adopted for the purpose of transposing the directive on the landfill of waste[66] into domestic German law. The *Verwaltungsgericht* (Administrative Court) Koblenz, before which the Deponie-zweckverband had brought a dispute, had doubts as to whether the national legislation was compatible with Article 5(1) and (2) of the directive. According to Article 5(1) of the directive, the Member States must develop a national strategy to decrease the amount of biodegradable waste which is transferred to the landfill sites. And according to the same provision this strategy must ensure that the amount of waste which is to be transferred to landfill sites is decreased before specific dates and by specific percentages. The German implementing legislation contains more 'stringent' environmental rules than the directive (tighter time-limits; higher percentages). The legal basis of the directive is Article 192 TFEU, which means that Article 193 TFEU also applies. Nevertheless, the *Verwaltungs-gericht* wished to know whether the directive would preclude the more stringent German implementing legislation. The Court ruled in paras. 31 and 32: 'Under

---

[64] To adopt less stringent standards Member States will have to rely on a specific clause in the directive/regulation. See e.g. Article 18(1) of Batteries Directive 2006/66 (OJ 2006 L 266/1) according to which Member States may exempt producers which place very small quantities of batteries or accumulators on the national market, from some requirements of the directive.

[65] Case C-6/03 *Deponiezweckverband Eiterköpfe* [2005] ECR I-2753.

[66] OJ 1999 L 182/1.

Article 5(1) of the directive, the Member States are to set up national strategies in order to reduce the amount of biodegradable waste going to landfills. Under the same provision, those national strategies must include measures to achieve the targets fixed in Article 5(2) of the directive. The last-mentioned provision states that those national strategies must provide that the amount of waste going to landfill should be reduced by certain percentages before certain fixed dates. The wording and broad logic of those provisions make it clearly apparent that they set a minimum reduction to be achieved by the Member States and they do not preclude the adopting by the latter of more stringent measures.

It follows that *Article 176 EC* [now Article 193 TFEU] *and the Directive* allow the Member States to introduce more stringent protection measures that go beyond the minimum requirements fixed by the Directive [...].' [emphasis added]

The Court thus put an end to an ambiguity concerning the concept 'more stringent protective measures'. Whenever the national rules are stricter than those required by a European measure, Article 193 TFEU is applicable.[67] National legislation concerning situations falling outside the scope of a European measure is, of course, not to be considered as 'more stringent protective measures'. In our view, the same would apply when the stricter national legislation finds its legal basis in 'Article 193-type' provisions in the directives concerned. Finally, there does not appear to be any reason why this conclusion would not apply to those cases where the stricter national measure is not legally based on *explicit* provisions in the Treaty or secondary law, but where the power to take more stringent measures follows *implicitly* from secondary law; i.e. directives for which it must be concluded from the wording – with terms such as 'at least', 'maximum', 'at most' – that they aim at minimum harmonisation.

More stringent protective measures must be compatible with the Treaties

More stringent protective measures must be compatible with the Treaties. This means in particular that the requirements of the free movement of goods,[68] the rules on competition and the provisions on taxation must be observed in national environmental rules.[69] Article 193 TFEU does indicate that Member States may still have some freedom to pursue national policies after the adoption of European measures, of course, under the same rules as if there had been no harmonisation, but Article 193 TFEU most definitely does not give Member States a licence to act in contravention of the provisions of Articles 34-36 TFEU,

---

[67] Cf. also Case C-100/08 *Commission v. Belgium* [2009] ECR I-140. This case concerned more stringent measures then those under CITES Regulation 338/97 on the protection of species of wild fauna and flora by regulating trade therein. See also Chapter 8, para. 19.3.

[68] Case C-389/96 *Aher-Waggon GmbH* [1998] ECR I-4473, provides an example where the Court tested more stringent German legislation to combat disturbances from air-traffic noise for compatibility with Article 34 TFEU.

[69] And, arguably, the rules of the WTO; Cf. Scott (2000) at 40-41.

or to fail to meet their commitments to the EU in other respects, for instance secondary legislation.

> A good example of this can be found in the *Dusseldorp* case.[70] The case concerned the question whether the principles of self-sufficiency and proximity could be applied to shipments of waste for recovery, given that Regulation 259/93 only provided for this in respect of waste for disposal. After noting that Regulation 259/93 was based on Article 130s EC, the precursor of Article 192 TFEU, the Court observed: 'It is therefore necessary to consider whether, in accordance with that provision, measures such as those adopted in the Long-term Plan for the application of the principles of self-sufficiency and proximity to waste for recovery are compatible with Article 34 of the Treaty [now Article 35 TFEU].'

After ruling that the Dutch measures were thus not compatible, the Court continued:

> 'It must therefore be concluded that the object and effect of application of the principles of self-sufficiency and proximity to waste for recovery, such as oil filters, is to restrict exports of that waste and is not justified, in circumstances such as those in the present case, by an imperative requirement relating to protection of the environment or the desire to protect the health and life of humans in accordance with Article 36 of the Treaty. A Member State cannot therefore rely on Article 130t [now Article 193 TFEU] of the Treaty in order to apply the principles of self-sufficiency and proximity to such waste.'

We have stated in the beginning of this chapter that many European environmental measures are not only aimed at attaining European *environmental* objectives, but can be aimed at the smooth functioning of the internal market as well. In Case C-64/09, *Commission* v. *France*, the Court of Justice ruled on more stringent French measures than the ones in the End-of-Life Vehicles Directive:

> 'Such measures must, however, be compatible with the provisions of the EC Treaty and, *inter alia*, must not frustrate the achievement of the objective pursued in the second instance by that directive, namely to ensure the smooth functioning of the internal market and to avoid distortions of competition in the Union.'[71]

Therefore, more stringent protective measures should not only be in line with the *environmental* objectives of the directive concerned, but also with all secondary non-environmental objectives.

Furthermore, recent case law of the Court of Justice seems to suggest that also the environmental principles mentioned in Article 192 TFEU – for instance

---

[70] Case C-203/96 *Dusseldorp* [1998] ECR I-4075.

[71] Case C-64/09 *Commission* v. *France* [2010] ECR I-3283, para. 35.

the 'polluter pays principle' – may preclude Member States to take more stringent protective measures.[72]

More stringent measures and the proportionality principle
When Member States fulfil *obligations* laid down in minimum directives, there is no doubt that they are obliged to take account of the proportionality principle when doing so – this is evident from the case law of the Court.[73] But, are they also obliged to respect the principle of proportionality when they make use of their *competence* to take stricter national measures?

Although the proportionality principle is enshrined in Article 5(4) of the EU Treaty, the Court made clear in the *Deponiezweckverband* case that the more stringent national legislation adopted does not have to be reviewed in the light of the Union principle of proportionality.[74] The paragraphs 61-64 relating to this are quoted here:

'It is clear from the broad logic of Article 176 EC [now Article 193 TFEU] that, in adopting stricter measures, Member States still exercise powers governed by Community law, given that such measures must in any case be compatible with the Treaty. Nevertheless, it falls to the Member States to define the extent of the protection to be achieved.

In that context, in so far as it is a matter of ensuring that the minimum requirements laid down by the Directive are enforced, the Community principle of proportionality demands that measures of domestic law should be appropriate and necessary in relation to the objectives pursued.

In contrast, and inasmuch as other provisions of the Treaty are not involved, that principle is no longer applicable so far as concerns more stringent protective measures of domestic law adopted by virtue of Article 176 EC [now Article 193 TFEU] and going beyond the minimum requirements laid down by the Directive.

As a result, the reply to the second question has to be that the Community-law principle of proportionality is not applicable so far as concerns more stringent protective measures of domestic law adopted by virtue of Article 176 EC [now Article 193 TFEU] and going beyond the minimum requirements laid down by a Community directive in the sphere of the environment, inasmuch as other provisions of the Treaty are not involved.'

This conclusion – more stringent national legislation adopted on the basis of Article 193 TFEU does not have to be reviewed in the light of the principle of

---

[72] Case C-188/07 *Commune de Mesquer* [2008] ECR I-4501, para. 82, final sentence.

[73] Case C-293/97 *Standley* [1999] ECR I-2603.

[74] Case C-6/03 *Deponiezweckverband Eiterköpfe* [2005] ECR I-2753. See also Case C-2/97 *Società italiana petroli* [1998] ECR I-8597, which also demonstrates that the principle of proportionality does not play a role in the review of more stringent national measures if such measures do not form an obstacle to free movement.

proportionality – is not only relevant for the interpretation of Article 193 TFEU, but seems to us also to be significant for all other cases of minimum harmonisation.

Can the use of Article 193 TFEU be restricted by the European measure itself?
These observations lead us to a possible third restriction on the use of Article 193 TFEU. Can the content of secondary European environmental legislation as such prevent Member States invoking Article 193 TFEU?[75]

> Let us present the following example to illustrate the importance and practical relevance of this question. According to Article 16(3) of Directive 2003/87 establishing a scheme for greenhouse gas emission allowance trading within the EU 'Member States shall ensure that any operator who does not surrender sufficient allowances by 30 April of each year to cover its emissions during the preceding year shall be held liable for the payment of an excess emissions penalty. The excess emissions penalty shall be €100 for each ton of carbon dioxide equivalent emitted by that installation for which the operator has not surrendered allowances'.[76] The penalty is fixed by the directive on €100 for each ton of carbon dioxide emitted. Would the Member States, in view of their powers under Article 193 TFEU, be allowed to apply a penalty of say €150 for each ton emitted?
>
> Or take the following, may be even more important, example from Article 9 of the Industrial Emissions Directive where its relation with the Emissions Trading Directive is explained.[77] Article 9 explicitly states that the Member States shall not impose emissions limit values for greenhouse gasses for installations within the emissions trading scheme.[78] The reason for this is that the latter requires the operators decisions on whether or not to reduce greenhouse gas emissions to be dependent only on the market price for the greenhouse gas allowances that need to be surrendered for every unit of greenhouse gas emitted. Both the IE Directive and the Emissions Trading Directive are based on Article 192 TFEU and an emission limit values for greenhouse gasses could arguably be qualified as a stricter environmental protection measure. Recital 10 of the preamble further complicates this by confirming that, in accordance with Article 193 TFEU, this directive does not stand in the way of the introduction by the Member States of stricter measures, such as greenhouse gas emission requirements. So the question is, are emission limit values allowed or not?

Legal writers differ on the subject. The prevailing view is that Member States can *always* adopt more stringent measures following harmonisation under Article 192 TFEU.[79] A strong argument in favour of this view is that the Treaty

---

[75] Cf. Krämer (2007) at 127 *et seq.*

[76] OJ 2003 L 275/32.

[77] See also Chapter 8, section 6.

[78] Such emission limit values are, however, allowed if this is necessary to avoid significant local pollution.

[79] Cf. Winter (1998), Winter (2000) 666.

at all times takes precedence over secondary legislation. If the Treaty states that stricter measures are allowed, this competence cannot then be restricted by a legal instrument of a lower order. Another strong argument is that Article 193 TFEU would otherwise have hardly any significance at all.[80] After all, only where there is 'no room' in the directive itself does the question of more stringent measures arise. A third argument is that environmental directives based on Article 192 TFEU are aimed at achieving the *environmental* objectives of Article 191(1) and based on the environmental principles of Article 191(2) TFEU. If an environmental directive were to preclude Member States from taking more stringent measures, this could never be justified for environmental reasons. This argument, however, lost its strength in view of recent case law of the Court of Justice.[81]

Another view, also taken by the present authors, is the following. If a measure based on Article 192 TFEU implicitly or expressly provides that Member States shall not adopt certain protective measures, a Member State cannot then invoke Article 193 TFEU to justify adopting such a measure after all. This argument is based on the fact that Article 193 TFEU must be considered a codification of legislative practice before the Single European Act. As stated above, 'more stringent protective measures' clauses were frequently included in directives on the environment prior to the entry into force of the Single European Act. On the other hand, total harmonisation was possible then, under the 'old' Articles 100 and 235 (now Articles 115 and 352 TFEU). The inclusion of Article 193 TFEU by the Single European Act was designed solely to give the practice of using minimum harmonisation clauses a basis in the Treaty, without thereby implicitly making total harmonisation impossible. This view implies that the inclusion of Article 193 in the Treaty was not really intended to have legal consequences. According to this interpretation, Article 193 TFEU merely expresses the principle that, in general, decision-making under Article 192 TFEU takes the shape of minimum harmonisation, but does not limit the power of the Union legislature, by way of 'self-binding', of restricting Member States to take more stringent standards. In other words it is up to the Union legislature to decide to what extent Member States are allowed to adopt more stringent standards than those set in a directive. This argument is also supported by the fact that otherwise, Article 193 TFEU would give a Member State the power unilaterally and without any control *ex ante* from the Commission to disregard standards set by the Union legislature. This seems strange, particularly in view of the procedure set out in paragraphs 4 to 6 of Article 114 TFEU. In *Dusseldorp* the Court was asked to give its opinion on this issue. The parties were totally divided on the point, as is clear from the following quote from the judgment:

---

[80] Cf. Winter (1998), Winter (2000) 666.

[81] Cf. in particualr Case C-64/09 *Commission* v. *France* [2010] ECR I-3283, were the Court of Justice refers to 'the smooth functioning of the internal market' and avoiding 'distortions of competition' being objectives of Directive 2000/53 on end-of-life vehicles. The ELV Directive is an 'Article 192' directive.

'According to Dusseldorp and the Commission, the Regulation brought about full harmonisation of the rules on shipments of waste between Member States, so that in principle the latter can object to such shipments only on the basis of that Regulation. Furthermore, Article 130t [now Article 193 TFEU] of the Treaty permits Member States to adopt rules only if they are compatible with, *inter alia*, Article 30 [now Article 34 TFEU] *et seq.* of the Treaty. They maintain that the Long-term Plan contains measures having equivalent effect to quantitative restrictions on export prohibited by Article 34 [now Article 35 TFEU] of the Treaty, which are not justified either by imperative requirements relating to the protection of the environment or under Article 36 of the EC Treaty [now Article 36 TFEU].

According to the Netherlands Government, it can be concluded from the wording and the general scheme of the Regulation and from Article 130t [now Article 193 TFEU] of the Treaty that the measures adopted pursuant to Article 130s [now Article 192 TFEU] constitute minimum harmonisation. In those circumstances, there is nothing to prevent Member States from seeking to achieve a higher level of protection on the basis of Article 130t [now Article 193 TFEU]. Furthermore, the Plan is not contrary to the Treaty and, in particular, does not contain any prohibition on export.

In the alternative, the Netherlands Government submits that, if the Long-term Plan does contain a prohibition on export for the purposes of Article 34 [now Article 35 TFEU], that prohibition is justified under Article 36 of the Treaty [now Article 36 TFEU] by the pursuit of the best method of disposal of waste and by the need for continuity of disposal, which are intended to protect the health and life of humans.'

The Court expressly did not address the question of whether Article 193 TFEU could be relied on in the event of total harmonisation. Indeed, in his Opinion, Advocate General Jacobs advised the Court not to. In his view this was unnecessary in this case as the policy rules of the Netherlands Government would not withstand the test of Articles 35 and 36 TFEU anyway. The fact that the Court proceeded to examine the compatibility of the measures with Articles 35 and 36 TFEU without considering whether it was possible to apply Article 193 TFEU suggests that the Court did not, *a priori*, regard this as impossible.[82] On the other hand, it could also be argued that the Court did not yet want to rule on the matter in this case.

In a judgment rendered after *Dusseldorp,* the Court seems to have settled this doctrinal dispute. In the *Fornasar* case the Court, referring to Article 193 TFEU, stated in very broad terms that 'it must be observed that the European rules do not seek to effect complete harmonisation in the area of the environment'.[83] And

---

[82] Winter (2000) 666, who argues that the Court in *Dusseldorp* has implicitly accepted the use of Article 193 TFEU in the context of total harmonisation.

[83] Case C-318/98 *Fornasar* [2000] ECR I-4785, para. 46. Cf. also Case C-82/09 *Dimos Agiou Nikolaou* [2010] ECR I-3649, par. 24.

as a consequence the Court ruled that the old Hazardous Waste Directive did not prevent the Member States from classifying as hazardous waste other than that featuring on the list of hazardous waste laid down by the so-called Hazardous Waste Liste[84], and thus from adopting more stringent protective measures in order to prohibit the abandonment, dumping or uncontrolled disposal of such waste.[85]

However, the discussion can be re-opened again in view of the judgment in *Deponiezweckverband*[86] and even more important, the *ERG II* case.[87]

In the *ERG II* case, the Court of Justice ruled that a Member State cannot validly rely on the 'more stringent measures' clause in Article 16(1) of the Environmental Liability Directive 2004/35, to maintain or adopt provisions or authorises a practice enabling the competent authority to disregard, first, the operators' right to be heard and the obligation to invite the persons on whose land remedial measures are to be carried out to submit their observations and, second, the obligation to carry out a detailed examination of the potential options for environmental recovery. According to the Court of Justice, the operators' right to be heard and the right of the persons whose land is affected by remedial measures to submit their observations clearly constitute a minimum level of protection guaranteed by Directive 2004/35, which cannot reasonably be called into question.

As appears from this judgment, a Member State cannot rely on a 'more stringent measures' clause in a directive if this is incompatible with the explicit content of the directive itself. There is no reason why this judgment cannot be applied by analogy to Article 193 TFEU.

Article 193 TFEU and local and regional authorities

A problem of an entirely different order is posed by the possible application of Article 193 TFEU in the relations between the central government of a Member State and its local or regional authorities. Can such a local authority, relying on Article 193 TFEU, apply stricter protective measures than allowed by the central government, thus ignoring any restrictions imposed by that government? The answer to this question will depend on the legal relations Article 193 TFEU was intended to regulate. It seems clear that Article 193 TFEU was drafted to allow Member States to take stricter protective measures in their relations with the Union. It was designed to regulate relations between the Member States and the EU, and not those between central government and local government. Local authorities should not therefore be permitted to invoke Article 193 TFEU in support of stricter protective measures than those laid down by a central government. It goes without saying that a local or regional authority

---

[84] See now Decision 2000/532, OJ 2000 L 226/3.

[85] See also Chapter 8, section 17.

[86] Case C-6/03 *Deponiezweckverband Eiterköpfe* [2005] ECR I-2753.

[87] Joined Cases C-379/08 and C-380/08 *ERG and others* [2010] ECR I-2007 (*ERG II*).

may invoke Article 193 TFEU in respect of the Union where what is involved is the application of environmental law within their competence.[88] As long as the national laws allow this, there is no problem at all.

Notification under Article 193 TFEU

The final point that must be discussed in connection with Article 193 TFEU concerns the requirement that Member States must notify the Commission of stricter protective measures. Unlike notification in the context of Article 114 TFEU, there is no standstill requirement here and it does not make implementation of the national measures conditional upon agreement by the Commission or its failure to object. Therefore, non-notification will not preclude application of national rules in the national legal order.[89]

> In *Azienda Agro-Zootecnica Franchini* the Court of Justice ruled that neither the wording nor the purpose of Article 193 TFEU 'provides any support for the view that failure by the Member States to comply with their notification obligation under Article 193 TFEU in itself renders unlawful the more stringent protective measures thus adopted.[90]

Questions as to whether or not national rules can be applied before notification and whether or not the obligations are directly effective are therefore not at issue. On the other hand, the Commission will be able to institute proceedings for violation of the Treaty. Finally, if Article 193 TFEU is interpreted literally, the requirement to notify the Commission applies not only to stricter measures adopted *after* a directive has come into force, but also to *existing* provisions laying down stricter standards.

6 Derogation ex Article 114 TFEU

In Chapter 2 we have argued that Article 114 (1) TFEU is the legal basis for Union harmonisation measures having as their object the establishment and the functioning of the internal market and that these measures may contribute to environmental protection as well. Paragraphs 4-6 of Article 114 establish a procedure whereby Member States may be authorised by the Commission to respectively maintain or introduce national provisions incompatible with the newly adopted Union measure. Paragraphs 4 and 5 of Article 114 TFEU read as follows:

---

[88] The same applies *mutatis mutandis* with respect to the derogation procedure of Article 114(4-6) TFEU; cf. Case T-366/03 and T-235/04 *Land Oberösterreich und Österreich v. Commission* [2005] ECR-II-4005:

[89] Cf. Scott (2000) at 39.

[90] Case C-2/10 *Azienda Agro-Zootecnica Franchini*, Judgment of 21 July 2011, para. 53.

'4. If, after the adoption of a harmonisation measure by the European Parliament and the Council, by the Council or by the Commission, a Member State deems it necessary to maintain national provisions on grounds of major needs referred to in Article 36, or relating to the protection of the environment or the working environment, it shall notify the Commission of these provisions as well as the grounds for maintaining them.

5. Moreover, without prejudice to paragraph 4, if, after the adoption of a harmonisation measure by the European Parliament and the Council, by the Council or by the Commission, a Member State deems it necessary to introduce national provisions based on new scientific evidence relating to the protection of the environment or the working environment on grounds of a problem specific to that Member State arising after the adoption of the harmonisation measure, it shall notify the Commission of the envisaged provisions as well as the grounds for introducing them.'

The Court of Justice has held that the procedure of Article 114 TFEU allows a Member State to *maintain*[91] (para. 4) or to *introduce* (para. 5) national rules derogating from a harmonisation measure taken in the framework of the internal market.[92] Article 114(4-5) TFEU provides an exception to the principles of uniform application of European law and the unity of the market and therefore must be strictly interpreted. It seems self-evident that the procedure can only be used to derogate from measures that have Article 114 TFEU as legal basis and cannot be used for other 'internal market related' environmental measures, for instance measures taken in the framework of the Energy Title (Article 194 TFEU).

It is for the Member State which invokes Article 114(4-5) TFEU to prove that the conditions for application of those provisions have been met.[93] The Commission taking decisions under this procedure has a duty of care as well as a duty to state the reasons for the decision.[94]

However, it hardly seems tenable that Article 114(4-5) TFEU must be invoked in all cases where a Member State desires to take more stringent protective measures. Article 114(4-5) TFEU aims at approving or rejecting national measures that *derogate* from a harmonisation measure. Where the harmonisation measure itself leaves room for such measures, it is not necessary to invoke these paragraphs, because in that case there is no *derogation* from the European

---

[91] In general national provisions which, at the moment of adoption of the measure, exist only in draft will have to be examined under Article 114(5) TFEU. See for exception to that rule, Commission Decision 2002/884, OJ 2002 L 308/30.

[92] Case C-41/93 *France* v. *Commission* [1994] ECR I-1829.

[93] Case T-366/03 *Land Oberösterreich and Austria* v. *Commission* [2005] ECR II-4005, para. 63 and Case C-3/00 *Denmark* v. *Commission* [2003] ECR I-2643, para. 84. Cf. also Case T-182/06 *Netherlands* v. *Commission* [2007] ECR II-1983, para. 50.

[94] Cf. in particular Case C-405/07 P *Netherlands* v. *Commission* [2008] ECR I-8301, para. 72.

measures.[95] It appears from the case law of the Court of Justice that when more stringent national measures are still within the range laid down by the internal market directives, they are permitted without there being the necessity to use the procedures provided for in the fourth and fifth paragraphs of Article 114 TFEU.[96] National provisions that are falling outside the scope of a harmonisation directive will not be assessed under this procedure either.[97] Notification of such national measures should be declared inadmissible by the Commission.[98]

In view of the judgment of *Deponiezweckverband*, discussed above, the somewhat paradoxical result is that more stringent measures based on Article 193 TFEU must be reported to the Commission, but more stringent measures that fall within a European measure based on Article 114 TFEU do not have to be reported.

The two paragraphs of Article 114 TFEU, paragraph 4 in respect of *maintaining* existing national provisions and paragraph 5 in respect of *introducing* new provisions, make it clear that it is permitted to introduce new and to maintain existing national legislation which derogates from European harmonisation measures. Article 114(4-5) TFEU must be interpreted in the sense that any Member State, irrespective of how it voted in Council, can in principle be allowed to rely on the derogation procedure.

More stringent or less stringent national standards?

As has been demonstrated above, Article 193 TFEU allows Member States to take more stringent protective measures. In view of the wording 'more stringent protective measures', we ruled out that Member States are able to invoke the article to avoid meeting European standards implying a higher degree of protection than they regard as necessary. The article permits a more stringent national environment policy, not one that is less stringent. However, Article 114(4-5) TFEU does not contain this phrase. Does this therefore imply that a Member State may invoke Article 114(4-5) TFEU if it believes that the level of harmonisation sought by the Union legislature is too high? There are two arguments against this view.

In the first place, Article 114(3) TFEU provides that the Commission, in its proposals concerning environmental protection and pertaining to the establishing and functioning of the internal market, will take as a base a high level of protection. Allowing Member States to derogate from this high level would contravene the aim of the article. In the second place, the text of Article 114(4-5) TFEU does not contain anything to support this, either. It would be hard to imagine how a less stringent national provision could be 'necessary' for the protection of the environment. On the other hand, it is not inconceivable that

---

[95] This can be derived from Case C-52/00 *Commission* v. *France* [2001] ECR I-3827, paras. 13-16.

[96] Case C-11/92 *Gallaher*, para. 43.

[97] Cf. Case T-234/04 *Netherlands* v. *Commission* [2007] ECR II-4589.

[98] E.g. Commission Decision 2002/65 OJ L 25/47.

a Member State might invoke one of the *other* exceptions referred to in Article 114 TFEU and so fails to fulfil an obligation in an environmental directive. In short, Article 114(4-5) TFEU can only be applied to justify national measures which aim to achieve a greater degree of protection than does a harmonisation measure which has been adopted by the Union legislature. The only, somewhat theoretical, exception to this rule might be where application of a less stringent environmental standard could be offset by improvements in other sectors of the environment. The following might serve as an example. Suppose that a directive imposes emission limit values for the discharge of substances in air or water. Suppose also that certain discharges could be avoided altogether by means of a new production process. This would, however, entail minor infringements of the emission limit values laid down by the directive. If it were assumed, for the purpose of the example, that these minor infringements were more than offset in environmental terms by the other benefits, a derogation based on Article 114(4-5) TFEU might be possible.

Introducing national provisions

Although the *introduction* of legislation is indeed covered by Article 114(5) TFEU, the cumulative[99] conditions under which this is possible are not altogether clear. First of all, paragraph 5 requires that Member States must prove that there is 'new scientific evidence' justifying their behaviour. *New* evidence requires that the scientific evidence on which the request is based was not available at the time of adoption of the directive in question.[100] However, it is not quite clear whether 'new' must be understood as evidence produced and/or published after the adoption of the European measure only, or that it also includes 'older' evidence but which has not been taken into account, or which for some reason has been overlooked of deemed irrelevant, by the European institutions during the decision-making procedure.

> In general both the Court of Justice and the Commission have favoured the more narrow interpretation of the requirement to submit 'new' evidence.[101] In *Land Oberösterreich* the Court did not accept the so-called 'Müller report' dated before the adoption of the directive as new evidence.[102]
>
> A case where a somewhat more flexible approach was taken is the following. In a case concerning emissions of particulate matter by diesel powered vehicles, the Dutch Government produced recent scientific studies to show that susceptible population groups are subject to higher health risks associated with particulate

---

[99] Case C-512/99 *Germany v. Commission* [2003] ECR I-845 (*German man-made mineral fibres*), para. 81.

[100] Case C-3/00 *Denmark v. Commission* [2003] ECR I-2643, para. 56 *et seq.* See Fleurke (2008), 269-270 in particular.

[101] Cf. Fleurke (2008) at 269.

[102] Case C-439/05 P and C-454/05 P *Land Oberösterreich und Österreich v. Commission* [2007] ECR I-7141, para. 63.

matter.[103] Although the Commission noted that the environmental and health effects related to particulate matter concentrations were already known to a certain extent before the adoption of the directive, it did accept the studies as *new* evidence. Since the adoption of the directive, a large number of new epidemiological studies on many aspects of exposure and health effects of particulate matter have been completed which led the World Health Organisation to produce updates of its air quality guidelines.

Watertight proof should not be necessary, as this clause must be interpreted in the light of the precautionary principle.[104] However, a mere policy change would not seem sufficient.[105] Secondly, paragraph 5 requires that this evidence relate to the protection of the environment or the working environment. The 'public policy' grounds of Article 36 TFEU are omitted. This clearly restricts the Member States options to derogate from European standards in the area of chemicals, dangerous substances, biocides and so on. This of course seems odd, particularly given that the 'public policy' grounds can be used for maintaining existing national standards. Introducing new national standards is therefore more difficult than maintaining existing ones. The reason for this has been explained by the Court in the *German Man-made Mineral Fibres* case:[106]

'The difference between the two cases provided for in Article 95 EC [now Article 114 TFEU] is that, in the first, the national provisions predated the harmonisation measure. They were therefore known to the Community legislature but it could not or did not seek to be guided by them for the purpose of harmonisation. It was therefore considered acceptable for the Member State to request that its own rules remain in force. To that end, the EC Treaty requires that such national provisions must be justified on grounds of the major needs referred to in Article 30 EC [now Article 36 TFEU] or relating to the protection of the environment or the working environment. By contrast, in the second case, the adoption of new national legislation is more likely to jeopardize harmonisation. The Community institutions could not, by definition, have taken account of the national text when drawing up the harmonisation measure. In that case, the requirements referred to in Article 30 EC [now Article 36 TFEU] are not taken into account and only grounds relating to protection of the environment or the working environment are accepted, on condition that the Member State provides new scientific evidence and that the need to

---

[103] Commission Decision 2006/372, OJ 2006 L 142/16.

[104] See point 104 of Decision 1999/832, OJ 1999 L 329/25 (*Dutch creosote*). See on the precautionary principle also Chapter 1, section 3.2.

[105] The precautionary principle does not imply that either; Cf. Case C-3/00 *Denmark v. Commission* [2003] ECR I-2643, para. 103: 'a Member State cannot unilaterally invoke the precautionary principle in order to maintain derogating national provisions. In an area where Member State legislation has been harmonised, it is for the Community legislature to apply the precautionary principle.'

[106] Case C-512/99 *Germany v. Commission* [2003] ECR I-845 (*German man-made mineral fibres*), para. 41.

introduce new national provisions results from a problem specific to the Member State concerned arising after the adoption of the harmonisation measure.'

We are not completely convinced by this line of reasoning, particularly not by looking at it from a non-discrimination point of view. This imbalance in the Treaty, and sanctioned by the Court, could result in a certain national measure being allowed in one Member State (as existing national legislation covered by an Article 36 TFEU ground) but not in another (because it was being introduced there). However, this problem can be solved, to a certain extent, if we either interpret 'the protection of the environment' to include 'the protection of health and life of humans, animals or plants' mentioned in Article 36 TFEU[107] or interpret it in light of the more broadly formulated objectives of Article 191 TFEU. 'Environment' in Article 191 TFEU does include the protection of human health. It remains to be seen if the the Commission and the Court are willing to embark on this line of reasoning.

A problem specific to that Member State and Article 114(5) TFEU
Under Article 114(5) TFEU, the Member State must show that the new national measures are necessary to tackle a problem that is specific to that Member State, for instance, because of its high population density, highly concentrated infrastructure, special geological, metrological or geomorphological circumstances, etc. In other words, there have to be circumstances specific to that Member State justifying the more stringent environmental measures. This means that a simple statement: 'we want stricter environmental legislation', would not be sufficient. The *Land Oberösterreich* case made this quite clear.[108]

> The case concerned a notification under Article 114(5) TFEU of a draft law of the *Land Oberösterreich* (Province of Upper Austria in Austria) banning genetic engineering altogether. The decision of the Commission rejecting Austria's request for derogation was challenged at the Court under Article 263 TFEU. The Court upheld the Commission's decision in view of Austria's failure to establish that the territory of the *Land Oberösterreich* contained 'unusual or unique ecosystems that required separate risk assessments from those conducted for Austria as a whole or in other similar areas of Europe.' Consequently, the Court held that the arguments by which the applicants have disputed the findings made by the Commission on the condition relating to the existence of a problem specific to the notifying Member State had to be rejected.

---

[107] This does not however seem very logical. Article 114(4) TFEU uses the term 'environment' in addition to the grounds mentioned in Article 36 TFEU. This shows that the two concepts are – at least in the context of Article 114 TFEU – not identical.

[108] Case T-366/03 and T-235/04 *Land Oberösterreich und Österreich* v. *Commission* [2005] ECR II-4005; Judgment upheld by the Court of Justice in Case C-439/05 P and C-454/05 P *Land Oberösterreich und Österreich* v. *Commission* [2007] ECR I-7141.

In the *Dutch Diesel Engine* case, the Court further clarified this requirement.[109] It argued that it is not possible to rely on Article 114(3) TFEU 'in order to deal with a general environmental danger in the Union':

> 'Any problem which arises in terms which are on the whole comparable through-out the Member States and which lends itself, therefore, to harmonised solutions at Community level is general in nature and is, consequently, not specific within the meaning of Article 95(5) EC [now Article 114(5) TFEU].'
>
> [...]
>
> 'It is therefore necessary, in order correctly to interpret Article 95(5) EC [now Article 114(5) TFEU], to envisage the requirement of national specificity of a prob-lem essentially from the angle of the aptness or inaptness of the harmonisation of the applicable Community rules to confront adequately the difficulties encoun-tered locally, since the established inaptness of those rules justifies the introduc-tion of national measures.'

In other words, the justification for Member State action lies in the fact that, due to the local nature of the problem, a solution at European level is unsuitable to resolve the problem established. However, this requirement does not necessarily mean that a Member State would be precluded from taking more stringent mea-sures simply because the same problem occurred elsewhere also. In the *Dutch Diesel Engine* case, the Dutch Government complained that the Commission made the grant of the derogation requested subject to the requirement that the air quality problem relied upon in support of its request affects the Netherlands exclusively. After stating, as a matter of principle, 'for a problem to be specific to a Member State within the meaning of the relevant provision, it is not neces-sary that it is the result of an environmental danger within that State alone', the Court found that the Commission did not apply such an exclusivity test and rejected the Netherlands Government as lacking any factual basis.[110] Indeed, specific does not mean exclusive or unique.

A problem specific to that Member State and Article 114(4) TFEU
This criterion cannot be found, at least not explicitly, in the text regard-ing existing national legislation and this seems to imply another imbalance. However, there is a point in saying that this condition must be met with respect to Article 114(4) TFEU as well. When national environmental legislation has been harmonised, the presumption must be that the level of protection result-ing from harmonisation is adequate.[111] If Member States want to derogate from a directive, either by introducing new legislation or by maintaining existing

---

[109] Case T-182/06 *Netherlands* v. *Commission* [2007] ECR II-1983. See however the appeal in Case C-405/07 P *Netherlands* v. *Commission* [2008] ECR I-8301.

[110] Case T-182/06 *Netherlands* v. *Commission* [2007] ECR II-1983, paras. 65 and 72 in particular.

[111] The famous *Inter-Huiles* case seems to point in the same direction. Case 172/82 *Inter-Huiles* [1983] ECR 555.

stricter standards, they have to show that this is justified on grounds specific to that Member State.[112] However, in the *Danish Foodstuffs* case, the Court decided

> 'that neither the wording of Article 95(4) EC [Article 114(4) TFEU] nor the broad logic of that article as a whole entails a requirement that the applicant Member State prove that maintaining the national provisions which it notifies to the Commission is justified by a problem specific to that Member State.'[113]

Exit, the 'specific ground' criterion one might presume? Wrong, as the Court in the next paragraph of the same judgment acknowledges,

> 'when a problem specific to the applicant Member State in fact exists, that circumstance can be *highly relevant* in guiding the Commission as to whether to approve or reject the notified national provisions. It is a factor which, in the present case, the Commission should have taken into account when it adopted its decision.' [emphasis added]

In other words, Article 114(4) TFEU does not make approval of the Commission conditional of the existence of a problem specific to that Member State, but it is 'highly relevant'. And because the Commission considered the possible existence of a situation specific to Denmark merely as a useful element in assessing what decision to adopt and not as a condition of approval the decision of the Commission was upheld. With all respect to the Court of Justice, but it looks as if the Court is playing with words in particular if we have look at the decision of the Commission itself.[114] At point 32 of the decision we read that '[I]n the light of the information supplied by Denmark, the Commission also examined whether sulphites constituted a particular health problem for the Danish population as compared with the populations of the other Member States.' This was followed by: 'Consequently, the information available to the Commission has not made it possible to conclude that the Danish population is in a specific situation compared with the populations of other Member States, notably its immediate neighbours, as regards this question of allergies related to sulphites' and concluded 'that the Danish measures, though based on public health considerations, are still not justified by the need to protect public health.' In other words, the Commission was looking for specific circumstances in Denmark, could not find them and concluded that the derogating measures could not be justified for reasons of public health protection. So it may be the case that *de jure* the 'specific ground' criterion is not being applied with respect to Article 114(4) TFEU; the Commission does apply this criterion *de facto*[115] and the Court has accepted this.

---

[112] Cf. Case C-389/96 *Aher-Waggon GmbH* [1998] ECR I-4473.

[113] Case C-3/00 *Denmark* v. *Commission* [2003] ECR I-2643, para. 59. Analogous considerations apply to the requirement for new scientific evidence, para. 62 of the judgment.

[114] OJ 1999 L 329/1.

[115] See also the Commission Decision approving stricter Dutch legislation on creosote in the light of the specific geographic situation of the Netherlands. Decision 1999/832, OJ 1999 L 329/25 (*Dutch creosote*).

The role of the Commission under Article 114(6) TFEU
Article 114(6) TFEU reads as follows:

'The Commission shall, within six months of the notifications as referred to in paragraphs 4 and 5, approve or reject the national provisions involved after having verified whether or not they are a means of arbitrary discrimination or a disguised restriction on trade between Member States and whether or not they shall constitute an obstacle to the functioning of the internal market.

In the absence of a decision by the Commission within this period the national provisions referred to in paragraphs 4 and 5 shall be deemed to have been approved.

When justified by the complexity of the matter and in the absence of danger for human health, the Commission may notify the Member State concerned that the period referred to in this paragraph may be extended for a further period of up to six months.'

Given the procedural framework, the Commission normally has to limit itself to examining the relevance of the elements, which are submitted by the requesting Member State, without having itself to seek possible reasons or justifications. The responsibility of proving that the national measures are justified lies with the Member State making the request.[116]

Two further issues have to be discussed in this context. The first concerns the grounds the Commission must take into account in its assessment. The second concerns the legal consequences of notification.

Article 114(6) TFEU states the conditions which must be met before the Commission is allowed to approve national derogating measures, In addition to the familiar[117] conditions of 'no arbitrary discrimination' and 'no disguised restriction to trade', another condition is that there should be 'no obstacle to the functioning of the internal market'. Such an the assessment is a matter for the Commission, and the Court will not, in an application for annulment, substitute its assessment for that of the Commission.[118]

'No arbitrary discrimination' is interpreted by the Commission as meaning that no different treatment should be give to similar situations, nor similar treat-

---

Cf. also one of the Dutch creosote cases: Commission Decision 2002/884, OJ 2002 L 308/30, point 66 in particular. Similar observations can be made with respect to submitting scientific evidence. Although only required under Article 114(5) TFEU, a Member State is well advised to submit relevant and convincing scientific evidence with its notification. Otherwise, Member States will run the risk of not convincing the Commission of the necessity of the derogating measures. Cf. for instance Commission Decision 2003/829 (*German azodyes*). OJ 2003 L 311/46, point 47 in particular.

[116] Case T-366/03 *Land Oberösterreich and Austria* v. *Commission* [2005] ECR II-4005, para. 63 and Case C-3/00 *Denmark* v. *Commission* [2003] ECR I-2643, para. 84. Cf. also Case T-182/06 *Netherlands* v. *Commission* [2007] ECR II-1983, para. 50.

[117] See Article 36 TFEU.

[118] Case C-3/00 *Denmark* v. *Commission* [2003] ECR I-2643, para. 125.

ment to different situations.[119] According to the Commission the 'no disguised restriction to trade' provision is intended to prevent the restrictions based on the criteria of paragraph 4 being applied for inappropriate reasons, and in reality constituting economic measures introduced to impede the import of products from other Member States in order to protect indirectly national production.[120] In other words: is there a real and genuine concern for the protection of human health and the environment or not?

According to the Commission the condition 'no obstacle to the functioning of the internal market' cannot be interpreted in such a way that it prohibits the approval of any national measure likely to affect the establishment of the internal market.[121] In fact, any national measure derogating from a harmonisation measure aiming at the establishment and operation of the internal market, constitutes in substance a measure that is likely to affect the internal market. This of course raises the interesting question of what the condition does mean? The first series of Commission decisions applying this clause give the impression that the Commission interprets it as a special application of the proportionality principle. In the *Dutch Creosote* case the Commission stated that the concept of obstacle to the functioning of the internal market 'has to be understood as a disproportionate effect in relation to the pursued objective.'[122] The Commission went on to discuss the possible effects of the Dutch legislation on production, sales and trade of creosote. In this case the Dutch legislation met the Commission requirements. This way of applying the proportionality principle seems to differ in two respects from the manner in which it is normally applied in the context of the assessment of national measures affecting the free movement of goods.[123] First, it includes effects on the market other than barriers to trade and, second, the effects on the internal market are weighed in the same basket as the environmental objectives pursued (proportionality *stricto sensu*).[124]

The conclusion seems to be that the 'no obstacle' clause has a meaning of its own. The decisions of the Commission show that the Commission has been given a fairly wide discretionary power to block derogating national standards even if the national measures are justified from an environmental point of view and even if there is no arbitrary discrimination or disguised restriction to trade.

[119] Decision 1999/832, OJ 1999 L 329/25 (*Dutch creosote*).

[120] Decision 1999/832, OJ 1999 L 329/25 and Decision 2002/59, OJ 2002 L 23/37 (*Dutch creosote II*). See also Chapter 6, section 4.3.

[121] Decision 1999/832, OJ 1999 L 329/25.

[122] Decision 1999/832, OJ 1999 L 329/25. Other decisions confirm this. See e.g. Commission Decision 2006/372, OJ 2006 L 142/16.

[123] In other words, is the measure 'suitable and necessary', see point 105 in the Dutch Creosote Decision 1999/832, OJ 1999 L 329/25. See on the proportionality principle in the context of Articles 34-36 TFEU, Chapter 6, section 4.5.

[124] Cf. for instance Decision 94/783, OJ 1994 L 316/43 (*German PCP*). See on the concept of proportionality *stricto sensu*, also Chapter 6, section 4.5.

In assessing the national measures the Commission can take into account any effect on the internal market and has therefore been given a power to balance, rather intensive, different objectives and interests going well beyond the standard way of applying the proportionality principle.

As far as the consequences of notification are concerned, the first thing to note is that the Commission must take[125] a decision within six months of notification, failing which the measures are deemed to have been approved. However, the text does not state what the consequences are of non-notification by the Member State. Two judgments of the Court of Justice relating to the precursor of Article 114 TFEU, the 'old' Article 100a(4) EC, must be mentioned in this respect, the *PCP* case[126] and the *Kortas* case.[127]

> In the *PCP* case, Germany had invoked Article 100a(4) EC to justify national provisions prohibiting pentachlorophenol (PCP), which were stricter than those provided for in the PCP directive.[128] The Commission decided to approve the German provisions on the grounds that Germany had voted against the directive, that it had notified the Commission of the provisions, that the German provisions were already in force before the directive was adopted and that they were not discriminatory, as they applied without distinction to both national and imported products.[129] France appealed against the Commission's decision to the Court of Justice. The Court held that the Commission's decision must be annulled, because it did not satisfy the obligation to state reasons.

Two points to note are that, in the first place, the Court regarded the Commission's decision to approve or reject national legislation as a decision, which is amenable to an action for annulment under Article 263 TFEU.[130] Secondly, the legal consequence of the Commission's decision is plain:

> 'A Member State is not, therefore, authorized to apply the national provisions notified by it until after it has obtained a decision from the Commission confirming them.'

---

[125] And *notify* the decision to the Member State whithin that period: Case T-69/08 *Commission v. Poland*, Judgment of 9 December 2010.

[126] Case C-41/93 *France v. Commission* [1994] ECR I-1829.

[127] Case C-319/97 *Kortas* [1999] ECR I-3143.

[128] Directive 91/173, OJ 1991 L 85/34.

[129] OJ 1992 C 334/8.

[130] See however Case T-234/04 *Netherlands v. Commission* [2007] ECR II-4589. A Member State cannot on the basis of Article 114(4) TFEU request the Commission to take a decision on the extent of harmonisation under a Union measure and/or on the compatibility of national legislation with such a measure. Any position adopted by the Commission pertaining such a request is not capable of being the subject of an application for annulment.

Until the national provisions have been approved, a standstill requirement applies. In the *Kortas* case, the Court went a step further.[131] The interesting thing about *Kortas* is that the Commission had not responded to Sweden's notification for several years. In this respect we have to mention that Article 100a(4) of the old EC Treaty did not provide for any time-limit within which the Commission was to confirm the provisions notified to it. This was only introduced by the Treaty of Amsterdam. In its judgment the Court concluded in *Kortas* that the aim of the procedure is to ensure that no Member State applied national rules derogating from the harmonised legislation without obtaining due confirmation from the Commission. Referring to the *PCP* case, the Court observed that harmonisation measures would be rendered ineffective if Member States retained the right unilaterally to apply national rules derogating from those measures.

Although Article 114(6) TFEU now does provide for a time limit within which the Commission must have taken a decision, failing which national provisions will be deemed to have been approved, the general rule in *Kortas* is still good law. A Member State is not authorised to apply the national provisions notified by it until after it has obtained an approval, either by an explicit decision from the Commission or implicitly by the expiration of the six months time limit of Article 114(6) TFEU.

Based on this case law we may also conclude that after expiry of the implementation period of an Article 114 measure, Member States must refrain from applying any legislation derogation from the Union measure that has been notified to the Commission without receiving approval. The same applies to new legislation that has been notified but not received approval, even before expiry of the implementation deadline of the Union measure.[132] It should be added that the same applies to legislation which has not been notified, but which should have been under Article 114(4-6) TFEU.

7   Inherent Competence to Derogate?

An entirely different question arises if there is an inherent general competence in European law for Member States to derogate from environmental standards in directives, even where the directive does not provide for such a competence and neither Article 114(4-6) TFEU nor Article 193 TFEU are applicable.

In principle, obligations entered into within the framework of an environmental directive have to be fulfilled. Member States have no freedom to derogate from the level of protection required by a directive beyond the provisions of the

---

[131] See on this case Sevenster (2000) at 296-298.

[132] Cf. also Sevenster (2000) at 308.

directive itself.[133] It is thus European law which determines whether, and if so to what extent, Member States may depart from common levels of protection. Many environmental directives contain safeguard clauses allowing Member States to derogate temporarily from the requirements ECR of the directive.[134]

The next question to be addressed is whether derogations from the requirements of a directive can be accepted, which are not provided for by the directive in question. The case law of the Court of Justice does indeed contain indications that this might be the case under certain circumstances.

> In the *Leybucht* case, German dredging, filling and dyke-building operations in the Leybucht area were at issue.[135] Germany had designated the area a protected area under Article 4 of the Wild Birds Directive.[136] According to Article 4(4) of the directive, Germany had to take appropriate steps to avoid pollution or deterioration of habitats or any disturbances affecting the birds. The dyke-reinforcement work would result in a reduction in the size of the special protection area. The Court seemed to have accepted 'exceptional grounds' to justify an alteration in the extent of the protected area.
>
> The Court subsequently held that those 'exceptional grounds' must correspond to a general interest which is superior to the general interest represented by the ecological objective of the directive. In this case the Court held that the danger of flooding and the protection of the coast constitute sufficiently serious reasons to justify the dyke works and the strengthening of coastal structures as long as those measures are confined to a strict minimum and involve only the smallest possible reduction of the special protection area. Economic considerations, for example to ensure that fishing vessels had access to the harbour, were not however acceptable.

The more general conclusion that can be drawn from this judgment seems to be that even in cases where a directive does not provide for derogations from its requirements, there is apparently an inherent competence to derogate in those cases where higher interests are involved than those the directive is designed to protect. In each individual case it will have to be considered which higher interests are acceptable in European law. In addition, this judgment seems to imply that economic and recreational interests cannot necessarily be regarded as falling under this inherent competence.

Finally, there is another point of interest in the judgment. That is the introduction of the concept of 'offsetting ecological benefits'. After the Court had noted that securing access to the fishing harbour of Greetsiel could not be

---

[133] Cf. e.g. Case 228/87 *Pretore di Torino* v. *Persons unknown* [1988] ECR 5099: 'Derogations from the directive are permitted only under the conditions provided for in Articles 9, 10 and 20 thereof. These provisions must be interpreted strictly.'

[134] See on this Chapter 1, section 3.2.

[135] Case C-57/89 *Commission* v. *Germany* [1991] ECR I-883.

[136] OJ 1979 L 103/1, later amended.

regarded as a superior interest, it reflected that the work in question might also have positive ecological effects. The ecological disadvantages would be offset by the formation of new salt meadows of ecological importance. The Court was thus applying the principle of 'offsetting ecological benefits' as a condition under which a Member State might derogate from the obligations contained in Article 4(4) of the directive. The question is however if, and to what extent, this principle is generally applicable to European environmental law. More recent case law seems to suggest that it is not. In a case concerning the implementation in Austria of the Waste Directive, the Court ruled that the directive 'cannot be interpreted as meaning that the Member States are released from adopting transposing measures where they consider that their national provisions are better than the European provisions concerned and that the national provisions are therefore better able to ensure that the objective pursued by the directive is achieved.'[137] We will have to wait on further case law to clarify this issue.

In sum: laying down environmental standards in directives therefore has an important stabilizing function. They prevent unilateral steps by Member States in derogation from the required level of protection – this is prevented by the pre-emptive effect of European environmental law. Derogation is possible where:
- the Commission has approved national legislation according to Article 114(6) TFEU, or
- the directive in question allows it, or
- interests superior to the environmental interest are involved, or ecological benefits are offset.

European environmental law differs from national environmental law in this respect. If a national legislature decides to lower its environmental standards, it is competent to do so. All that is required is that the national laws and policies are altered in accordance with new ideas and policy considerations and according to the relevant national decision-making procedures.

---

[137] Case C-194/01 *Commission v. Austria* [2004] ECR I-4579, para. 39. See also Case C-103/02 *Commission v. Italy* [2004] ECR I-9127, para. 33. Cf. on this issue also Pagh (2005) at 8-9.

CHAPTER 4

Implementation

1 General Remarks

Complying with obligations arising under Union environmental law and, in particular, under regulations and directives, is often referred to as 'implementation'. This chapter will consider the main features of this process.[1] In theory four different phases can be distinguished in the process of implementation. First, there is the *transposition* of directives into national law, whereby the directive is, as it were, translated into national law. Regulations do not require transposition; in fact, it is not permitted to transpose regulations into national law.[2] The transposition of a directive requires the adoption of binding rules of national law. The second phase is the *operationalisation* of the regulation or directive. Normally, this will mean designating the national authorities that are to be responsible for the further implementation and application of the Union rules, and adopting enforcement and procedural measures. As *operationalisation* is closely linked with *transposition* we will treat both phases together.[3] The third phase consists of the *application* of the regulation or directive in specific cases – or, more precisely as regards directives, application of the national rules implementing them. Finally, the Union provisions – or the national law implementing them – must be *enforced*: observance of the regulation or national rules based on the directive must be monitored and, if necessary secured by means of sanctions. We will deal with *application* and *enforcement* of Union environmental law in section 5 of this chapter.

2 The Duty to Transpose Environmental Directives into National Law

Obligations under directives are generally formulated as instructions to the Member States. For example, Article 4(1) of Directive 2006/66 on batteries and accumulators and waste batteries and accumulators stipulates the following:

'1. Without prejudice to Directive 2000/53/EC, Member States shall prohibit the placing on the market of:
a) all batteries or accumulators, whether or not incorporated into appliances, that contain more than 0,0005% of mercury by weight; and
b) portable batteries or accumulators, including those incorporated into appliances, that contain more than 0,002% of cadmium by weight.'[4]

---

[1] This section builds upon Jans et al. (2007), Chapter 1, section 5.

[2] See more in detail section 3.7 of this chapter.

[3] See sections 2 and 3 of this chapter.

[4] OJ 2006 L 266/1.

Such obligations have to be transposed into the national legal system, within the time limits[5] set by the directive. To that end a directive will contain a provision like:

> 'Member States shall bring into force the laws, regulations and administrative provisions necessary to comply with this Directive by 1 March 2007 and forthwith inform the Commission thereof. When Member States adopt those provisions, they shall contain a reference to this Directive or be accompanied by such a reference on the occasion of their official publication. Member States shall determine how such reference is to be made.'

It is true that the third paragraph of Article 288 TFEU provides that a directive shall be binding, as to the result to be achieved, upon each Member State to which it is addressed, but shall leave to the national authorities a broad discretion regarding the choice of form and methods.[6] However, this power has been somewhat restricted by judgments of the Court of Justice in connection with the principle of sincere cooperation contained in Article 4(3) TEU. This provides that Member States shall take all appropriate measures, whether general or particular, to ensure fulfilment of their European obligations.

As early as the *Royer* case the Court had held that the freedom left to the Member States by Article 288 TFEU as to the choice of forms and methods of implementation of directives does not affect their obligation to choose the most appropriate forms and methods.[7] This seems to suggest that consequently, the Commission can impose the form or method which it considers the most appropriate for implementing a provision. That view, however, is incorrect. Its only task is to check whether the national legislation corresponds to the objective which the Union legislature intended to achieve.[8]

Furthermore, the Court has also repeatedly held that the transposition of a directive into national law does not necessarily require the provisions of the directive to be enacted in precisely the same words in a specific express legal provision.[9]

> As an example we may point at the Luxembourg implementation of the Water Framework Directive 2000/60. In Case C-32/05 the Court of Justice dealt with the question whether the directive obliges Member States to adopt *framework* legislation in order to implement the requirements of the directive in national law.[10] The

---

[5] Cf. on possible extensions of time limits Case C-236/99 *Commission* v. *Belgium* [2000] ECR I-5657.

[6] Cf. for instance on the Wild Birds Directive Case C-418/04 *Commission* v. *Ireland* [2007] ECR I-10947.

[7] Case 48/75 *Royer* [1976] ECR 497.

[8] Case C-392/99 *Commission* v. *Portugal* [2003] ECR I-3373, concerning the implementation in Portugal of the old Waste Oils Directive.

[9] Case C-339/87 *Commission* v. *Netherlands* [1990] ECR I-851 and Case C-32/05 *Commission* v. *Luxembourg* [2006] ECR I-11323.

[10] Case C-32/05 *Commission* v. *Luxembourg* [2006] ECR I-11323.

Court found that the provisions of the directive did not show that Member States are under a duty to adopt such framework legislation in order to implement its provisions correctly. Although the Court acknowledged, that adopting framework legislation may be an appropriate, or even more straightforward, method of implementing the directive, it nevertheless concluded that adopting framework legislation is not the only way in which Member States may ensure that the directive is fully applied. Had the Union legislature intended to require Member States to adopt framework legislation in their national legal systems in order to implement the directive, it would have been open to it to insert a provision to that effect in the text of the directive, the Court finally argued.

Here the Court is respecting the freedom left to the Member States by Article 288 TFEU. The competence to choose the most appropriate forms and methods implies that a general legal context may be sufficient if it actually ensures the full application of the directive in a sufficiently clear and precise manner.

In the *Traen* case the Court stated that the exercise of a discretionary power is qualified only by the requirement that the objectives of the directive, namely the protection of human health and of the environment, must be complied with.[11]
In Case C-6/04 the Commission argued that the United Kingdom did not transpose the Habitats Directive appropriately into its legal order.[12] The United Kingdom's argument that the most appropriate way of implementing the Habitats Directive was to impose on nature conservation bodies on them *a general duty* to exercise their functions so as to secure compliance with the requirements of the Habitats Directive was rejected by the Court. The Court found the UK legislation 'so general that it does not give effect to the Habitats Directive with sufficient precision and clarity to satisfy fully the demands of legal certainty'.

Consequently, there is a fine balance between the freedom left to Member States in implementing directives and the constraints imposed on them. On the one hand it is recognised that it must be for each Member State to determine how the provisions of Union law can best be enforced in the light of its own particular institutions. On the other hand, this must be in compliance with Article 288 TFEU. Moreover it is considered essential that the measures taken by the different Member States should be applied with the same effectiveness and rigour as in the application of their national law.

In several judgments relating to the Wild Birds Directive, the Court has added the requirement that the precision of transposition is of particular importance. This requirement is generally expressed in words such as the following:

---

[11] Joined Cases 372-374/85 *Traen* [1987] ECR 2141.
[12] Case C-6/04 *Commission* v. *UK* [2005] ECR I-9017.

'However, a faithful transposition becomes particularly important in a case such as this in which the management of the common heritage is entrusted to the Member States in their respective territories.'[13]

'The directive is based on the consideration that effective bird protection, and in particular protection of migratory species, is typically a transfrontier environment problem entailing common responsibilities for the Member States.'[14]

Thus as far as the transposition of the Wild Birds Directive is concerned, and the same could also be said of the Habitats Directive,[15] the Court seems to take a very strict view of the adequacy of national implementing legislation.

These judgments may also be important for the way other 'transboundary' provisions in environmental directives are implemented, in particular for the many provisions on conducting consultations, providing information etc. where transboundary environmental effects are involved.[16] Even without explicit reference to the Wild Birds Directive, it is clear from its judgments that the Court also attaches great importance to the proper transposition of such obligations into national law.[17]

Thus Member States retain the freedom to adapt the content of a directive to their national systems of environmental law, and in doing so may utilise their own legal instruments, legal terminology and division of public law powers. As long as an environmental directive is transposed fully and accurately into national law within the deadlines set by the directive, the legal relations it covers are primarily governed by the national measures taken to implement it. Nevertheless, until the deadline has expired, the Member State to which the directive is addressed must refrain from taking any measures liable seriously to compromise the result prescribed.[18]

Finally it must be noted that the Court is very reluctant to accept Member States' 'excuses' for not being able to comply with their obligations under EU law. Although acknowledged by the Court in theory, pleading *force majeure* will

---

[13] Case 252/85 *Commission* v. *France* [1988] ECR 2243.

[14] Case 262/85 *Commission* v. *Italy* [1987] ECR 3073. Cf. also more recently Case C-418/04 *Commission* v. *Ireland* [2007] ECR I-10947.

[15] Case C-6/04 *Commission* v. *UK* [2005] ECR I-9017, para. 25: 'that threatened habitats and species form part of the European Community's natural heritage and that the threats to them are often of a transboundary nature, so that the adoption of conservation measures is a common responsibility of all Member States. Consequently [...], faithful transposition becomes particularly important in an instance such as the present one, where management of the common heritage is entrusted to the Member States in their respective territories.'

[16] Cf. Case C-365/93 *Commission* v. *Greece* [1995] ECR I-499, concerning the implementation of directives intended to accord rights to nationals of other Member States.

[17] Case C-186/91 *Commission* v. *Belgium* [1993] ECR I-851.

[18] Case C-129/96 *Inter-Environnement Wallonie ASBL* v. *Waals Gewest* [1997] ECR I-7411. This case will be discussed more extensively in Chapter 5, section 2.1.

not be accepted easily.[19] Nor can a Member State plead that the national measures are better able to protect the environment than the European measures.[20]

3   Aspects of Transposition

3.1   Must Every Provision be Transposed?

European legislative practice shows that there may be great
differences in the types of obligations which directives impose on the Member
States and therefore in the results which must be achieved.[21] Some directives
require *legislative* measures to be adopted at national level and compliance with
those measures to be the subject of judicial or administrative review. Other
directives lay down that the Member States are to take the necessary measures
to ensure that certain objectives formulated in general and unquantifiable terms
are attained, whilst leaving them some discretion as to the nature of the measures to be taken.[22] Yet other directives require the Member States to obtain very
precise and specific results after a certain period.[23]

A question that has to be answered before discussing what requirements
national implementing legislation should be required to fulfil is whether every
provision of an environmental directive has to be transposed into national
legislation. An examination of various environmental directives shows that they
contain many different kinds of provisions. Essential for understanding the
Court's case law on the Member States' duty to transpose provisions of environmental directives into binding national law is that it is applicable to all provisions 'intended to create rights and obligations for individuals'.[24] This case law,
to be discussed more exhaustively below, also shows that the Court interprets
the concept of 'rights and obligations' in a fairly broad and flexible manner.

So what provisions do have to be transposed into national law and what
provisions do not? In the first place, some provisions are not directed at the
Member States, but at the Council or the European Commission. For example,
the Commission can be required to review the implementation of the European
measure and to produce implementation reports and/or feasibility studies.[25]

---

[19]   Cf. e.g. Case C-297/08 *Commission v. Italy*, Judgment of 4 March 2010, on the Italian 'struggle' to implement and enforce European waste law in the Campania region.

[20]   Case C-194/01 *Commission v. Austria* [2004] ECR I-4579. Cf. however also our remarks on the *Leybucht*
case in Chapter 3, section 7, Case C-57/89 *Commission v. Germany* [1991] ECR I-883.

[21]   Case C-60/01 *Commission v. France* [2002] ECR I-5679, para. 25.

[22]   Cf. Case C-365/97 *Commission v. Italy* [1999] ECR I-7773, to be discussed below.

[23]   Cf. Case C-56/90 *Commission v. United Kingdom* [1993] ECR I-4109, to be discussed below.

[24]   Case C-361/88 *Commission v. Germany* [1991] ECR I-2567.

[25]   E.g. Article 14 of the 'new' Shellfish Water Directive: '[...] The Commission shall publish a Community
report on the implementation of this Directive within nine months of receiving the reports from the
Member States'; Directive 2006/113 on the quality required of shellfish waters, OJ 2006 L 376/14.

By their very nature, such provisions, which are not addressed to the Member States, do not require transposition into national law by the Member States.

In the second place there are provisions which concern exclusively the relations between the Member States and the European institutions, in particular the Commission.[26] This category includes all kinds of obligations for the Member States to provide the Commission with information, such as the obligation to notify the Commission of the texts of implementing legislation, or to send the Commission brief factual reports or situation reports. Of course, the Member States must fulfil the obligations contained in such provisions. In other words, they must send the Commission required reports and provide it with the required information. Rights and obligations for individuals are not at issue here.[27] However, there is no need to have these kind of provisions transposed into national law.

> This conclusion is supported by the case law of the Court.[28] For instance, Article 12(1) of the Wild Birds Directive 79/409 requires the Member States to draw up every three years a report on the implementation of national provisions taken under that directive and forward it to the Commission so that it can check that the directive has been complied with by the Member States. According to the Court, that provision concerns only the relations between those Member States and the Commission.[29]

Of course, the above categories do not contain the most essential elements of a directive. The core of a directive is formed by the concrete and specific provisions. And in the case of environmental directives, these are specific substantive and operational provisions directed at the objectives[30] of environmental protection and/or market integration. In general these provisions will be designed to regulate more than simply the legal relations between the Member States and the Union institutions. Environmental directives are bound to have some measure of external impact and are designed to regulate relations between individuals and between individuals and the state. In other words, they will generally

---

[26] Case C-32/05 *Commission* v. *Luxembourg* [2006] ECR I-11323, para. 35.

[27] Cf. Case 380/87 *Balsamo* [1989] ECR 2491 in respect of the Member States' obligation to notify the Commission of draft rules on waste disposal under Article 3 of Directive 75/442.

[28] E.g. Case C-58/89 *Commission* v. *Germany* [1991] ECR I-4983; Case C-296/01 *Commission* v. *France* [2003] ECR I-13909, paras. 92 and 35.

[29] Case C-72/02 *Commission* v. *Portugal* [2003] ECR I-6597, paras. 19 and 20.

[30] Provisions of directives which merely specify the particular objectives the directive seeks to achieve – like Article 1 of the Water Framework Directive 2000/60 – do not require transposition; Case C-32/05 *Commission* v. *Luxembourg* [2006] ECR I-11323, para. 44. According to Article 1, its purpose is 'to establish a framework for the protection of inland surface waters, transitional waters, coastal waters and groundwater'. On the other hand, we would argue that definitions in the directive of key legal concepts (like 'waste' or 'surface waters') do require transposition, in view of legal certainty. See on the latter point also Krämer (2007) at 420-421.

be intended to create rights and obligations for individuals. Rights are granted to those who are confronted with the effects of pollution while obligations are imposed on those who cause it. Such provisions must be fulfilled not only *in fact*, but also *in law*. In other words, they must be given a legal basis and transposed into national law. There is in fact only one reason why an environmental directive containing rights and obligations for individuals should not result in further national legislative activity, and that is where national law already fully meet the requirements of the directive in every respect.

The judgments of the Court indicate that rights for individuals are readily implied. Thus *procedural* rules may also contain rights and obligations for individuals.[31] Case C-131/88 involved the procedural obligations under the old Groundwater Directive.[32] It required, e.g., prior investigations of the hydrogeological conditions of the area concerned before authorisations are issued. The Court held that the procedural provisions of the directive intend to create rights and obligations for individuals.

In Case C-361/88, in interpreting the European air quality standards, the Court also took a broad view of the question of when an individual's rights are at stake.[33] It pointed out that the obligation on Member States to prescribe air quality limit values not to be exceeded, was imposed 'in order to protect human health in particular', and that it therefore implies rights for individuals.

Another example in this context is the judgment in Case C-186/91, where the Court rejected the Belgian argument that the obligation to hold transboundary consultations contained in a directive on air quality standards for nitrogen dioxide did not contain rights for individuals and therefore did not require incorporation into national law.[34]

More examples in the case law of the Court of Justice concern the way France implemented the old Waste Incineration Directives.[35] The Court ruled that both directives require legislative measures to be adopted at the national level and compliance with those measures is to be the subject of judicial or administrative review. It stated that Directives 89/369 and 89/429 impose on the Member States obligations, formulated in clear and unequivocal terms, to achieve a certain result, in order that their incineration plants meet detailed and precise requirements within the stated time-limits and rejected the French Government's assertions that it is sufficient for a Member State to take all reasonably practicable measures.

---

[31] Case C-131/88 *Commission* v. *Germany* [1991] ECR I-825.

[32] The 'old' Groundwater Directive will be repealed from 21 December 2013 by the Water Framework Directive 2000/60, OJ 2000 L 327/1.

[33] Case C-361/88 *Commission* v. *Germany* [1991] ECR I-2567. Cf. also Case C-13/90 *Commission* v. *France* [1991] ECR I-4327; Case C-14/90 *Commission* v. *France* [1991] ECR I-4331; Case C-64/90 *Commission* v. *France* [1991] ECR I-4335 and Case C-58/89 *Commission* v. *Germany* [1991] ECR I-4983.

[34] Case C-186/91 *Commission* v. *Belgium* [1993] ECR I-851. Cf. also on transboundary EIA consultations Case C-435/09 *Commission* v. *Belgium*, Judgment of 24 March 2011, para. 92.

[35] Case C-60/01 *Commission* v. *France* [2002] ECR I-5679. See now also Directive 2000/76, OJ 2000 L 332/91.

Generally, the default choice will be transposition of the material and operational requirements of directives into national law. And where a directive prohibits certain activities, such as the marketing of environmentally harmful products which do not meet the requirements of the directive or emissions of certain pollutants, legislation is perhaps the only possible solution.

Other directives provide that the Member States are to take the necessary measures to ensure that certain objectives formulated in general and unquantifiable terms are attained, whilst leaving the Member States some discretion as to the nature of the measures to be taken. An example of this can be found in the *San Rocco* case.[36]

> This case involved the enforcement of Article 4 of the old Waste Framework Directive, according to which Member States are required to take the necessary measures to ensure that waste is disposed of without endangering human health and without harming the environment.[37] The Commission accused the Italian Government of having failed to take measures to repair the ecological situation in the San Rocco valley. As far as the alleged infringement of Article 4 of the directive was concerned, the Court observed that even though this provision does not say anything about the actual content of the measures to be taken, it is nevertheless binding on the Member States in respect of the objective to be achieved, albeit that they are allowed some measure of discretion in assessing the need for such measures.
>
> A more recent example, on the Water Framework Direcitve, is provided in Case C-32/05.[38] The Commission argued that the directive requires Member States to adopt both general and specific measures in order to render their national legal system compatible with the objectives laid down under the directive. With respect to the general measures to be taken, the Commission was of the opinion that the directive obliges Member States to adopt 'framework legislation' for water. However, the Court relying on its *San Rocco* judgment, ruled that Member States are not under a duty to adopt such framework legislation in order to implement its provisions correctly: 'It is true [...] that adopting framework legislation may be an appropriate, or more straightforward, method of implementing the directive, since it may provide the competent authorities with clear legal bases, in a single document, for drawing up the various measures laid down by the directive as regards water and whose implementation is to be spread over a period of time. The adoption of such framework legislation may also facilitate the work of the Commission, which has to ensure that the obligations imposed on Member States by the directive are complied with.

---

[36] Case C-365/97 *Commission* v. *Italy* [1999] ECR I-7773 and more recently Case C-135/05 *Commission* v. *Italy* [2007] ECR I-3475. See on this case law also Chapter 8, section 17.1.

[37] OJ 1975 L 194/47. See now Directive 2008/98 on waste, OJ 2008 L 312/3.

[38] Case C-32/05 *Commission* v. *Luxembourg* [2006] ECR I-11323, para. 34.

Nevertheless, adopting framework legislation is not the only way in which Member States may ensure that the directive is fully applied and provide for an organised and coherent system for complying with the objectives laid down under the directive.

Had the Community legislature intended to require Member States to adopt framework legislation in their national legal systems in order to implement the directive, it would have been open to it to insert a provision to that effect in the text of the directive. It did not do so.'

Also difficult are those cases where the directive actually requires something to be done, such as the establishment of collecting systems for urban wastewater[39] or the drawing up of waste management plans.[40] Although such directives require the Member States to obtain very precise and specific results after a certain period, they do not seem to require legislative measures to be adopted at national level.

The *Blackpool* case should be mentioned in this respect.[41] In this case the United Kingdom was held to have failed to take all the necessary measures to ensure that the quality of bathing water in the bathing areas in Blackpool and adjacent to Formby and Southport conformed to the limit values set in accordance with the old Bathing Water Directive.[42] The Court observed that it was clear from Article 4(1) of the directive that the Member States are to take all necessary measures to ensure that, within 10 years following the notification of the directive, bathing water conforms to the limit values set in accordance with Article 3 of the directive. The provision requires a particular result to be achieved, but not necessarily by way of adopting legislative measures.

A final category which could be distinguished includes those provisions referred to in section 2 above, which relate to transboundary environmental issues. As has been said earlier, the Court attaches great importance to the precision of their transposition in national legislative measures by the Member States.

3.2   Legally Binding Rules

In essence, the case law of the Court means that provisions of a directive containing rights and obligations for individuals has to be transposed into binding provisions of national law, in a manner which fully satisfies the requirements of clarity and legal certainty, and affords interested parties

---

[39]   Article 3 of Directive 91/271 concerning urban waste water treatment, OJ 1991 L 135/40, as amended.

[40]   Cf. Article 28 of the 'new' Waste Framework Directive 2008/98 (OJ 2008 L 312/3).

[41]   Case C-56/90 *Commission* v. *UK* [1993] ECR I-4109, paras. 42-44. See also Case C-268/00 *Commission* v. *Netherlands* [2002] ECR I-2995, paras. 12 to 14; Case C-198/97 *Commission* v. *Germany* [1999] ECR I-3257, para. 35 and Case C-307/98 *Commission* v. *Belgium* [2000] ECR I-3933, paras. 48 and 49.

[42]   Cf. also the new Bathing Water Directive 2006/17, OJ 2006 L 64/37.

recourse to the courts. It is important that the result intended by the directive is ensured not only in *fact*, but also in *law*.[43]

> An example of the terms in which the Court frames these requirements is the following, from the judgment in Case C-415/01 concerning the way Belgium had implemented the Wild Birds Directive.[44] The case was about the question whether the maps used in Belgium demarcating special protection areas were legally binding. The Court outlined that: 'according to consistent case-law, the provisions of directives must be implemented with *unquestionable* binding force, and the specificity, precision and clarity necessary to satisfy the requirements of legal certainty [...]. The principle of legal certainty requires appropriate publicity for the national measures adopted pursuant to Community rules in such a way as to enable the persons concerned by such measures to ascertain the scope of their rights and obligations in the particular area governed by Community law' [emphasis added]. With regard to those maps the Court ruled that they must be invested with binding force. If not, the boundaries of SPAs could be challenged at any time.
>
> And in Case C-32/05 concerning the way Luxembourg implemented the Water Framework Directive 2000/60, the Court ruled: '[...] the Court has repeatedly held that it is not always necessary formally to enact the requirements of a directive in a specific express legal provision, since the general legal context may be sufficient for implementation of a directive, depending on its content. In particular, the existence of general principles of constitutional or administrative law may render superfluous transposition by specific legislative or regulatory measures provided, however, that those principles actually ensure the full application of the directive by the national authorities and that, where the relevant provision of the directive seeks to create rights for individuals, the legal situation arising from those principles is sufficiently precise and clear and that the persons concerned are put in a position to know the full extent of their rights and, where appropriate, to be able to rely on them before the national courts'.[45]

---

43 Cf. Case C-83/97 *Commission* v. *Germany* [1997] ECR I-7191 on the implementation of the Habitats Directive. Germany did not deny that it had not adopted all the measures necessary for implementation of the directive. It stated, however, that since the passing of the deadline for transportation, the directive had been directly applied by the competent authorities and existing national provisions have been interpreted in accordance with European law. The Court: 'Since the directive has not been transposed into national law by the Federal Republic of Germany within the prescribed period, the action brought by the Commission must be held to be well founded.'

44 Case C-415/01 *Commission* v. *Belgium* [2003] ECR I-2081, para. 21. Cf. also Case C-159/99 *Commission* v. *Italy* [2001] ECR I-4007, para. 32 and Case C-225/97 *Commission* v. *France* [1999] ECR I-3011, para. 37.

45 Case C-32/05 *Commission* v. *Luxembourg* [2006] ECR I-11323, para. 34. Cf. also Case C-361/88 *Commission* v. *Germany* [1991] ECR I-2567 where the Court ruled in the event a directive intends to create obligations for individuals, transposition of European legislation into a provision whose binding nature is undeniable is also necessary in order that all those whose activities are liable to give rise to nuisances may ascertain precisely the obligations to which they are subject.

Legislation is an instrument of implementation of environmental directives which meets this requirement as regards its binding nature.[46] Or, as the Court put it in Case C-339/87, in respect of the use of ministerial rules adopted pursuant to the Dutch *Jachtwet* (Hunting Act), the rules are 'published in the Nederlandse *Staatscourant* (Dutch official gazette), are of a general nature and capable of creating rights and obligations for individuals.'[47] Thus provisions of directives which require transposition cannot in principle be transposed by means of rules which are not legally binding. This means that, generally speaking, directives have to be transposed by means of legislation adopted by the central government or by other administrative authorities. It would not, for example, be acceptable to implement a directive using plans which were not strictly binding.

> Dutch *Indicatieve Meerjaren Programma's* (Prospective Multiennial Programmes) clearly fall under that category, as the Court held in Case 96/81, as such a programme is 'nothing more than a set of guidelines for those responsible for the supervision of water quality and had no legally binding force.'[48] This implies that if a measure is only effective in respect of a Member State's internal authorities, this will be insufficient to create rights and obligations for individuals.[49]

Another element is that the national measures must ensure a complete and full transposition. In the *German TA Luft* cases, which will be discussed more in detail below, the Court had to decide on the way Germany implemented air quality standards. The area of application of the air quality standards in Germany was limited to industrial plants for which a licence was required, within the meaning of the German legislation on protection against pollution. The Commission argued that the nuisance created by sulphur dioxide may originate elsewhere than in the plant subject to a requirement of authorisation, for example in a high density of road traffic, private heating systems or pollution from another State. The Court accepted these arguments:

> 'The general nature of the directive cannot be satisfied by a transposition confined to certain sources of the exceeding of the limit values which it lays down and to certain measures to be adopted by the administrative authorities.'

These judgments indicate that when quality standards are transposed, it is not sufficient to link the standards to activities for which an authorisation is required. It is also required that provisions be adopted which are binding in

---

[46] Draft legislation will, of course, not suffice: Case C-65/00 *Commission* v. *Italy* [2002] ECR I-1795.

[47] Case C-339/87 *Commission* v. *Netherlands* [1990] ECR I-851.

[48] Case 96/81 *Commission* v. *Netherlands* [1982] ECR 1791.

[49] Another environmental case where the Court was not satisfied with the binding force of the transposition measures include Case C-239/03 *Commission* v. *France* [2004] ECR I-9325.

respect of the other activities which might cause air pollution.[50] The same could be said in respect of the implementation of emission limit values. Polluters who do not require authorisation must also in one way or another be obliged to comply with European standards. A full implementation must be guaranteed.

However, it can be implied that binding national legislation to implement an environmental directive may refer to standards, which are not as such binding,[51] for example, those of private standards organisations such as ISO, CEN and CENELEC. In that case the legislation containing the reference would have to make it clear that the standards have binding force in this particular context.

3.3 Transposition by Means of Administrative Circulars

An important question is to what extent a national government may make use of circulars, policy rules and other instruments which are binding only on the administration itself and have no effect in respect of third parties. 'Mere administrative practices', which by their nature are alterable at will by the authorities and are not given the appropriate publicity, cannot be regarded as constituting the proper fulfilment of obligations arising under the Treaty.[52]

Relevant cases in this respect are, *inter alia*, the *German TA Luft* cases, the *French Air Quality* cases and Case C-58/89 in the field of water quality.[53] The Court had great difficulty with the manner in which France and Germany had transposed the European air quality limit values and guide values for sulphur dioxide and suspended particulates and the limit values for lead in the air into their national legal systems.

In the *TA Luft* cases, the manner of transposition of European air quality directives by Germany was at issue. The air quality standards prescribed by the directives had been transposed by means of the *Technische Anleitung zur Reinhaltung der Luft (TA Luft)*. There was no clear indication in German legal writing and case law as to the precise legal nature of the instrument. In the first place, the Court pointed out that the obligation to prescribe limit values not to be exceeded is imposed in order to protect human health in particular. It implies, therefore, that whenever the exceeding of the limit values could endanger human health, the persons concerned must be in a position to rely on mandatory rules in order to be able to assert their rights. Furthermore, the fixing of limit values in a provision

---

[50] See also with respect requirements to the quality of water intended for human consumption Case C-316/00 *Commission v. Ireland* [2002] ECR I-10527, para. 49. The Court required Ireland to impose 'direct duties' on water distribution companies to comply with the provisions of the directive concerned.

[51] Case 208/85 *Commission v. Germany* [1987] ECR 4045.

[52] Cf. e.g. Case C-75/01 *Commission v. Luxembourg* [2003] ECR I-1585, para. 28.

[53] Case C-361/88 *Commission v. Germany* [1991] ECR I-2567; Case C-59/89 *Commission v. Germany* [1991] ECR I-2607; Case C-13/90 *Commission v. France* [1991] ECR I-4327; Case C-14/90 *Commission v. France* [1991] ECR I-4331; Case C-64/90 *Commission v. France* [1991] ECR I-4335 and Case C-58/89 *Commission v. Germany* [1991] ECR I-4983.

whose binding nature is undeniable is also necessary in order that all those whose activities are liable to give rise to nuisances may ascertain precisely the obligations to which they are subject. In view of the differences in German case law, as to the extent to which such technical circulars are recognised as binding, the Court took the view that the *TA Luft* did not meet these criteria: 'It must be stated that, in the particular case of the technical circular 'air', the Federal Republic of Germany has not pointed to any national judicial decision explicitly recognising that that circular, apart from being binding on the administration, has direct effect vis-à-vis third parties. It cannot be claimed, therefore, that individuals are in a position to know with certainty the full extent of their rights in order to rely on them, where appropriate, before the national courts or that those whose activities are liable to give rise to nuisances are adequately informed of the extent of their obligations.'

Environmental quality standards are established to protect the health of man and are in that sense intended to create rights for individuals. Transposition by means of binding provisions is therefore essential. Rules which are binding only on the administration and do not have any direct effect in respect of third parties do not meet the criteria. Nor do circulars which are binding only on the administrative hierarchy but nowhere else and which do not contain obligations for polluters.[54] The *French Air Quality* cases confirm the *German TA Luft* decisions.[55] Any person whose activities may cause pollution must be able to know precisely what obligations he has.

In sum: rules which bind only the administrative authorities but otherwise neither have binding effect nor are enforceable are not adequate as transposition instruments. The mere fact that they have been published does not detract from this. Similarly, circulars which only have binding force *within* the administrative hierarchy but not otherwise and which do not impose obligations on polluters are also inadequate as a means of implementing European environmental directives.[56]

3.4 Transposition by Means of Environmental Agreements

An environmental agreement is a voluntary agreement between the administrative authorities and industry in which the realisation of certain environmental objectives is agreed in a given field, generally in relation to a

---

[54] Cf. also Case C-95/92 *Commission* v. *Italy* [1993] ECR I-3119. This case concerned the transposition by Italy of Euratom Directive 84/466 (repealed by Directive 97/43, OJ 1997 L 180/22). Here the Court held that transposition by means of circulars, which have never been officially published and were subject to amendment by the Italian administration at will, only made recommendations which had no binding force. The Court reiterated its standpoint that Member States must transpose directives in a manner which fully meets the requirement of legal certainty and must consequently transpose their terms into national law as binding provisions.

[55] Case C-13/90 *Commission* v. *France* [1991] ECR I-4327.

[56] See for instance Case C-262/95 *Commission* v. *Germany* [1996] ECR I-5729. Cf. also Case C-315/98 *Commission* v. *Italy* [1999] ECR I-8001, para. 10.

particular substance or a particular product. The way the Court of Justice has stressed the importance of the legally binding nature of implementing measures and the guarantee that the obligations imposed by a directive are fully implemented raises the question whether the Court will approve the use of such environmental agreements for transposition purposes.[57]

A possible exception to the basic rule is where the directive itself provides for implementation by means of a voluntary agreement.[58]

> Article 27 of the Batteries Directive gives us an example of the use of voluntary agreements as an instrument to implement, albeit some and not all, provisions of the directive.[59] Article 27 of Directive 2006/66 states: '1. Provided that the objectives set out in this Directive are achieved, Member States may transpose the provisions set out in Articles 8, 15 and 20 by means of agreements between the competent authorities and economic operators concerned. Such agreements shall meet the following requirements:
> a) they shall be enforceable;
> b) they must specify objectives with the corresponding deadlines;
> c) they must be published in the national official journal or an official document equally accessible to the public and transmitted to the Commission.
> 2. The results achieved must be monitored regularly, and reported to the competent authorities and the Commission, and made available to the public under the conditions set out in the agreement.
> 3. The competent authorities shall ensure that the progress made under such agreements is examined.
> 4. In cases of non-compliance with the agreements, Member States shall implement the relevant provisions of this Directive by legislative, regulatory or administrative measures.'

The example provided in the Batteries Directive is very much in line with Commission Recommendation 96/733 concerning environmental agreements implementing European directives.[60] The Commission, followed by the Council,

---

[57] This might be otherwise if such a voluntary agreement was accompanied by binding public law measures, such as the Dutch *algemeen verbindend verklaring*, an instrument by which the applicability of a collective agreement is extended to cover an entire industry. The judgment of the Court in Case 215/83 indicates that this might be the case; Case 215/83 *Commission* v. *Belgium* [1985] ECR 1055.

[58] This would seem to have been confirmed with respect to the repealed Directive 85/339 on containers of liquids for human consumption by the Court's judgment in Case C-255/93 *Commission* v. *France* [1994] ECR I-4949.

[59] OJ 2006 L 266/1. See for other examples Article 22(3a) of Directive 94/62 as amended by Directive 2004/12 on packaging and packaging waste, OJ 2004 L 47/26; Article 17(3) of Directive 2002/96 on waste electrical and electronic equipment, OJ 2003 L 37/24 and Article 10(3) of Directive 2000/53 on end-of-life vehicles, OJ 2000 L 269/34.

[60] Commission Recommendation 96/733 concerning environmental agreements implementing Community directives, OJ 1996 L 333/59 and Council Resolution on environmental agreements, OJ 1997 C 321/6.

has announced that it wants to promote the use environmental agreements as a policy instrument to achieve environmental objectives. It has provided guidelines for the use of such agreements as a means of implementing European directives in the field of the environment and stated them in fairly uncompromising terms. Agreements should in all cases:

· take the form of a contract, enforceable either under civil or under public law;
· specify quantified objectives and indicate intermediary objectives with the corresponding deadlines;
· be published in the national Official Journal or as an official document equally accessible to the public;
· provide for the monitoring of the results achieved, for a regular reporting to the competent authorities and for appropriate information to the public;
· be open to all partners who wish to meet the conditions of the agreement.

Agreements should, where appropriate:

· establish effective arrangements for the collection, evaluation and verification of the results achieved;
· require the participating companies to make available the information regarding the implementation of the agreement to any third person under the same conditions applying to public authorities under Council Directive 90/313[61] on the freedom of access to information on the environment;
· establish dissuasive sanctions such as fines, penalties or the withdrawal of a permit, in case of non-compliance.

There would seem to be little difference between environmental agreements and 'normal' legislation once all these conditions have been met. Nevertheless, we believe it is right that the conditions should be so stringent. It could be argued that Article 288 paragraph 3 TFEU not only deals with the manner in which Member States implement directives, but also imposes constraints on the legislative competence of the Union legislature. Or do the principles of legal certainty and legal protection not apply where the Union legislature specifies the choice of implementation instruments in directives on the environment? Arguably they do.

As yet the Court has not ruled explicitly to what extent environmental agreements are an acceptable instrument of implementation.[62] It seems questionable

---

[61] See now however Directive 2003/4 on public access to environmental information and repealing Council Directive 90/313/EEC, OJ 2003 L 41/26.

[62] An indication that they might be acceptable can be implied from Case C-340/96 *Commission* v. *UK* [1999] ECR I-2023. On the other hand in Case C-96/98 *Commission* v. *France* [2001] ECR I-779, para. 26, the Court held that the agri-environmental measures concerned (in fact contracts concluded between the State and farmers which are designed to develop environmentally conscious farming methods), were 'voluntary and purely hortatory' in nature in nature and therefore not capable of supplementing effectively the protection regime for the classified special conservation areas for wild birds.

that they can be used to implement those provisions of environmental directives which require – in the words of the Court – implementation with *unquestion- able* binding force.[63] On the other hand, it is arguable that they might under certain conditions be used. Not only the conditions mentioned by the European Commission in its Recommendation 96/733 must be met. It is the authors' opinion that such an agreement would also have to be enforceable before the courts, applicable to the entire sector targeted (including newcomers on the market!) be entered into for an indefinite period and not be unilaterally termi- nable by the industry concerned. It would also have to provide for guarantees of legal protection for third parties, if the directive was intended to create rights for third parties. But even where all these criteria have been met, the directive would itself – like the Batteries Directive – have to allow sufficient room for implementation by environmental agreement.

3.5 'Transposition' by Compliance in Fact?

A defence frequently employed by national governments during infringement procedures is that no measures have been adopted *in practice* which are in breach of the directive in question. This defence occurs in two kinds of situation. The first is where implementing legislation does exist, but the administrative powers granted under that legislation are too wide in comparison with the underlying directive. The second is where the particular practice that is prohibited by the directive does not occur in that Member State, and there would thus seem no reason to pass legislation.

If the national implementing provisions allow the national authorities in question too much discretion, the directive may well prove not to have been properly implemented.[64] This area is fraught with problems.

An example is the judgment of the Court in Case 291/84, concerning the manner in which the Netherlands had implemented the Groundwater Directive.[65] Article 6 concerns artificial recharges of groundwater, which are subject to a special author- isation issued by the Member States on a case-by-case basis and on condition that there is no risk of polluting the groundwater. According to the Commission, that second condition was not included in Netherlands legislation. Article 14 of the *Grondwaterwet* (Law on groundwater) merely provided that the authorisation may be issued on terms such as to ensure the proper management of groundwater,

---

[63] Case C-415/01 *Commission v. Belgium* [2003] ECR I-2081, para. 21.

[64] Cf. e.g. Case C-6/04 *Commission v. UK* [2005] ECR I-9017; Case C-508/04 *Commission v. Austria* [2007] ECR I-3787, para. 88; Case C-526/08 *Commission v. Luxembourg*, Judgment of 29 June 2010, para. 60. Cf. also Case C-427/07 *Commission v. Ireland* [2009] ECR I-6277, para. 94, with respect to discretion- ary practices on the part of the *courts* in the context of the Aarhus Directive 2003/35. Cf. also more in general on an emerging principle of transparency in EU law, De Leeuw & Prechal (2007).

[65] Case 291/84 *Commission v. Netherlands* [1987] ECR 3483. The 'old' Groundwater Directive 80/68 will be repealed from 21 December 2013 by the Water Framework Directive 2000/60, OJ 2000 L 327/1.

and thus leaves the national authorities issuing the authorisation greater latitude than is permitted by the directive. The Netherlands Government contended that as a matter of policy such authorisation was granted only when there was no danger of pollution. However, the Court accepted the Commission's argument: 'As the Commission maintains, the possibility under the Netherlands legislation of making authorization conditional on proper groundwater management cannot be held to satisfy the requirement that the risk of groundwater pollution must be examined when an authorization is issued under Article 6 of the directive. Article 6 of Directive 80/68/EEC has therefore not been transposed into national law with sufficient precision.'

If a statutory provision leaves the national authorities too much discretionary power, it cannot successfully be argued that the obligations contained in a directive have been implemented by legislation. In that case implementation is only effected when an authorisation is issued under the legislation. The Court will not accept this.[66] Therefore, the conclusion is clear. If the legislation implementing the directive grants too much administrative freedom, this cannot be compensated by bringing the practice of issuing authorisations into line with the requirements of the directive.[67] Further legislative action is required.

Case C-339/87 concerning the implementation of the Wild Birds Directive in the Dutch legal system is also illustrative of the second kind of situation referred to above. Under Article 5(c) of the Wild Birds Directive, Member States are required to take measures prohibiting taking birds' eggs in the wild and keeping them, even if empty. Under the provisions of the Dutch *Jachtwet* it was permitted to seek, collect or possess the eggs of the wood pigeon, the carrion crow, the jackdaw, the jay and the magpie. The Dutch Government argued that in fact eggs of these species were not sought or collected in the Netherlands and that legislation was therefore unnecessary. The Court rejected this defence: 'The fact that a number of activities incompatible with the prohibitions contained in the directive are unknown in a particular Member State cannot justify the absence of appropriate legal provisions. In order to secure the full implementation of directives in law and not only in fact, Member States must establish a specific legal framework in the area in question.'

In other words, it is important not only that an activity that is prohibited by directive does not occur in *fact*, but also that it *may not occur in law*. This is not mere legal formalism on the part of the Court. It is a requirement of legal

---

[66] Another example is Case C-339/87 concerning the transposition of the Wild Birds Directive in the Dutch legal system; Case C-339/87 *Commission v. Netherlands* [1990] ECR I-851.

[67] Cf. also Case C-392/99 *Commission v. Portugal* [2003] ECR I-3373, para. 79 *et seq.* on the permitting conditions of the old Waste Oils Directive. The Court speaks of 'implementation of the requisite measures must constitute a *sine qua non* for issue of the permit', leaving no doubt about the required clarity of the implementing legislation.

certainty. In the case in question, the Advocate General considered that a Member State would only be relieved of its obligation to implement the provisions of the directive if the practices in question could not occur on its territory. In that case national legislation would not be required.

> In Case C-290/89 it is apparent that the Commission has adopted this view.[68] This case concerned the defective implementation by Belgium of Directives 75/440 and 79/869 concerning the quality and methods of measurement of surface water intended for the abstraction of drinking water in the Member States.[69] The Commission accepted the Belgian position that no measure of transposition was required for the Brussels Region since there is no surface water in that region intended for the production of drinking water. Although the Court did not explicitly consider the matter, it is clear from the operative part of the judgment that Belgium was only held to have failed to fulfil its obligations under the Treaty because it had not taken the measures necessary to implement the directives in the Flemish and Walloon Regions. No reference was made to the Brussels Region.
>   The fact that there is no titanium dioxide industry on Portuguese territory does of course not mean that Portugal is not required to submit to the Commission a report on the implementation of the TiO2 Directive. According the Court, Portugal must indicate that fact in its report, which it may not dispense with under any circumstances.[70]

This seems a sensible solution. If a situation cannot in fact occur, there is no need for legislative measures.

> This applies, for example, to the Netherlands in respect of implementation of Article 4(2) of Directive 91/271 concerning urban waste water management.[71] This provides for measures in respect of discharges to waters situated in high mountain regions (over 1500 m above sea level). As the highest point in the Netherlands is only 300 m above sea level, this provision is totally irrelevant in the Netherlands. The difference between this provision and the ones in Article 5 of the Wild Birds Directive discussed above is clear. Seeking and collecting certain eggs may not occur in the Netherlands now but it cannot be ruled out that this might change in the future. The practice referred to in the Urban Waste Water Directive not only does not occur, but also could not occur. That is why the Netherlands does have to implement the provisions of the former, but not of the latter, directive.

Legal writers have severely criticised the Court's strict approach as being unduly formalist. This criticism is not really justified. If the Court were not to adopt such a strict approach to the formal side of implementation, it would become

---

[68] Case C-290/89 *Commission v. Belgium* [1991] ECR I-2851.

[69] Both directives are repealed by the Water Framework Directive by 22 December 2007.

[70] Case C-435/99 *Commission v. Portugal* [2000] ECR I-11179.

[71] OJ 1991 L 135/40.

impossible for the European Commission to exercise any kind of effective control on compliance with directives inside the Member States. After all, the Commission would then be unable to rely on national laws, but would have to take on the actual control of compliance. In view of the limited size of the Commission apparatus and its extremely limited investigative powers within the territory of the Member States, such *de facto* control can hardly be regarded as a realistic proposition. In terms of the European legal order it is therefore of great importance that obligations imposed by directives are properly transposed into national laws. In this light the Court's case law should be regarded not as unduly formalistic, but as providing legal certainty in European environmental law.

3.6   Use of Different Wording in National Legislation

It has been stated above that incorporation of a directive into national law does not necessarily require the formal repetition of its rules word for word in an express, specific, statutory provision. Depending on its content a 'general legal context' may be satisfactory, provided that it effectively ensures full application of the directive in a way which is sufficiently clear and precise so that, if the directive aims to create rights for individuals, they will be able to ascertain the full extent of their rights and to rely on them before the national courts, if necessary.[72] One of the reasons for a national legislature not to adopt the definitions from a directive word for word is to avoid causing confusion. There is no need to adopt the definitions contained in a directive if the national store of concepts is wide enough to include the concepts used in the directive. However, if the national legislature chooses not to adopt the provisions of a directive formally and word for word, or if it takes the view that the existing legal framework is adequate to satisfy the requirements of the directive, there is a danger that the national concepts will not provide a seamless fit with those used in the directive. There may be some slight divergence between the obligations set out in the directive and the requirements of the national provisions. In other words there will be a greater danger that implementation is not complete.

The Court does not always explain why one provision of a directive should be incorporated into national law and another not. In that regard, it is important to note that the Court of Justice will determine in each individual case the nature of the provision in the directive, in order to gauge the extent of the obligation to transpose imposed on the Member States.[73]

---

[72] Case C-190/90 *Commission v. Netherlands* [1992] ECR I-3265. Cf. also more recent Case C-50/09 *Commission v. Ireland*, Judgment of 3 March 2011.

[73] Cf. Case C-233/00 *Commission v. France* [2003] ECR I-6625, para. 77. Sometimes, however, the Court of Justice takes a much more global approach to the question of whether obligations under a directive have been properly implemented: Case C-190/90 *Commission v. Netherlands* [1992] ECR I-3265 on the transposition in the Netherlands of the Post-Seveso Directive.

Case 412/85 is interesting in this connection.[74] The case concerned a provision in the German *Bundesnaturschutzgesetz*. Paragraph 22(3) allowed a departure from the prohibitions in respect of bird protection where the acts take place in the course of 'the normal use of the land for agricultural, forestry or fishing purposes'. According to Article 5 of the Wild Birds Directive, Member States are required to prohibit deliberate killing or capture and deliberate destruction of nests and eggs. Unintentional acts are not prohibited by the directive. The German Government argued that the derogations provided for in Paragraph 22(3) presuppose the absence of any intentional acts. The activities defined by Paragraph 22(3), such as the normal use of land, could never be regarded as constituting a deliberate failure to protect birds, because actions performed with the intention of killing, capturing, disturbing, keeping or selling wild birds cannot be described as forming part of normal agricultural, forestry or fishing activities. The Court was not prepared to accept this interpretation. It held that Paragraph 22(3) does not provide a precise indication of the extent to which damage to the environment is permitted. The concept of the normal use of the land and the concept of an unintentional infringement of the provisions for the protection of birds belong to two different legal planes. Since the German legislation does not define the concept of 'normal use', unintentional damage to the life and habitat of birds is not excluded from the scope of Paragraph 22 (3) of the *Bundesnaturschutzgesetz* in so far as such damage is necessary in the course of the normal use of the land. Thus the German Government's attempt to translate the concept of 'unintentional infringement' using the national concept of 'the normal use of the land' foundered. The Court held that these were not equivalent, and that German law therefore conflicted with the provisions of the Wild Birds Directive.

Another example of Court of Justice case law relates to the implementation of Article 9 of the same directive. Under this provision Member States are permitted to derogate from the provisions on bird protection contained in Articles 5 to 8 of the directive for various reasons. For example, 'to prevent serious damage to crops, livestock, forests, fisheries and water'. The question is to what extent the concept of 'serious damage' has to be incorporated into the national legal systems. In Case 247/85 the Commission argued that it was essential that the expression should be used in the Belgian legislation, but the Belgian Government disputed this.[75] The Court stated: 'In this regard it must be noted that the aim of this provision of the directive is not to prevent the threat of minor damage. The fact that a certain degree of damage is required for this derogation from the general system of protection accords with the degree of protection sought by the directive.

It must, however, be noted that the Commission has not proved that the concept of 'damage' in the Belgian rules is not interpreted and applied in the same way as the concept of 'serious damage' in the third indent of Article 9(1)(a) of the directive. This part of the complaint cannot therefore be upheld.'

---

[74] Case 412/85 *Commission v. Germany* [1987] ECR 3503.

[75] Case 247/85 *Commission v. Belgium* [1987] ECR 3029.

In other words, literal transposition is not necessary, as long as the provision is interpreted and applied as intended in the directive. However, as we have said already, too much discretion will not be acceptable for the Court. The above examples in the case law of the Court of Justice also show that is stricter in some cases than in other, apparently similar, cases. Bearing in mind the unpredictability of the Court, if a national legislature wishes to apply its own national concepts when implementing a directive, it is advised to operate with extreme care and precision.

3.7 Transposition of Environmental Regulations?

A regulation is the appropriate legal instrument where precise requirements must be imposed directly on the parties concerned, which are to be implemented at the same time and in the same manner throughout the Union. In spite of the fact that regulations are, according to the first paragraph of Article 288 TFEU, directly applicable in the Member States and thus do not generally have be transposed into the national legal systems to be effective, national authorities may nevertheless have to issue rules, particularly in the areas of enforcement and the designation of competent public authorities. The problem of which national implementing instrument to choose is therefore also relevant where European environmental law is enacted by regulation.

> A good example can be found in Regulation 995/2010 laying down the obligations of operators who place timber and timber products on the market.[76] The regulation contained numerous provisions which had to be worked out by the Member States. Thus Member States had to take appropriate measures on penalties applicable to infringements of the provisions of the regulation, to designate one or more competent authorities responsible for the application of the regulation and they also had to make all kinds of other organisational arrangements. Where details of important provisions in a regulation are left to be worked out by the Member States, the dividing line between directives and regulations becomes very hard to draw. It is therefore not surprising that this regulation entered 'into force' on the 20th day following its publication in the Official Journal of the EU on 20 November 2010, but that most of its provisions do not become applicable before 3 March 2013 (Article 21). In fact this gave the Member States some months to produce the necessary 'implementing' legislation.

Because substantive law does not have to be incorporated into the national legal systems in order to implement a regulation, the following consequence should be noted. The legal consequences of annulment of an environmental regulation are generally much more far-reaching than in the case of a directive.[77] Suppose, for example, that the Court had held in the *Basel Regulation* case that Regulation

---

[76] OJ 2010 L 295/23.

[77] Cf. in general on invalid directives: Vandamme (2005).

259/93 must be regarded as invalid.[78] In that case there would be no provisions left which could be applied and enforced at a national level, as there would be with a directive. Only in exceptional circumstances the Court of Justice is willing to use its powers under Article 264, second paragraph TFEU. The annulment of the TiO2 Directive in the *TiO2* case[79] did not mean that national implementing measures could no longer be applied. In so far as these measures were in conformity with the rules of European law (and national law!), they could be applied without any problem. The danger of a legal vacuum at the national level in the event of the annulment of a European regulation on the environment is therefore all the greater.

An important difference between regulations and directives is that regulations may have direct legal consequences for individuals. Environmental directives, on the other hand, cannot impose obligations on individuals unless there are national rules implementing them. In other words, they have no 'direct horizontal effect'.[80] Environmental regulations do, in principle. Once a regulation has entered into force (or, as the case may be, from the date on which it has to be applied), it directly binds individuals. It is therefore very important to determine whether a provision of European law must be regarded as a provision in a directive or one in a regulation. Generally this will not be a problem, as the Council's decision will clearly indicate whether a measure is a directive or a regulation. However, it is sometimes less easy to determine the legal nature of a European environmental provision.

> Take, for example, Article 16 of Regulation 304/2003 concerning the export and import of dangerous chemicals:[81] 'Chemicals that are intended for export shall be subject to the measures on packaging and labelling established in, or pursuant to, Directive 67/548/EEC, Directive 1999/45/EC, Directive 91/414/EEC and Directive 98/8/EC, or any other specific Community legislation'. In fact Article 16 of the *regulation* was here extending the scope of application of *directives*. It is not clear whether such an extension has the characteristics of a directive or of a regulation. As has been stated, the distinction is important for the purpose of establishing whether the measure has direct horizontal effect.[82]

---

[78] Case C-187/93 *EP v. Council* [1994] ECR I-2857.

[79] Case C-300/89 *Commission v. Council* [1991] ECR I-2867.

[80] See Chapter 5, section 2.2.

[81] OJ 1992 L 251/13, now repealed by Regulation 689/2008 concerning the export and import of dangerous chemicals, OJ 2008 L 204/1.

[82] Case C-37/06 *Viamex Agrar Handel and ZVK* [2008] ECR I-69, paras. 27-28, seems to suggest that in such a case the provisions of a directive do become directly applicable.

4 Implementation by Local or Regional Authorities

As the Court of Justice has frequently stated, each Member State is free to attribute or delegate powers to its public authorities as it considers fit and to implement directives by means of measures adopted by regional or local authorities. Where the constitutional system of a Member State provides that local and/or administrations are to have legislative competence, the mere adoption by those administrations of different standards does not constitute discrimination contrary to Union law.[83]

> Only occasionally does a directive try to limit national discretion in this respect. See for instance Article 3 of Directive 2008/50 on ambient air quality and cleaner air for Europe: 'For the implementation of this Directive, the Member States shall designate *at the appropriate levels* the competent authorities and bodies responsible for [...]'.[84] Emphasis added.

That division of powers does not however release it from the obligation to ensure that the provisions of the directive are properly implemented in national law.[85] It is thus irrelevant in European law whether a directive is implemented by the central government by means of legal rules which are universally applicable within its territory, or by local or regional authorities such as the German *Länder*, the Dutch *provincieën*, devolved administrations in the United Kingdom[86], the *Comunidades Autónomas* in Spain[87], or the Belgian *Gewesten*. Union law makes only one condition. The Member State must ensure that European environmental law is adopted and applied throughout its territory in accordance with the provisions of the directive.[88]

---

[83] Cf. Case C-428/07 *Horvath* [2009] ECR I-6355.

[84] OJ 2008 L 152/1. Cf. Case C-417/99 *Commission v. Spain* [2001] ECR I-6015.

[85] Joined Cases 227-230/85 *Commission v. Belgium* [1988] ECR 1, Case C-225/96 *Commission v. Italy* [1997] ECR I-6887 and Case C-236/99 *Commission v. Belgium* [2000] ECR I-5657.

[86] Case C-428/07 *Horvath* [2009] ECR I-6355.

[87] Cf. Case C-474/99 *Commission v. Spain* [2002] ECR I-5293, with respect to the implementation of the EIA Directive.

[88] Cf. Case C-260/93 *Commission v. Belgium* [1994] ECR I-1611 and also Case C-225/96 *Commission v. Italy* [1997] ECR I-687, where it was shown that only 11 of Italy's 20 regions had made a designation of shellfish waters, covering little more than 50% of the national territory. See also Case C-365/97 *Commission v. Italy* [1999] ECR I-7773, para. 69, where the Court ruled that the fact that Italy had failed to fulfil its obligation under the Waste Framework Directive only in the San Rocco valley, cannot have a bearing on any finding of an infringement. Cf. also Case C-292/99 *Commission v. France* [2002] ECR I-4097, where the Court ruled 'a failure to fulfil the obligation to draw up waste management plans must be regarded as serious, even if the failure relates to only a very small part of a Member State's territory, such as a single department [...], or a single area within a valley'.

The Commission has indeed occasionally attempted to restrict decentralisation it has considered to be too extreme. According to Article 5 of the 'old' Waste Directive, Member States had to designate the competent authority or authorities to be responsible 'in a given zone' for organizing waste disposal operations. These will generally be regional or local authorities. The Court had already stated in the *Traen* case that this provision does not lay down any restrictive criteria concerning the choice of competent authorities to be responsible for the planning, organisation, authorisation and supervision of waste disposal operations.[89]

In later proceedings the Commission argued that a Member State, to avoid excessive fragmentation of the relevant powers, must not allocate these powers to an excessive number of local authorities.[90] This argument also seemed to appeal to Advocate General Jacobs. Though it is true that the Member States are competent to designate the competent authorities, this competence is limited by the need to ensure respect for the aims of the directive, namely, the protection of human health and the environment. In his opinion, Member States should not therefore divide responsibility for designating the competent authorities to such an extent that the achievement of these aims is jeopardised. The Court did not refer to these remarks at all, but relied on the express text of the directive, which allowed the issue of authorisations by local and regional authorities.

If it were decided that a directive was to be implemented by autonomous measures on the part of local authorities, it would be necessary for the national legislatures to make provision for the event the local authorities should fail to fulfil the obligations under European law.

In Case C-237/90, Germany was held to have failed to comply with its obligations under the now repealed Directive 80/778 relating to the quality of water intended for human consumption.[91] According to Article 10(1), the competent national authorities could, in the event of emergencies, allow the maximum admissible concentration to be exceeded. Article 10(3) provided that Member States which have recourse to this derogation shall immediately inform the Commission thereof, stating the reasons for and probable duration of such derogation. In Germany, application of this derogation was delegated to the *Länder*. Germany was held to have failed to meet its obligations because it had not ensured its national laws contained provisions to require the *Länder* to notify the central government of such derogations, so that it in turn could comply with its obligation to notify the Commission. The Court took a similar judgment in Case C-301/95.[92] The case concerned the manner in which Germany had transposed the EIA Directive. The directive was implemented partly at federal level and partly at the level

---

[89] Joined Cases 372-374/85 *Traen* [1987] ECR 2141.

[90] Case C-359/88 *Zanetti* [1990] ECR I-1509.

[91] Case C-237/90 *Commission v. Germany* [1992] ECR I-5973. Cf. now Directive 98/83 on the quality of water intended for human consumption, OJ 1998 L 330/32.

[92] Case C-301/95 *Commission v. Germany* [1998] ECR I-6135.

of the *Länder*. The Court ruled that all of the national provisions, including those of the *Länder*, had to be communicated to the Commission. In this respect it was irrelevant that federal law takes precedence over regional provisions.

Regional implementation has also given rise to problems in Belgium. For example, waste management legislation there has been delegated to the regional authorities. Meanwhile the central government does not have the power to require the regional authorities to implement European legislation on waste, or to take alternative measures if the regional authorities fail to fulfil their obligations. In Joined Cases 227 to 230/85, this omission did not prevent the Court finding the State of Belgium had failed to meet its obligations under the directives on waste.[93] The Court has consistently held that a Member State may not plead provisions, practices or circumstances existing in its internal legal system in order to justify a failure to comply with its obligations under European law.[94]

5 Application and Enforcement of European Environmental Law

The mere transposition of environmental directives into national law is, of course, not enough. The obligations they contain have first to be applied and then enforced. This is primarily, but certainly not exclusively, a responsibility of the Member States. Article 192(4) TFEU states in so many words that the Member States shall finance *and implement* the environment policy of the Union.[95] However, the Court has held in connection with the principle of loyal cooperation contained in Article 4(3) TEU that, to the extent that environmental directives and regulations do not provide for specific enforcement obligations, national enforcement measures must be effective, dissuasive and proportionate.[96] Furthermore, national rules dealing with infringements of European environmental standards should not be less favourable than those governing infringements of national environmental rules. Except for the principle of loyal cooperation, many of the environmental measures taken by the European legislature contain an obligation in this respect. In many cases the requirements are couched in fairly general terms in the sense that Member States must take appropriate legal or administrative action in case of infringement of the provisions of the directive or regulation. Therefore, enforcement of European environmental law can be characterised as a shared responsibility.

---

93 Joined Cases 227-230/85 *Commission v. Belgium* [1988] ECR 1.

94 Cf. also Case C-71/97 *Commission v. Spain* [1998] ECR I-5991; Case C-274/98 *Commission v. Spain* [2000] ECR I-2823 and Case C-297/95 *Commission v. Germany* [1996] ECR I-6739.

95 Or as the Court has held in the *San Rocco* case: 'it is primarily for the national authorities to conduct the necessary on-the-spot investigations'; Case C-365/97 *Commission v. Italy* [1999] ECR I-7773, para. 85.

96 Case 68/88 *Commission v. Greece* [1989] ECR 2965; Case C-186/98 *Nunes and de Matos* [1999] ECR I-4883. Cf. in general on 'effective, dissuasive and proportionate', Faure (2010).

For instance Article 8 of Directive 2005/35 on ship-source pollution and on the introduction of penalties for infringements states: '1. Member States shall take the necessary measures to ensure that infringements within the meaning of Article 4 are subject to effective, proportionate and dissuasive penalties, which may include criminal or administrative penalties.[97]

2. Each Member State shall take the measures necessary to ensure that the penalties referred to in paragraph 1 apply to any person who is found responsible for an infringement within the meaning of Article 4.'

Another example is Article 21 of the Regulation 2037/2000 on substances that deplete the ozone layer: 'Member States shall determine the necessary penalties applicable to breaches of this Regulation. The penalties shall be effective, proportionate and dissuasive.'[98]

In the absence of more concrete and specific provisions imposed upon the Member States by the Union legislature, it is in the first place for Member States to determine how the factual situation must be brought in line with the legally desired situation. European environmental measures sometimes do contain more specific provisions which require a certain type of enforcement by the Member States.[99]

Take, for instance, Article 4(9) of the Waste Incineration Directive: 'If an incineration or co-incineration plant does not comply with the conditions of the permit, in particular with the emission limit values for air and water, the competent authority shall take action to enforce compliance.'[100] This provision surely implies a duty for the authorities to shut down a plant, if necessary, when the emission limit values are exceeded by the undertaking.

Or take Article 16 of CITES Regulation 338/97 on the protection of species of wild fauna and flora by regulating trade therein.[101] The enforcement measures required by the Member States include confiscation of illegal traded specimens.

In other cases Union environmental measures require Member States to organise inspections and other control measures to ensure compliance with the directive.[102] The case law of the Court of Justice shows that the implementing

---

[97] OJ 2005 L 255/11. Cf. on the validity of this directive Case C-308/06 *Intertanko and others* [2008] ECR I-4057.

[98] OJ 2000 L 244/1.

[99] The competence of the Union legislature includes both reparatory and punitive enforcement measures. See already Case C-240/90 *Germany* v. *Commission* [1992] ECR I-5383 and, for environmental law, Case C-440/05 *Commission* v. *Council* [2007] ECR I-9097. The latter case is already discussed in Chapter 1, section 3.1.

[100] Directive 2000/76 on the incineration of waste, OJ 2000 L 332/91.

[101] OJ 1997 L 61/1.

[102] Recommendation 2001/331 providing for minimum criteria for environmental inspections in the Member States, OJ 2001 L 118/41. Cf. on this Recommendation, Blomberg (2008).

national legislation must 'ensure that the undertakings concerned are in fact inspected periodically'.[103]

> Article 23 of Directive 2010/75 on industrial emissions provides a very clear and detailed example.[104] Member States are required to set up a system of environmental inspections of installations. Member States shall ensure that all installations are covered by an environmental inspection plan at national, regional or local level.
>
> Based on the inspection plans, the competent authority shall regularly draw up programmes for routine environmental inspections, including the frequency of site visits for different types of installations. The period between two site visits shall be based on a systematic appraisal of the environmental risks of the installations concerned and shall not exceed 1 year for installations posing the highest risks and 3 years for installations posing the lowest risks. If an inspection has identified an important case of non-compliance with the permit conditions, an additional site visit shall be carried out within 6 months of that inspection.
>
> Non-routine environmental inspections shall be carried out to investigate serious environmental complaints, serious environmental accidents, incidents and occurrences of non-compliance as soon as possible and, where appropriate, before the granting, reconsideration or update of a permit.

Only occasionally did an environmental legislative measure contain an obligation to ensure criminal enforcement.[105] Member States were quick to regard such requirements as an incursion on their own competence.[106]

> An exception was Article 26(5) of Regulation 259/93, under which the Member States had to take appropriate legal action 'to prohibit and punish' illegal traffic of waste.[107] Another example can be found in Article 8(1) of Regulation 338/97 on the protection of species of wild fauna and flora by regulating trade therein: 'The purchase, offer to purchase, acquisition for commercial purposes, display to the public for commercial purposes, use for commercial gain and sale, keeping for sale, offering for sale or transporting for sale of specimens of the species listed in Annex A *shall be prohibited*.'[108]

---

[103] Case C-392/99 *Commission* v. *Portugal* [2003] ECR I-3373, para. 168.

[104] OJ 2010 L 334/17.

[105] Cf. our observations in Chapter 1, section 3.

[106] See also Chapter 1, section 3.1.

[107] OJ 1993 L 30/1, later amended. Cf. however now Article 50 of the 'new' Regulation 1013/2006 on shipments of waste, OJ 2006 L 190/1. It speaks more generally on 'penalties' that 'must be effective, proportionate and dissuasive'. Regulation 1013/2006 has repealed Regulation 259/93 with effect from 12 July 2007.

[108] OJ 1997 L 61/1; emphasis added by the authors. Cf. Case C-344/08 *Rubach* [2009] ECR I-7033.

Since 2008 matters have changed as a result of Directive 2008/99 on the protection of the environment through criminal law.[109] Member States are required to ensure that a great number of conducts causing substantial damage to the environment constitute a criminal offence, when unlawful and committed intentionally or with at least serious negligence. Inciting, aiding and abetting the intentional conduct is punishable as a criminal offence as well. Member States shall also ensure that legal persons can be held liable for offences where such offences have been committed for their benefit by any person who has a leading position within the legal person, acting either individually or as part of an organ of the legal person.

> Another example is provided by Directive 2009/123 amending Directive 2005/35 on ship-source pollution and on the introduction of penalties.[110] According to Article 4(1) of the amended directive: 'Member States shall ensure that ship-source discharges of polluting substances, including minor cases of such discharges, into any of the areas referred to in Article 3(1) are regarded as infringements if committed with intent, recklessly or with serious negligence.' Article 4(2) continues: 'Each Member State shall take the necessary measures to ensure that any natural or legal person having committed an infringement within the meaning of paragraph 1 can be held liable therefor.' The directive also contains provisions in order to hold legal persons liable for criminal offences.

It will be clear that the differences between environmental directives as regards the action to be taken to enforce them are still great. Even ignoring the fact that some directives contain hardly any provision on enforcement at all, it seems there can be no question of a coherent European enforcement policy yet.

The manner in which European environmental law is enforced by the Member States is however under Commission control. Inadequate enforcement, once again in law and in fact, may be a reason for the Commission to initiate proceedings under Article 258 TFEU.[111] It should be noted that the Commission does not have any formal competence to ensure compliance with European environmental legislation on the territory of the Member States. And that the Commission does not currently have a formal inspectorate to assess implementation firsthand.[112] Only occasionally is the Commission given some investigative competences in secondary legislation.[113]

[109] OJ 2008 L 328/28.

[110] OJ 2009 L 280/52.

[111] Cf. for instance the unpublished judgment in Case C-317/02 *Commission* v. *Ireland*, Judgment of 18 November 2004. The Court ruled that Member States are required to ensure that the appropriate measures are taken, including administrative action or criminal proceedings, against those persons who have failed to comply with European rules.

[112] Commission Staff Working Document accompanying the Commission Communication on Implementing European Community Environmental Law, SEC (2008) 2876, 18 November 2008.

[113] Cf. Regulation 1005/2009 on substances that deplete the ozone layer, OJ 2009 L 286/1, Article 28(2).

On a voluntary basis Member States sometimes allow Commission officials in their territory for inspection. For instance, in 1998, Commission officials went on a mission to Zakinthos (Greece) to verify whether any measures for the protection, required by the Habitats Directive, of the sea turtle *Caretta caretta* had in fact been implemented. In the course of the mission, they visited the beaches at Laganas, Kalamaki, Sekania, Dafni and Gerakas, the places where that species lays its eggs.[114]

At a more practical level, we must note the importance of the IMPEL network. Since its inception in 1992, the informal EU Network for the Implementation and Enforcement of Environmental Law (IMPEL), consisting of European regulators and inspectors concerned with the implementation and enforcement of environmental law, has been a key instrument in discussing the practical application and enforcement of existing legislation.[115]

Enforcement in law and in fact

It was stated above that directives have to be implemented not only in fact, but also in law. Conversely, even where a directive is adequately transposed into national law, but the national provisions are not effectively enforced, even in an individual case,[116] this will not suffice either.

> Or in the words of the Court, with respect to the old Waste Incineration Directive: 'Accordingly, a Member State will comply with its obligations under Directive 89/369 and thus achieve the result prescribed therein only if, in addition to the correct implementation of the provisions of that directive into domestic law, the incineration plants located in its territory have in actual fact been commissioned and operate in accordance with the requirements of the provisions of Directive 89/369'.[117]
>
> With respect to Article 12(1)(d) Habitats Directive the Court stated that it 'requires the Member States not only to adopt a comprehensive legislative framework but also to implement concrete and specific protection measures'.[118]
>
> The first time this was confirmed, at least in the environment sector, was in Case C-42/89, in which the Court held that Belgium had failed to fulfil its obligations under the Treaty because the supply of drinking water to the city of Verviers did not in fact meet the required standards.[119]

This indicates that Member States are required not merely to do their best to enforce standards contained in a directive, but to produce the desired result.

---

[114] Case C-103/00 *Commission v. Greece* [2002] ECR I-1147.

[115] See http://impel.eu (last visited 7 October 2011). See also the critical remarks of Hedemann-Robinson, (2007, at 465) pointing that IMPEL seemed to have become a new venue for the Member States for lobbying the Commission on policy development, without the proper safeguards with respect to transparency and accountability.

[116] Case C-431/92 *Commission v. Germany* [1995] ECR I-2189.

[117] Case C-139/00 *Commission v. Spain* [2002] ECR I-6407.

[118] Case C-383/09 *Commission v. France*, Judgment of 9 June 2011.

[119] Case C-42/89 *Commission v. Belgium* [1990] ECR I-2821.

An example of a Court of Justice judgment where a Member State was held to have failed to implement a directive *in fact* is the *Blackpool* case.[120] In this case the United Kingdom was held to have failed to take all the necessary measures to ensure that the quality of bathing water in the bathing areas in Blackpool and adjacent to Formby and Southport conformed to the limit values set in accordance with the old Bathing Water Directive.[121] The main argument of the UK Government was that it had taken 'all practicable steps' to meet the limit values. The Court rejected this argument: 'It follows that the directive requires the Member States to take steps to ensure that certain results are attained, and, apart from those derogations, they cannot rely on particular circumstances to justify a failure to fulfil that obligation. Consequently, the United Kingdom's argument that it took all practicable steps cannot afford a further ground, in addition to the derogations expressly permitted, justifying the failure to fulfil the obligation to bring the waters at issue into conformity at least with the annex to the directive.' The operative part of the judgment makes it quite clear. The Court declared that, 'by failing to take all the necessary measures to ensure that the quality of the bathing water in Blackpool and of those adjacent to Southport conforms to the limit values set in accordance with Article 3 of Council Directive 76/160/EEC [...] the United Kingdom has failed to fulfil its obligations under the EEC Treaty.' In other words, there is nothing for it but to ensure that the bathing water conforms to the limit values set in the directive.[122]

Although Member States have some discretion with respect to their enforcement strategies and policies and must be allowed to prioritise their enforcement efforts, the *Blackpool* case makes it clear that a statutory system which allows the government to tolerate infringements of a directive is incompatible with European law.[123] In particular if the national enforcement authorities are engaged in a systemic and consistent tolerance of situations not in accordance with European environmental law.[124]

---

[120] Case C-56/90 *Commission* v. *UK* [1993] ECR I-4109. Cf. also Case C-427/00 *Commission* v. *UK* [2001] ECR I-8535.

[121] See now the consolidated version of the Bathing Water Directive, Directive 2006/7, OJ 2006 L 64/37.

[122] This strict approach is also apparent in a case concerning the failure in parts of Germany to comply with the standards in the Bathing Water Directive, Case C-198/97 *Commission* v. *Germany* [1999] ECR I-3257. See also, with respect to the old Bathing Water Directive Case C-268/00 *Commission* v. *Netherlands* [2002] ECR I-2995, para. 12: 'the Directive is not to be understood as meaning that the Member States need only *endeavour* to adopt all reasonably feasible measures. On the contrary, that provision imposes upon Member States an *obligation to achieve a particular result*'. Emphasis added by the authors.

[123] Cf. also Case 68/88 *Commission* v. *Greece* [1989] ECR 2965 and, on fisheries, Case C-232/08 *Commission* v. *Netherlands* [2009] ECR I-166. See also Case C-112/00 *Schmidberger* [2003] ECR I-5659. Cf. also, outside the field of environmental law, Case C-265/95 *Commission* v. *France* [1997] ECR I-6959 (*Spanish Strawberries*). See on the possible role of this latter judgment on Member States' duties to enforce environmental law Temmink (2000) at 77-80.

[124] Case C-494/01 *Commission* v. *Ireland* [2005] ECR I-3331, para. 27 in particular.

A good example can be found in Case C-215/06.[125] The Commission claimed that the Irish practice of 'retention permission' undermined the proper enforcement of the EIA Directive. In Ireland, the absence of an environmental impact assessment required by the EIA Directive could be remedied by obtaining such a retention permission which makes it possible to leave projects which were not properly authorised undisturbed. The Court of Justice: 'The consequence of that possibility [...] may be that the competent authorities do not take action to suspend or put an end to a project that is within the scope of Directive 85/337 as amended and is being carried out or has already been carried out with no regard to the requirements relating to development consent and to an environmental impact assessment prior to issue of that development consent, and that they refrain from initiating the enforcement procedure provided for by the PDA [the Irish Planning and Development Act], in relation to which Ireland points out that the powers are discretionary.' This demonstrated, in the rather frank words of the Court of Justice the 'inadequacy of the enforcement system set up by Ireland'.

It is not entirely clear to what extent the Court has adopted a more flexible approach for the Member States in the *San Rocco* case, already mentioned above in this chapter.[126] This case involved the enforcement of Article 4 of the 'old' Waste Framework Directive, according to which Member States were required to take the necessary measures to ensure that waste is disposed of without endangering human health and without harming the environment. The Commission accused the Italian Government of having failed to take measures to repair the ecological situation in the San Rocco valley. As far as the alleged infringement of Article 4 of the directive was concerned, the Court observed that even though this provision did not say anything about the actual content of the measures to be taken, it was nevertheless binding on the Member States in respect of the objective to be achieved, albeit that they were allowed some measure of discretion in assessing the need for such measures. However, the Court went on, where a factual situation is not consistent with the objectives set out in Article 4 it cannot in principle be concluded from this that the Member State in question has necessarily failed to fulfil its obligation to comply with Article 4. Continuation of such a factual situation, particularly where this results in a significant deterioration of the environment during a prolonged period without the competent authorities intervening, may however indicate that the Member State has exceeded the limits of its discretion. In other words, the key element is not the actual violation of the environmental objectives but the failure of the competent authorities to respond adequately.

This judgment seems to imply that the mere fact that the factual situation is not in accordance with the directive does not in itself mean that the Member State is infringing its environmental obligations. It should be noted however that the

---

[125] Case C-215/06 *Commission v. Ireland* [2008] ECR I-4911.

[126] Case C-365/97 *Commission v. Italy* [1999] ECR I-7773. Cf. for a similar case, and confirming *San Rocco*, concerning an illegal waste site in Greece, Case C-420/02 *Commission v. Greece* [2004] ECR I-11175. See also Chapter 8, section 17.1.

obligation in Article 4 of the old Waste Framework Directive was framed in very general terms and this may have been the reason the Court adopted this more flexible approach. Be that as it may, these judgments underline the fact that not only failure properly to transpose a directive into national law may cause the Court to hold that a Member State has failed to fulfil its obligations, but also a factual infringement of European standards.

General practices of non-compliance

Finally, we have to note that according to the judgment of the European Court of Justice in Case C-494/01 (*Commission* v. *Ireland*) on 12 specific factual infringements of the Waste Framework Directive, the Court ruled that 'in principle nothing prevents the Commission from seeking in parallel a finding that provisions of a directive have not been complied with by reason of the conduct of a Member State's authorities with regard to particular specifically identified situations and a finding that those provisions have not been complied with because its authorities have adopted a general practice contrary thereto, which the particular situations illustrate where appropriate.'[127] In other words, the Commission is entitled to deduct from a series of *individual* infringements, that there is a 'general practice' of non-compliance and non-enforcement. This implies that the Commission is not only entitled to demand that these individual infringements of the directive are remedied, but also that the public authorities in question change, more fundamentally and structurally, their enforcement policies.[128] To qualify as a general practice of non-compliance it must be, to some degree, of a consistent and general nature and must not be geographically confined to only a part of the territory of the Member State in question.[129]

6 Supervision by the Commission

Under Article 17 TEU, the Commission is charged with ensuring that the provisions of the Treaties and the measures taken by the institutions pursuant to the Treaty are applied.[130] This means the Commission has been given primary responsibility for monitoring the application of European law in

---

[127] Case C-494/01 *Commission* v. *Ireland* [2005] ECR I-3331, para. 27 in particular.

[128] Cf. Wennerås (2007) at 252 *et seq.*

[129] Case C-441/02 *Commission* v. *Germany* [2006] ECR I-3449, para. 50, and on the criterium of 'geographically confined' Case C-248/05 *Commission* v. *Ireland* [2007] ECR I-9261, para. 115. The two incidents in the *Finnish wolf hunting* case (Case C-342/05 *Commission* v. *Finland* [2007] ECR I-4713) can not not be seen as sufficient evidence for an administrative practice generally and persistently in violation of Union law.

[130] Cf. for a critical comment on the Commission's role in enforcement, Macrory (2005A) and Blomberg (2008).

the Member States.[131] According to the Commission[132] its task is to seek solutions to implementation challenges, by:

1) legislative and post-legislative work aimed at the prevention of breaches;
2) responding to the specific concerns of the European public;
3) more immediate and intensive treatment of the most important infringements;
4) enhanced dialogue with the European Parliament; and
5) enhanced transparency, communication and dialogue with the public and interested parties.

Even so, the full formal and substantive application of the law, as has been demonstrated in the previous section of this chapter, in the first place is a matter for the Member States. This is apparent from the principle of loyal cooperation, under which Member States must take all appropriate measures to ensure fulfilment of their European law obligations and from the first sentence of Article 192(4) TFEU, which requires the Member States to finance and implement the environment policy. Moreover it is clear from the use of the directive as an instrument of European environment policy that it is the Member States which are primarily responsible for implementation. In addition to the Commission's role in monitoring compliance with European law, it should not be ruled out for the future that the European Environment Agency[133] will play an increasingly important part in this respect. Figures and other details on the Commission's monitoring of the application of European law are to be found in the annual reports on that subject.[134]

6.1 The Treaty Infringement Procedure

The most important instrument at the Commission's disposal is the procedure laid down in Article 258 TFEU. This provides that the Commission may bring a matter before the Court of Justice if it considers that a Member State has failed to fulfil an obligation under the Treaties. Nevertheless, in terms of monitoring application of the law, the Commission only avails itself of this formal power as a last resort. The Court long ago established that private persons cannot compel the Commission to initiate infringement proceedings, nor do they have legal recourse against decisions of the Commission not to

---

[131] See Seventh Annual Survey on the Implementation and Enforcement of Community Environmental Law 2005, SEC (2006) 1143. See also Lee (2005) at 51.

[132] Cf. in general the Communication from the Commission on Implementing European Community Environmental Law, COM (2008) 773 final, 18 November 2008. See on this Communication, critically, Ballesteros (2009).

[133] Regulation 401/2009 on the European Environment Agency and the European Environment Information and Observation Network, OJ 2009 L 126/13.

[134] See e.g. 27th annual report on monitoring the application of EU law, COM (2010) 538. Cf. also the Commission website at http://ec.europa.eu/eu_law/index_en.htm (last visited 7 October 2011).

commence proceedings, or to discontinue or stay proceedings that have been instituted.[135]

The Commission distinguishes, from a legal perspective, three different types of infringement proceedings:

1) non-communication cases, for failure to adopt and communicate national implementing measures;
2) non-conformity cases, where Member State transposition measures do not conform to the requirements of the directive;
3) bad application cases, where a Member State, through action or inaction, fails to comply with EU environmental law requirements other than the requirements to adopt and communicate correct implementing legislation.[136]

The Article 258 procedure gives the Commission extensive powers in its relations with the Member States.

> Thus, in Case C-422/92, Germany disputed the Commission's admissibility in a proceeding for infringement of, the now repealed, Directive 84/631 on the supervision and control within the Union of the transfrontier shipment of hazardous waste.[137] The Commission brought its action long after the publication of the contested national provisions and did so at a time when developments in European policy and law on the environment were such as could give the impression that there was no longer any expectation that such action would be brought. The Court, however, argued that it is not necessary for the Commission to have a specific interest in bringing an action in order to commence proceedings under Article 258 TFEU.

However, in the light of the settled case law that the Commission is not obliged to act within a specified period, the Court came to the conclusion that the Commission is entitled to decide, in its discretion, on what date it may be appropriate to bring an action. And it is not for the Court to review the exercise of that discretion. Nor will a decision of the Commission not to start an infringement-procedure give rise to non-contractual liability on the part of the Union.[138]

> As a matter of policy the Commission will deal with the following three categories of infringements more immediately and intensively.[139] The first category includes

---

[135] Case 48/65 *Lütticke* [1966] ECR 19.

[136] Detailed data can be found the annual reports on monitoring the application of EU law.

[137] Case C-422/92 *Commission v. Germany* [1995] ECR I-1097.

[138] Case C-205/10 P *Eriksen* v. *Commission*, Judgment of 12 January 2011. The case concerned an action for compensation for damage suffered as a result of the alleged failure of the Commission to take measures necessary to ensure that Denmark complies with Euratom Directive 96/29.

[139] Communication from the Commission on Implementing European Community Environmental Law, COM (2008) 773 final, 18 November 2008.

non-communication of implementing measures for directives. The second
category concerns failures to comply with judgments of the Court of Justice within
a period of 12 to 24 months. The third category is breaches of Union environmental law raising issues of principle or having particularly far-reaching negative
impact for citizens, such as those concerning the application of Treaty principles
and main elements of framework regulations and directives.

The application of European environmental law is the subject of many and regular contacts of a less formal nature between the Commission and the Member
States. For example, after approval of a directive by the Council, the Commission writes an official letter to the Member States notifying them of the directive and the time limits within which national law must have been adjusted to
comply with the directive. About three months before expiry of the time limit for
incorporation into national law, the Commission writes a second letter to those
Member States which have not yet informed the Commission that the necessary
adjustments have been made. As the Member States are twice reminded by the
Commission of their obligations, a practice has evolved whereby the Commission will initiate Article 258 proceedings after expiry of the time limit if a
Member State has not informed it that the necessary measures have been taken.
The complaint addresses the formal aspect of failure to notify the Commission.
Later proceedings may deal with the substance of the case.

    Member States are required to give such notification, either under a specific
provision of the directive in question, or pursuant to the principle of loyal
cooperation.[140] The Commission requires the Member States to specify in detail
the provisions of national law in which each article and clause of the directive
is incorporated, for example in a synoptic table.[141] Most directives also require
Member States that their transposition legislation contains a reference to the
European measure or that the national legislation is accompanied by such a
reference on the occasion of their official publication.[142]

> Directive 91/692 standardizing and rationalizing reports on the implementation
> of certain directives relating to the environment is also relevant in this context.[143]
> This provision should lead to greater uniformity in the Member States' reports,
> and thus enable the Commission to carry out more effective control.

---

[140] See also Chapter 8, section 2.

[141] OJ 1991 C 338/1, Annex C, section 8. Where the directive is implemented by regional authorities, this
can cause severe problems, see Case C-474/99 *Commission* v. *Spain* [2002] ECR I-5293, with respect to
the implementation of the EIA Directive.

[142] Cf. e.g. Article 23 of Directive 2009/128 establishing a framework for Community action to achieve the
sustainable use of pesticides, OJ 2009 L 309/71.

[143] OJ 1991 L 377/48. Cf. on its limited success, Wennerås (2006) at 198. See also Commission Decision
94/741 concerning questionnaires for Member States reports on the implementation of certain Directives in the waste sector, OJ 1994 L 296/42 and Commission Decision 97/622, OJ 1997 L 256/13. Cf.
also the Interinstitutional Agreement on better law-making, OJ 2003 C 321/1, point 34.

In order to ensure effective implementation, the Commission also makes use of a wide range of non-legal instruments, for instance by producing so-called interpretation and guidance documents.[144] Better implementation is also promoted through multilateral contacts with Member States in expert groups and committees to discuss implementation issues. Such meetings are held in the chemicals, air, nature and waste sectors, but are more rare in the fields of noise and water.[145]

As indicated above, the Article 258 procedure is a final resort as regards the enforcement of European law. There are three stages in this procedure:
   1) a letter of formal notice from the Commission;
   2) a reasoned opinion from the Commission and
   3) referral to the Court of Justice.

The content of the letter of formal notice, though not bound by any formality, is important for the further procedure.[146] This is because the Court has decided that the scope of an application under Article 258 TFEU is delimited by the pre-litigation procedure.[147] The Commission is not permitted to introduce new grounds and pleas in law, either in its reasoned opinion or before the Court. Member States usually have two months to reply to the formal notice. If the response is not satisfactory, the Commission may decide to issue a reasoned opinion in which it details the alleged infringement and sets a new time limit. Should the Member State still fail to comply within the time limit, the Commission may refer the matter to the Court. In order to prove that the transposition of a directive is insufficient or inadequate, it is not necessary to establish the actual effects of the legislation transposing it into national law: it is the wording of the legislation itself which harbours the insufficiencies or defects of transposition.[148] In principle it is for the Commission to prove the existence of the alleged infringement and to provide the Court with the information necessary for it to determine whether the infringement is made out, and the Commission may not

---

[144] Cf. Commission Communication on Better monitoring of the application of Community law, COM (2002) 725 final.

[145] Some directives even provide for technical committees to be established, for instance the ORNIS Committee under Article 16 of the Wild Birds Directive, the Habitats Committee under Article 20 of the Habitats Directive and the standing Committee on Biocidal Products established by Article 28 of the Biocides Directive 98/8.

[146] See on the confidentiality of documents related to infringement proceedings Case T-105/95 *WWF UK v. Commission* [1997] ECR II-313; Case T-191/99 *Petrie a.o. v. Commission* [2001] ECR II-3677 and Case T-362/08 *IFAW Internationaler Tierschutz-Fonds v. Commission*, Judgment of 13 January 2011. Cf. Krämer (2003A). See also Article 4(2) Regulation 1049/2001 regarding public access to European Parliament, Council and Commission documents, OJ 2001 L 145/43. See also with respect to so called conformity-checking studies and implementation action plans, the pending Case T-111/11 *ClientEarth v. Commission*.

[147] Case C-52/90 *Commission v. Denmark* [1992] ECR I-2187.

[148] Case C-392/96 *Commission v. Ireland* [1999] ECR I-5901.

rely on any presumption for that purpose.[149] But if the Member State does not provide any indications to the contrary, the Court will deem that the Commission has proved the alleged infringement.[150]

A problem is, in particular in view of transparency, that the Commission has kept secret the letters of formal notice and the reasoned opinions. It argues that both phases of the infringement procedure as well as the phase before the Court of Justice are confidential in order to facilitate relations between the Commission and the Member States to solve compliance problems amicably.[151]

Another problem with respect to infringement proceedings is the length of the procedure and that, in view of Article 278 TFEU, actions brought before the Court of Justice do not have a suspensory effect. Recently however, the Commission seems to be willing to petition to the Court for suspension orders, where a Member State is violating its obligations under environmental directives.[152] The following, more or less successful, actions must be mentioned.

> In Case C-503/06 R, the President of the Court ordered the suspension of a regional Italian act on hunting, in Case C-76/08 R the Commission applied successfully for interim measures in a Maltese case of illicit bird hunting, and in Case C-193/07 R, the Polish government was ordered not to proceed with a reforestation project as this would be in violation of the Habitat Directive.[153]

Consequences of a declaration of infringement

A successful action results in a judgment in which the Court declares that the Member State has failed to fulfil its obligations under the Treaties. Article 260(1) TFEU provides that if the Court of Justice finds that a Member State has failed to fulfil an obligation under the Treaties, the State shall be required to take the necessary measures to comply with the judgment of the Court.[154] The Treaty of Lisbon, however, introduced an interesting innovation. The innovation concerns the second paragraph of Article 260 TFEU, introducing a procedure

---

[149] Case C-376/09 Commission v. Malta, Judgment of 19 May 2011, para. 32.

[150] Cf. Case C-365/97 Commission v. Italy [1999] ECR I-7773. The case concerned an infringement of the Waste Directive. See also Case C-494/01 Commission v. Ireland [2005] ECR I-3331, para. 41: 'It is the Commission's responsibility to place before the Court the information needed to enable the Court to establish that the obligation has not been fulfilled, and in so doing the Commission may not rely on any presumption'. With regard more specifically to the EIA Directive, the Court held in Case C-117/02 Commission v. Portugal [2004] ECR I-5517, para. 85, that the Commission must furnish at least some evidence of the effects that the disputed project in question is likely to have on the environment.

[151] It has been argued that this is not in line with the Aarhus Convention. Cf. e.g. Ballesteros (2009) at 57

[152] Cf. Hedemann-Robinson (2010).

[153] Case C-503/06 R Commission v. Italy [2006] ECR I-141, [2007] ECR I-19, [2008] ECR I-74; Case C-76/08 R Commission v. Malta [2008] ECR I-64 and Case C-193/07 R Commission v. Poland, orders of 18 April 2007, 18 July 2007 and 28 January 2008. Cf. also Blomberg (2008) at 70 et seq.

[154] And the failure to comply with this can lead to another infringement procedure; Cf. Case C-291/93 Commission v. Italy [1994] ECR I-859. Cf. Article 260 TFEU.

that enables the European Commission to bring a case before the Court after having given the Member State in question the possibility to react. This means that the old procedure with a statement of objections and a reasoned opinion is reduced to just one exchange of views between the Commission and the Member State. The remainder of the procedure is identical with the Commission asking for and the Court being able to impose a lump sum or penalty payment.

Furthermore, a specialised procedure is introduced for infringement proceedings concerning non-communication of implementing measures for directives. Article 260(3) TFEU allows the Commission to directly ask for the imposition of a lump sum or penalty payment. The Court may then impose a lump sum or penalty payment not exceeding the amount requested by the Commission. The latter requirement is not to be found in the procedure on the basis of Article 260(2) TFEU which leads to the question whether that procedure enables the Court to impose a lump sum or penalty payment that exceeds the amount requested by the Commission. In view of the Court's standard jurisprudence according to which it is not bound by the Commission's suggestion for a lump sum or penalty payment, this should indeed be possible.[155] The Court deduced this from the wording of the old Article 228(2) EC, and the Treaty of Lisbon did not change the wording of that provision in this regard.

Imposing financial sanctions on a Member State[156]

Since the Treaty of Maastricht the Court has been able to impose a lump sum and/or[157] penalty payment on a Member State that has failed to implement a judgment establishing an infringement (Article 260(2) TFEU).[158] Although the decision on the imposition of the sanctions lies with the Court of Justice, which has full jurisdiction in this area, the Commission plays a determining role in so far as it is responsible for initiating such a procedure and bringing the case before the Court of Justice with a proposal[159] for the application of a lump sum and/or[160] penalty payment of a specific amount. In the meantime, the Commis-

---

[155] For example, Case C-387/97 *Commission v. Greece* [2000] ECR I-5047, para. 80; Case C-304/02 *Commission v. France* [2005] ECR I-6263 and Case C-121/07 *Commission v. France* [2008] ECR I-9159, para 61.

[156] Cf. Jack (2011).

[157] The judgment in Case C-304/02 *Commission v. France* [2005] ECR I-6263, confirmed that the two kinds of financial sanction (penalty and lump sum) can apply cumulatively for the same infringement. According to the Commission a combined sanction should be the rule, although the Commission does not exclude the possibility, in very specific cases, of recourse to the lump sum alone; Cf. Commission Communication, Application of Article 228 of the EC Treaty, SEC (2005) 1658 final, at 3.

[158] In Chapter 5, section 4 we will discuss the question of Member State liability for failing to comply with its obligations under the so called *Francovich* doctrine.

[159] This proposal 'cannot bind the Court and merely constitute a useful point of reference'; Case C-278/01 *Commission v. Spain* [2003] ECR I-14141, para. 41.

[160] A combination of the two is possible: Case C-304/02 *Commission v. France* [2005] ECR I-6263.

sion has published some guidelines on how to apply financial sanctions.[161] According to the Commission the fixing of sanctions should be based on three fundamental criteria:
  · the seriousness of the infringement;
  · its duration;
  · the need to ensure that the penalty itself is a deterrent to further infringements.

From the point of view of the effectiveness of the sanction, the Commission regards that it is important to fix amounts that are appropriate in order to ensure their *deterrent* effect. However, it should be noted that is not the Commission who imposes the sanctions, but the Court of Justice exercising 'a wide discretion'.[162] To date, there have been a couple of judgments of the Court of Justice imposing financial penalties in environmental cases.[163]

> In Case C-387/97, the Commission had requested that Greece be ordered to pay a penalty as long as it fails to take the necessary measures to ensure that toxic waste in the area around Chanià is disposed of without endangering human health and without harming the environment. The Court had already found in 1992 that Greece had failed to fulfil its obligations in this matter.[164] The Court agreed with the Commission and ordered Greece to pay a penalty of €20,000 per day as long as it failed to take the necessary measures. In particular the Court took into account that the failure to comply with the obligations resulting from the Framework Waste Directive could, by the very nature of that obligation, endanger human health directly and harm the environment and therefore had to be regarded as particularly serious.
>
> Case C-278/01 concerned the failure of Spain to comply with the Bathing Water Directive. The Court ordered Spain to pay to the Commission a penalty payment of €624,150 per year and per 1% of bathing areas in Spanish inshore waters which have been found not to conform to the limit values laid down under the directive for the year in question, as from the time when the quality of bathing water achieved in the first bathing season following delivery of this judgment is ascertained until the year in which the judgment in *Commission v. Spain* is fully complied with.
>
> Case C-121/07 concerned the failure of France to comply with GMO Directive 2001/18. The Court clarified the difference between an order for a penalty payment and the imposition of a lump sum payment. An order for a penalty payment, is

---

[161] Cf. Commission Communication, Application of Article 228 of the EC Treaty, SEC (2005) 1658 and its update Commission Communication, Application of Article 260 of the Treaty on the Functioning of the European Union, SEC(2010) 923/3.

[162] See in particular Case C-121/07 *Commission v. France* [2008] ECR I-9159, para. 63.

[163] Case C-387/97 *Commission v. Greece* [2000] ECR I-5047; Case C-278/01 *Commission v. Spain* [2003] ECR I-14141 and Case C-121/07 *Commission v. France* [2008] ECR I-9159.

[164] Case C-45/91 *Commission v. Greece* [1992] ECR I-2509.

essentially intended to be coercive as regards an *ongoing breach*. According to the Court of Justice, there is no requirement for the same approach to be adopted with regard to the imposition of a lump sum payment.

In its judgments the Court affirmed the importance of the proportionality principle and that therefore a penalty payment should be appropriate to the circumstances and proportionate both to the breach found and to the ability to pay of the Member State concerned. According to the Court in Case C-278/01, there may be infringement situations, for instance concerning quality standards for bathing water set by the directive, where, as the Court noted, 'it is particularly difficult for the Member States to achieve complete implementation', and where 'it is conceivable that the defendant Member State might manage significantly to increase the extent of its implementation of the Directive but not to implement it fully in the short term'. In those circumstances, the Court ruled, 'a penalty which does not take account of the progress which a Member State may have made in complying with its obligations is neither appropriate to the circumstances nor proportionate to the breach which has been found'.

The Commission acknowledged that it might be justified to provide for the suspension of a penalty. For instance, a Member State found against for having allowed an important nature site to deteriorate as a result of land drainage may carry out infrastructure works aimed at restoring the hydrological conditions that are ecologically necessary. A period of monitoring may be needed to determine whether the works have succeeded in remedying the harm done.[165]

In fixing the amount of the penalty, the importance of the European rules breached and the impact of the infringement on general and particular interests will be taken into account. '[S]erious or irreparable damage to human health or the environment' is explicitly mentioned by the Commission as such a factor.

6.2 Informal Complaints to the Commission

As has been noted, the Commission's decision whether or not to initiate Article 258 proceedings, or to terminate a proceeding that has already been started, is not open to review by the Court. Neither private individuals, local residents or environmental organisations can compel the Commission to initiate infringement proceedings.[166] However, a complaints procedure has been developed in practice, which, though having no basis in the Treaty, has nevertheless reached some degree of formalisation.[167]

---

[165] Commission Communication, Application of Article 228 of the EC Treaty, SEC (2005) 1658 final, at 5.

[166] Not to be confused with complaints under Regulation 1367/2006 on the application of the provisions of the Aarhus Convention on Access to Information, Public Participation in Decision-making and Access to Justice in Environmental Matters to Community institutions and bodies (OJ 2006 L 264/13). See on this regulation Chapter 5, section 5.3. See critically Krämer (2009A).

[167] See http://ec.europa.eu/eu_law/your_rights/your_rights_en.htm#1depot (last visited 7 October 2011).

Since September 2009 all complaints and enquiries are recorded in a central regis-try (CHAP). After registration and assessment, the Commission then decides how best to handle these. In most cases, the Commission will need to further inves-tigate the file. In complex cases, the Commission may need to request further clarification from the complainant. In the case of complaints concerning the bad application of one of the directives on nature protection, a special complaint form has been has been created to assist in guiding complainants in providing the sort of information the Commission would need in order to effectively assess such complaints which are often technically complex.

In other cases, it maybe necessary for the Commission to take contact with the Member State concerned outside the infringement process. This can be done through the Commission writing to the Member State or through so called package meetings between officials from the Commission and the Member State concerned.

In 2007, the Environment Directorate General requested the registration of 103 new complaint cases in the infringement database. In 2008 this number reduced to 62, but at the same time 75 cases were sent through to Member States via the pilot scheme for investigation. In 2009, the Environment Directorate General registered 27 new complaints in the infringement database, and in the same period launched 111 investigations through the EU pilot scheme. For the new CHAP complaints and enquiries registration system, which became operational in September 2009, 145 new complaints and enquiries were registered between September and the end of 2009.[168]

Clearly the complaints procedure does not remove the need for legal protection in the event of an incidental wrong application of European environmental law. Partly with a view to the principle of subsidiarity, it would be appropriate to create a system of legal protection, particularly for interested third parties, in the Member States themselves. However, access to the courts for third parties, including environmental organisations, is still rather problematic in many Member States.[169] However, the number of complaints still received in Brussels does however show the urgent need for legal protection in European environ-ment law.

---

[168] Information according to http://ec.europa.eu/environment/legal/law/complaints.htm (last visited 7 October 2011).

[169] See Chapter 5, section 5.2.

CHAPTER 5

Legal Protection

1 General Remarks

The European Court of Justice, that is now officially called the Court of Justice of the European Union, has consistently played an important role in European integration as well as the implementation of European environmental law.[1]

According to Article 2 TEU, the Union is founded on the values of respect for human dignity, freedom, democracy, equality, *the rule of law* and respect for human rights. We may also point at Article 19 TEU, which states that the Court of Justice of the European Union shall ensure that *the law* is observed in the interpretation and application of the Treaties. According to Article 47, first paragraph, of the Charter has everyone whose rights and freedoms guaranteed by the law of the Union are violated 'the right to an effective remedy before a tribunal'.[2] In its case law the Court of Justice has repeatedly held that the European Union is a community based on the rule of law.[3] The Court has also stated many times that individuals are entitled to effective judicial protection of the rights they derive from the Union legal order, and that the right to such protection is one of the general principles of law stemming from the constitutional traditions common to the Member States.[4]

This is not the place to discuss exhaustively all aspects of the *rule of law* and its significance to the European legal order. However as far as European environmental law is concerned, one aspect deserves our attention in particular, and that is the question of access to justice of individuals in case they feel that their 'environmental' rights have been infringed. But before doing so in section 5 of this chapter, we will first discuss three important mechanisms through which Union environmental law is applied by national courts: the direct effect of Union environmental law (section 2), the requirement to interpret national law in conformity with Union environmental law (section 3) and via the doctrine of state liability for infringements of Union environmental law (section 4).

2 The Direct Effect of Union Environmental Law[5]

General remarks
The Court of Justice established the foundations for its case law on the direct effect of Union environmental law in 1963, in *Van Gend & Loos*.[6] The Court ruled that European law, apart from legislation by Member States,

---

[1] Cf. Jans (2008).

[2] Cf. Case C-221/09 *AJD Tuna Ltd*, Judgment of 11 March 2011, para. 54.

[3] Cf. Case C-50/00 P *Unión de Pequeños Agricultores* v. *Council* [2002] ECR I-6677, para. 38.

[4] E.g. Case 222/84 *Johnston* [1986] ECR 1651, para. 18, and Case C-424/99 *Commission* v. *Austria* [2001] ECR I-9285, para. 45.

[5] This section partly builds upon Jans et al. (2007), Chapter III.

[6] Case 26/62 *Van Gend & Loos* [1963] ECR 1.

can confer rights on individuals, which are capable of being enforced before the national courts. Over the course of time the initial rather restrictive criteria have been significantly relaxed. In the Court's current case law these criteria are summarised as follows: provisions of Union law are directly effective if they are 'unconditional and sufficiently precise'.[7] A provision is *unconditional* where it is not subject, in its implementation or effects, to the taking of any measure either by the Union institutions or by the Member States. Moreover, a provision is *sufficiently precise* to be relied on by an individual and applied by a court where the obligations which it imposes are set out in unequivocal terms.

The most important condition which follows from the Court's case law is that discretionary powers in the implementation of a provision of Union law will prevent it from having direct effect. Examples are provisions allowing a certain degree of freedom of choice or ones that leave the exercise of powers to the discretion of the public authorities. In such cases powers can be relied upon only if they have been exercised. This will apply only if fulfilment of the obligation is conditional upon the implementing measures, and the discretion in question is 'real'. However, vagueness or imprecision in a provision of Union law need not be an obstacle to its having direct effect.

The way the Court has extended the concept of direct effect in recent years justifies the assertion that the crucial criterion is whether a provision provides a court with sufficient guidance to be able to apply it without exceeding the limits of its judicial powers. Viewed thus, a provision of Union law is directly effective if a national court can apply it without encroaching on the jurisdiction of national or European authorities. This implies that, even when Member States enjoy some discretion, some measures can have direct effect. After all, no discretionary power is ever totally unfettered; the rule of law implies that the exercise of State competence is conditioned by legal rules. Or, in the words of Dworkin: 'Discretion, like the hole in the doughnut, does not exist except as an area left open by a surrounding belt of restriction'.[8] In many cases a provision of Union law which confers discretionary powers will at the same time establish the conditions for their exercise. The case law of the Court, the *Kraaijeveld* case in particular, also offers indications that the doctrine of the direct effect of Union law is developing in that direction.[9]

Kraaijeveld concerned, among other things, the question to what extent certain works involving dykes should be subject to a prior environmental impact assessment under the EIA Directive. Article 2(1) of the directive lays down the general obligation that 'projects likely to have significant effects on the environment' are to be subject to an assessment. This general obligation is further specified in

---

[7] Case C-236/92 *Comitato di coordinamento per la difesa della Cava v. Regione Lombardia* [1994] ECR I-485 and more recently Case C-115/09 *Trianel Kohlekraftwerk Lünen*, Judgment of 12 May 2011.

[8] R.M. Dworkin, *Taking rights seriously* (Harvard University Press 1977) at 31.

[9] Case C-72/95 *Kraaijeveld* [1996] ECR I-5403. See also Case C-287/98 *Linster* [2000] ECR I-6917 and more recently Case C-237/07 *Janecek* [2008] ECR I-6221.

Article 4(1) in combination with Annex I of the directive, which states the projects for which an assessment is always required. There is no question of a discretion here. However, Article 4(2) in combination with Annex II clearly gives the national legislature more freedom when implementing the directive. So much so that the Dutch *Raad van State* (Council of State) denied its direct effect.[10] This was because it allows the national legislature to establish the criteria and/or thresholds necessary to determine whether or not a project is to be subject to an assessment. In the Netherlands, works involving dykes (among the projects listed in Annex II), were subject to an assessment if the dyke was 5 km or more in length, with a cross-section of at least 250 square metres. The Court of Justice concluded that Article 4(2) did allow Member States 'a certain discretion', namely to fix specifications, thresholds and criteria. However, it went on to say that this discretion was itself limited, namely by the obligation set out in Article 2(1) that projects likely to have significant effects on the environment are to be subject to an impact assessment. The national court was instructed to examine whether the legislature had remained within the limits of its discretion, and thus to review the national legislation in the light of the directive.

In *Landelijke Vereniging tot Behoud van de Waddenzee*,[11] the Court extended this approach. Where the national court was required in *Kraaijeveld* to examine whether the *national legislature* had remained within the limits of discretion allowed by the directive, in this case it became clear that even where there is no implementing legislation, the decisions of an *administrative authority* must also remain within those limits, and that the national courts must examine whether or not this is the case. This case concerned Article 6(2-3) Habitats Directive.

What the Court in fact did in cases like *Kraaijeveld* and *Waddenzee* was to acknowledge that individuals may also rely on provisions that allow discretion (in this case the freedom to make exceptions in certain cases). The national court must then examine whether the *national legislature* has stayed within the limits of the law when exercising its powers. In the literature this type of direct effect is referred to as 'legality review'.[12] We however agree with Prechal who notes that there is no need to distinguish legality review as a separate category.[13] We agree with her stating 'Direct effect is the obligation of a court or another authority to apply the relevant provision of Community law, either as a norm which governs the case or as a standard for legal review.'[14]

In summary, then, a provision of Union law can be said to have direct effect if it can be applied by the national courts, acting within their judicial powers. It is the responsibility of the courts to ensure that the national legislature and administrative authorities, when acting within the sphere of operation of Union

---

[10]   Dutch *Raad van State* 3 August 1993 [1994] AB 287.

[11]   Case C-127/02 *Landelijke Vereniging tot Behoud van de Waddenzee* [2004] ECR I-7405, para. 65.

[12]   See for an overview of the literature: Prechal (2005), at 234 *et seq.*

[13]   Prechal (2005) at 234-241.

[14]   Prechal (2005) at 241.

law, abide by their Union law obligations and do not exceed any discretion they may have. As far as environmental law is concerned, the direct effect of primary Union law has been accepted by the Court in respect of, *inter alia*, Articles 30, 34, 35, 36, 101, 102, 108(3) and 110 TFEU. The validity of national environmental law which is incompatible[15] with these provisions may be challenged before the national courts.

Direct effect and individual rights

In its case law the Court uses various formulations to describe the implications of direct effect. On the one hand, the Court observes that directly effective provisions of Union law can confer rights on private individuals which the national courts have to uphold, and, on the other hand, that a directly effective provision of Union law can be invoked before a national court. Both formulations stress the role of the national courts in enforcing direct effect. The second, more neutral formulation is to be preferred. The formulation that focuses on 'rights of individuals' is misleading, as it gives the impression that only those provisions of Union law are directly effective which confer, to a greater or lesser extent, rights on individuals. It is the authors' view that 'rights of individuals' should be seen in a procedural rather than a substantive light. Individual rights stem from Member States' obligations. In other words it is necessary to distinguish the concept of direct effect from the question of whether Union law creates rights for individuals.[16] Direct effect is concerned with the quality of the Union law provision being relied on. Has it been formulated so as to be 'unconditional and sufficiently precise', or not? Either way, this does not necessarily imply a substantive entitlement. Where the Court refers to direct effect in terms of creating 'rights for individuals' the Court is, in our view, acknowledging a procedural right, namely the right to rely on that provision before the national courts. Viewed thus, direct effect and the conferring of rights on individuals are distinct concepts. Nevertheless, it must be admitted that other scholars argue that substantive rights are indeed a prerequisite for direct effect.[17]

This doctrinal issue is of particular relevance in the field of environmental law. As Prechal & Hancher rightly noted, environmental law is different from other areas of law.[18] The diffuse interests which environmental law represents cannot easily be captured in the language of individual rights. It is the authors' view that individuals wanting to rely on an environmental directive do not have to show, as a condition of Union law, that their substantive rights under the

---

[15] The adoption of national measures correctly implementing a directive does not, however, preclude an individual to rely on the direct effect, according to Case C-62/00 *Marks & Spencer* [2002] ECR I-6325. According to the Court of Justice it would be inconsistent with the Union legal order for individuals not to be able to rely on a directive where the national authorities *apply* the national measures implementing the directive in a manner incompatible with it.

[16] Cf. also Case C-431/92 *Commission v. Germany* [1995] ECR I-2189.

[17] Cf. for a more comprehensive treatment of relevant case law and literature: Prechal (2005), Chapter 6.

[18] Prechal & Hancher (2002) at 109.

directive have been affected. This means that they can also rely on those provisions which do not as such confer rights on individuals, but are 'unconditional and sufficiently precise'. Any other view would imply that 'pure' environmental protection provisions could not be relied upon in national courts. Implicitly the Court seems to have accepted our view in its *Großkrotzenburg* and *Kraaijeveld* judgments.[19] Especially in the *Kraaijeveld* case it was quite clear that Kraaijeveld was affected in his business interests. Nevertheless it was, albeit again implicitly, accepted that he could rely on the EIA Directive, even though its objective is to prevent significant harm to the environment. On the other hand, there is national environment-related case law which seems to endorse a different view. Some argue that, as a matter of Union law, individuals can only rely on directly effective provisions of Union law if these provisions are meant to confer rights on individuals.[20]

2.1   Direct Effect of Provisions in Environmental Directives

Apart from the direct effect of provisions of primary Union law, the possibility of invoking the provisions of an environmental directive is particularly important in the sphere of the environment. After all, directives have to be transposed into national legislation and the question therefore arises what the legal significance is of an environmental directive in the national legal orders where it has not been implemented, or not within the requisite time limit, or otherwise incorrectly.

It is important to note that individuals can rely upon directly effective provisions of a directive only *after* expiry of the period for transposition. This is because Member States must be given the time to bring their legislation into line with the requirements of the directive. In the *Inter-Environnement* judgment, however, the Court of Justice introduced an important nuance.[21] Having acknowledged the basic rule that Member States cannot be faulted for not having transposed a directive into their internal legal order before expiry of the transposition period, it went on to observe that it followed from the principle of loyal cooperation in conjunction with Article 288 TFEU 'that during that period they must refrain from taking any measures liable seriously to compromise the

---

[19] Case C-431/92 *Commission* v. *Germany* [1995] ECR I-2189 and Case C-72/95 *Kraaijeveld* [1996] ECR I-5403.

[20] See for instance Advocate General Kokott in the *Waddenzee* case; Case C-127/02 *Landelijke Vereniging tot Behoud van de Waddenzee* [2004] ECR I-7405, points 142-144 of her Opinion. She argued that Article 6(2) and (3) of the Habitats Directive did not establish 'individual rights' and that accordingly individuals may rely on these provisions only in so far as avenues of legal redress are available to them under national law. In view of the judgment of the Court in that case, it must assumed that the Court did not agree with her. Cf. also the Dutch District Court 's-Gravenhage 24 November 1999 *Waterpakt* [2000] *MR* I.

[21] Case C-129/96 *Inter-Environnement* [1997] ECR I-7411. See also Case C-422/05 *Commission* v. *Belgium* [2007] ECR I-4749, on noise-related operating restrictions at Belgium airports.

result prescribed.' Recent case law shows that this doctrine is not only applicable to transposition periods, but also to other transitional regimes.

> In *Stichting Zuid-Hollandse Milieufederatie*, the Court applied this doctrine to the interpretation of Article 16 of the old Biocides Directive 91/414.[22] After having ruled that the words 'continue to apply its current system or practice of placing biocidal products on the market' in Article 16(1) the directive are not to be interpreted as constituting a standstill obligation, the Court continued by stating that the Member States' right to amend their systems for the authorisation of biocidal products cannot be regarded as unlimited either. During the implementation period they must refrain from taking any measures liable seriously to compromise the result prescribed by the directive.
> In *Stichting Natuur en Milieu* the Court applied the doctrine to the transition period of Article 4 of the National Emission Ceilings Directive.[23]

The question however remains if and to what extent this doctrine can be used as a substitute for direct effect.[24]

> The Dutch *Raad van State* (Council of State) has applied this rule – and therefore seems to have accepted that it is directly effective – in many cases involving the Habitats Directive.[25] It observed that the principle of Union loyalty meant that, in a case like the one before it, Member States and their national authorities must refrain from activities which could seriously jeopardise the result prescribed by the directive during the period between the transmission of a list as referred to in Article 4(1) of the directive and adoption of the list by the Commission. As the government had not taken this into account in its decision-making, the decision was annulled for lack of due care in its preparation. By examining whether the government had acted in conformity with its obligations under the principle of loyal cooperation, the Dutch *Raad van State* followed the example of the highest German administrative court, which had also carried out a similar *Inter-Environnement* test in relation to the same provision of the Habitats Directive.[26]

Clearly, it is impossible to examine here the many environmental directives, each containing numerous provisions, in order to ascertain their direct effect. A general approach will suffice. Various categories of provisions will be discussed. In this respect we will not only rely on the case law of the Court specifically

---

[22] Case C-316/04 *Stichting Zuid-Hollandse Milieufederatie* [2005] ECR I-9759 and Case C-138/05 *Stichting Zuid-Hollandse Milieufederatie* [2006] ECR I-8339.

[23] Joined Cases C-165/09 to C-167/09 *Stichting Natuur en Milieu a.o.*, Judgment of 26 May 2011.

[24] The judgment in *Rieser*, Case C-157/02 [2004] ECR I-1477, paras. 66-69 seems to suggest that this obligation is not directly effective. Cf. also Case C-212/04 *Adeneler a.o.* [2006] ECR I-6057.

[25] E.g. Dutch *Raad van State* 11 July 2001 [2001] MR 38.

[26] German *Bundesverwaltungsgericht* 19 May 1998 [1998] NVwZ (*Ostsee-autobahn*), 961 and German *Bundesverwaltungsgericht* 27 January 2000 BVerwGE 110, 302, 308 (*Hildesheimer Ortsumgehung*).

dealing with direct effect, but also on the Court's judgments in infringement proceedings under Article 258 TFEU. Although the Court of Justice stated in the *Großkrotzenburg* case that an obligation flowing directly from a directive is 'quite separate' from the question of whether individuals may rely on provisions of an unimplemented directive[27], we agree with Prechal who notes that if the Court of Justice is able to examine in infringement proceedings whether a Member State has remained within the limits of a directive, there are no fundamental reasons why a national court could not do the same.[28]

Direct effect of product standards

Environmental directives laying down precise and detailed conditions to which products harmful to the environment must conform before being placed on the market will normally be directly effective, as is illustrated by the Court's judgment in *Ratti*.[29]

> Directive 73/173 contained detailed provisions regarding the packaging and labelling of solvents.[30] However, Italian legislation imposed additional conditions and required publication of certain information not required by the directive. Ratti was prosecuted for an infringement of the Italian legislation, even though he had acted in compliance with the provisions of the directive. The Court held: 'It follows that a national court requested by a person who has complied with the provisions of a directive not to apply a national provision incompatible with the directive not incorporated into the internal legal order of a defaulting Member State, must uphold that request if the obligation in question is unconditional and sufficiently precise.'
>
> Ratti was acquitted because the provisions of the directive could indeed be considered unconditional and sufficiently precise. In the light of this judgment, product standards such as those contained in the Batteries Directive[31] must be regarded as producing direct effect. Article 4 of this directive requires Member States to prohibit the placing on the market of a) all batteries or accumulators, whether or not incorporated into appliances, that contain more than 0.0005% of mercury by weight; and b) portable batteries or accumulators, including those incorporated into appliances, that contain more than 0.002% of cadmium by weight. National provisions which are not of the required stringency but specify a value of, say, 0.05% may be challenged by invoking the directive. The standards of '0.0005% of mercury by weight' and '0.002% of cadmium by weight' are of course sufficiently precise and unconditional.

---

[27] Case C-431/92 *Commission* v. *Germany* [1995] ECR I-2189, para. 26. Cf. Case C-365/97 *Commission* v. *Italy* [1999] ECR I-7773 (*San Rocco*), para. 63.

[28] Prechal (2005) at 313. Cf. also Wennerås (2007) at 30.

[29] Case 148/78 *Ratti* [1979] ECR 1629.

[30] OJ 1973 L 189/7. See, until 31 May 2015, Directive 1999/45, OJ 1999 L 200/1. And after 31 May 2015: Regulation 1272/2008, OJ 2008 L 353/1.

[31] Directive 2006/66 on batteries and accumulators and waste batteries and accumulators, OJ 2006 L 266/1.

The reverse is also true, and a more stringent product standard may also be challenged. In that case the directive must contain a 'free movement' clause, as it did in the *Ratti* case. The Batteries Directive does contain such a clause: 'Member States shall not, on the grounds dealt with in this Directive, impede, prohibit, or restrict the placing on the market in their territory of batteries and accumulators that meet the requirements of this Directive' (Article 6). As is confirmed by, for example, the *Ratti* case, such a clause produces direct effect. A more stringent national provision would be incompatible with such a provision, unless the Commission has approved these more stringent measures under Article 114(4-6) TFEU.[32]

Direct effect and emission limit values and environmental quality standards

In Chapter 3 it was noted that most European environmental legislation can be characterised as effecting 'minimum harmonisation'.[33] Directives lay down minimum standards of protection, though more stringent national standards are allowed. This applies in particular to emission standards and environmental quality objectives. Does the fact that a directive allows the Member States to adopt more stringent environmental standards imply that the minimum standards of the directive do not produce direct effect? For instance, Directive 2000/76[34] lays down a number of emission limit values to waste incineration plants. It is quite clear that these emission limit values are directly effective in as far as the directive establishes sufficiently precise numerical minimum standards.[35] In the present example, measures which allowed emissions exceeding the standards of the directive would be in breach of the directive and could be challenged on the basis of the emission limit values laid down in the directive. However, national measures containing a more stringent standard are not problematic in the light of the directive, since in that case no provision of the directive would have been breached.

Provisions requiring further implementation

Environmental directives requiring further national or European implementation lack the necessary 'unconditionality' and therefore do not have direct effect. It has been noted in literature that environmental directives have become increasingly vague, open-ended and conditional.[36] There is indeed a shift, in

---

[32] See more extensively Chapter 3, section 6.

[33] See Article 193 TFEU and, for example, Case C-376/90 *Commission* v. *Belgium* [1992] ECR I-6153.

[34] OJ 2000 L 332/91.

[35] Cf. on the direct effect of minimum standards outside Union environmental law: Joined Cases C-6/90 and C-9/90 *Francovich* [1991] ECR I-5357. See for an opposite view the Opinion of Advocate General Elmer in *Arcaro*, Case C-168/95 *Criminal proceedings against Arcaro* [1996] ECR I-4705, who seems to suggest that minimum emission standards do not have direct effect in view of the 'substantial discretion' for the national authorities. His view is clearly untenable, as it would mean – in view of Article 193 TFEU – that almost all European environmental legislation based on Article 192 TFEU direct effect.

[36] Somsen (2003). Cf. on this trend of 'proceduralisation' also Lee (2005) 166 *et seq.*

particular in the area of water and air pollution, from exact numerical emission standards and quality limit values to an increased reliance on environmental framework directives requiring further implementation. Wennerås states that this trend of more flexible lawmaking may provide cost-efficiency benefits, but it does so at the expense of the direct effect of environmental directives and effective enforcement of Union environmental law.[37]

> In this respect a Dutch case regarding the IPPC Directive can illustrate the above. Instead of fixing, directly effective, emission standards in the directive itself, Article 9(4), delegates that to the Member States. They are required to set emission standards, which 'shall be based on the best available techniques, without prescribing the use of any technique or specific technology, but taking into account the technical characteristics of the installation concerned, its geographical location and the local environmental conditions.' The flexible nature of this provision provides a strong argument against it being directly effective. However, the Dutch *Raad van State* decided that the obligation to apply the best available techniques, also in view of the definition of BAT in Article 2 in combination with Annex IV, is sufficiently precise to be directly effective in the *Kraaijeveld* sense of the doctrine.[38]

Another question concerns the possible direct effect of broadly formulated provisions setting out the general scope of the directive. Arguably, they are not. Thus in the *Lombardia Waste* case the Court decided that Article 4 of the 'old' Waste Directive, although binding,[39] is not directly effective.[40]

> That provision stated in general terms that Member States should take the necessary measures to ensure that waste is disposed of without endangering human health and without harming the environment. According to the Court this provision did not meet the conditions for it to have direct effect. It must be regarded as a framework provision: 'Article 4 [...] indicates a programme to be followed and sets out the objectives which the Member States must observe in their performance of the more specific obligations imposed on them by Articles 5 to 11 of the directive concerning planning, supervision and monitoring of waste disposal operations.' The Court therefore concluded that: 'The provision at issue must be regarded as defining the framework for the action to be taken by the Member States regarding the treatment of waste and not as requiring, in itself, the adoption of specific measures or a particular method of waste disposal. It is therefore neither unconditional nor sufficiently precise and thus is not capable of conferring rights on which individuals may rely as against the State.'[41]

---

[37] Wennerås (2007) at 43-44.

[38] Dutch *Raad van State* 13 November 2002 [2003] *M&R* 39.

[39] Case C-365/97 *Commission v. Italy* [1999] ECR I-7773 (*San Rocco*).

[40] Case C-236/92 *Comitato di coordinamento per la difesa della Cava v. Regione Lombardia* [1994] ECR I-485.

[41] Cf. also Case C-60/01 *Commission v. France* [2002] ECR I-5679, were the Court makes a distinction between provisions 'formulated in general and unquantifiable terms' like in *Lombardia Waste* and provi-

With a reference to Case C-236/92 the Court also found the obligations imposed by Article 4 of the National Emission Ceilings Directive, not directly effective. According to the Court of Justice: 'that article is *purely programmatic* in nature, in that it merely lays down an objective to be attained, leaving the Member States wide flexibility as to the means to be employed in order to reach that objective'.[42] Article 4 of the NEC Directive requires Member States to ensure that the emission ceilings for e.g. sulphur dioxide (SO2), nitrogen oxides (NOx) are not exceeded in any year after 2010.

Such framework provisions are a regular feature of Union environmental law. They are those provisions which set out the general aim of an environmental directive. Another example is Article 1 of the Water Framework Directive 2000/60. According to Article 1, its purpose is 'to establish a framework for the protection of inland surface waters, transitional waters, coastal waters and groundwater'. According to the Court of Justice, provisions of directives, which merely specify the particular objectives the directive seeks to achieve, do not require transposition.[43] It is the authors' opinion that such provisions will in general not be directly effective either. Hence these general obligations cannot be invoked independently before national courts.

In the Netherlands the courts have had to decide on a number of questions arising in connection with the possible direct effect of Article 1(1) of Directive 78/176.[44] This provision provides: 'The aim of this Directive is the prevention and progressive reduction, with a view to its elimination, of pollution caused by waste from the titanium dioxide industry.' This general requirement is then worked out in more detail in a number of operative provisions. The Dutch court was asked to clarify whether, apart from the operative provisions of the directive, Article 1(1) should be afforded independent significance and, if so, whether it was directly effective. A number of environmental interest groups interpreted this provision as a 'standstill' requirement, in the light of which the Dutch licensing system could be reviewed. It was decided that the provision could not be invoked before a Dutch court.[45] In the light of the Court of Justice judgment in the *Lombardia Waste* case[46] this judgment would seem to be correct.

Derogation clauses and direct effect
The following construction is regularly found in environmental directives. Often Member States are required to fulfil a certain obligation, while at the

---

sions which 'require the Member States to obtain very precise and specific results after a certain period' like the *Blackpool* case.

[42] Case C-165/09 *Stichting Natuur en Milieu and others*, Judgment of 26 May 2011, para. 97. Emphasis added by the authors.

[43] Case C-32/05 *Commission* v. *Luxembourg* [2006] ECR I-11323, para. 44.

[44] OJ 1978 L 54/19.

[45] Decision of the Dutch Crown 13 May 1985 *Dutch TiO2* [1986] M&R, 90-94.

[46] Case C-236/92 *Comitato di coordinamento per la difesa della Cava* v. *Regione Lombardia* [1994] ECR I-485.

same the directive provides for derogations from these obligations, provided certain conditions are met.

> A good example from Dutch case law is the judgment of the *Raad van State* (Council of State) concerning the creation in Dutch legislation of an exemption from the requirement to carry out an environmental impact assessment. Under the EIA Directive, certain precisely defined projects are subject to an environmental impact assessment. This requirement, laid down in Article 4(1) of the directive, is unconditional and sufficiently precise, albeit that Article 2(3) gives the Member States a power to exempt specific projects in exceptional cases. In this case, the primary rule is the obligation to carry out an environmental impact assessment; the secondary rule gives a power to grant exemptions. Does the discretion given by the secondary rule stand in the way of the direct effect of the primary rule? According to the *Raad van State* in *Rosmalen-Geffen*, it does not:[47] 'The Council of State notes that Article 2(1) read together with Article 4(1) and the Annex I mentioned there precisely defines when there is an obligation to carry out an environmental impact assessment. It is true that Article 2(3) of the directive gives Member States a certain discretion to grant exemptions from this obligation, but this discretion is limited to exceptional cases, and for specific projects. Given the above, it is our view that Articles 2(1) and 2(3) read together with Article 4(1) of the directive are directly effective provisions'.

The direct effect of such a provision resides in the limitations it imposes on the exercise by a public authority of a particular competence. These limitations are subject to judicial control and therefore have direct effect. The power to derogate as such, in other words, whether or not actually to use the power, is not directly effective. As far as the direct effect of these limitations is concerned, the following should also be borne in mind. If the principal provision is directly effective, but the power of derogation is not, this may produce results which run counter to the objective and the intention of the directive.[48]

From the case law of the Court it appears that, where a directive contains both provisions which are directly effective and provisions which are not, an individual can invoke directly effective provisions which, owing to their particular subject matter, are capable of being severed from the general body of provisions and applied separately.[49] By extension it can be concluded that directly effective provisions contained in environmental directives cannot be invoked if they are not capable of being severed from the general body of provisions.

---

[47] Dutch *Raad van State* 11 November 1991, *Rosmalen-Geffen* [1992] AB 50.

[48] Cf. also C-53/02 *Commune de Braine-le-Château a.o.* [2004] ECR I-3251, para. 43 in particular. The Court ruled that a failure to draw up waste management plans does not imply that individual permits can no longer be issued, as this would result in the implementation of other provisions of the Waste Directive being unduly delayed, to the detriment of achieving the objectives pursued by the directive.

[49] Case 8/81 *Becker* [1982] ECR 53. Confirmed for environmental law in Case C-346/97 *Braathens Sverige AB* [1999] ECR I-3419 and Case C-115/09 *Trianel Kohlekraftwerk Lünen*, Judgment of 12 May 2011, paras. 55-56. See on the latter case also section 5.1 in this chapter.

The following may serve as an example. Article 3(1) of Directive 2003/4 on public access to environmental information[50] states that Member States shall make available environmental information held by or for them to any applicant at his request and without his having to state an interest. This provision is sufficiently precise and unconditionally formulated to produce direct effect. Article 4 of the directive gives Member States the power to refuse such a request for information where it affects, *inter alia*, public security or commercial and industrial confidentiality. Article 4 confers a discretionary power and does not impose an obligation on the Member State. There is therefore no question of direct effect in the sense that Member States are allowed to refuse a request for information relating to, for example, commercial and industrial confidentiality. Does this mean that if Article 4 of the directive has not been implemented correctly, all information relating to the environment must be made available as a consequence of the direct effect of Article 3(1)? All these questions presumably have to be answered in the light of *Becker*.[51] When is a provision, in view of the context in which it has been placed, capable of being separated from the general body of provisions in the directive concerned? This will require a close examination of the effects the direct effect of a single provision have and whether these effects coincide with the objective and scope of the directive. In the case of Directive 2003/4, it could be argued that a general obligation to provide information on the environment goes too far and would produce results which are in conflict with the general context of the directive. Public authorities should be given the opportunity to consider in each individual case whether any of the grounds for derogation apply. Denying the public authorities this margin of discretion is in conflict with the objective of the directive. In that case the direct effect of the directive can only be invoked when information is refused on grounds other than those contained in Article 4 of the directive.

Clearly wrong is Justice Tucker's view in *Wychavon District Council* v. *Secretary of State for the Environment and Velcourt Ltd.*[52] With respect to the direct effect of the EIA Directive, he held 'it is unnecessary for me to analyse each Article in the Directive in turn in order to determine whether it is unconditional or uncertain. It will suffice if in respect of any Article which offends against the principle it is identified'. He then identified a number of provisions in the directive which did not meet the threshold of 'unconditional and sufficiently precise' and held as a consequence that the EIA Directive was incapable of having direct effect.

Direct effect and licensing/permitting/authorisation requirements

Many directives contain licensing, permitting or authorisation requirements. Examples can be found in European waste, water pollution and air pollution directives in particular.

---

[50] OJ 2003 L 41/26.

[51] Case 8/81 *Becker* [1982] ECR 53. Cf. also Case C-365/98 *Brinkmann Tabakfabriken* [2000] ECR I-4619.

[52] English High Court, Queen's Bench Division, 16 December 1993 [1994] 2 Env. LR 239. Cf. on this case Davies (2004) at 105.

For instance, Article 4(1) of the Waste Incineration Directive 2000/76 states that 'no incineration or co-incineration plant shall operate without a permit to carry out these activities'.[53] Or take Article 4 of Directive 2006/11 on pollution caused by certain dangerous substances discharged into the aquatic environment of the Community which requires that, with respect to so-called 'List 1' substances, 'all discharges into the waters [...] which are liable to contain any such substance, shall require prior authorisation by the competent authority of the Member State concerned'.[54]

Of course, it could be that the competent national authorities have discretion in issuing authorisations under directives like the ones mentioned above. However, the prohibition on discharges without prior authorisation is as such clear, precise and unconditional and therefore directly effective, so that any interested party may rely on it before the national courts in an action to halt discharges which are not authorised in accordance with the procedure and criteria which it prescribes.[55]

Similar remarks can be made with respect to Article 2(1) of the EIA Directive according to which an environmental impact assessment must be carried out before the competent authority gives consent to a developer to proceed with a project which is likely to have significant effects on the environment. In the *Wells* case the Court of Justice ruled that an individual may rely on Article 2(1) of the EIA Directive before a national court.[56]

The requirement to draw up action plans

There are quite a few directives that require from the Member States to draw up so-called 'action plans' to improve the environment (e.g. water and/or air quality). An important question therefore is, whether this obligation can be relied upon before a national court. It was exactly this question which emerged in the *Janecek* case.[57]

The facts of the case were as follows. Mr Janecek lives close to Munich's central ring road. Measurements of an air quality measuring station taken nearby his home have shown that, in 2005 and 2006, the limit value fixed for emissions of 'particulate matter PM10' was exceeded much more than 35 times, even though that is the maximum number of instances permitted under the Federal Law on combating pollution. Although an air quality action plan exists in respect of the city of Munich, Janecek brought an action before the *Verwaltungsgericht* Munich for an order requiring the Freistaat Bayern to draw up an

---

[53]   OJ 2000 L 332/91.

[54]   OJ 2006 L 64/52.

[55]   Cf. Case C-213/03 *Pêcheurs de l'étang de Berre* [2004] ECR I-7357, para. 42 in particular.

[56]   Case C-201/02 *Wells* [2004] ECR I-723, para. 61. Cf. well before *Wells* at national level, English High Court, Queen's Bench Division (McCullough J) 26 October 1990 *Twyford Parish Council a.o. v. Secretary of State for the Environment and another* [1992] 1 C.M.L.R. 276.

[57]   Case C-237/07 *Janecek* [2008] ECR I-6221.

air quality action plan in order to ensure compliance with the maximum permitted number of instances (35 per year) being exceeded. The relevant provision of Union law on which Janecek relied was Article 7(3) of Directive 96/62 on ambient air quality assessment and management, which provided:

> 'Member States shall draw up action plans indicating the measures to be taken in the short term where there is a risk of the limit values and/or alert thresholds being exceeded, in order to reduce that risk and to limit the duration of such an occurrence. ...'

The *Verwaltungsgericht* Munich dismissed that action as unfounded. On appeal, the *Verwaltungsgerichtshof* held that the residents concerned may require the competent authorities to draw up an action plan, but that they are not entitled to insist that it must include the particular measures that would guarantee compliance in the short-term with the emission limit values. According to the *Verwaltungsgerichtshof*, the national authorities are required only to ensure that such a plan pursues that objective to the extent to which it is possible and proportionate for it to do so. Consequently, it ordered the Freistaat Bayern to draw up an action plan complying with those requirements. Janecek and the Freistaat Bayern appealed to the *Bundesverwaltungsgericht*. According to the *Bundesverwaltungsgericht*, neither the spirit nor the letter of Article 7(3) of Directive 96/62 confers a personal right[58] to have an action plan drawn up. However, the *Bundesverwaltungsgericht*, recognising that there is a school of thought which draws different conclusions from the rules in question, asked the European Court of Justice some preliminary questions.

With respect to the question whether an individual can require the competent national authorities to draw up an action plan in the case – referred to in Article 7(3) of Directive 96/62 – where there is a risk that the limit values or alert thresholds may be exceeded, the Court of Justice ruled that this is indeed the case. According to the Court, Article 7(3) places the Member States under a clear obligation to draw up action plans both where there is a risk of the limit values being exceeded and where there is a risk of the alert thresholds being exceeded. That interpretation follows 'from a straightforward reading'. In addition, the Court referred to its older case law on direct effect[59] and noted that it has consistently held that individuals are entitled, as against public bodies, to rely on the provisions of a directive which are unconditional and sufficiently precise. And that it is incompatible with the binding effect which Article 288 TFEU ascribes to a directive to exclude, in principle, the possibility of the obligation imposed by that directive being relied on by persons concerned. This applies in particularly in respect of a directive which is intended to control and reduce atmospheric pollution and which is designed, therefore, to protect public health. The Court also drew attention to the doctrine of consistent interpretation, by which it is for the competent national authorities and courts to interpret

---

[58] In German: *ein subjektives Recht*; see para. 18 of the judgment, German version.

[59] Case 148/78 *Ratti* [1979] ECR 1629, para. 20.

national law, as far as possible, in a way that is compatible with the purpose of that directive.[60] Finally the Court referred to its case law on the invocability of European air and water quality standards, stating that whenever the failure to observe the measures required by the directives which relate to air quality and drinking water, and which are designed to protect public health, could endanger human health, the persons concerned must be in a position to rely on the mandatory rules included in those directives.[61] The Court's conclusion with respect to Article 7(3) of Directive 96/62 is worth quoting:

> '39 It follows from the foregoing that the natural or legal persons directly concerned by a risk that the limit values or alert thresholds may be exceeded must be in a position to require the competent authorities to draw up an action plan where such a risk exists, if necessary by bringing an action before the competent courts.
>
> 40 The fact that those persons may have other courses of action available to them – in particular, the power to require that the competent authorities lay down specific measures to reduce pollution, which, as indicated by the referring court, is provided for under German law – is irrelevant in that regard.
>
> 41 Directive 96/62 does not place any restrictions on the measures which may be adopted pursuant to other provisions of national law; moreover, it contains wording that is quite specific with regard to planning for the purposes, as stated in the 12th recital in the preamble to the directive, of protecting the environment 'as a whole', taking account of all the factors to be considered, such as, in particular, the requirements for the operation of industrial installations or travel.
>
> 42 The answer to the first question must therefore be that Article 7(3) of Directive 96/62 must be interpreted as meaning that, where there is a risk that the limit values or alert thresholds may be exceeded, persons directly concerned must be in a position to require the competent national authorities to draw up an action plan, even though, under national law, those persons may have other courses of action available to them for requiring those authorities to take measures to combat atmospheric pollution.'[62]

The next couple of questions referred by the *Bundesverwaltungsgericht* concerned whether the competent national authorities are obliged to lay down measures which, in the short term, would ensure that the limit value is attained, or whether they can confine themselves to taking measures to ensure a reduction in instances of the limit value being exceeded or limits on their duration and which are, consequently, liable to make it possible for the situation to be improved gradually. The Court of Justice, looking at the wording of Article 7(3)

---

[60] Case C-106/89 *Marleasing* [1990] ECR I-4135, para. 8. Cf., more extensively: Jans et al. (2007), chapter IV.

[61] Case C-361/88 *Commission v. Germany* [1991] ECR I-2567; Case C-59/89 *Commission v. Germany* [1991] ECR I-2607 and Case C-58/89 *Commission v. Germany* [1991] ECR I-4983.

[62] In the same vein, with respect to the obligation to draw up programmes for the progressive reduction of national emissions covered by the NEC Directive (Article 6): Case C-165/09 *Stichting Natuur en Milieu and others*, Judgment of 26 May 2011, paras. 99-100.

concluded that the Member States are not obliged to take measures to ensure that those limit values and/or alert thresholds are never exceeded. On the contrary, the Court found it apparent from the broad logic of the directive that it is for the Member States to take measures capable of reducing to a minimum the risk of the standards being exceeded and the duration of such an occurrence, taking into account all the material circumstances and opposing interests. Consequently:

> '46 It must be noted in this regard that, while the Member States thus have a discretion, Article 7(3) of Directive 96/62 includes limits on the exercise of that discretion which may be relied upon before the national courts (see, to that effect, Case C-72/95 Kraaijeveld and Others [1996] ECR I-5403, paragraph 59), relating to the adequacy of the measures which must be included in the action plan with the aim of reducing the risk of the limit values and/or alert thresholds being exceeded and the duration of such an occurrence, taking into account the balance which must be maintained between that objective and the various opposing public and private interests.
>
> 47 Therefore, the answer to the second and third questions must be that the Member States are obliged, subject to judicial review by the national courts, only to take such measures – in the context of an action plan and in the short term – as are capable of reducing to a minimum the risk that the limit values or alert thresholds may be exceeded and of ensuring a gradual return to a level below those values or thresholds, taking into account the factual circumstances and all opposing interests.'

The proceedings before the German courts made it clear that there is still considerable doubt on the workfloor, so to speak, whether provisions of environmental directives are directly effective or not. The various positions taken by the *Verwaltungsgericht*, the *Verwaltungsgerichtshof* and the *Bundesverwaltungsgericht* illustrate this. In section 2 of this chapter, discussing the *Kraaijeveld* and *Landelijke Vereniging tot Behoud van de Waddenzee* cases,[63] we argued that in our opinion the view that there is 'policy discretion and therefore no direct effect' is too simple. The judgment in *Janecek* confirms this analysis. It is clear from paragraph 46 that the Court of Justice takes the view that Member States do have discretion when taking specific measures to implement action plans, but that the limits on the exercise of that discretion may be relied upon before the national courts. The fact that Members States have a certain discretion when determining the content of environmental action plans does not make the obligation to draw them up any less unconditional.[64]

---

[63] Case C-72/95 *Kraaijeveld* [1996] ECR I-5403; Case C-127/02 *Landelijke Vereniging tot Behoud van de Waddenzee* [2004] ECR I-7405.

[64] See for a similar approach with respect to Art. 6 of the National Emission Ceilings Directive (the obligation to draw up programmes for the progressive reduction of national emissions of e.g. SO2 and NOx), Joined Cases C-165/09 to C-167/09 *Stichting Natuur en Milieu a.o.*, Judgment of 26 May 2011.

Enforcement measures with direct effect

It follows from the case law of the Court that obligations arising from environmental directives should be considered obligations to attain certain results rather than merely requiring the Member States to take all practicable steps.[65] An individual will primarily be interested in whether or not he or she, by invoking the directive, can force public authorities to take certain measures which will result in compliance with the standards contained in the directive. In general, national law provides a wide range of instruments which public authorities can use to attain the appropriate level of environmental protection. Thus, a plant producing excessive emissions of dangerous substances can be closed down, subject to criminal sanctions, etc. The question here is to what extent an individual can rely upon the direct effect of environmental directives relating to enforcement mechanisms where the Member State has failed to comply with the standards set out in the directive.

It must be assumed that Member States enjoy considerable discretion, at least in respect of the question *how* standards contained in environmental directives are enforced, within the limits of the principle of loyal cooperation (effective, preventive, non-discriminatory and proportional). As a result of this discretion, an individual does not have a right (i.e. there is no direct effect) to demand *specific* enforcement action, unless this has been expressly provided for in the directive itself. Some directives do indeed prescribe in detail the inspection, supervision and other enforcement mechanisms. Whether this is the case will have to be examined from one directive to the next. If a directive does contain directly effective enforcement provisions they have to be applied.

> Take for instance Article 4(9) of the Waste Incineration Directive: 'If an incineration or co-incineration plant does not comply with the conditions of the permit, in particular with the emission limit values for air and water, the competent authority shall take action to enforce compliance.'[66] This provision clearly implies a duty for the authorities to shut down a plant, if necessary, when the emission limit values are exceeded by the undertaking.
>
> Another example of such a provision is Article 5(4) of Directive 2006/11.[67] This directive requires national authorities to establish emission standards in authorisations to prevent water pollution. The provision states: 'Should the emission standards not be complied with, the competent authority in the Member State concerned shall take all appropriate steps to ensure that the conditions of authorisation are fulfilled and, if necessary, that the discharge is prohibited.' This provision implies that it is not permitted to tolerate discharges which violate the emission standards contained in the directive.

---

[65] Case C-56/90 *Commission* v. *UK* [1993] ECR I-4109.

[66] Directive 2000/76 on the incineration of waste, OJ 2000 L 332/91.

[67] Directive 2006/11 on pollution caused by certain dangerous substances discharged into the aquatic environment of the Community, OJ 2006 L 64/52.

Most interesting are the enforcement obligations in Article 4(5) of Directive 1999/22 relating to the keeping of wild animals in zoos.[68] It states: 'If the zoo is not licensed in accordance with this Directive or the licensing conditions are not met, the zoo or part thereof:

a) shall be closed to the public by the competent authority; and/or

b) shall comply with appropriate requirements imposed by the competent authority to ensure that the licensing conditions are met.

Should these requirements not be complied with within an appropriate period to be determined by the competent authorities but not exceeding two years, the competent authority shall withdraw or modify the licence and close the zoo or part thereof.'

However, in the absence of concrete and specific provisions, it is primarily for the Member States to determine how the factual situation must be brought into line with the legal situation, although it appears from the relevant case law that the Court can subject this decision to rigorous review.[69] Where discretionary powers exist this presumably rules out the direct effect of the obligation to enforce European values. As regards the latter, it is worth noting the conclusion of Advocate General Mischo in the German *TA Luft* cases.[70] In his opinion Member States do enjoy discretion as to the choice concerning the measures which are necessary to enforce air quality standards. The European institutions would only be able to challenge the approaches adopted by Member States if it appeared from the facts that these were not capable of achieving the intended goals. As long as the factual and legal situations have not been brought into line it must be assumed that, even though the obligations imposed by a directive have not been fulfilled, individuals do not always have the right to invoke the directive by insisting that specific enforcement measures are taken by the public authorities.[71]

The designation of special protection areas

Another type of obligation arising out of environmental directives requiring further implementation and therefore apparently lacking direct effect, are provisions requiring Member States to designate geographical areas to which special protection measures will then apply. An example is the classification of special bird protection areas under the Wild Birds Directive. For protected species of birds, Article 4(1) requires Member States to 'classify in particular the most suitable territories in number and size as special protection areas for the

---

[68] OJ 1999 L 94/24.

[69] Cf. Case C-365/97 *Commission v. Italy* [1999] ECR I-7773 (*San Rocco*). See also outside the field of environmental law Case 68/88 *Commission v. Greece* [1989] ECR 2965; Case 326/88 *Hansen* [1990] ECR I-2911 and Case C-287/91 *Commission v. Italy* [1992] ECR I-3315.

[70] Case C-361/88 *Commission v. Germany* [1991] ECR I-2567 and Case C-59/89 *Commission v. Germany* [1991] ECR I-2607.

[71] See on questions regarding liability of public authorities in cases of non-enforcement, De Graaf & Jans (2007).

conservation of these species, taking into account their protection requirements in the geographical sea and land area where this directive applies'.[72] Failure to classify special protection areas while protected species of birds and migrating birds do occur in the territory of the Member State, constitutes a clear breach of the directive. This may result in the Commission initiating an infringement procedure under Article 258 TFEU.

> In Case C-334/89, Italy was brought before the Court of Justice because it had not classified any special protection areas.[73] The Court held: 'The Italian Government has not, either during or before the proceedings before the Court, reported any special conservation measures adopted by it at national level of the species listed in that annex. Nor has it made any claim to the effect that none of the species in question occurs in Italian territory. Accordingly, it should have established special protection areas and adopted special conservation measures in respect of the species present on its territory.' The Court ruled that Italy had failed to fulfil its obligations under the Treaty.

From this case it can be concluded that there is an obligation to classify special protection areas when specific species of birds occur in the territory of the Member State. A much more difficult question is whether, in a specific case, the directive also creates an obligation to classify a certain clearly identified area as a special protection area. From the early case law of the Court it appeared that Member States have some margin of discretion in the classification of special protection areas.

> In the *Leybucht* case the question was to what extent the Member States are entitled to reduce or modify the geographical size of a special protection area.[74] The Court observed that the Member states 'do have a certain discretion with regard to the choice of the territories which are most suitable for classification as special protection areas pursuant to Article 4(1) of the directive.'

On the basis of this judgment, the conclusion has been drawn that where the Member States do have a certain discretion, it would be difficult to establish an obligation to classify a particular area. This would only be otherwise if the discretion were restricted by the Member State itself, for example because the area in question had been given protected status on the basis of other, national or international, law. That a Member State's discretion could indeed be more limited than is suggested in the *Leybucht* case is evident from later judgments.

> Thus in Case C-3/96 the Commission argued that the Netherlands had wrongly failed to designate a number of specifically named areas as special protection

---

[72]   See on this more in detail Chapter 8, section 19.1.

[73]   Case C-334/89 *Commission* v. *Italy* [1991] ECR I-93.

[74]   Case C-57/89 *Commission* v. *Germany* [1991] ECR I-883. See on declassification also Thomas (2008).

areas.[75] The Court, while acknowledging that the Member States have a certain margin of discretion in the choice of SPAs, stated that the classification of those areas is nevertheless subject to certain ornithological criteria. It follows, the Court continued, that the Member States' margin of discretion in choosing the most suitable territories for classification as SPAs does not concern the appropriateness of classifying as SPAs the territories which appear the most suitable according to ornithological criteria, but only the application of those criteria for identifying the most suitable territories for conservation of the species listed in the directive. Member States are obliged to classify as SPAs all the sites which, applying ornithological criteria, appear to be the most suitable for conservation of the species in question, the Court concluded.

Although this case concerned a Treaty infringement procedure in which the question of direct effect was not as such at issue, the judgment is nevertheless pertinent. If the Court has restricted a Member State's discretion to designate SPAs to such an extent that this could amount to a concrete obligation to designate a specific area, it is hard to see why that obligation should not also be directly effective.[76] Furthermore, it must be assumed that also the obligations in directives in relation to these special protection areas can be directly effective as well and that therefore these obligations are not conditional upon prior designation. In the *Santoña marshes* case, for instance the Court ruled that the obligations ex Article 4(4) of the Wild Birds Directive to take appropriate steps to avoid pollution or deterioration of special protection areas are applicable to the *Santoña marshes*, although they were not designated as such.[77] With respect to the possible direct effect of the protective measures required by the Habitats Directive, the *Dragaggi* case must be mentioned.[78] The Court ruled that the protective measures prescribed in Article 6(2) to (4) of the directive are required only as regards sites which are placed on the list of sites selected as sites of Community importance. This rules out any direct effect of these provisions with respect to habitats erroneously not being designated.[79]

Other environmental directives contain similar obligations to designate special protection areas, for example, the Bathing Water Directive,[80] the Water Framework Directive[81] and Nitrates Directive.[82] For these directives too, it will

---

[75] Case C-3/96 *Commission v. Netherlands* [1998] ECR I-3031. Cf. also Case C-166/97 *Commission v. France* [1999] ECR I-1719 and Case C-355/90 *Commission v. Spain* [1993] ECR I-4221 (*Santoña marshes*).

[76] Cf. Prechal (2005) 313.

[77] Case C-355/90 *Commission v. Spain* [1993] ECR I-4221.

[78] Case C-117/03 *Dragaggi a.o.* [2005] ECR I-167, para. 25.

[79] See however C-244/05 *Bund Naturschutz in Bayern a.o.* [2006] ECR I-8445, where the Court ruled that the Member States are required to take all the measures necessary to avoid interventions which incur the risk of seriously compromising the ecological characteristics of the sites which appear on the national list transmitted to the Commission. See also Chapter 8, section 19.2.

[80] OJ 2006 L 64/37.

[81] OJ 2000 L 327/1.

[82] OJ 1991 L 375/1.

have to be determined in each individual case whether the criteria in the directive in question require that a particular area is classified or not.

As regards the old Bathing Water Directive, existing case law points to similar conclusions to those in the cases on the Wild Birds Directive discussed above. Under this directive bathing water in bathing areas is supposed to satisfy minimum standards. In the *Blackpool* case, one of the questions addressed was which waters had to be considered as bathing areas within the meaning of the directive.[83] The Court pointed out that the directive defines the term 'bathing water' as all running or still fresh waters, or parts thereof, and sea water in which bathing is not prohibited and is traditionally practised by a large number of bathers. The United Kingdom contended that it was not clear whether Blackpool and Southport fell within the scope of the directive. Here, too, the Member State appears to have little real discretion. It could be inferred from the presence of changing huts, toilets, markers and lifeguards that certain areas fell within the scope of the directive and that its quality objectives therefore had to be adhered to.

Similar conclusions can be drawn with respect to the duty to designate 'vulnerable zones' under the Nitrates Directive. Although the Member States have a 'wide discretion' to identity those vulnerable zones, France was nevertheless in violation because it did not designate the Seine bay under the directive.[84]

However, if the Member States do not have a genuine obligation to determine the areas to which stringent environmental quality standards apply, there can be no question of direct effect. For example, certain air quality directives allowed Member States to classify areas to which more stringent air quality standards apply.[85] Such areas are classified if 'the Member State concerned considers' these zones should be afforded special environmental protection. Where a provision of a directive does not impose an obligation on the Member States, such provision is clearly not directly effective.

Direct effect of procedural rules
Procedural rules do not always give individuals rights which they may enforce before the national courts. That was made clear by the Court in the *Balsamo* case.[86]

Article 3(2) of the 'old' Waste Directive required Member States to inform the Commission in good time of any draft rules concerning, *inter alia*, the use of prod-

---

[83] Case C-56/90 *Commission v. UK* [1993] ECR I-4109. Cf. for the new Bathing Water Directive 2006/17, OJ 2006 L 64/37.

[84] Case C-258/00 *Commission v. France* [2002] ECR I-5959. Similar rulings have been rendered to other Member States as well. Cf. e.g. with respect to Spain's failure to designate the Rambla de Mojácar as a vulnerable zone Case C-416/02 *Commission v. Spain* [2005] ECR I-7487.

[85] E.g. Article 4(2) of Directive 85/203 on air quality standards for nitrogen dioxide, OJ 1985 L 87/1.

[86] Case 380/87 *Balsamo* [1989] ECR 2491.

ucts which might be a source of technical difficulties as regards disposal or lead to excessive disposal costs.[87] The Italian Government did not notify the Commission of a decision of the Mayor of Cinisello Balsamo prohibiting the supply to consumers of non-biodegradable bags. The competent Italian court submitted several questions to the Court of Justice. One of the questions was whether Article 3(2) of the directive gave individuals a right which they could enforce before the national courts in order to obtain the annulment or suspension of national rules falling within the scope of that provision on the ground that those rules were adopted without having previously been communicated to the Commission. According to the Court, Article 3(2) was intended to ensure that the Commission is informed of any plans for national measures regarding waste disposal so that it can consider whether harmonising legislation is called for and whether the draft rules submitted to it are compatible with Union law. The Court held that neither the wording nor the purpose of the provision in question provides any support for the view that failure by the Member States to give prior notice to the Commission in itself renders unlawful the rules thus adopted. The Court concluded that Article 3(2) of the directive concerned relations between the Member States and the Commission and did not give rise to any right for individuals which might be infringed by a Member State's breach of its obligation to inform the Commission in advance of draft rules.[88]

In view of the *CIA Security* case law we cannot agree with Wennerås, who states that the notification requirement of Article 2(3) of the EIA Directive is directly effective.[89] That provision enables Member States, in exceptional cases, to exempt a specific project in whole or in part from the provisions of the directive. However, Member States must inform the Commission.

However, it is evident from another judgment of the Court that *procedural* rules can contain rights and obligations for private individuals.[90]

This case was, *inter alia*, about the formal obligations flowing from Articles 7 to 11 and Article 13 of the 'old' Ground Water Directive (80/68).[91] Article 7 requires prior examination of the hydrogeological conditions and Articles 8 to 11 and Article 13 impose further requirements on the issuing of authorisations. The authorisations may not be issued until it has been checked that the ground water, and in particular its quality, will undergo the requisite surveillance (Article 8). That is why Articles 9 and 10 of the directive lay down the information to be specified in

---

[87] See now also Article 6(4) of the Waste Framework Directive 2008/98 (OJ 2008 L 312/3). Cf. also Case C-159/00 *Sapod Audic* [2002] ECR I-5031, para. 61-63.

[88] See Dutch *Raad van State* 16 June 1995 [1995] *M&R* 93, applying the '*Balsamo* doctrine' on the duty to notify national legislation under Article 2(3) of the EIA Directive.

[89] Wennerås (2007) at 54.

[90] Case C-131/88 *Commission v. Germany* [1991] ECR I-825.

[91] OJ 1980 L 20/43. The 'old' Groundwater Directive will be repealed from 21 December 2013 by the Water Framework Directive 2000/60 (OJ 2000 L 327/1).

the authorisations. The authorisations may be granted for a limited period only, and are to be reviewed at least every four years (Article 11). Moreover, the directive requires the Member States to monitor compliance with the conditions laid down in the authorisations and the effects of discharges on groundwater (Article 13). According to the Court, it must be observed that the procedural provisions of the directive lay down, in order to guarantee effective protection of groundwater, precise and detailed rules 'which are intended to create rights and obligations for individuals'. In particular this judgment shows that the term 'rights and obligations' should be understood not only to include the rights and obligations of individuals, but far more in terms of 'having an interest in' or 'being affected by'. The conclusion must therefore be that in such cases the Member State must offer interested parties adequate legal protection against breaches of obligations imposed by directives.

Direct effect of provisions in environmental treaties concluded by the Union

It has been acknowledged by the Court that provisions of international treaties concluded by the Union could be directly effective, when these provisions contain clear and precise obligations which are not subject, in their implementation or effects, to the adoption of any subsequent measures.[92] In that case *national*[93] law can be reviewed directly, as a matter of Union law, in the light of the international environmental treaty concerned. This doctrine has been applied with respect to for the first time in the *Pêcheurs de l'étang de Berre* case.[94] The case involved, *inter alia*, Article 6(3) of the Protocol for the Protection of the Mediterranean Sea against Pollution from Land-based Sources.[95]

Under Article 6(1) and (3) of the Protocol provides: '1. The Parties shall strictly limit pollution from land-based sources in the Protocol Area by substances or sources listed in Annex II to this Protocol. [...] 3. Discharges shall be strictly subject to the issue, by the competent national authorities, of an authorisation taking due account of the provisions of Annex III [...].' The Court ruled that that provision clearly, precisely and unconditionally lays down the obligation for Member States to subject discharges of the substances listed in Annex II to the Protocol to the issue by the competent national authorities of an authorisation taking due account of the provisions of Annex III. In view of the Court, the fact that the national authorities have discretion in issuing authorisations under the criteria set out in Annex III in no way diminishes the clear, precise and unconditional nature of the prohibition on discharges without prior authorisation and that finding is also supported by the purpose and nature of the Protocol. In conclusion the Court

---

[92] Case 12/86 *Demirel* [1987] ECR 3719, para. 14. Cf. also Case C-240/09 *Lesoochranárske zoskupenie VLK*, Judgment of 8 March 2011, para. 44.

[93] According to Article 216(2) TFEU agreements concluded by the Union are binding upon the institutions of the Union *and on its Member States*.

[94] Case C-213/03 *Pêcheurs de l'étang de Berre* [2004] ECR I-7357.

[95] Approved by Council Decision 83/101, OJ 1983 L 67/1.

ruled that the provision has direct effect, so that any interested party is entitled to rely on it before the national courts.

In the *Slovak Bears* case the Court of Justice ruled that Article 9(3) of the Aarhus Convention is not directly effective. However, there is an obligation for the national court, in order to ensure effective judicial protection in the fields covered by EU environmental law, to interpret its national law in a way which, to the fullest extent possible, is consistent with the objectives laid down in Article 9(3) of the Aarhus Convention.[96]

But an international environmental treaty concluded by the Union can also be used as a standard of review to assess compliance of the *Union* with its obligations as a party to that agreement.[97] For instance in aaan application for annulment under Article 263 TFEU or, where the invalidity of a Union measure is pleaded before a national court, the Court of Justice exercises a review pursuant to the preliminary rulings procedure of Article 267 TFEU.[98]

In *Intertanko* the Court ruled that it is clear that the Union institutions are bound by agreements concluded by the Union and, consequently, that those agreements have primacy over secondary Union legislation.[99] It follows that the validity of a measure of secondary Union legislation may be affected by the fact that it is incompatible with such rules of international law. Where that invalidity is pleaded before a national court, the Court of Justice thus reviews the validity of the Union measure concerned subject to two conditions. First, the Union must be bound by those rules and second, the Court can examine the validity of Union legislation in the light of an international treaty only where 'the nature and the broad logic' of the latter do not preclude this and, in addition, the treaty's provisions appear, as regards their content, to be 'unconditional and sufficiently precise'. Nor MARPOL, nor UNCLOS meet those conditions, the Court ruled in *Intertanko*. Neither are provisions of the WTO agreements among the rules in the light of which the Court is to review the lawfulness of measures adopted by the European institutions.[100]

---

[96] Case C-240/09 *Lesoochranárske zoskupenie VLK*, Judgment of 8 March 2011.

[97] See for instance Case C-27/00 *Omega Air a.o.* [2002] ECR I-2569, where the Court reviewed the validity of Regulation 925/1999 on noise emissions of aeroplanes in the light of the 1944 Chicago Convention.

[98] See in particular, Case C-308/06 *Intertanko and others* [2008] ECR I-4057, para. 43. Cf. also Case C-377/98 *Netherlands* v. *EP and Council* [2000] ECR I-6229 where the Court seemed willing to review Directive 98/44 on the legal protection of biotechnological inventions (OJ 1998 L 213/13) in the light of the Unions's obligations under the Convention on Biological Diversity.

[99] Case C-308/06 *Intertanko and others* [2008] ECR I-4057, para. 42.

[100] See for instance Case C-27/00 *Omega Air a.o.* [2002] ECR I-2569.

2.2   Absence of Horizontal Direct Effect of Directives

Directives do not produce horizontal or third-party effect in the sense that, in the absence of national implementing measures, they directly result in obligations for private individuals.[101] Under Article 288, third paragraph, TFEU, directives are addressed to Member States and hence oblige the Member States to take the necessary steps. They therefore only have *vertical* direct effect. In principle therefore, direct effect cannot be invoked to establish a breach of a provision of a directive in relations between individuals. In the *Traen* case the Court was very explicit in deciding that provisions of the Waste Directive 'do not directly impose obligations upon persons or undertakings.'[102] Or, to give another clear example, it is out of the question that the obligations for the operator under the Environmental Liability Directive to take preventive and/or remedial measures can be enforced without national implementing legislation.[103] This doctrine has been applied consistently in national courts.

In the Dutch *Drenthe Crows* case, the issue was to what extent an environmental directive, in this case the Wild Birds Directive,[104] can impose obligations on private individuals.[105] A hunting association had called its members to hunt crows on a certain day. Dutch hunting laws allowed crow hunting even though the birds were in principle protected under the directive. An environmental interest group argued that the hunters were acting unlawfully because they were acting in breach of the directive. The judge in the case dismissed the application, observing that the directive created obligations for Member States, namely to adapt the national legislation. However, he added that, in legal relations between individuals, it would be going too far to accept that they should act as if the laws had already been adapted.

Another example is provided by the judgment of a Dutch court in interlocutory proceedings in which the Belgian firm of Cockerill Sambre was taken to court by several environmental interest groups in connection with discharges into the River Maas.[106] One of the arguments was that the discharges of so-called 'PACs' in

---

[101] Case 152/84 *Marshall* I [1986] ECR 737. Regulations however do have horizontal effect. In view of the Judgment in Case C-253/00 *Muñoz* [2002] ECR I-7289, it must be assumed that in national law a tort claim must be available to enforce environmental standards laid down in the regulation. Cf. on the relevance of the *Muñoz* case for environmental law Betlem (2005).

[102] Joined Cases 372-374/85 *Traen* [1987] ECR 2141.

[103] Directive 2004/35 on environmental liability with regard to the prevention and remedying of environmental damage, OJ 2004 L 143/56, in particular Articles 4 and 5. The question whether the obligation for public authorities take the necessary action vis-a-vis the operator is directly effective will be discussed below.

[104] OJ 1979 L 103/1, later amended.

[105] Dutch District Court Assen 11 April 1989 *Drenthe Crows* [1989] M&R 372-374.

[106] Dutch District Court Maastricht 3 February 1993 *Cockerill Sambre* [1993] MR 17.

particular were in breach of Directive 76/464.[107] The applicants alleged that Cockerill had abused the failure by the Belgian Government to comply with its obligations under the directive. The court dismissed the application, observing that the
directive addresses the Member States, and therefore does not have the effect of
binding individuals directly.

In short, an individual can invoke a directive vis-à-vis national authorities, but
not vis-à-vis another individual. This position is wholly in line with the case law
of the Court of Justice. Individuals do not therefore act unlawfully when they act
in breach of standards set by environmental directives, if these standards have
not been transposed into national legislation.

Directly effective provisions of a directive will therefore normally only be
invoked in respect of an 'emanation of the state'. It is important to note that
the term 'emanation of the state' must be interpreted in a broad sense. As was
observed in *Foster* v. *British Gas,* provisions of a directive having direct effect
may 'in any event' be relied on against a body, whatever its legal form, 'which
has been made responsible, pursuant to a measure adopted by the State for
providing a public service under the control of the State and has for that purpose
special powers beyond those which result from the normal rules applicable in
relations between individuals.'[108] Regional gas, water[109] and electricity companies, but probably also certain waste disposal companies may, depending on the
circumstances fall within this broad definition.

Inverse direct effect[110]

Apart from lacking horizontal effect, a directive *a fortiori* also lacks 'inverse
direct effect'.[111] In other words, a public authority cannot invoke a directive
against an individual and thereby require him to act in conformity with the
directive, where the obligations contained in the directive have not yet been
implemented in the national legal order. If the Member State is at fault, this
cannot be held against the individual. The State must be prevented from taking
advantage of its own failure to comply with Union law.

> The following example will serve to clarify what the consequences of this doctrine
> could be in the environmental law field. Suppose that a new directive requires
> Member States to introduce an energy-eco tax. Would the state be entitled to
> apply this directive and charge a tax on energy, even though the directive had not

---

[107] Now repealed by Directive 2006/11 on pollution caused by certain dangerous substances discharged
into the aquatic environment of the Community, OJ 2006 L 64/52.

[108] Case C-188/89 *Foster* v. *British Gas* [1990] ECR 3343.

[109] See English High Court 25 August 1994 *Griffin* v. *South West Water Services Ltd* [1995] IRLR 15.

[110] The notion 'inverse direct effect' was introduced by the Court in Case C-201/02 *Wells* [2004] ECR I-723,
para. 58.

[111] Case 14/86 *Pretore di Salò* v. *Persons unknown* [1987] ECR 2545, in particular para. 19. Cf. also Case
80/86 *Kolpinghuis* [1987] ECR 3969.

yet been implemented in the national legislation? The answer has to be that it could not. If the Member State has not fulfilled its obligations, it may not rely on the directive against an individual.

Horizontal side-effects of vertical direct effect

It has been explained above that the horizontal effect of environmental directives has been rejected by the Court of Justice. This does not mean that environmental directives which have not been properly implemented produce no horizontal legal effects between individuals at all. An environmental directive can give rise to obligations in a more indirect way. If the competent authorities grant a permit which is in conflict with a directive, an appeal by an interested third party will result in its annulment. Acts which were allowed by the permit before are no longer allowed once it has been annulled. This has obvious consequences in the sphere of civil liability. In this roundabout way, horizontal effects may after all arise.

There are other ways in which environmental directives can produce indirect horizontal effects. Thus, where an interested third party invokes a directly effective provision of an environmental directive, for example in an appeal against the grant of an environmental permit, a successful appeal would mean that the permit-holder would be placed in a less favourable position, because his permit would be void. There is nothing special about this, because a permit which contravenes national environmental law can be annulled. The Court of Justice addressed this problem in the *Wells* case.[112]

This case concerned a dispute between Mrs Wells and the Secretary of State for Transport, Local Government and the Regions concerning the grant of a new consent for mining operations at Conygar Quarry without an environmental impact assessment having first been carried out. In 1947 an 'old mining permission' had been granted for Conygar Quarry under the Town and Country Planning (General Interim Development) Order 1946. Conygar Quarry was divided into two sections, of slightly more than 7.5 hectares each, separated by a road on which Mrs Wells' house was situated. Mrs Wells had bought her house in 1984, that is to say 37 years after the permission had been granted, but at a time when the Quarry had long since been dormant. The site was recognised to be environmentally extremely sensitive. The area in or adjacent to which the quarry lay was subject to several designations of nature and environmental conservation importance. At the beginning of 1991, the owners of Conygar Quarry had applied to the competent Mineral Planning Authority (MPA) for registration of the old mining permission under the Planning and Compensation Act 1991. Registration was granted by a decision of 24 August 1992, which stated that no development could lawfully be carried out unless and until an application for the determination of new planning conditions had been made to the MPA and finally determined (the registration

---

[112] Case C-201/02 *Wells* [2004] ECR I-723. Confirmed in Case C-127/02 *Landelijke Vereniging tot Behoud van de Waddenzee* [2004] ECR I-7405.

decision). The owners of Conygar Quarry had therefore applied to the competent MPA for determination of new planning conditions. As the MPA, by decision of 22 December 1994, had imposed more stringent conditions than those submitted by the owners of Conygar Quarry, the latter exercised their right of appeal to the Secretary of State. By decision of 25 June 1997, the Secretary of State imposed 54 planning conditions, leaving some matters to be decided by the competent MPA. Those matters were approved by the competent MPA by decision of 8 July 1999. Neither the Secretary of State nor the competent MPA had examined whether it was necessary to carry out an environmental impact assessment pursuant to Directive 85/337.

According to the United Kingdom Government, acceptance that an individual was entitled to invoke Directive 85/337 would amount to inverse direct effect. The Court of Justice rejected this: 'mere adverse repercussions on the rights of third parties, even if the repercussions are certain, do not justify preventing an individual from invoking the provisions of a directive against the Member State concerned'. These adverse repercussions, the Court stated in paragraph 58, were 'not directly linked' to the performance of any obligation which would fall on the quarry owners under the directive. They were 'the consequence of the belated performance of [the Member State's] obligations.'

This case demonstrates that, where a third party successfully invokes the direct effect of the directive, this may put the permit holder at a disadvantage. However, it is impossible to regard this unacceptable: 'mere adverse repercussions on the rights of third parties' do not constitute inverse direct effect. The effects for the permit holder have to be seen as flowing from the rights which the third party has obtained under the directive vis-à-vis the competent authorities and are not 'directly linked'[113] with obligations of the permit holder. The adverse consequences of direct effect for the permit holder do not stem from the directive, but from the fact that the authorities have failed to fulfil their obligations under it. If the directive had been correctly implemented, the authorities would not have granted the authorisation in the first place. In so far as the additional burden results from the authorities' failure to fulfil their obligations under the directive vis-à-vis other individuals, this cannot be regarded as inverse direct effect. However, whenever the obligations of the authorities are *directly linked* with obligations of individuals stemming from the (non-implemented) directive, this would amount to inverse direct effect.

As an example for the latter we could point to the Environmental Liability Directive.[114] According to Article 5(1) of the directive an operator shall, in case of an imminent threat of environmental damage occurring, take the necessary preven-

---

[113] Case C-201/02 *Wells* [2004] ECR I-723, para. 56. This paragraph of the judgment is however lacking in Case C-127/02 *Landelijke Vereniging tot Behoud van de Waddenzee* [2004] ECR I-7405. Cf. on this Verschuuren (2005) and Lee (2005) at 63-64.

[114] OJ 2004 L 143/56. See on this directive also Chapter 8, section 9. Cf. also Wennerås (2007) at 49.

tive measures without delay. Article 12 states that natural or legal persons shall be entitled to request the competent authority to take action under this directive. In our view the obligations for public authorities under Article 12 are directly linked with the obligations of individuals, like the one in Article 5(1). This seems to exclude, under the *Wells* doctrine, that third parties can rely on the Environmental Liability Directive vis-à-vis public authorities to enforce the obligations of Article 5(1). As this would create, in absence of national implementing legislation, a direct obligation for individuals.

Although the Court's judgments in *Wells* and *Waddenzee* seem to be in line with the general case law of the Court of Justice, further case law needs to be awaited in order to establish a clear line between 'mere adverse consequences' and creating obligations for individuals.

2.3   Consequences of Direct Effect: Integral Application of Union Law

The Court repeatedly held that under the principle of sincere cooperation laid down in Article 4(3) TEU, the Member States are required to nullify the unlawful consequences of a breach of Union law.[115] Such an obligation is owed, within the sphere of its competence, by every organ of the Member State concerned.[116] However, it must be noted that the presence of direct effect does not release the Member State from its obligation to implement a directive.[117] Directives that have not been properly implemented cause uncertainty as to the legal position of those to whom they apply. This is why the Court insists on full and correct implementation.

In the *Simmenthal II* case the Court of Justice explained the implications of direct effect in combination with the principle of supremacy.[118] In a case within its jurisdiction, every national court must apply Union law in its entirety and protect the rights which it confers on individuals and must accordingly set aside any provision of national law which may conflict with it, whether prior or subsequent to the European rule. The consequences are thus twofold:

1) Union law must be applied in its entirety and
2) any provision of national law which is in conflict with it must be set aside.

In other decisions, it has also drawn attention to the implications of direct effect for authorities other than the judiciary. In *Fratelli Costanzo* the Court decided that all national administrative authorities, including regional and local authorities, are under an obligation to apply directly effective provisions of Union

---

[115] Case 6/60 *Humblet* [1960] ECR 559, at 569, and Joined Cases C-6/90 and C-9/90 *Francovich* [1991] ECR I-5357, para. 36.

[116] Case C-8/88 *Germany* v. *Commission* [1990] ECR I-2321, para. 13.

[117] Case C-208/90 *Emmott* [1991] ECR I-4269, in particular para. 20.

[118] Case 106/77 *Simmenthal* [1978] ECR 629.

law.[119] The *Costanzo* case is of great significance for national environmental law, in view of the competences regional and local authorities have in applying (implemented) environmental law. The case illustrates that regional and local authorities have an *independent* responsibility to ensure the fulfilment of Union law obligations. Regional and local authorities cannot 'hide' behind national legislation if this legislation is contrary to European rules. If necessary, they must independently set aside national legislation if its application would cause them to act in breach of directly effective provisions of Union law.

> A good example from Dutch administrative law is a judgment of the *Raad van State* (Council of State) in a case involving Directive 2000/53 (end-of-life vehicles). The *Raad van State* required the provincial authorities, in their decision-making, to take account of whether the legislation adopted in implementation of Directive 2000/53 was consistent with Article 35 TFEU. By simply assuming that the implementing legislation adopted by central government was lawful, the provincial authorities had acted without due care. It is hard to imagine a clearer illustration of local and regional authorities' own responsibility.[120]

In national environmental law however, we still encounter problems on how exactly this *Costanzo* doctrine should be applied in practice.

> The problems can be illustrated by referring to two judgments of the Dutch *Raad van State* relating to Article 3(4) of Directive 76/464 on pollution caused by certain dangerous substances discharged into the aquatic environment of the Community.[121] According to the *Raad van State*, this provision is directly effective in the national legal order. Authorisations to emit substances on the 'black list' which had been issued for an unlimited period were therefore contrary to Article 3(4) of the directive and were consequently revoked.[122] However, in a subsequent case where a public authority applied the rule in *Costanzo* and issued an authorisation for a limited period of time, the *Raad van State* annulled the decision, arguing that this would imply the horizontal direct effect of a directive not properly transposed into national law.

Depending on the proceedings, reliance on a directly effective provision of Union law can lead to full or partial annulment of the decision taken by the competent authority, to an award of damages, or to any other order the national

---

[119] Case 103/88 *Fratelli Costanzo* [1989] ECR 1839. Cf. on the *Costanzo* obligation Verhoeven (2011).

[120] Dutch *Raad van State* 26 November 2003 [2004] *M&R* 39.

[121] Directive 76/464 is repealed by Directive 2006/11 on pollution caused by certain dangerous substances discharged into the aquatic environment of the Community, OJ 2006 L 64/52.

[122] Dutch *Raad van State* 23 October 2002 [2003] *M&R* 4 and 5. The cases are also mentioned in Annex VI, Application of Community law by national courts: a survey. Twentieth annual report on monitoring the application of Community law (2002), COM (2003) 669. Similar problems occurred with respect to the duty to apply Article 6 (3) of the Habitat Directive, Dutch *Raad van State* 7 December 2005 [2006] *M&R* 19.

court is capable of imposing on the public authorities under national law. As far as environmental law is concerned the problem of direct effect will primarily arise in public law disputes before the various administrative courts. Where the competent authorities take concrete decisions, for example by granting, withdrawing or changing environmental permits, it will generally be the courts with jurisdiction over such matters that will be competent to decide disputes. Where directly effective provisions of Union law are at issue, this may result in the national law or decree in question being ignored or annulled.

In some Member States, in cases concerning actions based on the unlawfulness of acts by the State resulting from its failure to fulfil obligations under an environmental directive, the competent courts will be the civil courts. In principle this can lead to the award of damages, an injunction, etc. Dutch civil courts, for instance, have accepted that breaches of directly effective provisions of environmental directives by public authorities are unlawful.

When the direct effect of Union law is invoked in criminal proceedings, this will often involve a situation in which the national law prohibits something which ought not to have been prohibited according to a directive. Defendants who successfully invoke Union law will be acquitted, as the charges will not constitute a criminal offence. In such cases the national provision on which the charges were based will be set aside or held inapplicable.

> The *Ratti* case provides a clear example of this.[123] Similarly, in the *Red Grouse* case regarding the infringement of certain prohibitions in the Dutch *Vogelwet* concerning the sale of species threatened with extinction, the Court decided that these prohibitions were at variance with the Treaty.[124] In this case a restaurant in The Hague had sold red grouse, a protected bird under the *Vogelwet*. The owner argued that he had bought the birds in the United Kingdom, where the species is not protected. The Court held that the Dutch prohibitions breached the rules on the free movement of goods. Here, too, the decision of the Court resulted in acquittal in the criminal proceedings before the national court.[125]

Integral application of directives, protection of the rights of individuals and non-application of conflicting national laws are thus the most important legal consequences of the direct effect of directives. But what does this mean for environmental law in practice? What precisely has to be applied in its entirety? The answer to these questions depends on what exactly the environmental directive requires. In each instance it has to be borne in mind that the basis for direct effect resides in the obligations the directive imposes on the Member States. Thus each provision of each directive has to be examined to determine what obligations it imposes. This implies also that if a directive provides for various options out of which the Member States may choose, direct effect, in the

---

[123] Case 148/78 *Ratti* [1979] ECR 1629.

[124] Case C-169/89 *Gourmetterie v.d. Burg* [1990] ECR I-2143.

[125] Dutch *Hoge Raad* 20 November 1990 *Gourmetterie v.d. Burg* [1991] NJ 241.

Kraaijeveld meaning, does not require the national court to take the place of the national legislature on which alone it is incumbent to choose the option which it deems appropriate. The fact that directly effective provisions of environmental directives have to be applied in their entirety therefore implies a wide diversity of application modalities.

In the case of directives laying down product standards, which generally aim for total harmonisation, direct effect implies that a product which satisfies the environmental requirements contained in the directive must be allowed on the market, whereas a product which does not meet the requirements must be refused. Or, as was held in the *Braathens* case, which concerned a Swedish energy tax incompatible with Directive 92/81, individuals were entitled to rely on the directive to oppose the taxation.[126]

In environmental directives involving minimum harmonisation, for example directives concerning the quality of water and air, direct effect resides in the limits the directive establishes in respect of the maximum level of pollution. In such cases it is these minimum limits that must be applied. Application of directly effective emission standards or quality standards prevents the lawful application of national environmental law which is not sufficiently stringent in the light of European environmental standards.

In the derogation clauses described above, for example the exemptions from the obligation to carry out an environmental impact assessment, direct effect resides in the limitations of these powers of exemption. This means that the power of derogation as such is not subject to judicial control, but only the extent to which the authorities have remained within the limits allowed by the directive. The significance of this remark becomes apparent if a closer look is taken at the powers of exemption contained in the EIA Directive.

Above it was stated that the powers of exemption contained in Dutch EIA legislation were too wide by comparison with Article 2(3) of the directive. In proceedings before the competent Dutch court the Dutch exemption provisions were set aside on the ground that they were incompatible with the directly effective provision in the directive.[127] Consequently, the power to grant exemptions conferred by Dutch law could no longer be applied and all such projects had to be made subject to an EIA. In a situation like this the question arises whether the competent authorities can directly invoke the powers of exemption contained in the directive. If this is a case of direct effect, it could be argued that this provision should be applied. This need not, however, follow from the direct effect of Article 2(3) of the EIA Directive for the following reasons. The directive does not impose an obligation to grant an exemption when an exceptional case arises. It merely creates the power to do so. It does not give holders of a planning permit a right to be exempted. The question whether an exemption should be granted or not is not addressed by the directive. The directive has no direct effect in this respect. Direct effect, and hence the

---

[126] Case C-346/97 *Braathens Sverige AB* [1999] ECR I-3419. See on this case also section 7.4 of Chapter 2.

[127] Dutch *Raad van State* 11 November 1991 *Rosmalen/Geffen* [1992] AB 50.

obligation for Member States, resides in the limitation of the use of these powers to exceptional cases. In other words, the directive requires Member States to limit the exercise of their powers of exemption to exceptional cases. This limitation has direct effect and should be applied in the sense of *Fratelli Costanzo*.[128] Nothing more is meant by application than 'fulfilling obligations'. In view of the fact that the directive does not provide for an obligation to grant an exemption when an exceptional case occurs, a secretary of state or minister cannot directly invoke the directive. Such a form of 'application' of environmental law would amount to what has been referred to above as 'inverse vertical direct effect'. It would be the State which invoked an unimplemented provision of a directive as against an individual and not the other way round as is usually the case where direct vertical effect is concerned.

It must therefore be concluded that the obligations under a directive and the rights it aims to protect must be determined in each individual case. However, it will generally not be easy to determine what obligations the directive imposes and what rights it aims to protect. The conclusion must therefore be that the extent to which the national authorities can apply unimplemented provisions depends on what obligations the directive imposes and what rights of individuals it aims to protect. This requires careful examination by the national courts in each case and for each directive.

3   The Doctrine of Consistent Interpretation[129]

National courts are required, when applying national law,[130] to interpret that law, once the period for transposition has expired,[131] *as far as possible*,[132] so as to be consistent with Union[133] law. An interpretation which causes national law to conflict with European law must where possible be avoided. The national court is required to do its utmost when interpreting national law to reflect, as far as possible, the substance of Union law in question. In *Marleasing*, the Court observed:

'In applying national law, whether the provisions in question were adopted before or after the directive, the national court called upon to interpret it is required to do

---

[128] Case 103/88 *Fratelli Costanzo* [1989] ECR 1839.

[129] This section builds upon Jans et al. (2007), Chapter IV.

[130] Case C-131/97 *Carbonari* [1999] ECR I-1103, para. 48.

[131] Case C-212/04 *Adeneler* [2006] ECR I-6057.

[132] Or 'the fullest extent possible'; Case C-240/09 *Lesoochranárske zoskupenie VLK*, Judgment of 8 March 2011, para. 50.

[133] Including international treaties, like the Aarhus Convention, to which the EU is a party. Cf. with respect to the obligation to interpret national law consistent with Article 9(3) of the Aarhus Convention: Case C-240/09 *Lesoochranárske zoskupenie VLK*, Judgment of 8 March 2011, para. 50.

so, as far as possible, in the light of the wording and the purpose of the directive in order to achieve the result pursued by the latter and thereby comply with the third paragraph of Article 189 EC [now Article 288 TFEU].'[134]

In *Pfeiffer* the Court further specified this requirement by stating that 'if the application of interpretative methods recognised by national law enables, in certain circumstances, a provision of domestic law to be construed in such a way as to avoid conflict with another rule of domestic law or the scope of that provision to be restricted to that end by applying it only in so far as it is compatible with the rule concerned, the national court is bound to use those methods in order to achieve the result sought by the directive.'[135] The qualification *as far as possible* indicates that the requirement is not unlimited. In *Kolpinghuis* the Court of Justice observed that the obligation to interpret national law in the light of Union law is limited 'by the general principles of law and in particular the principle of legal certainty'.[136]

Consider the following example: in a given Member State, national rules explicitly permit discharges of certain substances into surface water, even though the relevant directive requires Member States to prohibit such discharges. In this kind of situation, individuals consulting the national rules are surely entitled to assume that they 'mean what they say'.

In such a case, consistent interpretation would imply a *contra legem* interpretation of national law. In *Pupino* the Court of Justice has explicitly ruled that, for reasons of legal certainty, interpretation *contra* the law should be rejected and made clear that national administrative courts are not in fact required to interpret national rules in this way.[137]

Remedial and non-remedial interpretation

The issue of interpretation in the light of EU law is particularly, but not exclusively,[138] relevant in relation to the transposition of provisions of directives. The third paragraph of Article 288 TFEU requires that directives be transposed into national law, but leaves the choice of 'form and methods' to the national authorities. This transposition requirement, in combination with some measure of discretion as regards implementation, may result in a degree of tension between European and national law. Provisions of directives often turn out not to have been incorporated word for word into national implementing legislation.

---

[134] Case C-106/89 *Marleasing* [1990] ECR I-4135.

[135] Joined Cases C-397/01 to C-403/01 *Pfeiffer* [2004] ECR I-8835, para. 116.

[136] Case 80/86 *Kolpinghuis* [1987] ECR 3969, para. 13.

[137] Case C-105/03 *Pupino* [2005] ECR I-5285, para. 47. Cf. also Case C-212/04 *Adeneler a.o.* [2006] ECR I-6057.

[138] Cf. Case C-165/91 *Van Munster* [1994] ECR I-4661 on the requirement for national courts to interpret domestic law in the light of the aims of the Treaty.

In such cases the national courts will consult the directive to ensure that EU law is properly applied.

But even where the national legislature has stuck literally to the text of the directive, national courts have to be constantly aware of EU law. Due in part to the influence of the case law of the Court of Justice, the meaning of terms contained in directives, and thus national law (because of the obligation to interpret national provisions in the light of the wording and purpose of the directive), may change significantly with time.

> To appreciate this it is sufficient to refer to the case law of the Court of Justice concerning the meaning of the terms 'waste' in Directive 75/442 and 'discharge' in Directive 76/464 and the consequences this has had for the substance of national legislation and thus for national implementation.[139] National courts have to be constantly aware of developments in European law to ensure they do not interpret these terms in national environmental legislation in a manner which would be at odds with the European directives. This also makes it clear that the necessity to interpret national law in the light of European law is not confined to cases where the text of national law actually conflicts with European law.

In addition, there are of course cases in which consistent interpretation is applied in a situation where national law does indeed conflict with European law. If the national court is able successfully to interpret the national rules so as to accord with European rules, this avoids a conflict with European law in the specific case. Whether or not it is possible in this kind of case to interpret the national rules in the light of European law depends largely on the nature of the conflict. Where the national norm is in line with the European norm, but the national implementing legislation is inadequate, it will generally be possible to resolve the conflict by means of consistent interpretation. This will be particularly true where the national norm contains terms which may be interpreted in several ways. However, where the national norm is diametrically opposed to the European norm, consistent interpretation is at some point likely to conflict with the principle of legal certainty.

Nevertheless, even where the national court is able to resolve the conflict between the national and the European rules satisfactorily, the national legislature is not released from its obligation to ensure that proper implementing legislation is put in place.[140] Courts can be said to interpret national law in conformity with a directive when they construe national provisions in a way which is different from the normal manner of interpretation and where a 'normal' interpretation would have produced a result which was at odds with the directive. This manner of interpretation is therefore in many ways artificial

---

[139] Cf. Chapter 8, section 17.1.

[140] Cf. Case C-50/09 *Commission* v. *Ireland*, Judgment of 3 March 2011, para. 47, concerning the practice of the Irish Supreme Court of interpreting the provisions of Irish law in the light of the EIA Directive.

and irregular and serves only as a makeshift for poor implementation. Full and correct implementation is necessary to put an end to legal uncertainty.

An example of this 'remedial'[20] variant is the judgment of the Dutch *Raad van State* (Council of State) in the *ATM* case.[21]

> This case concerned the relationship between the then Article 10.36a of the Dutch *Wet milieubeheer* (Environmental Management Act; *Wm*) and the second paragraph of Article 4(6) of Directive 84/631, as it then was, concerning transfrontier shipments of hazardous waste. The problem was that, under the Dutch statute, the export of waste could be prohibited if that might jeopardise the implementation of plans and programmes prepared by the Dutch environment minister for the disposal of hazardous waste. The directive only regarded an export ban as permitted if this 'would adversely affect the implementation of a plan prepared pursuant to Article 12 of Directive 78/319 or Article 6 of Directive 76/403.' The national court compared the two provisions and concluded that the Dutch legislation was drafted too broadly and allowed an obstruction of exports on grounds that were not consistent with those of the directive. It referred to a defect in the Dutch legislation regarding the implementation of the applicable Community law. In this case it decided to interpret the domestic legislation in the light of the European rules: the defect in the Dutch Act could 'given its nature and extent, be resolved by interpreting this part of the Article in the light of the wording and purpose of the applicable directives.'

Where the domestic court interprets the domestic rules so as to give full effect to European rules, it is using the 'superior' rule of EU law in order to be able to apply national law properly.

Consistent interpretation must thus be regarded as a means of ensuring a national court does not take a decision which is incompatible with Union law. It follows from the Court's case law that the duty of national courts to interpret national law in the light of Union law applies not only to relations between the State and the individual, but also to relations between individuals.[141] In such cases, some indirect horizontal effects would seem to be recognised.[142]

Consistent interpretation of private law

The significance of this doctrine for private environmental law is illustrated in the *Cockerill Sambre* case referred to above.[143] Although there was no question of the emission limit values laid down in Directive 76/464[144] having true horizontal direct effect, the question nevertheless arose to what extent inter-

---

[141] Case C-106/89 *Marleasing* [1990] ECR I-4135.

[142] See the Opinion of Advocate General Darmon in Case C-236/92 *Comitato di coordinamento per la difesa della Cava* v. *Regione Lombardia* [1994] ECR I-485, para. 28.

[143] Dutch District Court Maastricht 3 February 1993 *Cockerill Sambre* [1993] MR 17.

[144] Now repealed by Directive 2006/11 on pollution caused by certain dangerous substances discharged into the aquatic environment of the Community, OJ 2006 L 64/52.

pretation in the light of the directive might have given rise to an obligation for Cockerill Sambre to comply with the limit values. It should be remembered that since *Marleasing* the national courts are obliged to interpret national law 'as far as possible' in conformity with the directive. Although opinions may differ as to the precise meaning of the phrase, national law must presumably be sufficiently flexible to allow such an interpretation. If express environmental legislation had existed which would have allowed Cockerill Sambre to carry out certain environmentally harmful activities, this rule of interpretation would have been of little use. After all, the national courts can hardly change something which is expressly permitted into something which is prohibited. *Contra legem* interpretation is to rejected as this would conflict with the requirement of legal certainty.[145] Similarly, where a polluter acts in accordance with an authorisation which has been recently and validly granted, it would seem hard to defend the position that it is unlawful to act in accordance with its conditions because the limit values of the directive have been exceeded. This despite the fact that in some Member States, like the Netherlands, liability law does not automatically preclude an action for damages, even if the defendant has acted in conformity with the permit. In this type of case, direct action against the authorised discharge would be unlikely to succeed and interested third parties would be well advised to challenge any acts or decisions of the authorities by invoking the (vertical) direct effect of the limit values.

Under Union law direct action at the national level against an authorised polluter would only seem possible in a national legal situation which is open to multiple interpretations. In such a case the polluter could be required to act in accordance with the provisions and standards contained in a directive by interpreting the national law in conformity with the directive. In particular it could be argued that the 'duty of care', a central concept of liability law in many national legal systems, should be interpreted in the light of the limit values contained in the directive. The violation of limit values (or other obligations) contained in environmental directives which have not been implemented would constitute a breach of the duty of care, and hence be unlawful. As has already been observed, this would only be practicable if the courts have sufficient leeway to apply this rule of interpretation.

Consistent interpretation of criminal environmental law

Interpreting national criminal environmental law in this manner will obviously have to be approached even more cautiously than is the case with private and administrative law.[146] After all, it might result in an act becoming an offence which would not have been if the directive had not existed. As the Court of Justice has recognised, the principle that penal provisions may not have retroactive effect is one which is common to all the legal orders of the Member States.[147]

---

[145] Case C-105/03 *Pupino* [2005] ECR I-5285, para. 47.

[146] Case C-105/03 *Pupino* [2005] ECR I-5285, para. 47.

[147] Case 63/83 *Kent Kirk* [1984] ECR 2689.

It is incompatible with the requirement of legal certainty. The significance for the environment sector was made clear in the *Arcaro* case.[148]

> In this case the Court answered several question referred to it by the *Pretura di Vicenza* in connection with criminal proceedings before that court. Arcaro was suspected of having discharged cadmium into surface water in contravention of Italian rules on the subject. These rules were designed to implement a number of European directives concerning industrial discharges of dangerous substances into water. Under the Italian legislation only new plant was required to obtain an authorisation and not existing plant such as Arcaro's. This was in breach of the directive, the Court ruled, as it makes any discharge, irrespective of the date on which the plant from which it comes commenced operation, subject to the issue of a prior authorisation. The Court also confirmed that a directive may not by itself create obligations for an individual and that a provision of a directive may not therefore be relied upon as such against such a person. Referring to earlier judgments, it observed that this case law seeks to prevent a Member State from taking advantage of its own failure to comply with Union law. Consequently, a directive cannot, of itself and independently of a national law adopted by a Member State for its implementation, have the effect of determining or aggravating the liability in criminal law of persons who act in contravention of the provisions of that directive. A public authority may not therefore rely on the directive against an individual. The *Pretura* was still keen to know whether there were any means available to it which would enable it to apply the Italian legislation, despite the fact that the directive had not been fully transposed. Could the rules be interpreted otherwise than in the light of the directive? The Court replied in the following terms: 'the obligation of the national court to refer to the content of the directive when interpreting the relevant rules of its own national law reaches a limit where such an interpretation leads to the imposition on an individual of an obligation laid down by a directive which has not been transposed or, more especially, where it has the effect of determining or aggravating, on the basis of the directive and in the absence of a law enacted for its implementation, the liability in criminal law of persons who act in contravention of that directive's provisions.'

In other words, the national court's obligation to apply the law in such a way as to achieve the result intended by a directive may not be taken so far that it would cause or compound an individual's criminal liability for failing to comply with provisions of a directive which have not been properly transposed.[149]

Consistent interpretation of public environmental law

In the Netherlands the doctrine of consistent interpretation has frequently been applied with respect to implementing legislation which has been formu-

---

[148] Case C-168/95 *Arcaro* [1996] ECR I-4705.

[149] Case 80/86 *Kolpinghuis* [1987] ECR 3969. Cf. also Joined Cases C-387/02, C-391/02 and C-403/02 *Berlusconi* [2004] ECR I-3565, paras. 74 *et seq.*

lated too broadly in the light of the relevant directive. An example is the judgment of the Dutch *Raad van State* in the *ATM* case.[150]

> This case concerned the relationship between the then section 10.36a of the Dutch
> Environmental Protection Act (*Wet milieubeheer*) and the second paragraph of
> Article 4(6) of Directive 84/631,[151] as it then was, concerning transfrontier ship-
> ments of hazardous waste. The problem was that, under the Dutch statute, the
> export of waste could be prohibited if that might jeopardise the implementa-
> tion of plans and programmes prepared by the Dutch environment minister for
> the disposal of hazardous waste. The directive only regarded an export ban as
> permitted if this 'would adversely affect the implementation of a plan prepared
> pursuant to Article 12 of Directive 78/319/EEC or Article 6 of Directive 76/403/EEC'.
> The national court compared the two provisions and concluded that the Dutch
> legislation was drafted too broadly and allowed an obstruction of exports on
> grounds that were not consistent with those of the directive. It referred to a defect
> in the Dutch legislation regarding the implementation of the applicable Union
> law. In this case it decided to interpret the domestic legislation in the light of the
> European rules: the defect in the Dutch Act could 'given its nature and extent,
> be resolved by interpreting this part of the section in the light of the wording and
> purpose of the applicable directives.'
>
> Another example in Dutch environmental case law can be found in a judgment
> of the Council of State on Directive 2001/18 on the deliberate release into the
> environment of genetically modified organisms.[152] This directive had not been
> transposed precise enough into Dutch law, in particular with respect to the trans-
> position of the precautionary principle. Under the Environmentally Dangerous
> Substances Act (*Wet milieugevaarlijke stoffen*) authorisation had been granted for
> small-scale trials with flowering genetically modified rape. Pursuant to the second
> paragraph of section 26 of the Act, the authorisation could only be refused 'in the
> interest of the protection of man and the environment'. According to the court this
> statutory framework provided sufficient basis for the court to interpret in the light
> of the directive. The obligations set out in the directive, including the precaution-
> ary principle and the duty to carry out a specific environmental risk assessment
> in accordance with the criteria of Annex II of the directive, were 'read into' the
> national law.
>
> An interesting example from German law is the following. Under § 4 bs. 1 Satz
> 2 *Umweltinformationsgesetz* German administrative authorities have a certain
> discretion (*freies Ermessen*) as to whether they supply environmental information
> requested by a citizen by sending copies, or by allowing the citizen to inspect the
> documents on site. The *Bundesverwaltungsgericht* ruled that this discretion must
> be interpreted in the light of the objective of the directive on freedom of access to

---

[150] Dutch *Raad van State* 15 December 1994 [1996] AB 29.

[151] Cf. now Regulation 1013/2006 on shipments of waste, OJ 1993 L 30/1. See Chapter 8, section 17.7.

[152] Dutch *Raad van State* 28 June 2004 [2004] M&R 104.

information on the environment.[153] In this specific case it meant that the administrative body had to send the copies requested even though this was significantly more burdensome than allowing their inspection.

In England the judgment in *R* v. *Secretary of State for the Environment*, ex parte *Greenpeace* is worthwhile mentioning.[154] The case concerned the British Nuclear Fuels Ltd. nuclear waste reprocessing plant at Sellafield. According to the 'justification principle' of Article 6 of the directive 'every activity resulting in an exposure to ionising radiation shall be justified by the advantages which it produces'. The High Court acknowledged that the Radioactive Substances Act 1993 had to be interpreted in the light of Article 6 of the directive.[155]

4 The Significance of *Francovich* for Environmental Law[156]

In the *Francovich* case the Court of Justice ruled that Member States are obliged to make good the losses and damage caused to individuals by breaches of Union law for which they can be held responsible.[157] The doctrine developed in *Francovich* has been refined and elaborated in later cases.[158] Member States can be held responsible for legislative, executive or factual acts. Individuals who have suffered damage have a right to reparation where three conditions are met:

- the rule of law infringed must have been intended to confer rights on individuals;
- the breach must be sufficiently serious;
- and there must be a direct causal link between the breach of the obligation resting on the state and the damage sustained by the injured parties.

In developing its case law on the non-contractual liability of the Member States, the Court has had regard to its case law on liability under Article 340 TFEU. According to the Court's judgment in *Bergaderm*, the liability regimes for the Union institutions and the Member States are founded on the same basis.[159]

---

[153] BverwGE 102, 282, 286. See on this directive, Chapter 8, section 16.

[154] [1994] 4 All ER 352. Cf. on this case Davies (2004) at 107.

[155] Interestingly, in a Dutch case the Council of State relied on the doctrine of direct effect in order to apply the justification principle of Article 6 of the Directive; Dutch *Raad van State* 27 March 1991 [1991] AB 537.

[156] This section builds upon Jans et al. (2007), Chapter VIII. The national case law discussed in this chapter is largely taken from the various Annual Reports of the Commission on monitoring the application of Union law, and the *Francovich* Follow-up website at http://www.eel.nl (last visited 7 October 2011).

[157] Joined Cases C-6/90 and C-9/90 *Francovich* [1991] ECR I-5357.

[158] Joined Cases C-46/93 and C-48/93 *Brasserie du pêcheur and Factortame* [1996] ECR I-1029 and Joined Cases C-178/94, C-179/94, C-188/94, C-189/94 and C-190/94, *Dillenkofer a.o.*[1996] ECR I-4845.

[159] Cf. Case C-352/98 P *Bergaderm* [2000] ECR I-5291, para. 41.

Liability applies in respect of whatever organ of the State was responsible for the breach.[160] In terms of environmental law, this means that local and regional authorities must also ensure that they do not act in breach of Union law when applying national environmental rules.[161] This can give rise to problems, especially when such local or regional authorities are applying 'superior' national environmental rules in good faith. The question of who to hold liable, the State or the local or regional authority, is not easily answered. On the one hand it is the State which is the cause of the problem – it should have ensured the legislation was in order – but on the other hand local and regional authorities have a responsibility of their own, as is clear from the judgment in *Fratelli Costanzo*.[162] In principle, it could be argued that any person suffering loss or damage as a result of the application of legislation which is not in conformity with Union law can hold both the State and the local or regional authority in question liable.[163] The question which then arises, as to the relationship between the State and the local or regional authority, is a matter for national law.[164]

It is on the basis of the rules of national law of liability that the State must make reparation for the consequences of loss and damage caused. The procedural rules governing this Union-inspired state liability are hence governed by national law. National liability law, including its procedural rules, therefore serve as a 'vehicle' for a remedy of state liability based on Union law. However, national provisions which are more restrictive than the conditions formulated in *Francovich* must be ignored.[165] Since it is not a requirement for reparation that provisions have direct effect, breaches of provisions which lack direct effect may also give rise to liability. Below the various conditions for state liability and the manner in which they are applied in respect of European environmental law will be considered.

4.1   The Breach Must be Sufficiently Serious

In the context of the obligation to implement Union environmental law, a breach will be sufficiently serious if:
· a Member State has failed to take legislative measures, for instance to implement an environmental directive, unless the Member State was entitled to assume that its legislation was already satisfactory;
· a Member State has taken legislative measures, but not the right ones, while it could have known that the measures it had taken were not satisfactory.

---

[160] Joined Cases C-46/93 and C-48/93 *Brasserie du pêcheur and Factortame* [1996] ECR I-1029, in particular para. 32. Cf. Wennerås (2004).

[161] Cf. Case C-302/97 *Konle* [1999] ECR I-3099.

[162] Case 103/88 *Fratelli Costanzo* [1989] ECR 1839.

[163] Cf. Case C-424/97 *Haim II* [2000] ECR I-5123.

[164] Cf. Case C-302/97 *Konle* [1999] ECR I-3099.

[165] Cf. Case C-177/88 *Dekker* [1990] ECR I-3941.

In cases other than those where a Member State is required to implement Union environmental law, legislative activities of a Member State would initially have been regarded as involving a sufficiently serious breach if it could be concluded that the Member State could not, in good faith, believe that its action was compatible with Union law. Since *Bergaderm*, it must be assumed that the crucial element in relation to legislative acts is how broad the Member State's discretion is.[166] If the Member State has only considerably reduced or even no discretion, the mere infringement of Union law is sufficient. If it does have a real choice, the decisive test is whether there has been a manifest and grave disregard of the limits of that discretion.[167]

If the Member State has no discretion, as in respect of time limits for implementation (which must be met regardless), a mere breach will at the same time constitute a sufficiently serious breach. If there is discretion, application of the system developed by the Court of Justice amounts in practice to little more than a test of whether the Member State could reasonably have arrived at the assumption that the decision or act was compatible with Union law.

4.2   Conferring Rights on Individuals

As regards the condition that the rule infringed must be intended to create rights for individuals, the following remarks must be made. Firstly, the question of whether a rule of Union law implies 'rights for individuals' is not only relevant in relation to the liability of Member States for infringements. As has been demonstrated in Chapter 4, the Court of Justice also uses the concept 'rights for individuals' in order to determine which provisions from directives must be transposed into national law. Thus it emerges from the case law of the Court, in the context of infringement proceedings brought against a Member State for failure to transpose a directive, that the Court is fairly willing to accept that a directive creates 'rights for individuals'. All kinds of obligations in environmental directives have been held create 'rights for individuals', even where the scope of the protection afforded by these directives is very broad.[168]

The following example may help to clarify this. In Case C-186/91, the Belgian Government argued that the obligation set out in Article 11 of Directive 85/203 on air quality standards for nitrogen dioxide, requiring Member States to hold transboundary consultations, did not confer rights on individuals and therefore did not require incorporation into national law; the Court rejected this argument.[169]

---

[166] Cf. Case C-5/94 *Hedley Lomas* [1996] ECR 2553 and Case C-352/98 P *Bergaderm* [2000] ECR I-5291.

[167] Case C-352/98 P *Bergaderm* [2000] ECR I-5291, para. 43. Cf. on discretion Hilson (2005).

[168] E.g. Case C-361/88 *Commission v. Germany* [1991] ECR I-2567.

[169] Case C-186/91 *Commission v. Belgium* [1993] ECR I-851. See now Article 25 of Directive 2008/50 on ambient air quality and cleaner air for Europe, OJ 2008 L 152/1.

However, it hardly seems tenable to argue that the mere infringement of a procedural obligation to hold transboundary consultations could result in individuals being able to hold a Member State liable. This example makes it clear that a provision of a directive that has to be transposed into national law because it creates 'rights for individuals' does not necessarily have to be qualified as 'conferring rights on individuals' in terms of state liability.[170]

Secondly, complex problems concerning 'rights for individuals' were also discussed in section 2.1 of this chapter in relation to direct effect. In *Brasserie du Pêcheur*, concerning the infringement of the directly effective Article 34 and 49 TFEU, the Court stated that these provisions 'have direct effect in the sense that they confer on individuals rights upon which they are entitled to rely directly before the national courts. Breach of such provisions may give rise to reparation.' The question is whether the Court intended to say that directly effective provisions by definition create rights for individuals which are relevant in the context of the case law on liability. This seems highly doubtful, particularly in the light of the judgment in *Peter Paul*.[171] However, some authors still argue that '[...], infringements of Community provisions that are directly effective satisfy the first condition for state liability'.[172]

In summary, even though the case law is not entirely clear on the matter, it must be assumed that the Court of Justice does not always apply the concept 'rights for individuals' consistently. In other words, the term may have one meaning in the context of direct effect and another in the context of state liability and yet another in relation to the transposition of directives.[173]

Thirdly, it is the authors' opinion that this condition may be expected to cause some particular problems inside the field of Union environmental law. The point is that most of European environmental law does not *specifically* aims to protect the rights of individuals, but is intended to protect 'the public and/or the environment in general'. For instance, can one really say that the Habitats and Wild Birds Directives are intended to confer rights on individuals? This will be discussed in the next paragraph more extensively.

Also, but not specifically

From the case law of the Court of Justice, in particular from its judgment in *Peter Paul*, we must assume that it is not sufficient if the rule that had been infringed *also* protected the interests of the claimant, but that the rule infringed should *specifically* have the objective to protect individuals.[174] This case law

---

[170] See for an opposite view Wennerås (2007) at 152. In the authors' view, it is also unlikely that the mere infringement by a Member State of its obligation to notify the Commission under Article 193 TFEU will give rise to state liability.

[171] Case C-222/02 *Peter Paul a.o. v. Germany* [2004] ECR I-9425.

[172] Wennerås (2007) at 152.

[173] Cf. Prechal (2005), 97-111.

[174] Case C-222/02 *Peter Paul a.o. v. Germany* [2004] ECR I-9425. See for an opposite view Wennerås (2007) 154-155.

amounts to introducing a rather strict *Schutznorm* requirement into EU state liability law. However, the case law of the Court of Justice does not seem to be consistent in all respects. Take, for example, the directly effective obligations under the EIA Directive. Under this directive, an environmental impact assessment must have been carried out before consent is given for certain projects likely to have significant effects on the environment. From the case law of the Court of Justice it is clear that interested third parties may rely on these provisions before the national courts.[175] However, it cannot be said that the directive gives third parties a right to have an environmental impact assessment carried out. They are only affected indirectly by the obligations of the state. Nevertheless, in *Wells,* the Court of Justice stated, albeit in an *obiter,* that a Member State may be liable for a breach of the obligation not to grant a consent before an environmental impact assessment has been carried out.[176] Apparently it found that this was a provision 'intended to confer rights on individuals'. Be this as it may, a *Schutznorm* requirement can be found in most national laws on (state) liability. It is therefore not surprising that national courts have also applied a similar strict *Schutznorm* requirement.

In the first place, the Dutch *Gerechtshof Den Haag* (The Hague appeal court) in a judgment concerning Article 5 in combination with Annex III of the Nitrates Directive (91/676) must be mentioned.[177] Under this provision, Member States must establish and implement action programmes to reduce and prevent pollution caused by nitrates. The measures to be included in the action programmes must ensure that the amount of livestock manure applied to the land each year does not exceed 170 kg per hectare. In the view of the *Gerechtshof* these provisions were not intended to confer rights on individuals on the basis of which individuals could hold the state liable for the cost of purifying ground and surface water, or the cost of alternative drinking water. It held that the directive did not lay down the obligation to guarantee a particular quality of water, upon which individuals could base quality entitlements as against the state. This judgment seems to be at odds with a judgment of the French *Tribunal administratif* (administrative court) at Rennes.[178] In 1995, the *Tribunal d'instance* (district court) at Guincamp had ordered the Société Suez Lyonnaise des Eaux to pay compensation to 176 subscribers of its drinking water distribution network on account of the excessive nitrate content of the water it distributed. The Société accordingly brought proceedings before the *Tribunal administratif* to obtain compensation for the state's late transposition of Article 5 of Directive 91/676. The *Tribunal* accepted this argument and concluded that the state was liable.

---

[175] Case C-201/02 *Wells* [2004] ECR I-723, para. 66.

[176] Case C-201/02 *Wells* [2004] ECR I-723, para. 66.

[177] Dutch *Gerechtshof* Den Haag 27 October 2005 (*Waterpakt*) [2006] *M&R* 4.

[178] French *Tribunal administratif* Rennes, 2 May 2001, *Société Suez Lyonnaise des Eaux,* req. No 97182. Reported in the Nineteenth annual report on monitoring the application of Community law; COM (2002) 324.

In the second place we refer to an English judgment in *Bowden* v. *South West Water and Another*, where a mussel fisherman claimed that he had been driven out of business because his fishing waters had been classified under a directive and because of pollution of the waters.[179] The fisherman pleaded the breach of the Bathing Waters Directive, the Shellfish Waters Directive and the Urban Waste Water Directive. The Court of Appeal formulated the test to be applied as follows: 'The question is whether the provision was adopted in order to protect the interests of the person who claims to be entitled to a right under the directive [...].' The High Court judge who heard the case, whose conclusion was followed by the Court of Appeal, noted that the plaintiff's claim was as a fisherman and observed that neither the Bathing Waters Directive nor the Urban Waste Water Directive was intended to confer rights on mussel fisherman: 'There is nothing in either which could possibly be said to entail the grant of rights to shell-fisherman, or which would enable the content of any such a right to be identified. They are concerned with different subject matter. Of course, improvements in water quality for bathers, and in treatment standards of waste water, may assist other interest groups, but that is not enough to give them a right of action.' As regards the Shellfish Directives, the Court of Appeal agreed with the High Court judge that they were at least related to the plaintiff's activities and that it could be said that if there was a failure by the United Kingdom to implement or to comply with the requirements of those directives it could have contributed to the loss of the plaintiff's fishing grounds. However, if there was a breach, it would be a breach of an obligation owed to the public in general and there was nothing to tie such a breach to specific rights of individuals or which would enable the content of such a right to be ascertained. Accordingly, there was no basis for a claim for damages.

This judgment in *Bowden* v. *South West Water and Another* is particularly interesting because the court adopted the position that where the rule infringed aims to protect 'the public in general', it could not give rise to a successful claim for damages. If this position were correct, it would mean that infringements by the state of, for example, environmental (air and water) quality standards could not give rise to liability.

4.3   Direct Causal Link

At present there is no question of a clearly developed Union doctrine of causality. The Court refers to the requirement of a direct causal link. But though it is a matter for the national courts to decide whether there is a direct causal link, it is not clear to what extent causality may be interpreted according to national law. It is therefore not clear what exactly this requirement entails. Nor is it clear to what specific problems this may give rise in relation to environmental law. Nevertheless, the following is worth considering. It is possi-

---

[179] English High Court, 17 December 1997, *Bowden* v. *South West Water and Another* [1998] 3 C.M.L.R. 330 and Court of Appeal, 15 December 1998, [1999] 3 C.M.L.R. 180. Cf. on this case Lee (2005) at 65.

ble that in certain cases parties directly affected might be able to obtain compensation for loss or damage resulting from incorrect implementation. Suppose the authorities have granted a permit on the basis of national legislation which has not yet been adapted to conform with the directive. The permit may be revoked and ultimately the applicant will have to comply with the more stringent requirements. This may well involve additional investment in the production process. It seems likely that these costs, necessary to comply with the more stringent European standard, are not open to compensation. This is because they would have been incurred anyway if the directive had been correctly implemented and it would run counter to the polluter pays principle. On the other hand, costs which have been incurred by an individual relying in good faith on the correctness of national environmental law may qualify for compensation. Certain development costs might, for example, fall in this category.

Another potential problem is the compensation of damage to the environment. To what extent can environmental damage qualify for compensation where a Member State has, for instance, failed to designate special protection areas for birds? And who would be entitled to claim the damage? Or would this example fail by virtue of the simple fact that the standard breached must create rights for individuals?[180]

Francovich shows that an action for damages against the State is possible. However, it is unclear to what extent this embraces reparation for environmental damage other than mere pecuniary damage.[181] Future case law will have to clarify the situation. Moreover, an injunction or other court order will generally prove more useful to interested third parties than damages. To what extent can *Francovich* accommodate these needs? Probably it should not be interpreted too narrowly. *Francovich* after all concerned the detrimental financial consequences of the State's failure to act. As a matter of principle, there appear to be few objections against extending the remedies available to adversely affected individuals if this means that the effect of directives in Member States is strengthened. The significance of this would be that a breach of a provision of an environmental directive which lacked direct effect could also be challenged in court.

5   Access to Justice

5.1   Access to Justice and National Courts

According to Article 19(1) TEU Member States are responsible to provide remedies sufficient to ensure effective legal protection in the fields covered by Union law. We have demonstrated in the previous sections of this chapter that European environmental law is applied before national courts by means of three different mechanisms: through the direct effect of Union envi-

---

[180] Cf. also the Commission's White Paper on Environmental Liability, COM (2000) 66.

[181] Cf. Wennerås (2007) at 156.

ronmental law, through the requirement that national courts interpret national law in conformity with Union environmental law (consistent interpretation) and via the doctrine of state liability for infringements of Union environmental law. However, this presupposes that individuals have access to a national court in order to invoke Union environmental law.

The way in which a provision of Union environmental can be invoked in the national legal system and the form in which this occurs depend largely on national law. According to the established case law of the Court of Justice, it is, in the absence of Union law, for the national legal order of each Member State to designate the competent courts and to lay down the procedural rules for proceedings designed to ensure the protection of the rights which individuals acquire through the direct effect of Union law.[182] In other words, Union law does not in principle concern itself with the manner in which it is applied within the national legal orders. This is known in European law as the principle of procedural autonomy. As an expression of the subsidiarity principle, procedural autonomy implies a degree of variation in the manner in which substantive Union law is applied in the Member States.

However, the Court went on to introduce two requirements which these procedural rules must satisfy. In the first place the rules that govern a dispute with a Union dimension may not be less favourable than those governing similar domestic actions. This is known as the principle of equivalence. In the second place the rules must not render virtually impossible or, at the very least, excessively difficult the exercise of rights conferred by the Union legal order. This is known as the principle of effectiveness.

Hence, private individuals are first and foremost dependent on the legal procedures established by national law. The form in which the direct effect of a provision of Union law can be invoked is therefore primarily[183] determined by national law. Invoking a directly effective provision in interlocutory proceedings before a civil court will produce a different result from the result produced in administrative or criminal proceedings.

And indeed, it has emerged from research[184] that national procedural law varies from one country to the next. There are e.g. differences in time limits for appeal,[185] standing requirements in particular for NGOs, access to legal aid,

---

[182] Case 45/76 *Comet* [1976] ECR 2043; Case 33/76 *Rewe* [1976] ECR 1989 and Case 265/78 *Ferwerda* [1980] ECR 617. Cf. on this so-called *Rewe/Comet* case law: Jans et al. (2007), Chapter 2.

[183] Unless the directive has dealt with the issue. For instance, it must assumed that 'any natural or legal person' whose rights under Directive 2003/4 on public access to environmental information (OJ 2003 L 41/26) are violated has standing in national courts.

[184] See, for example, De Sadeleer et al. (2005).

[185] Cf. English Court of Appeal 12 April 2000 *Regina* v. *North West Leicestershire Country Council, East Midlands International Airport Ltd.*, ex parte *Moses* [2000] Env. L.R. 443. Reasonable time limits have been upheld as being compatible with the requirements of Union law; Case C-188/95 *Fantask* [1997] ECR I-6783.

intensity of judicial review,[186] court and other legal costs[187], differences in the length of judicial proceedings, etc. As a result comparable proceedings may produce very different outcomes.

On the basis of the principle of procedural autonomy, one might expect the Court of Justice to show deference to national rules on access to justice. That this is not always the case can be illustrated by the judgment in *Janecek*.[188]

> Janecek brought an action before the *Verwaltungsgericht* Munich for an order requiring the Freistaat Bayern to draw up an air quality action plan in order to ensure compliance with the relevant air quality directive. According to the German courts, neither the spirit nor the letter of the directive confers *ein subjektives Recht* (a personal right) to have an action plan drawn up. In order to have standing in a German administrative court the possible violation of such *ein subjektives Recht* is a pre-requisite. Relevant in this regard is § 42(2) of the German *Verwaltungs-gerichtsordnung* (German Administrative Procedure Statute) which provides that an action for annulment is only admissible '*wenn der Kläger geltend macht, durch den Verwaltungsakt oder seine Ablehnung oder Unterlassung in seinen Rechten verletzt zu sein.*' [Emphasis added]. Commencing an action for annulment without a violation of 'personal rights'[189] would generally speaking result in a declaration of inadmissibility by the competent administrative court.

According to the Court of Justice 'the natural or legal persons directly concerned by a risk that the limit values or alert thresholds may be exceeded' can rely on the directive. Although it is highly doubtful whether Janecek could be considered an interested party under German procedural law and whether his claim would be admissible, the decision of the Court of Justice certainly seems to imply that the German administrative court has to give a substantive ruling on

---

[186] Cf. with respect to the Aarhus Directive 2003/35 requiring courts to examine the substantive legality of a decision Case C-427/07 *Commission* v. *Ireland* [2009] ECR I-6277, paras. 87-89. Cf. outside environmental law Case C-120/97 *Upjohn Ltd.* [1999] ECR I-223.

[187] Cf. also Case C-427/07 *Commission* v. *Ireland* [2009] ECR I-6277, paras. 92-93.

[188] Case C-237/07 *Janecek* [2008] ECR I-6221. See also 'older' case law of the Court on air quality, the so-called German TA Luft cases (Case 361/88 *Commission* v. *Germany* [1991] ECR I-2567 and Case C-59/89 *Commission* v. *Germany* [1991] ECR I-2607). See on these latter cases also section 3.3 of Chapter 4.

[189] According to the prevailing *Schutznorm*-doctrine (doctrine of the protective scope of the norm) in German administrative law a legal norm must specifically aim at the protection of individuals in order to qualify as a *Schutznorm*. And without a *Schutznorm* there is no legal standing in administrative courts. It can and has been argued that applying a too restrictive *Schutznorm* requirement can be at odds with European law and the principle of effective judicial protection in particular. See for instance, referring to the *Streekgewest* case (Case C-174/02 [2005] ECR I-85) in particular, Jans et al. (2007), 289-293. The German literature on this is abundant. See, e.g., Schwerdtfeger (2007). See also the Opinion of Advocate General Sharpston in the *Trianel* case (Case C-115/09, Judgment of 12 May 2011), paras. 28-36 and the Judgment of the ECJ in *Trianel*, to be discussed below.

Janecek's contentions. The Court of Justice seems to require the German court to apply a wider interpretation of the concept 'interested party' than is usual in German law. The reason for this is that directly effective European law is involved; in that case it is sufficient that a person is 'directly concerned' to gain access to the national courts.

Finally, let us give another example, of a rather 'activist' approach of the Court of Justice reviewing national procedural law. This time from the case law on stating reasons for decisions. In *Mellor*, the simple question before the Court of Justice was whether the reasons for an administrative authority's decision determining that a project was not subject to an environmental impact assessment had to be made available to the public.[190] Under English law, reasons only have to be made public where a decision does require an environmental impact assessment and not otherwise.[191] In its decision, the Court seems to be running with the hare and hunting with hounds. It referred to earlier case law and concluded that an administrative authority's decision whether or not an EIA is required 'must contain or be accompanied by all the information that makes it possible to check that it is based on adequate screening, carried out in accordance with the requirements of Directive 85/337.' Nevertheless, it continued:

> 'It does not follow, however, from Directive 85/337, or from the case-law of the Court, in particular, [...] that a determination not to subject a project to an EIA must, itself, contain the reasons for which the competent authority determined that an assessment was unnecessary.'

The duty to state reasons for this kind of 'negative' screening opinion is above all necessary, it emerges from the judgment, in order to protect the interests of third parties. They must be able to satisfy themselves that the administrative authority has acted in accordance with the law, 'if necessary through legal action'. It is interesting that the Court not only refers to 'interested parties' in the generic sense, but in this context also explicitly refers to 'other national authorities concerned'. In the guise of a judgment about the duty to state reasons, it seems that the Court has also given a judgment, again via the back door, about access to the courts, in this case for national authorities.

The importance of Aarhus Directive 2003/35

It is important to note that the *Rewe/Comet* doctrine is applicable only *in the absence* of Union rules on procedural matters. Procedural autonomy applies 'in principle', but there are exceptions. If the Union legislature considers that these differences have become too great in any particular area, it may decide to take legislative action and harmonise national legislation in that area. In such cases, it is not only the substantive law that is harmonised but also the manner in which Member States must apply it. To comply with its obligations under Article

---

[190] Case C-75/08 *Mellor* [2009] ECR I-3799. See also Chapter 8, paragraph 3.2.
[191] See commentary by R. Macrory in ENDS Report 413, June 2009, 55-56.

9(2) and (4) of the Aarhus Convention on access to information, public participation in decision-making and access to justice in environmental matters[192]
the Union legislature enacted Directive 2003/35.[193] The directive more or less
'copy-pasted' Articles 9(2) and (4) of the Convention. This directive provides a
legal framework, for access to justice in the Member States as far as it concerns
decision-making on EIAs and with respect to IPPC installations. To that extent
Directive 2003/35 amended both the IPPC and the EIA Directives. One could
say that the framework of the directive replaces the principle of procedural
autonomy. EIA Directive 85/337, now reads:

> *'Article 10a*
>
> *Access to justice*
> Member States shall ensure that, in accordance with the relevant national legal
> system, members of the public concerned:
> (a) having a sufficient interest, or alternatively,
> (b) maintaining the impairment of a right, where administrative procedural law
> of a Member State requires this as a precondition,
> have access to a review procedure before a court of law or another independent
> and impartial body established by law to challenge the substantive or procedural
> legality of decisions, acts or omissions subject to the public participation provi-
> sions of this Directive.
> Member States shall determine at what stage the decisions, acts or omissions
> may be challenged.
> What constitutes a sufficient interest and impairment of a right shall be deter-
> mined by the Member States, consistently with the objective of giving the public
> concerned wide access to justice. To this end, the interest of any non-govern-
> mental organisation meeting the requirements referred to in Article 1(2), shall
> be deemed sufficient for the purpose of subparagraph (a) of this Article. Such
> organisations shall also be deemed to have rights capable of being impaired for
> the purpose of subparagraph (b) of this Article.
> The provisions of this Article shall not exclude the possibility of a preliminary
> review procedure before an administrative authority and shall not affect the
> requirement of exhaustion of administrative review procedures prior to recourse to
> judicial review procedures, where such a requirement exists under national law.
> Any such procedure shall be fair, equitable, timely and not prohibitively expen-
> sive.
> In order to further the effectiveness of the provisions of this Article, Member
> States shall ensure that practical information is made available to the public on
> access to administrative and judicial review procedures.'

---

[192] OJ 2005 L 124/4, concluded by Council Decision 2005/370, OJ 2005 L 124/1.

[193] OJ 2003 L 156/17. See on this directive more extensively, Chapter 8, sections 3.3, 5 and 7.3.

This directive has now 'produced' its first case law and could prove to have a major impact on national procedural environmental law. The *Djurgården* case can serve as an illustration.[194]

> The case concerned a reference for a preliminary ruling from the Swedish *Högsta domstolen*, which wanted to know whether the directive permitted national legislation that allowed access to a court of law or other independent and impartial body only to non-governmental environmental organisations with at least 2000 members. At the same time, the question arose whether access to the court could be limited on the ground that the persons concerned had already had the opportunity to express their views during the public participation phase of the decision-making procedure. As regards the latter question the Court of Justice observed:
>
> 'It is also apparent therefrom [Article 10a of Directive 85/337, as amended by Directive 2003/35] that any non-governmental organisations which promote environmental protection and meet the conditions which may be required by national law satisfy the criteria, with respect to the public concerned who may bring an appeal, laid down in Article 1(2) of Directive 85/337 read in conjunction with Article 10a.'
>
> '[...] participation in an environmental decision-making procedure under the conditions laid down in Articles 2(2) and 6(4) of Directive 85/337 is separate and has a different purpose from a legal review, since the latter may, where appropriate, be directed at a decision adopted at the end of that procedure. Therefore, participation in the decision-making procedure has no effect on the conditions for access to the review procedure.'[195]

This judgment does not have only serious consequences for Swedish procedural environmental law, but for the law of other Member States as well.

> Dutch law, for instance, contains a provision to the effect that a party may not rely on a breach of a legal rule before a court of law unless this was first raised during the preceding public participation procedure (section 6:13 Dutch General Administrative Law Act). And German administrative procedural law (what is known as *materielle Präklusion*) is comparable to Dutch law in this respect.[196]
>
> In fact, the situation in both Dutch and German law is the reverse of the situation in the Swedish case. As a result of the emphasis on the independent role and function of judicial protection and its separation from the public participation procedure, also in terms of purpose, the question arises to what extent section 6:13 of the Dutch General Administrative Law Act is consistent with the Aarhus

---

[194] Case C-263/08 *Djurgården-Lilla Värtans Miljöskyddsförening* [2009] ECR I-9967. See on this judgment also Reichl (2010).

[195] See also paragraph 48 of the judgment, from which it is clear that access to review procedures may not be limited on the ground that the persons concerned have already been able to express their views in the participatory phase of the decision-making procedure.

[196] Cf. Niedzwicki (2007).

Directive. The Court of Justice decision would seem to imply that as far as access to justice is concerned it is irrelevant whether or not an organisation has taken part in the decision-making procedure.

As regards the '2000-member limit' the Court of Justice ruled that this was also unacceptable. The Court stressed that while it was true that the words 'meet the conditions which may be required by national law' leave it to national legislatures to determine under what conditions environmental organisations may have access to justice, the national rules must both 'ensure 'wide access to justice' and 'render effective' the provisions of the EIA Directive on judicial remedies. The Court concluded:

'Accordingly, those national rules must not be liable to nullify Community provisions which provide that parties who have a sufficient interest to challenge a project and those whose rights it impairs, which include environmental protection associations, are to be entitled to bring actions before the competent courts.'

It is within the Member State's margin of discretion to require that the environmental organisation has as its object the protection of nature and the environment and:

'[I]t is conceivable that the condition that an environmental protection association must have a minimum number of members may be relevant in order to ensure that it does in fact exist and that it is active. However, the number of members required cannot be fixed by national law at such a level that it runs counter to the objectives of Directive 85/337 and in particular the objective of facilitating judicial review of projects which fall within its scope.'

Thus, judgment was passed on the '2000-member criterion':

'The Swedish Government, which acknowledges that at present only two associations have at least 2000 members and thereby satisfy the condition laid down in Paragraph 13 of Chapter 16 of the Environment Act, has in fact submitted that local associations could contact one of those two associations and ask them to bring an appeal. However, that possibility in itself is not capable of satisfying the requirements of Directive 85/337 as, first, the associations entitled to bring an appeal might not have the same interest in projects of limited size and, second, they would be likely to receive numerous requests of that kind which would have to be dealt with selectively on the basis of criteria which would not be subject to review. Finally, such a system would give rise, by its very nature, to a filtering of appeals directly contrary to the spirit of the directive which, as stated in paragraph 33 of this judgment, is intended to implement the Aarhus Convention.'

This part of the judgment might have effects for the law of many other Member States as well.

In this respect too there are parallels with Dutch administrative procedural law. Though Dutch law does not have a 2000-member rule, there are other impediments to environmental organisations desiring to bring a matter before the courts. Recent case law of the Dutch Council of State has made it clear that 'litigation-only' NGOs do not have standing.[197] Whether or not this case law is consistent with the Aarhus Directive is not completely clear.

In similar vein as in *Djurgården* the Court of Justice ruled on restrictions in German administrative procedural law in the *Trianel* case.[198] A judgment which could have significant impact on key topics of national administrative procedural law in many Member States.

In *Trianel*, a German administrative court referred the question whether environmental organisations should be allowed to argue infringement of rules of law that are intended to protect the legal interests of individuals. According to the German *Umweltrechtsbehelfsgesetz* (Environmental Appeals Act) environmental organisations have standing only in judicial review, under the condition that the decision challenged is in violation of legal rules that '*Rechte Einzelner begründen*' (establish individual rights). The Court of Justice found this incompatible with Directive 2003/35, implementing Article 9(2) of the Aarhus Convention. This Directive precludes legislation which does not permit non-governmental organisations to rely before the courts, in an action contesting a decision authorising projects 'likely to have significant effects on the environment' on the infringement of a rule flowing from the environment law of the European Union and intended to protect the environment, on the ground that that rule protects only the interests of the general public and not the interests of individuals. Such a non-governmental organisation has the right to rely before the courts, on the infringement of the rules of national law flowing from the Habitats Directive even where, on the ground that the rules relied on protect only the interests of the general public and not the interests of individuals, national procedural law does not permit this.

Other cases that can be referred to are a number of Belgian cases currently before the Court of Justice, such as Case C-177/09, in which one of the questions raised is to what extent a review procedure should be available before a court of law against decisions of the legislature falling within the scope of the Aarhus directive.[199]

The relevance of Article 9(3) Aarhus Convention

Above we mentioned that Directive 2003/35 regulates access to justice in respect of decisions by Member States on environmental impact assessment and IPPC installations. The preamble to that directive, however, shows that this directive is exclusively intended to implement Article 9 paragraphs 2 and 4 of

---

[197] Cf. Tolsma et al. (2009).

[198] Case C-115/09 *Trianel Kohlekraftwerk Lünen*, Judgment of 12 May 2011.

[199] Case C-177/09 *Le Poumon vert de la Hulpe and others*, pending.

the Aarhus Convention. So what about the legal framework for access to justice in the Member States with respect to environmental decision-making outside EIA and IPPC? Article 9(3) of the Aarhus Convention reads:

'In addition and without prejudice to the review procedures referred to in paragraphs 1 and 2 above, each Party shall ensure that, where they meet the criteria, if any, laid down in its national law, members of the public have access to administrative or judicial procedures to challenge acts and omissions by private persons and public authorities which contravene provisions of its national law relating to the environment'.

A proposal from the Commission to implement the access to justice provisions of Article 9(3) on a full scale via a directive is, politically speaking, 'dead'.[200] The question arises whether Article 9(3) can be relied upon, as a matter of Union law, to gain access to a national court. The Court of Justice dealt with this question in the *Slovak Bears* case, already discussed in section 2 of Chapter 2.[201]

In that case the Slovak Supreme Court referred preliminary questions on the interpretation of the Aarhus Convention to the Court of Justice. In particular, it wanted to know whether Art. 9(3) of the Aarhus Convention is directly effective within the meaning of settled case law of the Court of Justice. The Court denied any direct effect, as a matter of EU law, but continued by stating, that under the principle of effectiveness[202] 'if the effective protection of EU environmental law is not to be undermined, it is inconceivable that Article 9(3) of the Aarhus Convention be interpreted in such a way as to make it in practice impossible or excessively difficult to exercise rights conferred by EU law'. Consequently, 'it is for the national court, in order to ensure effective judicial protection in the fields covered by EU environmental law, to interpret its national law in a way which, to the fullest extent possible, is consistent with the objectives laid down in Article 9(3) of the Aarhus Convention.'

Although, under the principle of procedural autonomy, it is for the domestic legal system of each Member State to lay down the detailed procedural rules governing actions for safeguarding rights which individuals derive from EU law, their discretion seems to be restricted by the Aarhus Convention. In other words, as a matter of Union law there is an obligation on the Member States to interpret their access to justice laws in the light of Article 9(3) of the Aarhus

---

[200] COM/2003/0624 final.

[201] Case C-240/09 *Lesoochranárske zoskupenie VLK*, Judgment of 8 March 2011. See on this judgment also Chapter 2, section 2.

[202] See on this principle section 5.1 of this chapter. This triggers also the intriguing question of whether the LZV could not claim access to the Slovak court on the basis of the principle of effective judicial protection as enshrined in Article 47 of the Charter of Fundamental Rights of the European Union. Cf. Case C-279/09 *DEB Deutsche Energiehandels- und Beratungsgesellschaft*, Judgment of 22 December 2010.

Convention. Although Article 9(3) of the Aarhus Convention is too insufficiently clear and precise an obligation to have direct effect, but apparently, it is precise and clear enough to require the Slovak to court to interpret its laws so as to enable an environmental protection organisation, such as the LZV, to challenge the Slovak ministry's decisions. If this analysis is correct, this can only mean that through the use of consistent interpretation Article 9(3) of the Aarhus Convention is applicable across the full breadth of European environmental law.[203] Furthermore, those environmental groups should be allowed access to a court to challenge decisions that might conflict with the environmental law of the Union. This would not only improve access to justice for NGOs at national level, but would inevitably enhance the legal position of NGOs environmental organisations at the level of the European court(s).[204]

5.2   Legal Protection under Article 263 TFEU

Finally, it is important to devote some attention to another aspect of access to justice. As we have seen in the previous section, the protection of individuals against breaches of Union environmental law by public authorities of the Member States or by other individuals, through the doctrines of direct effect, consistent interpretation and state liability, is largely effected through national procedures. However, where an individual objects to the very substance of Union environmental law, there are few means of obtaining a remedy at national level. Even if the validity of an environmental directive could be challenged before a national court, under Union law the national court is not competent to pronounce on its validity.[205] In that case the national court will avail itself of the preliminary ruling procedure set out in Article 267 TFEU and refer the matter to the Court of Justice. The Treaties do not offer individuals any form of direct legal protection in such a case.

Neither will an action for annulment under Article 263 TFEU offer a solution. Actions for the annulment of legislative acts like *directives* or *regulations* brought by individuals will certainly be declared inadmissible.[206] However, according to the fourth paragraph of Article 263 TFEU '[A]ny natural or legal person may, [...] institute proceedings against an act addressed to that person or which is of direct and individual concern to them...[...]'.

---

[203] Cf. also Ebbeson (2011).

[204] In particular given the consistency argument in para. 42 of the judgment. See also section 5.1 of this chapter.

[205] Case 314/85 *Foto-Frost* [1987] ECR 4199.

[206] Case T-475/93 *Buralux* v. *Council* [1994] ECR 3229 and Case C-209/94 P *Buralux* v. *Council* [1996] ECR I-615. Cf. more recently Case T-16/04 *Arcelor*, Judgment of 2 March 2010, where steel giant company ArcelorMittal was declared inadmissible in its appeal against Directive 2003/87. However, national courts are allowed to refer to the Court of Justice under Article 267 TFEU for a ruling on the validity of such measures; See for instance Case C-27/00 *Omega Air a.o.* [2002] ECR I-2569 and Case C-221/09 *AJD Tuna Ltd*, Judgment of 11 March 2011.

Although the implementation of Union environmental law is largely a matter for the Member States, the Commission can increasingly be seen to possess powers to take acts in the field of or related to the environment. Sometimes these powers are conferred by the Treaties, in other cases by secondary legislation.

An example where the Commission derives its powers from the Treaty is provided by the provisions relating to state aid (Articles 107 and 108 TFEU). These articles are also relevant for the assessment of national aid for the protection of the environment. They give the Commission the power to approve national environmental aids, not to approve them or to make aid subject to certain conditions, and other, more procedural decisions can also be taken.[207]

Another example is provided by the Treaty provisions on competition law (Articles 101 and 102 TFEU). In practice, it has become clear that certain practices of undertakings, even when they concern environmental protection, can conflict with Treaty provisions. Here, too, the Commission has the power to take decisions.[208]

As far as the Commission's powers under secondary legislation are concerned, particular reference is made to the powers of the Commission under Directive 2001/18 on the deliberate release into the environment of genetically modified organisms.[209] Or take the powers of the Commission to allow (or not to allow) access to environmental information in documents under Regulation 1049/2001.[210] Finally, it should be noted that the Commission also has powers to finance projects in the context of the European Regional Development Fund, the European Social Fund and the Cohesion Fund.[211] As provided in Article 17 of Regulation 1083/2006, the objectives of the Funds shall be pursued in the framework of sustainable development and promotion of the goal of protecting and improving the environment. Here, too, the need may be felt for judicial protection against decisions by the Commission which take insufficient account of Union environmental law.

In any event, persons to whom acts of the Commission (or the Council) with an environmental impact are addressed may in any event appeal under Article 263 TFEU. Such an appeal must be lodged with the General Court. In the examples mentioned above, it is sometimes the Member State to which the act is addressed. It is the Member State which is given the option of granting aid for the protection of the environment or not and it is the Member State which can be considered the beneficiary of Structural Fund projects. However, in the case of the Ozone Regulation, it is the importer who should be considered the

---

[207] See Chapter 7, section 7.4.

[208] See on this issue Chapter 7, sections 3 and 4 in particular.

[209] OJ 2001 L 106/1, as amended.

[210] OJ 2001 L 145/43.

[211] Regulation 1083/2006 laying down general provisions on the European Regional Development Fund, the European Social Fund and the Cohesion Fund, OJ 2006 L 210/25.

applicant and the person addressed.[212] In the case of decisions based on the provisions of Articles 101 and 102 TFEU the undertakings concerned should be regarded as the persons addressed.

In addition to the persons to whom an act of the Council or Commission is addressed, third parties may also be admissible in Article 263 proceedings, if the act is of 'direct and individual concern' to them.

Individual concern

The case law of the European Courts, in particular regarding the meaning of 'individual concern' is known under the term '*Plaumann* doctrine'[213] and can briefly be summarised as follows: a third party is individually concerned and his action for annulment admissible if he is affected by the act in a manner which distinguishes him from others. Or, in the words of the Court of Justice:

'persons other than those to whom a decision is addressed may claim to be individually concerned only if that decision affects them by reason of certain attributes which are peculiar to them or by reason of circumstances in which they are differentiated from all other persons and, by virtue of those factors, distinguishes them individually just as in the case of the person addressed'.[214]

While the Union, then E(E)C, was more or less exclusively aimed at market integration, this criterion was sufficient. Where an importer, exporter or other market participant was affected in his particular private interests, the criterion of direct and individual concern would distinguish him from all other market participants. This means that where an 'environmental act' of the Commission (or Council) affects a market participant in his private market interests, there will often be no problem as regards admissibility.

A case in point is the judgment of the Court of First Instance in *Waterleiding Maatschappij 'Noord-West Brabant' NV v. Commission*.[215] The case involved a decision of the Commission not to open formal procedures under the state aid rules of the Treaty against certain environment-related tax relief in Dutch law. With respect to some of the tax relief the Court found that they directly affected the structure of the market in which the applicant operated and therefore affected its competitive position on that market. The applicant therefore had to be regarded as directly and individually concerned by the contested decision of the Commission.

---

[212] Admissibility is no problem whatsoever: cf. Case T-336/94 *Efisol* [1996] ECR II-1343.

[213] Case 25/62 *Plaumann* v. *Commission* [1963] ECR 95, 107. This case law is still very much alive: Case C-50/00 P *Unión de Pequeños Agricultores* v. *Council* [2002] ECR I-6677 and Case C-263/02 P *Commission* v. *Jégo-Quéré* [2004] ECR I-3425. See also Case T-94/04 *EEB a.o.* v. *Commission* [2005] ECR II-4919. Cf. Lee (2005) at 139 *et seq*. Cf. on this case law extensively Schwensfeier (2009).

[214] Cf. Case C-355/08 P *WWF-UK* v. *Council* [2009] ECR I-73, para. 41.

[215] Case T-188/95 *Waterleiding Maatschappij 'Noord-West Brabant' NV* v. *Commission* [1998] ECR II-3713.

The judgment of the Court in Case C-295/92 points in the same direction.[216] This case concerned the intention of the Dutch parliament to adapt taxes on fossil fuels in such a way that the energy content and the carbon content would each count for half. The measure contained a number of exemptions, including one for large-scale industrial users. The measure had been notified to the Commission as state aid within the meaning of Article 107(1) TFEU. The Commission considered the measure compatible with the internal market. The Dutch Agricultural Association (*Landbouwschap*) considered the exemption for large-scale industrial users unlawful and lodged an appeal. There was a background of many years of discussion about the price of gas for the glasshouse sector. The Court of Justice declared the Association inadmissible, because the aid in question would only benefit a group of large industrial undertakings, which were not in competition with either the Association or the glasshouse farmers it represented. According to the Court, the interests of the Association would not be affected in any way whether the Commission decision was upheld or annulled. *A contrario*, it could be inferred from this that if an interested third party is in direct competition and the interests of the third party have been affected by a decision, an appeal would be admissible. In the light of this case law, the legal protection of this category of interested parties would probably cause few problems. The most important condition is that there must be a competitive relationship between the party ultimately benefiting from the decision and the party lodging the appeal.

With respect to a decision of the Commission, which is addressed only to the Member States, concerning the non-inclusion of a certain substance in Annex I to Directive 91/414 and the withdrawal of authorisations for plant protection products containing that substance, the *Cheminova* ase illustrates that 'notifiers' under Directive 91/414 are directly and individually concerned by those decisions.[217] However, merely being a seller or user of such a substance is not sufficient to individualise them for the purposes of Article 263, fourth paragraph, TFEU.[218]

Matters are different however when the act is of a more general and normative character, like its decisions on national plans for the allocation of greenhouse gas emission allowances. An operator of an installation subject to compulsory emissions trading, cannot claim to be individually concerned by these decisions when the decision, addressed to a Member State, affects all undertakings subject to compulsory emission trading in more or less the same way.[219]

---

[216] Case C-295/92 *Landbouwschap* v. *Commission* [1992] ECR I-5003.

[217] Case T-326/07 *Cheminova and others* v. *Commission* [2009] ECR II-2685.

[218] Order T-326/07 R *Cheminova and others* v. *Commission* [2007] ECR II-4877. Upheld in appeal Order C-60/08 P(R) *Cheminova and others* v. *Commission* [2009] ECR I-43. Cf. also Order T-467/07 R *Du Pont de Nemours (France) and others* v. *Commission* [2008] ECR II-40.

[219] Case T-28/07 *Fels-Werke a.o.* v. *Commission* [2007] ECR II-98. Appeal dismissed in Case C-503/07 P *Saint-Gobain Glass Deutschland* v. *Commission* [2008] ECR I-2217.

In that respect we may also point at the *Sahlstedt* case. Private landowners challenged the decision of the Commission, taken under the Habitats Directive, adopting the list of sites of Community importance for the Boreal biogeographical region. Their property was included in the list. The Court of Justice ruled that since the contested decision was not adopted in the light of the specific situation of the landowners, it could not be regarded as a group of individual decisions addressed to each landowner and that appellants are not individually concerned by the decision.[220]

Much more complicated is the admissibility of individuals who object to an act on environmental grounds. Here there are no *private* or *specific* interests at issue but, on the contrary, the *public interest*.

The case law mentioned above, which required that a person's interests be specifically affected cannot, almost by definition, fulfil a distinguishing function here. In other words, the case law is 'private interest biased'.

To give just a very simple example of this bias. When an environmental organisation wants to challenge a measure of the Commission to include paraquat as an active substance under the Pesticide Directive 91/414, they will be declared inadmissible in their action for annulment.[221] However, when a producer of metalaxyl wants to challenge a Commission decision, also taken under the Pesticide Directive 91/414, concerning the non-inclusion of that substance, admissibility is no problem whatsoever.[222]

After all, the key feature of the public interest is that it is universal, applicable to all. If the criterion of 'direct and individual concern' is applied with full force this must inevitably produce the paradoxical result that the more serious the infringement (the harm to the environment) and the wider the group potentially affected the less is the likelihood that the criterion can be met.[223] The judgments of the General Court and the Court of Justice in the *Greenpeace* case discussed below show that both these courts have fallen into this paradoxical trap.[224] The leading case on the admissibility of interested third parties trying to annul decisions affecting the environment is still the *Greenpeace* case.

This case concerned two power stations on the Canary Islands, for which no environmental impact assessment had been prepared. Greenpeace had appealed

---

[220] Case C-362/06 P *Sahlstedt and others v. Commission* [2009] ECR I-2903. Cf. also Case T-150/05 *Sahlstedt and Others v. Commission* [2006] ECR II-1851.

[221] Case T-94/04 *EEB a.o. v. Commission* [2005] ECR II-4919.

[222] Case C-326/05 P *Industrias Químicas del Vallés v. Commission* [2007] ECR I-6557.

[223] Cf. Winter (1999).

[224] Case C-321/95 P *Greenpeace v. Commission* [1998] ECR I-1651. See also, in the same vein, Case T-219/95 R *Danielsson* [1995] ECR II-3051 and Case T-142/03 *Fost Plus v. Commission* [2005] ECR II-589.

against a judgment of the Court of First Instance (now General Court).[225] That Court had declared Greenpeace's action seeking annulment of a Commission decision to pay the Spanish Government ECU 12 million from the European Regional Development Fund for the construction of the two power stations inadmissible. The Court of First Instance had reached this decision referring to the settled case law of the Court of Justice according to which persons other than the addressees may claim that a decision is of direct concern to them only if that decision affects them by reason of certain attributes which are peculiar to them, or by reason of factual circumstances which differentiate them from all other persons and thereby distinguish them individually in the same way as the person addressed. The Court of First Instance observed that whilst this case law concerned essentially cases involving economic interests, the essential criterion which it applied remained applicable whatever the nature, economic or otherwise, of the applicants' interests which were affected.

Accordingly, the Court of First Instance held that the criterion proposed by the applicants for appraising their *locus standi*, namely the existence of harm suffered or to be suffered, was not in itself sufficient to confer *locus standi* on an applicant. This was because such harm might affect, in a general abstract way, a large number of persons who could not be determined in advance in such a way as to distinguish them individually just like the addressee of a decision, as required under the settled case law mentioned above.

There was thus no question of a special regime of *locus standi* in respect of environmental decisions, reflecting the public function of the environment. In this regard the Court of First Instance held that the status of a 'normal' interested third party, such as a 'local resident', 'fisherman' or 'farmer' or of persons concerned by the impact which the building of two power stations might have on local tourism, on the health of Canary Island residents and on the environment did not differ from that of all the people living or pursuing an activity in the areas concerned and that the applicants thus could not be affected by the contested decision otherwise than in the same manner as any other local resident, fisherman, farmer or tourist who was, or might be in the future, in the same situation.

As far as the *locus standi* of the organisation Greenpeace was concerned, the Court of First Instance observed that an association formed for the protection of the collective interests of a category of persons could not be considered to be directly and individually concerned, for the purposes of the fourth paragraph of Article 263 TFEU, by a measure affecting the general interests of that category, and was therefore not entitled to bring an action for annulment where its members could not do so individually.

On appeal the Court of Justice upheld the judgment of the Court of First Instance. It did however consider the argument that the Court of First Instance

---

[225] Case T-585/93 *Greenpeace* v. *Commission* [1995] ECR II-2205. Cf. also Case T-117/94 *Associazione Agricoltori della Provincia di Rovigo a.o.* v. *Commission* [1995] ECR II-455 and Case C-142/95 P *Associazione Agricoltori della Provincia di Rovigo a.o.* v. *Commission* [1996] ECR I-6669.

had failed to take account of the nature and specific characteristics of the environmental interests underpinning the action. It emphasised that it was the decision to build the two power stations in question which was liable to affect the environmental rights arising under the EIA Directive that the appellants sought to invoke. The contested decision, which concerned the Commision's financing of those power stations, could affect those rights only indirectly. As regards the appellants' argument that if they were denied *locus standi* before the Court of Justice, the rights which they derive from the EIA Directive would have no effective judicial protection at all, the Court noted that Greenpeace had also brought proceedings before the national courts challenging the administrative authorisations issued concerning the construction of those power stations. The Court of Justice added that although the subject-matter of those proceedings and of the action brought before the Court of First Instance was different, both actions were based on the same rights afforded to individuals by the EIA Directive, so that those rights were fully protected by the national courts which could refer a question to the Court of Justice for a preliminary ruling. This case law has been severely criticised, and in our opinion rightly.[226]

In fact it seems that the Court of Justice is applying a double standard here. While Member States are required to offer legal protection where rights and obligations under environmental directives are breached,[227] the standard seems to be applied far less strictly to acts and omissions of the Union itself. Furthermore, in these judgments the Court has failed adequately to appreciate that the old remedies, designed to protect private interests, are inadequate to protect public goods, such as the environment. As long as the Court fails to acknowledge this in its case law, the conclusion must be that legal protection against European decisions having significant environmental effects is seriously flawed.

In summary with respect to the notion of 'individual concern', the conclusion seems justified that third parties can rely on little judicial protection against acts taken by the European institutions affecting the environment. This rather bad track-record prompted the Aarhus Compliance Committee to the following statement:

> 'that if the examined jurisprudence of the EU Courts on access to justice were to continue, unless fully compensated for by adequate administrative review procedures, the Party concerned would fail to comply with article 9, paragraph 3, of the Convention.'[228]

---

[226] Cf. Ward (2000) at 154-156.

[227] Cf. cases like Case C-237/07 *Janecek* [2008] ECR I-6221; Case C-263/08 *Djurgården-Lilla Värtans Miljöskyddsförening* [2009] ECR I-9967; Case C-115/09 *Trianel Kohlekraftwerk Lünen*, Judgment of 12 May 2011 and Case C-240/09 *Lesoochranárske zoskupenie VLK*, Judgment of 8 March 2011.

[228] Findings and Recommendations of the Compliance Committee with regard to Communication Accc/C/2008/32 (Part I) Concerning Compliance by the European Union, adopted on 14 April 2011.

It is argued by the authors that the recent judgment in the *Slovak Bears* case makes a change in the case law of the Court of Justice unavoidable.[229] In that case the Slovak court was required to interpret its national law consistent with the objectives laid down in Article 9(3) of the Aarhus Convention, so as to enable an environmental protection organisation to challenge the Slovak ministry's decisions in question. Given the 'consistency argument' in para. 42 of the judgment, this should inevitably also enhance the legal position of environmental organisations at the level of the European court (s). There is no reason why the Court of Justice itself would not be subject to the requirement of an 'Article 9(3) Aarhus-proof interpretation' of Article 263, fourth paragraph, TFEU.

Direct concern

With respect to the condition of 'direct concern' the standard case law of the Court of Justice states:

> 'that for an individual to be directly concerned by a Community measure, [...] it must directly affect the legal situation of the individual and leave no discretion to the addressees of that measure, who are entrusted with the task of implementing it, such implementation being purely automatic and resulting from Community rules without the application of other intermediate rules'.

In the *Inuit Tapiriit Kanatami* case both seal hunters and trappers and those who are active in the processing and/or marketing of seal products challenged Regulation 1007/2009 on trade in seal products.[230] According to the General Court the regulation 'directly affects only the legal situation of those of the applicants who are active in the placing on the market of the European Union of seal products.' And that the regulation does not in any way prohibit seal hunting, which takes place outside the European Union market, or the use or consumption of seal products which are not marketed. Consequently, the seal hunters and trappers are not directly affected, but the market operators are!

Another example is the *Sahlstedt* case, discussed above, where private landowners challenged a decision of the Commission, taken under the Habitats Directive, adopting the list of sites of Community importance that included their lands.[231] The landowners argued that this decision had a significant effect, both legal and factual, on their property rights. The Court of First Instance ruled however that they were not directly concerned:

> 'it cannot be held that the contested decision – which designates, as sites of Community importance, areas of Finland in which the applicants own land –

---

[229] Case C-240/09 *Lesoochranárske zoskupenie VLK,* Judgment of 8 March 2011.

[230] Case T-18/10 *Inuit Tapiriit Kanatami a.o.,* Judgment of 6 September 2011. Regulation 1007/2009 will be discussed in Chapter 8, section 19.4.

[231] Case C-362/06 P *Sahlstedt and others* v. *Commission* [2009] ECR I-2903 and, in first instance, Case T-150/05 *Sahlstedt and Others* v. *Commission* [2006] ECR II-1851.

produces, by itself, effects on the applicants' legal situation. The contested decision contains no provision as regards the system of protection of sites of Community importance, such as conservation measures or authorisation procedures to
be followed. Thus, it affects neither the rights or obligations of the landowners nor
the exercise of those rights. Contrary to the applicants' argument, the inclusion
of those sites in the list of sites of Community importance imposes no obligation
whatsoever on economic operators or private persons.

Article 4(4) of the habitats directive states that once a site of Community
importance has been adopted by the Commission, the Member State concerned
is to designate that site as a 'special area of conservation' within six years at most.
In that regard, Article 6(1) of the habitats directive states that the Member States
are to establish the necessary conservation measures for special areas of conservation, the aim being to meet the ecological requirements of the natural habitat
types and species present on the sites.'

In sum, the CFI ruled that the Finnish landowners are not directly affected
by the decision of the Commission, but by the national measures implementing that decision. It is remarkable, that in appeal, the Court of Justice did not
mention 'direct concern' (or not) at all, but declared the landowners inadmissible
because they were not individually concerned by the Commission decision.

The add-on of the Lisbon Treaty

It remains also to be seen to what extent the amendment of Article 263,
fourth paragraph, by the Lisbon Treaty will improve the situation to challenge
acts of the EU institutions affecting the environment. After the amendment
Article 263, fourth paragraph, TFEU reads:

'Any natural or legal person may, under the conditions laid down in the first and
second paragraphs, institute proceedings against an act addressed to that person
or which is of direct and individual concern to them, *and against a regulatory act
which is of direct concern to them and does not entail implementing measures*.' [ital-
ics added by the authors]

In other words, there is no need to demonstrate that one is 'individually
concerned' under the final sentence of Article 263, fourth paragraph, TFEU.
According to the General Court, in its first case law, the meaning of 'regulatory act' must be understood as covering *all acts of general application apart from
legislative acts*.[232] This could broaden the possibilities of individuals to challenge
in particular delegated acts and implementing measures before the European
Courts.[233] Note however, that under this new provision there is still the require-

---

[232] Cf. the first case law on the new elements of this provision: Case T-18/10 *Inuit Tapiriit Kanatami a.o.*,
Judgment of 6 September 2011.

[233] See on 'delegated acts' and 'implementing measures', Chapter 2, section 6. See for a case where the
appellants might have benefited from this new provision, Case C-355/08 P *WWF-UK* v. *Council* [2009]
ECR I-73.

ment of 'direct concern'. Also, this provision only speaks of 'regulatory' acts, meaning that acts of a more individual nature do not 'benefit' from this provision. That would mean that under the new text Greenpeace as well as the European Environmental Bureau in the cases discussed above will still be declared inadmissible.[234]

5.3   Regulation 1367/2006[235]

On 25 June 1998 the Union signed the Convention on Access to Information, Public Participation in Decision-making and Access to Justice in Environmental Matters, the so-called 'Aarhus Convention'.[236] Provisions of Union law should therefore be consistent with the Aarhus Convention.[237] In view of the remarks made in section 5.2 of this chapter, it was not a big surprise that the Union felt it necessary to improve access to justice in environmental matters as far as it concerns acts of the European institutions. Article 9(3) of the Aarhus Convention requires access to judicial or other review procedures for challenging acts and omissions by private persons and public authorities which contravene provisions of law relating to the environment. Regulation 1367/2006 on the application of the provisions of the Aarhus Convention on Access to Information, Public Participation in Decision-making and Access to Justice in Environmental Matters to Community institutions and bodies (the 'Aarhus Regulation') is to ensure that European law is in sync with the Aarhus Convention. Therefore, let us have a look at its provisions.

The internal review procedure
According to Article 10(1) of the regulation, the internal review procedure is open to allow challenges to an 'administrative act' and omissions to take such an act. The concept of an 'administrative act' is defined in Article 2(1)(g) of the regulation as meaning: 'any measure of individual scope under environmental law, taken by a Community institution or body, and having legally binding and external effects'. Thus, in order to have access to this procedure for internal review, measures involved must be:
   1. of individual scope;
   2. legally binding and
   3. have external effects.

---

[234] Case C-321/95 P *Greenpeace* v. *Commission* [1998] ECR I-1651 and Case T-94/04 *EEB a.o.* v. *Commission* [2005] ECR II-4919.

[235] Regulation 1367/2006 on the application of the provisions of the Aarhus Convention on Access to Information, Public Participation in Decision-making and Access to Justice in Environmental Matters to Community institutions and bodies, OJ 2006 L 264/13. This section builds upon Jans (2006). Cf. also Pallemaerts (2011a).

[236] OJ 2005 L 124/4, concluded by Council Decision 2005/370, OJ 2005 L 124/1.

[237] Case C-240/09 *Lesoochranárske zoskupenie VLK*, Judgment of 8 March 2011.

These are cumulative criteria, which means that each and every one of these conditions must be met for the measures to be amenable to internal review.

Furthermore, Article 2(2) of the regulation makes it clear that not even all decisions are subject to the internal review procedure. Excluded are also measures taken by a institution or body in its capacity as an administrative review body, such as under:

a) Articles 101, 102, 106 and 107 TFEU (competition rules);
b) Articles 258 and 260 TFEU (infringement proceedings);
c) Article 228 TFEU (Ombudsman proceedings);
d) Article 325 TFEU (OLAF proceedings).

The use of the words 'such as' clearly indicates the non-exhaustive character of the list, which of course triggers the question of what is meant by 'its capacity as an administrative review body'. It is in particular questionable to see the Commission's decisions in the area of competition law on the same footing as its role in infringement proceedings. Can one really say that, in the area of competition law, the Commission is acting in an administrative review capacity? In our view the Commission is only exercising decision-making competences like in any other area where it possesses decision-making authority. What makes a decision of the Commission applying competition rules in individual cases so significantly different from any other decision it can take?

Furthermore, the regulation restricts the internal review procedure to administrative acts 'under environmental law'. The definition of 'environmental law' can be found in Article 2(1)(f) of the regulation:

'Community legislation which, irrespective of its legal basis, contributes to the pursuit of the objectives of Community policy on the environment as set out in the Treaty: preserving, protecting and improving the quality of the environment, protecting human health, the prudent and rational utilisation of natural resources, and promoting measures at international level to deal with regional or worldwide environmental problems.'

This definition is very restrictive. Can one really say that the Treaty rules on structural funds, agriculture, fisheries, industrial policy, development aid, etc. etc. contribute to the pursuit of the environmental objectives of the Union? If not, decisions taken in these policy areas fall outside the scope of application of the internal review procedure.

Article 10(1) opens the internal review procedure to challenge acts of a 'Community institution or body'. Article 2(1)(c) gives the following definition of the phrase: 'any public institution, body, office or agency established by, or on the basis of, the Treaty except when acting in a judicial or legislative capacity'. On the one hand, this definition is very broad indeed, as it does not limit the review procedure to the 'traditional' institutions of the Union mentioned in Article 13 TEU. Any 'organ' of the EU will be covered by this. But the limitation to non-judicial and non-legislative capacity is less clear.

It is also peculiar that only certain non-governmental organisations are entitled to make a request for internal review. Natural persons do not have access to it. Article 11 of the regulation lists the criteria:

a) it is an independent non-profit-making legal person in accordance with a Member State's national law or practice;
b) it has the primary stated objective of promoting environmental protection in the context of environmental law;
c) it has existed for more than two years and is actively pursuing the objective referred to under (b);
d) the subject matter in respect of which the request for internal review is made is covered by its objective and activities.

Standard of review

The internal review procedure was, according to the Commission's proposal (Article 9(1)), related to 'a breach of environmental law'. Environmental law was defined in Article 2(1)(g) of the proposal and 'means any Community legislation which has as its objective the protection or the improvement of the environment including human health and the protection or the rational use of natural resources.' However, the text was not clear on the standards of review to be applied: just a 'marginal' or 'discretionary' review, or rather a 'full' or 'merits' review? Surprisingly, in the final text of the regulation any reference to a standard of review is omitted. Article 10 of the regulation just states the entitlement to an internal review procedure, without mentioning the applicable standards for such a review. Therefore, it is now completely unclear when a request for internal review is substantiated of not. This makes the duty for the institution to 'consider any such request' an empty shell. And it makes the right of the institution not to consider a request if the request is 'clearly unsubstantiated' a *carte blanche* to disregard any request.

The first practice of the regulation

Practice shows that, up until now, a request for internal review has led to a final decision in only a couple of cases.[238] The vast majority of these cases, the request was declared inadmissible. In only one case did the relevant European institution come to a material and substantive examination of the request. This request, however, did not lead to an actual review, but was declared unfounded. The requirements of the regulation that the request must concern a decision of 'individual scope', or a legal measure with external effect, were in particular grounds for inadmissibility. The present authors are of the opinion that the conditions for admissibility of the regulation and the (broad) application thereof by the EU institutions, cannot be based on the Aarhus Convention itself. Therefore, we plead that the conditions for admissibility should be interpreted and applied in conformity with the Aarhus Convention, Article 9(3) in particular.

---

[238] Cf. Harryvan & Jans (2010) and Pallemaerts (2011a). Cf. e.g. Case T-396/09 R *Vereniging Milieudefensie a.o. v. Commission*, Order of 17 December 2009.

It is our opinion that only 'real' legislative acts within the meaning of Articles 289-292 TFEU should fall outside the scope of the internal review procedure. The newly created distinction between 'legislative acts' and 'non-legislative acts' in the Lisbon Treaty, enables the EU institutions to positively amend their restrictive approach so far.[239]

Above we referred to the findings of the Aarhus Compliance Committee with respect to the *Greenpeace* case limiting access to justice to the EU courts: 'unless fully compensated for by adequate administrative review procedures' this case law is not in compliance with Article 9(3), of the Aarhus Convention.[240] It is hard to see, in view of how the regulation is actually applied, how the internal review procedure can 'fully' compensate for the lack of standing under Article 263, fourth paragraph, TFEU. Once again, it is argued by the present authors that the judgment in the *Slovak Bears* case makes a change in either the case law of the Court of Justice or in the way the institutions apply the regulation, unavoidable.[241]

Review of the review-decision under Article 263 TFEU?

Article 12(1) of the regulation reads: 'The non-governmental organisation which made the request for internal review pursuant to Article 10 may institute proceedings before the Court of Justice in accordance with the relevant provisions of the Treaty.' Indeed, 'may institute proceedings', but is the original administrative act challenged or the decision of the institution taken in the internal review procedure? Although one may assume that it one has to challenge the decision taken in review, the current text is not clear at all.[242] By the way, this lack of clarity can trigger some rather awkward procedural complications. It is (is it?) conceivable that the initial decision is challenged directly at the Court under Article 263 TFEU by those who are 'directly and individually'[243] concerned, whilst, at the same time the act is being reviewed according to Article 10 of the regulation. It is also not quite clear to what extent parties with opposite interests can participate in this review procedure[244] and what constraints the principle of legal certainty will bring about.

Even more serious, though, is our second observation. According to Article 12 of the regulation may non-governmental organisations institute proceed-

---

[239] Also the judgment of the General Court in Case T-18/10 *Inuit Tapiriit Kanatami a.o.*, Judgment of 6 September 2011 supports this line of thought. See also our remarks on this case in section 5.2 of this chapter.

[240] Findings and Recommendations of the Compliance Committee with regard to Communication Accc/C/2008/32 (Part I) Concerning Compliance by the European Union, adopted on 14 April 2011.

[241] Case C-240/09 *Lesoochranárske zoskupenie VLK*, Judgment of 8 March 2011.

[242] According to Wennerås (2007) at 238 the written reply is the subject matter for judicial review. His main argument is that the regulation apparently aims to align with Regulation 1049/2001 regarding public access to European Parliament, Council and Commission documents, OJ 2001 L 145/43.

[243] For instance by individuals not having access to the internal review procedure.

[244] Our guess is that they cannot participate. In any case, the regulation should have addressed this point.

ings before the Court of Justice 'in accordance with the relevant provisions of the Treaty'. Being the addressee of the decision taken in review, *locus standi* at the Court of Justice will not be a problem for those organisations who have requested the review. However, it is the authors opinion that the Court of Justice will not be able to exercise a full review of the original decision. The problem with that is of course that Article 263, fourth paragraph, TFEU still requires that the applicant must be 'direct and individually' concerned by that decision. In other words, the regulation might be capable to provide for *administrative* review, but not for *judicial* review.

> This is supported by the judgment in the *EEB* case.[245] In that case the European Environmental Bureau tried to rely on the proposal for the Aarhus Regulation to have access to the General Court under Article 263 TFEU in order to challenge Commission Directive 2003/112 to include paraquat as an active substance. The Court ruled: 'The Court notes, first, that the principles governing the hierarchy of norms [...] preclude secondary legislation from conferring standing on individuals who do not meet the requirements of the fourth paragraph of Article 230 EC [now Article 263 TFEU]. A fortiori the same holds true for the statement of reasons of a proposal for secondary legislation.'

In view of this judgment, it is highly unlikely that the regulation will be capable of broadening the scope of Article 263, fourth paragraph, TFEU beyond the current *Greenpeace* case law of the Court of Justice. At best, the Court will accept actions of non-governmental organisations for annulments of decisions taken during the internal review procedure, but only in so far such an action seeks to safeguard the prerogatives of non-governmental organisation in such an internal review procedure: has there been a fair hearing of the complaints and other due process type of arguments.[246] For a Union that claims to be based on the rule of law, this is clearly insufficient.

---

[245] Case T-94/04 *EEB a.o. v. Commission* [2005] ECR II-4919.

[246] See for parallel case law: Case C-70/88 *EP v. Council* [1990] ECR I-2041, para. 27.

CHAPTER 6

Free Movement of Goods

1   General Remarks

The preceding five chapters have discussed in some depth the contours of Union environmental law as reflected in directives and regulations on the environment, and the consequences for the Member States. It has been demonstrated that the limits within which Member States may develop national environmental policy are primarily defined by such European secondary legislation. The first questions that have to be addressed, when endeavouring to establish what freedom the Member States do have when adopting national protective measures, are whether the field is already covered by European legislation, what the content of that legislation is and to what extent it leaves room for extensions, derogations, etc.[1]

Even though there is European legislation in almost every conceivable field of environmental policy, there are still major parts of environmental law which have not been harmonised. It must indeed be assumed, in the light of the principle of subsidiarity and of the provisions of Article 193 TFEU, that certain areas of national environmental law will never fully be harmonised. In these areas the Member States retain primary responsibility for the content of their environmental legislation. Only the restrictions flowing from European primary law – in particular the Treaty on the Functioning of the European Union – limit them. This chapter will examine in particular the extent to which the provisions on the free movement of goods, Articles 28 to 36 TFEU, are relevant. As far as other market freedoms are concerned, and occasionally they are,[2] our observations in particular relating to the exceptions in section 4.3 to 4.5 of this chapter are applicable *mutatis mutandis*.

There is another reason for considering these provisions, as the Court of Justice held in the *Inter-Huiles* case, which is that the European institutions are themselves also bound by these rules.[3] This means, for example, that the Council may not in its legislative capacity adopt measures which are incompatible with Articles 34-36 TFEU. However, the Union institutions may have a greater degree of discretionary power as regards the manner and form of legislation than do the Member States in implementing it.[4] In order that Union secondary legislation should not be incompatible with the Treaties, it must as far as possible be interpreted in the light of the Treaties.[5]

Article 34 TFEU however does not have horizontal effect. In *Sapod Audic* the Court ruled that a contractual obligation to affix the 'Green Dot logo' to products

---

[1]   See Chapter 3, sections 2 and 3 in particular.

[2]   See, e.g., Case C-400/08 *Commission* v. *Spain*, Judgment of 24 March 2011.

[3]   Case 172/82 *Inter-Huiles* [1983] ECR 555. Confirmed in Case C-341/95 *Gianni Bettati* [1998] ECR I-4355, para. 61: 'It is settled law that the prohibition of quantitative restrictions and of all measures having equivalent effect applies not only to national measures but also to measures adopted by the Community institutions'.

[4]   Cf. in general Mortelmans (2002) and Temmink (2000) at 71.

[5]   Case C-128/89 *Commission* v. *Italy* [1990] ECR 3239.

cannot be regarded as a barrier to trade for the purposes of Article 34 TFEU 'since it was not imposed by a Member State but agreed between individuals'.[6] Having said this, we have to take into account that according to the ruling in *Schmidberger*, the states have to take a certain responsibility for actions of individuals affecting the Treaty rules on goods.[7]

2 Environmental Charges and Article 30 TFEU[8]

Article 30 TFEU prohibits customs duties and all charges having equivalent effect on trading between the Member States. Since all 'genuine' customs duties on inter-state trading have been abolished since 1 January 1970, only charges having equivalent effect are now of any practical significance. In Case 24/68, the Court of Justice defined the extent of the prohibition as follows:[9]

> 'Any pecuniary charge, however small and whatever its designation and mode of application, which is imposed unilaterally on domestic or foreign goods by reason of the fact that they cross a frontier, and which is not a customs duty in the strict sense, constitutes a charge having equivalent effect within the meaning of Articles 9, 12, 13 and 16 EC [now Article 30 TFEU], even if it is not imposed for the benefit of the State, is not discriminatory or protective in effect and if the product on which the charge is imposed is not in competition with any domestic product.'
>
> A tax levied by the local municipality of Carrara on marble excavated in the territory of the municipality on its transportation across the boundaries of the municipal territory therefore constitutes a charge having effect equivalent to a customs duty.[10] Also the German legislation establishing a solidarity fund for the return of waste and requiring exporters of waste to contribute to the fund, including those exporting to other Member States, was to be considered a charge in the meaning of Article 30 TFEU.[11]

There are no derogations from the prohibition. Customs duties and charges having equivalent effect are prohibited regardless of the purpose for which they were introduced and the destination of the revenue from them. Unlike non-tariff restrictions, such charges cannot be justified by pleading protection of the

---

[6] Case C-159/00 *Sapod Audic* [2002] ECR I-5031, para. 74.

[7] Case C-112/00 *Schmidberger* [2003] ECR I-5659. See also section 4.1 of this chapter. Cf. also Case C-265/95 *Commission* v. *France* [1997] ECR I-6959, discussed in Chapter 4, section 5.

[8] See in general also Commission Communication on Environmental taxes and charges in the Single Market, OJ 1997 C 224/6.

[9] Case 24/68 *Commission* v. *Italy* [1969] ECR 193.

[10] Case C-72/03 *Carbonati Apuani* [2004] ECR I-8027.

[11] Case C-389/00 *Commission* v. *Germany* [2003] ECR I-2001. Cf. also Case C-173/05 *Commission* v. *Italy* [2007] ECR I-4917 on an environmental tax on gas pipelines installed in the Sicilian Region.

environment or protection of the health of humans, animals or plants. This does not mean that any environmental charge levied on an imported product must necessarily be incompatible with European law.

Certain charges are not regarded as charges having equivalent effect and are thus not prohibited as such. Thus the Court has allowed, *inter alia*, a recompense for a service actually rendered to an importer.[12] However, this exception has hardly any relevance in the field of environmental law. Where certain controls are necessary from the point of view of protection of the environment or of health, for example, tests for the presence of chemical residues on products, they will be regarded as necessary in the public interest and not as services rendered to an individual importer.[13] In that case, the Court held that the costs must be borne out of state funds. It could be added that the mere fact that certain environmental tests may be allowed on the basis of Articles 34 to 36 TFEU does not imply that a charge to cover the cost will also be allowed.

More relevant from a practical point of view is that charges which form part of a general system of domestic taxation must not be regarded as a charge having equivalent effect. If a charge does form part of such a system, it is not assessed in the light of Article 30 TFEU but in the light of Article 110 TFEU.[14] This is important because, as will be shown below, Article 110 TFEU allows Member States much more freedom than Article 30 TFEU.

The main criterion for distinguishing between the scope of application of Article 30 TFEU and that of Article 110 TFEU is that charges having equivalent effect are in principle levied only on imported products by reason of the fact that they cross the frontier or, in the case of a levy on exports, on domestic goods, whereas Article 110 TFEU applies to charges levied on both domestic and foreign goods.[15]

One rather special case is where an environmental charge within the general system of internal taxation applying systematically to domestic and imported products, according to the same criteria, can nevertheless constitute a charge having an effect equivalent to customs duty on imports, when such contribution

---

[12] Case 133/82 *Commission* v. *Luxembourg* [1983] ECR 1669. See also Case C-72/03 *Carbonati Apuani* [2004] ECR I-8027, para. 32, where the Court stresses the existence of a direct link between the tax at issue and the services provided for the operators on which the tax is imposed. Using the charge or tax to improve the environment will in general not satisfy this requirement. Cf. also Case C-389/00 *Commission* v. *Germany* [2003] ECR I-2001. The compulsory export charge did not confer on exporters of waste 'any specific or definite benefit'. That finding was supported by the fact that the charge as determined solely according to the type and quantity of the waste to be shipped. There was thus nothing given in return for any service actually provided to them, either as a category of operators or in an individual capacity, the Court argued.

[13] By analogy with Joined Cases C-277/91, C-318/91 and C-319/91 *Ligur Carni* [1993] ECR I-6621.

[14] Cf. with respect to a Romanian tax levied on the registration of motor vehicles Case C-402/09 *Tatu*, Judgment of 7 April 2011.

[15] This settled case law. Cf. e.g. Case C-213/96 *Outokumpu* [1998] ECR I-1777, para. 20 and Case C-313/05 *Brzeziński* [2007] ECR I-519, para. 22.

is intended exclusively to support activities which specifically benefit the taxed domestic product.[16] The taxed product and the favoured national product must be identical, and the tax burden on the domestic product must be fully compensated. These conditions will not easily be met.

> Consider the following, fictitious example. A charge is levied on certain environmentally harmful products, both imported and domestic products. This would normally be regarded as a tax within the meaning of Article 110 TFEU, and not as a charge having equivalent effect. This would only be otherwise if the proceeds of the charge were used exclusively to finance activities to promote sales of the domestic product.
>
> In that case only the imported product would in fact be taxed, and the tax might be regarded as a charge having equivalent effect within the meaning of Article 110 TFEU. If, however, the proceeds were used for a more general publicity campaign to promote environmentally friendly behaviour, there could be no question of there being such a charge. Domestic manufacturers would no longer be fully compensated, nor would there be a direct relation between the product taxed and the recipient of the proceeds. In that case the charge would have to be assessed in the light of Article 110 TFEU.

From these conditions it is evident that national legislators must have regard to the manner in which the proceeds of environmental charges are applied. Financial bonuses to national enterprises may make such a charge incompatible with the Treaty provisions prohibiting customs duties and charges having equivalent effect.

3 Article 110 TFEU

According to Article 110, first paragraph, TFEU, Member States are prohibited from imposing on the products of other Member States any internal taxation of any kind in excess of that imposed on similar domestic products. The Member States are moreover prohibited from imposing on the products of other Member States any internal taxation of such a nature as to afford indirect protection to other, domestic, products (Article 110, second paragraph, TFEU).

The aim of Article 110 TFEU is to guarantee the fiscal neutrality of imported products as compared with domestic production. The simple fact that a product crosses a border may not lead to a difference in fiscal treatment.[17] However, the Article 110 prohibition does not affect environmental taxes which hit domestic products harder than imported products.[18] In *Outokumpu* for instance the Court ruled that the fact that electricity of domestic origin is in some cases taxed more

---

[16] Case 77/72 *Capolongo* [1973] ECR 611.

[17] Cf. e.g. Case C-402/09 *Tatu*, Judgment of 7 April 2011.

[18] Case 86/78 *Peureux* [1979] ECR 897.

heavily than imported electricity is immaterial in this connection since, in order to ascertain whether the system in question is compatible with Article 110 TFEU, the tax burden imposed on imported electricity must be compared with the lowest tax burden imposed on electricity of domestic origin.[19] This *reverse* discrimination is in principle outside the scope of Article 110 TFEU.

In view of the case law of the Court of Justice it may be assumed that environmental taxes fall, without any question, within its scope of Article 110 TFEU. This applies not only to those taxes whose primary function is the *financing* of certain measures, such as water purification installations, rather than the promotion of environmentally friendly behaviour, but also to *regulatory* charges. Regulatory charges are expressly designed to discourage environmentally harmful behaviour, for example by taxing certain emissions or the use of certain raw materials. Behaving in an environmentally friendly manner thus becomes relatively cheaper, which will supposedly encourage polluters to move in the right direction. In the past it has been argued that such charges, not being 'taxes', fall outside the scope of Article 110 TFEU. This opinion seems nowadays no longer tenable, particularly in the light of the *Outokumpu* case, to be discussed below.[20]

For sake of completeness we must note that under special circumstances a national tax or charge can neither be reviewed in the light of Article 110 TFEU or Article 30 TFEU. The Danish Law on registration duty on motor provided for the levy of a charge, ('registration duty'), on new motor vehicles. Because there is no domestic car industry the charge was in fact imposed solely on imported new vehicles. However, this does not mean that the charge had to be characterised as a charge having equivalent effect since the charge was part of a general system of internal taxation. On the other hand, Article 110 TFEU cannot be invoked where there is no similar or competing domestic production. Under those circumstances the Court will examine the charge in the light of Article 34 TFEU.[21]

Similar products

In assessing the compatibility of a tax with Article 110 TFEU, the tax on an imported product must be compared with the tax on the equivalent domestic product. The first question to be answered is whether the products are similar, in which case the first paragraph of Article 110 TFEU applies, or competitive, in which case the second paragraph applies. It should be noted that the Court has not always made a clear distinction between the two paragraphs, and in cases of doubt has preferred to apply the second paragraph.

---

[19] Case C-213/96 *Outokumpu* [1998] ECR I-1801, para. 36

[20] Case C-213/96 *Outokumpu* [1998] ECR I-1801

[21] Case C-383/01 *De Danske Bilimportører* [2003] ECR I-6065. Cf. also Case C-402/09 *Tatu*, Judgment of 7 April 2011. Cf. also a rather peculiar case on a regional environmental tax on stopovers for tourist purposes by aircraft, Case C-169/08 *Presidente del Consiglio dei Ministri* [2009] ECR I-10821. The Court found that legislation in violation of the Treaty rules on services and state aid.

When assessing whether the products are similar within the meaning of first paragraph of Article 110 TFEU, the following specific problem arises, particularly in respect of regulatory charges. Such charges are imposed in order to encourage people to purchase products which cause less environmental harm. It may be asked whether a difference in terms of environmental features (degree of harm caused during production, use or disposal) is sufficient to make a product dissimilar. Is a car fitted with the latest 'diesel particulate filter' similar to one that is not? Is timber that has been produced sustainably similar to timber that has not? Are batteries that can be re-used similar to those that can only be used once?[22]

As yet the Court has not had to decide on this specific issue. However, the Court gives a broad interpretation of the term 'similar' in the sense of the first paragraph.[23] The comparison is not based on the products being completely identical, but on their having similar characteristics and meeting the same needs from the point of view of consumers. If this approach is applied to the environment sector, either of two arguments is possible. On the one hand it could be said, for example, that both a car that is fitted with the latest 'diesel particulate filter' and one that is not serve the same transport needs of the consumer and are thus similar. On the other hand it could be argued that a car without the latest 'diesel particulate filter' does not meet the needs of the environmentally conscious consumer and could not therefore be regarded as a true alternative. Indeed this distinction is made in Regulation 66/2010 on the EU Ecolabel, under which ecolabels can be awarded for products with the same function but with different ecological properties.[24] In any case, it would be hard to deny that the two types of product bear a certain competitive relationship with each other. From the case law, it can be deduced that when it is difficult to make a demarcation, the Court tends to judge the factual situation under the second paragraph of Article 110 TFEU. This provision requires that a Member State's internal taxation must not have the effect of protecting domestic products. In the assessment of this aspect, not only the actual situation but also the potential market for foreign products, if no protectionist measures were involved, should be taken into consideration. It is also necessary to take into account how the revenue from the levy is used. The Court has ruled that when the revenue from a levy is used to partly offset the burden borne by domestic products, the charge constitutes discriminatory taxation within the meaning of Article 110 TFEU.[25]

---

[22] Cf. Commission Communication on Environmental taxes and charges in the Single Market, COM (97) 9 final at 9.

[23] Cf. Case C-221/06 *Stadtgemeinde Frohnleiten* [2007] ECR I-2613, were the Court refused to apply the 'loose' discrimination test from the *Walloon Waste* case (Case C-2/90 *Commission* v. *Belgium* [1992] ECR I-4431; see below, section 4 of this chapter) to Article 110, first paragraph, TFEU.

[24] OJ 2010 L 27/1. See on this Regulation Chapter 8, section 8.1.

[25] Case C-17/91 *Georges Lornoy* [1992] ECR I-6523.

Neutrality of tax burdens

The tax burden on the imported and domestic products should be neutral and should not impede or hinder the importation. The non-discrimination should be evident in tariffs, tax basis, exemptions, means of payment, etc. Not only is there a range of case law on this issue, but also specifically for the environment sector, notably the *Italian Oil* case.[26]

> Under Italian legislation, regenerated waste petroleum products received certain tax advantages. The objective of the Italian law was to stimulate recycling of used oil. The preferential taxes were however not applicable to imported oil. The first question addressed by the Court was whether Article 110 TFEU allows any differentiation at all of taxes on broadly defined product groups in this type of case. The Court observed that it was clear:
> 'that at the present stage of the development of Community law and in the absence of any unification or harmonization of the relevant provisions, Community law does not prohibit Member States from granting tax advantages, in the form of exemption from or reduction of duties, to certain products or to certain classes of producers. The Treaty does not therefore forbid, as far as domestic tax laws are concerned, the taxation at differential rates of products which may serve the same economic ends, especially if, as in the case of regenerated mineral oils, it appears that the cost of production, objectively speaking, differs considerably from that of oils of primary distillation.'

Although the Court did not say so in as many words, this would seem to imply that environmental considerations – in this case a measure to promote the recycling of waste – could be a legitimate social or economic reason for applying differential taxation.[27] The next question the Court had to address was whether these tax advantages could be granted exclusively to the domestic products. The Court held that they could not:

> 'On the other hand pursuant to the first paragraph of Article 95 [now Article 110 TFEU] the tax advantages in question must also be granted without any discrimination to products from the other Member States which satisfy the same conditions as the domestic products which qualify for the exemptions or reductions allowed by national law.'

In the *Outokumpu* case the Court was given the opportunity to confirm its position in the *Italian Oil* case.[28] The Court indicated that Member States may apply different rates of duty to electricity, according to its manner of production. A lower rate for electricity produced by water power – as opposed to electricity

---

[26] Case 21/79 *Commission* v. *Italy* [1980] ECR 1.

[27] Cf. also our remarks on the principle of equal treatment in Chapter 1, section 2.

[28] Case C-213/96 *Outokumpu* [1998] ECR I-1801.

produced by conventional means – is permitted, provided this rate also applies to imported electricity. The Court ruled that:

> 'Community law does not restrict the freedom of each Member State to establish a tax system which differentiates between certain products, even products which are similar within the meaning of the first paragraph of Article 95 EC [now Article 110 TFEU], on the basis of objective criteria, such as the nature of the raw materials used or the production processes employed. Such differentiation is compatible with Community law, however, only if it pursues objectives which are themselves compatible with the requirements of the Treaty and its secondary legislation'.[29]
>
> In *Nádasdi* ruling on the compatibility of an Hungarian registration duty on motor vehicles, the Court of Justice accepted 'engine type, engine capacity and a classification based on environmental considerations' being objective criteria to be used for the purpose of differential taxation.[30]

Following these cases there can be no doubt that environmental considerations can be regarded as a legitimate reason for applying differential taxation. Furthermore, Article 110 TFEU would not appear to give the Union a right to judge whether a levy in a Member State is excessively high in relation to its environmental objective.[31] However, differential taxation may not lead to any form of discrimination, direct or indirect,[32] against imports from other Member States or any form of protection of competing domestic products[33] and any tax advantage granted to domestic products must also be granted without any discrimination to products from the other Member States which satisfy the same conditions as the domestic products which qualify for the exemptions or reductions allowed by national law.[34] As soon as the discriminatory character of national legislation has been established, there is no room to justify the measure for reasons of environmental protection.[35]

In summary, differential taxation based on the environmental characteristics of products is allowed, provided the differentiation also applies to imported products and any other form of discrimination or protectionism is avoided.[36]

---

[29] Case C-213/96 *Outokumpu* [1998] ECR I-1801, para. 30.

[30] Case C-290/05 *Nádasdi* [2006] ECR I-10115, para. 52.

[31] This seems to follow from Case C-132/88 *Commission* v. *Greece* [1990] ECR 1567, para. 17.

[32] See on *indirect* discrimination in particular Case C-402/09 *Tatu*, Judgment of 7 April 2011.

[33] Case C-213/96 *Outokumpu* [1998] ECR I-1801.

[34] Case 21/79 *Commission* v. *Italy* [1980] ECR 1 and Case C-313/05 *Brzeziński* [2007] ECR I-519, with respect to Polish excise duties on second-hand vehicles.

[35] Case C-313/05 *Brzeziński* [2007] ECR I-519, para. 39.

[36] Cf. Commission Communication on Environmental taxes and charges in the Single Market, OJ 1997 C 224/6 at 7-8.

4   Non-tariff Restrictions and Protection of the Environment

General remarks

In order to guarantee unobstructed movement of goods between the Member States, Article 34 TFEU prohibits national authorities from imposing quantitative import restrictions on the import of goods from other Member States, and all measures having equivalent effect. Article 35 TFEU contains a similar prohibition with respect to exports. Article 36 TFEU lists a number of exceptions to these two prohibitions.[37] In addition, the Court of Justice has formulated a number of supplementary grounds justifying barriers to imports of goods ('rule of reason' or *Cassis de Dijon* exception).[38] It is up to the national authorities to prove that the conditions allowing these exceptions have been met.

One of the consequences of harmonisation is that whenever a national measure has been the subject of *exhaustive* harmonisation at European level it must be assessed in the light of the provisions of the harmonising measure and not those of the Treaty concerning the free movement of goods or one of the other market freedoms.[39] After harmonisation the directive, or in some cases the regulation, provides the context for review of the national legislation.[40] It should however be noted that European environmental legislation is also required to be compatible with Articles 34 to 36 TFEU.[41]

All products?

The applicability of the rules on the free movement of goods has been at issue in several cases concerning waste. Thus, in the *Walloon Waste* case the Belgian Government contended that waste cannot be considered as goods within the meaning of Article 34 TFEU.[42] The Belgian Government added that the operations for disposing of waste are covered by the provisions of the Treaty relating to the freedom to supply services. It was argued that waste, in particular waste which cannot be recycled or re-used, did not have an intrinsic commercial value and could not therefore be sold. In itself this argument is not without merit. It could be argued that the disposal of waste, which has a negative economic value, is not primarily a commercial transaction directed at the purchasing of waste, but above all aimed at purchasing a service, namely

---

[37] See below, section 4.3.

[38] See below, section 4.4.

[39] See for a detailed discussion Chapter 3, section 2.

[40] Leading cases in this respect are: Case C-37/92 *Vanacker and Lesage* [1993] ECR I-4947; Case C-473/98 *Kemikalieninspektionen* v. *Toolex Alpha AB* [2000] ECR I-5681, para. 25 and Case C-324/99 *Daimler-Chrysler* [2001] ECR I-9897. See also Chapter 3, section 2.

[41] Case 172/82 *Inter-Huiles* [1983] ECR 555, para. 12. It should be noted that in this respect the Court seems to allow the institutions a wider margin of discretion than the Member States; Cf. Temmink (2000) at 71.

[42] Case C-2/90 *Commission* v. *Belgium* [1992] ECR I-4431.

the removal of waste. Although the practical significance of this distinction is limited – the rules and exceptions applying to the freedom to provide services are quite similar to those applying to goods[43] – the Court made it clear that there is no room for application of the treaty provisions on services:

> 'In reply to these arguments it is sufficient to point out that objects which are transported over a frontier in order to give rise to commercial transactions are subject to Article 30 [now Article 34 TFEU], irrespective of the nature of those transactions.'

Equally, the Court rejected a distinction based on the difference between recyclable and non-recyclable waste. It reasoned that, from a practical point of view, serious difficulties would arise, especially with respect to border control, if such a distinction was made. Such a distinction would also be based on uncertain characteristics – which, because of technical developments and the profitability of reused waste, could be changed in time. Because of these factors, the Court found that all waste should be treated as a 'good' under Article 34 TFEU.

In short, what is crucial for determining whether or not goods should be regarded as being subject to Article 34 TFEU is whether they may be the object of a commercial transaction.[44] This is also true of waste, even though it has negative value. As a result, waste is subject to the rules on the free movement of goods. This decision shows that measures which hinder intra-EU trade in waste are not covered by the rules on the freedom to provide services.[45]

4.1   The Scope of Application of Article 34 TFEU

The Dassonville *formula*

One of the most important restrictions on national, but also on EU, environment policy is the prohibition of measures having an effect equivalent to quantitative restrictions on imports and exports. A large number of national environmental measures are in principle covered by the definition given in the *Dassonville* case of a measure having equivalent effect to a restriction on imports.[46] There the Court defined such measures as national measures 'which are capable of hindering, directly or indirectly, actually or potentially, intra-Community trade.' Any measure which may in the slightest way be a

---

[43] Case C-76/90 *Säger* [1991] ECR I-4221. See also the Services Directive, Directive 2006/123 on services in the internal market (OJ 2006 L 376/36). The protection of the environment is regarded as one of the 'overriding reasons relating to the public interest' which may be relied upon by Member States to restrict access to or exercise of a service activity in their territory.

[44] Only products, like narcotic drugs, which are, because of their very nature, subject to a prohibition on importation and offering for sale in all the Member States, do not benefit from the free movement of goods rules. See Case C-137/09 *Josemans*, Judgment of 16 December 2010.

[45] The decision was implicitly confirmed in the *Vanacker* case; Case C-37/92 *Vanacker* [1993] ECR I-4947.

[46] Case 8/74 *Dassonville* [1974] ECR 837.

restriction in this sense is covered by the prohibition in Article 34 TFEU. These include not only measures affecting imports, such as import bans, import permits, tests and samples of goods which may be harmful to the environment, but also 'measures applicable without distinction'. In other words measures which are applicable both to imports and to domestic products, like for example, regulations on safety, packaging and labelling, marketing authorisation procedures, quality requirements etc. Regulations which, in the event of disparities between the legislation in the Member States, are clearly capable of hindering intra-Union trade. According to the judgment of the Court of Justice in the *Cassis de Dijon* case, products lawfully produced and marketed in one of the Member States must be granted market access in other Member States.[47] It should also be noted that in accordance with the settled case law of the Court of Justice, Article 34 TFEU is applicable without distinction to products originating in the EU and to those which have been put into free circulation in any of the Member States, irrespective of the actual origin of those products.[48]

The case law of the Court of Justice contains several examples of environmental measures which have been regarded as 'measures having equivalent effect'.

In the *Improsol* case the Court held that a prohibition, enforced by penalties in criminal law, of selling, storing or using any plant-protection product not authorised by a national law is capable of affecting imports from other Member States where the same product is admitted wholly or in part and thus of constituting a barrier to intra-EU trade.[49] Such rules therefore constitute a measure having an effect equivalent to a quantitative restriction. Similar, a general prohibition on the industrial use of trichloroethylene constitutes also a 'measure having equivalent effect'.[50]

In the *Danish Bottles* case a system requiring manufacturers and importers to market beer and soft drinks only in re-usable containers, which must be approved by a National Agency for the Protection of the Environment, was held to be subject to Article 34 TFEU.[51] The requirement implied a prohibition against the marketing of goods in containers other than ones which were returnable. The import of foreign beer and soft drinks which were legitimately marketed in other Member States, but did not meet the requirements of the country of importation, was thus not possible. Furthermore, the fact of having to establish a system for the

---

[47] Case 120/78 *Rewe-Zentral AG* [1979] ECR 649.

[48] Case C-131/93 *Commission* v. *Germany* [1994] ECR I-3303, pará. 10.

[49] Case 125/88 *Nijman* [1989] ECR 3533. Cf. also Case C-293/94 *Brandsma* [1996] ECR I-3159; Case C-400/96 *Harpegnies* [1998] ECR I-5121; Case C-443/02 *Schreiber* [2004] ECR I-7275; Case C-100/96 *British Agrochemicals* [1999] ECR I-1499 and Case C-201/06 *Commission* v. *France* [2008] ECR I-735.

[50] Case C-473/98 *Kemikalieninspektionen* v. *Toolex Alpha AB* [2000] ECR I-5681.

[51] Case 302/86 *Commission* v. *Denmark* [1988] ECR 4607. See also on German rules concerning deposit and return obligations for non-reusable packaging Case C-309/02 *Radlberger Getränkegesellschaft and S. Spitz* [2004] ECR I-11763 and Case C-463/01 *Commission* v. *Germany* [2004] ECR I-11705.

return of containers meant that foreign manufacturers would be obliged to incur relatively high transport costs.

Labelling requirements quite clearly fall under the scope of Article 34 TFEU. The Court ruled that Italy, by subjecting manganese alkaline batteries containing less than 0.0005% mercury by weight to a marking scheme which requires, in particular, an indication as to the presence of heavy metals, failed to fulfil its obligations under Article 34 TFEU.[52]

A Dutch measure which fell foul of Article 34 TFEU was one prohibiting the importation and keeping of red grouse. The Court held in the *Red Grouse* case that this could not be justified in respect of a bird which does not occur in the territory of the legislating Member State, but is found in another Member State (the United Kingdom) where it may be lawfully hunted.[53]

In the *Balsamo* case it was argued that the Mayor of Cinisello Balsamo's prohibition of the supply to customers of non-biodegradable bags in which to carry away their purchases was incompatible with Article 34 TFEU.[54] However, the Court was not required to give a preliminary ruling on this point, as the national court had not submitted a question on the matter. Since such a prohibition virtually amounts to a total prohibition on the sale of non-biodegradable bags, it should probably be regarded as falling within the scope of Article 34 TFEU.

A prohibition on the disposal of foreign waste also falls under the scope of application of Article 34 TFEU, as is clear from the judgment in the *Walloon Waste* case.[55]

From the *Bluhme* case it is clear that legislation prohibiting the keeping of a certain type of bee on the Danish island of Læsø constituted a restriction within the meaning of Article 34 TFEU.[56]

In *Aher-Waggon* the Court found that national legislation making the first registration in national territory of aircraft previously registered in a Member State conditional upon compliance with stricter noise standards than those laid down by a directive, restricted intra-EU trade.[57]

In *Schmidberger* Article 34 TFEU, in connection with Article 4(3) TEU, was applicable with respect to a decision of a local authority in Austria not to prohibit a demonstration by environmental protesters which resulted in the complete closure of the Brenner motorway for almost 30 hours.[58] The decision not to

---

[52] Case C-143/03 *Commission v. Italy*, unpublished Judgment of 14 October 2004.

[53] Case C-169/89 *Gourmetterie v.d. Burg* [1990] ECR I-2143.

[54] Case 380/87 *Balsamo* [1989] ECR 2491.

[55] Case C-2/90 *Commission v. Belgium* [1992] ECR I-4431.

[56] Case C-67/97 *Bluhme* [1998] ECR I-8033. Cf. however the Dutch *Raad van State*, which ruled that a national prohibition on the keeping of squirrels is not covered by Article 34 or 35 TFEU; 18 June 1998 [1999] *M&R* 12. In the light of the *Bluhme* ruling this would not seem correct.

[57] Case C-389/96 *Aher-Waggon* [1998] ECR I-4473. Cf. also, on Dutch legislation regarding identification and roadworthiness test prior to registration of vehicles, Case C-297/05 *Commission v. Netherlands* [2007] ECR I-7467.

[58] Case C-112/00 *Schmidberger* [2003] ECR I-5659.

intervene is capable of restricting intra-EU trade in goods and, in the words of the Court 'must, therefore, be regarded as constituting a measure of equivalent effect to a quantitative restriction which is, in principle, incompatible with the Community law'.

German legislation requiring electricity supply undertakings to purchase electricity produced from renewable energy sources at minimum prices was considered, in the *PreussenElektra* case, to be an import restriction.[59] Indeed, the German *Stromeinspeisungsgesetz* limits the possibility of importing the same product by preventing those undertakings from obtaining supplies in respect of part of their needs from traders situated in other Member States.

All these judgments demonstrate that if national environmental legislation in one way or another affects the access to the market, it is likely to be subject to the provisions of Article 34 TFEU. This does not mean that such measures will necessarily be prohibited, but it does mean they will have to be justified in the light of one of the exemptions to the article.

No de minimis

As the Court decided in the *Peralta* case, legislation is not incompatible with Article 34 TFEU where its purpose is not to regulate trade in goods with other Member States and the restrictive effects which it might have on the free movement of goods are too *uncertain* and too *indirect* for the obligation which it lays down to be regarded as being of a nature to hinder trade between Member States.[60]

The case concerned an Italian law which prohibited any vessel from discharging harmful substances into the sea. However some caution is advised here, as the uncertain and indirect restrictions referred to in *Peralta* are pertinent to the causal connection required between a measure and its consequences, but say nothing about the extent of those restrictions.

Another relevant case in this connection is *Bluhme*, which concerned Danish legislation prohibiting the keeping on the Danish island of Læsø of bees other than a certain sort.[61] Denmark argued that as the legislation applied to only 0.3% of its territory, it fell outside the scope of Article 34 TFEU. The Court rejected this argument, implicitly following the view taken by Advocate General Fennelly that a distinction had to be made between the 'scale' and the 'remoteness' of the effect on the movement of goods. The fact that the scale of the effects was limited did not imply that the measures were excluded from the scope of Article 34 TFEU.

In other words, Article 34 TFEU does not contain a *de minimis* rule.[62]

---

[59] Case C-379/98 *PreussenElektra* [2001] ECR I-2099.

[60] Case C-379/92 *Peralta* [1994] ECR I-3453, para. 24 and Case C-67/97 *Bluhme* [1998] ECR I-8033, para. 22.

[61] Case C-67/97 *Bluhme* [1998] ECR I-8033.

[62] Cf. on the issue of remoteness and the *de minimis* rule Oliver (1999) at 788-793.

The Keck *formula*

In the *Keck* case, the Court made a significant distinction as to what measures must be deemed to hinder trade:[63]

> 'However, contrary to what has previously been decided, the application to products from other Member States of national provisions restricting or prohibiting certain selling arrangements is not such as to hinder directly of indirectly, actually or potentially, trade between Member States within the meaning of the *Dassonville* judgment [...] provided that those provisions apply to all affected traders operating within the national territory and provided that they affect in the same manner, in law and in fact, the marketing of domestic products and of those from other Member States.

If national regulations on *selling arrangements* satisfy the criterion given in the *Keck* case, there is no need further to review the national measure in the light of the exemptions allowed by Article 36 TFEU or the rule of reason, nor of the principle of proportionality. It cannot yet be said what the consequences of this judgment for environmental law will be, particularly in the field of product policy.

> A possible example which might be regarded as falling under the *Keck* doctrine would be a measure whereby pesticides could be sold only on prescription, or only to certain persons. The same might apply to a ban on advertising certain environmentally harmful products.[64] Such measures might now be regarded as lawful without further review or justification.
>
> In *Bluhme* however, the Court made it quite clear that the Danish legislation prohibiting the keeping of bees 'concerns the intrinsic characteristics of the bees' and could not therefore be considered a 'selling arrangement'.[65]

Although Advocate General Kokott seemed to favour taking product *use* regulations outside the scope of Article 34 TFEU, in *Mickelsson & Roos* the Court of Justice refused to extend the *Keck* doctrine.[66]

> This case concerned Swedish legislation prohibiting, for environmental reasons, the use of jetski's. The Court of Justice ruled that this prohibition has the effect of preventing users of jetski's from using them 'for the specific and inherent purposes for which they were intended or of greatly restricting their use'. Indeed, why would somebody in Sweden want to buy a jetski when it is prohibited to use the product? The ECJ ruled that such a prohibition has 'the effect of *hindering the*

---

[63] Joined Cases C-267/91 and C-268/91 *Keck* [1993] ECR I-6097.

[64] Cf. Joined Cases 34, 35 and 36/95 *De Agostini* [1997] ECR I-3843, paras. 21 and 31.

[65] Case C-67/97 *Bluhme* [1998] ECR I-8033, para. 21.

[66] Case C-142/05 *Mickelsson and Roos* [2009] ECR I-4273. Cf. also Case C-110/05 *Commission* v. *Italy* [2009] ECR I-519. On this case law: Oliver (2010).

access to the domestic market in question for those goods'. [italics added] Therefore they constitute measures having equivalent effect to quantitative restrictions
on imports prohibited by Article 34 TFEU.

In general, it can safely be said that import bans (or restrictions) on 'dangerous'
products, import licensing systems, national environmental product standards
and also certain restrictions to the use of products affect the access of a product
to the market and will therefore continue to be considered a restriction on trade
falling whithin the scope of Article 34 TFEU.[67]

Trade restrictions within a Member State

Of course, the local or regional character of a measure does not mean by
definition that it cannot impinge on the internal market freedoms.[68] Another
question regarding the scope of Article 34 (and 35) TFEU is to what extent the
prohibition extends to trade restrictions *within* a Member State. For instance,
in terms of environmental law, is Article 34 TFEU applicable to regional waste
bans within a country or not?[69] According to the settled case law of the Court,
Article 34 TFEU does not apply to such internal trade restrictions.[70]

> For instance, in the *RI.SAN* case, concerning the organisation of a local solid
> urban waste collection service the Court stated that the free movement rules
> do not apply in a situation in which all the facts are confined to within a single
> Member State.[71]

This case law is completely in line with the text of Article 34 TFEU. The text of
Article 34 TFEU, and the same can be said with respect to Articles 30, 34 and
35 TFEU, seems crystal clear indeed. The articles prohibit restrictions '*between*
Member States' only. The problem however was that the case law of the Court of
Justice on customs duties and charges having equivalent effect gave support for
a more wider interpretation.[72] It seems however that the case law of the Court is
changing and that the doctrine on the non-applicability of Article 34 TFEU in
'internal situations' is due for overhaul.[73] Or to say it differently, that the Court

---

[67] Cf. Temmink (2000) at 74.

[68] Cf. Case C-67/97 *Bluhme* [1998] ECR I-8033; Case C-72/03 *Carbonati Apuani* [2004] ECR I-8027, para.
26 and Case C-169/08 *Presidente del Consiglio dei Ministri* [2009] ECR I-10821.

[69] National case law on this issue is somewhat scarce, although there is a judgment of the Dutch *Raad
van State* in which it refused to apply Article 34 TFEU with respect to inter-provincial restrictions on
the import of waste; Dutch *Raad van State* 24 December 1998 [1999] AB 153. See on this judgment
Temmink (2000) at 85-87.

[70] For example Case 314/81 *Waterkeyn* [1982] ECR 4337.

[71] Case C-108/98 *RI.SAN* [1999] ECR I-5219.

[72] Cf. Case C-163/90 *Legros* [1992] ECR I-4625; Case C-363/93 *Lancry* [1994] ECR I-3957; Case C-485/93
Simitzi [1995] ECR I-2655 and Case C-72/03 *Carbonati Apuani* [2004] ECR I-8027.

[73] See for instance, outside environmental law, Case C-321/94 *Pistre* [1994] ECR I-2343 and Case C-293/02
Jersey Produce Marketing Organisation [2005] ECR I-9543. Cf. Oliver (1999) at 786.

of Justice is capable of finding a 'transboundary nexus' to a case at hand with relative ease nowadays. Therefore, it looks more and more likely that the prohibitions of Article 34 and 35 TFEU will be capable of being applied in so-called 'internal situations'.

4.2 The Scope of Application of Article 35 TFEU

Restrictions on exports are prohibited by Article 35 TFEU. Although the prohibition is framed in identical terms to Article 34 TFEU, the Court has adopted a different approach to the interpretation of this article. Not just any restriction is covered by Article 35 TFEU, only those national measures which have as their specific object or effect the restriction of patterns of exports and thereby the establishment of a difference in treatment between the domestic trade of a Member State and its export trade, in such a way as to provide a special advantage for national products or for the domestic market of the State in question.[74]

In *Vanacker* the Court held that a prohibition on the export of waste oils was in breach of the rules on the free movement of goods.[75]

In the *Inter-Huiles* case, the question at issue was whether the French system of regulation of waste oils was in accordance with European law. The core of the French legislation was the requirement that waste oils should be delivered to approved disposal undertakings. It was not disputed that the French legislation prohibited, by implication, the export of waste oils to foreign countries, including other Member States. The French Government contended that their legislation was justified in the light of Article 5 of the old Waste Oils Directive 75/439.[76] However, having discussed the directive, the Court reached the conclusion that the directive does not automatically authorise the Member States to establish barriers to exports. It continued: 'That conclusion is reinforced by Article 34 of the EEC Treaty [now Article 35 TFEU], which prohibits all measures having an effect equivalent to quantitative restrictions on exports. As the Court has repeatedly held, the prohibition concerns all national measures which have as their specific object or effect the restriction of patterns of exports and thereby the establishment of a difference in treatment between the domestic trade of a Member State and its export trade, in such a way as to provide a special advantage for national products or for the domestic market of the State in question. Consequently, provisions which contravene those rules are also contrary to Article 34 EC [now Article 35 TFEU].'

---

74 Case 172/82 *Inter-Huiles* [1983] ECR 555.

75 Case C-37/92 *Vanacker* [1993] ECR I-4947; Case 172/82 *Inter-Huiles* [1983] ECR 555. Cf. also Case C-203/96 *Dusseldorp* [1998] ECR I-4075, to be discussed in more detail below.

76 OJ 1975 L 194/23, later amended.

The requirement that certain goods and/or products should only be delivered to domestic companies in fact means that the export of those products is prohibited.[77] Such requirements are thus covered by the prohibition contained in Article 35 TFEU.[78]

> In the *Dusseldorp* case, rules prohibiting the export of oil filters unless their processing abroad was superior to that in the Netherlands in combination with the requirement of insufficient capacity for the processing in the Netherlands, was held incompatible with Article 35 TFEU: 'It is plain that the object and effect of such a provision is to restrict exports and to provide a particular advantage for national production.'[79]

Unlike Article 34 TFEU, 'measures applicable without distinction' are not within the scope of application of Article 35 TFEU. This means that non-discriminatory measures which restrict exports do not require further justification by the Member States; they are simply allowed.

> In this light, the judgment of the Swedish Supreme Administrative Court in the *Barsebäck* case seems correct.[80] The circumstance alone that the export share of nuclear power electricity that is produced at the Barsebäck station is stated as being higher than at the other nuclear power stations is not a ground for considering that the decision of the Swedish Government to dismantle it is in violation of Article 35 TFEU.
>
> Another example of a measure which is not covered by Article 35 TFEU is the following. Suppose that, in order to limit the amount of waste produced, a national legislature were to prohibit the use of certain substances in the manufacture of a particular product. Such a measure would have the effect of restricting the export of that product to other Member States which do not have similar legislation. However, as the measure is non-discriminatory, it would not be prohibited under Article 35 TFEU. Nevertheless, as it would probably also operate to restrict imports, it would still have to stand up to review in the light of Article 35 TFEU. Thus, to determine the scope of Article 35 TFEU, it is crucial to examine whether or not a measure discriminates in favour of a Member State's domestic trade.

However it seems that the case law of the Court of Justice is in the process of changing bit by bit and that 'measures applicable without distinction' could also fall within the scope of application of Article 35 TFEU. The 'new' test seems to

---

[77] Cf. also Case C-209/98 *Sydhavnens Sten & Grus* [2000] ECR I-3743, para. 37.

[78] This approach is confirmed in the *Vanacker* case, Case C-37/92 *Vanacker* [1993] ECR I-4947. A similar approach is found in the *Nertsvoederfabriek* case, Case 118/86 *Nertsvoederfabriek* [1987] ECR 3883.

[79] Case C-203/96 *Dusseldorp* [1998] ECR I-4075.

[80] Judgment of the Swedish Supreme Administrative Court on 16 June 1999, case no. 1424-1998, 2397-1998 and 2939-1998, RÅ 1999 ref. 76, regarding the cessation of the right to operate the Barsebäck 1 nuclear power reactor.

be whether the national legislation 'is likely to hamper, at the very least potentially, intra-Community trade'.[81] This would broaden the scope of Article 35
TFEU considerably. However, we will have to wait on further developments in de
case law of the Court of Justice.

Once it has been established that a measure is within the scope of application of Article 35 TFEU, it must then be examined to what extent the measure
may nevertheless prove to be a justified restriction on the free movement of
goods.

4.3 Exceptions under Article 36 TFEU

General remarks
To the extent that national environmental legislation falls
within the scope of the prohibitions contained in Articles 34 and 35 TFEU, the
question arises whether this means that all this legislation must be set aside as
being incompatible with European rules. This is not the case. Article 36 TFEU
provides that restrictions on trade may be justified if they are necessary for the
protection of health and life of humans, animals or plants and do not constitute
a means of arbitrary discrimination or a disguised restriction on trade between
Member States.

The burden of proving that the criteria for application of Article 36 TFEU
have been met (and the same holds for application of the *rule of reason*) lies
primarily with the Member State wishing to rely on Article 36 TFEU.[82] It should
be noted however that Article 36 TFEU must be interpreted in the light of the
precautionary principle of Article 191(2) TFEU.[83] In other words, it would not
seem necessary in every case that there should be unambiguous scientific
evidence that the product or substance in question is harmful.[84] Protective mea-

---

[81] See Case C-205/07 *Gysbrechts and Santurel Inter* [2008] ECR I-9947 and Case C-161/09 *Kakavetsos-
Fragkopoulos*, Judgment of 3 March 2011. Cf. Barnard (2010) at 101.

[82] Cf. Case 251/78 *Denkavit Futtermittel* v. *Minister für Ernährung Landwirtschaft und Forsten* [1979] ECR
3369, para. 24. See also Advocate General Fennelly in the *Bluhme* case: 'In order to benefit from the
application of Article 36 of the Treaty, it is for a Member State to prove that a national measure is effective in attaining its protective objective'; Case C-67/97 *Bluhme* [1998] ECR I-8033. Cf. also more recent
Case C-249/07 *Commission* v. *Netherlands* [2008] ECR I-174, para. 45 *et seq.* and Case C-400/08 *Commission* v. *Spain*, Judgment of 24 March 2011, para. 85 in particular.

[83] Cf. Case C-463/01 *Commission* v. *Germany* [2004] ECR I-11705, para. 74: 'the precautionary principle and
the principle that preventive action should be taken, laid down in Article 174(2) EC [now Article 191(2)
TFEU], confer on the Member States a discretion in the interests of environment policy'.

[84] Cf. the Communication of the Commission, Single Market and the Environment, COM (99) 263. Cf.
also Case C-473/98 *Kemikalieninspektionen* v. *Toolex Alpha AB* [2000] ECR I-5681, para. 45. See also
Case C-121/00 *Hahn* [2002] ECR I-9193, para. 38: 'in so far as there are uncertainties at the present state
of scientific research, it is for the Member States, within the limits imposed by the Treaty, to decide what
degree of protection they wish to assure and, in particular, the stringency of the checks to be carried
out'.

sures are permissible if there is a strong suspicion that the substance in question poses a health threat.

Protection of health and life of humans, animals or plants

Although the Court repeatedly held that 'the health and life of humans rank foremost among the property or interests protected by' Article 36 TFEU[85] and that it is for the Member States to decide at what level they wish to set the protection of the life and health of humans,[86] the early case law of the Court of Justice has clearly shown that the scope of Article 36 TFEU, as an exception to a fundamental Treaty provision, had to be interpreted narrowly. As the protection of the environment is not included in the exhaustive list of exceptions contained in Article 36 TFEU, a restriction on imports or exports to protect the environment, without there being a real and actual threat to health and life of humans, animals or plants, was not capable of being justified by Article 36 TFEU.

> Import prohibitions of non-harmful wastes, which do not directly threaten life or health, cannot be justified on the grounds of Article 36 TFEU, as was made clear in the Court's judgment in the *Walloon Waste* case: 'So far as the environment is concerned, it should be observed that waste has a special characteristic. The accumulation of waste, even before it becomes a health hazard, constitutes a threat to the environment because of the limited capacity of each region or locality for receiving it.'[87] This case clearly makes a distinction between protecting the environment and protecting health.
>
> The same strict approach employed in the *Walloon Waste* case can also be found in the *Dusseldorp* case.[88] The Dutch Government argued that their export restrictions for oil filters could be justified under Article 36 TFEU. The Court did not agree: 'Such a justification would be relevant if the processing of oil filters in other Member States and their shipment over a greater distance as a result of their being exported posed a threat to the health and life of humans. The documents before the Court do not, however, show that to be the case. On the one hand, the Netherlands Government itself conceded that the processing of filters in Germany was comparable to that performed by AVR Chemie. On the other, it has not been established that the shipment of the oil filters posed a threat to the environment or to the life and health of humans.'

In line with this narrow and strict interpretation is the case law from the Court of Justice that an important criterion for application of Article 36 TFEU is that

---

[85] See for instance Case C-473/98 *Kemikalieninspektionen* v. *Toolex Alpha AB* [2000] ECR I-5681, para. 38.

[86] For instance Case 272/80 *Frans-Nederlandse Maatschappij voor Biologische Producten* [1981] ECR 3277 and Case 125/88 *Nijman* [1989] ECR 3533. Confirmed in Case C-293/94 *Brandsma* [1996] ECR I-3159, para. 11 and Case C-400/96 *Harpegnies* [1998] ECR I-5121, para. 33.

[87] Case C-2/90 *Commission* v. *Belgium* [1992] ECR I-4431.

[88] Case C-203/96 *Dusseldorp* [1998] ECR I-4075, para. 46. Cf. Case C-209/98 *Sydhavnens Sten & Grus* [2000] ECR I-3743, para. 45.

there must be a *real* and *actual* danger threatening life or public health. In particular national legislation restricting the placing on the market of plant protection products, pesticides, biocides and other dangerous substances has benefited from the exception of Article 36 TFEU.[89]

> One example is the *Fumicot* case, in which Dutch plant protection manufacturer, was fined in the Netherlands for an offence under the Dutch legislation on plant protection products) which prohibited the sale, storage or use as a plant protection product of a product which has not been approved.[90] The company concerned had imported, sold or supplied in the Netherlands a quantity of a plant protection product called 'Fumicot Fumispore'. That product had already been lawfully marketed in France but had not received the approval which is required in the Netherlands in accordance with Dutch law. The company contended that the system of approval was incompatible with Articles 34 and 36 TFEU: 'It should be noted that, at the time of the alleged offences, there were no common or harmonised rules relating to the production or marketing of plant protection products. In the absence of harmonisation, it was therefore for the Member States to decide what degree of protection of the health and life of humans they intended to assure and in particular how strict the checks to be carried out were to be [...], having regard however to the fact that their freedom of action is itself restricted by the Treaty. In that respect, it is not disputed that the national rules in question are intended to protect public health and that they therefore come within the exception provided for by Article 36. The measures of control applied by the Netherlands authorities, in particular as regards the approval of the product, may not therefore be challenged in principle.'[91]

From these judgments it appeared that the Court made a rather strict distinction between 'environmental protection' on the one hand and 'the protection of health and life of humans, animals or plants' on the other.[92] In view of this restrictive approach, it was doubtful whether measures not addressing a demonstrable direct interest to health and life of humans, animals or plants were covered by Article 36 TFEU. However, in the light of more recent case law it should not be ruled out that the Court now approves a wider interpretation of Article 36 TFEU.

> In the *Bluhme* case the Court observed that measures to preserve an indigenous animal population with distinct characteristics contribute to the maintenance of biodiversity by protecting the population concerned against extinction, 'or, even

---

[89] Case 94/83 *Albert Heijn* [1984] ECR 3263 and Case 54/85 *Mirepoix* [1986] ECR 1067.

[90] Case 272/80 *Frans-Nederlandse Maatschappij voor Biologische Producten* [1981] ECR 3277.

[91] This judgment was confirmed in the *Improsol* case, Case 125/88 *Nijman* [1989] ECR 3533. Cf. also Case C-400/96 *Harpegnies* [1998] ECR I-5121. Cf. also Case C-293/94 *Brandsma* [1996] ECR I-3159.

[92] There were however some cases where the Court seemed to apply a wider interpretation of Article 36 TFEU. See for instance Case 125/88 *Nijman* [1989] ECR 3533 and Case C-389/96 *Aher-Waggon* [1998] ECR I-4473, para. 19.

in the absence of such risk, on account of a scientific or other interest in preserving the pure population at the location concerned'. By so doing, they are aimed at protecting the life of those animals and are capable of being justified under Article 36 TFEU.[93] And in *PreussenElektra*, discussed above, the Court ruled that promoting the use of renewable energy sources for producing electricity 'is useful for protecting the environment in so far as it contributes to the reduction in emissions of greenhouse gases' and 'is also designed to protect the health and life of humans, animals and plants'.[94] It remains to be seen to what extent this wider interpretation of Article 36 TFEU will be pursued in future cases as well.

Finally, in *Mickelsson & Roos*, the Court of Justice argued that 'the protection of the environment', on the one hand, and 'the protection of health and life of humans, animals and plants', on the other hand, are, closely related objectives. In that case the Court decided to examine both grounds together in order to assess whether the Swedish restrictions on the use of jetski's were justified.[95] The noise caused by jetski's disturbs people and animals, including and above all certain protected species of birds. Furthermore, the easy transport of personal watercraft facilitates the spread of animal diseases. Under those circumstances a combined assessment is certainly justified.

Finally, it should be noted that, as far as animals and plants are concerned, not only species that are threatened with extinction or are extremely rare or uncommon qualify for protection. In principle, protection extends to all species of animals and plants.[96]

Arbitrary discrimination and disguised restrictions

According to the second sentence of Article 36 TFEU, national measures may not constitute a means of arbitrary discrimination or a disguised restriction on trade between Member States. The Court has not systematically addressed the question of what is and what is not a disguised restriction or an arbitrary discrimination. It could even be debated, in view of the requirement of the proportionality principle,[97] whether the second sentence adds anything at all. The most meaningful interpretation of the sentence is probably the following. Its wording indicates that it is possible, in principle, for domestic and foreign goods to be treated differently under Article 36 TFEU. In other words, the addition that there may be no arbitrary discrimination could be taken to mean that any difference must be based on grounds capable of objective justification.

---

[93] Case C-67/97 *Bluhme* [1998] ECR I-8033. Cf. also Case C-100/08 *Commission* v. *Belgium* [2009] ECR I-140 and Case C-249/07 *Commission* v. *Netherlands* [2008] ECR I-174.

[94] Case C-379/98 *PreussenElektra* [2001] ECR I-2099. Cf. also Case C-448/01 *EVN and Wienstrom* [2003] ECR I-14527.

[95] Case C-142/05 *Mickelsson and Roos* [2009] ECR I-4273, para. 33.

[96] See also Advocate General Van Gerven in Case C-169/89 *Gourmetterie v.d. Burg* [1990] ECR I-2143.

[97] See on this principle more in detail section 4.5 of this chapter.

Take the case where a Member State desired to restrict the import of certain dangerous substances, by introducing a system of import permits. This would be an arbitrary discrimination, if the domestic manufacture and marketing of the same substances was not subject to any restrictions. Any such measure in respect of foreign goods would have to be accompanied by corresponding, but not necessary identical, protective measures in respect of domestic goods.

Trading rules might constitute a disguised restriction on trade, if their restrictive effect is not limited to what is necessary to protect the interest referred to by the rules.[98] The dividing line between this requirement and the proportionality principle is not a sharp one.

An example from the environmental case law of the Court, where the term disguised restriction was discussed, is the *Fumicot* case referred to above.[99] After the Court had noted that, in the absence of harmonisation, it was for the Member States to decide what degree of protection of the health and life of humans they intended to assure, the Court continued: 'However, that leaves open the question whether the detailed procedures governing approvals, as indicated by the national court, may possibly constitute a disguised restriction, within the meaning of the last sentence of Article 36, on trade between Member States, in view, on the one hand, of the dangerous nature of the product and, on the other hand, of the fact that it has been the subject of a procedure for approval in the Member State where is has been lawfully marketed. Whilst a Member State is free to require a product of the type in question, which has already received approval in another Member State, to undergo a fresh procedure of examination and approval, the authorities of the Member States are nevertheless required to assist in bringing about a relaxation of the controls existing in intra-EU trade. It follows that they are not entitled unnecessarily to require technical or chemical analyses or laboratory tests where those analyses and tests have already been carried out in another Member State and their results are available to those authorities, or may at their request be placed at their disposal.'

4.4 The *Rule of Reason* and Environmental Protection

Apart from Article 36 TFEU, the Court's case law provides another means of considering certain trade restrictive measures admissible. In the *Cassis de Dijon* judgment and in subsequent cases it was decided that, in the absence of common rules, obstacles to free movement within the EU resulting from disparities between the national laws must be accepted, in so far as such rules, applicable to domestic and imported products without distinction, may be recognised as being necessary in order to satisfy a 'mandatory requirement' rec-

---

98 See Advocate General Van Gerven in Joined Cases C-1/90 and C-176/90 *Aragonesa* [1991] ECR I-4151.

99 Case 272/80 *Frans-Nederlandse Maatschappij voor Biologische Producten* [1981] ECR 3277.

ognised by Union law.[100] This is known as the 'rule of reason' exception. In that case the Court referred to public health, the fairness of commercial transactions and the defence of the consumer as examples of such mandatory requirements.

In the *Danish Bottles* case the Court added 'protection of the environment'[101] to this list.[102] In that case Danish legislation only allowed the marketing of beer and soft drinks if returnable containers were used and if the importer or manufacturer set up an approved system to ensure the collection and return of such containers. As a result the Danish market was virtually closed to foreign manufacturers of beer and soft drinks. The Commission decided to bring an action against Denmark for infringement of the Treaty. Recognizing that protection of the environment could justify a restriction of the free movement of goods, it contended that alternatives were available which would restrict trade less while still protecting the environment. In a key passage the Court held:

> '[...] that the protection of the environment is one of the Community's essential objectives, which may as such justify certain limitations of the principle of the free movement of goods. That view is moreover confirmed by the Single European Act. In view of the foregoing, it must therefore be stated that the protection of the environment is a mandatory requirement which may limit the application of Article 30 EC. [now Article 36 TFEU]'

In the light of the Court's earlier judgment on the status of environmental protection in the European legal order, this judgment was hardly surprising. It took the Court remarkably few words to establish that protection of the environment could justify import restrictions. This statement of principle was later confirmed in the *Walloon Waste* case.[103]

Environmental protection is clearly a more comprehensive concept than protection of health and life of humans, animals or plants, even if nowadays the Court seems to interpret Article 36 TFEU less strict than it used to.[104] The deposit-and-return system in the *Danish Bottles* case could probably not have been justified under Article 36 TFEU. The interests at stake – prevention of litter, energy conservation, promotion of re-use etc. – seem less easily encompassed by Article 36 TFEU.

More in particular the Court of Justice has accepted, e.g., the following environmental objectives under the rule of reason: protection of birds against noise

---

[100] Case 120/78 *Rewe-Zentral AG* [1979] ECR 649. Or 'imperative requirement': Case C-221/06 *Stadtgemeinde Frohnleiten* [2007] ECR I-2613, para. 66.

[101] Which has to be interpreted in the light of the principles mentioned in Article 191(2) TFEU; Cf. Case C-209/98 *Sydhavnens Sten & Grus* [2000] ECR I-3743, para. 48.

[102] Case 302/86 *Commission* v. *Denmark* [1988] ECR 4607 and confirmed by the Court of Justice in numerous cases afterwards.

[103] Case C-2/90 *Commission* v. *Belgium* [1992] ECR I-4431.

[104] See our remarks with respect to Article 36 TFEU in this chapter, section 4.3 above.

disturbances,[105] promoting the production of renewable energy,[106] biodiversity,[107] re-use and recycling of waste,[108] protection against aircraft noise,[109] to ensure the quality of ambient air,[110] town and country planning[111] and waste disposal in line with the self-sufficiency and proximity principles.[112]

In conclusion, the material scope of the rule of reason is still wider and thus offers the Member States more latitude to take protective measures.

Article 36 TFEU or a mandatory requirement?

It could be asked to what extent a national import restriction for environmental reasons should be regarded as a ground for justification in the sense of Article 36 TFEU, or as a 'mandatory requirement' in the sense of *Cassis de Dijon*[113] and the *Danish Bottles*[114] judgments? As the material scope of the rule of reason is wider and offers the Member States more leeway to take protective measures one could even argue that there is hardly any need to rely on Article 36 TFEU if the rule of reason is available to the Member States.

However, on the basis of older case law the rule of reason seemed more limited than Article 36 TFEU in a different respect. In principle, Article 36 TFEU allows an exemption for national measures which relate in particular to imported products only. In other words, it offers some room for 'measures applicable *with* distinction'. Such specific import restrictions may not, however, constitute an arbitrary discrimination. And prohibition of the importation of a harmful product will constitute an arbitrary discrimination if no restriction whatever is imposed on the domestic use of that product. It is not arbitrary however, if there is a valid and objective reason why the imported product is to be treated differently. In other words under Article 36 TFEU *differentiation* is allowed, but *discrimination* is not.

As far as the rule of reason is concerned, the measure in question had to be applied without distinction to domestic and foreign products. It was well-established case law that the rule of reason doctrine could not be relied on to justify national measures which were not applicable to domestic products and imported products *without* distinction.[115] This meant that national protective measures

---

[105] Case C-142/05 *Mickelsson and Roos* [2009] ECR I-4273.

[106] Case C-379/98 *PreussenElektra* [2001] ECR I-2099.

[107] Case C-67/97 *Bluhme* [1998] ECR I-8033.

[108] Case 302/86 *Commission v. Denmark* [1988] ECR 4607.

[109] Case C-389/96 *Aher-Waggon* [1998] ECR I-4473 and Case C-67/97 *Bluhme* [1998] ECR I-8033.

[110] Case C-320/03 *Commission v. Austria* [2005] ECR I-9871.

[111] Case C-400/08 *Commission v. Spain*, Judgment of 24 March 2011.

[112] Case C-2/90 *Commission v. Belgium* [1992] ECR I-4431.

[113] Case 120/78 *Rewe-Zentral AG* [1979] ECR 649.

[114] Case 302/86 *Commission v. Denmark* [1988] ECR 4607.

[115] See for instance, Joined Cases C-1/90 and C-176/90 *Aragonesa de Publicidad Exterior and Publivía* [1991] ECR I-4151, para. 13.

which might be justified on environmental grounds, but do not fall within the more limited scope of Article 36 TFEU, are only allowed if they can be regarded as measures applicable without distinction.

However, the judgment in the *Walloon Waste* case was the first case which caused some confusion as to the degree to which a measure must be applicable without distinction for the rule of reason to apply.[116]

> In that case, the lawfulness of a Walloon prohibition on the disposal of foreign waste was at issue. The Commission argued that these mandatory requirements of environmental protection could not be relied on to allow the Walloon restrictions. The Commission insisted that the measures at issue discriminated against waste coming from other Member States though that waste was no more harmful than that produced in Wallonia. The same line of reasoning was developed by Advocate General Jacobs in his Opinion. In the Advocate General's view, there was 'plainly' discrimination between foreign and Belgian waste and therefore the ruling of the Court in the Danish Bottles case could not serve as a precedent.[117] The Court of Justice first confirmed that the 'mandatory requirements' are to be taken into account only with regard to measures which apply to national and imported products without distinction. However, in order to determine whether the obstacle in question is discriminatory, the particular type of waste must be taken into account. The principle that environmental damage should as a priority be rectified at source – a principle laid down by Article 191(2) TFEU for action by the Union relating to the environment – means that it is for each region, commune or other local entity to take appropriate measures to receive, process and dispose of its own waste. Consequently waste should be disposed of as close as possible to the place where it is produced. It then observed that this principle is in conformity with the principles of self-sufficiency and proximity set out in the Basel Convention. The Court therefore concluded that, having regard to the differences between waste produced in one place and that in another and its connection with the place where it is produced, the Belgian measures could not be considered to be discriminatory.

What is interesting is, in the first place, that the Court has *de facto* equated the fact that a measure applies without distinction to the absence of discrimination. By thus equating the two, the Court has made the test of whether or not a measure applies without distinction a test of whether or not it is discriminatory. The relevance of this discussion could be that, for a national measure to benefit from the rule of reason exception, it no longer has to be framed as a measure applicable without distinction. Apparently, differential measures can also be excepted using the rule of reason, as long as there is an objective justification. More recent case law indeed seems to suggest that the criterion 'measure applicable

---

[116] Case C-2/90 *Commission* v. *Belgium* [1992] ECR I-4431.
[117] Case 302/86 *Commission* v. *Denmark* [1988] ECR 4607.

without distinction' is no longer a hard and fast rule in the case law of the Court of Justice.

> For example, it could be argued that the German rules in *Aher-Waggon* do indeed adversely affect foreign aircraft in particular, and it could also be argued that the Danish bee regulations in *Bluhme* are in essentially distinctly applicable measures.[118] The most clear example of an environmental case where the Court applied a rule of reason test, albeit not explicitly, with respect to a distinctly applicable measure is *PreussenElektra*.[119] The German rules clearly favoured domestic 'green energy' producing undertakings and it is hard to see those rules as being indistinctly applicable. It is the authors' opinion that the Court in that case applied the rule of reason and not Article 36 TFEU. The dictum of the judgment, where the Court ruled that the German measures 'are not incompatible' with Article 34 TFEU shows that the Court is not applying the exception of Article 36 TFEU. In that case the dictum of the judgment would entail something like '...is justified by Article 36 TFEU' or 'Article 36 TFEU does not preclude....'.
>
> We may also point to Dutch legislation requiring vehicles that have previously been registered in another Member State to undergo an identification check together with a roadworthiness test relating to their general condition prior to registration in the Netherlands.[120] Although the legislation, clearly not applicable without distinction, failed to meet the proportionality principle, the Court seemed to be willing to accept, at least in principle, that the Dutch government relied on 'environmental protection' as an overriding reason in the public interest capable of justifying a hindrance to the free movement of goods.
>
> Finally, we should mention Case C-320/03.[121] That case involved regional Austrian legislation prohibiting lorries of more than 7.5 tons, carrying certain goods, from being driven on a section of the A12 motorway in the Inn valley. This legislation had clearly discriminatory elements as the prohibition affected the international transit of goods – carried out as to more than 80% by non-Austrian undertakings – in particular. Nevertheless, the Court ruled – subject to the proportionality principle – that now the Austrian legislation was adopted in order to ensure the quality of ambient air the measure can be justified on 'environmental protection grounds'.

Taken together with indications in the Court's case law outside the field of the environment that the rule of reason will be applied where measures do make a distinction,[122] it cannot be ruled out that the relevance of the distinction between

---

[118] Case C-389/96 *Aher-Waggon* [1998] ECR I-4473 and Case C-67/97 *Bluhme* [1998] ECR I-8033.

[119] Case C-379/98 *PreussenElektra* [2001] ECR I-2099.

[120] Case C-297/05 *Commission v. Netherlands* [2007] ECR I-7467.

[121] Case C-320/03 *Commission v. Austria* [2005] ECR I-9871.

[122] Case C-385/99 *Müller-Fauré and van Riet* [2003] ECR I-4509; Case C-34/95 *De Agostini* [1997] ECR I-3843 and Case C-388/95 *Belgium v. Spain* [2000] ECR I-3123. Cf. on the shifting of the Court's case law in this respect Oliver (1999) at 804-806 and Timmermans (2006).

Article 36 interests and rule of reason exceptions has ceased to exist. Maybe it is time that the Court will rule on this explicitly.[123]

The rule of reason *and export restrictions*
Above it was stated that Article 35 TFEU applies only to discriminatory restrictions on exports. Measures applicable without distinction which have a restrictive effect on exports are therefore outside the scope of this provision. This means that there is no need to apply the rule of reason as far as Article 35 TFEU is concerned. There is thus no need for further review in the light of the requirement of the proportionality principle. However, if, as we have argued above, that the case law of the Court of Justice is changing and that 'measures applicable without distinction' might also fall within the scope of application of Article 35 TFEU, the 'rule of reason' is also relevant to Article 35 TFEU as well.

Under the 'old' rule that the rule of reason cannot be applied with respect to distinctly applicable measures, export restrictions which are within the scope of application of Article 35 TFEU may be justified only on the grounds contained in Article 36 TFEU. But also this case law of the Court of Justice seems to shifting. It was suggested above that the case law of the Court on the distinction between 'Article 36 interests' and 'rule of reason exceptions' is becoming blurred. And that there are indications that protection of the environment can also be relied on to justify measures other than those 'applicable without distinction'. If our interpretation of the direction the law is taking is correct, it is hard to understand why 'protection of the environment' should not be relied on to justify measures falling under the scope of Article 35 TFEU.

> A paragraph from the *Dusseldorp* judgment will illustrate this. In that case the Dutch Government had argued that a ban on the export of oil filters was justified by the imperative requirement of protection of the environment. Unlike Advocate General Jacobs, the Court apparently did not want to dismiss the possibility of applying Article 35 TFEU in this way out of hand: 'It must therefore be concluded that the object and effect of application of the principles of self-sufficiency and proximity to waste for recovery, such as oil filters, is to restrict exports of that waste and is not justified, in circumstances such as those in the present case, *by an imperative requirement relating to protection of the environment* or the desire to protect the health and life of humans in accordance with Article 36'.[124]
>
> However, in *Sten & Grus* the Court ruled 'that the protection of the environment cannot serve to justify any restriction on exports'.[125] This seems to have settled the case. On the other hand, the quoted phrase should be read in context of the facts of the case. The Court was quite clear that the waste in *Sten & Grus* was non-

---

[123] The Court has been invited to do so by Advocate General Jacobs in the *PreussenElektra* case; See point 229 of his Opinion. Cf. also the Opinion of Advocate General Geelhoed in Case C-320/03 *Commission* v. *Austria* [2005] ECR I-9871, point 106 of his Opinion.

[124] Emphasis added by the authors. Cf. the case note of Notaro in [1999] *CMLRev.* 1317-1319.

[125] Case C-209/98 *Sydhavnens Sten & Grus* [2000] ECR I-3743, paras. 48.

hazardous and intended for recovery and that nothing has been put forward to the Court to show that there is a danger to the health and life of humans, animals or plants. As some commentators rightly put it, this leaves open the possibility that a restriction on exports might be justifiable for environmental reasons if the waste in question would cause environmental damage.[126]

If our interpretation of the shifting case law of the Court of Justice is correct, the Court has not only broadened the scope of the prohibition of Article 35 TFEU, but also significantly extended the possibilities of imposing restrictions on the free movement of goods based on environmental considerations. Some caution must nevertheless be exercised in interpreting this more recent trends in the case law. We shall have to await further developments.

4.5   Other Aspects for the Application of the Exceptions

Non-economic purposes only
It is established case law of the Court that Article 36 TFEU and the rule of reason may only be used for non-economic purposes. It should not be ruled out that in some cases a particular measure, even though its primary function is protection of health or the environment, will also aim to achieve a certain economic objective. This is particularly true of export restrictions in the waste sector. One of the reasons for Member States to prohibit the export of waste is to ensure that their own national waste disposal installations can operate profitably. There is always the danger that, as a result of the export of large quantities of waste, the capacity of national disposal installations will be greater than the demand for waste disposal. This can result in under-utilised national waste disposal capacity, driving up prices of waste disposal, and creating even more waste exports. To avoid this, some Member States want to restrict the export of waste, improving the supply for their own national disposal installations.

The question which arises here is whether the economic profitability of waste disposal installations falls within the scope of Article 36 TFEU. The judgments of the Court, particularly in the *Inter-Huiles*, *Nertsvoederfabriek* and *Dusseldorp* cases, show that this poses its own problems.[127] The *Inter-Huiles* case concerned French legislation, according to which all waste oil must be delivered to officially authorised waste oil collectors. The French Government argued that the disputed legislation satisfied an economic requirement, since only the collection of all waste oils is sufficient to ensure the profitability of undertakings approved for the disposal of waste oils. The Court did not accept that argument: 'Articles 13 and 14 of the directive provide that, by way of compensation for the obligations imposed on the

---

[126] Davies (2004) at 208 and Notaro (2000) at 310-311.

[127] Case 172/82 *Inter-Huiles* [1983] ECR 555; Case C-203/96 *Dusseldorp* [1998] ECR I-4075 and Case 118/86 *Nertsvoederfabriek* [1987] ECR 3883.

undertakings for the implementation of Article 5, Member States may, without placing restrictions on exports, grant such undertakings "indemnities" financed in accordance with the principle of "polluter pays".'

It is impossible to draw any too far-reaching conclusions from this. In this particular case the argument that the measure was necessary to ensure the profitability of waste disposal installations was rejected because the directive itself provided for other instruments to protect this interest. The judgment cannot be seen as implying a general preference for financial incentives rather than non-tariff instruments.

> Another relevant Court judgment can be found in the *Nertsvoederfabriek* case. A Dutch law required poultry offal to be delivered only to licensed rendering plants. This law implied a prohibition of exports. The Netherlands Government argued that the law was essential in order to maintain the overall effectiveness of the system. As the Court acknowledged, referring to an earlier judgment: 'The mere fact that national provisions, justified by objective circumstances corresponding to the needs of the interests referred to therein, enable other objectives of an economic nature to be achieved as well, does not exclude the application of Article 36. That applies with greater force where the objective of an economic nature necessarily enables the objective relating to health to be attained.'

In this case the implied prohibition of exports could not be maintained, because another condition was not met. The Court held that it does not appear necessary to prohibit the exportation of poultry offal, provided that the conditions relating to health laid down by those provisions are satisfied with respect to removal and transport on national territory.

In the *Dusseldorp* case the Court explicitly rejected the Dutch Government's argument concerning the profitability of waste processing plant. The Netherlands had argued that the measures in question were necessary to provide the Dutch waste company with sufficient waste to be able to operate profitably, and to ensure that it received a sufficient supply of oil filters for use as fuel. In the absence of sufficient supply, the company would have been obliged to use a less environmentally friendly fuel. The Court responded as follows:

> 'Even if the national measure in question could be justified by reasons relating to the protection of the environment, it is sufficient to point out that the arguments put forward by the Netherlands Government, concerning the profitability of the national undertaking AVR Chemie and the costs incurred by it, are of an economic nature. The Court has held that aims of a purely economic nature cannot justify barriers to the fundamental principle of the free movement of goods'.

It is worth noting that the Court did not desire to link the profitability test with an underlying environmental objective. Surely it could be argued that, ultimately, the export ban was not designed to ensure AVR's profitability, but that it was a prerequisite to achieving certain environmental goals (adequate waste disposal). There are other judgments where the Court has indeed considered the underlying aims.[128]

In the light of all this case law, the conclusion must be that Article 36 TFEU and the rule of reason do not seem to allow Member States to restrict the export of waste to ensure the profitability of their national waste disposal installations. More general, the condition that Article 36 TFEU and the rule of reason may only be used for non-economic purposes can pose a serious obstacle for the Member States. However, Article 106(2) TFEU may be used to do just this.[129]

The proportionality principle

It is clear from the judgments of the Court that national measures restricting the free movement of goods, but which are in principle capable of being justified under Article 36 TFEU or the rule of reason, must be compatible with the proportionality principle. This principle involves two or possibly three different aspects, which are discussed below.

In the first place the national measure must be *suitable* actually to protect the interest to be protected. In the environment field this means there must be a causal link between the measure and the protection of the environment. It is hardly surprising that this hurdle rarely proves difficult to cross. After all, why should a Member State desiring to protect a particular interest not adopt an effective measure? Nevertheless, this criterion does give the Court a means of acting against measures which are presented as necessary for the protection of the environment, but are essentially protectionist. The measure taken or proposed must be appropriate actually to protect the interest that requires protection and to avert the danger to the health of humans, animals or plants. A national measure is certainly not allowed if it does not, or could not, have the desired effect.

The causal link between the measure and the environmental objective which is required should be demonstrated by the Member States by reference to relevant science. However the precautionary principle may in some cases justify a measure even where the causal link cannot be clearly established on the basis of the scientific evidence available.[130] It is not entirely clear how strict the Court is in respect of the required causal link. Is it sufficient that the measure has some positive effect on the interest to be protected, or must more be required?

In the *Red Grouse* case, Advocate General Van Gerven discussed the question whether the Dutch prohibition of imports would actually have a positive effect on

---

[128] For example, Case C-324/93 *Evans Medical* [1995] ECR I-563, Case 118/86 *Nertsvoederfabriek* [1987] ECR 3883 and, on waste disposal (!), Case C-209/98 *Sydhavnens Sten & Grus* [2000] ECR I-3743.

[129] Cf. Chapter 7, section 6.2.

[130] Cf. Case C-473/98 *Kemikalieninspektionen* v. *Toolex Alpha AB* [2000] ECR I-5681, paras. 41-45.

the protection of the species outside the Netherlands.[131] His reply was affirmative: 'There is a possibility that the prohibition of imports into the Netherlands may reduce demand for dead birds of the species in question from the United Kingdom and thereby exert a positive influence on the population of that species in the Member State in which it occurs; in other words, there may to some extent be a causal connection between the measure in question and the objective pursued.'

'Positive influence' and 'to some extent a causal connection' were thus sufficient, in his view, to regard the measure as acceptable in this respect.

In the *Danish Bottles* case the Court was particularly concerned to assess whether the measure could be regarded as necessary.[132] The Court examined the connection between the mandatory deposit-and-return system and the attainment of environmental objectives:

'First of all, as regards the obligation to establish a deposit-and-return system for empty containers, it must be observed that this requirement is an indispensable element of a system intended to ensure the re-use of containers and therefore appears necessary to achieve the aims pursued by the contested rules.'

The causal connection is not always explicitly examined, as it was in this case. In most cases the causal relation is so obvious and unproblematic that the Court does not need to examine it explicitly.

Secondly, a measure must be *necessary* in the sense that it restricts trade as little as possible; there must be no measures less restrictive, but adequate, available. Or, in other words: the means which the Member States choose must be limited to what is actually necessary.[133] Possible alternative national instruments will first be assessed in the light of the question: would they or would they not protect the interest similar[134] or equally effective? If the answer is that they would, the question must then be addressed which of these instruments would entail the least negative effects for market integration. This also implies that the mere fact that other Member States have less strict rules or have chosen a different system of protection, does not necessarily mean that the proportionality principle has been violated.[135]

In the *Danish Bottles* case the Court expressed the necessity requirement as follows: 'Such rules must also be proportionate to the aim in view. If a Member State has a choice between various measures for achieving the same aim, it

---

[131] Case C-169/89 *Gourmetterie v.d. Burg* [1990] ECR I-2143.

[132] Case 302/86 *Commission v. Denmark* [1988] ECR 4607.

[133] Case C-333/08 *Commission v. France* [2010] ECR I-757.

[134] Cf. Case C-297/05 *Commission v. Netherlands* [2007] ECR I-7467, para. 79.

[135] Cf. Case C-227/02 *EU Wood Trading* [2004] ECR I-11957, paras. 51-52 and Case C-219/07 *Nationale Raad van Dierenkwekers en Liefhebbers and Andibel* [2008] ECR I-4475, para. 31.

should choose the means which least restricts the free movements of goods.'
And, referring to its judgment in the *ADBHU* case: 'Measures adopted to protect
the environment must not "go beyond the inevitable restrictions which are justified by the pursuit of the objective of environmental protection".'[136]

The Court then proceeded to review the compatibility of the mandatory system
of collection and return of containers with the principle of proportionality it
had thereby formulated. Having observed, as regards the obligation to establish
a deposit-and-return system for empty containers, that this requirement was
an indispensable element of a system intended to insure the re-use of containers and therefore appeared necessary to achieve the aim pursued, it concluded:
'That being so, the restrictions which it imposes on the free movement of goods
cannot be regarded as disproportionate.' Here the causal connection was examined simultaneously with the test of proportionality.

> In the *Crayfish* case, German legislation fell foul of the Court's review of a measure
> in the light of the necessity test.[137] According to the Federal Law on the Protection
> of Nature (*Bundesnaturschutzgesetz*) the importation of live crayfish for commer-
> cial purposes is in principle prohibited. However, the competent public authority
> may, on application, derogate from that prohibition where the application of the
> law would, contrary to the legislator's intention, lead to excessive hardship. The
> German Government argued that the import restrictions were needed for the
> effective protection of native species of crayfish against disease and the risks of
> faunal distortion. The Commission submitted that this objective could have been
> achieved by measures having less restrictive effects on intra-EU trade. For exam-
> ple, instead of simply prohibiting imports of all species of live freshwater crayfish,
> Germany could have confined itself to making consignments of crayfish from other
> Member States or already in free circulation in the EU subject to health checks
> and only carrying out checks by sample if such consignments were accompanied
> by a health certificate issued by the competent authorities of the dispatching
> Member State certifying that the product in question presented no risk to health,
> or instead confined itself to regulating the marketing of crayfish in its territory,
> in particular by subjecting to authorisation only the restocking of national waters
> with species likely to be carrying the disease and restricting release of animals in
> the wild and restocking areas in which native species are to be found. The Court
> of Justice agreed with the Commission: 'However, the Federal Government has
> not convincingly shown that such measures, involving less serious restrictions
> for intra-Community trade, were incapable of effectively protecting the interests
> pleaded.' In view of the *Crayfish* case one could argue that there exists a presump-
> tion against total bans.
> In *Toolex* however the Court was more lenient towards Swedish legislation
> which laid down a general prohibition on the use of trichloroethylene for industrial

---

[136] Case 240/83 *ADBHU* [1985] ECR 531.

[137] Case C-131/93 *Commission* v. *Germany* [1994] ECR I-3303. Cf. also Case C-249/07 *Commission* v. *Netherlands* [2008] ECR I-174.

purposes and established a system of individual exemptions, granted subject to conditions.[138] In particular the Court accepted the so-called 'substitution principle' according to which an exemption is granted only on the condition that no safer replacement product is available and provided that the applicant continues to seek alternative solutions which are less harmful to public health and the environment.

The more general conclusion that can be drawn from these judgments is that *general prohibitions* on imports of goods and products which will be harmful to the environment or pose a threat to health will not easily pass the proportionality test. Most of the time, the Court lays the burden of proof on the Member States. They must be able to show convincingly that the less stringent alternatives suggested by for instance the Commission are not adequate to protect the environment or health equally effectively. By implication, Member States are also under a duty to examine carefully the possibility of using measures less restrictive.[139] In other words, Member States who did not even contemplate the possibility of taking less restrictive measures *ex ante* will fail this part of the proportionality test already at the beginning.

In the area of national legislation on pesticides and biocides we come across the following, very specific, application of the necessity test. Although the Court allowed restrictions on the marketing of such products and held that Member State are free to require such products which have already received approval in another Member State to undergo a fresh procedure of examination and approval, the proportionality principle requires:

> 'that technical or chemical analyses or laboratory tests are not unnecessarily required when the same analyses and tests have already been carried out in that other Member State and their results are available to the competent authorities of the importing Member State or can, at their request, be made available to them.'[140]

Some authors argue that there is a third criterion to the application of the principle of proportionality. Would a measure be disproportionate if the obstacles resulting for intra-EU trade were not proportionate to the object intended or the result achieved (proportionality *stricto sensu*)? The problem will become clear if placed against the background of the Court's considerations in the *Danish Bottles* case.[141]

> The different arguments put forward in the case are both interesting and of practical relevance. The Commission considered that it follows from the principle of proportionality that the level of protection should not be fixed exaggeratedly high

---

[138] Case C-473/98 *Kemikalieninspektionen* v. *Toolex Alpha AB* [2000] ECR I-5681.

[139] Case C-320/03 *Commission* v. *Austria* [2005] ECR I-9871, para. 87. See on the 'proceduralization' of the proportionality principle also Barnard (2010) at 186.

[140] Case C-400/96 *Harpegnies* [1998] ECR I-5121, para. 36.

[141] Case 302/86 *Commission* v. *Denmark* [1988] ECR 4607.

and that other solutions should be accepted even if they are a little less effective in assuring the aim pursued.[142] By implication, this means that interests such as the environment and public health must be weighed in the same balance as the interest of free movement of goods. The United Kingdom supported this view. Protection of the environment is indeed one of the important objectives of the Union, but it does not follow that every measure adopted for the protection of the environment is *prima facie* justified and that it only remains to examine whether the same results could be achieved by alternative means. The effect of such a view would be that measures to eliminate all forms of pollution would always be justified, since it would be obvious that very often similarly effective results could not be obtained by other means: 'It is submitted that there must be a point beyond which measures for the protection of the environment can no longer be regarded as fulfilling one of the Community's essential objectives and that a balance between protection of the environment and the free movement of goods must be sought in accordance with the case law of the Court.' Advocate General Slynn expressed a similar view: 'There has to be a balancing of interests between the free movement of goods and environmental protection, even if in achieving the balance the high standard of the protection sought has to be reduced. The level of protection sought must be a reasonable level.'

Advocate General Van Gerven took more or less the same view in the *Red Grouse* case.[143] In his view, two tests of proportionality ought to be carried out in connection with Article 36 TFEU. He referred to the first of these as the criterion of the least restrictive alternative. Together, review in the light of this criterion and examination of the causal connection between the measure adopted and attainment of the aim pursued constituted the requirement of necessity. In addition, in his view, another test of proportionality was required. A measure which has a causal connection with the objective it pursues, and to which there is no less restrictive alternative, must subsequently be assessed in the light of the criterion of proportionality between the obstacle introduced and the objective pursued and/or the result actually achieved thereby. As a result of the application of that criterion, a Member State may be obliged to dispense with the measure in question or resign itself to a less effective one, where the restrictive effect of the first measure is disproportionate so far as the free movement of goods is concerned to the objective pursued by the measure or to the result actually achieved thereby. In other words, a measure taken to protect the life and health of humans, animals and plants may lose its lawfulness if its contribution to the protective aim is too little in the light of its restrictive effect on trade, even if there are no less restrictive measures available. In this view, proportion-

---

[142] See however Commission Decision 98/523, OJ 1998 L 233/25 concerning certain noise-related restrictions affecting air carriers' access to the new Karlstad airport in Sweden. According to the Commission the proportionality principle requires merely 'an *adequate* level of protection against aircraft noise', para. 38 of the decision.

[143] Case C-169/89 *Gourmetterie v.d. Burg* [1990] ECR I-2143.

ality implies that the interests named in Article 36 TFEU should be weighed against the free movement of goods. Van Gerven invoked the Court's decision in the *Danish Bottles* case to support his view.[144] The Court's considerations with respect to the requirement that only approved containers should be used do indeed seem to support this view:

> 'It is undoubtedly true that the existing system for returning approved containers ensures a maximum rate of re-use and therefore a *very considerable degree of protection of the environment* since empty containers can be returned to any retailer of beverages. Non-approved containers, on the other hand, can be returned only to the retailer who sold the beverages, since it is impossible to set up such a comprehensive system for those containers as well. Nevertheless, the system for returning non-approved containers *is capable of protecting the environment* and, as far as imports are concerned, affects only limited quantities of beverages compared with the quantity of beverages consumed in Denmark owing to the restrictive effect which the requirement that containers should be returnable has on imports.'[145]

There is much to be said for applying the principle of proportionality only in the form of the suitability and necessity tests. This view receives support from considerations of the Court that, in the absence of common or harmonised rules on health and/or the environment, it was for the Member States to decide upon the level at which they wished to protect the health and life of animals, and the environment.[146] The precautionary principle also points in this direction. In its guidelines on the precautionary principle the European Commission argues that the Union has the right to establish the level of protection of the environment, human, animal and plant health that it deems appropriate.[147] If the Union is entitled to set its own level of protection, in particular vis-à-vis the other WTO members, it is hard to see how this right can be denied the Member States.

Other reasons for restricting the application of the proportionality principle are of a more 'constitutional' nature. The third variant (proportionality *stricto sensu*) is problematic, as it requires a weighing of interests, normally reserved for the legislature. The proper functioning of the internal market must be balanced against protection of the environment. This is not simply a matter of

---

[144] Case 302/86 *Commission* v. *Denmark* [1988] ECR 4607. See also, outside environmental law, where the Court seemed to have applied the proportionality *stricto sensu* test: Case C-169/91 *Council of the City of Stoke-on-Trent and Norwich City Council* v. *B & Q Plc* [1992] ECR I-6635 and Case C-112/00 *Schmidberger* [2003] ECR I-5659, para. 81. Cf. also Case C-413/99 *Baumbast* 2002 ECR I-7091.

[145] Cf. also the way the Court applied the proportionality principle with respect to German rules concerning deposit and return obligations for non-reusable packaging in Case C-309/02 *Radlberger Getränkegesellschaft and S. Spitz* [2004] ECR I-11763.

[146] See Case C-131/93 *Commission* v. *Germany* [1994] ECR I-3303, para. 16, and Case 272/80 *Frans-Nederlandse Maatschappij voor Biologische Producten* [1981] ECR 3277, para. 12. Cf. Krämer (2007) at 106-110.

[147] Communication from the Commission on the *Precautionary principle*, COM (2000) 1 final.

a proper separation of the functions of the judiciary and the legislature. In the European context, application of the proportionality principle also impinges on the division of powers between the Union and its Member States. After all, application of Article 36 TFEU, the rule of reason, etc. is by definition[148] only at issue where the European legislature has not yet taken any action. A weighing of interests in the context of the proportionality principle therefore implies that the courts must first decide on the level of protection in the Union and then balance this against the interest of market integration. This, moreover, in a situation in which the Union legislature has not yet proved able to adopt legislation on the matter. This fact leads us to conclude that the courts should apply this variant of the proportionality principle with extreme caution.

This does not, of course, mean that all kinds of trade restrictions may now be introduced in the guise of environmental protection. In the first place, the 'no arbitrary discrimination and no disguised restriction on trade' tests can be applied to avoid this. At the same time the Court may require a degree of causal connection between the national measure and the environmental aim pursued. Such an assessment may be appropriate to measures which only indirectly and without any close connection produce a positive effect on the environment. But where an environmental interest is at stake which needs protection and the national measure in question is indeed capable of providing it, the lawfulness of the measure should not be capable of being questioned merely because the free movement of goods is seriously restricted.

Proportionality after harmonisation?

In Chapter 3, section 5 with respect to harmonisation we have noted that whenever Member States exercise their discretion by taking more stringent national environmental standards, this is made subject to an important condition. More stringent measures are permitted inasmuch as other provisions of the Treaty are not involved. Should the more stringent measures come into conflict with the Treaty prohibitions regarding the internal market, for instance, then a review of proportionality is in fact carried out; this occurs as part of the examination whether the national measures are justified. An example from the case law is the judgment of the Court of Justice in *Aher-Waggon*.[149]

In 1992, Aher-Waggon bought a propeller-driven Piper PA 28-140 aircraft in Denmark which had been registered in that State since 1974. Subsequently, it requested the German *Bundesamt* to register the aircraft in Germany. This request was refused, on the ground that the aircraft exceeded the noise limits permitted in Germany. The aircraft did comply with the relevant European standard (73 dB(A)), however, with a sound level of 72.2 dB(A), it exceeded the German thresholds (69

---

[148] See for a detailed discussion Chapter 3, section 2.

[149] Case C-389/96 *Aher-Waggon* [1998] ECR I-4473. Cf. also Case C-510/99 *Tridon* [2001] ECR I-7777, where stricter national rules in the area of endangered species of animals and plants were reviewed in the light of the rules on free movement of goods.

dB(A)). Aher-Waggon was unsuccessful in its action before the *Verwaltungsgericht* (Administrative Court) and on appeal. In an application for review on a point of law (*Revision*) before the *Bundesverwaltungsgericht*, Aher-Waggon held that the refusal to register the aircraft in Germany was a breach of European law. It based this on the fact that aircraft of the same type and sound level that were already registered in Germany retained their registration.

The Court first determined that the directive only laid down minimum require-ments, and thus allowed the Member States to adopt stricter noise limits.[150] Here, however, the possibility of applying the principle of proportionality is not excluded. The reason is that in this case the stricter limits have a negative effect on the free movement of goods, and should in principle be considered measures having equivalent effect under Article 34 TFEU. The question that then arises is what influence the minimum level of protection laid down in the directive has, or should have, on the manner in which the proportionality principle is applied. We would argue that in such cases a stricter review on the basis of the propor-tionality principle is appropriate. After all, from the moment there is a direc-tive with minimum standards, these standards must be considered to offer an adequate or even 'a high level of protection'. Otherwise the directive itself might be considered to fail the 'suitability' test and infringe the principle of proportion-ality! But, if the standards of the directive provide an adequate level of protec-tion, how can stricter national measures be *necessary*? Surely it must be assumed that a Member State infringes the principle of proportionality when in fact there is nothing to protect. Member States may in principle be allowed to determine the desired level of protection, but obviously there must be something to protect. This aspect, in particular, could be reviewed more intensively by the Court in cases of European minimum standards.

So, what is the best way of dealing with the review – in light of the principle of proportionality – of stricter national measures that involve a breach of one of the free movement provisions of the Treaties? As mentioned, in such cases a more intensive review in light of the principle of proportionality seems appropri-ate, precisely because account must be taken of the level of protection already realised by the relevant directive.[151] In order to demonstrate the necessity of the national measures, the Member State will usually have to demonstrate why the protection offered by the directive does not offer a solution in its specific case. In other words, is there such an exceptional situation that the Member State feels it must disregard the level of protection of the directive, and adopt more stringent

---

[150] Case C-389/96 *Aher-Waggon* [1998] ECR I-4437.

[151] See also, but then in the framework of Article 114 TFEU [then Article 100a EC Treaty], Advocate General Tesauro: 'The control entrusted to the Community institutions by Article 100a(4), on the other hand, seems necessarily to be inspired by more stringent criteria than those underlying the provisions of Article 36, in that there is no possibility of not taking account of the standards of protection already laid down by the harmonization rules'; Case C-41/93 *France v. Commission* [1994] ECR I-1829, para. 6 of his Opinion.

measures? In such cases, therefore, we would advocate a similar proportionality review to that laid down by the Treaty in the framework of Article 114(5) TFEU for national measures derogating from harmonisation measures. This is notwithstanding the fact that it may be questioned whether the Court actually does carry out a more intensive proportionality review in these kinds of cases.[152]

Diagonal proportionality?

A problem which has likewise not been solved in the Court's interpretation of the principle of proportionality is the extent to which the principle should be applied *diagonally*, in other words across Treaty provisions. What this means can be illustrated as follows. It has been noted above that where national authorities impose justified trade restrictions, they should in any event choose the least restrictive policy instrument. A system of authorisations is to be preferred above a total prohibition; an obligation to give notification above a system of authorisations. However, these examples concern instruments which have been applied within the context of a particular Treaty provision (or group of provisions). Diagonal proportionality assumes that it is important that there should be no 'less restrictive alternative' not only in the light of Articles 34 to 36 TFEU, but also in the light of the other Treaty provisions. Thus, in the case of a non-tariff restriction, in the light of Article 110 or Articles 107 and 108 TFEU. In other words, a given non-tariff restriction might conflict with the proportionality principle, even if there were no less restrictive non-tariff instrument, where there was an appropriate tariff instrument which would produce a less restrictive effect. Diagonal proportionality presupposes that public authorities examine a wide range of potential alternatives each time they wish to use certain restrictive policy instruments. It is not clear from the case law of the Court of Justice whether, and if so to what extent, the principle of proportionality operates in this way.

The transfrontier application of the exceptions

To what extent can Member States justify trade restrictions by invoking the grounds for justification formulated in the *Cassis de Dijon*[153] and *Danish Bottles*[154] cases, where it is not their own protective interests which are at stake, but those of other states or Member States, or even global environmental interests? In other words, to what extent can Article 36 TFEU and the rule of reason be applied 'extraterritorially'?

Obviously, many environmental interests are of a transfrontier nature. In many cases, protection of the environment can no longer be regarded as a strictly national matter. The transfrontier nature of the environment has been acknowledged by the European legislature, for example in the many directives that have been enacted in which the Member States undertake obligations to

---

[152] Neither in *Aher-Waggon*, nor in *Tridon* did the Court clarify whether it carried out a more intensive review of proportionality than normal. Cf. also Case C-100/08 *Commission* v. *Belgium* [2009] ECR I-140.

[153] Case 120/78 *Rewe-Zentral AG* [1979] ECR 649.

[154] Case 302/86 *Commission* v. *Denmark* [1988] ECR 4607.

prevent and control transfrontier pollution. It would be in contradiction of this if the lawfulness of national measures implying trade restrictions were again to be sharply divided into national categories. In this connection, Article 191(1) TFEU, fourth indent, is relevant, where dealing with regional or worldwide environmental problems is defined as a Community environmental objective. This demonstrates that responsibility for the environment is not tied to strict national boundaries.

On the one hand it could be argued that the grounds for justification should be interpreted strictly and that only measures to protect the interests of the Member State in question are covered. In this view Member States should 'mind their own business'. This was the view taken by Advocate General Trabucchi. Article 36 TFEU allows every State the right to protect exclusively its own national interests, he stated in his Opinion in *Dassonville*.[155] He elaborated this view in the *Kramer* case.[156] Talking of the spirit and purpose of this exempting clause, he referred to 'the genuinely unilateral character', confined to a particular State, which results from the fact that the interest for which Article 36 TFEU provides protection is essentially national and internal to the State. In his view, this particular function of Article 36 TFEU resisted a broader interpretation. He was, however, prepared to make an exception for those interests which, though not strictly national interests, could be regarded, by their nature, as common to all the Member States and which should therefore be regarded as Community interests. The interest involved in the *Kramer* case was the protection of fishery resources.

The Court seems to have endorsed Trabucchi's view on the use of Article 36 TFEU to protect the common interests of the Member States or even the world community as such in the *PreussenElektra* case.[157] The Court ruled that promoting the use of renewable energy sources for producing electricity 'is useful for protecting the environment in so far as it contributes to the reduction in emissions of greenhouse gases'. It also referred explicitly, in accepting the German rules, to United Nations Framework Convention on Climate Change and the Kyoto Protocol.

Arguably the same can be said with respect to the application of Article 36 TFEU in cases related to the protection of endangered or migratory species and protected habitats. In Chapter 3 we have discussed the case law of the Court of Justice regarding the implementation of the Wild Birds and Habitats directives. In view of the Court's opinion that those directives concern typically 'a transfrontier environment problem entailing common responsibilities for the Member States',[158] we must assume that Member States must also be allowed to rely on Article 36 TFEU to protect their common heritage. In his Opinion in

---

[155] Case 8/74 *Dassonville* [1974] ECR 837.

[156] Joined Cases 3, 4 and 6/76 *Kramer* [1976] ECR 1279.

[157] Case C-379/98 *PreussenElektra* [2001] ECR I-2099.

[158] E.g. Case 262/85 *Commission v. Italy* [1987] ECR 3073 and Case C-6/04 *Commission* v. *UK* [2005] ECR I-9017.

the *Red Grouse* case, Advocate General Van Gerven argued that the transfrontier nature of the protection of birds was such that he considered it sufficient to assume that a Member State could rely on the concern for animal life in another Member State to justify a restriction on the free movement of goods.[159]

> That case concerned a prohibition on keeping or selling birds, including red grouse, under Article 7 of the Dutch *Vogelwet* (Law on Birds). The Netherlands *Hoge Raad* had referred the matter to the Court for a preliminary ruling on whether such a prohibition was justified under Article 36 TFEU. In principle, like the Commission and the Netherlands Government, Van Gerven regarded transfrontier application as possible, though he felt that the proportionality principle must be assessed even more stringent in such cases. He assumed that a Member State would adopt a restrictive measure 'having regard to the requirements of mutual confidence under the legislation of other Member States, where the measure adopted relates primarily to an interest located in those States.'

The Court might have given further clarification of the possibilities of transfrontier application of Article 36 TFEU in this case but it did not.[160] It observed that the Court had consistently held that a directive providing for exhaustive harmonisation of national legislation deprives a Member State of recourse to Article 36 TFEU. After discussing the directive in question, the Court concluded that the directive did regulate exhaustively the Member States' powers with regard to the conservation of wild birds. Member States are not authorised to adopt stricter protective measures in respect of a species of bird which does not occur in the territory of the legislating Member State but is found in another Member State where it may lawfully be hunted under the terms of the directive and under the legislation of that other State, and which is neither migratory nor endangered within the meaning of the directive. In other words, the directive's regulation of the conservation of wild birds, not being migratory birds nor birds threatened with extinction, is exhaustive for those Member States where the birds in question do not normally occur. Application of Article 36 TFEU is therefore not at issue. The Court's approach is thus not clear on this point. At best it could be argued that the distinction made by the Court between migratory birds and endangered birds does not entirely rule out the transfrontier application of Article 36 TFEU.

> With respect to endangered species, the *Tridon* case, is also of particular interest.[161] The case concerned French stricter measures than those laid down by the CITES Regulation. According to the French Government, the protection of captive born and bred specimens was necessary because the breeding of those species

---

[159] Case C-169/89 *Gourmetterie v.d. Burg* [1990] ECR I-2143.

[160] Case C-169/89 *Gourmetterie v.d. Burg* [1990] ECR I-2143.

[161] Case C-510/99 *Tridon* [2001] ECR I-7777. Cf. also Case C-219/07 *Nationale Raad van Dierenkwekers en Liefhebbers and Andibel* [2008] ECR I-4475 and Case C-100/08 *Commission v. Belgium* [2009] ECR I-140.

for commercial purposes could have marked negative effects on the conservation in the natural state of the species concerned. Such breeding would enable a real market to be created. To meet the demand created by such a market, there would be a great temptation to collect birds or eggs in their natural habitat. In *Tridon* the Court seemed to have accepted the French plea, subject to the proportionality principle only.

When 'common responsibilities' are absent, the extra-territorial application of Article 36 TFEU seems more problematic. Old and new case law of the Court of Justice is not clear in this respect.

The *Inter-Huiles* case may offer some indication that the Court takes a wider view of the territorial extent of grounds which will justify trade restrictions.[162] In that case the French Government refused to allow the import of waste oil in part because it feared environmental damage in Belgium. The Court, considering the French Government's argument that the rules in question were justified by the need to protect the environment, stated: 'That argument cannot be accepted. Clearly, the environment is protected just as effectively when the oils are sold to an authorized disposal or regenerating undertaking of another Member State as when they are disposed of in the Member State of origin.'

This could be taken to imply that, if the interest invoked by the state of origin was not already adequately protected in the receiving state, protective measures might be justified. This is however somewhat speculative. Although the *Inter-Huiles* case could be said to provide some support for the transfrontier application of Article 36 TFEU, the *Nertsvoederfabriek* case does not.[163] That case concerned a prohibition on the exportation of poultry offal. This could not be justified on the grounds of public health, because 'it does not appear necessary to prohibit the exportation of poultry offal, provided that the conditions relating to health laid down by those provisions are satisfied with respect to removal and transport on national territory.' Protection of foreign territory is apparently exclusively a matter for the foreign state.

Most interesting are also the following cases. Advocate General Léger discussed the issue of extraterritorial application at length in *Hedley Lomas* and *Compassion in World Farming*.[164] In his view a Member State can rely on Article 36 TFEU only to ensure protection of an interest safeguarded by that provision within its own national territory. However, the Court again refused to answer the question whether extraterritorial application of Article 36 TFEU was possible.[165] In *Compassion in World Farming* it repeated its position in *Hedley*

---

[162] Case 172/82 *Inter-Huiles* [1983] ECR 555.

[163] Case 118/86 *Nertsvoederfabriek* [1987] ECR 3883.

[164] Case C-5/94 *Hedley Lomas* [1996] ECR I-2553 and Case C-1/96 *Compassion in World Farming* [1998] ECR I-1251.

[165] Case C-5/94 *Hedley Lomas* [1996] ECR I-2553.

Lomas and *Red Grouse* that recourse to Article 36 TFEU is no longer possible where European directives provide for harmonisation of the measures necessary to achieve the specific objective which would be furthered by reliance upon that provision.[166] However, it may be possible to detect a shift in the Court's position in *Dusseldorp*, a case in which Dutch restrictions on the export of oil filters were held incompatible with Article 193 TFEU in the light of Articles 35 and 36 TFEU. The Dutch Government argued that the restrictions could be justified under Article 36 TFEU as concerning the protection of the health and life of humans. The Court did not agree, stating: 'Such a justification would be relevant if the processing of oil filters in other Member States and their shipment over a greater distance as a result of their being exported posed a threat to the health and life of humans.'[167] The interesting thing is, of course, that this observation, placed in the context of the possible justification of an export ban, might imply that Member States were also entitled to restrict the free movement of goods, even if the threat was to the health and life of persons in other Member States. Let it suffice to note that, again, the Court has not explicitly ruled on this form of extraterritorial application of Article 36 TFEU and we shall have to await further developments on this point, too.

In our view transfrontier application of Article 36 TFEU and the rule of reason should in principle be possible in particular where common interests are at state. However, Member States must bear in mind that the protection of health and/or the environment in other states is primarily the responsibility of those states. It could be added that this primary responsibility will tend to blur the greater the transfrontier, and thus common, nature of the interest to be protected.

There is an additional problem in respect of states outside the EU. Free movement of goods also applies to products coming from third countries which are in free circulation in Member States, according to Article 28(2) TFEU. Applying Article 36 TFEU more widely than allowed under the WTO rules is thus problematic. This should therefore be taken into account where Article 36 TFEU is applied in a transfrontier fashion.[168]

---

[166] Case C-1/96 *Compassion in World Farming* [1998] ECR I-1251.

[167] And repeated in Case C-209/98 *Sydhavnens Sten & Grus* [2000] ECR I-3743, para. 45. Cf. Davies (2004) at 214.

[168] Cf. on this issue Wiers (2002).

CHAPTER 7

Environment and Competition

1 General Remarks

In the first chapter we have seen that one of the fundamentals of European environmental policy is the 'polluter pays' principle. When fully applied, this principle means that the negative effects of production and consumption are translated into costs. This is called the internalisation of environmental costs. This internalisation allows the price mechanism to perform its signaling function.[1] More polluting products will become more expensive, and as a result there will be less consumption of these environmentally unfriendly products. This in turn will encourage more environmentally friendly production as well as research and development of more environmentally friendly production methods and products, thus putting the economy on a structurally less polluting path and leading to sustainable development.[2]

From the point of view of environmental protection, some competitive pressure is therefore necessary, as this pushes firms most effectively to minimise their environmental costs and thus reduce environmental pressure.

However, the polluter pays principle is by no means fully applied at the present time. Because adequate standards do not exist, some environmental costs are still not, or only partially, reflected in the price. Moreover, some environmental effects are partially internalised in some jurisdictions whereas other impacts on the environment may not be internalised and other jurisdictions may not apply the 'polluter pays' principle at all. In those cases there will be a distortion of the level playing field. Consider for example the situation in which the environmental effects of steel production have been internalised in one Member State while the environmental impact of the production of other metals has not been translated into costs. The result will be that steel production in one Member State will be more expensive compared to steel production in other Member States. Furthermore, the production of aluminium, which may be just as polluting, will be relatively cheaper.[3] As a result, measures that internalise environmental costs in one Member State will not come about, as no government would willfully put its own industry out of business. The only way to make such a scheme palatable to both the people suffering from the pollution and the industry would be compensate the industry for the extra costs arising from the internalisation. However, such compensation may very well constitute state aid within the meaning of Article 107 TFEU. This is just one example of an internalisation of environmental costs leading to a distortion of the level playing field which in turn leads to a distortion or restriction of competition covered by the competition provisions in the TFEU.

---

[1] XXIInd Competition Report, point 77 and XXIIIrd Competition Report, point 164.

[2] XXIIIrd Competition Report, point 164.

[3] The *Arcelor* case (Case C-127/07 *Arcelor Atlantique and Lorraine and others* [2008] ECR I-9895; see Chapter 1, section 2) concerning the scope of the EU ETS, deals with this point whereas the carbon leakage provisions of the EU ETS address the distortion of competition between the EU and third countries.

The competition rules in the TFEU have two addressees: undertakings and Member States. Undertakings, a term that roughly translates into business enterprises, may conclude environmental agreements or they may abuse a dominant market position for environmental reasons. Such practices fall within the compass of Articles 101 and 102 TFEU.

Member States may also restrict or distort competition for environmental purposes, as the example above shows. They may grant exclusive rights on environmental grounds, which would make Article 106 TFEU applicable or they could grant state aids, in which case Article 107 TFEU is relevant. The relation between environmental protection and Articles 101, 102, 106 and 107 TFEU as well as the useful effect doctrine will be examined below.[4] However, first the fundamentals of competition law will be examined for their relation with environmental protection. The confines of this book make it impossible to give a complete overview of EU competition law. For this the reader is referred to other works.[5]

2 The Fundamentals of EU Competition Law

2.1 Market Definition

Determining whether a restriction or distortion of competition takes place requires a definition of the relevant market first.[6] The relevant market consists of a relevant product market and the relevant geographical market. Basically, the product market consists of all products that are substitutable or interchangeable from the perspective of the consumer and the producer.[7] This substitutability is determined by various practicalities such as the price, intended use for certain groups of consumers or rules to which the treatment of certain waste is subject.[8] Furthermore, environmental considerations may also play a role in defining the relevant product market. If, for example, consumers are willing to pay 10% more for organic vegetables, this would point at organic fruit constituting a separate product market with only limited substitutability from non-organic fruit.[9] Similar considerations may also be relevant in defining the geographical market. In the *CECED* case the Commission found that the percentage of energy inefficient washing machines was higher in the UK and the southern Member States compared to the other Member States.[10] This could point to the fact that consumers in certain Member States did not consider

---

4 See also Kingston (2009).

5 See, for example, Jones & Sufrin (2010), Monti (2008), Whish (2008).

6 See for example, Case 27/76 *UBC* v. *Commission (United Brands)* [1978] ECR 207, para. 10.

7 See for more details: Commission Notice on the Definition of the Relevant Market, OJ 1997 C 372/5.

8 Case C-209/98 *Sydhavnens* [2000] ECR I-3743, para. 61. See on this case also Chapter 6.

9 See, for example, the merger decision in Case M.5046, *Friesland Foods / Campina*, paras. 48-52.

10 Decision 2000/475 *CECED*, OJ 2000 L 187/47, para. 17.

energy efficiency of washing machines as important, which could make these states a separate geographical market.

2.2 Undertaking

EU competition law applies only to undertakings. An undertaking has been defined as an entity engaged in an economic activity.[11] This raises the question to what extent environmental activities constitute economic activities. In *Diego Calì*, the Court was confronted with an Italian entity, SEPG, that was responsible for environmental protection in the port of Genoa.[12] According to Calì, SEPG was an undertaking that had abused its dominant position when it presented him with the bill for preventive environmental surveillance activities while no pollution whatsoever had occurred. According to the Court the preventive environmental surveillance constituted a task in the public interest which forms part of the essential functions of the State as regards protection of the environment in maritime areas.[13] It is important to note that the Court expressly distinguished between *preventive* surveillance and *curative* environmental services (which would be used once actual pollution had occurred).[14] The latter would probably constitute an economic activity, whereas it is indeed very difficult to envisage a market for or competition in preventive environmental surveillance. Finally, experiences with the liberalisation of markets have shown that competition is indeed possible in areas of the economy that were previously thought to be domain of public service obligations and state intervention. As a result of the internalisation of environmental costs, environmental protection may indeed increasingly constitute an economic activity.

3 Article 101 TFEU

3.1 Why Environmental Agreements exist and Restrict Competition

In a nutshell Article 101(1) TFEU prohibits coordination between undertakings that has as the object or effect to distort or restrict competition.[15] This prohibition may be declared inapplicable on the basis of the third paragraph in case the agreement has certain positive effects that are considered more important than the restriction of competition. Before the details and elements of Article 101 are examined we will first establish why Article 101 TFEU is relevant in the environmental sphere.

---

[11] Case C-41/90 *Höfner and Elser* v. *Macrotron* [1991] ECR I-1979, para. 21.

[12] Case C-343/95 *Diego Calì & Figli* v. *SEPG* [1997] ECR I-1547.

[13] Case C-343/95 *Diego Calì & Figli* v. *SEPG* [1997] ECR I-1547, para. 22.

[14] Case C-343/95 *Diego Calì & Figli* v. *SEPG* [1997] ECR I-1547, para. 20.

[15] See Townley (2009) for an overview of cases and decisions concerning this provision.

Above it was shown how an internalisation of environmental costs may lead to a distortion of the level playing field that may in turn result in a reaction that falls under EU competition law. The same can happen with so-called environmental agreements. This term is used to describe agreements between undertakings in order to protect the environment. These agreements may be purely voluntary, because companies realise that the environment is increasingly becoming a sales point, or they may be the result of government intervention. The ACEA environmental agreement, for example, was concluded among the European car manufacturers in order to avoid European legislation on this topic.[16] Environmental agreements may also be the result of legislation. The WEEE Directive, for example, explicitly envisages collective action from the industry as part of its implementation.[17]

So when a group of companies decides to collectively organise the collection and recycling of waste products, in order to meet the producer responsibility under the WEEE Directive,[18] this will entail costs. In a competitive business environment all the parties will want to minimise their actual costs. Thus in order to achieve economies of scale and to prevent free riding, the situation where one or more companies do not make the actual investments themselves, but take a free ride on the investments of others, the companies will want to include some mutual obligations in the environmental agreement. These obligations may restrict competition. They could relate to the passing on of the costs of the collection and recycling.[19] They could also concern the fixing of the price charged for the use of a collective take back and recycling system.[20] Finally, in the *CECED* case the restriction of competition took the form of a restriction of production, since the agreement prohibited the parties from manufacturing or importing energy inefficient washing machines. Again, this clause in the agreement was necessary because there is a demand for energy inefficient washing machines and in a stagnant market,[21] no company will willfully give up a business opportunity unless it is certain that its competitors will do the same.

3.2   Article 101(1) TFEU

Given that they want to prevent free riding, most environmental agreements will be in writing and signed by the parties. Alternatively, they will take the form of a decision of an industry association, an association of undertakings in Article 101 terminology. This hardly leads to questions concerning the applicability of Article 101(1) TFEU. Most competition problems with

---

[16]   See press release IP/06/1134, where the Commission threatens to come with legislation should the agreement not lead to the results.

[17]   Directive 2002/96, OJ 2002 L 37/24, notably recital 20 and Article 8(3) and 5(2)(c).

[18]   See further Chapter 8, section 17.4.

[19]   This occurred in the Dutch *Wit en Bruingoed* case; see Vedder (2003) at 376 *et seq.*

[20]   This was one of the restrictions in the *FKS* case; see Vedder (2003) at 383 *et seq.*

[21]   Decision 2000/475 *CECED*, OJ 2000 L 187/47, para. 31.

environmental agreements are the result of so-called horizontal agreements, i.e. agreements between competing undertakings in the same stage of production, be it manufacture, distribution, retail or disposal. Examples of this kind of agreement in the field of the environment are:

. agreements in the sphere of *research and development* with a view to developing more environmentally friendly products, production processes or methods of disposal. See, for example, the *BBC Brown Boveri* case, concerning cooperation in developing sodium-sulphur high-performance batteries intended primarily for use in electrically driven vehicles. This was considered to restrict competition because the parties could no longer conclude research and development agreements with third parties in this field;[22]

. agreements that set up collective systems for waste collection, sorting and treatment. Pursuant to the Packaging Waste Directive, the packaging industry in most Member States has opted for collective systems to organise the collection and treatment of packaging waste.[23] Examples are: the *Duales System Deutschland (DSD)*,[24] *Eco-emballages*,[25] *ARA/ARGEV/ ARO*.[26] These systems allow companies that use packaging to pay a fee and then a green dot on their products, showing that the packaging will normally be sorted and can be recycled.[27] Competition concerns in these cases essentially involve exclusivities that have a foreclosure effect in that they foreclose the market for sorting and recycling of packaging waste. Participating companies should be free to exit such green dot systems or joint a green dot system for only a part of their packaging waste. Furthermore, the companies that collect or treat the packaging waste on behalf of the green dot organisation should be free to decide how they market the processed waste;[28]

. agreements to protect the environment, for example to use the same environmentally friendly production processes, or not to use or manufacture certain harmful substances. An example may be the system created by the International Fruit Container Organization (IFCO) promoting re-usable plastic crates for the transport of fresh fruit and vegetables[29] or agreements between water bottlers to standardize bottles so as to enable

---

[22] Decision 88/541 *BBC Brown Boveri*, OJ 1988 L 301/68.

[23] It must be noted that most of these collective waste management schemes will also entail vertical restrictions of competition, because of exclusivities agreed with other undertakings responsible for the actual collection, sorting and recycling. Cf. Case T-419/03 *Altstoff Recycling Austria AG v. Commission*, Judgment of 22 March 2011.

[24] Decision 2001/837 *DSD* (Article 101), OJ 2001 L 319/1.

[25] Decision 2001/663 *Eco-Emballages*, OJ 2001 L 233/37.

[26] Decision 2004/208 *ARA/ARGEV/ARO*, OJ 2004 L 75/59.

[27] XXIIIrd Competition Report, point 168.

[28] See also Pons (2001).

[29] XXIIIrd Competition Report, point 168.

them to comply with legislation requiring these bottles to be re-usable if a system for their recycling did not exist.[30]

The above examples show the diversity of competition problems arising from environmental agreements. For an agreement to be caught by Article 101(1) TFEU a number of further requirements needs to be fulfilled.

The most obvious requirement is that the agreement must entail a restriction of competition. Case law has specified this in that a restriction must be qualitatively or qualitatively appreciable. With quantitative appreciability the market share of the parties to the agreement is the guiding criterion. In its *de minimis* notice the Commission has set out that a horizontal agreement will appreciably restrict competition if the market share of the parties exceeds 10%.[31] In determining qualitative appreciability the substance of the agreement has to be analysed with regard to the question of to what extent the parties are still free to decide for themselves what their actions on the market will be. Both approaches to appreciability can be found in the decisions of the Commission and the 2001 Guidelines on Horizontal Agreements, which contain a chapter devoted to environmental agreements and Article 101 TFEU.[32]

Agreements that do not directly limit the technical solutions open to parties and impose on the parties only loosely defined industry-wide targets will not appreciably restrict competition irrespective of the market share of the parties. The ACEA Agreement that imposes a general energy efficiency target on the European car manufacturers without limiting the means by which this target is to be achieved is an example of this type of agreement.[33] Needless to say, the environmental effectiveness of such agreements can be doubted.

Agreements that do have a direct effect on the parties' choice of means to achieve environmental objectives or that influence marketing decisions, production processes or products may fall under Article 101(1) TFEU dependent on the market share of the parties. This is the reasoning that has been used in the *CECED* case, where the agreement involved a reduction of output in the form of restriction to market energy inefficient washing machines.[34]

Finally, the Commission is of the opinion that environmental agreements that 'serve as a tool to engage in a disguised cartel' almost always fall under the prohibition. In this regard the Commission points to environmental agreements

---

[30] XXIIIrd Competition Report, points 169 and 240.

[31] Commission Notice on Agreements of Minor Importance (*De Minimis*), OJ 2001 C 368/13.

[32] OJ 2001 C 3/2, Chapter 7. These Guidelines have been replaced by the 2011 Guidelines on the applicability of Article 101 of the Treaty on the Functioning of the European Union to horizontal co-operation agreements, OJ 2011 C 11/1, hereafter the 2011 Horizontals Guidelines, which do not contain a separate chapter on environmental agreements anymore, see footnote 1 of the 2011 Guidelines. Instead, environmental agreements are treated as research & development agreements, specialisation agreements or standardisation agreements.

[33] See further Vedder (2003) at 142.

[34] Decision 2000/475 *CECED*, OJ 2000 L 187/47.

that involve price fixing or market sharing. An example of this type of case is the *VOTOB* case that involved tank storage undertakings in the Netherlands, which had agreed to impose a uniform environmental surcharge upon their consumers, in order to recoup the costs of environmental investments.[35]

Apart from non-appreciability, environmental agreements can also be outside the scope of Article 101(1) TFEU on the basis of the *rule of reason* or because they benefit from a so-called state action defence.

Whether or not there is a rule of reason or an exception for inherent restrictions is uncertain, partly because of gnomic and contradictory judgments by the General Court and Court of Justice, and partly because of the Babel-like confusion between legal writers. In a nutshell, the rule of reason boils down to a balancing of pro-competitive and anti-competitive effects within Article 101(1) TFEU. Even though the European Courts have never explicitly recognised the existence of such a thing,[36] the Court of Justice has certainly employed reasoning that can best be characterised as a rule of reason. The *Wouters* case is an example of this approach. This case involved a restriction of competition for members of the bar that served the good functioning of their profession. In *Wouters* the Court balanced the restriction of competition with these public interest-related positive effects within the framework of Article 101(1) TFEU.[37] As a result, it would also seem possible to balance environmental effects with restrictions of competition as part of the first paragraph of Article 101 TFEU.[38] The integration principle laid down in Article 11 TFEU lends further support for this.[39]

The 'state action defence' is available for so-called compulsory cartels. This refers to environmental agreements that have been forced upon the parties by public authorities.[40] Given the often close relation between government regulation and environmental agreements, it is conceivable that an environmental agreement is the result of 'conduct [that] was unilaterally imposed upon them by the national authorities through the exercise of irresistible pressures, such as, for example, the threat to adopt State measures likely to cause them to sustain substantial losses'.[41]

---

[35] XXIInd Competition Report, point 177-186, see further Vedder (2003) at 157.

[36] In fact, the General Court has explicitly rejected this in Case T-112/99 *Métropole* [2001] ECR II-2459, para. 72.

[37] Case C-309/99 *Wouters* [2002] ECR I-1577, paras. 97-110. See further paras. 99-107 of the Opinion of Advocate General Léger. This was confirmed in Case C-519/04 P *Meca-Medina* [2006] ECR I-6991, paras. 42-55.

[38] See further Vedder (2003) at 145 *et seq.*

[39] See Kingston (2010), at 783 for an overview of the various legal arguments, not just regarding Article 101 TFEU, in relation to the integration principle and EU competition law.

[40] See for an application outside the environmental context: Case C-198/01 *CIF* [2003] ECR I-8055.

[41] Case T-387/94 *Asia Motor France v. Commission* [1996] ECR II-961, para. 65. In Joined Cases C-359/95 P and C-379/95 P *Commission and France v. Ladbroke* [1997] ECR I-6265, the Court employed a more stringent test.

Even if an environmental agreement is covered by the prohibition of Article 101(1) TFEU this does not mean that there is no room whatever for environmental protection in competition law. Such an interpretation would be contrary to the integration principle laid down in Article 11 TFEU, under which environmental protection requirements must be integrated into the definition and implementation of the Union's policies and activities. 'Competition must therefore, as much as any other Union policy, take account of environmental considerations'.[42] These environmental considerations could also be taken into account in the application of Article 101(3) TFEU.

3.3   Article 101(3) TFEU

On the basis of Article 101(3) TFEU, in connection with Regulation 1/2003,[43] the prohibition of Article 101(1) TFEU may be declared inapplicable by the Commission, Member State competition authorities and national judges. This can only happen if the following cumulative conditions are met:

- the agreement contributes to improving the production or distribution of goods or to promoting technical or economic progress;
- it allows consumers a fair share of the resulting benefit;
- the restriction of competition is indispensable to the attainment of the benefits;
- competition is not eliminated in respect of a substantial part of the products in question.

The application of Article 101(3) TFEU can take place in an individual case, or for an entire category of agreements. The latter is referred to as a block exemption.[44] Concerning the application of the integration principle of Article 11 TFEU in connection with Article 101(3) TFEU, two consequences are worth noting. In the first place it can be said that, under the integration principle, environmental protection aims should play a part in the normal criteria that have to be taken into account in assessing an agreement on the basis of Article 101(3) TFEU. The degree to which Article 101(3) TFEU allows this will be discussed below. In the second place it is legitimate to ask whether Article 101(3) TFEU could be applied to an agreement that have serious negative environmental effects. In principle it could be argued that this would be inconsistent with the integration principle.[45] Such negative environmental effects would certainly have to be taken into account, but this does not mean that the applicability of Article 101(3) TFEU is ruled out completely. These effects should be taken into account and carefully balanced against the other interests involved. Following the entry into force of Regulation 1/2003 an interesting question is to what extent national judges are

---

[42]   XXIIIrd Competition Report, point 162.

[43]   OJ 2003 L1/1.

[44]   See further below.

[45]   Cf. Vedder (2003) at 185 et seq.

bound by the integration principle. Article 11 TFEU does not have any particular addressees, but is confined to 'definition and implementation of the Union's policies and activities'. The question therefore is to what extent national judges directly applying EU law are in fact defining and implementing EU policies and activities. The Court's case law that characterises national judges as decentralised Union judges when they apply directly effective EU law probably indicates an affirmative answer to this question.

Promoting technical or economic progress

The question at issue here is whether – and to what extent – environmental protection can be regarded as 'technical or economic progress'. Even without an integration principle, environmental improvements can be seen as technical improvements for the simple reason that such products are technically more advanced.[46] These technical/environmental improvements may relate to a relatively 'clean' production process, an environmentally friendly use of a product, or a less polluting form of disposal. The so-called life-cycle approach is a central feature of both national and European[47] product policy. The presence of the integration principle only strengthens this, as is evidenced by the Commission's decision-making practice, where even prior to the introduction of the integration principle, environmental considerations were taken into account. In the 1983 *Carbon Gas Technologie* decision, concerning a cooperation agreement for the purpose of developing a combined pressure gasification process using run-of-mine coal, the fact that the Commission regarded the process as 'less harmful to the environment' was one of the arguments for deciding that the prohibition on competition contributes to the promotion of technical and economic progress.[48] The Commission also found that environmental improvements contributed to technical and economic progress in *BBC Brown Boveri*,[49] *Assurpol*,[50] and *Ford/Volkswagen*.[51] In *ARA/ARGEV/ARO*, however, Article 101(3) TFEU was applied to an environmental agreement on primarily economic grounds.[52]

Much more interesting is the *CECED* case where the environmental improvements were not just taken into account, but in fact constituted the technical and economic progress by themselves.[53] The Commission first translates the environmental benefits into an economic benefit.[54] In *CECED* this meant

---

[46]   See Decision 2000/182 *GEAE/P & W*, OJ 2000 L 58/16, para. 79 concerning aircraft engine environmental performance as technical and economic progress.

[47]   E.g. Regulation 66/2010 on the EU Ecolabel, OJ 2010 L 27/1.

[48]   Decision 83/669 *Carbon Gas Technologie*, OJ 1983 L 376/17.

[49]   Decision 88/541 *BBC Brown Boveri*, OJ 1988 L 301/68.

[50]   Decision 92/96 *Assurpol*, OJ 1992 L 37/16.

[51]   Decision 93/49 *Ford* v. *Volkswagen*, OJ 1993 L 20/14, see further Vedder (2003) at 163.

[52]   Decision 2004/208 *ARA/ARGEV/ARO*, OJ 2004 L 75/59, notably para. 270.

[53]   Decision 2000/475 *CECED*, OJ 2000 L 187/47.

[54]   2011 Horizontals Guidelines, para. 329, where the *CECED* decision is mentioned. See for a discussion Vedder (2003) at 164.

that the phasing out of energy inefficient washing machines resulted in avoided carbon dioxide emissions and thus avoided costs. Moreover, the Commission also calculated individual economic benefits in *CECED* when it considered that the average consumer would recoup the higher purchasing costs within 6 to 40 months because of the reduced energy usage.

Allowing consumers a fair share

On the basis of the first requirement, discussed above, the environmental and economic benefits of the agreement have been established. The second requirement of Article 101(3) TFEU ensures that these benefits flowing from an environmental agreement are passed on to consumers. It should be noted that in the light of the integration principle the term consumer should be interpreted widely. It should be taken to include third parties who benefit from the positive effects, in terms of reduced environmental pressure, of the environmental agreements, or even the society as a whole.[55] With true environmental benefits, this should not be a problem, as all consumers invariably benefit from better protection of the environment. However, improved quality of the environment will often also mean that prices are higher. In this case the higher price must be balanced with the environmental or economic benefit, for example in the form of lower running costs that will result in the initial investment being recouped.[56]

> Furthermore, in its decision in the *KSB/Goulds/Lowara/ITT* case, concerning an agreement for the joint research, development and production of a single-stage, single-flow radial centrifugal pump, the energy conservation and the fact that the fluids handled by the water pumps are not polluted were regarded as environmentally beneficial and thus as constituting an improvement in operating characteristics.[57] The agreement would therefore also benefit consumers.
>
> The decision in the *Assurpol* case referred to above is also relevant. The Commission regarded the fact that victims of environmental damage can be compensated and the environment repaired as a benefit for consumers.

One of the clearest decisions given by the Commission in this respect is that concerning a set of agreements between chemical companies of the Exxon and Shell Groups related to establishing, financing, constructing, managing and operating a production joint venture.[58] The principal aim of the joint plant is production of linear low-density polyethylene. Reduction in the use of raw materials and of plastic waste and the avoidance of environmental risks involved in transport will be perceived 'as beneficial by many consumers at a time when the limitation of natural resources and threats to the environment are of increasing public concern.'

---

[55] Vedder (2003) at 170.

[56] Decision 2000/475 *CECED*, OJ 2000 L 187/47, para. 52.

[57] OJ 1991 L 19/25.

[58] OJ 1994 L 144/20.

Restrictions must be indispensable

From the text of Article 101(3) TFEU, and as the Commission explicitly stated in its XXIInd Competition Report, point 77, it is clear that the restrictions of competition must be *indispensable* to the alleged environmental benefits. An objective evaluation of these benefits must be supported with a cost-effectiveness analysis showing that alternative means of attaining the expected environmental benefits would be more economically or financially costly, under reasonable assumptions.[59] In its XXIIIrd Competition Report the Commission reaffirmed that it will examine carefully all agreements between companies to see if they are indispensable to attain the environmental objectives.

> In respect of the *Spa Monopole/GDB* case[60] the Commission noted that it will be particularly vigilant to ensure that such agreements do not foreclose market entry to outsiders and that where membership of the system is necessary for market access because there is no viable alternative, then this membership will be given on non-discriminatory terms. Other cases concerning collective waste management systems set up by industry foreclosure proved similarly important, with the Commission focusing on the duration of exclusive contracts.[61]
>
> In *CECED* the Commission investigated whether the environmental objectives could be achieved using alternative means. According to the Commission possible alternative means such as setting an industry-wide target, informing the consumers and or ecolabeling would not deliver the same benefits.[62]

With regard to those environmental agreements characterised by the Commission as disguised cartels, the indispensability requirement may be very difficult to fulfil. For example, environmental agreements, which contain uniform fees, charged irrespective of individual costs for e.g. waste collection, are highly suspect. Such an agreement would more or less amount to a price cartel. Moreover, price cartels are always prohibited, because their purpose is to pass on the cost rather than to protect the environment. It does not, therefore, matter that a price agreement is disguised as an environmental agreement.

> Relevant in this connection is the *VOTOB* case.[63] The association, Vereniging van Onafhankelijke Tankopslag Bedrijven (VOTOB), groups six undertakings offering tank storage facilities (land tanks) in the Netherlands. They decided to increase prices charged to their customers by a uniform, fixed amount. This 'environmental charge' was to cover the costs of investment required to reduce vapour emissions from members' storage tanks. The Commission objected to this charge as being incompatible with Article 101 TFEU for three reasons.

---

[59] 2011 Horizontals Guidelines, para. 329.

[60] XXIIIrd Competition Report, point 240.

[61] E.g. Decision 2004/208 *ARA/ARGEV/ARO*, OJ 2004 L 75/59, para. 277.

[62] Decision 2000/475 *CECED*, OJ 2000 L 187/47, paras. 59-63.

[63] XXIIrd Competition Report, points 177-186.

Firstly, the environmental charge was fixed. All members of VOTOB were to apply it regardless of their own considerations. When a price or an element of it is fixed, competition on that price element is excluded. By fixing the charge members of VOTOB have less incentive to make investments as cheaply and efficiently as possible. Secondly, it was a uniform charge. Though varying from product to product, the increase was identical for all VOTOB members. Uniform adaptation of the charge ignores differences in each individual member's circumstances. Some VOTOB members were already very close to achieving the required reductions in vapour emissions, while others were not. Furthermore, members of VOTOB employed different techniques to reduce emissions, and did not expend investment costs simultaneously. The charge ignored this. In addition, all VOTOB members retained the proceeds of the charge individually. The Commission therefore maintained that had there been no horizontal fixing of this particular cost element, individual members could have calculated the cost of necessary investment, decided whether to meet it from their own profit or to pass it on to their customers, and, if they decided to pass it on to their customers, determined by how much to increase their prices. This would have been done by the companies independently, having regard to prevailing market conditions and according to their own competitive position. Thirdly, the charge was invoiced to customers as a separate item, suggesting it was a 'charge' imposed by the government. Prior to the Commission's proceeding to a decision, VOTOB agreed to renounce its separate charging system and not to apply the uniformly fixed charge. In the light of these developments the Commission agreed to suspend proceedings.

This case makes clear that the Commission is not *a priori* opposed to the possible passing on to customers of environment-related investment costs, since this makes them more aware of environmental problems and their implications. However, customers should not be barred from challenging price increases and shopping around for the smallest increase. A system whereby members invoiced a total price, stating that it included the additional environmental investment cost, would be acceptable to the Commission. Customers reluctant to accept a higher price would remain in a position to negotiate conditions.

In this regard the WEEE Directive and the private system set up to implement it in the Netherlands provide an interesting example. The WEEE Directive contains a so-called 'old-for-new' obligation, on the basis of which retailers (and ultimately importers and producers) must take back old appliances whenever a consumer buys a new appliance. This means that for the waste products collected initially, constitute so-called historical waste, i.e. products that were marketed before the entry into force of the WEEE Directive. Moreover, it may very well be that the producer of that waste no longer exists, in which case the waste is classified as orphan historical waste. For this type of waste, the WEEE Directive allows a fixed uniform fee which may be mentioned separately on the invoice. A similar system

in the Netherlands was initially rejected by the Netherlands Competition Authority, but following the entry into force of the WEEE Directive it was allowed.[64]

Competition must not be eliminated

The Commission has to investigate on the one hand to what extent the
companies concerned in the agreement still compete with each other (internal
competition) and on the other what position they occupy in the relevant market
and to what extent the market has been affected by the agreement (external
competition). In particular it must be noted that whatever the environmental
gains, the agreement must not eliminate competition in terms of product or process differentiation, technological innovation or market entry.

On the latter point the *Spa Monopole/GDB* case is illustrative.[65] Because the
agreement hindered access by foreign water producers to the German market,
external competition was almost completely excluded. The decision in *Assurpol*[66] and in *BBC Brown Boveri*[67] both imply that the condition that competition
is not entirely eliminated is met if the more environmentally friendly products
are in competition with more traditional products.[68] Finally, *CECED* shows that
environmental cooperation by undertakings representing more than 90% of the
industry will still not completely eliminate competition because the undertakings will still be able to compete with regard to other aspects of their products,
such as price, quality and service.[69]

Block exemptions

Article 101(3) TFEU can also be applied to entire categories of agreements in
the form of so-called block exemptions. There exist block exemptions for *inter
alia* vertical agreements, research and development agreements and specialisation agreements and know-how licensing.[70] Again, by application of the integration principle, regulations containing these group exemptions should also
preferably be interpreted in the light of the environmental objectives of Article
191(1) TFEU. The decisions in *BBC Brown Boveri* and *KSB/Goulds/Lowara/ITT*
show that the environmentally friendly interpretation of block exemption agreements does not mean that the scope of the block exemption can be extended on
environmental grounds. In these cases the Commission took the environmental
benefits into account, but nevertheless considered the block exemption inapplicable because the requirements laid down in the regulation were not met. As a
result the Commission applied Article 101(3) TFEU on an individual basis.

---

[64] See for further details Vedder (2002).

[65] XXIIIrd Competition Report, point 240.

[66] OJ 1992 L 37/16.

[67] OJ 1988 L 301/68.

[68] This of course presumes that they are part of the same relevant product market.

[69] Decision 2000/475 *CECED*, OJ 2000 L 187/47, para. 64.

[70] Respectively, Commission Regulation 330/2010, OJ 2010 L 102/1, Commission Regulation 2659/2000,
     OJ 2000 L 304/7, Commission Regulation 2658/2000, OJ 2000 L 304/3.

The environmentally friendly interpretation in view of the integration principle should also mean that negative effects are taken into account. However, this cannot result in automatic non-applicability of the block exemption for the simple reason that the requirements for the applicability of these regulations, a market share cap and a so-called black list, do not envisage a balancing of environmental factors. However, the regulations do contain a provision on the basis of which the Commission or a national competition authority may withdraw the block exemption benefit if an agreement or a group of agreement no longer fulfils the criteria of Article 101(3) TFEU. As a result, the Commission may find that the negative environmental effects negate possible economic or technical advantages so that the first requirement of Article 101(3) TFEU no longer is met which would justify withdrawal of the block exemption benefit.

4 Article 102 TFEU

Article 102 TFEU provides that any abuse by one or more undertakings that occupy a dominant position within the internal market or in a substantial part of it is prohibited as incompatible with the internal market in so far as it may affect trade between Member States. It lists a number of examples of such abuse: imposing unfair purchase or selling prices or unfair trading conditions, limiting production or markets to the prejudice of consumers. Unlike Article 101 TFEU, this provision does not explicitly allow for exceptions. Nevertheless the doctrine of the objective justification may save behaviour that *prima facie* resembles abuse. For example, might not an undertaking which has a dominant position, and whose environmental image is important to it, require that its suppliers also act in an environmentally friendly manner, whether in the area of production, distribution or waste disposal? The dominant undertaking may well have an interest in protecting or improving its image. It is normally an abuse of a dominant position for an agreement to contain requirements which are not connected with the subject matter of the contract. Superficially, requiring suppliers to act in an environmentally friendly manner could be regarded as such an abuse. However, under the integration principle the question whether or not there had been an abuse of a dominant position should be answered in the light of the environmental objectives. An undertaking's protecting or improving its environmental image and attempting to achieve this by requiring suppliers to act in a certain manner would then not necessarily have to be regarded as abuse of a dominant position. The older example in which Article 102 TFEU was referred to was the *Spa Monopole/GDB* case, where the Commission found that, in view of the dominant position of the GDB in the market for mineral water containers, its refusal to grant foreign EU water producers access to its pool of standardised refillable glass bottles and crates, despite the fact that such access was essential in order to be able compete effectively in the mineral water market, constituted an abuse of a dominant position within the meaning of Article 102 TFEU.[71] Even though environmental issues were at stake, they did not play a decisive role for the Commission.[72] It simply applied its standard rules on the abuse of a dominant position. Much the same happened in the *DSD* case.[73] DSD *(Duales System Deutschland)* is the undertaking set up by the German packaging industry to meet the collection and recycling obligations imposed upon them by the German Packaging Ordinance.

> DSD works with a green dot that is placed on products in return for a fee that producers must pay to DSD and that is differentiated on the basis of the recyclability of the products. This green dot signifies to consumers that they must collect that waste through a separate waste collection system that exists alongside the municipal waste collection (hence dual system). At this moment the DSD system works in such a way that producers are under a *de facto* obligation to mark all of their products with a green dot and pay the fee for this, even if the products will not be returned using DSD's collection infrastructure. The hairdressing supplies association complained about this to the Commission, which resulted in a decision that found DSD to have abused its dominant position on the market for the collection of packaging waste in Germany.

DSD collects nearly all the packaging waste in Germany, has a market share exceeding 90% and was thus found to be dominant. The abuse arose from the fact that DSD required a fee from the hairdressing supplies companies, even if the empty shampoo bottles were taken back through a special system for the collection of shampoo bottles from professional hairdressers since the same bottles were also sold to consumers and thus had a green dot printed on them. Setting up a separate packaging line and distribution network for shampoo without the green dot would entail extra costs. According to the Commission this meant that unfair prices were charged since the shampoo manufacturers would have to pay the fee even for products that would never be collected through the DSD system.[74] In its decision the Commission does not refer to the integration principle or the protection of the environment, even when it investigates the possible objective justification. The Commission's approach to private environmental monopolies (Article 102 TFEU) may be contrasted with the Court's approach to environmental public monopolies pursuant to Article 106(2) TFEU, examined below.

---

[71] XXIIIrd Competition Report, point 240.

[72] A similar situation occurred in the *COBAT* case, concerning an Italian consortium responsible for collecting and recycling lead batteries. See press release IP/00/1351 and Kingston (2009) at 215.

[73] Commission Decision 2001/463 *DSD*, OJ 2001 L 166/1. This decision was unsuccessfully appealed in Case C-385/07 P *Duales System Deutschland* v. *Commission* [2009] ECR I-6155.

[74] In addition the Commission considered this amounted to a discriminatory or unfair trading condition and tying which would keep competing undertaking from becoming active on the market for the collection of packaging waste.

5 The *Useful Effect* Doctrine

5.1 The Position of the Member States

Apart from undertakings, the EU competition rules are also addressed at the Member States. Above it has been noted that in many cases environmental agreements are not completely 'voluntary'. Such agreements may be the result of the threat of legislation, or they may actually be reinforced by legislation. With regard to the precise definition of responsibilities between the undertakings and the Member State the Commission has also noted that measures taken by public authorities may compromise the effect of the competition rules, 'for example by requiring firms to engage in behaviour which restricts competition.'[75]

> VOTOB, for example, took the decision to charge their customers a uniform 'environmental charge' after concluding a covenant with the Dutch Government to improve environmental standards.[76] A further example of state actions that may be relevant under the *useful effect* doctrine is the system which exists in the Netherlands, whereby the minister can extend the applicability of a collective agreement to cover an entire industry. This could also be applied to environmental agreements which include a disposal fee, like the one in the *Wit en Bruingoed* case.[77] Declaring such an agreement generally binding would mean that also companies which were not a party to the original agreement would now have to charge this fixed fee to their customers. In these cases Article 101 TFEU applies to the underlying agreement between the companies in question, and the useful effect doctrine, consisting of Article 4(3) TEU read in conjunction with Articles 101 or 102 TFEU, would apply to the Member State's actions.

According to settled case law, Member States are required not to introduce or maintain in force measures, even of a legislative or regulatory nature, which may deprive the competition rules applicable to undertakings from their useful effect.[78] Such is the case, according to that case law:

> 'if a Member State requires or favours the adoption of agreements, decisions or concerted practices contrary to Article 101 or reinforces their effects, or deprives its own legislation of its official character by delegating to private traders responsibility for taking decisions affecting the economic sphere.'

An example of the first indent could be a government's extending the application of an environmental agreement to cover an entire industry. An example of

---

[75] Commission, XXIInd Competition Report, at point 77.

[76] XXIInd Competition Report, point 179.

[77] See further Vedder (2002) at 24 *et seq.*

[78] Case C-379/92 *Peralta* [1994] ECR I-3453, para. 21.

the second might be the extensive privatisation of parts of a country's environ-ment policy, for example by allowing the industry in question to set its own emission standards or product standards.

As far as environmental law is concerned, the Court's judgment in *Peralta* can be taken to imply that the sole fact that a government environmental mea-sure has anti-competitive effects will not cause it to be in breach of the useful effect doctrine. The case concerned Italian legislation prohibiting vessels from discharging harmful substances into the sea. The Court came to the conclu-sion that the useful effect doctrine may not be relied upon as against legisla-tion like the Italian legislation since '[t]hat legislation does not require or foster anti-competitive conduct since the prohibition which it lays down is sufficient in itself. Nor does it reinforce the effects of a pre-existing agreement.'

Any other conclusion would have led to a totally unacceptable result since environmental regulation invariably has anticompetitive effects. When emission standards are adopted by a government, this in fact means it is no longer possi-ble to use an environmentally harmful process. To some degree environmental legislation makes it impossible to exploit competitive advantages at the expense of the environment. These anti-competitive effects can be quite considerable, as was shown in the TiO_2 case.[79] In that case the increase in the cost of produc-tion as a result of the environmental standards in question was of the order of 20% of the total costs. Government regulation can thus have a significant effect on competition. The mere fact that this is the case does not, however, make the legislation incompatible with the useful effect doctrine.

Member State actions will only be incompatible with the useful effect doctrine if the underlying environmental agreement or practice is prohibited by Article 101 or 102 TFEU. This means that the exceptions provided for in Article 101(3) TFEU and the *Wouters* case are also relevant.[80] Even though this is not as such required by EU law, it is wise to notify the Commission of government involvement that is possibly contrary to the useful effect doctrine on the basis of Article 4(3) TEU.

5.2   The Position of the European Institutions

The European institutions are also indicating that they would like to see undertakings taking more responsibility for the environment. In Chapter 1 reference was made to the proportionality principle, which has been regarded as implying a preference for the use of voluntary agreements. The Fifth Environmental Action Programme[81] also indicates a preference for self-regula-

---

[79]   Case C-300/89 *Commission* v. *Council* [1991] ECR I-2867.

[80]   See, for example, Case C-67/96 *Albany* [1999] ECR I-5751, where a government measure declaring an agreement generally binding was found not to infringe the useful effect doctrine because the underly-ing agreement itself was compatible with Article 101 TFEU.

[81]   OJ 1993 C 138/1. This is essentially repeated in Article 3(5) of Decision 1600/2002 laying down the Sixth Environmental Action Programme.

tion by industry and for more indirect steering by public authorities, including the European authorities.

> The best-known example of European action in this field concerns the ozone prob-
> lem. In resolutions and recommendations the Member States and the industries
> concerned (organisations, manufacturers and importers) are urged to limit the
> use of certain ozone-depleting substances and products. A good example is the
> Council Resolution of 14 October 1988 on the limiting of the use of chlorofluoro-
> carbons and halons.[82] The Council invited the Commission: 'In cooperation
> with the Member States, to initiate discussions on voluntary agreements at the
> Community level with all the industries concerned, wherever feasible to substitute
> chlorofluorocarbons and halons in products, such as aerosols, or in equipment
> or processes using them, or if such substitution is not feasible, to reduce the use
> of these substances, so that the total amounts of these substances used will be
> reduced to the maximum possible extent.' Another example is that the Commis-
> sion is a party to the ACEA Agreement to reduce carbon dioxide emissions by
> cars.[83]

The compatibility of the behaviour of the institutions with Article 4(3) TEU taken in conjunction with Articles 101 and 102 TFEU should be reviewed in this area too. It should not be regarded as permissible for the EU institutions to act in breach of the competition rules.[84] However, here too, applying the integration principle, the competition rules should be interpreted so as to take account of the environmental objectives mentioned in Article 191(1) TFEU.

6   Article 106 TFEU

Article 106(1) TFEU deals with so-called public undertakings (or public monopolies) and provides that in the case of public undertakings and undertakings to which Member States grant special or exclusive rights, Member States shall neither enact nor maintain in force any measure contrary to the rules contained in the Treaty, in particular to those rules provided for in Article 18 and Articles 101 to 109 TFEU. Article 106(2) TFEU provides that undertak-ings entrusted with the operation of services of general economic interest are subject to the rules of the Treaty, *'in so far as the application of such rules does not obstruct the performance, in law or in fact, of the particular tasks assigned to them.'*

The importance of these provisions has been greatly enhanced thanks to the case law of the Court of Justice. From this it is clear that Article 106 TFEU is often applied in combination with Article 102 TFEU (abuse of a dominant posi-

---

[82]   OJ 1988 C 285/1.

[83]   Cf. Bongaerts (1999) and Commission Communication on Implementing the Community Strategy to Reduce Carbon Dioxide Emissions from Cars, COM (98) 495.

[84]   See, for example, Case C-341/95 *Bettati* [1998] ECR I-4355, at para. 61.

tion). Given the complexity of the material, it is impossible to discuss the case law in detail in this context. In general terms it can be said that Article 106(1) TFEU, taken in combination with Article 102 TFEU, prohibits a Member State from conferring special rights on an undertaking where that undertaking would be abusing its dominant position simply by exercising those rights, or where those rights could create a situation in which the undertaking would be brought to such an abuse. However, Article 106(2) TFEU may be used to justify this situation. We will now first consider the case law in which Article 106 TFEU played a part in relation to the environment.

6.1   Article 106(1) TFEU and Environmental Protection

As concerns Article 106(1) in connection with Article 102 TFEU, there have been several cases. Most of these involve national monopolies dealing with waste management that somehow limit the export of waste. The *Inter-Huiles* case, for example, involved a French system set up pursuant to the Waste Oils Directive which required collectors of waste oil to deliver their waste oils to authorised disposal companies.[85] One of the arguments put forward was that collection and disposal companies could be regarded as undertakings entrusted with the operation of services of general economic interest. The implicit prohibition on exports was said to be essential in order to fulfil this task, while the negative effect on inter-state trade would be kept to a minimum.

In *Dusseldorp* the Court was asked whether Article 106 TFEU, in conjunction with Article 102 TFEU, precludes national rules that require undertakings to deliver their dangerous waste for recovery to a national undertaking on which it has conferred the exclusive right to incinerate dangerous waste, unless the processing of their waste in another Member State is superior to that performed by the public undertaking.[86] According to the Court, the grant of exclusive rights for the incineration of dangerous waste on the territory of a Member State as a whole must be regarded as conferring on the undertaking concerned a dominant position in a substantial part of the internal market. Merely creating a dominant position is not, in itself, incompatible with Article 102 TFEU.[87] So far the Court is applying existing case law and in that sense the judgment can hardly be said to be remarkable. A Member State is only breaching Article 106 TFEU in conjunction with Article 102 TFEU if it adopts a measure which enables an undertaking to abuse its dominant position. In this case the Court

---

[85] Case 172/82 *Inter-Huiles* [1983] ECR 555; Case C-37/92 *Vanacker* [1993] ECR I-4947. See also Chapter 6.

[86] Case C-203/96 *Dusseldorp* [1998] ECR I-4075. See also Chapter 6.

[87] Cf. the judgment of the Swedish Supreme Administrative Court on 16 June 1999, case no. 1424-1998, 2397-1998 and 2939-1998, RÅ 1999 ref. 76, regarding the cessation of the right to operate the nuclear power reactor Barsebäck 1, which ruled that the EU competition rules do not preclude a closure by the Government of a nuclear power station-a decision dictated by public interests-even if this would lead to the strengthening of a competitor's dominant position on the market. Cf. also Case C-209/98 *Sydhavnens Sten & Grus* [2000] ECR I-3743, paras. 66-68.

found the abuse to follow from the fact that AVR Chemie (the public undertaking that was granted the exclusive rights) received waste for recovery that was intended for processing by a third undertaking, even though the quality of processing by that third undertaking was comparable with that provided by AVR Chemie. This favouring of the national undertaking resulted in the restriction of outlets, which can be regarded as abuse of a dominant position.[88] The Court's strict approach in *Dusseldorp* may be contrasted with that in *Sydhavnens*. In *Sydhavnens* a regulation by the Municipal Authorities of Copenhagen meant that only one public undertaking could process the building and construction waste generated in that municipality. The Court's approach to Article 106(1) TFEU in connection with Article 102 TFEU was much less straightforward than that in *Dusseldorp*.[89] Here, the Court explicitly takes us through the motions of market definition as well as the need to determine the position of the undertaking on the market. Moreover, in an obiter dictum the Court indicates that it does not see any abuse,[90] eventhough the applicant in the national case refers to the restriction of output reasoning that the Court itself used in *Dusseldorp*.[91]

6.2 Article 106(2) TFEU and Environmental Protection

In *Inter-Huiles* and *Vanacker* only the Advocates General explicitly addressed the applicability of Article 106(2) TFEU. Only in the *Almelo* case did the Court shed some light in the relation between Article 106(2) TFEU and environmental concerns. In that case the Court held that undertakings entrusted with the operation of services of general economic interest may be exempted from the application of the competition rules contained in the Treaty in so far as this is necessary to ensure the performance of particular tasks assigned to them.[92] In that regard, it is necessary to take into consideration the economic conditions in which the undertaking operates, in particular the costs which it has to bear and the legislation, particularly concerning the environment, to which it is subject.[93] Thus in *Almelo* the Court considered that environmental protection is one of the reasons that could justify an exception to the competition rules. In *Sydhavnens Sten & Grus* however the Court decided that the treatment of waste could be regarded as a service of general economic interest in the meaning of Article 106(2) TFEU.[94] Following *Sydhavnens* environmental protection can thus be considered to justify an application of Article

---

[88] Additionally, it also restricts exports contrary to Article 35 TFEU; see Chapter 6, section 4.2.

[89] Case C-209/98 *Sydhavnens Sten & Grus* [2000] ECR I-3743, paras. 57-65, see further Vedder (2003) at 255 *et seq.*

[90] Case C-209/98 *Sydhavnens Sten & Grus* [2000] ECR I-3743, para. 82.

[91] Case C-209/98 *Sydhavnens Sten & Grus* [2000] ECR I-3743, para. 72.

[92] Case C-393/92 *Gemeente Almelo v. NV Energiebedrijf IJsselmij* [1994] ECR I-1477.

[93] See also Case C-159/94 *Commission v. France* [1997] ECR I-5815, paras. 70-71.

[94] Case C-209/98 *Sydhavnens Sten & Grus* [2000] ECR I-3743, para. 75.

106(2) TFEU without any additional considerations.[95] Furthermore, the necessity or proportionality of an exception to the competition rules can be founded upon the profitability of the public environmental undertaking. In *Sydhavnens* a statutory monopoly was considered necessary in order for the public undertaking to be able to recoup its investment in setting up a high capacity waste treatment installation. This high capacity centre was in turn considered necessary to attain the environmental objective of a higher percentage of recycling, because it would bring the costs down. It is interesting to note that the Court refused to accept similar profitability-based reasoning in *Dusseldorp*.[96] This absence of clarity is even more problematic in view of the Court's case law on the impossibility to allow a justification of a restriction of the free movement of goods on 'purely economic reasons'.[97]

7   State Aid and Articles 107 and 108 TFEU

7.1   Why There is Environmental Aid and Why it Distorts Competition

It has already been noted that the polluter pays principle is one of the fundamentals of European environmental policy. When applied, this allows the price mechanism to perform its signalling function by translating into costs the negative effects of a particular product or production process on the environment. However, when a Member State decides to increase the level of environmental protection, this will result in increased costs and thus a deterioration of the position of the national industry. No Member State will therefore have an incentive to make the first move with the internalisation of environmental costs, for example in the form of the introduction of an ecotax or the introduction of more stringent emissions standards. In fact, most national attempts at implementing the polluter pays principle go hand in hand with a partial exception for the industries that are particularly polluting and would thus have to pay considerably more. The decisions of the Commission show that state aid cannot be given if it conflicts with the polluter pays principle laid down in Article 191(2) TFEU.[98]

---

[95] See, however, Decision 2003/814 concerning state aid for a UK waste paper recycling scheme, paras. 94-101, where the Commission critically examines the applicability of the term service of general economic interest.

[96] Case C-203/96 *Dusseldorp* [1998] ECR I-4075. See further Vedder (2003) at 272 *et seq.*

[97] See also Chapter 6, section 4.5.

[98] See, for example, the Decision concerning state aid measure N383/2008, an Austrian land remediation scheme, and notably para. 27 where the Commission indicates that the aid was allowed because it could only be granted where the polluter is not liable under EU or national law, could not be identified or cannot be made to bear the costs.

Its decision in respect of aid to *Cartiere del Garda*, which will be discussed in more detail below, is exemplary.[99] In that case the Commission concluded that the proposed aid to Cartiere del Garda does not meet the polluter pays principle contained in Article 191(2) TFEU. Applying this principle, the costs of measures required to reduce nuisances and pollution to an acceptable level should be borne by the firms whose activities are responsible for them. The general grant of state aid simply means that the public and not the polluter pays in the end. State aid should be granted only when the objectives considered essential for the environment are seriously in conflict with other social or economic objectives also of priority importance or when market forces by themselves are not sufficient to cause people to act in such a way that environmental objectives are attained.

As the primary institution responsible for enforcing the provisions on state aid, the Commission addressed the problem of state aids for environmental protection for the first time in 1974 when it drew up the first environmental aid guidelines.[100] These guidelines were applied, with certain amendments, until the end of 1993. At the end of 1993 the Commission drafted new rules for assessing national aid measures.[101] These were replaced by the 2001 Guidelines on Environmental Aid.[102] Currently, the 2008 Guidelines on Environmental Aid are in force.[103]

Just as with the other competition provisions, the integration principle does not mean that environmental state aid is not *a priori* exempted from the prohibition of state aids contained in Article 107(1) TFEU. This is not more than logical given the role that undistorted competition may play in attaining environmental objectives. This view can also be seen in the Commission decision amending German aid schemes for the motor vehicle industry.[104] In that case the German Government decided not to apply the Commission Guidelines on state aid to the motor vehicle industry.[105] One of the arguments for this was that incentives for global environmental protection aid schemes represented a top political priority in Germany, and the EU itself pursues the same objectives according to Article 191 TFEU. According to the Commission, the development of environmentally friendly and energy-saving vehicles is a standard requirement for the motor industry, partly imposed by European legislation, and should, as a general principle, be financed by the company's own resources. The reduction of motor vehicle pollution and the associated technologies have become a major aspect of competition between manufacturers, and their importance should

---

[99] OJ 1993 L 273/51.

[100] The 'old' Guidelines; IVth Competition Report, points 175-182.

[101] The 1994 Guidelines; OJ 1994 C 72/1. Cf. also Case T-150/95 *UK Steel Association* v. *Commission* [1997] ECR II-1433 on environmental aid and the ECSC Treaty.

[102] OJ 2001 C 37/3.

[103] OJ 2008 C 82/1.

[104] OJ 1990 L 188/55.

[105] OJ 1989 C 123/3.

increase further in the future. The Commission seeks to avoid that competition is distorted through the granting of aid to manufacturers in order to assist them in catching up with existing technologies in this domain.[106]

The most important legal consequence of a measure being a grant of aid within the meaning of Article 107(1) TFEU is that it has to be notified to the Commission according to Article 108(3) TFEU. The Commission can then decide whether the proposed aid is compatible with the internal market. Until the Commission has taken a final decision in its favour, the Member State may not put its proposed measures into effect pursuant to the so-called standstill clause. Environmental aid which is granted without the Commission being informed or without its approval is granted unlawfully.[107] Moreover, the standstill clause, contained in the final sentence of Article 108(3) TFEU is directly effective.[108]

7.2   The Scope of Article 107(1) TFEU

Article 107(1) TFEU provides that any aid granted by a Member State which distorts competition by favouring certain undertakings is, in so far as it affects trade between Member States, incompatible with the internal market. Under certain circumstances aid will be compatible with the internal market or may be considered compatible with the internal market, according to Article 107(2) or 107(3) TFEU. Before considering the question under what circumstances the Commission may consider state aid compatible with the internal market, it must be decided when environmental aid has to be regarded as aid within the meaning of the Treaty. The definition in Article 107(1) TFEU gives some indications, which are discussed below.

Aid granted through state resources
From the case law of the Court it is clear that the term aid must be interpreted broadly. Whenever companies benefit from relief which is funded from public resources, the measure will generally be regarded as aid. Not only *direct* aid in the form of grants etc., but also *indirect* aid is regarded as aid in this sense. Indirect aid may be involved in any case where the state does not receive income it otherwise would, as in the case of preferential tariffs, tax remissions, accelerated depreciation for tax purposes, guarantees, interest subsidies, tax relief, etc. The Commission has also regarded a reduction in the cost price of electricity as aid.[109] The Commission has regarded the following as examples of aid schemes:

---

[106] See also the remarks above on the scope of the prohibition on cartels contained in Article 101(1) TFEU.

[107] Regulation 659/1999, and notably Chapter III of that Regulation contain some of the rules concerning unlawful aid. Ultimately, this could result in a Commission decision ordering the recovery of the unlawfully granted aid, see Case T-62/08 *ThyssenKrupp Acciai Speciali Terni*, Judgment of 1 July 2010, paras. 223-252 concerning an Italian environmental aid measure.

[108] Case 47/69 *Steinike & Weinlig* [1977] ECR 595.

[109] OJ 1994 C 32/37.

. tax relief for companies using a minimum of 50% recycled material as raw material in their production;[110]
. a scheme to promote the recycling of surplus manure;[111]
. subsidies to stimulate investment in wind power;[112]
. a reduction in the waste-collection tax paid to the city of Wiesbaden in return for a commitment to purchase from the city at current market prices, all waste paper collected;[113]
. subsidised loans for effluent treatment, waste management, air pollution control and energy conservation;[114]
. interest subsidies on loans for investments for energy savings and the rational use of energy;[115]
. partial tax relief from CO2/energy taxes for energy-intensive firms.[116]

As far as the financing of an aid measure is concerned, Article 107(1) TFEU requires that the aid be financed from state resources. Even aid which is funded from levies imposed on the companies in question can be regarded as aid within the meaning of Article 107(1) TFEU, as was shown in the case concerning aid to Dutch manure processors.[117]

The Dutch Government argued that there was no question of aid, as the aid would be wholly funded by levies paid by the farmers themselves. The fact that the funds were raised by means of a levy on the production of surplus manure was no reason for the Commission not to consider the measure an aid measure. In reaching this decision, the Commission took into account that the levy was introduced by a regulation of the *Landbouwschap* (Agricultural Board), in other words as an obligatory measure under public law, and that payment of the levy could be enforced. More generally, the fact that a subsidy is financed by a parafiscal charge levied on production in a certain sector is not sufficient to divest the system of its character as aid granted by a Member State within the meaning of Article 107 TFEU.[118]

In *PreussenElektra* the limits to this line of reasoning were clarified by the Court.[119] At stake was a German measure according to which privatised regional electricity distributors were obliged to buy all the renewable energy produced in their region at a price that was higher than the market price. Despite the fact

---

[110] XXIIIrd Competition Report, point 420.

[111] XXIInd Competition Report, point 449; OJ 1991 C 82/3 en OJ 1992 L 170/34.

[112] XXIInd Competition Report, point 449.

[113] XXIInd Competition Report, point 452.

[114] XXIInd Competition Report, point 453.

[115] OJ 1991 L 156/39.

[116] XXIInd Competition Report, point 451.

[117] Decision 92/316, OJ 1992 L 170/34.

[118] Case 259/85 *France v. Commission* [1987] ECR 4393. See further Case C-206/06 *Essent Netwerk Noord* [2008] ECR I-5497, paras. 60-75.

[119] Case C-379/98 *PreussenElektra* [2001] ECR I-2099. See on this case also Chapter 6.

that this clearly conferred an economic advantage upon the producers of renew-able energy, as the Court explicitly recognised, it was considered to fall outside the scope of Article 107(1) TFEU, because at the end of the day this benefit was paid by private regional energy distributors and consumers. Thus no state resources were involved and Article 107(1) TFEU did not apply.[120] However, as soon as the funds pass through some public authority, they will become state resources.[121]

This results in an interesting question concerning tradable emission rights schemes. Here a commodity (an emission right) is created that can be traded and thus represents a market value. The commodity, however, is created by the state and depending on the method of initial distribution (allocation free of charge – grandfathering – or auctioning), the emissions rights will be handed out for free or distributed at a market price. Where the initial distribution involves grandfathering, there may be an advantage for the industry concerned. This advantage flows essentially from the fact that the state has handed out for free something that is tradable.[122]

> Concerning tradable emission rights a distinction is often made between credit trading and permit trading. Permit trading involves a fixed amount of available permits (the cap), that correspond to an amount of pollution and that may be traded. In order to achieve the emissions reduction the amount of permits is reduced over the years. In credit trading a dynamic cap is set in the shape of an energy efficiency criterion (e.g. a certain amount of emissions relative to the ther-mal capacity). Emissions reductions are then achieved through a tightening of the efficiency criterion. A potential disadvantage of credit trading is that there is no fixed emissions cap, and increased economic activity could still go hand in hand with increased emissions.[123]

The state aid analysis of emissions trading schemes provides an interesting perspective on the sharing of responsibility for environmental protection between the Member State and the industry. One of the arguments put forward in the *Netherlands NOx* case was that the economic advantage represented by the tradability of emissions rights in that case was nothing more than a compensa-tion for the efforts of the companies to reduce emissions. This argument, that essentially holds that environmental protection is a service provided by compa-

---

[120] Case C-379/98 *PreussenElektra* [2001] ECR I-2099, paras. 54-60. This line of reasoning appears to also underlie the *Dutch Car Wrecks* case, press release IP/01/1518, Competition Policy Newsletter 2002/2, at 87.

[121] See Decision 2010/460 concerning aid measures C 38/A/04 (ex NN 58/04) and C 36/B/06 (ex NN 38/06), paras. 163-165.

[122] See on this point regarding a Dutch NOx trading scheme Case C-279/08 P *Commission v. Netherlands*, Judgment of 8 September 2011, paras. 86-95.

[123] From a competition perspective this is also an advantage as the absence of a cap also means that market access is not restricted, see Vedder (2009).

nies to the member State, was rejected by the Court.[124] The idea behind this is that the costs of reducing emissions are normal costs of business. This may be different where the provision of a specific (environmental) service is entrusted to a specific undertaking.[125]

Favouring certain undertakings

Article 107(1) TFEU applies only if the measure favours certain undertakings or products. In other words: there must be an advantage that must furthermore benefit a selected group of undertakings. These two requirements, *favouring* and *selectivity*, are closely related and will be treated together in this section.

It can sometimes be difficult to draw the dividing line between 'aid that favours' an undertaking by putting it at an advantage and genuine compensation by the government for actual costs incurred. This was an issue in the *ADBHU* case on the compatibility of the former Articles 13 and 14 (currently Articles 14 and 15) of Directive 75/439 on the disposal of waste oils[126] with Articles 107 and 108 TFEU.[127] In the preamble to the directive the Council considers that in cases where certain undertakings are required to collect and/or dispose of waste oils, compensation by indemnities of that part of their costs relating thereto and not covered by their earnings should be possible. These indemnities might, *inter alia*, be financed by a charge on new or regenerated oils. Article 13 of the directive read as follows: 'As a reciprocal concession for the obligations imposed on them by the Member States pursuant to Article 5, indemnities may be granted to collection and/or disposal undertakings for the service rendered. Such indemnities must not exceed annual uncovered costs actually recorded by the undertaking taking into account a reasonable profit. The amount of these indemnities must be such as not to cause any significant distortion of competition or to give rise to artificial patterns of trade in products.' Article 14 continued: 'The indemnities may be financed, among other methods, by a charge imposed on products which after use are transformed into waste oils, or on waste oils. The financing of indemnities must be in accordance with the 'polluter pays' principle.' The validity of these articles was disputed before the Court in connection with their possible incompatibility with the provisions of Articles 107 to 109 TFEU on state aid. It was argued that the financial indemnities should have been regarded as aid. The Court clearly felt otherwise:

'In that respect the Commission and the Council, in their observations, rightly argue that the indemnities do not constitute aid within the meaning of Article [107 *et seq.* TFEU], but rather compensation for the services performed by the collection or disposal undertakings.'

---

[124] Case C-279/08 P *Commission v. Netherlands*, Judgment of 8 September 2011, para. 89.

[125] See below in this section concerning the *Altmark Trans* case, Case C-280/00 *Altmark Trans* [2003] ECR I-7747.

[126] OJ 1975 L 194/31. See now Directive 2008/98, OJ 2008 L 312/3, discussed in Chapter 8, section 17.1.

[127] Case 240/83 *ADBHU* [1985] ECR 531. See also Chapter 1, section 1.

Financial indemnities such as those provided for in the Waste Oils Directive, as well as in some other directives, are not to be regarded as aid to the waste disposal companies, but as remuneration for services performed on behalf of the government. A Commission decision which is relevant in this respect is that to approve a Danish scheme to pay firms engaged in the collection of waste oils.[128] The Commission, like the Court in the *ADBHU* case, considered that the payments were straightforward remuneration for services, and not aid.

This reasoning was further elaborated in the *Altmark Trans* case.[129] This case involved the compatibility of a subsidy that would compensate the extra costs arising from the fulfilment of a service of general economic interest pursuant to Article 106(2) TFEU. According to the Court such a compensatory scheme would not constitute state aid provided that the public service obligations have been clearly defined and the public undertaking is actually charged with providing these services. The compensation must take place in a transparent manner and may not entail any overcompensation. Finally, if public service obligation is not tendered the costs should be established using an objective benchmark.[130]

A related question is whether damages payable in compensation for damage suffered are to be considered aid. This is a type of payment regularly encountered in the field of environmental law. In general a distinction is made between damages which have to be paid for an *unlawful* act, whether by a private polluter or by public authorities, and compensation for a *lawful* act on the part of the public authorities. In terms of European law, the issue of unlawfulness hardly poses a problem. In *Asteris* the Court held that compensation paid on the grounds of liability for an unlawful act by public authorities was not aid within the meaning of Article 107 TFEU:[131]

> 'State aid, that is to say measures of the public authorities favouring certain undertakings or certain products, is fundamentally different in its legal nature from damages which the competent national authorities may be ordered to pay to individuals in compensation for the damage they have caused to those individuals.'

Nor can payment of damages by private individuals, on the ground of their liability for pollution caused by them unlawfully, be regarded as aid for the

---

[128] XXIIIrd Competition Report, point 421. See also XXIVth Competition Report, point 388. With respect to a Danish scheme introducing an environmental charge on the sale of tyres to finance collection and disposal of used tyres in an environmentally friendly way, the Commission considered that payment to the collecting companies constituted compensation for the service rendered and therefore did not involve any state aid. See also Case N 638/02, OJ 2003 C82/10, on the compensation of the costs arising from the collection of CFCs and halons.

[129] Case C-280/00 *Altmark Trans* [2003] ECR I-7747; see also Case C-53/00 *Ferring* [2001] ECR I-9067.

[130] See further Case C-206/06 *Essent Netwerk Noord* [2008] ECR I-5497, paras. 78-85.

[131] Case 106/87 *Asteris* [1988] ECR 5515.

simple reason that there is no funding through State resources, as required by Article 107.

More difficult, however, is the case of compensation for *lawful* acts by public authorities, something which occurs in many Member States.[132] Generally this involves a direct contribution from the public authorities to the polluter, often intended to avoid endangering a company's competitive position where it has to meet disproportionately high costs to fulfil new or stricter environmental provisions. Most of these cases hinge on the degree of discretion the public authorities have in furnishing compensation. Thus the Commission has decided that an amendment to German legislation providing for a levy on effluent discharges was an improvement from the point of view of undistorted competition, because a discretionary power to waive the levy for economic reasons was abolished.[133] Applied to the problem of compensation for lawful acts by public authorities, this case justifies the conclusion that such compensation should as far as possible be given in accordance with objective criteria and that too much administrative latitude should be avoided.

This ties in rather nicely with the second requirement, namely that a measure must be selective if it is to constitute aid. Aid that is awarded to *every* company is not aid within the meaning of Article 107(1) TFEU. The benefits must be awarded to specific industries or undertakings and thus contain an element of selective favouring. The financial position of these specific industries is then favoured in comparison with their competitors. A good example of the degree of specificity required was the proposed aid to Dutch manure processing factories. The aid envisaged was to be given to a specific industry and would have distorted competition in various ways. In the first place, foreign manure processing plants, which have to operate without such aid, would be put at a disadvantage. In the second place, the competitive position of the artificial fertilizer industry, which manufactures a competitive product, would be adversely affected. And in the third place, competition between Dutch farmers and their foreign counterparts might be distorted. The aid to manure processing plants would inevitably mean that not all the environmental consequences of intensive animal husbandry in the Netherlands would be charged to the producer, which might be the case abroad. The Commission also acknowledged that the aid measures might very well increase the competitiveness of Dutch factory farms and processed manure.[134] German aid to the chemical company Riedel for the construction of a bromine-recovery plant was held to distort competition in two ways. First, because it would allow Riedel to process its residues more cheaply than other chemical companies and, second, because aid for investment in the

---

[132] Whether or not EU law also *requires* to pay compensation for damage caused by lawful actions of the state will not be discussed here; Cf. e.g. Case C-120/06 P *FIAMM and FIAMM Technologies v. Council and Commission* [2008] ECR I-6513.

[133] XVIth Competition Report, point 261.

[134] Decision 92/316, OJ 1992 L 170/34, at IV.

recovery plant would give Riedel a competitive advantage over companies which did not receive such state aid.[135]

Ecotaxation can also lead to problems concerning selectivity in two ways. Firstly, ecotaxation schemes often include exceptions or rebates for industries that would face a particularly high tax burden and thus a reduction of competitiveness. These rebates/exceptions may be selective and thus constitute aid.[136] The *Adria-Wien* case contains a good example of this type of measure.[137]

> At hand was an Austrian energy tax that contained a rebate for undertakings primarily producing goods where the tax would exceed a certain threshold. Undertakings supplying services could not qualify for this rebate no matter how much energy tax they would have to pay. According to the Court the tax rebate constituted 'aid granted through state resources', so selectivity was the most important element. A measure is selective if it favours certain undertaking or productions that are in a comparable position to other undertakings or productions in a similar factual and legal position in the light of the objective the measure. This means that any differentiation in the tax burden must be objectively justified in the light of the objectives of the tax scheme.[138] Thus the Court investigated whether the environmental objectives of the energy tax could justify the rebate for goods producing industries only. As the Court rather dryly noticed: energy consumption by companies supplying services is equally damaging to the environment as energy consumption by undertakings producing goods.[139] As a result the rebate was not objectively justified and thus selective. This conclusion was also borne out by the statement of reasons for the Austrian energy tax, according to which the rebate was intended to preserve the international competitiveness of the Austrian industry.[140]

The second problem concerning selectivity and ecotaxation schemes arises from the fact that any functioning ecotax will make environmentally unfriendly production methods or products more expensive compared to environmentally friendly production methods or products. As a result there may be companies claiming that the ecotaxation confers a selective benefit on the companies selling the environmentally friendly products or using less polluting production methods. These companies will then want to challenge the ecotax measure

---

[135] Decision 1999/671, OJ 1999 L 267/51.

[136] See further, Commission Guidelines on Environmental Aid, OJ 2008 C 82/1, para. 57 and section 4. For an application see Commission Decision 2009/972, Danish tax relief for the CO2 tax on quota-regulated fuel consumption in industry, paras. 38-47.

[137] Case C-143/99 *Adria-Wien* [2001] ECR I-8365.

[138] Case C-143/99 *Adria-Wien* [2001] ECR I-8365, paras. 41, 42.

[139] Case C-143/99 *Adria-Wien* [2001] ECR I-8365, para. 52.

[140] Case C-143/99 *Adria-Wien* [2001] ECR I-8365, para. 54.

under the state aid rules of the EU.[141] The *BAA* saga provides a textbook example of such a case and just how difficult it is to apply the selectivity criterion.[142]

> This dealt with the Aggregates Levy, which is a tax imposed on the use of certain aggregates (granulated materials used in construction etc.) in the UK. As the objective of the Aggregates Levy was to come to a more rational use of virgin aggregates and to encourage the recycling of aggregates, the Levy contained an exemption for recycled aggregates and aggregates that are essentially byproducts. The General Court found that the Commission was right to conclude that this exemption could be justified in the light of the environmental objectives of the Levy, meaning that as a non-selective measure, no state aid was involved.[143] The Court, however, disagreed and found that the environmental objectives of the aggregates levvy could not justify classification of the measure as non-selective.[144] According to the Court the environmental objectives should be taken into account in the application of Article 107(3) TFEU.

> A final case worth mentioning here deals the possible selectivity of emissions trading schemes. In order to implement the NEC Directive, the Netherlands enacted an emissions trading scheme for nitrogen oxides. Under this scheme the undertakings subject to an emissions reduction recieved credits for free which they could sell on a market if their energy efficiency exceeded a benchmark. According to the Commission the gratis provision of these credits by the state entailed a selective advantage. The General Court, however, was of the opinion that the scheme was non-selective because the free allocation took place only to the companies subject to the scheme. According to the General Court the companies outside the scheme (and thus not subject to an abatement objective) were not in a comparable situation and the installed thermal capacity was an objective criterion in line with the environmental objective.[145] This was rejected by the Court of Justice, that held that the selectivity was to be determined by the effects of the measure.[146] In this case all companies emitting NOx were subject to an emissions abatement target, but only large emitters, those with an installed thermal capac-

---

[141] Case T-359/04 *British Aggregates Association III*, Judgment of 9 September 2010, provides a nice example of how an eco-tax can be adjusted to take account of reduced competitiveness of the industry concerned (in this case the Northern Irish aggregates industry, para. 14, 19-21) which then distorts competition with aggregates producers in another member state (Ireland, paras. 60-61). The Commission decision declaring this aid measure to be compatible with the internal market was annulled by the General Court, paras. 96-103.

[142] Case T-210/02 *British Aggregates Association I (BAA)* [2006] ECR II-2789. This judgment was set aside in Case C-487/06 P *British Aggregates Association II* [2008] ECR I-10505.

[143] Case T-210/02 *British Aggregates Association (BAA)* [2006] ECR II-2789, paras. 115-128.

[144] Case C-487/06 P *British Aggregates Association II* [2008] ECR I-10505, paras. 81-92.

[145] Case T-233/04 *Netherlands v. Commission* [2008] ECR II-591, paras. 84-100 (*NOx trading scheme*). Cf. also the appeal in Case C-279/08 P. See further Vedder (2009) 62-64 and Weishaar (2009) 145-188.

[146] Case C-279/08 P *Commission v. Netherlands*, Judgment of 8 September 2011, paras. 50-67.

ity exceeding 20 MWth, would benefit from the emissions trading scheme. This means that companies in a similar situation are treated differently.[147]

The effect of the Court's judgment in *Netherlands NOx* is that an aid measure will be state aid, irrespective of the (environmental) objective. Whilst this may be regarded as an unwanted interference in national environmental policy, the advantage of this approach is that the Commission may thus supervise the compatibilty of the measure with Article 107(3) TFEU. Part of this appraisal under Article 107(3) TFEU is also whether or not the measure is effective in achieving the environmental objective.[148]

Adverse effect on trade between member States
     Only state aid that affects trade between Member States is prohibited. The Courts generally give a wide interpretation to this requirement.[149] Despite this, the Commission has issued a *de minimis* regulation according to which state aid not exceeding €200,000 over a three-year period is outside the scope of Article 107 TFEU and thus does not require prior notification.[150]

7.3   Application of Article 107(2) and (3) TFEU to Environmental Aid

General remarks
     The second and third paragraphs of Article 107 TFEU provide for an exhaustive list of grounds on which aid may be considered compatible with the internal market. Here, too, the mere fact that protection of the environment is involved will not as such result in compatibility by virtue of the integration principle. This means that it must be examined to what extent the normal grounds for exemption can be used to make aid compatible. In the light of the integration principle such exemptions should be interpreted in an environmentally friendly way.[151]
     Finally it should be noted that, in assessing aid by Member States in fields other than that of the environment, the environmental effects of the aid should be taken into account.[152] Equally, aid for projects which entail disproportionate effects for the environment should be avoided.

---

[147] Case C-279/08 P *Commission* v. *Netherlands*, Judgment of 8 September 2011, paras. 63, 64.

[148] See further Vedder (2009) at 62-63.

[149] See, for example, Case C-280/00 *Altmark Trans* [2003] ECR I-7747, which dealt with an aid measure concerning local public transport from a municipality in the middle of Germany, paras. 77-82.

[150] Regulation 1998/2006, OJ 2006 L 379/5.

[151] See also the remarks made earlier in this chapter on exemption from the prohibition on cartels.

[152] See further Vedder (2003) at 315 *et seq.* Interestingly, only the previous Guidelines on Environmental Aid, OJ 2001 C 37/3, explictly mentioned this, see para. 83. The Guidelines that are currently in force no longer contain a similar provision.

Member States desiring to grant aid will have to show that the aid does indeed benefit the environment. From its decision on proposed aid to Hoff-mann-La Roche it is clear that the Commission will look closely at the objectives of the aid.[153] In that case the Austrian Government indicated that part of the aid was intended for environmental purposes. By this it meant aid for measures to reduce the risk of accidents and combat air and water pollution. The Commission held aid for the latter measures allowable, but regarded the measures to reduce the risk of accidents as a normal obligation for the company. Such measures were not therefore viewed as environmental measures and aid for them would be regarded as general investment aid.

Article 107(2) TFEU

Article 107(2) TFEU provides for three exemptions which will make aid compatible with the internal market. Article 107(2)(b) TFEU may well be relevant for the environment, as it provides for aid to make good the damage caused by natural disasters or other exceptional occurrences. Flooding caused by the River Maas in the southeast of the Netherlands gave rise to aid approved under this provision.[154]

Article 107(3) TFEU

Article 107(3) TFEU contains essentially two grounds for exemptions that are relevant for environmental state aids. Firstly, Article 107(3)(b) TFEU provides that aid 'to promote the execution of an important project of common European interest' may be considered compatible with the internal market. Secondly, Article 107(3)(c) TFEU is relevant. Just as with Article 101(3) TFEU, the Commission has limited the discretion inherent in these provisions and provided more legal certainty by issuing block exemptions as well a guidelines.[155] The block exemptions mean that certain categories of state aid no longer need to be notified to the Commission. The guidelines have a legal effect in that they bind the author (the Commission), on the strength of the principle of legitimate expectations.[156]

Concerning Article 107(3)(b) TFEU, the Court recognised in *Glaverbel* that this provision might be used for environmental purposes.[157] It held 'that a project may not be described as being of common European interest for the purposes of Article 92(3)(b) [now Article 107(3)(b)] unless it forms part of a transnational European programme supported jointly by a number of governments of the Member States, or arises from concerted action by a number of Member States to combat a common threat such as environmental pollution.' The current Guidelines on environmental aid state that the exemption provided

---

[153] Decision 98/251, OJ 1998 L 103/28.

[154] Cf. XXIVth Competition Report, point 354.

[155] For an overview and discussion of the previous Guidelines see Vedder (2003) at 301 *et seq.* and Seinen (2005). The current guidelines are discussed in Weishaar (2009) 154-161.

[156] Case C-351/98 *Spain* v. *Commission* [2002] ECR I-8031 (*Plan Renove*), para. 76.

[157] Case 62/87 *Glaverbel* [1988] ECR 1573.

for in Article 107(3)(b) TFEU applies only as a secondary ground. It allows for aid to projects that 'must contribute in a concrete, exemplary and identifiable manner to the Community interest in the field of environmental protection, such as by being of great importance for the environmental strategy of the European Union. The advantage achieved by the objective of the project must not be limited to the Member State or the Member States implementing it, but must extend to the Community as a whole.' The Commission explicitly states that the mere fact that companies from more than one Member State are involved does not suffice in this regard.[158] Where these strict criteria are met, the Commission may authorise aid at higher rates than normally allowed pursuant to Article 107(3)(c) TFEU.

Article 107(3) TFEU is currently the primary ground for an exemption. It forms the basis for the General Block Exemption Regulation.[159] This Regulation has the effect of declaring entire categories of state aid to be compatible with the internal market, thus exempting these aid measures from the notification requirement.[160] The Regulation also applies to aid for environmental protection. Such aid qualifies for the block exemption if it fulfills the criteria listed in Chapter I and Section 4 of Chapter II. In this regard it is relevant that according to Article 5 of the Regulation only transparent aid qualifies. This essentially means that the amount of aid involved should be easily identifiable.[161] Furthermore, Chapter I distinguishes between individual aid and aid schemes as well as investment and operating aid. Whereas the former distinction is self-explanatory, the difference between investment aid and operating aid may not be as evident.[162] Investment aid entails a one-off subsidy for an environmental investment, whereas operating aid is used to cover the increased operating costs on a day to day basis. A further general rule derived from Chapter I is that individual environmental investment aid exceeding € 7.5 million per project per undertaking will always have to be notified.[163] A final requirement worth mentioning here is that aid must have an 'incentive effect'. This means that it must be shown that the subsidised activity would not have taken place in the absence of the state aid.

The further requirements for environmental aid can be found in Section 4 of Chapter II. Here we see that Article 18 allows for investment aid to allow undertakings to go beyond EU environmental standards or in the absence of EU standards. The amount of aid that may be granted is determined by means of so-called aid intensities. This refers to the percentage of eligible costs that may

---

[158] Commission Guidelines on Environmental Aid, OJ 2008, C 82/1, para. 147.

[159] Regulation 800/2008, OJ 2008 L 214/3, Article 3.

[160] It may be noted that the Regulation does not apply to certain sectors of the economy, Article 1(3), notably the fishery and aquaculture sector.

[161] Regulation 800/2008, OJ 2008 L 214/3, Article 2(6).

[162] See, concerning the previous Guidelines: Case C-351/98 *Spain* v. *Commission* [2002] ECR I-8031 (*Plan Renove*), para. 77.

[163] Regulation 800/2008, OJ 2008 L 214/3, Article 6(1)(b). Notice that this threshold can also be exceeded when more aid measures cumulate, cf. Article 7.

be subsidised. These eligible costs must be strictly confined to the extra investment costs necessary to meet environmental objectives.[164] General investment costs not attributable to environmental protection must be excluded. Thus, in the case of new or replacement plant, the cost of the basic investment involved merely to create or replace production capacity without improving its environmental performance is not eligible.[165] In any case aid ostensibly intended for environmental protection measures but which is in fact for general investment is not covered by the guidelines. This is true, for example, of aid for relocating firms to new sites in the same area.[166]

Articles 19-23 allow, in similar vein, for investment aid for the purchase of new transport vehicles, early adaptation to EU standards for SMEs, energy saving, high-efficiency co-generation and renewable energy. Concerning all of these aid categories the aid intensity to small enterprises is increased with 20% whereas medium-sized undertakings qualify for a 10% bonus.[167] Furthermore, aid for environmental studies is exempted up to an aid intensity of 50%, which may again be increased with an extra 10 or 20% depending on the size of the undertaking.

Article 25 of the Regulation provides for a group exemption for reductions in environmental taxes. Environmental taxes are defined in Article 17(10) of the Regulation as a tax 'whose specific tax base has a clear negative effect on the environment or which seeks to tax certain activities, goods or services so that the environmental costs may be included in their price and/or so that producers and consumers are oriented towards activities which better respect the environment'. This means that most environmental taxes will result in increased daily operating costs, so that a reduction in those costs entails operating aid.[168] The aid involved in this is exempted provided that the conditions laid down in Directive 2003/96 are met and the tax reduction is granted for a maximum of ten years after which the appropriateness of the reduction is examined by the Member State. Directive 2003/96 contains minimum rates for the taxation of energy products and electricity.[169]

Any aid measure that does not qualify for a group exemption must be notified to the Commission on the basis of Article 108(3) TFEU. The Commission will then see whether the aid could be brought under one of the headings of Article 107(3) TFEU. The Commission has set out it's policy in this regard in the 2008 Guidelines on Environmental Aid. Here we see the same distinction between operating aid and investment aid as well as the general framework for the Commission's appraisal in the form of the balancing test. In a nutshell, this

---

[164] See for example Case T-166/01 *Lucchini* [2006] ECR II-2875 on environmental investments in the coal and steel sector.

[165] Regulation 800/2008, OJ 2008 L 214/3, Article 18 (5)-(8).

[166] See, for example, Decision 93/564, OJ 1993 L 273/51 on the relocation of the Cartiere del Garda.

[167] These terms are defined in Annex I to the Regulation.

[168] Cf. Case C-143/99 *Adria-Wien* [2001] ECR I-8365.

[169] OJ 2003 L 283/51, as amended by Directive 2004/75, OJ 2004 L 195/31.

balancing test means that the Commission will first investigate whether the aid measure aims at a well-defined objective of the common interest. This objective obviously includes increased environmental protection.[170] If there is such a well-defined objective the second step investigates whether the state aid is the right instrument to address the market failure. This means that the incentive effect, appropriateness and proportionality of the state aid are investigated. Finally, the Commission will examine whether the effects on competition and trade are limited.

The Guidelines basically contain the same typology of state aid measures that we have seen in the General Block Exemption Regulation, however, with slightly higher aid intensities and more guidance on the application of the various conditions attached to the applicability of Article 107(3)(c) TFEU.[171] An important innovation compared to the General Block Exemption Regulation is the possibility to subsidise up to 100% of the eligible costs if the aid is granted in a bidding process.[172] The Guidelines are notably more elaborate on the topic of environmental operating aid, where General Block Exemption Regulation only deals with reductions from ecotaxes.[173] As far as tax reductions are concerned, the *Adria-Wien* case shows that they may constitute state aid. The Commission, however, explicitly recognises the need to protect the competitiveness of industries subject to national ecotaxation schemes that impose a higher tax burden than that laid down in Directive 2003/96. The Commission will allow such tax exemptions if the Member State shows that the ecotax reduction is granted on the basis of objective and transparent criteria whilst, in the absence of the reduction, the ecotax itself should have an effect on sales because the increased costs could not be passed on to consumers.[174] Furthermore the Member State must ensure that the tax reduction for an individual company is proportionate to that company's environmental performance compared to an EU-wide benchmark. In addition the beneficiaries should pay at least 20% of the tax and the tax must result in environmental protection, for example because environmental agreements are concluded.[175]

The Guidelines allow for operating aid for energy saving,[176] renewables and high-efficiency cogeneration. Concerning the last two categories the Commission provides three options to overcome the fact that the high investments involved may make market entry difficult due to the price differences between renewable or high-efficiency co-generated energy and traditional energy.[177] The

---

[170] Commission Guidelines on Environmental Aid, OJ 2008, C 82/1, para. 16.

[171] The Annex to the Guidelines contains an overview of the various aid intensities.

[172] E.g. para. 97, 104, 116 and 123 of the Commission Guidelines on Environmental Aid, OJ 2008, C 82/1.

[173] Chapter 4 of the Guidelines contain more detailed rules for this type of aid.

[174] Para. 158 of the Commission Guidelines on Environmental Aid, OJ 2008, C 82/1.

[175] Para. 159 of the Commission Guidelines on Environmental Aid, OJ 2008, C 82/1.

[176] Commission Guidelines on Environmental Aid, OJ 2008, C 82/1, paras. 99, 100.

[177] Operating aid for these two categories is basically treated identically in accordance with section 3.1.6.2 of the Commission Guidelines on Environmental Aid, OJ 2008, C 82/1.

first option is to compensate the difference between the extra production costs and the market price. The second option is to provide support through market based mechanisms such as a tender or tradable green certificates and the third option is to provide degressive operating aid for a period of five years. Member States are therefore allowed to subsidise the higher production costs of renewable energy for example through direct subsidies or so-called green certificates. Member States may also choose to subsidise renewable energy production using the *PreussenElektra* method, when they oblige private parties to buy all renewable energy produced.[178] In this method no state aid is involved, and thus the national measure will not have to be notified in the first place.

The Guidelines also contain rules on aid for the relocation of undertakings[179] and the aid involved in tradable permit schemes.[180] The rules for investment aid in general also apply to aid for investment to repair past damage to the environment, for example by making polluted industrial sites again fit for use.[181] Cleaning up polluted industrial sites at the government's expense must in principle be regarded as aid to the person responsible for causing the pollution. Under the polluter pays principle, that person should pay for the costs of repair himself.[182] However, in cases where the person responsible for the pollution cannot be identified or called to account, aid for rehabilitating such areas may not fall under Article 107(1) TFEU in that it does not confer a gratuitous financial benefit on *particular* firms or industries. The Commission will examine such cases on their merits. In the *Kiener Deponie Bachmanning* case, the Commission was prepared to allow the clean-up of the landfill with part State funding, but only subject to the condition that everything possible was done to recover the costs from the polluter.[183]

7.4   European Aid for Environmental Protection

Aid for the protection of the environment is not only provided by the Member States. The European institutions also have means of supplying aid. Below follows a brief overview of the main provisions in this respect.

---

[178] See above, section 7.2.

[179] Section 3.1.1.1 of the Commission Guidelines on Environmental Aid, OJ 2008, C 82/1.

[180] Section 3.1.1.2 of the Commission Guidelines on Environmental Aid, OJ 2008, C 82/1. It may be noted that this assumes that aid within the meaning of Article 107(1) TFEU is involved. The discussion of Case T-233/04 *Netherlands v. Commission* [2008] ECR II-591 (*NOx trading scheme*) above, has shown that this may not necessarilly be the case.

[181] Section 3.1.10 of the Commission Guidelines on Environmental Aid, OJ 2008, C 82/1. See for example The decision in case N 620/2009, Aid Scheme for the Remediation of Contaminated Sites in Saxony.

[182] See also Chapter 8, section 9 on the Environmental Liability Directive.

[183] Decision 1999/272, OJ L 109/51. See on cleaning-up costs also Decision 1999/646, OJ L 260/1.

The Structural Funds

In the first place there are the Structural Funds – the European Regional Development Fund (ERDF), the European Social Fund (ESF) and the Cohesion Fund.[184] Under Article 11 TFEU, the TFEU's environment policies should be fully integrated into these funds. However, that stage had not yet been reached under Regulation 1260/99,[185] the predecessor of the current regulation. It remains to be seen to what extent the current legislation, Regulation 1083/2006,[186] in particular its Articles 3, 17, 40(f), 47 and 52(c) and the strategic guidelines on cohesion[187] adopted pursuant to Article 25 of Regulation 1083/2006 will improve in practice the integration of environmental considerations in the structural polices.[188]

Life+

The general objective of Regulation 614/2007 establishing a financial instrument for the environment ('Life+') is to contribute to the development and implementation of European environmental policy and legislation by financing all kinds of environmental actions in the European Union.[189] Life+ is the EU's only financial instrument specifically focusing on environmental protection as it repeals a number of other sources of EU environmental funding.[190]

Life is now in its fourth phase with the entry into force of the Life+ Regulation. The first phase lasted until 1996 and was concluded with the entry into force of Regulation 1404/96. The changes made in the second phase were designed to produce more concentrated efforts and increase the efficiency and transparency of application procedures and promote joint national action and cooperation. To this end the second and third phase acknowledged three areas of activity eligible for financial support from Life: Life-Nature, Life-Environment and Life-Third Countries.

Life+ operates solely on the basis of co-financing. The rates of assistance vary depending on the area of activity supported and are different from those contained in the guidelines on state aid for environmental protection.[191] Moreo-

---

[184] For the period 2007-2013, the European Fisheries Fund (EFF) and the European Agricultural Fund for Rural Development (EAFRD) have been moved to a different heading of the Financial Perspectives.

[185] OJ 1999 L 161.

[186] OJ 2006 L 210/25, as most recently amended by Regulation 539/2010, OJ 2010 L 158/1.

[187] OJ 2006 L 291/11.

[188] See COM (2006) 639 on the relation between the SEA Directive, see Chapter 8, section 3.4 below, and the assessment of the environmental effects under the Community funds. In this regard we may point to, *inter alia*, the European Parliament's resolution on the implementation of the structural funds, point 15, OJ 2010 C 117E/79.

[189] OJ 2007 L 149/1. This Regulation repeals Regulation 1655/2000.

[190] Regulation 614/2007, OJ 2007 L 149/1, Article 16. COM (2010) 516 contains the mid-term review of the functioning of Life+.

[191] Regulation 614/2007, OJ 2007 L 149/1, Article 5 allows for financing up to 50% of eligible costs. However, under the nature and biodiversity component up to 75% of the costs may be funded.

ver, the Life+ expressly states that this funding may not be cumulated with funding from other EU sources, such as the structural funds or the Cohesion Fund.[192]

The fourth phase changes the division into three thematic components: Nature and Biodiversity, Environment Policy and Governance and Information and Communication.[193] In essence this change concerning the last component reflects the fact that environmental protection must be integrated in everyday decision-making and administration. Interestingly, the second component of Life+ also allows for the support of NGOs.[194]

The Cohesion Fund

Another important source of European environmental aid is the Cohesion Fund referred to in Article 177 TFEU.[195] The Cohesion Fund is a structural instrument that helps Member States to reduce economic and social disparities and to stabilise their economies since 1994. The Cohesion Fund finances up to 85% of eligible expenditure of major projects involving the environment and transport infrastructure. At present Greece, Portugal, Spain, Cyprus, Czech Republic, Estonia, Hungary, Latvia, Lithuania, Malta, Poland, Slovakia and Slovenia qualify for payments from this fund.

The Council Regulation establishing the Cohesion Fund[196] provides that the fund can provide assistance for 'the environment within the priorities assigned to the EU environmental protection policy under the policy and action programme on the environment. In this context, the Fund may also intervene in areas related to sustainable development which clearly present environmental benefits, namely energy efficiency and renewable energy and, in the transport sector outside the trans-European networks, rail, river and sea transport, intermodal transport systems and their interoperability, management of road, sea and air traffic, clean urban transport and public transport.' (Article 2(1)(b)). Interestingly, the 'old' Cohesion Fund Regulation contained Article 8 according to which the projects financed by the Cohesion Fund 'shall be in keeping with the provisions of the Treaties, with the instruments adopted pursuant thereto and with Union policies, including those concerning environmental protection.' A similar provision has been omitted from the current regulation. However, the fact that its objective is to improve cohesion as well as sustainable development (Article 1(1)) in connection with the fact that Regulation 1083/2006[197] partly governs the Cohesion fund (Article 1(2)), an environmentally unfriendly application of the Cohesion fund seems unlikely. The new Cohesion Fund Regulation entered into force on 1 August 2006.

---

[192] Regulation 614/2007, OJ 2007 L 149/1, Article 9.

[193] Regulation 614/2007, OJ 2007 L 149/1, Article 4(1).

[194] Regulation 614/2007, OJ 2007 L 149/1, Article 4(3)(e) in connection with 7 and point 15 of Annex II.

[195] Cf. Coffey & Fergusson (1997) and Evans (1999).

[196] Regulation 1084/2006, OJ 2006 L 210/79, repealing Regulation 1164/94, OJ 1994 L 130/1.

[197] See above in this section.

8 Conclusions

All the cases discussed above in the context of Articles 101 and 102 TFEU lead to the conclusion that, even though environmental considerations are relevant in the sense that they are taken into account, the Commission has still to take a decision in which environmental reasons are in themselves the *decisive* factor.[198] Integration may well require a more active, more creative attitude on the Commission's part in this respect. Moreover, protection of the environment can no longer be seen purely as a responsibility of government. This is reflected in the increasing use of environmental agreements as an instrument of environmental protection. These have been acknowledged at the European level, too, and their use is encouraged. In this context the traditional black-and-white approach on which European competition policy and law were founded is becoming increasingly inappropriate. This approach assumed that it was up to public authorities to establish and pursue environmental policy by means of legislation and its application through prohibitions and permits, and up to 'the market' to respond by operating as profitably as possible within these constraints. In this climate, competition policies which allowed only marginal room for environmental considerations were appropriate. However today, where the market is very much expected to act responsibly on its own account, environmental objectives should play a greater part in competition policy than is currently the case. This is a necessary consequence of the integration principle of Article 11 TFEU.

This may be contrasted with the application of Article 106 and 107 TFEU in an environmental context. Here we see that the Commission and Court provide ample room for manoeuvre for Member States that want to encourage industry to go beyond the minimum environmental standards. Moreover, EU and Member State subsidies that do not have a specific environmental objective are also scrutinised concerning their environmental impact.

---

[198] Vedder (2003) at 166.

CHAPTER 8

Substantive European Environmental Law

The preceding chapters have dealt with a number of general aspects of European environmental law, mainly in terms of primary European law in its relation with environmental protection. In the following sections an overview will be given of substantive European environmental law as created through legal acts of the European Parliament, Council and the Commission. Relevant case law of the Court of Justice will specifically be discussed. The chapter will begin with a brief discussion of the broad outlines of the EU's policy on the environment as set out in the Environmental Action Programmes that have been adopted over the years. After this, the so-called 'horizontal' environmental legislation is examined. This refers to legislation which, in contrast with sectoral legislation, relates not only to a single sphere of the environment (water, air, noise, soil, radiation etc.) but which examines a given activity from a variety of environmental viewpoints. Finally, sectoral legislation is examined.

1 The Environmental Action Programmes

The European institutions have produced six action programmes on the environment since 1973. These contain priority policy plans for the coming years. The programmes give a good picture of the opinions – at least those held by the EU institutions – on the importance and possible role of a European environment policy, as these have changed with the years.

Thus, in 1973, the first programme[1] spelled out the objectives and principles of environment policy and went on to list a large number of essentially remedial actions that were seen to be necessary at European level. The second programme,[2] in 1977, largely updated and extended the first and elaborated on the ideas contained in it. However, by 1983, when the third programme was adopted,[3] more emphasis was placed on a preventive approach, in other words, an approach requiring economic and social developments to be undertaken in such a way as to avoid the creation of environmental problems. The resources of the environment were recognised as constituting the basis of, but also setting the limits to, further development.

By the time of the fourth programme,[4] it was the view of the Commission that the context had again changed. The Commission had become convinced that, in view of the continuing deterioration of the environment, the establishment of strict standards for environmental protection was no longer merely an option, but had become essential. It had also become convinced that, in view of the growing public demand for improved standards of environmental protection and for environmentally friendly goods, European industry would not be successful unless it increasingly geared itself towards meeting that demand.

---

[1] OJ 1973 C 112/1.

[2] OJ 1977 C 139/1.

[3] OJ 1983 C 46/1.

[4] OJ 1987 C 328/1.

High standards of environmental protection had thus become an imperative, and an economic imperative at that. On the basis of this perception, the
Commission had designated a number of policy areas as priority areas. This
meant that in establishing its priorities, the Commission would give preference
to measures which would result in an improvement in the functioning of the
internal market.

In 1993 the Commission drafted the Fifth Environmental Action Programme, titled 'Towards Sustainability'. The general approach and strategy
contained in this programme were approved by the Council in a Resolution of 1
February 1993. The Fifth Action Programme represented a departure from its
predecessors in several respects. The central objective was 'sustainable development'. As used in the programme, the word 'sustainable' was intended to reflect
a policy and strategy for continued economic and social development without
detriment to the environment and the natural resources on the quality of which
continued human activity and further development depend. The programme
aimed to achieve such changes in society's patterns of behaviour necessary
for sustainability through the optimum involvement of all sectors of society in
a spirit of shared responsibility, including public administration, public and
private enterprise, and the general public. The emphasis on joint responsibility required a broadening of the range of instruments used in environment
policy. Not only traditional instruments such as prohibitions and permits, but
also market-based instruments (taxes, fiscal incentives) should be employed
and so-called horizontal, supporting instruments such as public information
and education. Thus, in contrast with its predecessors, the Fifth Environmental
Action Programme[5] was much more a strategic programme and much less a
list of concrete measures that ought to be taken in the short term. By Decision
2179/98 of the European Parliament and of the Council the Fifth Environmental Action has been reviewed.[6] This review process has resulted in the adoption of the Sixth Environmental Action Programme.[7] Like its predecessor, this
programme is strategic, but it also recognises four priority areas where action is
necessary. These are: climate change, nature and biodiversity, environment and
health and quality of life and sustainable management of resources and wastes.[8]
As far as the instruments are concerned the Sixth Action Programme envisages ten basic strategies:[9] introducing and amending legislation, improving the
implementation of legislation,[10] integrating environmental concerns into other
policies,[11] using market-based instruments to achieve sustainable development,
involving the industry and social partners to achieve sustainable development,

---

[5] OJ 1993 C 138/1.

[6] OJ 1998 L 275/1.

[7] Decision 1600/2002, OJ 2002 L 242/1, adopted on the basis of Commission proposal COM (2001) 31.

[8] Decision 1600/2002, OJ 2002 L 242/1, Article 1(4).

[9] Decision 1600/2002, OJ 2002 L 242/1, Article 3.

[10] See Chapter 4.

[11] See, for example, Chapter 7 on the integration of environmental considerations in competition policy.

making environmental information available for consumers in order to make consumption more sustainable, integrating environmental concerns in the financial sector, creating an environmental liability scheme, improving environmental governance and integrating environmental considerations in land-use planning and management decisions. Unless indicated otherwise, these basic strategies and their further implementation will be discussed in this chapter. In addition the Sixth Environmental Action Programme envisages the adoption of so-called thematic strategies by the Commission and Council and the European Parliament within three years from the adoption of the action programme.[12] Thematic strategies are envisaged in the following areas: soil protection, the protection of the marine environment, sustainable use of pesticides, integrated and coherent policy on air pollution, improvement of the urban environment, sustainable use of resources and waste recycling. Again, these strategies and their implementation will be discussed in this chapter below. Finally the action programme contains provisions on international cooperation, policy making on the basis of the programme and on the monitoring and evaluation. The programme began on 22 July 2002 and will be valid for ten years.[13] In the meantime, a mid-term review has been conducted and the European Parliament has adopted a resolution that is by and large critical on the progress made in implementing the programme.[14] The European Parliament notes, *inter alia*, that not all thematic strategies have been accompanied by specific targets and calls for more attention to the correct implementation and enforcement of EU environmental law.

2   The Notification Directive and other Notification Obligations

In the discussion of Articles 193 and 114(4-6) TFEU in Chapter 3, it became clear that national environmental measures which are more stringent than the European ones generally have to be notified to the Commission. Moreover, directives always contain provisions requiring Member States to notify the Commission of national implementing legislation. However, European environmental law also contains a large number of such provisions apart from the cases just mentioned. In the past national environmental measures had to be notified under the Notification Agreement of 5 March 1973.[15] This requires that the Commission shall be informed as soon as possible of any draft legislative, regulatory or administrative measures and of any international initiative concerning the protection or improvement of the environment which. In practice, although as far as we are aware it has never officially been withdrawn,

---

[12]   Decision 1600/2002, OJ 2002 L 242/1, Article 4.

[13]   Decision 1600/2002, OJ 2002 L 242/1, Article 1(3).

[14]   Resolution of 10 April 2008, 2007/2204(INI) OJ 2009 C 247E/18.

[15]   OJ 1973 C 9/1.

the Notification Agreement has lost much of its significance since the adoption of Directive 83/189, as amended by Directive 94/10 and now consolidated
by Directive 98/34 laying down a procedure for the provision of information
in the field of technical standards and regulations, the so-called Notification
Directive.[16] Under this directive Member States are required to notify the Commission of legislative proposals in the field of technical regulations applying
to products. Article 1 defines 'technical regulation' as meaning the following:
'technical specifications and other requirements, including the relevant administrative provisions, the observance of which is compulsory, *de jure* or *de facto,* in
the case of marketing or use in a Member State or a major part thereof'. *De facto*
technical regulations include voluntary agreements to which a public authority
is a contracting party and which provide, in the public interest, for compliance
with technical specifications. For example, voluntary agreements whereby product standards are agreed upon between the public authorities and an industry.
'Technical specification' is defined as: a specification contained in a document
which lays down the characteristics required of a product such as levels of quality, performance, safety or dimensions, including the requirements applicable
to the product as regards the name under which the product is sold, terminology, symbols, testing and test methods, packaging, marking or labelling and
conformity assessment procedures. Environmental product specifications will
therefore often fall within the scope of application of this directive, and will
therefore have to be notified.

> Two cases in which the Court of Justice has ruled on the matter in an environmen-
> tal context are *Bic Benelux* and Case C-279/94.[17] In *Bic Benelux* the Court had to
> answer the question of to what extent the Notification Directive was applicable
> to a Belgian law which introduced an environmental tax on disposable razors. In
> addition the legislation required a marking to be placed on products subject to
> the environmental tax. Bic, which marketed integral disposable razors in Belgium
> before the environmental tax arrangements came into force, asked the Belgian
> *Council of State* to annul this legislation, on the ground that the law had not
> been notified to the Commission prior to its adoption. According to the Belgian
> Government the obligation to mark the razors had to be regarded as an environ-
> mental protection measure falling outside the scope of the Notification Directive.
> The Court disagreed in no uncertain terms, stating that the fact that a national
> measure was adopted in order to protect the environment does not mean that
> the measure in question falls outside the scope of the directive. Its final conclu-
> sion was that an obligation to affix specific distinctive signs to products which are
> subject to a tax levied on them on account of the environmental damage which

---

[16] OJ 1998 L 204/37, as amended by Directive 98/48, OJ 1998 L 217/18. The preamble to this directive
contains a reference to the Notification Agreement of 1973 where it speaks of its inadequate time limits.
The Commission has issued a proposal to repeal this directive, COM (2010) 179.

[17] Case C-13/96 *Bic Benelux* v. *Belgium* [1997] ECR I-1753 and Case C-279/94 *Commission* v. *Italy* [1997]
ECR I-4743.

they are deemed to cause, constitutes a technical specification within the meaning of the Notification Directive.

Case C-274/97 concerned Italian legislation on asbestos. More particularly the legislation dealt with the extraction, importation, processing, use, marketing, treatment and disposal in the national territory, as well as the exportation, of asbestos and products containing asbestos, and laid down rules for the cessation of the production and trade, extraction, importation, exportation and use of asbestos and products containing asbestos. It also prohibited the extraction, importation, exportation, marketing and production of asbestos, asbestos products and products containing asbestos after a period of one year after the date of entry into force of the Italian legislation. The Court ruled as follows: 'Such a provision, in prohibiting the marketing and use of asbestos, constitutes a technical regulation which the Italian Government ought to have notified in accordance with the first subparagraph of Article 8(1) of the directive.'

If national legislation contains provisions some of which are within the scope of the directive, but others are not, the Commission can nevertheless require that it is notified of the legislation as a whole. Only full communication will enable the Commission to evaluate correctly the exact scope of any technical regulations contained in that law.[18]

If the Commission should have any objections to the national regulations, the Member States may be required to postpone their adoption for a certain period (Article 9). Breach of the obligation to notify renders the technical regulations concerned inapplicable, so that they are unenforceable against individuals and individuals may rely on them before the national court, which must decline to apply a national technical regulation which has not been notified in accordance with the directive.[19]

Environmental directives may themselves also contain specific information requirements. One example is Article 3(2) of the 'old' Waste Directive,[20] which provided that the Commission must be informed of draft national rules concerning, inter alia, waste prevention, the development of clean technologies, recycling and re-use. The question of whether such a requirement also applied to measures adopted by local and regional authorities has been addressed by the Court of Justice in the Balsamo case.[21] In that case the Italian Government had

---

[18] Case C-279/94 Commission v. Italy [1997] ECR I-4743. However, the mere fact that all the provisions have been notified to the Commission does not prevent the Member State from bringing provisions which do not constitute technical regulations into force immediately, and therefore without waiting for the results of the examination procedure provided for by the directive.

[19] Case C-194/94 CIA Security [1996] ECR I-2201. See also Case C-303/04 Lidl Italia [2005] ECR I-7865 on an Italian rule holding a prohibition to market non-biodegradable cotton buds.

[20] Directive 75/442, OJ 1975 L 194/47, before its amendment by Directive 91/156, OJ 1991 L 377/48.

[21] Case 380/87 Balsamo [1989] ECR 2491. Cf. with respect to the notification requirement of Article 7(3) of the 'old' Waste Directive, Case C-209/98 Sydhavnens Sten & Grus [2000] ECR I-3743, paras. 96-102, where the same approach was being followed.

contended that the obligation under Article 3(2) of the directive to inform the Commission related only to 'measures of a certain degree of importance and could not cover provisions whose practical effects are extremely limited, such as those adopted by a small municipality.' The Court rejected this argument:

> 'It need merely be stated that the directive does not provide for any derogation or limitation regarding the obligation to inform the Commission of the draft rules referred to in Article 3. Consequently, that obligation extends to draft rules drawn up by all authorities in the Member States, including decentralized authorities such as municipalities.'

Thus where the obligation is unconditional, the Member States must also notify the Commission of measures adopted by local and regional authorities. Be that as it may, in the *Balsamo* case the failure to comply with the obligation did not affect the lawfulness of the national rules in question:

> 'Neither the wording nor the purpose of the provision in question provides any support for the view that failure by the Member States to observe their obligation to give prior notice in itself renders unlawful the rules thus adopted. It follows from the foregoing that the above mentioned provision concerns relations between the Member States and the Commission and does not give rise to any right for individuals which might be infringed by a Member State's breach of its obligation to inform the Commission in advance of draft rules.'[22]

This decision does not imply that failure to comply with an obligation to notify the Commission of a measure could *never* affect the enforceability of that measure. The arguments for deciding the local measure was not unlawful in this case had to do with the nature of the notification obligation in question. In this case there was no question of European monitoring, nor did the directive make implementation of the national measures conditional upon the Commission's not having any objections. It is clear from the judgment in the *CIA Security* case that if there is a monitoring procedure, and the Commission is entitled to raise objections, failure to notify does have consequences for the national measures in question.[23]

Other provisions containing specific notification requirements are those relating to the application of safeguard clauses by the Member States. Especially in directives laying down total harmonisation of product standards, Member States are often empowered to depart from the directive in emergencies. Application of such clauses generally requires that the Commission be notified. Incidentally, in Case C-43/90 it was held that, even if a national measure is

---

[22] Cf. also with respect to the notification requirement of Article 193 TFEU, Case C-2/10 *Azienda Agro-Zootecnica Franchini*, Judgment of 21 July 2011. See on this case also Chapter 3, section 5.

[23] Case C-194/94 *CIA Security* [1996] ECR I-2201.

provisional, there is no obligation to state in so many words that it is.[24] Simple notification is sufficient.

Where the application of such a safeguard clause is delegated to local or regional authorities, the national legislation must contain provisions requiring those authorities to inform the central government of the measures in question, so that it in turn can notify the Commission. This emerged in Case C-237/90, where implementation in Germany of the safeguard powers under Articles 9 and 10 of Directive 80/778 relating to the quality of water intended for human consumption were at issue.[25] This is inherent in the Court's case law on implementation by decentral authorities according to which the central government is ultimately responsible.[26]

Finally, there is the duty of sincere cooperation of Article 4(3) TEU, by which the Member States are required to facilitate the achievement of the EU's tasks. In order to fulfil this task properly the Commission must be fully informed of the measures adopted by Member States for the purpose of implementing decisions of the EU institutions. The practical significance of this became apparent in the Court's judgment in the *Campania* case.[27] Under the Waste Directives, Member States must draw up a report on the measures taken to implement their obligations in respect of waste disposal and send it to the Commission. The Commission had asked the Italian Government for information concerning the quantities produced, the methods employed and the importation of waste into the region of Campania. The Italian Government maintained that it was not obliged to furnish the information requested, because this went beyond the obligation to produce the reports. The Court rejected this argument and held that Italy had failed to meet its obligations under the duty of sincere cooperation:

'In so far as it concerned the disposal of waste covered by the directive on waste and the directive on toxic and dangerous waste and the competent authority for disposal operations, that request for information came within the scope of the Commission's power to supervision. The inaction on the part of the Italian Government, which thus prevented the Commission from obtaining an accurate picture of conditions in Campania, must be treated as a refusal to cooperate with that institution.'

The Court added that the Italian Government was in any case obliged to explain its position further. This case could be taken to imply an obligation on the Member States to provide information to the Commission, even where there are no explicit provisions, where the information relates to matters within the scope of application of a directive and the information would enable the Commission to exercise its task of monitoring compliance with the directive.[28]

---

[24] Case C-43/90 *Commission v. Germany* [1992] ECR I-1909.

[25] Case C-237/90 *Commission v. Germany* [1992] ECR I-5973.

[26] See Chapter 4, section 4, e.g. Case C-87/02 *Commission v. Italy* [2004] ECR I-5975 (*Lotto Zero*), para. 38.

[27] Case C-33/90 *Commission v. Italy* [1991] ECR I-5987 *(Campania)*.

[28] The Court seems to have confirmed this in Case C-285/96 *Commission v. Italy* [1998] ECR I-5935.

3 Environmental Impact Assessment

Environmental impact assessment was first introduced by the US National Environmental Policy Act 1969.[29] It is a procedural instrument that implements the prevention principle by requiring an assessment of the environmental effects of certain decisions in advance.[30] In the EU environmental assessment is required for certain projects and plans. For *projects* the legal framework consists of the Environmental Impact Assessment (EIA) Directive.[31] Environmental assessment for *plans* and *programmes* is governed by the Strategic Environmental Assessment (SEA) Directive.[32] Below, first the EIA Directive will be discussed.

3.1 The EIA Directive

The scope of the EIA directive
Article 2(1) of the EIA Directive is one of the central provisions and requires that, before consent is given, projects likely to have significant effects on the environment by virtue, *inter alia*, of their nature, size or location are made subject to a requirement for development consent[33] and an assessment with regard to their effects. Article 1(1) states that the directive shall apply to public and private projects which are likely to have significant effects on the environment.[34] For the purposes of the directive, 'project' means the execution of construction works or of other installations or schemes, or other interventions in the natural surroundings and landscape including those involving the extraction of mineral resources. The term project is consistently interpreted widely and the Court is clear about the fact that splitting of projects and failure to take into account cumulative effects of connected projects are incompatible with the directive.[35] Moreover, beneficial environmental effects do not exclude a project

---

[29] 42 USC 4321-4347.

[30] See on the subject in general Holder (2004) and Moreno (2005). See, concerning the EIA Directive, Case C-392/96 *Commission* v. *Ireland* [1999] ECR-5901, para. 62.

[31] Directive 85/337 on the assessment of the effects of certain public and private projects on the environment, OJ 1985 L 175/40, as amended by Directive 97/11, OJ 1997 L 73/5 and Directive 2003/35, OJ 2003 L 156/17.

[32] Directive 2001/42 on the assessment of the effects of certain plans and programmes on the environment, OJ 2001 L 197/30. An assessment under the EIA Directive is without prejudice to the requirements of the SEA Directive; Case C-295/10 *Valčiukienė and others*, Judgment of 22 September 2011, para. 59.

[33] On the definition of this concept see Case C-290/03 *Barker* [2006] ECR I-3949, paras. 39-41.

[34] These projects are listed in Annex I and II.

[35] See on the wide interpretation of the projects listed Case C-2/07 *Abraham et al.* [2008] ECR I-1197, paras. 29-37 and Case C-142/07 *Ecologistas en Acción-CODA* [2008] ECR I-6097, paras. 28-45. Case C-2/07 *Abraham et al.* [2008] ECR I-1197 further shows that an agreement between the public authorities and a private party to extend a runway does not constitute a project, as this requires works or physi-

from the scope of the directive.[36] Article 2(1) of the directive thus results in a very wide scope, that is limited in a number of ways.

Firstly, Article 1(4) allows for the Member States to decide that 'projects serving national defence purposes' are outside the scope of the EIA Directive.[37] In the *Bozen* case the Court ruled:

> 'That provision thus excludes from the directive's scope and, therefore, from the assessment procedure for which it provides, projects intended to safeguard national defence. Such an exclusion introduces an exception to the general rule laid down by the directive that environmental effects are to be assessed in advance and it must accordingly be interpreted restrictively. Only projects which mainly serve national defence purposes may therefore be excluded from the assessment obligation.
>
> It follows that the directive covers projects, such as that at issue in the main proceedings which, as the file shows, has the principal objective of restructuring an airport in order for it to be capable of commercial use, even though it may also be used for military purposes.'[38]

Here we see the Court's traditional method of approaching such questions concerning the scope of environmental measures. In line with a teleological approach, exceptions to the rule are interpreted narrowly in order not to jeopardise the environmental objective. Secondly, Article 1(5) provides that the directive is not to apply to projects the details of which are adopted by a specific act of national legislation, since the objectives of the directive, including that of supplying information, are achieved through the legislative process. In the *Bozen* case the Court clarified its position.[39] In order to be able to apply the exemption two conditions have to be met. The first requires the details of the project to be adopted by a specific legislative act; under the second, the objectives of the directive, including that of supplying information, must be achieved through the legislative process. With regard to the first condition the Court

---

cal interventions (para. 23). Such an agreement may, however, constitute development consent (paras. 25-28). This is essentially confirmed in Case C-275/09 *Brussels Hoofdstedelijk Gewest*, Judgment of 17 March 2011.

[36] Case C-142/07 *Ecologistas en Acción-CODA* [2008] ECR I-6097, para. 41.

[37] These decisions must be taken on a case-by-case basis. Moreover, this may only take place if the Member States consider that applying the EIA Directive would adversely affect the national defence purposes. The fact that this exemption has to take place on a case-by-case basis excludes blanket-decisions exempting all national defence projects from the scope.

[38] Case C-435/97 *World Wildlife Fund v. Autonome Provinz* [1999] ECR I-5613, paras. 65-66.

[39] Case C-435/97 *World Wildlife Fund v. Autonome Provinz* [1999] ECR I-5613, paras. 55-63. Cf. for some national case law on Article 1(5): the Danish Supreme Court ruling of 2 December 1998 on the building of the Öresund bridge, *Greenpeace v. Minister of Traffic*, EfR. 1999.367 H (referred to by Peter Pagh in *YEEL* (2000) at 474-475 and the Dutch *Raad van State* 16 June 1995 [1995] *M&R* 93 on the *Deltawet Grote Rivieren*, legislation containing rules on the reinforcement of river-dykes.

argued that the legislative act, which grants the developer the right to carry out the project, must be specific and display the same characteristics as the development consent and must lay down the project in detail. It is only by complying with such requirements that the objectives referred to in the second condition can be achieved through the legislative process.

Concerning the temporal scope of the directive there have been a number of cases dealing with the so-called 'pipeline-problem'.[40] This refers to the fact that the projects the EIA Directive refers to can take many years to complete. In the meantime the balance between (economic) progress and environmental protection may have shifted, leading to requests for assessments.[41] As a result there have been questions on the applicability of the EIA Directive to projects that were said to have started before the deadline for implementation of the EIA Directive had passed. The applicability of the EIA Directive hinges on whether or not the application for development consent was lodged before the deadline for implementation, 8 July 1988 for Directive 85/337.

This was ruled in the *Bund Naturschutz* case in response to questions from the *Bayerische Verwaltungsgerichtshof* on the permissibility of national transitional rules, the Court pointed out that:[42]

> 'there is nothing in the directive which could be construed as authorizing the Member States to exempt projects in respect of which the consent procedures were initiated after the deadline of 3 July 1988 from the obligation to carry out an environmental impact assessment. On the contrary, all the provisions in the directive were formulated on the basis that it was to be transposed into the legal systems of the Member States by 3 July 1988 at the latest.
>
> Accordingly, regardless whether the directive permits a Member State to introduce transitional rules for consent procedures already initiated and in progress before the deadline of 3 July 1988, the directive in any case precludes the introduction in respect of procedures initiated after that date of rules such as those at issue in the main proceedings by a national law, which, in breach of the directive, transposes it belatedly into the domestic legal system. Such an interpretation would result in an extension of the deadline of 3 July 1988 and would be contrary to the obligations under the directive.'[43]

The Court added to that in the *Großkrotzenburg* case that informal contacts between the competent authority and the developer, even relating to the content and proposal to lodge an application for consent for a project, cannot be treated for the purposes of applying the directive as a definite indication of the date on

---

[40] See for this terminology Case C-201/02 *Wells* [2004] ECR I-723, para. 48.

[41] See, for example, the reverie by Advocate General Mischo in Case C-81/96 *B en W Haarlemmerliede en Spaarnwoude v. GS van Noord-Holland* [1998] ECR I-3923, para. 32.

[42] Case C-396/92 *Bund Naturschutz v. Bayern* [1994] ECR I-3717.

[43] Case C-396/92 *Bund Naturschutz v. Bayern* [1994] ECR I-3717. Cf. also Case C-301/95 *Commission v. Germany* [1998] ECR I-6135.

which the procedure was initiated. The date when the application for consent was *formally* lodged constitutes the sole criterion which may be used.[44]

Following the amendment by Directive 97/11, the EIA Directive makes clear that the EIA Directive in its current form will only apply if a request for development consent is submitted after 14 March 1999 (the deadline for implementation of Directive 97/11).[45]

Projects subject to an EIA

Even when a project is within the scope of the directive, an assessment is not always required. The directive distinguishes between so-called Annex I projects which are always made subject to an assessment (Article 4(1)) and Annex II projects where the Member States shall determine through a case-by-case examination, and/or thresholds or criteria set by the Member State whether the project shall be made subject to an assessment (Article 4(2)).

When a case-by-case examination is carried out or thresholds or criteria are set, the relevant selection criteria set out in Annex III shall be taken into account in a screening procedure.[46] These include both the characteristics of the project (its size, the accumulation with other projects, the use of natural resources, the production of waste, pollution and nuisances, the risk of accidents), its location (the environmental sensitivity of geographical areas likely to be affected) and the characteristics of the potential impact (the extent of the impact, the transfrontier nature, the magnitude and complexity, the probability and the duration, frequency and reversibility of the impact).[47]

Under the 'old' directive the Court set clear limits on the Member States' powers when setting thresholds. Ruling on Belgian legislation which excluded certain whole classes of projects listed in Annex II from the requirement of an impact assessment, the Court held that the criteria and/or the thresholds mentioned in Article 4(2) were designed to facilitate examination of the actual characteristics of any given project in order to determine whether it is subject to the requirement of assessment, not to exempt in advance from that obligation certain whole classes of projects listed in Annex II which may be envisaged as taking place on the territory of a Member State.[48] In the *Kraaijeveld* case

---

[44] Case C-431/92 *Commission* v. *Germany* [1995] ECR I-2189 *(Großkrotzenburg)*.

[45] Directive 97/11, OJ 1997 L 73/5, Article 3(3).

[46] See Case C-75/08 *Mellor* [2009] ECR I-3799, paras. 48-61, where the Court concludes that the decision resulting from a screening obligation does not have to include all the reasons for that decision. However, such information should be made available upon request. Cf. also Case C-255/08 *Commission* v. *Netherlands*, Judgment of 15 October 2009 and Case C-66/06 *Commission* v. *Ireland* [2008] ECR I-158.

[47] Case C-2/07 *Abraham et al.* [2008] ECR I-1197, paras. 41-46, further shows that the increased use and thus nuisance as a result of the project should also be taken into account. It appears that the Court considers that this should not only be taken into account in assessing the effects (the actual EIA), but also in determining whether or not a project is within the scope of the EIA Directive.

[48] Case C-133/94 *Commission* v. *Belgium* [1996] ECR I-2323. Cf. on the question of the interpretation of the concept of classes of projects, Case C-301/95 *Commission* v. *Germany* [1998] ECR I-6135, paras. 38-46.

the Court confirmed this position and stated it more precisely.[49] The Court acknowledged that Article 4(2) of the directive conferred on Member States a measure of discretion to specify certain types of projects which would be subject to an assessment. However, the limits of that discretion are to be found in the obligation set out in Article 2(1) that projects likely to have significant effects on the environment are to be subject to an impact assessment. The question of whether, in laying down such criteria, the Member State went beyond the limits of its discretion cannot be determined in relation to the characteristics of a single project. It depends on an overall assessment of the characteristics of projects of that nature which could be envisaged in the Member State.

In Case C-392/96 the Court ruled against the way Ireland had made use of its discretion to set thresholds. On the setting of 'absolute thresholds' the Court ruled that 'a Member State which established criteria or thresholds taking account only of the size of projects, without also taking their nature and location into consideration, would exceed the limits of its discretion under Articles 2(1) and 4(2) of the directive'.[50] On the 'cumulative effect' of projects the Court ruled in the same case that the Member States must ensure that the objective of the legislation would not be circumvented by the splitting of projects:

> 'Not taking account of the cumulative effect of projects means in practice that all projects of a certain type may escape the obligation to carry out an assessment when, taken together, they are likely to have significant effects on the environment within the meaning of Article 2(1) of the Directive.'[51]

Annex I projects include crude-oil, thermal power stations and other combustion installations, various nuclear installations, integrated works for the initial smelting of cast-iron and steel, installations for the extraction of asbestos, integrated chemical installations, construction of lines for long-distance railway traffic,[52] construction of motorways,[53] inland waterways and ports, waste disposal installations, groundwater abstraction or artificial groundwater recharge schemes, waste water treatment plants, extraction of petroleum and natural gas for commercial purposes, dams, pipelines for the transport of gas, oil or chemicals, installations for the intensive rearing of poultry or pigs,[54] quarries and open-cast mining, construction of overhead electrical power lines, and installations for storage of petroleum, petrochemical, or chemical products. Some of these projects are subject to a threshold. Where the threshold is

---

[49] Case C-72/95 *Kraaijeveld* [1996] ECR I-5403.

[50] Case C-392/96 *Commission v. Ireland* [1999] ECR I-5901, para. 65; Case C-435/09 *Commission v. Belgium*, Judgment of 24 March 2011, paras. 48-65.

[51] Case C-392/96 *Commission v. Ireland* [1999] ECR I-5901, para. 76. See further Case C-205/08 *Umwelt-anwalt von Kärnten* [2009] ECR I-11525, paras. 51-55 where the Court states that this applies in a trans-boundary context as well.

[52] Case C-227/01 *Commission v. Spain* [2004] ECR I-8253 (*Valencia-Tarragona railway*), paras. 48-54.

[53] Case C-87/02 *Commission v. Italy* [2004] ECR I-5975 (*Lotto Zero*), paras. 41-49.

[54] Case C-121/03 *Commission v. Spain* [2005] ECR I-7569 (*Pig Farms in Baix Ter*), paras. 86-98.

not exceeded the project will generally be covered by Annex II. Annex II also contains a whole list of projects, ranging from reclamation of land from the sea and installations for the slaughter of animals, tourism and leisure projects[55] such as ski-runs, ski lifts and cable-cars to urban development projects.[56]

Annex II also covers any change or extension of projects listed in Annex I or Annex II, already authorised, executed or in the process of being executed, which may have significant adverse effects on the environment (changes or extensions not listed in Annex I).[57] The same applies to projects in Annex I.[58]

The Court's case law already clarified that modifications to projects listed in Annex II are not *a priori* exempted from the directive.[59]

The EIA procedure

The directive allows Member States considerable freedom as to the manner in which the assessment should be carried out. Article 5(3) provides that the information to be provided should include at least:

· a description of the project comprising information on the site, design and size of the project;
· a description of the measures envisaged in order to avoid, reduce and, if possible, remedy significant adverse effects;
· the data required to identify and assess the main effects which the project is likely to have on the environment;
· an outline of the main alternatives studied by the developer and an indication of the main reasons for his choice, taking into account the environmental effects;
· a non-technical summary of the information.

Annex IV contains details of the information to be supplied. Besides this the directive lays down rules that have to be complied with before consent for a project is given. Consultation of the public is inherent in the EIA-instrument,

---

[55] Case C-117/02 *Commission v. Portugal* [2004] ECR I-5517 (*Hotels in the Sintra-Cascais site of Community importance*). This case shows that the mere fact that a project takes place in a national park does not mean that it will have significant effects on the environment, paras. 80-88.

[56] Case C-332/04 *Commission v. Spain* (*Cinema in Paterna*) [2006] ECR I-40, paras. 70-88. This case shows that the mere fact that a project is implemented in an urban area is not enough to rule out possible environmental effects, particularly if the cinema is presented to be the second-largest in Europe attracting more than 60,000 people per week. Cf. also the intensity of review to be exercised by national courts the English Court of Appeal 14 February 2003 *Goodman and Hedges* v. *LB Lewisham and Big Yellow Property Co. Ltd.* [2003] EWCA Civ 140.

[57] See for instance Case C-431/92 *Commission v. Germany* [1995] ECR I-2189.

[58] Annex I, point 22.

[59] Case C-435/97 *World Wildlife Fund* v. *Autonome Provinz* [1999] ECR I-5613, para. 39: 'the mere fact that the Directive did not expressly refer to modifications to projects included in Annex II, as opposed to modifications to projects included in Annex I, did not justify the conclusion that they were not covered by the Directive'. Cf. also Case C-72/95 *Kraaijeveld* [1996] ECR I-5403, para. 40.

and has been reinforced by the amendments to the EIA Directive by Directive 2003/35 on public participation.[60] Member States are required to ensure that any request for development consent and any information in that connection is made available to the public within a reasonable time in order to give the public concerned the opportunity to express an opinion before the development consent is granted (Article 6(2)). Even though Article 6(2) is silent on this point, the Court has ruled that Member States may require a reasonable sum for this information.[61] They must also take the measures necessary to ensure that the authorities likely to be concerned by the project by reason of their specific environmental responsibilities are given an opportunity to express their opinion on the information supplied by the developer and on the request for development consent (Article 6(1)).[62] The logical consequence of these provisions is that the results of consultations and the information gathered must be taken into consideration in the development consent procedure (Article 8).

According to Article 2(2) the EIA may be integrated into the existing procedures for consent to projects in the Member States. The question to what extent an *ordinary* environmental authorisation procedure, in other words one that is not a specific EIA procedure, complies with the directive's requirements was addressed by the Court in Case C-431/92.[63] The Court seems to have accepted this as long as all the requirements of the directive have been complied with.[64] The same rationale – one that hinges on the effectiveness of the EIA Directive – can also be seen in the case law on the time of an EIA in a multi-stage procedure. Normally, an EIA should be carried out at the earlier stage, but when the actual environmental effects can only be known at the later stage, the EIA should also be conducted at that later stage.[65]

Article 2(3) provides that Member States may, in exceptional cases, exempt a specific project in whole or in part from an EIA. However in that case the Member States shall consider whether another form of assessment would be appropriate and whether the information thus collected should be made avai-

---

[60] See further section 6.3 below.

[61] Case C-216/05 *Commission* v. *Ireland* [2006] ECR I-10787, paras. 42-47, where a fee of €20 or €45 was considered reasonable and not to constitute an obstacle to the participation rights.

[62] However, according to Article 6(3) the Member States can determine the details for such information and consultation; cf. Case C-216/05 *Commission* v. *Ireland* [2006] ECR I-10787, paras. 24-28.

[63] Case C-431/92 *Commission* v. *Germany* [1995] ECR I-2189.

[64] Confirmed in Case C-435/97 *World Wildlife Fund* v. *Autonome Provinz* [1999] ECR I-5613, para. 52 and Case C-278/98 *Linster* [2000] ECR I-6817, paras. 49-58. See for an application at national level of this doctrine the judgment of the Swedish Supreme Administrative Court of 16 June 1999, case nos. 1424-1998, 2397-1998 and 2939-1998, RÅ 1999 ref. 76, regarding the cessation of the right to operate the nuclear power reactor Barsebäck 1.

[65] Case C-201/02 *Wells* [2004] ECR I-723, paras. 42-52 and Case C-508/03 *Commission* v. *UK* [2006] ECR I-3969, paras. 104-106 and Case C-290/03 *Barker* [2006] ECR I-3949, paras. 46-48.

lable to the public. They must also provide the Commission with the relevant information prior to granting consent.[66]

In case of projects with transboundary effects, the Convention on Environmental Impact Assessment in a Transboundary Context, the so-called Espoo Convention, signed by the EC on 25 February 1991, is relevant. This convention was implemented at the EU level in the form of changes to Article 7 of the EIA Directive.

Where a Member State is aware that a project is likely to have significant transboundary effects or where a Member State likely to be significantly affected so requests, the Member State in whose territory the project is intended to be carried out shall send to the affected Member State as soon as possible and no later than when informing its own public, *inter alia:*

· a description of the project, together with any available information on its possible transboundary impact;
· information on the nature of the decision which may be taken;
· and shall give the other Member State a reasonable time in which to indicate whether it wishes to participate in the EIA procedure.

If a Member State which receives the above information indicates that it intends to participate in the EIA procedure, the Member State in whose territory the project is intended to be carried out shall, if it has not already done so, send to the affected Member State all information to be given pursuant to Article 6(2). The Member States concerned shall also arrange for the information to be made available pursuant to Article 6(3)(a) and (b). They shall ensure that those authorities and the public concerned are given an opportunity, before development consent for the project is granted, to forward their opinion within a reasonable time on the information supplied to the competent authority in the Member State in whose territory the project is intended to be carried out.

Finally, the Member States concerned shall enter into consultations regarding, *inter alia,* the potential transboundary effects of the project and the measures envisaged to reduce or eliminate such effects and shall agree on a reasonable time frame for the duration of the consultation period.

National legislation transposing the obligations of Article 7 of the directive must contain explicit provisions requiring the authorities to transmit the information to the other Member States.[67]

---

[66] Irish legislation failed to meet these requirements; Case C-392/96 *Commission* v. *Ireland* [1999] ECR I-5901, para. 87. According to the Dutch *Raad van State* 16 June 1995 [1995] *M&R* 93, a failure to notify does not affect the legality of the legislation concerned or permits granted on the basis of it. The Commission has published a guidance document concerning this provision on the D-G environment website http://ec.europa.eu/environment/eia/pdf/eia_art2_3.pdf (last visited 7 October 2011).

[67] Case C-392/96 *Commission* v. *Ireland* [1999] ECR I-5901, para. 94. Cf. also Case C-435/09 *Commission* v. *Belgium,* Judgment of 24 March 2011, para. 92.

When a decision to grant or refuse development consent has been taken,[68] Article 9 of the EIA Directive requires the competent authority to inform the public thereof and to make available to the public the following information:
· the content of the decision and any conditions attached thereto;
· having examined the concerns and opinions expressed by the public concerned, the main reasons and considerations on which the decision is based, including information about the public participation process;
· a description of the main measures to avoid, reduce and, if possible, offset the major adverse effects.

Article 10a was introduced by Directive 2003/35 and requires that the Member States grant access to a judicial review procedure for members of the public concerned.[69]

3.2   The Strategic Environmental Assessment Directive

The SEA Directive implements the idea that the environmental effects of certain actions should be identified in advance at an even earlier stage than the EIA Directive.[70] Where the latter requires an EIA for projects, the former applies to the strategic or planning stage that precedes the action project-stage. The integration of environmental concerns at this stage is generally considered to contribute to sustainability.[71] The initial proposal for the SEA Directive dates from 1996,[72] was amended in 1999[73] and resulted in the SEA Directive in 2001.[74] According to Article 13 the SEA Directive had to be implemented before 21 July 2004.[75] The framework of the SEA Directive closely follows that of the EIA Directive.

The scope of the SEA Directive
The SEA Directive applies to plans and programmes. Article 2(a) defines this as 'plans and programmes, including those co-financed by the EU, as well as any modifications to them, which are subject to preparation and/or adoption by an authority at national, regional or local level or which are prepared by an authority for adoption, through a legislative procedure by Parliament or Government,

---

[68] Such a decision must be explicitly taken, so-called tacit authorisation according to which a positive decision as deemed to have been taken after the expiry of a certain time-limit is not compatible with the EIA Directive, Case C-230/00 *Commission v. Belgium* [2001] ECR-4591.

[69] See section 6.3 below and Chapter 5, section 5.

[70] See for an appraisal of the SEA Directive in the light of the EIA Directive, Sheate (2003).

[71] Marsden & De Mulder (2005).

[72] COM (1996) 511, OJ 1997 C 128/14.

[73] COM (1999) 73, OJ 1999 C 83/13.

[74] Directive 2001/42, OJ 2001 L 197/30.

[75] Several Member States failed to implement the SEA Directive on time: see e.g. infringement Case C-159/06 *Commission v. Finland* [2006] ECR I-114.

and which are required by legislative, regulatory or administrative provisions'. This very wide definition is narrowed down by Article 3(8).[76] On the basis of this provision, plans and programmes the sole purpose of which is to serve national defence or civil emergency and financial or budget plans and programmes are excluded from the scope of the directive.[77]

For co-financed plans and programmes Article 13(9) contains an exception for plans and programmes co-financed under the 2000-2006 programming period for the 'old' Cohesion Fund Regulation 1260/1999 and the 2000-2006 and 2000-2007 programming periods for the European Agricultural Fund for Rural Development Regulation 1257/1999.[78]

Contrary to the EIA Directive, the SEA Directive contains provisions as regards its temporal scope. According to Article 13(3) the obligation to conduct a prior environmental assessment applies only to plans and programmes of which the first formal preparatory act is subsequent to the deadline for implementation (21 July 2004). Furthermore, for plans and programmes initiated before 21 July 2004 (i.e. pipeline plans and programmes), the environmental assessment obligation applies if these plans and programmes are finally approved only after 21 July 2005. For the pipeline plans and programmes, the Member States can decide that the environmental assessment obligation does not apply on a case-by-case basis if they consider this 'not feasible'.[79]

Plans and programmes subject to SEA

According to Article 3(1) all plans and programmes likely to have significant environmental effects are subject to the environmental assessment obligation. Article 3(2) further specifies this by making an environmental assessment mandatory for two categories of plans and programmes. Firstly those which are prepared for agriculture, forestry, fisheries, energy, industry, transport,[80] waste management, water management, telecommunications, tourism, town and country planning or land use and which set the framework for future development consent of projects listed in Annexes I and II to Directive 85/337. Secondly the plans and programmes which, in view of the likely effect on sites, have been

---

76 It will, for example, also include action programmes adopted as part of the implementation of the Nitrates Directive, see below paragraph 10.9, cf. Joined Cases C-105/09 and C-110/09 *Terre wallonne ASBL and Inter-Environnement Wallonie ASBL* v. *Région wallonne*, Judgment of 17 June 2010, paras. 35-42.

77 This provision can be compared to Article 1(4) of the EIA Directive which will probably result in a narrow interpretation of this exception, see by analogy: Case C-435/97 *World Wildlife Fund* v. *Autonome Provinz* [1999] ECR I-5613, paras. 65-66.

78 See further COM (2006) 639 on the relationship between the SEA Directive and Community Funds.

79 On the basis of the *Kraaieveld* case law of the Court this provision can probably be invoked in order to ascertain whether or not a Member State has exceeded the limits to its discretion set by Article 13(3).

80 Article 8(1) of Decision 661/2010 of the European Parliament and of the Council of 7 July 2010 on Union guidelines for the development of the trans-European transport network requires an assessment for all projects that form part of the trans-European transport network, OJ 2010 L 204/1.

determined to require an assessment pursuant to Article 6 or 7 of the Habitats Directive.[81] These categories of plans and programmes are always subject to the environmental assessment obligation unless they involve only minor modifications or small areas at local level (Article 3(3)); *de minimis* exception) and the Member States have determined that they are not likely to have significant environmental effects.

Environmental assessment is optional for all other plans and programmes which set the framework for future development consent of projects, insofar as these are likely to have significant environmental effects (Article 3(4)). Article 3(5) requires the Member States to establish a so-called screening mechanism on the basis of which it will be determined whether or not there is a likelihood of significant environmental effects in case of the *de minimis* exception or in their application of the optional environmental assessment.[82] On doing so the Member States have to use the (non-exhaustive) criteria in Annex II. This situation resembles that with regard to Annex II-projects under the EIA Directive and is thus likely to lead to comparable case law. The first indent of point 1 of Annex II, for example, allows the Member States to set quantitative thresholds, similar to the thresholds allowed under Article 4(2) of the EIA Directive.

The SEA procedure

The SEA procedure is also comparable to the EIA procedure. Basically, an environmental report that will become part of the plan or programme (Article 2(c)) needs to be completed according to Article 5 in connection with Annex I. This report must be completed during the preparation of the plan or programme (Article 4(1)) and is subject to consultation (Article 6(1)). The consultation on the basis of the SEA Directive can be transboundary as well (Article 7).[83] The SEA procedure may be integrated into existing procedures or it may take the form of a special procedure to implement the directive (Article 4(2)). As the usefulness of SEA hinges on the quality of the environmental assessment, Article 12(2) constitutes a major step forward compared to the EIA Directive because it requires the Member States to implement some form of quality control for the environmental reports.

Because the plan or programme subject to SEA may also set the framework for future projects subject to EIA, the SEA Directive contains Article 4(3) dealing with so-called 'tiering' of environmental assessment. This addresses the desire to avoid unnecessary duplication of environmental assessments. During the negotiations leading up to the SEA Directive, an amendment was introduced according to which only one environmental assessment (either an SEA or an EIA) would be required. This was rejected, and Article 11(1) explicitly states that

---

[81] See further section 17.2 of this chapter.

[82] Cf. Case C-295/10 *Valčiukienė and others*, Judgment of 22 September 2011.

[83] This implements the Espoo convention and the ECE Protocol on strategic environmental assessment to the Espoo convention (Kiev 2003).

the fact that there has been an SEA for a plan does not rule out the requirement of an EIA for a project implementing that plan. This does, however, highlight the problems arising from a wide definition of plans and programmes in connection with an equally wide definition 'project'.[84] This will probably have to be resolved in the form of an integration or consolidation of the EIA and the SEA Directives.

According to Article 8, the environmental report and results of the (transboundary) consultations have to be taking into account in the preparation of the plan or programme. Indications that SEA is more than just a purely procedural tool[85] can be found in Articles 9 and 10. Article 9 requires the final decision on the plan or programme to be communicated to the authorities, the public concerned and the parties in the (transboundary) consultation. Importantly, it also requires the communication of a statement summarising how the environmental considerations have been integrated, thus presuming a duty to integrate them, rather than a duty to take them into account. Moreover, the decision should also include a monitoring mechanism so that the unforeseen significant environmental effects of the implementation of the plan or programme are identified and remedial action is possible (Article 10). The introduction of a monitoring mechanism is a major step forward compared to the EIA Directive where the introduction of a similar obligation met with strong opposition.[86]

According to the wording of Article 11(1) an environmental assessment carried out under the SEA Directive is without prejudice to any requirements under EIA Directive 85/337. It follows that an environmental assessment carried out under the EIA Directive is in addition to an assessment carried out under the SEA Directive.[87] Similarly, an assessment under the EIA Directive is without prejudice to the requirements of the SEA Directive and cannot dispense with the obligation to carry out an environmental assessment pursuant to the SEA in order to comply with the environmental aspects specific to that directive. As assessments carried out pursuant to the SEA Directive and the EIA Directive differ for a number of reasons, it is necessary to comply with the requirements of both of those directives concurrently.

4   The Seveso II Directive

Directive 82/501 on the major-accident hazards of certain industrial activities,[88] better known as the Post-Seveso Directive, provided for measures to protect the public and the environment from the consequences

---

[84] See further Sheate (2003) at 345.

[85] Lee (2005) at 171.

[86] Sheate (2003) at 346.

[87] Cf. Case C-295/10 *Valčiukienė and others*, Judgment of 22 September 2011.

[88] OJ 1982 L 230/1, later amended. See on the interpretation of some of its provisions Case C-190/90 *Commission v. Netherlands* [1992] ECR I-3265.

of possible major industrial accidents. The immediate reason for drafting the directive was the dioxin disaster in the Italian town of Seveso. The directive was mainly concerned with the prevention of such accidents.

After a number of amendments the directive has been replaced by Directive 96/82 on the control of major-accident hazards involving dangerous substances the so-called 'Seveso II Directive'.[89] Directive 96/82 is intended to implement the Convention on the Transboundary Effects of Industrial Accidents.[90]

According to Article 1 the directive aims at the prevention of major accidents which involve dangerous substances, and the limitation of their consequences for man and the environment, with a view to ensuring high levels of protection throughout the EU in a consistent and effective manner. The directive is applicable to establishments where dangerous substances are present in quantities equal to or in excess of the quantities listed in Annex I. Article 4 states that the directive does not apply to, for instance, military establishments, hazards created by ionizing radiation, the transport of dangerous substances outside establishments, the transport of dangerous substances in pipelines outside establishments, the activities of the extractive industries concerned with exploration for minerals in mines and quarries and waste land-fill sites.

Under the general obligations of the directive, Member States are required to ensure that the operator is obliged to take all measures necessary to prevent major accidents and to limit their consequences for man and the environment (Article 5(1)) and that the operator is required to prove to the competent authority, at any time, that he has taken all the measures necessary as specified in the directive (Article 5(2)).

The operator is also required to send a notification to the competent authority, containing all kinds of information on the establishment (Article 6). He is required to draw up a document setting out his major-accident prevention policy and to ensure that it is properly implemented (Article 7).[91] To avoid dangers caused by the 'domino effect' the competent authority must, using the information received from all operators, identify establishments or groups of establishments where the likelihood and the possibility or consequences of a major accident may be increased because of the location and the proximity of such establishments (Article 8).

The additional requirements of Articles 9, 11 and 13 apply in respect of certain establishments. Member States must require the operator to produce a safety report (Article 9)[92] and draw up an internal emergency plan (Article

---

[89] OJ 1997 L 10/13, amended by Directive 2003/105, OJ 2003 L 345/97, in the light of some serious industrial accidents.

[90] Decision 98/685 concerning the Convention on the Transboundary Effects of Industrial Accidents, OJ 1998 L 326/1.

[91] See on the supervision of the implementation Case C-336/97 *Commission v. Italy* [1999] ECR I-3771, paras. 23-25.

[92] The dispensation from this obligation (Article 9(6)(a)) should be subject to the criteria in Decision 98/433, OJ 1998 L 192/19.

11) and must ensure that comprehensive information on safety measures is supplied to the relevant authorities so that they can draw up external safety plans. This also applies in the case of transboundary effects (Article 13).

Article 12 on land-use planning provides an example of application of the integration principle. Member States are required to ensure that the objectives of preventing major accidents and limiting the consequences of such accidents are taken into account in their land-use policies and/or other relevant policies.[93]

As soon as practicable following a major accident, the operator shall be required to send detailed information to the competent authorities (Article 14), which are then required to inform the Commission of their findings (Article 15).[94] Articles 17 and 18 are particularly relevant in terms of the actual application of the directive in the Member States. The first paragraph of Article 17(1) provides that Member States *shall* prohibit the use or bringing into use of any establishment, installation or storage facility, or any part thereof where the measures taken by the operator for the prevention and mitigation of major accidents are *seriously deficient,* while the second paragraph provides that they may prohibit the use or bringing into use of any establishment, installation or storage facility, or any part thereof if the operator has not submitted the notification, reports or other information required by the directive within the specified period. Finally, under Article 18 the Member States are required to organise a system of inspections, or other measures of control appropriate to the type of establishment concerned.

Currently a proposal to amend the Seveso II Directive is pending.[95] The main reason for this proposal is to bring the directive in line with the 2008 Regulation on the classification, labelling and packaging of dangerous substances,[96] the Industrial Emissions Directive[97] as well as the Aarhus Convention.[98]

5   The IPPC Directive

Directive 2008/1 concerning integrated pollution prevention and control, the so-called IPPC Directive, represents an important step towards a more integrated and horizontal approach.[99] As stated in its preamble, diffe-

---

93 See also Chapter 1, section 4.

94 The form for transmitting this information has been adopted by means of Decision 2009/10, OJ 2009 L 6/64.

95 COM (2010) 781. The procedure can be followed under number 2010/0377/COD.

96 Regulation 1272/2008, OJ 2008 L 353/1.

97 Directive 2010/75, OJ 2010 L 334/17, see section 6 below.

98 See paragraph 7 below. This relates primarily to Articles 14 and 22 of the proposal.

99 OJ 2008 L 24/8. This directive codifies and replaces the old IPPC Directive 96/61, OJ 1996 L 257/26, as that was amended by Directive 2003/35, OJ 2003 L 156/17, Directive 2003/87, OJ 2003 L 275/32 and Regulation 166/2006, OJ 2006 L 33/1. See, on the IPPC Directive in general: Lange (2008).

rent approaches to controlling emissions into the air, water or soil separately may encourage the shifting of pollution between the various environmental media rather than protecting the environment as a whole. The IPPC Directive establishes a general framework for integrated pollution prevention and control. Further steps towards an integrated approach to emissions from industrial installations have been taken in the form of the adoption of the Industrial Emissions Directive (IE Directive).[100]

The scope of the IPPC Directive

The IPPC Directive applies only to installations, defined in Article 2(3), as stationary technical units in which one of the activities listed in Annex I are carried and any other directly associated and technically connected activities. The effect of Annex I is to basically confine the scope of the IPPC Directive to large (defined in terms of production capacity) industrial installations producing, *inter alia*, energy, metals, minerals (cement), chemicals and various other categories such as intensive animal husbandry.[101] The directive applies to all new permits and changes in permits.

The temporal scope of the directive is defined in Articles 4 and 5. Basically all installations in operation before the deadline for implementation of the directive (30 October 1999, Article 2(4) in connection with 5 and 21(2)) are subject to an eight-year transitional period (Article 5(1)). New installations, i.e. those not already in operation before 30 October 1999 must have an integrated permit (Article 4).

The integrated approach

The integrated approach follows from the fact that the environment is more than the sum of its component parts (air, land, water) together with the realisation that environmental improvements in one area may actually result in environmental deterioration in another area. Installing a more effective filter on a chimney may, for example, result in cleaner air as well as the production of more waste (when the filter cleaned). To ensure that this balance takes account of all areas or sectors of the environment an integrated approach is required. This integrated approach can be seen in the numerous references to 'the environment taken as a whole'[102] in the directive as well as in the general obligations upon the operator contained in Article 3 of the directive.[103] Member States are required to ensure that installations are operated in such a way that:

---

[100] Directive 2010/75, OJ 2010 L 334/17, see section 6 below.

[101] See on this category and the wide interpretation Case C-473/07 *Association nationale pour la protection des eaux et rivières-TOS and Association OABA* v. *Ministère de l'Ecologie, du Développement et de l'Aménagement durables* [2009] ECR I-319, paras. 19-27. The same wide interpretation rules out a scheme that exludes entire categories of agricultural activities if these have an environmental impact (excretion) equivalent or larger than the installations covered by the IPPC Directive, paras. 42-44.

[102] See for example Article 1 of the IPPC Directive.

[103] See for an overview of the difficulties in achieving an integrated approach: Bohne & Dietze (2004).

- all the appropriate preventive measures are taken against pollution, in particular through application of the best available techniques;
- no significant pollution is caused;
- waste production is avoided in accordance with the Waste Framework Directive; where waste is produced, it is recovered or, where that is technically and economically impossible, it is disposed of while avoiding or reducing any impact on the environment;
- energy is used efficiently;
- the necessary measures are taken to prevent accidents and limit their consequences;
- the necessary measures are taken upon definitive cessation of activities to avoid any pollution risk and return the site of operation to a satisfactory state.

The integrated approach should be implemented by means of permits. Article 6 requires Member States to take the necessary measures to ensure that an application to the competent authority for a permit includes a description of:
- the installation and its activities;
- the raw and auxiliary materials, other substances and the energy used in or generated by the installation;
- the sources of emissions from the installation;
- the conditions of the site of the installation;
- the nature and quantities of foreseeable emissions from the installation into each medium as well as identification of significant effects of the emissions on the environment;
- the proposed technology and other techniques for preventing or, where this not possible, reducing emissions from the installation;
- where necessary, measures for the prevention and recovery of waste generated by the installation;
- further measures planned to comply with the general principles of the basic obligations of the operator as provided for in Article 3;
- measures planned to monitor emissions into the environment.

To ensure an integrated approach to issuing permits, Article 7 requires *substantive* as well as *procedural* integration.[104] As regards the latter, Member States are required to ensure that the procedure for the grant of the permit is *fully coordinated* where more than one competent authority is involved. The substantive integration is to be ascertained by a requirement of full coordination of the conditions of the permit. The permit must contain conditions that guarantee that the installation complies with the IPPC Directive; otherwise the permit must be refused (Article 8).

---

[104] Bohne and Dietze (2004) at 199.

The most important of these conditions take the form of the requirement in Article 9(3) to include in the permit emission limit values for pollutants likely to be emitted from the installation.[105] The rules on the emissions limits values reflect the difficulty in finding a compromise between the protection of the environment by ensuring good environmental quality standards on the one hand and subsidiarity considerations that result in local (geographical) considerations playing a role on the other.[106] Emission limit values shall be based on 'the best available techniques',[107] without prescribing the use of any technique or specific technology, but taking into account the technical characteristics of the installation concerned, its geographical location and the local environmental conditions. In all circumstances, the conditions of the permit shall contain provisions on the minimisation of long distance or transboundary pollution and ensure a high level of protection for the environment as a whole (Article 9(4)). However, where an environmental quality standard requires stricter conditions than those achievable by the use of the best available techniques, additional measures shall in particular be required in the permit (Article 10). The European Parliament and Council can set European-wide emissions limit values if the setting of emissions limit values on the basis of the best available techniques proves insufficient (Article 19).

Competent authorities must periodically reconsider and, where necessary, update permit conditions (Article 13(1)).

Finally, the directive contains provisions on compliance (Article 14), access to information and public participation in the permit procedure (Article 15),[108] access to justice (Article 16),[109] transboundary effects (Article 18) and various

---

[105] Article 9(3) was amended by Directive 2003/87 so as to preclude emissions limit values for greenhouse gasses subject to the emissions trading scheme. A similar prohibition of ELVs foor greenhouse gasses can be found in the IED, see further sections 6 and 11.4 below.

[106] See recitals 17 and 18 of the preamble. See further: Doppelhammer (2000) at 203.

[107] Often abbreviated as BAT. See for a definition Article 2(11) of the directive: 'the most effective and advanced stage in the development of activities and their methods of operation which indicate the practical suitability of particular techniques for providing in principle the basis for emission limit values designed to prevent and, where that is not practicable, generally to reduce emissions and the impact on the environment as a whole'. Note that the second indent effectively introduces economic/cost considerations. Guidance as to what are best available techniques is provided by so-called BAT Reference Documents (BREFs), drawn up by the European IPPC Bureau in Seville (http://eippcb.jrc.es; last visited 7 October 2011), see also Article 17(2). Such BREFs have no binding or interpretative effect on the provisions of the IPPC Directive, cf. Case C-473/07 *Association nationale pour la protection des eaux et rivières-TOS and Association OABA* v. *Ministère de l'Ecologie, du Développement et de l'Aménagement durables* [2009] ECR I-319, para. 30.

[108] Article 15(3), containing the obligation to publish an inventory of all emissions from IPPC-installations was repealed with effect from 24 February 2006 on the basis of Article 21(2) of Regulation 166/2006, OJ 2006 L 33/1, the so-called PRTR Regulation, see further section 7.2 below.

[109] The provisions on public participation and access to justice were introduced by Directive 2003/35, see further section 7 below.

transitional provisions, particularly relevant in respect of Directive 76/464 on pollution caused by certain dangerous substances discharged into the aquatic environment of the Community[110] and Directive 84/360 on the combating of air pollution from industrial plants.[111] The IPPC Directive will be repealed from 7 January 2014 onwards and replaced by the Industrial Emissions Directive.[112]

6   The Industrial Emissions Directive

Directive 2010/75 on industrial emissions (IE Directive) essentially integrates and codifies no less than seven Directives. These are the directives on waste from the titanium dioxide industry,[113] Directive 1999/13 on the limitation of emissions of volatile organic compounds due to the use of organic solvents in certain activities and installations,[114] Directive 2000/76 on the incineration of waste,[115] Directive 2001/80 on the limitation of emissions of certain pollutants into the air from large combustion plants[116] and finally, the IPPC Directive is recast into the IE Directive.[117] The directive consists of seven chapters, of which Chapters I, II and VII apply generally whereas the remaining chapters contain specific rules for, respectively, combustion plants, waste incineration plants, installations and processes using organic solvents and the titanium dioxide industry. By and large the structure of the IPPC Directive is employed and compared to the directives that are replaced, environmental standards have been raised.[118]

Chapter I contains the common provisions, such as the definition of terms used and the obligation for the Member States to require a permit for all installations covered by the IE Directive.[119] Moreover, the directive contains rules on incidents and accidents (Article 7) and non-compliance (Article 8). An interesting provision can be found in Article 9, where the relation with the Emissions Trading Directive is explained. Article 9 explicitly states that the Member States shall not impose emissions limit values for greenhouse gasses for installations within the emissions trading scheme.[120] The reason for this

---

[110] OJ 1976 L 129/23, later amended.

[111] OJ 1984 L 188/20, later amended.

[112] Directive 2010/75, OJ 2010 L 334/17, Article 81.

[113] Directive 78/176, OJ 1978L 54/19, Directive 82/883, OJ 1982 L 378/1, Directive 92/112, OJ 1992 L 409/11, see below section 11.10.

[114] OJ 1999 L 85/1, see below section 12.2.

[115] OJ 2000 L 332/91, see below section 12.2.

[116] OJ 2001 L 309/1, see below section 12.2.

[117] OJ 2008 L 24/8, See above section 5.

[118] See, for example, recital 29 of the preamble to the IE Directive.

[119] It may be noted that Article 6 IE Directive allows the Member States to lay down the requirements for installations in general binding rules to which the permit can refer.

[120] Such emission limit values are, however, allowed if this is necessary to avoid significant local pollution.

is that the latter requires the operators decisions on whether or not to reduce greenhouse gas emissions to be dependent only on the market price for the greenhouse gas allowances that need to be surrendered for every unit of greenhouse gas emitted. How this accords with Article 193 TFEU, according to which environmental harmonisation does not stand in the way of stricter environmental protection measures, is being discussed in Chapter 3, section 5.

The directive contains an extensive and complex set of transitional rules and rules on transposition and entry into force (Article 80-82). It shall be reviewed by 7 January 2016 in particular with regard to intensive cattle rearing and the spreading of manure

The scope of the directive

The scope of the IE Directive is confined to the industrial activities referred to in chapters II to VI of the IE Directive. It does not apply to research and development activities (Article 2). This begs the question on how to distinguish industrial activities from other activities. The directive remains silent on this point, though the heading of Annex I prescribes that the Commission shall provide guidance on the industrial scale of the activities mentioned in that Annex.

The directive contains a fairly complicated regime as regards its temporal scope. Essentially, the directive applies from 7 January 2014 onwards, however, for certain activities and installations the application of the directive is postponed untill 2016 (Article 82). Moreover, for large combustion plants, Article 32 entails a possibility for the Member States to hand in with the Commission transitional national plans for combustion plants that were permitted before 27 November 2002 (date of entry into force of the LCP Directive) and active before 27 November 2003. Such plans must be notified to the Commission before 1 January 2013 (Article 32(5)) and the Commission must decide whether or not to accept the plan on the basis of compliance with the implementing rules adopted on the basis of Article 41(b).[121] The directive remains silent on the exact legal implications of a negative decision on the part of the Commission, other than referring to the possibility of a new version of such plans. This probably makes the status of such plans and the Commission's decision concerning these plans comparable to that of the National Allocation Plans under the first two trading phases of the EU Emissions Trading Scheme.[122]

Annex I activities

Chapter II of the IE Directive contains the general rules for all Annex I activities. This Annex I is an almost literal copy of Annex I to the IPPC Directive, with the notable exception that now installations for the gassification or lique-

---

[121] The Commission had to submit a proposal before 1 July 2011

[122] See further below section 13.1. On the status of such plans and the Commission decision see, *inter alia*, Case T-374/04 *Germany* v. *Commission* [2007] ECR II-4431.

faction with a rated thermal input between 20 and 50 MW are also included.[123] The IE Directive also centers around four central figures: a permit, best available techniques, emissions limit values and environmental quality standards. The rules on permits are by and large comparable to those in the IPPC Directive. The general principles governing the basic obligations for the operator require the Member State to ensure that the best available techniques (BAT) are used (Article 11(b)) and that no significant pollution is caused (Article 11(c)). The relation between the Member State and the operator of the installation is defined by the permit, which is to ensure compliance with the general principles mentioned above, as well as Article 18 (Article 14(1)).[124] Article 18 repeats the rule already found in the IPPC Directive according to which environmental quality standards ultimately determine operating conditions because they should result in extra measures.[125]

What constitutes BAT is unchanged compared to the IPPC Directive,[126] however, how this is determined is now much more elaborately described in the directive. Article 13 IE Directive now states that the exchange of information in best available techniques shall take place between the Member States, industries concerned and, interestingly, environmental non-governmental organisations.[127] The information exchange shall then draw up documents on what constitutes the best available technique which are turned into BAT conclusions by means of a Commission decision (Article 13(5)).[128] The Commission is assisted in this task by a forum made up of representatives of the Member States, industries and environmental NGOs (Article 13(3)). Until the adoption of such new BAT conclusions, the old BAT reference documents shall apply as BAT conclusions.[129]

The fourth central concept is that of the emissions limit value. This is described in the IE Directive as the mass of an emission that may not be exceeded during one or more periods of time (Article 3(5)). Article 14 requires the permit conditions to include at least emissions limit values for the substances listed in annex II. These conditions must be set in reference to the BAT conclusions (Article 14(3)). Article 15(3) more specifically requires that the emissions limit values be set on the basis of the BAT conclusions. Essentially three exceptions exist to this binding character of the BAT conclusions. Firstly, less stringent emission limit values are authorised by Article 15(4) of the directive in case the imposition of BAT would lead to disproportionately

---

[123] Annex I, point 1.4(b); the IPPC and LCP Directives both have a threshold of 50 MW.

[124] The same applies to general binding rules, Article 17 IE Directive.

[125] Cf. Article 10 IPPC Directive.

[126] Cf. Article 3(10) IE Directive with Article 2(12) IPPC Directive.

[127] It may be noted that the IPPC Directive did not envisage involvement of environmental NGOs in the process of establishing BAT, Article 17(2) IPPC Directive.

[128] The Commission will take this decision in accordance with the examination procedure, Article 75(2) IE Directive in connection with Article 13(1)(c) of Regulation 182/2011, OJ 2011 L 55/13. This was the old regulatory comitology procedure.

[129] Article 13(7). This does not apply to Article 15(3) and (4).

higher costs compared to the environmental benefits due to the geographical location or the local environmental conditions of the installation concerned or the technical characteristics of the installation concerned. This provision thus enables an extra cost-benefit-analysis,[130] provided that the emissions limit values specified in the IE Directive are observed. This finding must be substantiated with reasons that are to be annexed to the permit. Secondly, Article 18, that was already mentioned above, requires stricter emissions limit values than those associated with BAT where this is required by an environmental quality standard. Thirdly, Article 15(5) authorises a derogation for the testing of emerging techniques for a maximum of nine months.[131]

Finally, the directive contains rules on the possibility of having generally binding rules instead of individual permits (Article 17), provided that the same level of integrated environmental protection is ascertained. Furthermore, we find rules on the communication of advances in BAT (Article 19), the updating of permits in the light of new BAT conclusions (Article 21), site closure (Article 22) and environmental inspections (Article 23). Both provisions contain major innovations compared to the IPPC Directive, which contains only minimal rules on inspections and no rules on site closure. Chapter II concludes with provisions on transbounday effects (Article 26) and the implementation of the Aarhus rules on access to environmental information and public participation in connection with the IE Directive permits (Article 24) and provisions on access to justice (Article 25). These provisions do not entail substantial changes compared to those in the IPPC Directive.[132]

Combustion plants

Chapter III of the IED contains the special provisions for combustion plants with a thermal input of 50 MW or greater and thus codifies and recasts the Large Combustion Plants Directive.[133] With regard to the scope, it must be noted that the second paragraph of Article 28 excludes a significant category of combustion plants, including, most significantly, waste incineration plants with the exception of plants where biomass is combusted.[134] Compared to the LCP Directive, some innovations worth mentioning are Article 29 on the aggregation of combustion installations that share a smokestack[135] and the stricter emissions limit values and desulphurisation rates. With regard to the latter, a distinction

---

[130] It is additional in that the concept of BAT already includes an appraisal of the economic availability of a technique, Article 3(10)(b) IE Directive.

[131] Note that Article 27 contains further provisions regarding emerging techniques allowing for Commission guidance

[132] Articles 15 and 16 of Directive 2008/1. The provision on access to information and public participation in the IE Directive is slightly more elaborate, Cf. Article 24(2) IE Directive.

[133] Directive 2001/80, the LCP Directive, see below, section 12.2,

[134] Article 28(j) in connection with 3(31) IE Directive.

[135] This elaborates Article 2(7)(j), last sentence, of the LCP Directive.

must be made between the emissions limit values that apply to plants permitted before 7 January 2013 and put into operation no later than 7 January 2014 (pre 2014 combustion plants) and all other (post 2014) combustion plants. Pre 2014 combustion plants must comply with the emissions limit values in Annex V, Part 1, whereas Part 2 of the same annex applies to post 2014 plants.[136] With regard to the pre-2014 combustion plants a further distinction must be made between those that have already been exempted under Article 4(4) of the LCP Directive and all other plants. With regard to the former, the pre-exempted plants, compliance with the emissions limit values in Annex V, Part 1 is required. All other plants have two options: apply of the limited lifetime derogation or opt-in the Transitional National Plan. The limited lifetime derogation essentially continues the exemption regime established under Article 4(4) of the LCP Directive.[137] Operators of such plants may apply for a limited lifetime derogation under Article 33(1) of the IE Directive. This derogation essentially means that the emissions limit values in the LCP Directive must be complied with (Article 33(1)(c)) whilst the plant may only be operated for 17,500 hours untill 31 December 2023 (Article 33(1)(a)). An alternative may be to opt-in the Transitional National Plan.[138] This Plan allows the plants to continue to comply with the emissions limit values prescribed by the LCP Directive that are, however, to become stricter with a view to compliance with the emissions limit values of Annex V, Part 1, on 1 July 2020. Such plans are to be drawn up by the Member States, subject to approval by the Commission (Article 32(5)).

The IE Directive further contains special rules for small isolated systems and district heating plants, malfunction of monitoring equipment as well as the calculation of emissions limit values for multi-fuel plants. Furthermore, operators of electricity plants with an output equal or exceeding 300 megawatts are required to investigate whether or not carbon capture and storage is a feasible option (Article 36). If this turns out to be feasible, the competent authority is to ensure that the installation is 'capture-ready', which essentially means that some space is reserved on the site where the necessary equipment can later be placed. Finally, some implementing rules are envisaged (Article 41). It may be recalled that the combustion plants within the meaning of Chapter III are also Annex I activities and thus the permit must comply with, *inter alia*, the provisions on BAT.

---

[136] A comparison between Parts 1 and 2 of Annex V reveals that on average the emissions limit values in Part 2 are slightly stricter, cf. *inter alia* the emissions limit value for NOx for a combustion plant using coal with a thermal input > 300 MW. Part 1 contains a limit value of 200 mg/Nm3, whereas Part 2 lays down an emissions limit value of 150 mg/Nm3. The emissions limit values in Annex V to the IE Directive are significantly stricter than those laid down in the Annexes to the LCP Directive.

[137] This also explains why such pre-exempted plants cannot benefit from a further lifetime derogation.

[138] It may be noted that this option excludes plants with a limited lifetime derogation (Article 32(1)(a)) as well as pre-exempted plants under the LCP Directive (Article 32(1)(d)).

Waste (co) incineration plants

Chapter IV contains the special rules for waste incineration and waste co-incineration plants and thus recasts Directive 2000/76 on waste incineration.[139] Compared to the Waste Incineration Directive some emissions limit values have become stricter, but the IE Directive by and large copies the Waste Incineration Directive. One notable exception to this is the inclusion of rules on the classification of gasification and pyrolysis plants connected to combustion installations (Article 42(1), second paragraph) as well as the scope of the installations that qualify as waste (co)-incinerators (Article 42(1), third to fifth paragraph). These changes reflect the Court's case law on these concepts.[140]

Installations and activities using solvents and the titanium dioxide industry

Chapter V of the IE Directive contains the special provisions for activities and installations using solvents. This chapter recasts Directive 1999/13. Chapter VI of the IE Directive recasts the Titanium Dioxide Directive.[141] The IE Directive contains no significant changes as far as these Directives are concerned.

7 Environmental Governance and the Aarhus Convention

According to Article 1 TEU and Article 10(1) TEU decisions in the Union shall be 'taken as openly as possible and as closely as possible to the citizen'. Article 10(1) TEU also states that 'every citizen shall have the right to participate in the democratic life of the Union'. Throughout the Sixth Environmental Action Programme references to environmental governance can be found. For the purposes of this book environmental governance is equated with:[142]

· access to environmental information;
· public participation in decision-making in environmental matters;
· access to justice in environmental matters.

These three main headings correspond to the so-called three pillars of the UNECE Aarhus Convention.[143] Below these three pillars and their implementation by the EU as well as the Member States will be discussed.

---

[139] See further below, section 12.2.

[140] See further below, section 17.1.

[141] Directive 82/883 and Directive 92/112, see further below, section 11.10.

[142] See for a discussion: Lee (2005) at 113.

[143] Concluded on behalf of the EC by Decision 2005/370, OJ 2005 L 124/1. Cf. Jendroska (2005).

7.1   Access to Environmental Information at Member State Level

The steps announced in the Fourth Environmental Action Programme to improve public access to information[144] resulted in the adoption of Directive 90/313.[145] From 14 February 2005 Directive 90/313 has been replaced with Directive 2003/4,[146] partly with a view to implementing the Aarhus Convention.[147] The new directive also consolidates the Court's case law concerning Directive 90/313 and expands the existing access to environmental information according to the second recital of the preamble. The scope of the directive is confined by essentially two concepts: 'environmental information' and 'public authorities'. Article 2(1) contains a very wide definition of 'environmental information', that encompasses all media and forms and every aspect of the environment.

> With respect to the case law under the old Directive 90/313 we might point to the judgment in *Mecklenburg v. Kreis Pinneberg*, where the Court ruled that the directive is to be interpreted as covering a statement of views given by a countryside protection authority in development consent proceedings if that statement is capable of influencing the outcome of those proceedings as regards interests pertaining to the protection of the environment.[148]
>
> In Case C-266/09 the Court ruled that information, relating to residues of a plant protection product on food, and submitted within a national authorisation procedure for a plant protection product with a view to setting the maximum quantity of a pesticide, falls within the scope of 'environmental information' of Article 2 of Directive 2003/4.[149]
>
> However in *Ville de Lyon*, the Court of Justice ruled that trading information under the Emissions Trading Directive cannot be seen as 'environmental information'.[150] The Court clarified that pursuant to Article 17 of Directive 2003/87 only decisions relating to the allocation of allowances and the reports of emissions required under the greenhouse gas emissions permit and held by the competent authority are to be made available to the public in accordance with Directive 2003/4. All other data, and notably the data on the trading of allowances is subject

---

[144] OJ 1987 C 328/1 point 2.6.2.

[145] OJ 1990 L 158/56.

[146] Case C-266/09 *Stichting Natuur en Milieu*, Judgment of 16 December 2010, provides that the date on which a decision concerning access to information was taken determines whether Directive 2003/4 or its predecessor is applicable. All such decisions taken after 14 February 2005 are thus subject to the current Directive, even when the information in question was filed before that date, para. 34, 35.

[147] OJ 2003 L 41/26, see COM (2000) 402 for the proposal.

[148] Case C-321/96 *Mecklenburg* v. *Kreis Pinneberg* [1998] ECR I-3809, paras. 21 and 22.

[149] Case C-266/09 *Stichting Natuur en Milieu and Others* v. *College voor de toelating van gewasbeschermingsmiddelen en biociden*, Judgment of 16 December 2010, paras. 39-42.

[150] Case C-524/09 *Ville de Lyon*, Judgment of 22 December 2010.

to a specific access regime under Regulation 2216/2004. In essence this regime entails confidentiality of this data for a period of five years following the year to which the data relates.

The term 'public authority' is similarly widely defined in Article 2(2), to also include bodies without a specific environmental function or objective at all levels of government as well as private entities having public functions or responsibilities.[151] This is further expanded because also environmental information held on behalf of the public authorities should be accessible; Article 2(4) in connection with Article 3(1). It should, however, be noted that special regimes on access to environmental information exist, as will be explained in more detail below.

The central provision is Article 3, paragraph 1 of which requires the Member States to make environmental information available upon request without the applicant having to state an interest. This request must be sufficiently precise, because requests that are too general may be refused, provided that the authority has invited the applicant to specify his request (Article 4(1) (c) in connection with Article 3(3)). A similar duty to set up a dialogue with the applicant applies to requests sent to the wrong public authority (Article 4(1)(a)). Finally, Article 3(5) requires the Member States to set up registers and lists of environmental information in order to facilitate access to this information.

The access to environmental information is subject to exceptions listed in Article 4 of the directive. The first paragraph of Article 4 contains a list of exceptions that relate primarily to the internal working of the authority. The exceptions in the second paragraph of Article 4 involve interests of third parties or a more general nature, such as confidentiality of commercial information (Article 4(2)(d)). According to the last paragraph of Article 4(2) whenever one of the exceptions is invoked by an authority a balance must be struck between the public interest served by free access to the information and the interests protected by the exceptions.[152] In all cases the exceptions must be interpreted narrowly[153] and in conformity with the Aarhus Convention.[154] Furthermore, with the exception of the interests listed in paragraph 1 and 2 (b), (c) and (e), there

---

[151] See, again concerning Directive 90/313, Case C-217/97 *Commission* v. *Germany* [1999] ECR I-5087. The Court made it clear that even authorities, like for instance courts, acting normally in the exercise of their judicial powers and therefore not in principle covered by the directive, may also have responsibilities relating to the environment or be in possession of information on the environment within the meaning of the directive when they act outside their strictly judicial functions. If that is the case they must be regarded as public authorities for the purposes of the directive.

[152] Case C-266/09 *Stichting Natuur en Milieu*, Judgment of 16 December 2010, clarifies that such a balance must be struck in every individual case, even if general criteria are provided, paras. 56-59.

[153] Article 4(2) last paragraph, see also, concerning Directive 90/313, Case C-321/96 *Mecklenburg* v. *Kreis Pinneberg* [1998] ECR I-3809, para. 25.

[154] See Advocate General Kokott in Case C-524/09 *Ville de Lyon*, Judgment of 22 December 2010, and by analogy Case C-240/09 *Lesoochranárske zoskupenie VLK*, Judgment of 8 March 2011.

will always be an overriding public interest in disclosure of the information if it relates to emissions into the environment. Emission-related information must thus always be made public. Unfortunately, the term 'emissions' is not further defined. However, in view of the Court's case law concerning Directive 90/313, it seems likely that this concept will receive a wide interpretation, leading to environmental information being as widely available as possible. Particularly in connection with the PRTR Regulation this is interesting.[155] Information held by public authorities shall be supplied in part where it is possible to separate out information that is subject to one of the exceptions in Article 4.[156]

Taken together with the intention of the directive, Article 193 TFEU would seem to leave the Member States room to restrict the number of grounds for refusing information even further; it seems likely that the more stringent protective measures referred to there are better ensured by greater freedom of information. The wording of Article 4(1) and (2) – 'may provide' – seems to allow for this. That 'Member States *may* provide for a request for such information to be refused' makes it clear that they are not under a duty to maintain confidentiality, but merely have a discretionary power. The directive does not itself provide protection for a person who feels that the authorities have exceeded their competence by, for example, publishing confidential commercial or industrial data, or breaching the confidentiality of his personal data and/or files, assuming these grounds for confidentiality had been transposed in the relevant national legislation.

Article 5(1) prohibits the Member States from imposing any charges for access to the lists referred to in Article 3(5). However, Article 5(2) expressly permits Member States to impose a charge for supplying the information, but goes on to state that such charge may not exceed a reasonable cost. Concerning the nearly identical provision in Directive 90/313, the Court held that in the absence of more details in the directive itself, what constitutes a reasonable cost must be determined in the light of the purpose of the directive:

> 'any interpretation of what constitutes "reasonable cost" for the purposes of Article 5 of the directive which may have the result that persons are dissuaded from seeking to obtain information or which may restrict their right of access to information must be rejected. Consequently, the term "reasonable" for the purposes of Article 5 of the directive must be understood as meaning that it does not authorise Member States to pass on to those seeking information the entire amount of the costs, in particular indirect ones, actually incurred for the State budget in conducting an information search.'[157]

---

[155] See further below section 6.2.

[156] Article 4(4) of Directive 2003/4. Concerning a similar provision in Directive 90/313, the Court has held that it must be transposed explicitly in national law; Case C-217/97 *Commission* v. *Germany* [1999] ECR I-5087.

[157] Case C-217/97 *Commission* v. *Germany* [1999] ECR I-5087.

A person who considers that his request for information has been unreasonably refused or ignored, was inadequately answered, or otherwise not dealt with in accordance with Articles 3, 4 or 5 by a public authority, may seek a judicial or administrative review of the decision in accordance with the relevant national legal system (Article 6). Compared to the similar provision in Directive 90/313, the current wording is significantly wider.[158] This will probably mean that judicial review is not limited to the statement of reasons alone and could also involve a review of the reasons invoked.

In addition to a right – freedom of access to information – the directive also provides for a corresponding duty: Member States are required to provide general information to the public on the state of the environment by such means as the periodic publication of descriptive reports (Article 7).

Apart from the provisions of Directive 2003/4, there are many other directives containing information requirements. These may differ markedly from the requirements of the freedom of information directive. Under Directive 67/548[159] (as amended by Directive 92/32[160]) on the packaging and labelling of dangerous preparations, any manufacturer intending to place certain dangerous substances on the market must notify the competent authority. Article 19 provides that if he considers that there is a confidentiality problem, the notifier may indicate the information which he considers to be commercially sensitive and disclosure of which might harm him industrially or commercially, and which he therefore wishes to be kept secret from all persons other than the competent authorities and the Commission. Here there is no question of a discretionary power to maintain confidentiality, but of a duty. The European Ecolabel Regulation also requires non-disclosure of certain information.[161] Other such requirements are to be found in e.g. Article 20 of the Seveso II Directive[162] and Article 25 of Directive 2001/18 on the deliberate release of GMOs.[163] Finally, the regime for public availability of data relating tot the European Emissions Trading Scheme for greenhouse gases also differs from that laid down in Directive 2003/4.[164]

---

[158] Article 4 of Directive 90/313 only speaks of the 'request for information [that] has been unreasonably refused or ignored, or has been inadequately answered by a public authority'.

[159] OJ 1967 L 196/1.

[160] OJ 1992 L 154/15.

[161] Point 3 of Annex V to Regulation 66/2010, OJ 2010 L 27/1.

[162] See also Article 13(4) of the Seveso II Directive, see further section 4 above.

[163] OJ 2001 L 106/1. See on the relation between the access regime in this directive and that in Directive 2003/4, Case C-552/07 *Commune de Sausheim* v. *Pierre Azelvandre* [2009] ECR I-987, paras. 47-54, where the Court states that the reasons for confidentiality provided for under Directive 2003/4 do not apply to information to be disclosed under the directive on the deliberate release of GMOs.

[164] Case C-524/09 *Ville de Lyon*, Judgment of 22 December 2010.

7.2   Access to Environmental Information at EU Level

According to Article 15(3) TFEU shall 'any citizen of the Union, and any natural or legal person residing or having its registered office in a Member State, [...] have a right of access to documents of the Union's institutions, bodies, offices and agencies, whatever their medium [...]'. As it is a signatory itself, the European Union must also implement the Aarhus Convention. It has done so in the form of Regulation 1367/2006 (the Aarhus Regulation).[165] Title II of the Aarhus Regulation concerns access to environmental information and Article 3 declares the general Regulation 1049/2001 on access to information held by the EU institutions, applicable.[166] In view of the *Slovak Bears* case, mentioned above, it must be assumed that Regulation 1049/2001 needs to be interpreted in conformity with the Aarhus Convention if applied with respect to 'environmental information'.[167]

The Aarhus Regulation contains additional provisions on access to environmental information. For example, Article 6(1) of the Aarhus Regulation ensures that information on emissions into the environment shall always be disclosed.[168] Interestingly, the duty to always disclose emissions-related information also applies to intellectual property related information, whereas for environmental information held by the Member States a similar duty does not apply.[169] The EU is also obliged to set up registers and to disseminate environmental information.

Whereas the Member States are not allowed to pass on the complete costs of complying with a request for information, the EU is allowed to do exactly this for copies of more than 20 pages.[170] According to the regulation shall these charges 'not exceed the real cost of producing and sending the copies'. However, the Aarhus Convention, Article 4(8), only allows to charge for 'a reasonable amount'. Finally, concerning review of decisions refusing access to information, Articles 7 and 8 of Regulation 1049/2001 provide for a two-stage administrative procedure and access to the European Ombudsman or a Court.[171]

---

[165] Regulation 1367/2006 on the application of the provisions of the Aarhus Convention on Access to Information, Public Participation in Decision-making and Access to Justice in Environmental Matters to Community institutions and bodies, OJ 2006 L 264/13.

[166] Regulation 1049/2001 Regarding Public Access to European Parliament, Council and Commission Documents, OJ 2001 L 145/43.

[167] See however, in this respect Case T-362/08 *IFAW Internationaler Tierschutz-Fonds*, Judgment of 13 January 2011, where the public interests as regards to 'economic policy', as allowed by Article 4 Regulation 1049/2001, were being taken into account. The Aarhus Convention does not provide such a ground for refusal. See also the different approaches by the Court and the Advocate General in Case C-524/09 *Ville de Lyon*, Judgment of 22 December 2010.

[168] Cf. Article 4(2) last paragraph of Directive 2003/4.

[169] See Article 4(2), last paragraph, of Directive 2003/4 since the duty to always disclose emissions related information does not apply to Article 4(2)(e).

[170] Article 10(1) of Regulation 1049/2001.

[171] ClientEarth has filed two actions against the Commission on the basis of the Aarhus Regulation: Case T-120/10, OJ 2010 C 134/42 and Case T-111/11, OJ 2011 C 130/16.

A very important type of environmental information relates to emissions into the environment. The gathering of this type of information was the subject of the so-called EPER Decision (European Pollutant Emission Register).[172] Because it is a signatory, the European Union had to implement the UNECE Protocol on Pollutant Release and Transfer Registers to the Aarhus Convention. This has taken place in the form of Regulation 166/2006, the Pollutant Release and Transfer Register (PRTR) Regulation.[173] According to Article 5(1) the report-ing obligation applies to all releases from installations mentioned in Annex I of pollutants mentioned in Annex II for which a certain threshold is exceeded. The list in Annex I is nearly identical to that in Annex I to the IPPC Direc-tive. In this regard PRTR Regulation hardly goes beyond the EPER Decision it builds upon. In addition to true releases, transfers of hazardous waste are also subject to a reporting obligation. The information thus collected by the national authorities has to be reported to the Commission on the basis of Article 7(2). With assistance from the European Environment Agency, the Commission will then incorporate the information in a European PRTR (Article 5(3)). The PRTR will also include information on releases from diffuse sources, but only insofar as this information has already been reported by the Member States (Article 8). The PRTR shall be freely accessible from the internet (Article 10) and possible exceptions to the free access to the information contained therein or in the Member State report must comply with Article 4 of Directive 2003/4 (Article 11). The PRTR Regulation apparently allows for confidentiality of information on releases. In view of the fact that emissions-related information must always be disclosed, this leads to the question of what the exact relation is between the 'release' within the meaning of Article 2(10) of the PRTR Regulation and 'emissions' as referred to in Article 4(2) of Directive 2003/4. It would seem that the European legislature considers that emissions are not to be equated with, for example, discharging. It appears doubtful whether this narrow concept of emission is tenable. The regulation provides for public participation (Article 12) as well as access to justice (Article 13). Article 15 may just be of greatest practi-cal importance, as it can be construed as containing an obligation on the part of the Member States and the Commission to 'translate' the technical information contained in the PRTR into layman's terms, thus making the information truly accessible.[174]

7.3 Public Participation in Decision-making at Member State Level

Environmental information is interesting if it can be used to influence the decision-making. This requires access to decision-making pro-cedures, in other words public participation. This pillar of the Aarhus Conven-

---

[172] Decision 2000/479, OJ 2000 L 192/36.

[173] OJ 2006 L 33/1, for a discussion on the compatibility of the EPER Decision with the PRTR Protocol see Lee (2005) at 132.

[174] See on this problem Lee (2005) at 132.

tion is implemented, as far as the Member States are concerned, by Directive 2003/35, the Public Participation Directive.[175] The Public Participation Directive consists of two main parts. Firstly, Article 2 contains provisions for a general public participation procedure. Secondly, Articles 3 & 4 amend the EIA and IPPC Directives in order to improve the public participation as part of those directives.

The scope of the general public participation procedure is defined primarily by Annex I. The following plans and programmes are subject to the public participation requirement:

· waste management plans and waste prevention programmes pursuant to the Waste Framework Directive (Article 31 of the Waste Framework Directive);
· packaging waste management plans pursuant to Article 14 of the Packaging Waste Directive 94/62;
· air quality plans for zones where the air quality exceeds the limit values pursuant to Directive 2008/50;
· programs for vulnerable zones pursuant to Article 5(1) the Nitrates Directive 91/676.

Article 2(5) excludes all plans and programmes that fall under the SEA Directive[176] as well as those subject to public participation on the basis of the Water Framework Directive. As was said above, the IPPC- and EIA Directives have their own specific provisions on public participation. Provisions on public consultation can also be found in the field of GMO-legislation.[177]

The actual obligation to allow for public participation applies only to natural and legal persons and, but only insofar as national law allows for this, associations or groups of natural and legal persons (Article 2(1)). The first stage of public participation involves informing the public about the proposals and the possibility of participation (Article 2(2)(a)). After this there must be possibility for effective participation. This refers to the stage in the decision-making process when the options are still open. The central obligation according to Article 2(2)(c) is to take due account of the views of the results of the public consultation. Under Article 2(2)(d) the public must be informed of the final decision and public participation process.

The provisions on public participation in the EIA and IPPC Directive are quite similar, but they have a wider scope in that they also provide for cross-border public participation[178] and provisions on access to justice.[179]

---

[175] Directive 2003/35 providing for public participation in respect of the drawing up of certain plans and programmes relating to the environment, OJ 2003 L 156/17.

[176] See above, section 3.4.

[177] Articles 9 and 24 of the GMO Deliberate Release Directive 2001/18, OJ 2001 L 106/1.

[178] Article 7 of the EIA Directive and Article 17 of the IPPC Directive.

[179] Article 10a of the EIA Directive and Article 15a of the IPPC Directive.

7.4   Public Participation in Decision-making at EU Level

The provisions on public participation in decision-making by the European institutions can be found in Title III of the Aarhus Regulation.[180] Public participation is open to natural or legal persons as well as associations of these and concerns the preparation, modification or review of plans or programmes relating to the environment (Article 9(1)). Article 2(1)(e) gives a wide definition of plans and programmes relating to the environment that is significantly narrowed down by the last paragraph of that provision. According to this financial or budget plans are outside the scope of the Title on public participation. Just as the national authorities, the European institutions and bodies are under a obligation to inform the public of the proposals and the possibility of public participation. Secondly, they have a duty to take due account of the results of the public participation. Finally the public must be informed of the final decision and the public participation. It is interesting to note that the last information obligation is formulated differently for the Member States and the EU. Only the Member States are obliged to inform the public of the public participation *process*,[181] whereas the EU institutions must inform the public of the public participation. This could mean that Member States must only inform the public of the procedure followed (time-limits etc.) and not of the actual impact the public consultation has had.

7.5   Access to Justice at Member State Level

In order to implement the third pillar (access to justice) on the Member State level a directive has been proposed by the Commission.[182] This directive would contain the general provisions on access to justice in addition to the specific rules on access to justice resulting from the public participation in the EIA and IPPC Directives and the specific rules on access to environmental information.[183]

The provisions on access to justice in the EIA Directive and the IPPC Directive are identical.[184] Essentially they require the Member States to grant access to justice for the public concerned insofar as they have a sufficient interest or maintain the impairment of a right. The public concerned is defined as 'the public affected or likely to be affected by, or having an interest in, the taking of a decision on the issuing or the updating of a permit or of permit conditions' The

---

[180] Regulation 1367/2006, OJ 2006 L 264/13.

[181] Article 2(2)(d) of Directive 2003/35, OJ 2003 L 156/17.

[182] COM (2003) 624 final, Co-decision procedure COD/2003/246.

[183] The provisions on access to justice in Directive 2003/4 have already discussed above, section 7.1.

[184] Article 10a of the EIA Directive and Article 15a of the IPPC Directive. See, for a wide and purpose-oriented interpretation of Article 10a of the EIA Directive Case C-263/08 *Djurgården-Lilla Värtans Miljöskyddsförening* [2009] ECR I-9967 and Case C-115/09 *Trianel Kohlekraftwerk Lünen*, Judgment of 12 May 2011. See also Chapter 5, section 5.1.

directives state that non-governmental organisations promoting environmental protection and meeting any requirements under national law are considered to be public concerned. It is important to note that national requirements still ultimately determine whether or not an NGO qualifies as public concerned. What constitutes a sufficient interest or impairment of a right is determined by the Member States, again leaving the definition of the exact scope to the Member States. However, in doing so they must act consistently with the objective of giving the public concerned wide access to justice. As far as the actual procedures are concerned, the directive does not exclude the possibility of a preliminary review procedure and confines itself to stating that the procedure must be fair, equitable, timely and not prohibitively expensive.[185]

The proposal for the directive is currently still undergoing the first reading and much is still uncertain. Article 4 of the Commission proposal requires the Member States to grant access to justice to all natural and legal persons that have a sufficient interest or maintain the impairment of a right. In addition, so-called qualified entities have a right to judicial review even if they cannot show a sufficient interest or the impairment of a right (Article 5). This is subject to the requirement that the qualified entity is acting within its statutory and geographic area of activities. Article 8 contains the requirements for recognition as a qualified entity whereas Article 9 lays down a procedure for this. Access to justice is available only if the natural or legal person or the qualified entity has first submitted a request for internal review (Article 6). Only when this request for internal review is not taken within 12 to 18 weeks or when the decision is insufficient to ensure compliance with environmental law is there a right to start 'environmental proceedings'. This is defined as the administrative or judicial review proceedings in environmental matters, other than proceedings in criminal matters, before a court or other independent body established by law, which is concluded by a binding decision (Article 2(1)(f)).

The European Parliament has approved the proposal, albeit with some rather far-going amendments. For one it considers that criminal procedures should not be excluded from the scope of the concept of environmental proceedings. Furthermore, the qualified entity is controversial since it considered to go beyond what is required by the Aarhus Convention and may open up environmental procedures to a very great extent. The future of the proposal is uncertain as it still needs to undergo the first reading in the Council.

7.6 Access to Justice at EU Level

The provisions on access to justice at the EU level can be found in Title IV of the Aarhus Regulation 1367/2006.[186]

---

[185] The last requirement excludes a discretionary power for the courts not to order costs to be paid by the unsuccessful party, Case C-427/07 *Commission* v. *Ireland* [2009] ECR I-6277, paras. 93-94.

[186] See on this regulation Chapter 5, section 4.2.

8 Integrated Product Policy

In each phase of their life cycle, products have an impact on the environment. The manufacture, use and ultimate disposal of a product cause a greater or lesser degree of harm to the environment. Today, a life-cycle approach to environmental product policy is increasingly being adopted. This means that a number of environmental issues must be addressed. These range from the energy efficiency of the production process and distribution, the environmental impact a product will have during its usage by the consumer to the waste the product becomes once it reaches its end of life. This means that a number of pieces of European environmental law can be brought under the heading of integrated product policy (IPP) or life cycle analysis (LCA).[187] This section will deal the Ecolabel Regulation, the Eco-audit Regulation and the Ecodesign Directive.[188] An integrated product policy also includes, among others, initiatives to internalise external costs and efforts at greening public procurement.

8.1 The Ecolabel Regulation

The Ecolabel Regulation links the life-cycle approach to a scheme whereby the reduced environmental impact is visualised through a sign (the flower logo).[189] A system of ecolabels awarded for products with reduced environmental impact is intended to draw the consumers' attention to environmentally friendly options, enabling them to take reasoned decisions when purchasing products. Recital 5 of the Preamble to the Ecolabel Regulation specifies that it is part of the EU's sustainable consumption and production policy which aims at reducing the negative environmental impact of consumption and production. The Court's judgment in *Energy Star* shows that this link between, on the one hand, the actual impact on purchasing decisions and thus trade and, on the other, creating environmental awareness and environmental protection is not always clear.[190]

> This case concerns the legal basis for the Council decision approving the EC's accession to the US Energy Star Program. The Council opted for Article 175 EC, currently Article 192 TFEU, whereas the Commission considered Article 133 EC,

---

[187] See the Commission Green Paper on Integrated Product Policy, COM (2001) 68 final, follow-up in Communication on Integrated Product Policy – Building on Environmental Life-Cycle Thinking, COM (2003) 302 final.

[188] The energy efficiency related legislation is addressed below in section 7.3. Waste related legislation is dealt with below in section 15.

[189] Regulation 66/2010, OJ 2010 L 27/1, repealing Regulation 1980/2000, OJ 2000 L 237/1. The flower logo is specified in Annex II to the regulation.

[190] Case C-281/01 *Commission v. Council* [2002] ECR I-12049 (*Energy Star*). Cf. on this case also Chapter 2, section 5.

currently Article 207 TFEU the appropriate legal basis. According to the Court the Energy Star Program encourages the supply of, and demand for, energy-efficient products and therefore promotes energy conservation. Furthermore, the extension of the program to the EU by means of the Energy Star Agreement helps to achieve that objective. Nevertheless the Court held that the fact remains that the Energy Star Agreement itself does not contain new energy-efficiency requirements but merely renders existing standards applicable.[191] The effect on energy conservation is seen as merely an indirect and distant effect, in contrast to the effect on trade in office equipment which is direct and immediate.[192] As a result the Court comes to the conclusion that it is a predominantly commercial policy-instrument. The fact that ecolabelling schemes have only an indirect and uncertain environmental impact compared to a direct impact on trade could be taken more generally – and the Court appears to do so as well – to mean that the Ecolabel Regulation should have been based on Article 114 TFEU.[193] In our opinion this does not reflect the fact that the environmental impact and the effect on consumption and trade are reciprocal in that the effect on trade is directly related to the environmental impact and vice versa. In that regard a dual legal basis (internal market and environment) would better reflect the nature of ecolabelling. This is also reflected in the difficulties encountered by public authorities seeking to introduce green or sustainability-based criteria in their public procurement policy.[194]

The EU Ecolabel is a voluntary award, not a requirement. In other words, products which meet certain requirements may bear the European Ecolabel, but are not required to do so. Existing or future national ecolabels are not affected by the regulation and may therefore co-exist, provided that the criteria for the award of the national ecolabel are at least as strict as those for the EU Ecolabel (Article 11(1)). Medical and veterinary products as well as organic agricultural products are outside the scope of the Ecolabel Regulation.[195]

---

[191] Case C-281/01 *Commission v. Council* [2002] ECR I-12049 (*Energy Star*), para. 42.

[192] Case C-281/01 *Commission v. Council* [2002] ECR I-12049 (*Energy Star*), para. 41.

[193] Case C-281/01 *Commission v. Council* [2002] ECR I-12049 (*Energy Star*), para. 46. In fact the Energy Star Regulation, Regulation 106/2008, OJ 2008 L 39/1, was adopted on the basis of Article 175 EC, currently Article 192 TFEU, whilst taking into account the need to ensure a properly functioning internal market, see recital 4 of the preamble.

[194] Cf. with regard to Member State public procurement Case C-513/99 *Concordia Bus Finland* [2002] ECR I-7213, paras. 54-86; Case C-448/01 *EVN AG and Wienstrom GmbH* [2003] ECR I-14527, paras. 32-71. On green procurement by EU institutions see Case T-331/06 *Evropaïki Dynamiki – Proigmena Systimata Tilepikoinonion Pliroforikis kai Tilematikis AE*, Judgment 8 July 2010, paras. 74-78. The Commission has dedicated a website to green public procurement, http://ec.europa.eu/environment/gpp/index_en.htm (last visited 7 October 2011). See furthermore Article 12(3) of the Ecolabel Regulation, where the possibility is considered of including the EU Ecolabel in the Manual for authorities awarding public contracts.

[195] Article 2(2) and 9(5) of the Ecolabel Regulation and recital 6 of the preamble. Note, furthermore, that the possibility of including food and feed products is considered, with the option of awarding the label

An Ecolabel can be awarded to products which meet the criteria established for a given product group (Article 9).[196] However, the Ecolabel shall not be awarded to certain products, namely those which have already been classified as dangerous under European legislation or those manufactured by processes which are likely to harm significantly man and/or the environment (Article 6(6)).[197] The decision to establish product groups and the specific ecological criteria for each group will be taken by the Commission (Article 8), assisted by a committee (Article 16) and the European Union Ecolabeling Board (EUEB; Article 8(2)).[198] Up until now ecological criteria have been established by Commission decision for, *inter alia,* bed mattresses,[199] dish washers,[200] refrigerators[201] and growing media.[202]

Applications for the award of an Ecolabel must be made to the competent national body designated for the purpose. It decides whether to award a label (Article 9). Every application is subject to the payment of the costs of processing the application.[203] The competent body concludes a contract with the applicant covering the terms of use of the label (Article 9). In the meantime, a standard contract has been established by Commission Decision 2000/729.[204]

To avoid 'ecolabel shopping', the regulation provides that the application may be made only in the Member State in which the product is manufactured or first marketed or into which the product is imported from a third country (Article 9(1)). It should be noted that the regulation does not provide for legal

---

to organically produced food and feed only.

[196] The criteria are mentioned in Article 9(3).

[197] This provision is in line with Article 2(4) of the previous Ecolabel Regulation, Regulation 1980/2000, with the notable exception that Article 6(7) now authorises the award of an ecolabel to goods containing dangerous substances if the replacement of these dangerous substances is technically not feasible and provided that the substances have not been identified as substances to be included in Annex XIV to the Reach Regulation. Article 2(4) of Regulation 1980/2000 did not contain such an exception.

[198] See Article 5 for the EUEB. This board is set up by Decision 2010/709, OJ 2010 L 308/53. This decision replaces Decision 2000/730, OJ 2000 L 293/24. The EUEB consists of representatives of the national certification authorities and representatives from the various branches of the industry, trade unions, traders, retailers, importers, environmental protection groups and consumer organisations.

[199] Decision 98/634, OJ 1998 L 302/31, as amended by Decision 2002/740, OJ 2002 L 236/10.

[200] Decision 98/483, OJ 1998 L 216/12, as amended by Decision 2001/397, OJ 2001 L 139/21.

[201] Decision 2000/40, OJ 2000 L 13/22, as amended by Decision 2004/669, OJ 2004 L 306/16.

[202] Decision 2007/64, OJ 2007 L 32/14, 137, as amended by Decision 2009/888, OJ 2009 L 318/43. The 2009 decision extends the validity of several ecolabel decisions.

[203] Article 9(5), third paragraph, and Annex III to the Ecolabel Regulation. See further Decision 2000/728, OJ 2000 L 293/18, as amended by Decision 2003/393, OJ 2003 L 135/31.

[204] OJ 2000 L 293/20. Interestingly, Annex IV to the current Ecolabel Regulation contains a new and more elaborate standard contract. The entry into force of the current Ecolabel Regulation does not affect contracts concluded under the previous Ecolabel Regulation except for the provisions on fees, which are aligned with those in the current Ecolabel Regulation, cf. Article 19.

protection against decisions concerning the award of ecolabels, though the need will no doubt be felt, particularly by applicants whose request has been refused. Whether the same applies to the improper *award* of an ecolabel is less clear. Given the fact that environmental organisations and consumer organisations are expressly named as principal interest groups in recital 8 of the Preamble to the regulation, it seems arguable that these organisations at least should be able to appeal against decisions of a competent authority improperly awarding an ecolabel.

Finally, the Ecolabel Regulation contains an elaborate regime on false or misleading advertising and general supervision on the use of the ecolabel.[205] In general, the improper use of the ecolabel or the use of any label which leads to confusion with the EU Ecolabel is to be prohibited by the national competent authorities (Article 10(1) and (5)). The use of the word 'prohibited' gives rise to the presumption that the regulation envisages a criminal sanction and that civil or administrative law sanctions by Member States will not suffice.

8.2   The Eco-audit (EMAS) Regulation

Regulation 1221/2009 provides for rules allowing voluntary participation by organisations in a European eco-management and audit scheme (EMAS Regulation).[206] This is based on the assumption that organisations have their own responsibility to manage the environmental impact of their activities. The eco-management and audit scheme introduced by the regulation is designed to assess and improve the environmental performance of organisations, and provide information about this performance to the public. Participation in the EMAS under the current Regulation is open to all organisations that have their own functions and administration, irrespective of the public or private ownership, legal form and whether or not it is for profit (Article 2(22) in connection with Article 4(1)). In order to qualify for EMAS the organisation must be willing to continually improve the environmental performance.[207] The organisation must furthermore conduct an environmental review, adopt an environmental management system, carry out environmental auditing and prepare

---

[205] Article 10 of the Ecolabel Regulation. Note that this provision is noticeably more elaborate than the corresponding provision (Article 9(2)) in the previous Regulation.

[206] Regulation 1221/2009 on the voluntary participation by organisations in a Community eco-management and audit scheme (EMAS), OJ 2009 L 342/1. It replaces the old EMAS Regulation 761/2001, OJ 2001 L 114/1, and Commission Decisions 2001/681 and 2006/193 adopted on the basis of that old Regulation.

[207] This follows from Article 4(1)(d) of the EMAS Regulation which requires an environmental statement in accordance with Annex IV. Point (B)(b) of Annex IV requires an environmental policy which is defined in Article 2(1) to include a 'commitment to continuous environmental improvement. Note that under the old EMAS Regulation this was explicitly stated in Article 3(1) which has been removed according to the correlation table in Annex VIII.

an environmental statement (Article 4(1)). The requirements for the environmental review, the environmental management system, environmental auditing and the environmental statement are set out in Annex II and III.[208] The outcome of this must be verified (Article 4(5)) and be sent to the competent authority of the Member State (Article 5(2)).

Chapter V gives more detailed rules for the tasks, accreditation and supervision of the environmental verifiers and Chapter IV provides the detailed rules for the competent bodies to be set up by the Member States. If the competent national authority is satisfied that an organisation satisfies all the conditions of the regulation, and a validated environmental statement has been received, the organisation is registered and placed on a list of registered sites (Articles 13 and 15). A fee may be required for registration (Article 39).

The site will be deleted from the register if an organisation fails to submit a validated environmental statement and registration fee or if at any time the competent body concludes that the organisation is no longer complying with all the conditions of the regulation (Article 15(3)). The same applies if a competent body is informed by the competent enforcement authority of a breach of relevant environmental requirements (Article 15(4)). Refusal or suspension shall be lifted if the competent body has received satisfactory assurances from the competent enforcement authority that the breach has been rectified and that satisfactory arrangements are in place to ensure that it does not recur.

Organisations may use the EMAS-logo provided their registration is valid (Article 10). The logo may further be used on all recent and verified environmental information disseminated by the organisation (Article 10(5)). The EMAS logo may not be used on products or their packaging and in comparative advertising (Article 10(4)).[209]

8.3 The Ecodesign Directives

Directive 2009/125 contains the framework for the setting of ecodesign requirements for energy-using products.[210] It is based on Article 95 EC, currently Article 114 TFEU, and contains the general framework for setting ecodesign requirements for energy-using products as part of the new approach to harmonisation. Energy-using products is defined as all products dependent on energy (in whatever form) and thus defined in a rather wide sense, excluding only transportation means (Article 1(3)). Ecodesign is defined in Article 2(23) of the directive as 'the integration of environmental aspects into product design

---

[208] The Commission has provided further guidance in the form of Commission recommendations, OJ 2001 L 247/1 and 2003 L 184/19 and Decision 2001/681, OJ 2001 L 247/24.

[209] It may be noted that under the old EMAS Regulation the Commission adopted a decision authorising the use of the logo on transport packaging or tertiary packaging, see Decision 2006/193, OJ 2006 L 70/63. Since this decision is repealed by the current EMAS Regulation such use is now no longer allowed.

[210] OJ 2009 L 285/10. It recasts the old Eco design Directive 2005/32, OJ 2005 L 191/29.

with the aim of improving the environmental performance of the [product] throughout its whole life cycle'. As part of the new approach the directive itself does not contain the actual rules with which the products must comply. Instead, it contains the general rules (essential requirements, Article 15 in connection with Annex I and II) for setting ecodesign standards which will then have to take place on the basis of so-called implementing measures.[211] In this regard it is interesting to note that the directive allows for voluntary agreements or self-regulation by the industry as an alternative to Commission implementing measures (Article 17, in connection with Annex VIII). A further element of the new approach is the procedure for assessing conformity of products with the rules established in the implementing measures (Article 8). This assessment can take place through internal design control or through a management system (Article 8(2)). The management system of an organisation participating in EMAS shall be presumed to comply with the directive if the design function is included in the EMAS. Moreover, products qualifying for the European Ecolabel are presumed to be in conformity with the directive if the design requirements are part of that ecolabel. Given that both the EMAS and the Ecolabel Regulation use the life-cycle analysis, the design-function should be included.[212] Any product complying with the ecodesign parameters should benefit from the free movement of goods (Article 6).

9   The Environmental Liability Directive

Another example of a horizontal measure is Directive 2004/35 on environmental liability.[213] It is horizontal because it covers a range of environmental sectors that may be damaged. Moreover, it is the result of protracted negotiations and constitutes a careful compromise.[214] Moreover, the implementation proved to be difficult as well.[215] It implements the principle that the polluter should pay, by making the polluter liable for the environmental damage

---

[211] The Ecodesign Directive regards the following Directives as implementing measures: Directive 92/42 on hot-water boilers, OJ 1992 L 167/17, as amended, Directive 96/57 on freezers and refrigerators, OJ 1996 L 236/36 and Directive 2000/55 on ballasts in fluorescent lighting, OJ 2000 L 279/33.

[212] Ecolabel Regulation 66/2010, OJ 2010 L 27/1, Art. 6(3) and EMAS Regulation 1221/2009, OJ 2009 L 342/1, Art. 2(7) in connection with Annex I, point 2(b)(i).

[213] Directive 2004/35 on environmental liability with regard to the prevention and remedying of environmental damage, OJ 2004 L 143/56, as amended by Directive 2006/21, OJ 2006 L 102/15 and Directive 2009/31, OJ 2009 L 140/114. These two amending Directives included the management of extractive waste and the operation of a carbon storage site in the list of activities subject to the directive. See in general on the directive: Roller (2005).

[214] The Commission proposal, COM (2002) 17 final, was preceded by white paper, COM (2000) 66 final, and a green paper, COM (93) 47 final.

[215] COM (2010) 581 contains the evaluation of the directive's effectiveness and notes that there were significant delays with the implementation of the directive, see paragraph 2.

caused.[216] The idea of environmental liability should also have preventive effects in that operators of installations that could potentially damage the environment will now have an incentive to minimise the chances of environmental damage actually occurring. As the directive is based on Article 175 EC, currently Article 192 TFEU, Member States are allowed to adopt more stringent measures, such as the extension of the scope or a stricter liability regime.[217] Given that this would only be detrimental to the national industry (reverse discrimination), this will probably not lead to problems concerning the compatibility with the Treaties.

The scope of the directive

The scope of the Environmental Liability Directive is limited in three ways.[218] First, the personal scope is limited to 'operators' of 'occupational activities' (Article 3(1)). Article 2(6) defines operator as 'any natural or legal, private or public person who operates or controls the occupational activity'. Occupational activity is similarly widely defined in Article 2(7) as any activity carried out in the course of an economic activity, a business or an undertaking, irrespectively of its private or public, profit or non-profit character. This definition may be problematic with regard to public entities that are active in the field of environmental protection, as they may not be involved in an economic activity.[219] As a result they would be outside the scope of the directive even though their activities may very well result in environmental damage. Another interpretation would risk a divergence of the concept of an undertaking and the notion of economic activity in the directive from that used in EU competition law.

Second, the material scope is limited to 'environmental damage'. This is defined in Article 2(1) as damage to protected species and habitats, water damage and land damage. Damage, in turn is defined as a measurable adverse change in a natural resource or a measurable impairment of a natural resource service. The latter concept refers to function that natural resources may have for other natural resources (e.g. migrating birds need a quiet and unpolluted area to

---

[216] Recital 2 of the preamble to the directive, see on the polluter pays principle, Chapter 1, section 3.3 above.

[217] On the basis of Article 193 TFEU and Article 16(2) of the directive. See, on such more stringent measures Case C-378/08 *ERG and others* [2010] ECR I-1919 (*ERG I*), para. 68. Note, however, that such more stringent measures must be in accordance with the polluter pays principle and may thus not result in liability for a person who does not qualify as a polluter in the first place, Case C-378/08 *ERG I*, para. 67.

[218] Note that non-applicability of the directive does not rule out the applicability of the Treaties or other secondary EU law, cf. Case C-378/08 *ERG I*, para. 44. See also Joined Cases C-379/08 and C-380/08 *ERG and others* [2010] ECR I-2007 (*ERG II*), para. 37. The questions referred in Joined Cases Cases C-478/08 and C-479/08 *Buzzi Unicem SpA and Others* v. *Ministero dello Sviluppo economico and Others and Dow Italia Divisione Commerciale Srl* v. *Ministero Ambiente e Tutela del Territorio e del Mare and Others* [2010] ECR I-31, were answered by reference to the two *ERG* cases. An example of such a liability regime on the basis of other secondary EU law, the Waste Framework Directive, can be seen in Case C-188/07 *Commune de Mesquer* [2008] ECR I-4501.

[219] See, for example, the SEPG in Case C-343/95 *Diego Calì & Figli* v. *SEPG* [1997] ECR I-1547.

rest) or the public. Defining a natural resource service as the function a natural resource may have for the public would appear to be risky, in that the public utility of a natural resource may very well be at odds with the natural utility. Lower groundwater levels, for example, may be devastating to the natural utility, but because the area will also become more accessible, the public utility may actually increase. As regards damage to protected species and habitats, the directive refers to the Habitats and Wild Birds Directives[220] (Article 2(1)(a), in connection with 2(3) and Annex I). The further definition of this type of damage turns on the term conservation status (defined in Article 2(4)). Concerning damage to water the directive refers to the Water Framework Directive.[221] According to Article 2(1)(b) water damage exists if there are significant adverse effects for the ecological, chemical and/or quantitative status and/or ecological potential, unless Article 4(7) of the Water Framework Directive applies.[222] For land damage the directive does not refer to other secondary European law, because this does not exist at this moment.[223] The directive defines land damage as land contamination that creates a significant risk of human health being adversely affected. Contrary to the damage to nature and water damage, land damage thus employs an ethnocentric concept of environment, focusing on the risk to humans and not the environment as a whole. Furthermore, it is interesting to note that damage exists when there is a *measurable* adverse effect, whereas water damage and damage to nature damage all require *significant* adverse effects and for land damage simple adverse effects on human health suffice. It remains to be seen whether this choice of words was deliberate and indeed intends to put the bar for damage to nature and water higher than for land damage. Concerning the material scope, regard must also be had to Article 4 of the directive. This excludes liability on the basis of the directive for damage caused by armed conflicts and natural phenomena. Furthermore, the directive does not apply to activities subject to a special liability regime (Article 4(2) and (4))[224] and it is without prejudice to the right of an operator to limit his liability in accordance with the international conventions on limitation of the liability for maritime claims and inland navigation (Article 4(3)).

Third, the temporal scope is restricted to damage caused by an event taking place after 30 April 2007, the deadline for implementation. For damage caused by an event after 30 April 2007 there is no liability on the basis of the directive if the event derives from an activity that took place and was finished

---

[220] See below section 17.

[221] See below section 10.1.

[222] According to Article 4(7) reasons of overriding public interest can justify failure to reach the environmental objectives of the Water Framework Directive, subject to conditions.

[223] Note that a proposal for a Framework Directive on Soil Protection, COM (2006) 232, is still pending.

[224] Referred to in Annex IV. This includes liability for oil spills, transport of dangerous substances and nuclear damage. See, on the liability regime for oil spills Case C-188/07 *Commune de Mesquer* [2008] ECR I-4501, paras. 87 *et seq.*

before 30 April 2007 (Article 17 in connection with Article 19(1)).[225] Concerning the second indent it is interesting to note that the directive does not define the causal relation (derives from) between the event and the activity that was finished. The fact that no further qualification, such as directly deriving from, was included appears to indicate that operators may also be liable for environmental damage caused by third parties, for example entering a poorly fenced off abandoned industrial installation. Finally, the directive limits the liability to 30 years following the event that caused the damage.

Environmental liability and preventive and remedial action

The actual extent of the environmental liability depends on the liability regime applicable and possible exceptions or justifications available to the person held liable. In this regard, the directive distinguishes between two liability regimes. For so-called Annex III activities, there is strict liability, whereas all other occupational activities are subject to fault liability.[226] The activities in Annex III could be summarised as activities that are inherently dangerous to the environment. They include all installations requiring IPPC-permits, waste management operations and installations dealing with dangerous substances and the use of genetically modified organisms. For non-Annex III activities, liability exists only for damage to protected species and natural habitats. Land damage and water damage will thus not lead to liability on the basis of the directive.[227] Furthermore, the operator must have been at fault or negligent. For liability arising from pollution of a diffuse character, a term not further define in the directive,[228] the directive requires a causal link between the damage and the activities of the individual operators. The question of causation was addressed in the *ERG* cases, dealing with an Italian liability scheme according to which several industrial operators active in the petrochemical industry were held liable for the pollution in the Augusta Roadstead. This roadstead was a place where there have been naval and petrochemical activities long before the entry into force of the directive, and as a result the companies claimed that the Italian liability regime infringed the directive essentially because they would be held liable for diffuse damage caused by others. This liability took the form of a presumption that there is a causal link between the pollution found and the activities of the companies due to the fact that their installations are located close to that pollution.[229] The Court points out that in view of the polluter pays principle, this may not lead to a liability for companies that does not reflect their

---

[225] Cf. Case C-378/08 *ERG I*, para. 40, 41. See also Joined Cases C-379/08 and C-380/08 *ERG II*, para.33, 34.

[226] Cf. Case C-378/08 *ERG I*, paras. 61-63.

[227] However, more stringent measures adopted on the basis of Article 193 TFEU and/or 16(1) of the directive can result in such liability, Case C-378/08 *ERG I*, paras. 68-69.

[228] It seems likely that the Court will refer to similar definitions provided in its case law concerning other pieces of secondary Union law, such as Case C-232/97 *Nederhoff* [1999] ECR I-6385.

[229] Case C-378/08 *ERG I*, para. 56.

contribution to the pollution. This means that the competent authorities must
have plausible evidence capable of justifying this presumption, such as the fact
that the operator's installation is located close to the pollution found and that
there is a correlation between the pollutants identified and the substances used
by the operator in connection with his activities.[230]

Mere liability will not necessarily protect the environment. For this reason
the directive contains provisions on preventive and remedial action. According
to Article 5 the operator shall take all the necessary preventive measures where
there is an imminent threat of environmental damage occurring. Article 6 on
remedial action requires the operator to take all practicable steps to limit or to
prevent further environmental damage (containment action). In addition, the
operator is required to take all necessary remedial measures. The difference in
wording between Article 5(1) (all *necessary* steps) and Article 6(1)(a) (all *practicable* steps for containment action) appears to indicate a greater degree of freedom
on the part of the operator in case of remedial actions. Determining necessity
accepts the environmental protection objective whereas practicability involves
a balance between the environmental protection objective and the practical
(economic) possibilities of the operator and may thus result in a less ambitious
environmental objective. The costs for the preventive and remedial actions shall
be borne by the operator (Article 8(1)).

Implementing environmental liability
The Commission initially envisaged a system of private liability, where
private parties would effectuate the liability. The current directive has opted for
a system of public liability, with a competent authority being primarily responsible for making the environmental liability work in practice. Article 11 requires
the Member States to designate the competent authority. This competent authority must be informed of environmental damage or the threat of environmental
damage by the operator (Article 5(2) and 6(1)). Once it has been informed, the
competent authority can request further information from the operator. It may
give the operator instructions to prevent or limit the environmental damage and
it may require the operator to take the necessary preventive and remedial measures (Article 5(3)(b) and Article 6(2)(c)). Furthermore, the competent authority
can itself take the necessary preventive and remedial measures (Article 5(3)(d)
and Article 6(2)(e)). It follows from Article 6(3) that the competent authority
can only take the remedial measures itself as a means of last resort.[231] Concerning both remedial and preventive measures the directive makes it clear that the
initial obligation rests with the operator. Only if the operator does not comply
with the instructions and obligations, cannot be identified or is not obliged to
bear the costs under the directive will the competent authority be able to take

---

[230] Case C-378/08 *ERG I*, para. 57. The causality requirement also applies to the imposition of remedial
measures by the competent authorities, Case C-378/08 *ERG I*, para. 64.

[231] A similar provision does not exist for preventive measures, leading to the conclusion that the competent
authority could take these itself also when it is not a measure of last resort.

the measures itself. The directive thus vests the ultimate responsibility on the competent authority and thus puts it in a superior position compared to that of the operator. This is confirmed by the Court in *ERG II*, where it held that the authority may also unilaterally amend remedial measures proposed and even put into effect by the operators.[232] This power may, however, only be used if the previous remedial measures are ineffective and other measures are necessary to remedy the environmental damage whilst procedural safeguards, such as the operators right to be heard, must be observed.[233] The measures thus imposed by the competent authority must not result in the operators incurring manifestly disproportionate costs compared to the original measures, unless it can be shown by the authority that the original measure was inappropriate from an environmental perspective.[234] This in our view clearly shows that the costs are or secondary importance to the environmental objectives, something that should also impact upon cost recovery decisions pursuant to Article 8 of the directive.[235]

According to Article 8(2), the competent authority is obliged to recover the costs arising from preventive or remedial measures[236] it has implemented itself. However, the competent authority may decide not to recover the costs if this would not be cost-effective or where the operator cannot be identified. In our opinion the criterion of cost-effectiveness is misplaced in this context. In this connection we refer to the fact that public authorities go to great lengths to recover fines (even if the costs of doing so outweigh the actual fine) because not recovering them would diminish the effect of the fine, thus reducing its preventive effect. Since the environmental liability should have a similar preventive effect and implements the polluter pays principle, it is our opinion that the costs should always be recovered.

Article 8(3) contains two further exceptions to the general rule that the operator shall bear the costs or the preventive or remedial actions. For the first exception the operator needs to prove that a third party caused the damage despite the fact that appropriate safety measures were in place. The second exception requires the operator to prove that the damage resulted from an order or an instruction coming from a public authority insofar as this order was not consequent upon an incident caused by the operator. This refers to the scenario where water used to extinguish a fire pollutes nearby land or water. If the fire was caused by a natural phenomenon within the meaning of Article 4(1)(b) the

---

[232] Joined Cases C-379/08 and C-380/08 *ERG II*, para. 50, 51.

[233] Joined Cases C-379/08 and C-380/08 *ERG II*, para. 51, 52. Dispensing with such procedural safeguards in the absence of situations of urgency, para. 56, cannot be regarded as a more stringent measure, para. 65.

[234] Joined Cases C-379/08 and C-380/08 *ERG II*, para. 64.

[235] This is also reflected in the Court's considerations concerning the infringement of the right to property, where the prevention and precautionary priciples are the guiding principles, Joined Cases C-379/08 and C-380/08 *ERG II*, paras. 83-91.

[236] The directive refers to preventive and remedial *actions*. It is assumed that this is sloppy drafting and that this term can be taken to mean preventive and remedial measures.

operator will not be liable. If, however, the fire was caused by the operator, the costs will have to be recovered. In these situations the Member States must take the appropriate measures to allow the operator to recover the costs.

Article 8(4) contains two exceptions that will result in the operator not having to bear the costs of remedial actions. This provision differs from Article 8(3) in that it applies only to remedial actions and does not require the operator to *prove* anything, but simply demands that he *demonstrates* that he was not at fault or negligent. The operator must further demonstrate that the damage was caused by an emission or event expressly authorised on the basis of national laws implementing the directives and regulation in Annex III. This is referred to as the 'permit defence'. Even though Article 8(4)(a) does not explicitly mention this, it is to be assumed that the permit defence will only be available for permits given on the basis of national laws that correctly implement the directives in Annex III. Anything else would only increase the disparities arising from incorrect implementation. The second exception in Article 8(4) exonerates the operator from the damage caused by emissions or use of a product when he demonstrates that this emission or that use was not considered likely to cause environmental damage according to the state of the scientific and technical knowledge at that time. This raises the question to what extent the precautionary principle applies to this provision, making it applicable to the operators' assessment of the state of the scientific and technical knowledge. Recital 20 of the preamble to the directive speaks of a potential for damage that 'could not have been known' at the time the emission or event took place. In our opinion this exception to the general rule that the polluter should pay should be interpreted narrowly in the light of the precautionary principle. This means that even inconclusive scientific evidence of the potential for environmental damage can rule out the applicability of Article 8(4)(b).

Given that the directive wants to implement the polluter pays principle, it may seem surprising that it requires the Member States to encourage the development of financial security instruments with the aim of enabling operators to use financial guarantees to cover their responsibilities. On second thought, however, this is all but surprising since the insurance premium may well function as a very effective risk indicator creating an incentive for the operators to minimise risks and thus premiums.

Article 10 contains a limitation period of five years during which the competent authority can initiate recovery procedures.

Because the directive relies on the competent authority to actually implement the liability there are also rules on the possibilities for natural or legal persons to file requests for action. In a way that closely resembles the provisions on access to justice in the proposal for a directive implementing the Aarhus Convention,[237] Article 12 gives natural or legal persons the right to make the

---

[237] See above section 7.5.

competent authority aware of environmental damage or the threat thereof.[238] More importantly, they are also entitled to request the competent authority to take action under the directive (Article 12(1)). On the basis of Article 13 the same natural or legal persons must have access to justice to review the procedural and substantive legality of the decisions, acts or failure to act of the competent authority.

A final consequence of the choice for a public liability system has found its way into Article 16(2) according to which the directive does not prevent the Member States from prohibiting double recovery of costs in case of concurrent action by the competent authority and a person whose property is affected by environmental damage.

10 The European Environment Agency

At the beginning of May 1990, the Council adopted Regulation 1210/90 on the establishment of the European Environment Agency and the European Environment Information and Observation Network.[239] The Agency is based in Copenhagen[240] and it is the Agency's task to provide the EU and the Member States with objective, reliable and comparable information at the European level enabling them to take the requisite measures to protect the environment, to assess the results of such measures and to ensure that the public is properly informed about the state of the environment. The information in question is scientific and technical information about the present and foreseeable state of the environment (quality, sensitivity, pressures). The regulation designates a number of priority areas of work, with particular emphasis on transfrontier, plurinational and global phenomena. The Agency is also open to countries which are not members of the European Union (Article 19). The powers and duties of the Agency were a particular bone of contention when it was set up. It was decided not to give it powers of inspection of its own in the Member States. Its tasks have been kept limited and relate primarily to the gathering, analysis and dissemination of environmental information. To this end it forms a part of the European Environment Information and Observation Network set up on the basis of Article 4 of the regulation.[241]

---

[238] See Joined Cases T-236/04 and T-241/04 *EEB and Stichting Natuur en Milieu v. Commission* [2005] ECR II-4945, where the parties relied unsuccessfully on, *inter alia*, this provision to get standing under Article 263, fourth paragraph, TFEU. Cf. also Chapter 5, section 5.2.

[239] OJ 1990 L 120/1, as amended by Regulation 933/1999, OJ 1999 L 117/1, Regulation 1641/2003, OJ 2003 L 245/1. The 1990 regulation has been replaced by a codified regulation, Regulation 401/2009, OJ 2009 L 126/13.

[240] See: http://www.eea.europa.eu (last visited 7 October 2011).

[241] See: http://eionet.europa.eu (last visited 7 October 2011).

11 Legislation on Water Protection

European environmental legislation designed to protect both fresh water and seawater generally aims to prevent pollution at its source whilst also laying down environmental quality standards. Incidentally, it also addresses water quantity issues. As early as 1976 the Council adopted a directive to prevent pollution by products which, in view of their toxicity, persistence and bioaccumulation, constitute a particular and permanent threat to the environment and public health. Since then, European environmental water law has steadily evolved in what has been called four waves.[242]

The first wave started with the 1975 Drinking Water Directive[243] and can be said to have lasted until the adoption of the 1980 Groundwater Directive.[244] This group of water directives protects the European water resources by virtue of the various uses that it may have, such as drinking water, shellfish water or water for freshwater fish. The second wave occurred in 1991 when the Urban Waste Water Directive[245] and the Nitrates Directive[246] were adopted. The adoption of the 2000 Framework Directive on Water Protection (hereafter Water Framework Directive)[247] can be characterised as the third wave and the 2008 Marine Strategy Framework Directive can be seen as the fourth and last wave.

In addition to the legislation mentioned in this paragraph there are many other pieces of European environmental law that relate (indirectly) to the protection of water, such as the EIA Directive, the Habitats Directive and the Industrial Emissions Directive.[248]

The transfrontier and international character of water pollution means that European action alone is often not sufficient. The EU is therefore a party to a large number of regional and international conventions on the subject. The most important are:

- the 1974 Paris Convention for the prevention of marine pollution from land-based sources and the 1986 Paris Protocol amending the Convention;[249]
- the 1974 Helsinki Convention on the protection of the environment of the Baltic Sea area (HELCOM; as revised in 1992);[250]
- the 1976 Barcelona Convention for the protection of the Mediterranean Sea against pollution, and various Protocols to the Convention;[251]

---

[242] Grimeaud (2001) at 41 and 43.

[243] Directive 75/440, OJ 1975 L 194/26.

[244] Directive 80/68, OJ 1980 L 20/43.

[245] Directive 91/271, OJ 1991 L 135/40.

[246] Directive 91676, OJ 1991 L 375/1.

[247] Directive 2000/60 establishing a framework for Community action in the field of water policy, OJ 2000 L 327/1.

[248] See above, sections 17.2 and 5 respectively.

[249] OJ 1975 L 194/5 and OJ 1987 L 24/47.

[250] OJ 1994 L 73.

[251] OJ 1977 L 240/3, see, e.g. Case C-239/03 *Commission v. France* [2004] ECR I-9325.

· the 1976 Bonn Agreement on the protection of the Rhine against chemical pollution;[252]
· the 1983 Bonn Agreement for cooperation in dealing with pollution of the North Sea by oil and other harmful substances;[253]
· the 1990 Lisbon Accord of Cooperation for the protection of the coasts and waters of the Northeast Atlantic against pollution (OSPAR);[254]
· the Convention on the International Commission for the Protection of the Elbe[255] and
· the United Nations Convention on the Law of the Sea (UNCLOS).[256]

11.1   The Water Framework Directive 2000/60

The Water Framework Directive[257] is the result of fairly protracted negotiations and represents a complete overhaul of the water protection legislation of the EU.[258] Contrary to older water protection legislation the Water Framework Directive adopts a more holistic approach to water that is reflected in the river basin approach. This means that all interconnected waters in a river basin are protected by this one instrument. This holistic approach can also been seen in the fact that it replaces most of the fragmented first wave water protection instruments.[259] On the basis of Article 22 the following directives and decisions were repealed in December 2007:
· Directive 75/440 on water for the abstraction of drinking water;
· Decision 77/795 on the exchange of information concerning water quality;
· Directive 79/869 on measuring and analysis of water for the abstraction of drinking water.

In December 2013 the following directives will be repealed:
· Directive 78/659 on freshwaters for fish;
· Directive 79/923 on shellfish waters;
· Directive 80/68 on groundwater;
· Directive 76/464 on the pollution caused by dangerous substances.[260]

---

[252] OJ 1977 L 240/53.

[253] OJ 1984 L 188/9.

[254] OJ 1994 L 73/20.

[255] OJ 1991 L 321/25.

[256] Decision 98/392 concerning the conclusion of the United Nations Convention of 10 December 1982 on the Law of the Sea and the Agreement of 28 July 1994 relating to the implementation of Part XI thereof, OJ 1998 L 179.

[257] Cf. on this directive in general and on the implementation in the Netherlands and Germany in particular, Van Rijswick (2003).

[258] Formally starting with Commission proposal COM (1997) 49, see, however, Grimeaud (2001) at 43.

[259] The Bathing Water Directive 76/160, for example, will not be repealed by the Water Framework Directive, see further section 11.5 below.

[260] This directive has been replaced by Directive 2006/11, see below, section 11.3.

Concerning Directive 76/464 a special transitional regime applies. The provision in that directive enabling the Council to adopt so-called daughter directives has been replaced by Article 16 of the Water Framework Directive with effect from the entry into force of this directive. The remainder of Directive 76/464 continues to apply, but it has in the meantime been replaced with Directive 2006/11 subject to some transitional provisions (Article 22(3)).

As was mentioned above, the Water Framework Directive adopts the river basin approach. This means that water protection measures attach to 'the area of land from which all surface run-off flows through a sequence of streams, rivers and, possibly, lakes into the sea at a single river mouth, estuary or delta' (Article 2(13)). The Member States have to designate river basin districts and competent authorities for the river basins (Article 3(1) and (2)). Moreover, the Member States are under a duty to assign river basins extending to more than one Member State to an international river basin district.[261] In such an international river basin district, the Member States shall ensure the coordination of their national measures (Article 3(4)).[262] Article 12 provides for a procedure according to which the Commission can help resolve issues between Member States that cannot be resolved between the Member States. Finally, river basins extending into non-Member States are subject to a less strict duty to ensure coordination (Article 3(5)). The last sentence of Article 3(5) appears to indicate that the fact that a river basin extends to non-Member States does not exonerate the Member States for the purposes of this directive. This may be problematic given that it may be difficult to meet the directive's environmental objectives in a downstream Member State where pollution originates in an upstream non-member state. The environmental objectives are laid down in Article 4 of the Water Framework Directive. The directive contains such objectives for surface water (Article 4(1)(a)), groundwater (Article 4(1)(b)) and protected areas (Article 4(1)(c)). Moreover, within the category of surface water there is a separate category for artificial and heavily modified bodies of surface waters. Surface water is defined in Article 2(1) as inland waters, transitional waters and coastal waters. Groundwater is defined as all water which is below the surface of the ground in the saturation zone and in direct contact with the ground (Article 2(2)). Protected areas are defined in Annex IV of the directive as those areas that are designated for the abstraction of drinking water, areas designated for the protection of economically significant aquatic species, bathing waters, nutrient-sensitive areas[263] and areas protected by virtue of European nature protection legislation. An artificial water body is a body created by human activity. Heavily modified bodies of water are those that as a result of human activity are substantially changed in character. Such artificial and heavily modified bodies of water must

---

[261] See, for a critical analysis of the river basin approach, Keessen et al. (2010)

[262] This can take place through an instruction of national delegations to international commissions, see Case C-32/05 *Commission v. Luxembourg* [2006] ECR I-11323, paras. 71-72.

[263] This includes, but is not confined to, vulnerable zones pursuant to the Nitrates Directive and sensitive areas pursuant to the Urban Waste Water Directive,

be designated by the Member State. This designation has to take place using the procedure set out in Annex II on the basis of the following criteria (Article 4(3)):
· the changes to the body of water necessary for achieving good ecological status (as opposed to good ecological potential) would have significant adverse effects on the wider environment, navigation, purposes for which water is stored (e.g. abstraction of drinking water), water management or other equally important sustainable human development activities and
· there is no technically or economically viable alternative to the water body where that alternative is a significantly better environmental option.

All in all the criteria for designating a body of surface water as heavily modified are quite open and leave the Member States considerable leeway in designating waters as such. This has important consequences for the environmental objectives that apply.

For all surface waters, including those that are artificial and heavily modified, a standstill obligation applies according to which the Member States must implement the necessary measures to prevent deterioration (Article 4(1)(a) (i)). Similarly, irrespective of the type of surface water, pollution from priority (hazardous) substances is subject to regulation on the basis of Article 16 of the Water Framework Directive, discussed below.[264] For non-artificial and non-heavily modified surface water the Member States must protect, enhance and restore with the aim of achieving *good surface water status* before 2015 (Article 4(1)(ii)). Member States must further take measures with the aim to reduce pollution from priority substances and to cease or phase out emissions, discharges and losses of priority hazardous substances (Article 4(1)(iii)). For artificial and heavily modified waters the Member States must implement measures in order to achieve *good ecological potential* and *good surface water chemical status* by 2015. The surface water status is determined by the ecological and chemical status, and good surface water status requires good ecological status as well as a good chemical status (Article 2(17) and (18)). The precise criteria for determining the ecological and chemical status are laid down in Annex V, though this does not contain any limit values or environmental quality indicators.[265]

Groundwater is also subject to a standstill obligation (Article 4(1)(b)(i)) and Member States are obliged to take the necessary measures to prevent or limit the input of pollution into groundwater. Furthermore, Member States must protect, enhance and restore all bodies of groundwater and ensure a balance between the abstraction and recharge of groundwater with the aim of achieving *good*

---

[264] See, on the relation between the Water Framework Directive and EU Plant Protection Products legislation Van Rijswick and Vogelezang-Stoute (2008) as well as Case T-75/06 *Bayer CropScience AG et al.* v. *Commission* [2008] ECR II-2081, paras. 181-186

[265] Commission Decision 2005/646, OJ 2005 L 243/1 establishes a register of sites for the intercalibration network that is used to establish ecological potential and chemical status. The results of this have been laid down in Decision 2008/915, OJ 2008 L 332/20.

groundwater status by 2015 (Article 4(1)(b)(ii)). Again the criteria for determining the groundwater status are laid down in Annex V, without any specific environmental quality values. Article 4(1)(b)(ii) is interesting because it addresses, when it refers to the balance between abstraction and recharge, water quantity aspects. Quantitative water management is of course subject to a special decision-making procedure and a separate legal basis (Article 192(2)(b), second indent, TFEU), begging the question whether the quantitative aspects are indeed subordinate to the quality aspects so that the Water Framework Directive could indeed be based on Article 192(1) TFEU.[266] In our opinion the Water Framework Directive clearly has the primary objective of protecting water quality. Finally, the Member States have a duty to reverse significant and sustained upwards trends in groundwater pollution (trend reversal duty, Article 4(1)(b)(iii)).

Finally, the environmental objectives for protected areas are those laid down in the Water Framework Directive or – if these are more stringent – those laid down in the specific pieces of environmental law. For protected areas the 2015 deadlines also applies.

Much of the complexity of the Water Framework Directive is due to the exceptions contained in it. According to Article 4(4) the 2015 deadline may be extended if certain criteria are met. These criteria, laid down in points i to iii of Article 4(4) contain a wide margin of discretion for the Member States. Article 4(4)(a)(ii), for example, allows an extension if the measures needed to be complied with 'would be disproportionately expensive'. Such extensions must be limited to two further updates of the river basin management plan, i.e. 12 years (Article 4(4)(c) in connection with 13(7)). According to Article 4((4)(c) the extension can be for an indefinite period if the natural conditions are such that the objectives cannot be achieved on time.

Apart from the extension of the 2015 deadline there are further exceptions in Article 4(5), (6) and (7). Article 4(5) allows the Member States to aim for less stringent environmental objectives if achieving these objectives would be infeasible or disproportionately expensive, provided the cumulative conditions in (a) to (d) are met. Interestingly, Article 4(5) refers to 'feasibility' whereas other provisions (such as Article 4(4)(a)(i) and 4(7)(d)) refer to 'technical feasibility' are a reason for an exception. It is possible that, for example, reasons of political feasibility would allow the application of Article 4(5). Article 4(5) only applies to surface waters, not to groundwater or protected areas. Article 4(6) contains an exception for temporary deteriorations of the status of water bodies as a result of exceptional and not reasonably foreseeable circumstances, such as floods, droughts or accidents. The application of this exception is subject to the cumulative criteria contained in Article 4(6)(a) to (e). It may be noted that Article 4(6)(e) ensures that these circumstances will not allow for an exception in the future, as the management plans have to be adapted to include them. As a result, they will no longer be unforeseen in the future. The increased probability of flooding as

---

[266] See Case C-36/98 *Spain v. Council* [2001] ECR I-779 (*Danube Convention*).

a result of climate change can probably be brought under this heading. Article 4(6) does not apply to protected areas. Finally, Article 4(7) allows an exception from the environmental objectives and the duty to prevent deterioration of the status of a body of water if this is the result of new modifications to the physical characteristics of the surface water or alterations of the groundwater level or new sustainable human development activities. With regard to the latter reason for an exception, it may be noted that the term 'sustainable human development activities' is not defined anywhere. Again application of this exception is subject to four cumulative conditions (Article 4(7)(a) to (d)). As Article 4(7)(c) shows, this provision probably fulfils the same role as Article 6(4) of the Habitats Directive (an exception for overriding public interests), it can therefore be assumed that the Court's interpretation of this provision will be similar.[267] Concerning this provision, it is probable that pipeline-problems[268] will emerge, as the cumulative criteria in Article 4(7) will not apply to alterations and modifications that are not 'new'. It cannot be excluded that Member States will want to classify an alteration as not new. The Court will probably apply its case law concerning the pipeline problem in the EIA Directive, meaning that new alterations are those that have formally started after the deadline for implementation (22 December 2003).

Concerning all the exceptions and derogations, the bottom line is laid down in Article 4(8). This provision stipulates the application of Article 4(3) (artificial and heavily modified bodies), 4(4) (extension of the deadline), 4(5) (less stringent objectives), 4(6) (derogation for exceptional circumstances) and 4(7) (new activities and changes). Moreover, Article 4(9) obliges the Member States to take steps to ensure that the application of Article 4 guarantees at least the same level of protection as existing European legislation. The complexity of the environmental objectives has resulted in some scholars questioning the possibility to invoke this directive in a national court. Indeed, the Court has characterised most of the provisions of the directive as requiring the Member States to take the necessary measures to ensure that certain (more or less generally) formulated objectives are attained, whilst leaving the Member States some discretion as to these measures.[269] This probably means that these obligations will not be directly effective or that the Court's test will be confined to a review whether the limits to the discretion have been exceeded or not.

Article 5 requires the Member States to review the river basins, the effects of human activities on those basins and an economic analysis of the water use. Furthermore, pursuant to Article 6 the Member States must keep a register of protected sites. For drinking water, Article 7 contains special rules. Article 8 lays down the rules for monitoring the status of surface waters and groundwater

---

[267] See, concerning a similar concept in the Wild Birds Directive, Case C-57/89 *Commission* v. *Germany* [1991] ECR I-881 (*Leybucht*).

[268] See section 3 of this chapter, concerning the EIA Directive.

[269] Case C-32/05 *Commission* v. *Luxembourg* [2006] ECR I-11323, para. 43.

and protected areas.[270] The monitoring programmes had to be implemented before 2009 (Article 8(2)). Article 9 contains an implementation of the polluter pays principle and requires the Member States to ensure that by 2010 water pricing policies contain 'adequate incentives' for efficient water usage. All of this is part of the principle that the costs of water services should be recovered. 'Water services' is defined in Article 2(38) as encompassing all services which provide for households and any other (economic or public) activity abstraction, impoundment, storage, treatment and distribution of surface water or groundwater as well waste-water collection and treatment. In our opinion this definition includes water quantity management (such as emergency storage of excessive rainfalls), leading to the question whether the costs arising from this (dyke reinforcement) should also be recovered. In our opinion the second sentence of Article 9(1) makes it clear that the idea behind all this is that costs are to be recovered from the final users of water. As a result costs for water quantity management, insofar as they are not connected to water use, do not have to be recovered. Furthermore, the Member States must ensure that water prices are differentiated for, at least, industry, households and agriculture. In setting up such a differentiated pricing scheme the Member States may have regard to the social, environmental and economic effects that the recovery of costs will have. This provides Member States with a possibility to mitigate the effects of a straightforward application of the polluter pays principle. A further exception can be seen in Article 9(4), according to which the duty to set up a differentiated water-pricing scheme does not apply where this would be incompatible with 'established practices'. However, this may not compromise the purposes and the achievement of the environmental objectives of the Water Framework Directive. Finally, it is worth recalling that, although Article 9(3) states that this directive does not stand in the way of government funding of measures in order to achieve the objectives of the directive, this is without prejudice to the state aid provisions contained in. Article 107 and 108(3) TFEU.[271]

Article 10 contains the so-called combined approach for point and diffuse sources. This means that point sources should be subject to emissions controls supplemented with environmental quality standards. In the emission limit values prove insufficient to achieve the environmental quality standards, the emissions limit values should be made more stringent (Article 10(3)). The emission controls should based on the best available techniques (Article 10(2)(a)) or the relevant emission limit values (Article 10(2)(b)) whereas diffuse sources should be subject to the controls set out in the IPPC Directive,[272] the Urban Waste Water Directive,[273] the Nitrates Directive,[274] the so-called Daughter Direc-

---

[270] Directive 2009/90, OJ 2009 L 201/36, adopted pursuant to Article 8(3) of the Water Framework Directive, contains the specific rules on monitoring and chemical analysis.

[271] See Chapter 7 above.

[272] See above, section 5. Note that the IPPC Directive will be replaced by the Industrial Emissions Directive, section 6 above.

[273] See below, section 11.8.

[274] See below, section 11.9.

tives[275] and any other relevant European legislation. Such controls must be in place before 2012, i.e. one year before the Water Framework Directive replaces the last batch of Directives.

Articles 11 to 15 contain the provisions that deal with the procedural side of the Water Framework Directive. On the basis of Article 11 the Member States must implement a programme of measures in order to achieve the environmental objectives of Article 4. A distinction is made between so-called basic measures and supplementary measures (Article 11(2)), with the former certainly being mandatory. An important change compared to the old regime can be found in Article 11(3)(g) and (h), according to which point and diffuse sources of pollution may now also be subject to regulation on the basis of general binding rules, and not necessarily a specific permit. The programme of measures must be established before 2009 and be operational before 2012. Finally, the programme must be reviewed before 2015 and every six years thereafter (Article 11(7) and (8)). Article 13 requires the Member States to draw up river basin management plans before 2009, and to be reviewed by 2015 at the latest and every six years thereafter (Article 13(6) and (7)). In case of river basins covering more than one Member State the Member States are required to coordinate their river basin management plans (Article 13(2)). For river basins covering non-Member States as well, there is a less far-going obligation to 'endeavour to produce' a single river basin management plan (Article 13(3)). Details about the river basin management plans can be found in Annex VII. Article 14 contains rules on public information and consultation in connection with the production and review of river basin management plans.[276] Article 15 requires the Member States to report to the Commission on the river basin management plans and submit summaries of the analyses conducted pursuant to Article 5 and the monitoring programmes set up under Article 8.[277]

Article 16 is a more substantive provision that replaces Article 6 of Directive 76/464. On the basis of the latter provision the Council, acting on a proposal from the Commission, could set emission limit values for List I substances in the form of so-called Daughter Directives. Thus far this has resulted in five such directives, which can hardly be called a success given that the Commission list was several times longer.[278] Article 16 contains a similar enabling clause, but requires the European Parliament and the Council to adopt the daughter

---

[275] These are the directives adopted pursuant to Article 16 of the Water Framework Directive and those adopted pursuant to Directive 76/464, now replaced by Directive 2006/11, see below, section 11.3.

[276] The Court held that this provision is intended to confer rights upon individuals and interested parties, Case C-32/05 *Commission v. Luxembourg* [2006] ECR I-11323, para. 80, 81.

[277] The Commission started infringement proceedings against a number of Member States for non-compliance with this requirement.

[278] Directive 82/176 on mercury discharges (OJ 1982 L 81/29), Directive 83/513 on cadmium discharges (OJ 1983 L 291/1), Directive 84/156 on mercury (OJ 1984 L 74/49), Directive 84/491 on hexachlorocyclohexane discharges (OJ 1984 L 274/11) and Directive 86/280 on discharges of dangerous substances (OJ 1986 L 181/16), listed in Annex IX to the Water Framework Directive.

directives to reduce discharges, emissions and losses priority substances and
to completely phase out all emissions and discharges of priority hazardous
substances (Article 16(1)). These measures should be taken on the basis of a
Commission proposal. The list of priority (hazardous) substances can be found
in Annex X to the Water Framework Directive,[279] and replaces the list in the
Commission communication pursuant to Directive 76/464.[280] As a follow up
to this list of priority (hazardous) substances, the Commission has proposed a
directive on environmental quality standards.[281] Pursuant to Article 16(6) the
Commission will propose measures to completely phase out priority hazardous
substances within 20 years from the adoption of these measures by the Council
and European Parliament. As was mentioned above, the adoption of daughter
directives up until today can hardly be considered successful and the lack of
action on the basis of Directive 76/464[282] has resulted in a safety net provision
in the form of Article 16(8). According to this provision lack of action on the part
of the Council and the European Parliament before 2006 will mean that the
Member States will become responsible for establishing environmental quality
standards themselves. However, following the adoption of Directive 2008/105,
there are now EU wide environmental quality standards laid down for the priority substances and other substances.[283]

Article 17 contains a comparable enabling clause for the protection of
groundwater. This provision requires the Council and the European Parliament to adopt before December 2002, on the basis of a Commission proposal,
specific measures to prevent and control the pollution of groundwater. These
measures consist of two main components: criteria for the assessment of good
groundwater chemical status (Article 17(2)(a)) and criteria for the identification
of significant and sustained upward trends and for the definition of starting
points for trend reversals in groundwater chemical status (Article 17(2)(b)). In a
similar vein to the safety net provision in Article 16(8), Article 17(4) makes the
Member States individually responsible to define the above mentioned criteria
before 2005 in case the EU fails to do so. Interestingly, Article 17(5) adds to this
another safety net in that failure to apply Article 17(4) will result in 75% of the
current quality standards[284] becoming the norm for trend reversal. However,

---

[279] Note that this Annex was amended by Directive 2008/105, OJ 2008 L 348/84. The list was adopted by
the Council and the European Parliament on the basis of Article 16(11) of the Water Framework Directive by Decision 2455/2001, OJ 2001 L 331/1.

[280] Communication of 22 June 1982, OJ 1982 C 176/3.

[281] COM (2006) 397 final (2006/0129/COD).

[282] This absence of Daughter Directives effectively means that Black list substances (a term that more or
less equates to priority hazardous substances within the meaning of the Water Framework Directive)
would only be subject to the much lighter Grey list-regime (the regime for priority substances in the
Water Framework Directive).

[283] OJ 2008 L 348/84. This directive further amends Annex X to Directive 2000/60.

[284] Laid down in the Groundwater Directive 80/68, see below, section 10.4.

with the adoption of Directive 2006/118, the criteria mentioned in Article 17(2) have been set, so that recourse to Article 17(4) and (5) is no longer necessary.[285]

Articles 18 and further again contain more procedural rules, concerning reporting, adaptations, comitology etc.[286] Article 22, as was noted above, contains the repeals and transitional provisions.

11.2 The Flood Risk Directive

Directive 2007/60 on the assessment and management of flood risks closely follows the framework approach that can be seen in the Water Framework Directive and complements the latter with measures concerning flood risk management.[287] The objectives of the directive are to reduce the adverse consequences for human health, the environment, cultural heritage and economic activity associated with floods (Article 1). Interestingly, the definition of floods allows the Member States to exclude floods from sewage systems (2(1)). This is problematic given that such sewage overflows are particularly dangerous for human health and the environment.[288] It does so by adopting a four-stage procedure whereby Member States first have to conduct a preliminary flood risk assessment before 22 December 2011 (Article 4). However, Member States may also choose to use flood risk assessments conducted at an earlier stage (Article 13(1)). The preliminary flood risk assessment must use the river basin approach also adopted by the Water Framework Directive (Article 4(1)).

The second stage consists of the identification of those areas where a potential significant flood risk exists or might be considered likely to occur (Article 5(1)).

The third stage is laid down in Article 6(1) and involves the drawing up of flood hazard maps and flood risk maps. The flood hazard maps must distinguish three categories of flood scenarios ((a) low probability or extreme event scenarios; (b) medium probability which is defined as an event with a likely return period equal to or exceeding 100 years and (c) flood with a high probability. For these categories the flood extent, water depth and water flow must be shown on the map. The flood risk maps must reflect the combination of flood risk and potential adverse effects on human health, the environment, cultural

---

[285] Directive 2006/118, OJ 2006 L 372/19, see below, section 10.4.

[286] In addition to the comitology procedures, the Commission has also issued an extensive amount of guidance documents to clarify specific aspects of the Water Framework Directive, see http://circa.europa.eu/Public/irc/env/wfd/library?l=/framework_directive/guidance_documents&vm=detailed&sb=Title (last visited 7 October 2011).

[287] OJ 2007 L 288/27.

[288] The Urban Waster Water Directive, however, requires waste water treatment installations to be designed in a way that will limit the pollution of receiving waters due to storm water overflows, insofar as this does not entail excessive costs (Annex I under A). It may also be noted that leaked sewage qualifies as waste and thus falls within the scope of the Waste Framework Directive, see Case C-252/05 *Thames Water Utilities* [2007] ECR I-3883.

heritage and economic activity (Article 5(5) in combination with Article 2(2)). The directive provides that flood risk must be expressed as (a) the number of inhabitants affected; (b) the type of economic activity involved; (c) IPPC installations and protected areas affected and (d) other information considered relevant by the Member States. As the directive is based on Article 175 EC, it must be possible for the Member States to take further elements into account when drawing up their flood risk maps as part of adopting a more stringent approach. However, the directive allows for less stringent measures for coastal waters where adequate protection is in place and for floods from groundwater sources (Articles 5(6) and (7)). Flood risk maps and flood hazard maps must be drawn up before 22 December 2013.

The fourth and final stage requires the Member States to establish flood risk management plans that should contain appropriate objectives and focus on the reduction of potential adverse effects of flooding on human health, the environment, cultural heritage and economic activity. The Member States may decide to include non-structural initiatives and/or the reduction of the likelihood of flooding when they consider this appropriate. Such plans must take into account the costs and benefits, flood extent, flood conveyance routes, flood retainment areas, the environmental objectives of the Water Framework Directive, soil and water managements, land use and spatial planning, nature conservation and navigation and port facilities (Article 7(3)). The aspects to be addressed in such plans are also quite widely set out in the third subparagraph. All in all this provision appears to give the Member States considerable leeway when they draw up such plans. This discretion is exacerbated by the fact that Member States may extend the list of factors taken into account when drawing up flood risk maps. It is also limited in an important way by the solidarity requirement imposed upon the Member States by Article 7(4). According to this provision flood risk management plans shall not include measures which, by their extent and impact, significantly increase flood risks in upstream or downstream countries, unless such measures have been coordinated and agreed upon by the states concerned pursuant to Article 8 of the directive. A more stringent implementation of the flood risk criterion in a downstream state could thus result in less room for manoeuvre for upstream states. The flood risk management plans should be completed before 22 December 2015. The directive contains provisions on coordination with the Water Framework Directive,[289] public information and consultation (Article 10), comitology (Articles 11 and 12), transitional measures (Article 13) and reporting and review (Articles 14-16). The directive entered into force on 26 November 2007 and must be implemented before 22 November 2009 (Articles 17 and 18).

---

[289] In this regard we may also refer to the coordination with climate change policies, see the Commission's white paper on adapting to climate change, COM (2009) 147.

11.3 Directive 2006/11 on Pollution by Dangerous Substances

Directive 2006/11[290] on pollution caused by certain dangerous substances discharged into the aquatic environment of the Community replaces and codifies Directive 76/464.[291] It applies only to the waters listed in Article 1, which are (a) inland surface water, (b) territorial waters, and (c) internal coastal waters. Article 7 protects waters outside the scope of the directive by requiring the Member States to ensure that these waters are not subjected to increased pollution. Moreover, the Member States must ensure that the provisions of the directive are not circumvented.

Central to the directive is the distinction between so-called List I substances and List II substances (also referred to as Black and Grey-list substances). Pollution by List I substances must ultimately be completely eliminated by the Member States. Pollution by List II substances must be reduced. List I contains particularly dangerous substances selected mainly on the basis of their toxicity, persistence and bioaccumulation and includes mercury and cadmium and their compounds, carcinogens, persistent mineral oils and hydrocarbons and certain persistent synthetic substances. List II includes certain heavy metals, biocides, cyanides and fluorides.

In order to eliminate the pollution by List I substances, Article 4(a) requires the Member States to ensure that all discharges of these substances require prior authorisation. This authorisation should include emissions standards and may be granted for a limited period only (Article 4(a) and (b)). The term 'discharge' defined in Article 2(d) means the introduction into the waters referred to in Article 1 of any List I or II substances, with the exception of discharges of dredgings, operational discharges from ships in territorial waters and dumping from ships in territorial waters.[292] With respect to pollution from other significant sources, including multiple and diffuse sources, Member States have the obligation to avoid or eliminate them, by means of specific programmes according to Article 5(1) of Directive 86/280.[293] It follows that European law has established two distinct systems for combating pollution of surface water by dangerous substances: first, a system of authorisation, applicable where the pollution derives from an act attributable to a person in the form of a discharge, and, second, a system of specific programmes, applicable where the pollution cannot be attributed to a person because it derives from multiple and diffuse sources.[294]

---

[290] OJ 2006 L 64/52.

[291] OJ 1976 L 129/23, later amended.

[292] See, on the meaning of discharge in Directive 76/464, Case C-232/97 *Nederhoff* [1999] ECR I-6385, para. 37, concerning the placing by a person in surface water of wooden posts treated with creosote. Cf. also Case C-231/97 *Van Rooij* [1999] ECR I-6355 concerning the emission of contaminated steam which is precipitated on to surface water.

[293] OJ 1986 L 181/16, later amended.

[294] Case C-232/97 *Nederhoff* [1999] ECR I-6385, para. 42.

The greater part of the directive, however, must be regarded as a framework directive. In the 'old' directive, Article 6 required the Council to lay down in implementing directives (so-called 'daughter directives') the limit values which the emission standards must not exceed. Directive 2006/11 no longer contains this obligation, as it has been moved to Article 16 of the Water Framework Directive.[295] Article 6 now requires the establishment of implementation programmes to reduce pollution by List II substances. To constitute a programme within the meaning of Article 6, the national measures

> 'must embody a comprehensive and coherent approach, covering the entire national territory of each Member State and providing practical and coordinated arrangements for the reduction of pollution caused by any of the substances in List II which is relevant in the particular context of the Member State concerned, in accordance with the quality objectives fixed by those programmes for the waters affected. They differ, therefore, both from general purification programmes and from bundles of ad hoc measures designed to reduce water pollution'.[296]

According to Article 6(3) these programmes must contain quality objectives for water, to be laid down in accordance with Council directives, where these exist. The Council has not adopted any implementing directives containing quality objectives for these substances. In addition, all discharges of such substances require prior authorisation, in which emission standards shall be laid down (Article 6(2)). This requirement is interpreted strictly by the Court. It rules out, for example, tacit approval or general authorisation schemes.[297] Moreover, this is not altered by the fact that the Water Framework Directive allows for a transitional rule on the way in which the authorities are to deal with (low polluting) point sources.[298] The laying down by a Member State of limit values for emissions of List II substances does not constitute in itself a more stringent instrument than the implementation programmes and is therefore not sufficient to exempt that Member State from drawing up the implementation programmes.[299] As to the argument that so long as there is no water *pollution* there is no requirement for quality objectives to be laid down, the Court noted

---

[295] See above, section 10.1.

[296] See, concerning Article 6 of Directive 76/464, Case C-207/97 *Commission* v. *Belgium* [1999] ECR I-275, para. 40. Cf. also Case C-184/97 *Commission* v. *Germany* [1999] ECR I-7837; Case C-214/96 *Commission* v. *Spain* [1998] ECR I-7661; Case C-384/97 *Commission* v. *Greece* [2002] ECR I-3823; Case C-261/98 *Commission* v. *Portugal* [2000] ECR I-5905 and Case C-282/02 *Commission* v. *Ireland* [2005] ECR I-4653, para. 68.

[297] Case C-381/07 *Association nationale pour la protection des eaux et rivières – TOS* v. *Ministère de l'Écologie, du Développement et de l'Aménagement durables* [2008] ECR I-8281, paras. 26-30.

[298] Article 22(3)(b) Water Framework Directive, see Case C-381/07 *Association nationale pour la protection des eaux et rivières – TOS* v. *Ministère de l'Écologie, du Développement et de l'Aménagement durables* [2008] ECR I-8281, paras. 33, 34.

[299] Case C-184/97 *Commission* v. *Germany* [1999] ECR I-7837, paras. 40 and 29.

that the purpose of the implementation programmes is to reduce water pollution. The requirement to draw up programmes extends therefore to waters affected by discharges, as any discharge will inevitably lead, sooner or later, to pollution of the aquatic environment affected by it.[300] In similar vein, the Court held that there is a duty to set up pollution reduction programmes for all List II substances.[301]

The directive further contains a standstill requirement (Article 8)[302] and a provision expressly allowing Member States to take more stringent measures (Article 9). The possibility to take more stringent measures is understandable given that the directive has Article 175 EC (now Article 192 TFEU) as a legal basis. However, it appears to be at odds with the fourth recital in the preamble.[303] Article 9 permits Member States to make the authorisation for a discharge subject to additional requirements not provided for in the directive, in order to protect the European aquatic environment against pollution, even if these requirements have the effect of making the grant of authorisation impossible or altogether exceptional.[304] The additional requirements may include the obligation to investigate or choose alternative solutions which have less impact on the environment.

The provisions of Directive 2006/11 will remain applicable to existing installations until the measures required pursuant to Article 5 of the IPPC Directive have been taken by the competent authorities.[305] For new installations the relevant provisions concerning authorisation systems in Directive 2006/11 will not be applied now the IPPC Directive has been brought into effect.[306] The directive, like Directive 76/464, does not contain any provision on the deadline for transposition, but according to the Court this does not rule out the possibility to hold a Member State responsible if transposition did not take place in a reason-

---

[300] Case C-184/97 *Commission v. Germany* [1999] ECR I-7837, para. 60.

[301] See, concerning Article 7 of Directive 76/464, Case C-282/02 *Commission v. Ireland* [2005] ECR I-4653, paras. 35-43.

[302] See, concerning Article 9 of Directive 76/464, Case C-282/02 *Commission v. Ireland* [2005] ECR I-4653, paras. 88-91, according to which failure to implement a the directive is not a violation of the standstill obligation if there is a deterioration of water quality.

[303] This recital ('Discrepancies between the provisions applicable in the various Member States with regard to the discharge of certain dangerous substances into the aquatic environment may give rise to unequal conditions of competition and thus have a direct influence on the functioning of the internal market.') appears to be left over from the 'old' directive that had Articles 100 (now 115 TFEU) and 235 (now 352 TFEU) EC as a legal base.

[304] Case C-232/97 *Nederhoff* [1999] ECR I-6385, para. 61.

[305] Article 20(1) of the IPPC Directive. Cf. also Case C-207/97 *Commission v. Belgium* [1999] ECR I-275, para. 36.

[306] Article 20(2) of the IPPC Directive. The Industrial Emissions Directive no longer contains a similar rule.

able period.[307] Finally, as references to Directive 76/464 have to be construed as references to Directive 2006/11 (Article 13), the latter will be repealed in December 2013 on the basis of Article 22 of the Water Framework Directive.

11.4 Groundwater Protection

The preamble to Directive 76/464[308] had already referred to the adoption of specific European rules on discharges into groundwater. Directive 80/68 provides just those rules.[309] Furthermore, Directive 2006/118, a daughter directive to the Water Framework Directive, contains rules on pollution of groundwater by priority (hazardous) substances. This directive requires Member States to take the necessary measures to *prevent* the discharge into groundwater of certain substances (contained in List I in the Annex to the directive) and to *limit* the discharge into groundwater of other substances (contained in List II in the Annex; Article 3). From the judgment in Case 360/87, it is apparent that the national legislation implementing the directive must make the distinction between substances in lists I and II in so many words.[310] The Court held 'the distinction between the two types of substances is mandatory in view of the objective of the directive. It follows that it must be incorporated in national legislation with the requisite precision and clarity in order to meet the requirement of certainty.'

From the case law of the Court it is also clear that the prohibition on direct discharges of List I substances in Article 4(1) 'is general and absolute':

> 'and applies to discharges of substances in list I without distinguishing between the substances themselves and solutions thereof. That article does not empower the competent authorities of the Member States to determine, on a case-by-case basis and having regard to the circumstances, whether or not discharges have a detrimental effect.'[311]
>
> The Court noted that Article 2(b), which provides that the directive shall not apply to discharges of substances in such a small quantity as to exclude any danger to the groundwater, makes no difference in this respect.

The two lists of the Groundwater Directive do not correspond entirely with those of Directive 2006/11. For the purposes of the directive, 'direct discharge' means the introduction into groundwater of substances without percolation through the ground or subsoil (Article 1(2)(b)), while 'indirect discharge' means the introduction into groundwater of substances after percolation through the ground or subsoil (Article 1(2)(c)). Member States must prohibit all direct

---

[307] Case C-282/02 *Commission* v. *Ireland* [2005] ECR I-4653, para. 33.

[308] OJ 1976 L 129/23, later amended.

[309] OJ 1980 L 20/43, later amended.

[310] Case 360/87 *Commission* v. *Italy* [1991] ECR I-791.

[311] Case C-131/88 *Commission* v. *Germany* [1991] ECR I-825.

discharge of substances in list I (Article 4). Any disposal or tipping for the purpose of disposal of these substances which might lead to indirect discharge shall be subject to prior investigation,[312] and depending on the results of that investigation be prohibited or require authorisation. The investigation shall include examination of the hydrogeological conditions of the area concerned, the possible purifying powers of the soil and subsoil and the risk of pollution and alteration of the quality of the groundwater from the discharge (Article 7). It must establish whether the discharge into groundwater is a satisfactory solution from the point of view of the environment. Authorisations may be granted only if all technical precautions have been taken to prevent indirect discharges (Article 4). Member States must take all appropriate measures they deem necessary to prevent any indirect discharge due to other activities. Direct discharge of substances in list II and disposal or tipping for the purpose of disposal of these substances which might lead to indirect discharge must also be made subject to prior investigation (Article 5). Member States may grant an authorisation in the light of that investigation, provided that all the technical precautions for preventing groundwater pollution have been observed. From 16 January 2009 onwards all authorisations pursuant to Articles 4 and 5 of this directive will have to take into account the requirements laid down in Articles 3, 4 and 5, of the Groundwater Daughter Directive.[313] Article 6 of the directive contains provisions on the artificial recharge of groundwater subject to which a special authorisation may be issued for the artificial recharge of groundwater, namely 'if there is no risk of polluting the groundwater'.[314]

Articles 9 to 12 deal with the content of authorisations.[315] A system of 'tacit authorisation' is not allowed. According to Italian legislation a provisional authorisation was deemed to have been granted if the application for grant of authorisation had not been rejected within six months. According to the Court, the directive provides that the refusal, grant or withdrawal of authorisations must take place by way of an express measure in accordance with precise rules of procedure which comply with a number of necessary conditions, which create rights and obligations on the part of individuals. Consequently, tacit authorisation cannot be considered compatible with the requirements of the directive, since such authorisation does not make it possible to carry out prior inquiries, subsequent inquiries or checks.

---

[312] See on this Case C-131/88 *Commission* v. *Germany* [1991] ECR I-825. In this context Germany referred, *inter alia*, to the general procedures in its law on administrative procedure *(Verwaltungsverfahrensgesetz)*. These provisions were also not sufficiently precise and specific to withstand the scrutiny of the Court.

[313] Directive 2006/118, Article 7, see below in this section.

[314] This provision must be expressly transposed into national law; Case 291/84 *Commission* v. *Netherlands* [1987] ECR 3483.

[315] Case C-360/87 *Commission* v. *Italy* [1991] ECR I-791. See further Case C-416/02 *Commission* v. *Spain* [2005] ECR I-7487, paras. 106-109, according to which the use of agricultural slurry from farms is not subject to the authorisation regime on the basis of the Groundwater Directive.

Article 11 requires Member States to grant authorisations for a limited period, which must be reviewed at least every four years. The grant of authorisations for an indefinite period, even if they can be withdrawn or amended at any time, is incompatible with the directive. And as the Court held in Case C-131/88, the requirement contained in Article 11 is not met where the 'administrative authorities are free to decide whether or not to restrict the period of validity of the authorization'.[316]

Article 13, which requires Member States to monitor compliance with the conditions laid down in each authorisation and the effects of discharges on groundwater, was considered in Case C-360/87.[317] The Italian Government's argument that the fact that failure to observe the conditions laid down in authorisations constitutes a criminal offence automatically entails a duty of surveillance and monitoring on the part of the authorities responsible for investigating offences was not accepted by the Court. From this it appears that the national implementing legislation must contain explicit and specific instructions to carry out the necessary control and monitoring. For the same reason a German administrative provision requiring individuals to permit monitoring was held not to be sufficient, because it did not 'itself impose an obligation to monitor compliance with the conditions laid down in the authorizations'.[318] The scope of the standstill obligation in Article 18 was considered by the Court in Case 291/84.[319] Article 18 requires that the application of the measures taken pursuant to the directive may on no account lead, either directly or indirectly, to pollution of the water referred to in Article 1 of the directive. The Commission argued that Article 18 must be regarded not only as implying a standstill requirement, but as prohibiting any increase in the pollution of groundwater, even that caused by other substances. The Court rejected the Commission's argument stating that Article 18 refers to 'the measures taken pursuant to this Directive', causing the standstill obligation in turn to be confined to the pollution of groundwater by List I en II substances.

The Groundwater Directive will be repealed in December 2013,[320] but given that the Water Framework Directive already applies, this should not be a problem. As was already mentioned, a daughter directive on the basis of Article 17 of the Water Framework Directive has been adopted. This Groundwater Daughter Directive contains the criteria for the assessment of groundwater chemical status and the criteria for trend reversal. It complements the Water Framework Directive. The criteria for assessing groundwater chemical status are laid down in Article 3 in connection with Annex I. The specific criteria/threshold values

---

[316] Case C-131/88 *Commission v. Germany* [1991] ECR I-825.

[317] Case C-360/87 *Commission v. Italy* [1991] ECR I-791.

[318] Case C-131/88 *Commission v. Germany* [1991] ECR I-825.

[319] Case 291/84 *Commission v. Netherlands* [1987] ECR 3483, para. 21.

[320] Article 22(2) Water Framework Directive, see above, section 11.1.

have to be established by the Member States before 22 December 2008 (Article 3(5)). The detailed rules for trend reversal can be found in Article 5 in connection with Annex IV. Article 6 implements the duty contained in Article 4(1)(b)(i) of the Water Framework Directive to take measures to prevent inputs into the groundwater of any pollutants. Article 6(3) allows for exemptions from this duty on the grounds listed in points (a) to (f). The Groundwater Daughter Directive had to be implemented before 16 January 2009.

11.5 The Protection of Bathing Water

Directive 2006/7 (hereafter the new Bathing Water Directive) lays down rules for the quality of bathing water.[321] It replaces Directive 76/160 (hereafter the current Bathing Water Directive) with effect from 31 December 2014 (Article 17(1)) and complements the Water Framework Directive (Article 1(2)).[322] Many of the core elements of the current Bathing Water Directive have found their way into the new directive.

Central to the new Bathing Water Directive is the concept of bathing water. The definition in Article 1(3) is slightly narrower compared to that in the current Bathing Water Directive. In the new definition, bathing water exists if the authority expects a large number of people to bathe therein and has not prohibited bathing or issued a warning against bathing. The current directive does not require any expectations on the part of the authority and simply referred to waters where bathing is not prohibited and traditionally practised by a large number of bathers (Article 1(2)(a)).

Under the current Bathing Water Directive, Member States must ensure that the quality of bathing water conforms to the set limits within ten years (Article 4).[323] However, it does not provide for what should be done if Member States fail to comply with the values set out. Of course the Member States are required to take measures to ensure that the values are achieved, but it is does not require that bathing should be prohibited or restricted if the values are exceeded.[324] Such a prohibition is only required if public health is endangered.

The current directive also contains provisions on sampling (Articles 5 and 6)[325] and a standstill requirement (Article 7). Article 8, finally, indicates in what cases the directive may be waived, for example in the case of exceptional weather

---

[321] OJ 2006 L 64/37.

[322] OJ 1976 L 31/1, later amended.

[323] Cf. Case C-198/97 *Commission* v. *Germany* [1999] ECR I-3257. See further Case C-278/01 *Commission* v. *Spain* [2003] ECR I-14141, where the Court imposed a penalty payment for breach of Articles 3 and 4 of the current Bathing Water Directive.

[324] Case C-307/98 *Commission* v. *Belgium* [2000] ECR I-3933, paras. 59-63.

[325] On sampling, see Case C-198/97 *Commission* v. *Germany* [1999] ECR I-3257, paras. 44-47. See on this case also Chapter 4, sections 3.1 and 5.

or geographical conditions.[326] In no case may exceptions be made which disregard the requirements 'essential for public health protection'.

An important judgment which clarifies certain aspects of the current Bathing Water Directive was given by the Court in the *Blackpool* case.[327] In the first place the Court rejected the United Kingdom's argument that the directive did not provide a precise definition of the term 'bathing water' and that Member States thus had a discretionary power in that respect. The Court ruled that the objectives of the directive could not be achieved:

> 'if the waters of bathing resorts equipped with facilities such as changing huts, toilets, markers indicating bathing areas, and supervised by lifeguards, could be excluded from the scope of the directive solely because the number of bathers was below a certain threshold. Such facilities and the presence of lifeguards constitute evidence that the bathing area is frequented by a large number of bathers whose health must be protected.'

If certain areas fulfil these criteria, as was the case with Blackpool and Southport in this case, the water in question is bathing water and the quality standards laid down in the directive apply.

The judgment also clarifies the legal nature of the obligations under the current directive. The UK contended that the directive merely required the Member States to take 'all practicable steps' to comply with its obligations. The Court rejected this argument. More is required:

> 'It follows that the directive requires the Member States to take steps *to ensure* that certain results are attained, and, apart from those derogations [the ones in Articles 4(3), 5(2) and 8], they cannot rely on particular circumstances to justify a failure to fulfil that obligation.'[328]

In other words, best endeavours are not enough: the directive imposes an obligation to achieve a result. The new Bathing Water Directive contains a similar set of environmental objectives, albeit in a more elaborate framework. The first step the Member States must annually identify all bathing waters and the length of the bathing season (Article 3(1)) before the start of the first bathing season after March 2008. In addition the Member States have to ensure that monitoring of

---

[326] Cf. Case C-92/96 *Commission* v. *Spain* [1998] ECR I-505, concerning abnormal drought. However in this case the Spanish Government had not provided any specific evidence, either of the abnormal nature of the alleged drought or of the resultant inability on the part of the authorities to achieve the minimum standard for bathing water imposed by the directive, even by undertaking further efforts.

[327] Case C-56/90 *Commission* v. *UK* [1993] ECR I-4109. Cf. also Case C-307/98 *Commission* v. *Belgium* [2000] ECR I-3933.

[328] Emphasis added by the authors.

the bathing waters takes place in conformity with the directive.[329] On the basis of the results of the monitoring the bathing water quality assessment takes place (Article 4). This assessment will in turn result in a classification of the bathing water as poor, sufficient, good or excellent. This classification takes place on the basis of the microbiological criteria monitoring rules in Annex I and II. The first such classification must take place before the end of the 2015 bathing season (Article 5(2)) and the Member States must ensure that at that time all bathing waters are of at least sufficient quality (Article 5(3)). Article 5(3) also requires the Member States to take the 'realistic and proportionate measures' they consider appropriate to increase the number of bathing waters classified as good or excellent. Article 5(4) contains a derogation allowing the Member States to classify bathing waters as poor without being in breach of the directive. The Member States will then have to alert the public to this status and identify the cause of the pollution and take adequate measures. Classification as poor for five consecutive years will result in a permanent bathing prohibition or a permanent advice against bathing, unless achievement of sufficient status would be infeasible or disproportionately expensive. In sum, the Member States are allowed a derogation on economic grounds. Member States have a duty to monitor and inform the public in cases of cyanobacterial risks (algal bloom, Article 8). Interestingly, Article 9 requires the Member States to ensure visual inspection of bathing waters for pollution such as tarry residue, glass or any other waste and to take adequate management measures. Notwithstanding that the adequacy of measures may be open to discussion, this would appear to be a provision that has direct effect and could form the basis of a claim for damages suffered as a result of, for example, injury sustained because of glass that was in the bathing water. Article 10, on transboundary cooperation, corresponds to Article 4(4) in the current Bathing Water Directive. An important change in the new Bathing Water Directive relates to the information of the public. Under the current directive, there is only a duty to report to the Commission, and the Commission will then publish a report (Article 13). The new Bathing Water Directive, in line with the Aarhus Convention, contains more elaborate provisions on public information and consultation (Articles 11 and 12[330]) in addition to the duty to report to the Commission (Article 13). Finally, the deadline for implementation is 24 March 2008 (Article 18(1)), and from this date onwards, the new Bathing Water Directive is be applicable, replacing Directive 76/160. As a result, anyone wishing to rely on the Bathing Water Directive will, from the date of implementation onwards, have to rely on the new Bathing Water Directive, even if the current directive is not repealed at that time.

---

[329] Commission Decision 2009/64, OJ 2009 L 23/32, specifies the standards in this regard for microbiological methods.

[330] The symbols to be used for informing the public have been adopted by means of Commission Implementing Decision 2011/321, OJ 2011 L 143/38.

11.6   The Protection of Shellfish Waters and Fresh Water for Fish

There are two directives concerning waters designated by the Member States as needing protection or improvement in order to support shellfish life and growth[331] and freshwater fish life.[332] Both directives codify amendments to earlier directives and follow a nearly identical scheme. The scope of both directives is restricted by the fact that the Member States first have to designate waters as needing protection in order to support freshwater fish life or shellfish life. Concerning the latter, the directive is confined to coastal or brackish waters (Article 1 of Directive 2006/113). By not designating waters, a Member State could easily avoid its obligations. However, in the light of the decisions the Court has given on the basis of the 'old' directives, it would no longer seem possible to uphold such a literal interpretation. In Case 322/86, Italy failed to designate certain waters under the Fresh Water for Fish Directive:[333]

> 'No salmonid or cyprinid waters situated on Italian territory have been designated other than those in the autonomous province of Bolzano. The government has also failed to set, for these waters, specific values for the parameters laid down in Annex 1 of the directive, and to draw up programmes in order to ensure that these parameters conform to the values set. It must therefore be held that by failing to adopt within the prescribed period the measures necessary in order to comply with Council Directive 78/659/EEC of 18 July 1978 the Italian Republic has failed to fulfil its obligations under the EEC Treaty.'

From this it must be concluded that, although the wording of the directives suggests otherwise, the Member States' power to designate waters under the directives is not unlimited.[334] The Court's judgment does not, however, indicate what the limits are. Perhaps a parallel can be drawn with the Court's case law on the designation of special protection areas under the Wild Birds Directive.[335] This would then result in an obligation to designate those waters that support fish life or shellfish life or could support such life once pollution is reduced to such an extent that these fish or shellfish can grow and be of a high quality edible by man. When waters have been designated the Member States must observe values for certain pollutants or parameters (such as temperature, salinity and heavy metals; Article 3 in connection with Annex I). The directives lay down both I values which Member States are required to observe and G values

---

[331] Directive 2006/113, OJ 2006 L 376/14, repealing with effect from 15 January 2007 Directive 79/923, OJ 1979 L 281/47.

[332] Directive 2006/44, OJ 2006 L 264/20, repealing with effect from 14 October 2006 Directive 78/659, OJ 1978 L 222/1.

[333] Case 322/86 *Commission* v. *Italy* [1988] ECR 3995.

[334] See further Case C-148/05 *Commission* v. *Ireland* [2007] ECR I-82, paras. 46-48.

[335] Case C-3/96 *Commission* v. *Netherlands* [1998] ECR I-3031, see further section 17.1 below.

which they must endeavour to observe (Article 3(2)). The Member States then have to set up programmes[336] to ensure that within five years from the designation pollution is reduced so that the fresh waters comply with these values (Article 5). For shellfish waters the Member States have six years (Article 5).

The directives also contain provisions regarding monitoring (Article 6) sampling (Article 7), and a standstill requirement (Article 8). More stringent national measures are allowed on the basis of Article 9 and Article 10 contains rules on cross-border consultation. Furthermore a derogation is possible in the event of exceptional weather or geographical conditions (Article 11). Both directives will be repealed in December 2013.[337]

11.7 The Protection of Drinking Water

The protection of drinking water took place through two directives. Directive 75/440 concerning the quality of surface water intended for the abstraction of drinking water in the Member States contains the quality requirements which surface fresh water used or intended for use in the abstraction of drinking water must meet.[338] Directive 98/83,[339] which covers the area where consumer protection and protection of the environment converge, lays down product standards which have to be met by water intended for human consumption. Directive 75/440 was repealed in December 2007 by the Water Framework Directive.[340] As a result, Article 7 of the Water Framework Directive now constitutes the legal framework for the protection of water intended for abstraction of drinking water.[341]

Directive 98/83 lays down product standards which have to be met by water intended for human consumption.[342] Compared to its predecessor, Directive 98/83 shows signs of the influence of the subsidiarity principle when it focuses on compliance with essential quality and health parameters, leaving Member States free to add other parameters if they see fit. Furthermore, the directive seems to have broadened the scope of derogations. This is probably a late

---

[336] Once again 'specific programmes' are required. General water purification programmes are not sufficient, Case C-298/95 *Commission v. Germany* [1996] ECR I-6747, para. 24.

[337] Article 22(2) of the Water Framework Directive, in connection with Article 16, second paragraph, of the Shellfish Water and Freshwater Fish Directive.

[338] OJ 1974 L 194/34, later amended. An interesting case that deals with several aspects of this directive is Case C-58/89 *Commission v. Germany* [1991] ECR I-4983.

[339] OJ 1998 L 330/32, repealing Directive 80/778, OJ 1980 L 229/11.

[340] Article 22(1) of the Water Framework Directive.

[341] See above section 11.1.

[342] See, concerning the 'old' Directive 80/778, Case C-42/89 *Commission v. Belgium* [1990] ECR I-2821. The directive does not cover water from private wells. The Court held that it follows from Article 2 of the directive that the directive applies only to water supplied for human consumption and to water used in foodstuffs by a food production undertaking, but not to water from private sources, see further Article 3(2)(b) of Directive 98/83.

response by the Council to the Court's judgments in Case 228/87 and Case C-337/89.[343]

11.8   The Urban Waste Water Directive

Directive 91/271 concerns the collection, treatment and discharge of urban waste water and the treatment and discharge of waste water from certain industrial sectors.[344] Article 3 requires Member States to ensure that all agglomerations are provided with collecting systems for waste water, and lays down requirements such a system must meet. The period within which such a system must have been implemented is linked to population equivalents and the existence of 'sensitive areas'.[345] Article 4 sets criteria which the treatment of waste water must meet before it may be discharged into the collecting systems. Here, too, the periods by which implementation must have been fulfilled are linked to population equivalents. Discharges from urban waste water treatment plants must satisfy certain requirements.

Article 5 deals with 'sensitive areas', which must be identified by the Member States according to certain criteria including, *inter alia*, propensity for eutrophication.[346] Discharges of urban waste water into these areas are required to undergo more stringent treatment than other discharges. The same applies to discharges into catchment areas of sensitive areas. Article 5(8), in particular, is important. Member States do not have to identify sensitive areas if they implement the treatment for sensitive areas over all their territory.

Article 9 concerns the problem of discharges with transfrontier effects and provides for notification and consultation in such cases. Member States must ensure that pollution caused by discharges does not exceed the limits laid down in the directive. However, the second paragraph of Annex II B provides that Member States must recognize the presence of sensitive areas outside their national jurisdiction. This could imply that the existence of transfrontier effects might result in stricter standards being applied than if there were only national effects.

Article 11 provides that the discharge of industrial waste water into collecting systems and treatment plants is subject to prior regulations and/or specific authorisations. Article 13 similarly provides that biodegradable industrial waste water from certain industrial sectors which is discharged directly into surface waters is subject to prior regulations and/or specific authorisations. The compe-

---

[343] Case 228/87 *Pretore di Torino* v. *Persons unknown* [1988] ECR 5099; Case C-337/89 *Commission* v. *UK* [1992] ECR I-6103.

[344] OJ 1991 L 135/40, later amended. Cf. on the relation with the Waste Directive also Case C-252/05 *Thames Water* [2007] ECR I-3883 and section 15 of this chapter *infra*.

[345] These will also constitute protected areas under the Water Framework Directive; Cf. Article 4(1)(c) in connection with Annex IV under 1(iv).

[346] Eutrophication is defined in Article 2(11), a concept further explained in, *inter alia*, Case C-390/07 *Commission* v. *United Kingdom* [2009] ECR I-214, paras. 26-39.

tent authority or body must set requirements appropriate to the nature of the industry concerned.

Article 14 is designed to ensure that sludge arising from waste water treatment is re-used wherever possible. The disposal of such sludge must be made subject to general rules or registration or authorisation before 31 December 1998, and the disposal of sludge to surface waters is prohibited as of that date. Until then, Member States must ensure that the total amount of toxic, persistent or bioaccumulable materials is licensed and progressively reduced.

The directive also requires Member States to carry out monitoring (Article 15) and publish reports (Article 16).

11.9   The Nitrates Directive

It is a fact that modern intensive farming methods are a cause of many environmental problems. One of the consequences of applying livestock manure to land is the pollution of water by nitrates. The use of fertilizers containing nitrates is one of the main causes of pollution from diffuse sources affecting Europe's waters. Directive 91/676 aims to reduce water pollution caused or induced by nitrates from agricultural sources.[347]

The Member States are required to have identified the waters which were affected (or could be affected) by nitrate pollution before the end of 1993 (Article 3(1)).[348] The criteria for this are set out in Annex I, which sets the threshold for nitrates at 50 mg/l. According to the Court in the *Standley* case, Member States are not required to determine precisely what proportion of the pollution in the waters is attributable to nitrates of agricultural origin or that the cause of such pollution must be exclusively agricultural.[349] Indeed, in a later case the Court held that a 17% to 19% contribution by Walloon agriculture to nitrogen levels in several basins flowing into the North Sea was 'minor', but by no means insignificant. Any other solution would of course undermine the protection of the North Sea, which is one of the directive's objectives.[350]

Article 3(2) provides that Member States must designate as vulnerable zones all known areas of land in their territories which drain into the waters identified according to paragraph 1.[351] Once these zones have been designated, Member States must establish action programmes consisting of certain mandatory mea-

---

[347] OJ 1991 L 375/1. Cf. on the implementation COM (98) 16 and COM (97) 473.

[348] Case C-258/00 *Commission v. France* [2002] ECR I-5959, paras. 45-54, shows that the Member States cannot restrict the scope of the directive when they consider that other substances than nitrogen trigger eutrophication.

[349] Case C-293/97 *Standley* [1999] ECR I-2603.

[350] Case C-221/03 *Commission v. Belgium* [2005] ECR I-8307, paras. 84-89.

[351] These will also constitute protected areas under the Water Framework Directive, cf. Article 4(1)(c) in connection with Annex IV under 1(iv).

sures (Article 5 in conjunction with Annex III).[352] The limit for the application of livestock manure is, for example, set at 170 kg of nitrate per hectare (Annex III, paragraph 2).[353] There are a number of Commission decisions concerning the possibility of a derogation from this maximum.[354]

Outside the vulnerable zones, the general obligation contained in Article 4 applies. The Member States were supposed to have established a 'code of good agricultural practice', to be implemented by farmers on a voluntary basis, before the end of 1993. The items such a code should cover are contained in Annex II.

The directive provides for a special consultation procedure in the event of transfrontier pollution (Article 3(3)).

The directive does not preclude the Member States from applying the provisions of the directive in cases not covered by it.[355]

11.10   The Titanium Dioxide Directive

The manufacture of titanium dioxide (TiO_2), a whitener used in paints and toothpaste, among other things, is particularly harmful to the environment. It is responsible for producing a large quantity of highly acidic waste. This waste largely ends up in water as a result of dumping or discharge. For this reason the EU has been actively engaged in imposing specific measures on this particular industry since 1978. Moreover, the cost of waste disposal has a significant impact on the price of the product. From the point of view of the internal market, this is an additional reason for European action.

Directive 78/176 sets general targets for the prevention and reduction of waste produced by the TiO_2 industry.[356] Thus the Member States are required in a general sense to take the necessary measures to ensure that waste is disposed of without endangering human health and without harming the environment, and in particular without risk to water, air, soil and plants and animals and without deleteriously affecting beauty spots or the countryside (Article 2). They must also take appropriate measures to encourage the prevention, recycling and processing of waste, the extraction of raw materials and any other process for the reuse of waste (Article 3).

More specific is the obligation to issue authorisations contained in Article 4. The discharge, dumping, storage, tipping and injection of waste must be

---

[352] See, on the limits to national action programmes, Case C-322/00 *Commission v. Netherlands* [2003] ECR I-11267.

[353] See, on the way in which the amount of manure should be calculated, Case C-161/00 *Commission v. Germany* [2002] ECR I-2753, paras. 36-47.

[354] For example, Decision 2002/915, OJ 2002 L 319/24 (*Denmark*) Decision 2005/889, OJ 2005 L 324/89 (*Netherlands*) and Decision 2006/189, OJ 2006 L 66/44 (*Austria*). Many of these decisions are subsequently amended.

[355] Case C-293/97 *Standley* [1999] ECR I-2603.

[356] OJ 1978 L 54/19.

prohibited unless prior authorisation is issued by the competent authority of the Member State in whose territory the waste is produced. Prior authorisation must also be issued by the competent authority of the Member State in whose territory the waste is discharged, stored, tipped or injected or from whose territory it is discharged or dumped. The authorisation may be granted for a limited period only, though it may be renewed.

Articles 5 (discharge or dumping) and 6 (storage, tipping or injection) lay down the conditions under which authorisations may be granted. These are that:
- the waste cannot be disposed of by more appropriate means;
- an assessment carried out in the light of available scientific and technical knowledge shows that there will be no detrimental effect, either immediate or delayed, on underground waters, the soil or the atmosphere;
- there is no deleterious effect on leisure activities, the extraction of raw materials, plants and animals on regions of special scientific importance or on *other legitimate uses of the environment* in question.

New industrial establishments are also subject to authorisation (Article 11). An authorisation must be preceded by an environmental impact survey. The authorisation may be granted only to firms which give an undertaking to use only such of the materials, processes and techniques available on the market as are least damaging to the environment.

The directive contains several monitoring requirements (Article 7), which are further specified in Directive 82/883.[357] If the conditions laid down in the authorisation have not been fulfilled, the Member State concerned must take all appropriate steps to remedy the situation and may, if necessary, require the suspension of the discharge, dumping, etc. Member States are required to supply information and prepare reports (Articles 13 and 14). They are expressly permitted to adopt more stringent national regulations (Article 12).

Articles 9 and 10 concern the drawing up of programmes for the reduction and elimination of pollution. These programmes, which were supposed to have been sent to the Commission before 1 July 1980, were to have formed the basis for further legislation by the Council on the matter. However, it was not until December 1992 that the Council was able to introduce the further harmonisation measures announced in Article 9(3) of the directive, when it introduced Directive 92/112.[358] If it had not been for the Court's judgment in the *TiO2* case[359] annulling Directive 89/428[360] because it had been adopted on an inappropriate legal basis, this could have been done three years earlier. It should be added that Directive 92/112 is virtually identical to the directive that was annulled.

---

[357] OJ 1982 L 378/1.

[358] OJ 1992 L 409/11.

[359] Case C-300/89 *Commission* v. *Council* [1991] ECR I-2867.

[360] OJ 1989 L 201/56.

Under Article 3, the dumping of any solid waste, strong acid waste, treatment waste, weak acid waste, or neutralised waste is prohibited with effect from 15 June 1993. For the purposes of the directive, dumping means any deliberate disposal of substances and materials by or from ships or aircraft. The discharge of solid waste and strong acid waste, in particular, is prohibited from that date (Article 4). Articles 6 and 7 set emission limit values for other discharges of waste, in particular weak acid waste and neutralised waste. As an alternative to these limit values, Member States may choose to make use of quality objectives (coupled with appropriate limit values), if they are applied in such a way that the effects in terms of protecting the environment and avoiding distortions of competition are equivalent to that of the limit values laid down in the directive (Article 8). In that case the Commission must give its consent (Article 8(2) in conjunction with Article 10 of Directive 78/176). The directive also contains provisions requiring Member States to prevent air pollution (Article 9), to monitor each establishment (Article 10), to take preventive measures and to promote the re-use of waste (Article 11). Member States are permitted to take more stringent national measures, though this is noted in the preamble to the directive rather than in an express provision. Finally, this directive will be replaced by the Industrial Emissions Directive from 7 January 2014.[361]

11.11   Protection of the Marine Environment

The protection of the marine environment takes place through three sets of rules. Firstly, there are the rules on the prevention of accidents at sea and the remedying of the consequences of such accidents. Secondly, there is the EU's own Thematic Marine Strategy, that will function in a setting formed by international treaties.[362] Thirdly, part of the EU's fisheries policy also pertains to protecting the marine environment.[363]

Concerning the first limb, international policy in respect of the prevention of accidents at sea and the environmental problems connected with them are embodied above all in IMO Resolutions and the SOLAS and MARPOL Conventions.[364] The first European rules are to be found in Directive 79/116 concerning minimum requirements for certain tankers entering or leaving EU ports.[365] However, this directive is replaced by Directive 2002/59 concerning minimum requirements for vessels bound for or leaving EU ports and carrying dangerous or polluted goods.[366] Furthermore, Directive 95/21 contains rules on port state control concerning vessels and the protection of, *inter alia*, pollution

---

[361] Directive 2010/75, OJ 2010 L 334/17, Article 81(1).

[362] See above, section 4.

[363] This will not be dealt with here, see for information on this topic: Wolff (2002).

[364] At EU level the Commission's policy is set out in COM (93) 66 final.

[365] OJ 1979 L 33/33. This directive was repealed by Directive 93/73.

[366] OJ 2002 L 208/10, repealing Directive 93/75, OJ 1993 L 247/19.

prevention.[367] Pursuant to Regulation 1406/2002 the European Maritime Safety Agency has been established.[368] This Agency is (co-)responsible for monitoring many of the maritime safety rules. Following the Erika tanker disaster it has also been given powers in the field of pollution control.[369] Finally in this context it is worth mentioning Council Decision 2007/162 setting up a Civil Protection Financial Instrument that will cover, among others, cooperation in the fields of accidental marine pollution.[370] Concerning deliberate pollution from ships, Directive 2005/35[371] and Framework Decision 2005/667[372] make it an infringement to discharge a polluting substance from a ship in the internal waters, territorial waters, international straits or the exclusive economic zone if this discharge is committed intentionally, recklessly or by serious negligence (Article 4 in connection with Article 3(1) of Directive 2005/35). Moreover, such discharges are considered criminal offences if the conditions of Framework Decision 2005/667 are fulfilled.[373]

The EU's Thematic Strategy on the Protection and Conservation of the Marine Environment is the result of the Sixth Environmental Action Programme[374] and envisages a further integration of the above mentioned marine protection initiatives.[375] Moreover, the Marine Strategy Framework Directive has adopted.[376] This directive essentially applies the methodology of the Water Framework Directive to the protection of the marine environment. This too is protected in a fragmented way and in need of an integrated protection instrument. As a result, the proposal envisages the designation of marine regions as sub-regions and the development of marine strategies that will have to be coordinated if a marine (sub)region is shared by more than one Member State. The marine strategies will have to include measures necessary to attain good environmental status. In the meantime a Directive on the criteria and methodology for determining good environmental status has been adopted.[377]

---

[367] OJ 1995 L 175/1, amended by Directive 2002/84, OJ 2002 L 324/53.

[368] OJ 2002 L 208/1.

[369] Regulation 724/2004, OJ 2004 L 129/1.

[370] OJ 2007 L 71/9. This instrument takes over following the expiry of Decision 2850/2000 setting up a Community framework for cooperation in the field of accidental or deliberate marine pollution, OJ 2000 L 332/1.

[371] OJ 2005 L 255/11.

[372] OJ 2005 L 255/164; see Case C-440/05 Commission v. Council [2007] ECR I-9097, where the Commission contends that the measure should have been adopted pursuant to the EC transport provisions.

[373] For an overview and a critical discussion see: Pereira (2008).

[374] See above, section 1 of this chapter.

[375] COM (2005) 504 final. This is to take place through an integrated maritime policy, see, inter alia, Council Conclusions of the 2973rd General Affairs Council meeting, Brussels, 16 November 2009, available from: http://www.consilium.europa.eu/uedocs/cms_Data/docs/pressdata/en/gena/111184.pdf (last visited 7 October 2011).

[376] Directive 2008/56, OJ 2008 L 164/19.

[377] Directive 2010/477, OJ 2010 L 232/14.

12 Legislation on Air Pollution

European legislation concerning air pollution can be divided into instruments regarding sources of such pollution and air quality standards. A further distinction would be the on the basis of the various layers of the atmosphere, with the EU's efforts to protect the ozone layer in the stratosphere falling in a different category than all other measures that are concerned with the (lower) troposphere. Within the legislation concerning sources of pollution another distinction would be between stationary and mobile sources.

This legislation was adopted partly to fulfil the European obligations resulting from international treaties concluded by it, for example the 1979 Geneva Convention on Long-range Transboundary Air Pollution and the Protocols of Geneva (1984: monitoring and evaluation), Helsinki (1985: sulphur compounds), Sofia (1988: oxides of nitrogen),[378] and Gothenburg (1999: Acidification, Eutrophication and Ground-Level Ozone),[379] the 1985 Vienna Convention for the Protection of the Ozone Layer, MARPOL 73/78[380] and the 1987 Montreal Protocol on Substances which Deplete the Ozone Layer.[381]

12.1 Ambient Air Quality Directives

In the 1980s the Council adopted three directives laying down minimum air quality standards for various substances.[382] In 1992 the Council adopted a further Directive on ozone in ambient air.[383] These directives have lost much of their significance since the entry into force of Framework Directive 96/62 on ambient air quality assessment and management.[384] This directive has now been replaced with effect from 11 June 2010 by Directive 2008/50/EC on ambient air quality and cleaner air for Europe.[385]

The general aim of the Framework Directive is to (Article 1):
· define and establish objectives for ambient air quality designed to avoid, prevent or reduce harmful effects on human health and the environment as a whole;
· assess the ambient air quality in Member States on the basis of common methods and criteria;
· obtain information on ambient air quality in order to help combat air pollution and nuisance and to monitor long-term trends and improve-

---

[378] OJ 1981 L 171/13; OJ 1986 L 181/2; OJ 1993 L 149/16.

[379] Decision 2003/507, OJ 2003 L 179/1.

[380] Annex VI of the MARPOL convention addresses air pollution from ships.

[381] OJ 1988 L 297/10 and OJ 1988 L 297/21.

[382] Directive 80/779 (sulphur dioxide), OJ 1980 L 229/30, Directive 82/884 (lead), OJ 1982 L 378/15 and Directive 85/203 (nitrogen oxide), OJ 1985 L 87/1.

[383] Directive 92/72, OJ 1992 L 297/1.

[384] OJ 1996 L 296/55. Cf. Lefevere (1997).

[385] OJ 2008 L 152/1.

ments resulting from national and EU measures;
· ensuring that such information on ambient air quality is made available
to the public;
· maintain ambient air quality where it is good and improve it in other
cases, and
· promoting increased cooperation between the Member States in reducing
air pollution.

Whereas the predecessor of this directive did not contain any emissions limit
values, and could thus be characterised as a true framework directive, the
current directive does contain limit values and target values (Chapter III in
connection with the various annexes). This is a result of the integration of the
so-called 'daughter directives'[386] in the current directive.[387] The integration
of the daughter directives has not resulted in significant changes to the limit
values contained therein, with the regulation of very fine particulate matter
(often referred to as PM2.5) as a notable exception.

The structure of the directive consists of six chapters, with the first containing general objectives and definitions of terms. Chapter II contains the provisions on the assessment regime for sulphur dioxide, nitrogen dioxide and oxides
of nitrogen, particulate matter, lead, benzene and carbon monoxide. These
provisions are essentially copied from the various old daughter directives. Chapter III, on ambient air quality management contains the rules on the actual air
quality. It starts with the standstill obligation in Article 12 according to which
air quality must be maintained below the limit levels in those areas where air
quality standards comply with the limit values laid down in the directive. In
this regard we may note that reductions of air quality are allowed insofar as the
limit values are not exceeded. This means that the standstill obligation is not
complete, but in fact allows for measures resulting in poorer air quality up to the
limit values.

The directive distinguishes between alert values, limit values and critical
levels, whereby the latter relates to the effects of air pollution on trees, plants
and other ecosystems, but not on humans (Article 2(6)). For effects on human
health the alert values and limit values are relevant. Article 13 in connection
with Annex XI contains the limit values that are not to be exceeded for sulphur
dioxide, PM10, lead, carbon monoxide, nitrogen dioxide and benzene. For Ozone
and PM2.5 there is a similar regime, with the exception that attainment of the

---

[386] These are: Directive 1999/30 relating to limit values for sulphur dioxide, nitrogen dioxide and oxides
of nitrogen, particulate matter and lead in ambient air, OJ 1999 L 163/41; Directive 2000/69 relating
to limit values for benzene and carbon monoxide in ambient air, OJ 2000 L 313/12; Directive 2002/3
relating to ozone in ambient air, OJ 2002 L 67/14 and Directive 2004/107 relating to arsenic, cadmium,
mercury, nickel and polycyclic aromatic hydrocarbons in ambient air, OJ 2004 L 23/3.

[387] Cf. recital 3 of the preamble. Directive 2004/107 on arsenic, cadmium, mercury, nickel and polycyclic
aromatic hydrocarbons in ambient air has not been repealed, cf. recital 4 of the preamble to Directive
2008/50.

target values laid down for these substances must only be attained insofar as the measures do not entail any disproportionate costs (Article 16(1) and 17(1)). This proportionality test is absent for the other pollutants.

Concerning PM2.5 we have already noted the innovation consisting of the fact that this substance is now regulated at the EU level. We see, however, that this regulation does leave the Member States a considerable amount of leeway, for example as a result of the fact that the limit value only applies from 1 January 2015 (Article 16(2) in connection with Annex XIV, part E). Until that date there is only a target value, which entails an obligation to take all necessary measures not entailing disproportionate costs (Article 16(1) in connection with Annex XIV, part D).[388] One particularly disconcerting observation regarding PM2.5 is the fact that as yet no safe threshold has been identified, below which PM2.5 would no longer be dangerous to human health (recital 11 of the preamble). As a result of this, the target and limit value have been supplemented with an obligation for the Member States to take all measures not entailing disproportionate costs to reduce exposure to PM2.5 (Article 15 in connection with Annex XIV).[389]

The regime for ozone in ambient air is similar to that for PM2.5, with target values and long-term objectives (Article 17). It may be noted that there is a similarly qualified standstill obligation that allows increased ozone concentrations up to the long-term objective (Article 18).

Serious exceedances of the limit values may qualify as exceedances of the alert or information thresholds. In case of ozone, the information threshold will first be exceeded, resulting in a duty to inform the public. This information threshold as the level at which particularly sensitive sections of the population would be at risk from brief exposure (Article 2(11) in connection with 19 and Annex XII, part B). The next threshold is the alert threshold, where there is a risk for the population as a whole (Article 2(10)). For sulphur dioxide and nitrogen dioxide and ozone, where no information threshold has been defined, the exact thresholds may be found in Annex XII.

Another innovation providing more leeway to the Member States is the provision on contribution from natural sources (Article 20). This allows a Member State to claim that exceedances are attributable to natural sources. Following a notification of the Commission, such exceedances will not be considered exceedances within the meaning of the directive. This means that such exceedances will not trigger any information duties, despite the fact that air quality may well be below the prescribed levels. Moreover, it may be noted that the Commission does not have to approve or accept the notification by the Member State in order for the exceedances to fall outside the scope of the directive. Similar leeway is provided for the exceedances of the limit values for PM10 as a result of winter-sanding or salting of roads (Article 21). Finally, Article 21 provides for

---

[388] In addition, a margin of tolerance applies, cf. Annex XIV, part E.

[389] Article 32 explicitly includes the regime for PM2.5 in the Commission's review, with a view to possibly establishing binding exposure reduction obligations on the part of the Member States as well as a more ambitious limit value.

a possibility to postpone the deadlines attached to reaching certain limit values or to be exempted from applying certain limit values. Here we need to distinguish between nitrogen dioxide and benzene on the one hand and PM10 on the other. For the former, the deadlines mat extended for a maximum of five years, provided that an air quality plan is established. Concerning the latter, there is a possibility to exempted from the limit values, where these cannot be attained as a result of site-specific dispersion characteristic, adverse climatic conditions or transboundary contributions.[390] Again, an air quality plan must be drawn up and the Member State must show that all appropriate measures have been taken, at all levels of government. As far as the procedural side of things is concerned, the Member States involved are required to inform the Commission, which then has nine months to raise objections as part of which it may require the Member State to adjust the air quality plans it has submitted. It may be noted that this provision shows some similarity to that applicable to the approval of national allocation plans as part of the initial Emissions Trading Directive, probably resulting in a similar legal character of the Commission decision in this regard.[391]

Exceedances of target values or limit values, including the margin for tolerance trigger a duty to establish an air quality plan (Article 23(1)). Such plans shall contain the appropriate measures to attain the relevant values. Where the attainment deadline for a certain limit value has already passed the plans shall contain the appropriate measures limit the duration of the exceedance. In case there is a risk that alert thresholds are exceeded, a slightly more stringent duty to establish action plans is triggered.[392] Such action plans must contain the measures to be taken in the short term in order to reduce the risk or duration of the exceedance.[393] All the information on air quality must be made available to the public and the Commission pursuant to Articles 26 and 27. Finally, the directive contains provisions on implementing measures, the committee assisting the Commission and repeals and transitional provisions.

There are considerable differences concerning the application of these rules in the various Member States.[394] One of the solutions to the difficulty that certain Member States face in reaching the air quality objectives is the so-called balancing of slight reductions in air quality in one area where the air quality is

---

[390] This is particularly relevant for the, *inter alia*, The Netherlands, where it has been shown that particulate matter from British coal fired power plants ends up as particulate matter in The Netherlands, see: http://www.snm.nl/pdf/rapporttnonatuurenmilieuukcentrales.pdf (last visited 7 October 2011). It may be noted that this results in a duty to cooperate between the Dutch and British authorities on the basis of Article 25 of the directive.

[391] See below section 13.1.

[392] The predecessor of this provision, Article 7 of Directive 96/62, was found to be directly effective in Case C-237/07 *Janecek* [2008] ECR I-6221, paras. 34-47.

[393] For ozone, however, there is an exception, cf. the second paragraph of Article 24(1).

[394] Cf. Backes et al. (2005).

good with improvements of air quality in other areas with poor air quality. The standstill provisions in Articles 12 and 18 of the directive allows such a balancing method, provided that the limit values are not exceeded as a result of the reduction in air quality.

12.2   Directives on Emissions into the Air

As was mentioned above, part of European law on air pollution deals with the sources of air pollution. Here we find Directive 2001/81 on national emission ceilings (the National Emissions Ceilings Directive) that was adopted in part to implement the Gothenburg Protocol to the UNECE Convention on long-range transboundary air pollution.[395] Furthermore, there are directives covering emissions from various sources. With regard to the latter a distinction can be made between emissions from industrial plants (e.g. energy generation, waste incineration) and emissions from mobile sources (cars, boats, aircraft).

Overarching emissions ceilings can be found in the National Emissions Ceilings Directive. The objective this directive is to limit emissions of acidifying and eutrophying pollutants and ozone precursors in order to protect human health and the environment in the EU (Article 1). The directive covers all emissions resulting from human activity from the territory of the Member States and their exclusive economic zones irrespective of the source. There are, however, exceptions for international maritime traffic and aircraft emissions beyond the landing and take-off cycle (Article 2(a) and (b)). The landing and take-off cycle is defined in Article 3(g) as a 32,9 minute period in which the aircraft approaches, lands, taxies, takes-off and climbs. The preamble to the directive is quite clear when it states that the WHO guideline values are substantially exceeded in all Member States (recital 5), so that complete protection of the environment and human health are not possible at this time for reasons of technical and economic feasibility. As a result the directive contains in Article 5 the following interim objectives to be attained in 2010:

- for acidification the areas where the critical load is exceeded shall be reduced by 50% compared to the 1990 situation;
- for ozone the load above the critical level for human health shall be reduced by two-thirds compared to the 1990 situation;
- for ozone the load above the critical level for crops shall be reduced by one-third compared to the 1990 situation;
- for ozone there are absolute limits for human health and crops.

This interim objective is to be attained through the national emissions ceilings for sulphur dioxide, nitrogen oxides, volatile organic compounds and ammonia

---

[395] OJ 2001 L 309/22.

to be found in Annex I (Article 4).[396] Interestingly, Article 5 contains no interim objective for eutrophication, as would be expected on the basis of Article 1. The footnote to Annex I shows that the emissions ceilings are expected to result that is subject to nitrogen deposits in excess of the critical load will be reduced by 'about 30%' compared to 1990. The Member States must draw up national emission reduction programmes (Article 6) and make an inventory of the emissions taking place on their territory (Article 7).[397] These programmes and the inventories must be reported to the Commission and the European Environment Agency (Article 8). This will in turn lead to a Commission report (Article 9). This report may also contain a reconsideration of the scope of the directive (relating to the exclusion of international maritime traffic and flying aircraft) and the possibility of further reductions. Member States may prescribe more stringent national emissions ceilings (Article 4(1)) and Article 4(2) contains a standstill provision. Indeed, the Member States will have to go beyond their emissions ceilings prescribed in Annex I if they want to reach the environmental objectives in Article 5. Annex II contains the EU's 15 emissions ceiling designed to attain the interim objectives and these ceilings are consistently lower than the sum of the 15 Member States' national emissions ceilings in Annex I.

The national emissions ceilings are to be attained through reductions of the emissions of various sources. Rules on emissions from industrial plants and can be found in the following directives:

- Directive 2001/80 on the limitation of emissions of certain pollutants into the air from large combustion plants;[398]
- Directive 2000/76 on the incineration of waste;[399]
- Directive 2008/1 on integrated pollution prevention and control (IPPC);[400]
- Directive 2010/75 on Emissions from industrial installations.[401]

---

[396] The Court has characterised this provision as 'purely programmatic', thus effectively sidelining the emissions ceilings as a relevant factor to be taken into account in the permitting process, Joined Cases C-165/09 to C-167/09 *Stichting Natuur en Milieu and Others v College van Gedeputeerde Staten van Groningen and College van Gedeputeerde Staten van Zuid-Holland*, Judgment of 26 May 2011, para. 75.

[397] These obligations were also characterised as programmatic, excluding any particular measure, Joined Cases C-165/09 to C-167/09 *Stichting Natuur en Milieu and Others v College van Gedeputeerde Staten van Groningen and College van Gedeputeerde Staten van Zuid-Holland*, Judgment of 26 May 2011, para. 87.

[398] OJ 2001 L 309/1, This directive repeals Directive 88/609, OJ 1988 L 336/1.

[399] OJ 1994 L 365/34.

[400] This directive will not be dealt with here, see section 5 above.

[401] See section 6 above. Note that this directive will replace Directive 2001/80, the Large Combustion Plants Directive from 7 January 2016 onwards. It will replace Directive 2008/1, on integrated pollution prevention and control and Directive 2000/76 on waste incineration from 7 January 2014 onwards.

The Large Combustion Plants Directive 2001/80[402] repeals Directive 88/609[403] and applies to all combustion plants intended for the production of energy having a rated thermal input of 50 MW or more irrespective of the type of fuel used.[404] However, waste and hazardous waste are excluded from the concept of fuel, because there is a separate directive for the incineration of waste (Article 2(6), see below). At the heart of the directive are emission limit values for sulphur dioxide, oxides of nitrogen and dust. These must be included in all licenses for the construction or operation of plants (Article 4 in connection with Annex III to VII) or extensions to existing plants (Article 10). Member States may set more stringent emission limit values than those set out in the directive, or for other pollutants (Article 4(5)). Article 5 contains a derogation from the emission limit value for sulphur dioxide subject to conditions. Compared to the 'old' directive, the Large Combustion Plants Directive is more stringent because such plants will have to be phased out.[405] Furthermore, the directive contains detailed rules on abnormal operating conditions, such as a breakdown of the abatement equipment (Article 7(1)) or problems with the supply of the environmentally friendly fuels (Article 7(2) and (3)). The directive requires Member States to draw up programmes for the reduction of emissions (Article 3), ensure monitoring (Articles 12, 13 and 14) and provides for cross-border information and consultation in accordance with the Environmental Impact Assessment Directive (Article 11). The CCS Directive has amended the Large Combustion Plants Directive in that the feasibility of carbon capture and storage must be investigated and space must be set aside for the capture installation should the assessment be positive.[406] The Large Combustion Plants Directive will be replaced by the Industrial Emissions Directive from 7 January 2016 onwards.

The Waste Incineration Directive 2000/76 repeals the 'old' Municipal Waste Incinerators Directives[407] and the Hazardous Waste Incineration Plants Directive[408] with effect from 28 December 2005 (Article 18).[409] According to recital 15 of the preamble, Directive 2000/76 is more stringent than its predecessors. The

---

[402] OJ 2001 L 309/1, as most recently amended by Directive 2009/31, OJ 2009 L 140/114.

[403] OJ 1988 L 336/1, as last amended by Directive 94/66, OJ 1994 L 337/83. The repeal is with effect from 27 november 2002 and includes transitional rules for plants licensed before 27 November 2002 (Article 17).

[404] Note that the Court has endorsed a strict interpretation of Article 2(7) of the directive, which entails an exception to the scope of the directive for combustion processes where the combustion products are directly used in the production process. This concerned a combustion plant that produced electricity that was used in an aluminium production process, Case C-346/08 *Commission* v. *United Kingdom* [2010] ECR I-3491 *(Lynemouth)*, paras. 33-53.

[405] Article 5(1), second indent requires these plants to be used less after 1 January 2016, cf. Article 5(1) of Directive 88/609.

[406] Article 9a, as introduced by Article 33 of Directive 2009/31, OJ 2009 L 140/114.

[407] Directive 89/369, OJ 1989 L 163/32 and Directive 89/429, OJ 1989 L 203/50.

[408] Directive 94/67, OJ 1994 L 365/34.

[409] Article 20 contains transitional provisions.

directive covers incineration as well as co-incineration plants (Article 2(1)),[410] subject to exceptions for plants treating vegetable waste, radioactive waste, animal carcasses and off-shore oil exploration residues that are incinerated on board (Article 2(2)). An incineration plant is one that is dedicated to the thermal treatment of waste (Article 3(4)), whereas a co-incineration plant is one the main purpose of which is the generation of energy and which uses waste as a fuel or in which waste is thermally treated for the purpose of disposal (Article 3(5)).[411] This is particularly relevant with regard to waste gasification, where waste is gassified and the resulting gases are incinerated in a connected installation. This leads to the interesting question to what extent the gasses resulting from the gasification are still waste, and thus to what extent the installation is to be classified as a (co-)incineration plant or even a large combustion plant. Needless to say, the rules applying to the former are more stringent than those applying to the combustion plants and effectively rule out the use of such plants to generate electricity. The exact demarcation between incineration, co-incineration and combustion within the meaning of the large combustion plants directive has been clarified in the two *Lahti Energia* cases.[412] Here the Court held that a plant that subjects waste to a thermal treatment in order to produce a gas that can be used – after cleaning – as fuel classifies as a co-incineration plant.[413] The power plant that then uses the gas as a fuel does not fall within the scope of the Waste Incineration Directive because gaseous substances are excluded from the concept of waste.[414] Such power plants may well classify as large combustion plants. When, however, the gas emanating from the gasification plant is not cleaned and suitable as a fuel, the combined gasification and power plant must be classified jointly as a co-incineration plant.[415]

Incineration plants may only operate with a permit (Article 4(1) and should contain rules on the emissions limit values, the measurement techniques required to monitor the observance of these values and the types of waste that may be treated. Article 4(9) obliges the competent authority to take action to enforce compliance with the permit conditions. The exact rules to which

---

[410] The meaning of the word 'plant' was clarified in Case C-251/07 *Gävle Kraftvärme* [2008] ECR I-7047, para. 21-33 as meaning that every seperate boiler and associated equipment must be individually classified as a plant within the meaning of the directive.

[411] The Court has classified the main purpose of the plant as the sole criterion for distinguishing between incineration and co-incineration, Case C-251/07 *Gävle Kraftvärme* [2008] ECR I-7047, para. 40-43. This purpose is then to be identified by of an assessment that takes into account, in particular, of the volume of energy generated or material products produced by the plant in question in relation to the quantity of waste incinerated in that plant and the stability and continuity of that production (para. 46).

[412] Case C-317/07 *Lahti Energia I* [2008] ECR I-905 and Case C-209/09 *Lahti Energia II*, Judgment of 25 February 2010.

[413] Case C-317/07 *Lahti Energia I* [2008] ECR I-905, paras. 29-37.

[414] Case C-317/07 *Lahti Energia I* [2008] ECR I-905, paras. 38-42.

[415] Case C-209/09 *Lahti Energia II*, Judgment of 25 February 2010, paras. 17-31.

the plants are subject depend on whether or not they will be treating hazardous waste (Article 3(2)). The rules on, for example, the delivery and reception
of waste (Article 5) are stringent for hazardous waste (Article 5(4)), as are the
operating conditions (Article 6). This relates to higher temperatures required
for the incineration of hazardous wastes (1100°C instead of 850°C) and a higher
frequency for measurements (Article 11(7)).

Central to the directive is the obligation to operate the plant in such a way
that the emission limit values in Annex V are not exceeded (Article 7(1)). For
co-incineration plants the values in Annex II apply, unless more than 40% of the
heat release comes from hazardous waste. These values are equally stringent,
but take into account that in co-incineration only a fraction of the fuel is made
up of waste. Article 8 concerns the discharges of water used for cleaning exhaust
gases, and tries to prevent a shift from atmospheric pollution to water pollution
by requiring that such emissions must at least comply with the values in Annex
IV. There are also rules on the residues resulting from the incineration (Article
8). Article 12 contains special rules on access to information and public participation. Article 13 contains rules on abnormal operating conditions.

Another source of emissions into the atmosphere are motor vehicles, aircraft
and maritime traffic. It may be recalled that emissions from maritime traffic and aircraft, other than during the take-off and landing cycle, are excluded
from the Emissions Ceiling Directive. The first European measures to limit
and prevent air pollution by emissions from motor vehicles date from as early
as 1970. Directive 70/220[416] has been amended and updated many times since
then, both in the light of the technical advances in the manufacture of motor
vehicles and of new insights into environmental protection. The directive
provides that no Member State may refuse type-approval to vehicles whose emissions meet the standards laid down in the annexes to the directive. There are
similar directives for diesel engines and engines using liquefied natural gas[417] as
well as heavy duty vehicles like lorries.[418]

These directives will be replaced by Regulation 715/2007 on 1 January
2013.[419] This regulation contains the rules for the harmonised introduction of
the Euro 5 and Euro 6 emissions standards. In an effort to influence consumer
decisions involved in purchasing cars the Council and the EP adopted Directive 99/94 relating to the availability of consumer information on fuel economy
and CO2 emissions in respect of the marketing of new passenger cars.[420] The
sulphur content of certain liquid fuels was regulated in Directive 75/716, which
was replaced on 1 October 1994 by Directive 93/12. From that date Member

---

[416] OJ 1970 L 76/1, amended many times since then.

[417] Directives 72/306, OJ 1972 L 190/1, as amended by Directive 2005/21, OJ 2005 L 61/25 and Directive
2005/55, OJ 2005 L 275/1.

[418] Regulation 595/2009 OJ 2009 L 188/1. This regulation concerns the introduction of the Euro VI-emis-
sions norm.

[419] OJ 2007 L 171/1, as amended by Regulation 595/2009 OJ 2009 L 188/1.

[420] OJ 2000 L 12/16, as amended by Directive 2003/73, OJ 2003 L 186/34.

States were required to prohibit the marketing of diesel fuels in the EU if their sulphur compound content exceeded 0.2% by weight. Directive 93/12 has been amended a number of times and was ultimately replaced with Directive 2009/30.[421] This directive contains rules on the specifications various fuels have to meet so that they can be marketed throughout the European Union.[422]

Finally, the Paints Directive merits mentioning here.[423] This directive intends to limit emissions of volatile organic compounds from paints and varnishes. These volatile organic compounds pose an environmental problem *inter alia* because they increase the formation of ozone in ambient air.[424] The directive contains limit values for volatile organic compounds and requires the Member States to ensure that only paints that meet the limit values are placed on the market (Article 3). This is combined with a free movement clause for all paints that comply with the limit values (Article 8). The directive allows for the marketing of limited quantities of non-compliant paints for restoration purposes (Article 3(3)).

12.3   Protection of the Ozone Layer

Europe's involvement in protecting the ozone layer dates from 1978. In that year the Council adopted a resolution on fluorocarbons in the environment, urging that all appropriate measures should be taken to ensure that the European industry did not increase its production capacity in respect of chlorofluorocarbons.[425]

However, it was not until 1980 that legally binding measures were taken. In Council Decision 80/372 concerning chlorofluorocarbons in the environment,[426] the Member States were required to take all appropriate measures to ensure that industry situated in their territories did not increase its production capacity of certain chlorofluorocarbons.

The current law in respect of the protection of the ozone layer is laid down in Regulation 1005/2009, that recasts the various amendments to the previ-

---

[421] OJ 2009 L 140/88, Cf. recital 43 of the preamble to Directive 2009/30.

[422] This directive also entails a maximum limit on the concentration of MMT in automotive fuels as well as a labelling requirement intended to protect consumers and human health. In Case C-343/09 *Afton Chemical*, Judgment of 8 July 2010, the Court found that there was nothing affecting the validity of these rules.

[423] Directive 2004/42, OJ 2004 L 143/87. This directive replaces Directive 1999/13 on the reduction of emissions of volatile organic compounds (VOCs), OJ 1999 L 85/1.

[424] This is referred to a tropospheric ozone, which is covered by the Air Quality Directive, see section 12.1 above. VOC emissions are also subject to the National Emission Ceilings Directive, see section 12.2 above.

[425] OJ 1978 C 133/1.

[426] OJ 1980 L 90/45.

ous Regulations.[427] The current en preceding regulations were adopted in order to fulfil the obligations under the Vienna Convention for the Protection of the Ozone Layer and the Montreal Protocol on Substances that Deplete the Ozone Layer[428] and under the second amendment of the Montreal Protocol of 25 November 1992 on Substances that Deplete the ozone layer,[429] to which instruments the Member States and the EU are parties. Regulation 1005/2009 is more stringent than its predecessor, Regulation 2037/2000, and the Montreal Protocol. This is reflected in, *inter alia*, the complete cessation of production and consumption of methyl bromide, subject to derogations for critical uses, as well as the ban on using ozone depleting substances in the maintenance and servicing of equipment.

The subject matter and scope of the regulation are determined by Articles 1 and 2. The scope of the regulation is confined to ozone depleting substances that are referred to as controlled substances (Article 2 in connection with 3(4) and annex I). A special category of ozone depleting substances is referred to as new substances (Article 3(10) in connection with Annex II), these are subject to the requirements laid down in Chapter VI of the regulation. Production and marketing of controlled substances are prohibited (Articles 4 and 5), but products containing controlled substances may be put on the market provided that the use of the controlled substance is authorised (Article 6).

This seemingly simply scheme is complicated by Articles 7-13, which contain exemptions and exceptions. Under Article 7 marketing of controlled substances as feedstock, where the controlled substances will be chemically altered (Article 3(11)), is authorised. Article 8 contains a similar scheme for the placing on the market of controlled substances as process agents. This scheme is stricter in that there is a maximum amount of controlled substances that may be used and emitted in the EU every year (Article 8(4)). To this end the Commission has issued a decision containing quota for the specifically named companies that are allowed to use controlled substances in this way.[430] Article 9 allows placing on the market for destruction. Article 10-13 contain special rules for specific types of controlled substances. Article 10 contains an exception for the essential use for laboratory purposes[431] of controlled substances other than HFCs.[432] Article 11 allows for the production, marketing and use of products and equipment using HFCs as part of the complete phasing out of this production by 31 December

---

[427] OJ 2009 L 286/1. This regulation entered into force on 20 November 2009, replacing Regulation 2037/2000, OJ 2000 L 244/1, as amended by Regulation 1791/2006, OJ 2006 L 363/1.

[428] Decision 88/540, OJ 1988 L 297/8, which was amended on 29 June 1990; see Council Decision 91/690, OJ 1991 L 377/28; see Council Decision 94/68 of 2 December 1993, OJ 1994 L 33/1.

[429] Decision 94/68, OJ 1994 L 33/1.

[430] Commission Decision 2010/372, OJ 2010 L 169/17. This decision was adopted on the basis of Article 8(4) of the regulation.

[431] Such essential use is defined in Commission Regulation 291/2011, OJ 2011 L 79/4.

[432] The quota in this regard are allocated by means of Commission decisions on the basis of Article 10(6). See, most recently, Commission Regulation 537/2011, OJ 2011 L 147/4.

2019 (Article 11(1)(d)), unless this production is for laboratory purposes. Whilst exemptions from the timetable for phasing out are possible, such exemptions may not extend beyond 31 December 2018 (Article 11(8)). Article 12 authorised the use of methyl bromide on an exceptional basis until 18 March 2010, however emergency use is still possible after that date (Article 12(3)). Finally, Article 13 allows for the continued critical use of halons.[433] Article 14 allows for the transfer of the usage rights between these companies.[434]

Under the regulation, the release for free circulation in the EU of controlled substances and the export are subject to a licence, issued by the Commission (Article 18).[435] All trade in controlled substances with a state which is not party to the Protocol of Montreal is prohibited (Article 20). Moreover, Article 16 establishes a quota scheme for the release within the EU for free circulation of controlled substances.[436] Despite this being a highly restrictive scheme, it is most probably compatible with EU law in the light of the Court's judgment in the *Betatti* case.[437] The restrictive nature of the scheme can also be seen in the provisions on emissions monitoring, reporting and inspections. These very clearly put the Commission in the central position. The most interesting provisions are those on inspection (Article 28). When the Commission requests information from an undertaking, it must at the same time forward a copy of the request to the competent authority of the Member State within whose territory the undertaking's head office is situated (Article 28(3)). Article 28(1) provides that the competent authorities must carry out the investigations the Commission considers necessary. This indicates that the Member States have little or no discretion in the matter. Though this article does not actually confer formal powers of investigation on the Commission within the territory of the Member States, it goes a long way towards it, as Article 28(2) provides that, subject to the agreement of the competent authority of the Member State within whose territory the investigations are to be made, the officials of the Commission shall assist the officials of that authority in the performance of their duties. This situation is remarkably similar to that concerning the enforcement of Articles 101 and 102 TFEU, where the Commission enjoys far-going powers of inspection.[438]

---

[433] The critical use is defined in Commission Regulation 744/2010, OJ 2010 L 218/2, see on this critical use Case C-376/09 *Commission v. Malta*, Judgment of 19 May 2011, paras. 28-37.

[434] This is also allowed within the context of the use of controlled substances as process agents: Commission decision 2010/372, OJ 2010 L 169/17, Article 3.

[435] See, on the predecessor of this provision: Case T-336/94 *Efisol* [1996] ECR II-1343.

[436] See Commission Decision 2011/185, OJ 2011 L 79/18.

[437] Case C-341/95 *Gianni Bettati* [1998] ECR I-4355. See further Case T-216/05 *Mebrom* [2007] ECR II-1507, unsuccessfully appealed in Case C-373/07 P *Mebrom v. Commission* [2009] ECR I-54, para. 86, where the General Court finds that the Commission's quota system does not distort competition.

[438] Cf. the rules on inspection laid down in Chapter V of Regulation 1/2003, OJ 2003 L1/1.

13   Legislation on Climate Change

The EU is a member to the Kyoto Protocol to the UNFCCC, as are the Member States.[439] This means that the EU as well as the Member States have to reduce emissions of greenhouse gases as agreed in the Kyoto Protocol. For the fifteen old Member States this has resulted in the so-called burden sharing, according to which they have to contribute to a European-wide emissions reduction target of 8%.[440] As the Kyoto Protocol already envisages flexible instruments that will allow a Member State to achieve its emissions reduction in another Member State, a similar trading scheme has also been implemented in the EU.[441] In addition to legislation dealing directly with emissions reductions, the EU has also adopted legislation on energy efficiency as part of its package to meet the 'Kyoto challenge'. This is often referred to as the energy and climate package.[442] This package is designed around the 20, 20 by 2020 target as well as the desire to ensure sustainable security of energy supply.[443] In practical terms it means that the EU has set itself a 20% greenhouse gas abatement target, a 20% renewable energy target and a 20% energy efficiency target. Below these three pillars of the EU climate change policy will be examined in greater detail.

13.1   Implementing the Kyoto Protocol in the EU

Decision 2002/358 approves the Kyoto Protocol and contains the so-called burden sharing agreement. The respective emissions limit values for the EU and its Member States are laid down in Commission Decision 2006/944.[444] The data necessary to come to these emissions levels were gathered by national monitoring mechanisms set up pursuant to the Monitoring Mechanism Decision.[445]

The Monitoring Mechanism Decision repeals Decision 93/389[446] and establishes a fourfold framework. Firstly for monitoring anthropogenic greenhouse gas emissions. Secondly for evaluating the progress made by the Member States and the EU. Thirdly for setting up the national and European registries and programmes required by the Kyoto Protocol. Fourthly for ensuring timely, transparent and correct reporting on these issues by the EU and the Member States. Article 2 contains the framework for the national and European programmes. Article 3 contains rules on reporting by the Member States. Reporting should

---

[439] Decision 2002/358, OJ 2002 L 130/1. Cf. on the subject in general, Peeters & Deketelaere (2006) and Streck & Freestone (2005).

[440] Cf. recital 10 of the preamble to Decision 2002/358, OJ 2002 L 130/1.

[441] For an overview see: Yamin (2005).

[442] A large part of the package can be found in OJ 2009 L 140.

[443] See COM (2008) 30 final for an overview.

[444] OJ 2006 L 358/87, corrected in OJ 2006 L 367/80, as amended by Decision 2010/778, OJ 2010 L 332/41.

[445] Decision 280/2004, OJ 2004 L 49/1.

[446] OJ 1993 L 167/31, as amended by Decision 1999/296. OJ 1999 L 117/35.

take place concerning the emissions of the greenhouse gases listed in Annex A to the Kyoto Protocol (Article 3(1)(a)), but also on emissions of other gases and substances (Article 3(1)(b)). Apart from having to report on sources of greenhouse gases, the Member States must also report on so-called sinks of greenhouse gasses (Article 3(1)(c)). Sinks is the Kyoto Protocol-terminology for anything that removes greenhouse gases from the atmosphere, such as forests. On the basis of these reports the EU shall compile a greenhouse gas inventory (Article 4). The Commission will then annually assess the progress of the Member States and the EU in meeting the Kyoto targets (Article 5(1)) and report on this to the Council and the European Parliament (Article 5(2)). On the basis of the data gathered and the reports both the EU and the Member States have to report to the UNFCCC Secretariat on so-called demonstrable progress. Because the Kyoto Protocol and the implementation thereof by the EU allow for emissions trading a registry is necessary. Article 6 requires the EU and the Member States to set up such registries that will allow for accurate accounting of the emissions reductions and the trading of emissions. Article 7 contains provisions on the assigned amounts. This corresponds roughly to a quota for greenhouse gases that may be emitted in order to meet the reductions target agreed in the Kyoto Protocol and the burden sharing agreement.[447] The fact that both the EU and its Member States are signatories to the Kyoto Protocol also necessitates a provision on full and effective cooperation between these two in the international negotiations (Article 8). The Monitoring Decision is further implemented by Commission Decision 2005/166.[448]

The Kyoto Protocol recognises that emissions of greenhouse gases contribute to a global environmental problem. This means that the actual place where the emissions reductions take place is not relevant and this in turn opens up possibilities of achieving emissions reductions at places where the costs of doing so are relatively lower. This is called emissions trading and it takes place on an international scale and between the member States. Internationally, emissions trading can take place between a Member State and a developing country through the Clean Development Mechanism (CDM) and between a Member State and a developed third state Joint Implementation (JI). The credits thus created can also be used within the EU. This may take place in one of two contexts that correspond to the two major instruments used by the EU to abate greenhouse gas emissions. The first is the emissions trading scheme and the second is the effort sharing decision, that regulates the combined effort of the Member States to reduce emissions outside the sectors and industries covered by the emissions trading scheme.

---

[447] Decision 2002/358, OJ 2002 L 130/1.
[448] OJ 2005 L 55/57.

13.1.1   The Effort Sharing Decision

As was already mentioned above, this decision implements the EU and Member States effort to reduce greenhouse gas emissions outside the EU emissions trading scheme. To that end it establishes greenhouse gas emissions limits for the Member States (Article 3 in connection with Annex II). These limits are set as a percentage of the greenhouse gas emissions of the Member States in 2005 to be attained in 2020 by means of a linear reduction (Article 3(2), third subparagraph). A look at the table in Annex II reveals that most Member States have a reduction target (a negative percentage), whereas some are allowed to increase greenhouse gas emissions compared to the 2005 levels. This is the result of the desire to have some solidarity between the Member States and to ensure sustainable economic growth throughout the EU taking into account that economic growth is coupled to greenhouse gas emissions.[449] In practical terms it means that Member States with low GDPs are allowed to increase emissions or face limited reduction targets, whereas high-GDP Member States face stricter reduction targets. Again, this simple scheme is complicated in order to ensure increased flexibility for the Member States. A first source of flexibility comes from the possibility to carry forward emissions reductions up to 5% (Article 3(3)). Moreover, Member States may also engage in trading such emissions reductions with other Member States (Article 3(4) and (5)). Finally, the Member States may use the credits generated using the international trading mechanisms (JI and CDM) up to a maximum of 3% of the 2005 emissions (Article 5(4)). However, a higher percentage is allowed if the Member State can show that meeting the abatement target laid down in the Effort Sharing Decision would be – to put it bluntly – expensive (Article 5(5)).[450] Using credits in such a case is attractive because emissions reductions are generally cheaper in less developed countries, meaning that buying the credit representing a one tonne greenhouse gas emissions reduction in a developing country is often cheaper than actually reducing greenhouse gas emissions in the Member State with one tonne. Finally, Article 7 may be mentioned. Under the slightly enigmatic title 'corrective action' we find what is essentially a punitive scheme for those Member States that fail to meet their greenhouse gas abatement targets. The greenhouse gas emissions subject to the Effort Sharing Decision account for approximately 60% of all greenhouse gas emissions in the EU. The other 40% is subject to the emissions trading scheme.

---

[449] See recital 8 of the preamble to the effort sharing decision.

[450] For an analysis of this trade-off between costs and competitiveness on the one hand and climate change on the other see: Vedder (2011).

13.1.2 The Emissions Trading Scheme Directive

Directive 2003/87 regulates emissions trading for greenhouse gases (hereafter the Emissions Trading Scheme Directive (ETS Directive)).[451] With regard to this directive we need to distinguish between greenhouse gas emissions from stationary installations and those from certain aviation activities. A further distinction relates to the various deadlines or phases in the implementation of the ETS. Concerning stationary installations, all large industrial plants (by and large those that also require a permit on the basis of the IPPC and IE Directive (Annex I) require a Greenhouse gas emissions permit (Article 4), but only for the greenhouse gas[452] listed in Annex I (carbon dioxide).[453] The conditions for the application and the contents of the greenhouse gas emissions permits are laid down in Articles 5 and 6. As many of the Annex I installations will also require an IPPC permit, Article 8 provides for coordination with that directive. It may be recalled that the IPPC Directive was amended so as to preclude the inclusion of conditions relating to greenhouse gas emissions.[454] The central provision concerning the greenhouse gas emissions permit can be found in Article 6(2)(c) and (e) and relates to the obligation imposed on the operator to monitor the emissions of greenhouse gases and surrender allowances equal to the total emissions of the installation in the previous calendar year. It is with regard to these allowances that the trading takes place. These allowances are described as allowances to emit one ton of carbon dioxide during a specified period (Article 3(a)). Under the ETS Directive the Member States must first allocate the allowances in so-called national allocation plans (NAPs) pursuant to Article 9. The NAPs must be approved by the Commission on the basis of Article 9(3) in accordance with the criteria laid down in Annex III.[455] The total amount of allowances to be allocated must correspond to the Member State's emissions ceiling laid down in Decision 2006/944 and the emissions reductions objective of that Member State.[456] The total amount of available allowances must then be distributed over the Annex I installations pursuant to the NAP. In this regard the ETS Directive distinguishes three phases: the start-up or learning phase (January 2005-January 2008), the current operational phase

---

[451] OJ 2003 L 275/32, as amended by Directive 2004/101, OJ 2004 L 338/18 and Directive 2009/29, OJ 2009 L 140/63.

[452] A list of greenhouse gasses subject to the ETS Directive can be found in Annex II.

[453] See, on the scope of the EU ETS and the sectors included and the effect of that on competition Case C-127/07 *Arcelor* [2008] ECR I-9895.

[454] See above, section 5.

[455] See Case T-178/05 *UK* v. *Commission* [2005] ECR II-4807 on some formalities surrounding this decision; Case T-374/04 *Germany* v. *Commission* [2007] ECR II-4431, on the scope of Commission discretion and Case T-183/07 R *Poland* v. *Commmission* [2007] ECR II-152. Cf. Case T-28/07 *Fels-Werke a.o.* v. *Commission* [2007] ECR II-98, making it clear that undertakings have no *locus standi* at the General Court in an action for annulment of the decision of the Commission; see also section 5.2 of Chapter 5.

[456] Point 1 of Annex III to the ETS Directive. Article 1(32) of Directive 2009/29 repealed this Annex.

from January 2008 until December 2012 and the third phase from 1 January 2013 onwards. In the start-up phase at least 95% of the allowances are to be allocated free of charge ('grandfathering'); in the operational phase at least 90% of the allowances are to be grandfathered. This means that after January 2008 some Member States may chose to auction up to 20% of the allowances. The choice for grandfathering or auctioning and the general allocation is problematic with regard to the correct functioning of the emissions trading system, the need to maintain undistorted competition as well as the possibility of entry on to the market of a Member State. For one, grandfathering does not ensure that a market price is paid for the allowances.[457] Furthermore, over allocation of allowances may mean that a company receives an advantage from the state without having to pay for this, which may constitute state aid. Thirdly, a company wanting to establish a new Annex I installation will need to obtain allowances to cover for its emissions. These could either be unavailable (because the Member State NAP has handed out allowances corresponding to its emissions ceiling) or it may have to buy them on the market whereas the incumbent companies received the allowances free of charge. This is part of the reason why the Commission has to approve the NAPs and this includes an appraisal on the basis of the Treaty's state aid provisions (Articles 107 and 108 TFEU) as well as the need to allow for market entry (Points 5 and 6 of Annex III[458] and Article 11(3)[459]).[460]

After the allocation of the allowances on the basis of the NAPs, the actual trading can take place. The idea behind this is that the Member States will gradually reduce the available amount of allowances so as to attain the emissions reduction targets. As a result the allowances will become scarce and, since these are tradable, this means that the price will increase. A company that has reduced its emissions will thus have an excess of allowances that it could sell on the market to companies that have not reduced emissions and thus need to surrender allowances pursuant to their greenhouse gas emissions permit. As the amount of allowances is further reduced, scarcity and price increase leading to a greater incentive to actually reduce emissions. Because the allowances can be traded, the emissions reduction takes place most efficiently, i.e. by the company that can reduce emissions at the lowest costs. Companies can buy allowances from other participants in the EU emissions trading scheme, but they can also use so-called CERs and ERUs, which are the international tradable credits. CER stands for Certified Emissions Reduction (Article 3(n)) and ERU refers to an Emissions Reduction Unit (Article 3(m)). CERs and ERUs

---

[457] For a full discussion of this problem see Woerdman, Clò & Arcuri (2008).

[458] This annex is now repealed.

[459] This article was repealed by Article 1(13) of Directive 2009/29.

[460] See Case T-387/04 *EnBW Energie Baden-Württemberg AG* v. *Commission* [2007] ECR II-1195, concerning the legal nature of such a decision. According to the General Court, the Commission decision does not qualify as a state aid decision pursuant to Article 108 TFEU. Undertakings that consider their competitive position harmed by an approved NAP may institute national proceedings on the basis of a violation of the directly effective standstill obligation in Article 108(3) TFEU.

both represent emissions reductions as a result of the Kyoto protocol's project mechanisms (CDM and JI). The inclusion of CERs and ERUs in the ETS is made possible by Directive 2004/101, which introduced, *inter alia*, Article 11a and 11b in the ET Directive.[461] It is interesting to see that, in line with what has been prescribed in the Effort Sharing Decision, the EU has set limits to the use of these CERs and ERUs, resulting in the obligation to achieve a certain amount of the emissions reduction within the EU. This is closely connected with the obligation following from the Kyoto Protocol to ensure that JI and CDM are supplemental to domestic action, as it has been implemented in the Monitoring Mechanism Decision.[462] Moreover, there are also more substantive restrictions on the use of CERs and ERUs, resulting from the environmental impact that the generation of such credits may have in the third states concerned. We see this in Article 11b(6) of the directive, that intends to ensure that hydroelectric dams are constructed taking into account, *inter alia*, local needs. On a more general basis Article 11a(9) allows for the adoption of rules restricting the use of credits from specific activities.[463]

The allowances, including CERs and ERUs, thus generated must be tradable within the EU and internationally (Article 12(1)(a) and (b)). The allowances must then be surrendered before 30 April each year to cover for the emissions in the preceding calendar year, after which the allowances are cancelled. If a company fails to surrender sufficient allowances it will have to pay a fine and the name of the company will be made public (Article 16(2)). The amount of the fine is currently €100 for every tonne of carbon dioxide equivalent for which no allowances have been surrendered (Article 16(3)). In addition, the company will have to surrender the missing amount of allowances the next year.

From January 2013 onwards, the EU ETS changes considerably for stationary installations. For one, the NAPs disappear and are replaced by an EU-wide amount of allowances (Article 9).[464] This thus sets the cap on greenhouse gas emissions at an EU level. In order to ensure that the EU reduces greenhouse gas emissions, the cap is lowered with 1.74% every year. Moreover, allowances are in principle no longer to be grandfathered but instead to be auctioned (Article 10). To this end an Auctioning Regulation has been adopted.[465] This regulation intends to ensure that the auctioning platform will ensure all operators under the ETS have full, fair and equitable access to the auction and that the auction is transparent and cost-effective (Article 10(4)). It may be noted that the Auctioning Regulation envisages a common EU-wide auctioning platform, but also provides for an opt-out, whereby Member States can set up their own auctioning platform that should comply with the principles laid down in the ETS and

---

[461] This directive links the EU ETS with the CDM and JI project mechanisms; OJ 2004 L 228/18.

[462] Article 2(2) of Decision 280/2004, see above in this section.

[463] See, e.g., Commission Regulation 550/2011, OJ 2011 L 149/1.

[464] This quantity is set by means of Commission Decision 2010/634, OJ 2010 L 279/34.

[465] Commission Regulation 1031/2010, OJ 2010 L 302/1.

the Auctioning Regulation.[466] In view of the fact that what is auctioned are national allowances distributed on the basis of an EU-wide basis, the auctioning is to take place by the Member States and auctioning revenues can be spent by the Member States as well. These are no completely free in this, as Article 10(3) states that at least 50% of auctioning revenues should be spent on climate related objectives. The wording of Article 10(3) does not require such climate-related spending as the would 'should' indicates. Member States are, however, required to determine the use of the auction revenues, which will enhance transparency in this regard. Auctioning is supposed to lead to a functioning EU carbon market, but market oversight mechanism is put in place to prevent excessive price fluctuations (Article 29a). Interestingly, this provision only deals withy excessively high prices whereas the problem with the EU allowance market thus far have been the relatively low prices.[467]

Auctioning will mean that allowances can only be obtained at a market price. This will raise costs for the industries subject to the ETS considerably compared to the situation until 2012, where allowances overwhelmingly were grandfathered. As a result, there are a number of options to mitigate these effects on costs and thus international competitiveness. Article 10a allows for continued grandfathering on the basis of a harmonised EU-wide system, whereby only those installations that meet an EU-wide efficiency benchmark set at the level of the top 10% most efficient installation in a sector (Article 10a(2)).[468] Moreover, the amount of allowances to be grandfathered in accordance with this procedure only corresponds to 80% of historical emissions and it will decrease with a view to attain 30% grandfathering in 2020 and full auctioning in 2027. Because allowances are grandfathered, a reserve for new entrants is provided for (Article 10a(7)), whereas 300 million allowances from that reserve are available as a subsidy for CCS and renewable energy demonstration projects (Article 10a(8)). Finally, worth mentioning in this regard is the fact that electricity generation does not qualify for free allocation and will thus be subject to full auctioning from 2013 onwards (Article 10a(3) en (7)). Because of fears that energy intensive industries that would face high climate costs as a result of the ETS would leave the EU to third countries where the climate costs are lower, a regime for carbon leakage has been included in the ETS. The thresholds for determining whether an industry is subject to a risk of carbon leakage have been set out in Article 10a(15) and (16) and this basically involves an appraisal of estimated cost increases in relation to trade intensity from third countries.[469] If an industry is determined to be subject to a carbon leakage risk, the percentage of allowances free of charge increases to 100% (Article 10a(12)). As a result of the 100%

---

[466] Chapter VIII of the Auctioning Regulation. At this moment Germany, Poland and the UK have decided to opt-out of the EU auctioning scheme.

[467] For an overview of the economics of the ETS see Kuik & Oosterhuis (2008)

[468] These benchmarks have been set by means of Commission Decision 2011/278, OJ 2011 L 130/1.

[469] This has resulted in the Carbon Leakage Decision, that contains the list of industries concerned, Commission Decision 2010/2, OJ 2010 L 1/10.

grandfathering, the costs will drop and the risk of carbon leakage disappears. Because allowances for the electricity sector are to be auctioned, electricity costs are expected to rise. This has resulted in Article 10a(6), whereby the Member States may grant state aid to offset such costs, in accordance with the state aid rules.[470] The rules on carbon leakage are completed by Article 10b, that states that the Commission shall review the carbon leakage regime in the light of the international climate change negotiations.[471] This review can include the percentage of grandfathered allowances, the benchmark for grandfathering and the inclusion of importers. Article 10c is somewhat of an odd provision in that it was essentially written for a closed group of Member States who feared that 100% auctioning from 2013 onwards would put their electricity production at risk. As a result, Article 10c allows for transitional free allocation to electricity production in those Member States, provided that a plan for upgrading production and infrastructure is submitted.

Much of these rules apply also to the aviation sector, though the regime here is slightly different in that there is, for example, no greenhouse gas emissions permit. Instead, the ETS applies to all aviation activities listed in Annex I.[472] This means that all aircraft operators whose aircraft land in or depart from the EU are subject to the scheme. These aircraft operators are then appointed an administering state on the basis of Article 18a of the ETS Directive.[473] Article 3c sets the total amount of allowances available at 95% of the historical aviation emissions, multiplied by the number of years the scheme is in force since 2013.[474] Between January and December 2012, the available amount of allowances shall be 97% of historical aviation emissions and in that period 15% of the allowances shall be auctioned and 85% will be distributed free of charge. Again, there is a benchmark to ensure that only the most efficient operators qualify for the highest percentage of grandfathered allowances (Article 3e(3)(e)).[475] From 2013 onwards, the amount of grandfathered allowances corresponds to 82% of all available allowances, but there is a possibility to increase the percentage of auctioned allowances (Article 3d(2)). Again, the Auctioning Regulation applies.[476] The procedure for distribution of allowances free of charge is set out in Article 3e and involves a benchmark that is to ensure that only those aircraft

---

[470] This is expected to result in new (or amended) Guidelines on Environmental Aid (see Chapter 7, section 7.3).

[471] For an analysis of the carbon leakage regime, also in the light of the international negotiations, see: Vedder (2011A) and Vedder (2011B).

[472] According to Article 3b, the Commission is to issue detailed guidelines on this concept. These have been published in Decision 2009/450, OJ 2009 L 149/69.

[473] The most recent list of aircraft operators and the administering states can be found in Commission Regulation 394/2011, OJ 2011 L 107/1.

[474] Historical aviation emissions, defined in Article 3(s) of the ETS Directive, have been set by Commission Decision 2011/149, OJ 2011 L 61/42.

[475] The benchmark has been set by means of Commission Decision 2011/638, OJ 2011 L 252/20.

[476] Regulation 1031/2010, OJ 2010 L 302/1, see Article 3d(3) for the legal basis in this regard.

that have relatively limited emissions per tonne-kilometre receive allowances for free (Article 3e(3)(e)). The directive further establishes a special reserve (3% of all available allowances) for new entrants and aircraft operators whose tonne-kilometre increase by more than 18% annually compared to the benchmark year. This reserve thus tries to counter the negative effects that the ETS may have on the market. Finally, these operators are subject to a monitoring regime (Article 3g)).[477] The inclusion of aviation in the ETS is highly controversial because it includes aircraft operators established outside the EU and of an extraterritorial nature and thus resulted in action at ICAO-level,[478] as well as legal actions before the EU Court.[479] The international competitiveness and relation between EU action and international action is further evidenced by Article 25a. This allows the EU ETS to take into account third country measures to deal with climate change effects of aviation.

The ETS Directive further contains provisions on the competent authorities, the administrator in charge of the allowance administration and verification and monitoring.[480] Somewhat odd is Article 24 on the unilateral inclusion of additional activities and gases. This refers to so-called more stringent measures whereby a Member State could expand the scope of the ETS to installations not listed in Annex I and more greenhouse gases. Such measures are subject to the Commission's approval. This is surprising given that the directive is based on Article 175 EC, currently 192 TFEU, which results in the Member States always being able to adopt more stringent measures pursuant to Article 193 TFEU. The procedure in Article 24 of the ETS Directive effectively restricts the Member State's power pursuant to Article 193 TFEU along the lines of Article 114(4)-(6) TFEU.[481] With respect to the question whether the use of Article 193 TFEU can

---

[477] Monitoring requirements are further specified in Commission Decision 2009/339, OJ 2009 L 103/10.

[478] Resistance from the US would have resulted in a Resolution that would have blocked the EU's desire to include aviation, Resolution A36-22, Appendix L. However, a reservation entered by Portugal on behalf of the EU prevented this resolution from entering into force, Extracts of A36-Min. Ex/11 and A36-Min. Ex/10 (Minutes of the Eleventh and Tenth Meetings of the Executive Committee) Reservations Made to Assembly Resolutions A36-22 and A36-28. See also: Extracts of A36-Min. P/9 (Minutes of the Ninth Plenary Meeting) – Reservations made to Assembly Resolutions A36-22, A36-24 and A36-28. All available at http://www.icao.int (last visited 7 October 2011).

[479] Case C-366/10 *Air Transport Association of America*, pending preliminary reference, OJ 2010 C 260/9.

[480] Furthermore, it is supplemented by a number of decisions, directives and regulations. Decision 2006/780 was adopted pursuant to Article 11b(7) of the ETS Directive and wants to avoid double counting of ERUs, CERs and allowances, OJ 2006 L 316/12. Decision 2007/589 was adopted pursuant to Article 14(1) of the ETS Directive and contains guidelines for the monitoring and reporting of greenhouse gas emissions, OJ 2007 L 229/1. Commission Regulation 2216/2004, amended since then, was adopted pursuant to Article 19(3) of the ETS Directive and Article 6(1) of the Monitoring Mechanism Decision and contains the rules for a standardised and secured system of registries allowing for the administration of the trade in allowances, OJ 2004 L 386/1. A proposal for a new regulation is pending with the Council and European Parliament.

[481] See above Chapter 3, sections 5 and 6.

be restricted or altered by secondary law, such as the ETS Directive, we refer to our observations in Chapter 3, section 5 in particular. Moreover, the possibility for Member States to exclude certain small installations (Article 27) deserves mention here. Finally, the ETS Directive contains a number of provisions that link the EU ETS to the outcome of the international climate change negotiations. In this regard we may refer to the possibility of raising the EU's greenhouse gas abatement target to 30% (Article 28), a restriction that only credits from third countries that have ratified this agreement may be used in the ETS (Article 11a(7)) and a revision of the carbon leakage regime (Article 10b(1)).

13.2 The Renewable Energy Sources Directive

Another important part of the EU's climate change policy concerns the 20% renewable energy target to be attained in 2020. To this end the Renewable Energy Sources (RES) Directive lays down binding targets for the Member States.[482] Article 3 in connection with Annex I (A) stipulates that the Member States shall ensure that the share of renewable energy sources in gross final energy consumption is met in 2020. In contrast with the differentiated targets in Annex I, there is a uniform 10% target for renewable energy in transport (Article 3(4)). To this end a trajectory is provided for in Annex I (B) and the Member States are obliged to introduce various measures as well as a renewable action plan (Article 4). The directive furthermore contains detailed and complicated rules on the calculation of the share that renewables have in the total energy consumption (Article 5 in connection with various annexes). To increase the flexibility of the scheme, statistical transfers and joint projects are possible. Statistic transfers relate to the transfer of a certain amount of renewable energy from one Member State to another, so that the receiving Member State can take this amount of renewable energy into account in the efforts to meet the renewables targets. Joint projects may take place between Member States (Articles 7 and 8) and between Member States and third countries (Articles 9 and 10). In such joint projects the total amount of renewable energy produced can be divided among the parties involved, who may then take the amount of energy produced into account when calculating whether or not the renewables target has been met. Concerning joint projects with third countries an important restriction is that such projects only fall within the EU scheme if they relate to electricity. Moreover, that electricity must have been consumed in the EU by a new installation that has not received support from a third country (Article 9(2) (a)-(c)). To facilitate such joint projects Article 11 envisages joint support schemes. Completely separate from these flexibility mechanisms function the guarantees of origin (Article 15). These are designed to inform consumers of the share of renewable energy in a suppliers energy mix. Such guarantees must be determined on the basis of objective, transparent and non-discriminatory criteria and they must be transferrable between the Member States (Article 15(4)

---

[482] Directive 2009/28, OJ 2009 L 140/16.

and (5)). To encourage renewable electricity production, Article 16(2) provides
that such electricity shall have priority access to the electricity grid. This means
that in times of congestion, renewable electricity can always be fed into the
grid insofar as this does not jeopardise the reliability and safety of the grid.[483]
The directive further contains an elaborate set of rules designed to ensure the
sustainability of biofuels and bioliquids (Article 17). These rules are a response
to the often-heard criticism according to which biofuel production leads to
unsustainable production circumstances in many developing countries. To this
end, the RES Directive provides that biofuels shall not be taken into account for
meeting the renewables targets if they were produced in what is called land with
a high biodiversity value (Article 17(3)) or land with a high carbon stock (Article
17(4)). Moreover, social protection is ensured through a bi-annual Commission
report on social sustainability (Article 17(7)). Article 18 contains a verification
procedure.[484]

13.3 Energy Efficiency Measures and other Instruments to Combat Climate Change

The ETS Directive is the flagship instrument used by the EU
to combat climate change. Nonetheless there are various other instruments that
deal with other greenhouse gases and try to improve energy efficiency.

Regulation 842/2006 aims to reduce emissions of fluorinated greenhouse
gases.[485] The term fluorinated greenhouse gases covers so-called hydrofluoro-
carbons (HFCs), perfluorocarbons (PFCs) and Sulphur hexafluoride listed in
Annex I to the regulation.[486] All substances already covered by the regulation on
the protection of the ozone layer are outside the scope of Regulation 842/2006
(Article 2(1)).[487] In order to reduce these emissions the regulation contains rules
on the use, containment, recovery and destruction of these gases as well as rules
on the labelling and marketing of these gases and equipment containing these
gases. This has resulted in a dual legal basis for this regulation. The bulk of
the regulation has been based on Article 175 EC, currently 192 TFEU, but the
provisions dealing with labelling, control of use and marketing (Articles 7-9)
were based on Article 95 EC, currently Article 114 TFEU. Article 3 is directed
at the operators of stationary refrigeration, air conditioning, heat pump and fire
protection equipment insofar as this equipment contains fluorinated green-

---

[483] Note that for green gas no similar regime exists and that recital 12 of the RES Directive notes the environmental benefits of green gas whereas recital 26 of the Gas Directive, Directive 2009/73, OJ 2009 L
211/94, only contains an obligation to assist the wider use of such gas.

[484] The Commission can recognise compliance programmes in third countries on the basis of Article 18(4),
see, e.g., Commission Decision 2011/441, OJ 2011 L 190/85.

[485] OJ 2006 L 161/1.

[486] These groups of chemical substances feature also in Annex II to the ETS Directive, and may thus eventually be included in the ETS.

[487] See above, section 11.3.

house gases. It requires them to use all technically available measures that do not entail disproportionate costs to prevent leakage and repair detected leakages as soon as possible (Article 3(1)). Moreover, when the equipment contains more than 3 kg of these gases the operators are also required to check their equipment for leakage at certain intervals depending on the amount of gases contained (Article 3(2)). If more than 300 kg of these gases are contained a leakage detection system must be installed (Article 3(3)). This means that operators of, for example, air conditioning equipment containing less than 3 kg of fluorinated greenhouse gases, are under the general duty pursuant to Article 3(1) of the regulation to prevent leakage and to repair detected leakages. There is nothing in the regulation to suggest that this excludes final consumers of household air conditioning equipment.[488] Many of these aircos are filled with R-410A. Article 4 contains a duty for the operator of various types of stationary equipment to ensure that the gases contained in them are recovered. Given that the regulation applies without prejudice to the WEEE Directive (Article 1 third paragraph), this should not entail any costs for final consumers.[489] Article 5 contains rules on training and certification of personnel involved in the installation, maintenance etc. of equipment containing fluorinated greenhouse gases. Article 6 lays down reporting obligations for producers, importers and exporters of fluorinated greenhouse gases. Article 7 contains rules on the labelling of equipment containing fluorinated greenhouse gases. Article 8 prohibits certain applications of sulphur hexafluoride, such as the filling of vehicle tyres. Article 9(1) prohibits the marketing of products and equipment containing fluorinated greenhouse gases. The types of products and equipment, the gases contained in them and the date on which the marketing prohibition enters into force is laid down in Annex II. However, products that are shown to have been manufactured before the date of entry into force may still be marketed (Article 9(2)). Article 9(3) contains what could be called a specialised implementation of the possibility for a derogation pursuant to Article 114(4) TFEU. More stringent measures that have been adopted before 31 December 2005 may be maintained until 31 December 2012, provided that these measures are notified to the Commission before 4 July 2007 and these measures are compatible with the Treaty. It is interesting to note that, contrary to Article 114(6) TFEU, no explicit authorisation by the Commission is required for this. It may be wondered whether this is compatible with the Treaty as secondary European law cannot detract from primary European law and the effect of Article 9(3) is to effectively rob the Commission of its powers to ensure that the application of Union law (Article 17(1) TEU). Moreover, the test of compatibility with the internal market is arguably less strict than the test required by Article 114(6) TFEU. The special position of Article 9 is reaffirmed by Article 14, that accidentally is the only provision without a title. This declares the standard Treaty procedures for more stringent measures applicable

---

[488] Many of these aircos are filled with R410A, which is a mixture of the HFCs listed in Annex I to the regulation.

[489] Directive 2002/96, see below, section 17.4.

to the various provisions of the regulation, however, without prejudice to Article 9(3). The marketing prohibition entered into force on 4 July 2006 and the rest of the regulation entered into force on 4 July 2007. For fluorinated gasses in airconditioning systems of cars a special regime is laid down in the so-called MAC Directive.[490] This basically means that such gasses with a greenhouse gas potential exceeding 150 are banned.

Energy efficiency and energy saving is the focus of many initiatives, such as SAVE: Specific Action for Vigorous Energy Efficiency. More concrete rules can be found in Directive 2006/32 on energy end-use efficiency[491] and Directive 2010/31 on the energy performance of buildings.[492]

Directive 2006/32 replaces Directive 93/76 (Article 17)[493] and aims to enhance cost-effective improvements in energy-efficiency. The directive applies to companies involved in the distribution and sale of energy and final consumers of energy. Member States may, however, exclude small energy companies (Article 2(a) in connection with Article 3(r)). Furthermore, the directive does not apply to companies subject to the ET Directive. It does so by providing for a national indicative energy savings target of 9% to be achieved in 2015 (Article 1(a) in connection with Article 4(1)).[494] Annex I contains the detailed rules for calculating the target. Further means to achieve this objective boil down to the creation of a market for the efficient end use of energy (Article 1(a)) and a market for energy services and other energy efficiency improvement measures for final consumers (Article 1(b)). The directive envisages intermediary energy savings targets (Article 4(2)) that will be included in the so-called Energy Efficiency Action Plans (EEAPs) to be submitted by the Member States to the Commission (Article 14). Furthermore, the public sector is to play an exemplary role (Article 5(1)).[495] The public sector is to fulfil this role in part by greening its public procedures (Article 5(1) and seventh recital of the preamble). The market that the directive aims to create deals with so-called energy services and other energy efficiency improvement measures. These energy services may be provided by energy distributors, distribution system operators and other natural or legal persons. Interestingly, the Member States must refrain from any activities that might impede the creation of a market for energy services (Article 6(1)(b)) and they are under a duty to ensure that there is equal competition on this market (Article 6(3)). This effectively means that the directive contains specialised competition rules addressed at companies as well as the Member States that may have a wider scope than the general competition rules.[496] The market for energy

---

[490] This stands for Motor vehicle Air Conditioning Directive 2006/40, OJ 2006 L 161/12.

[491] OJ 2006 L 114/64.

[492] OJ 2010 L 153/13, replacing Directive 2002/91, OJ 2003 L 1/65.

[493] OJ 1993 L 237/28.

[494] This assumes that the directive will be applied from its entry into force (May 2006), if the first year of application is in 2007 (when the first plans must be submitted), the target is to be achieved in 2016.

[495] The public sector includes the armed forces, which are in principle subject to the directive, Article 2(c)).

[496] See Chapter 7.

services may also be created by voluntary agreements or a market based scheme involving tradable so-called white certificates (Article 6(2)(b) in connection with Article 3(s)). The directive further contains provisions on the exchange of information, such as best practices (Article 7), and the certification of technical experts (Article 8). Very interesting are the provisions that deal with the financial incentives and tariff structures. According to Article 9(1) the Member States are to repeal or amend legislation that disproportionately impedes or restricts the use of financial instruments for energy saving. This may in effect lead to a greening of all state operated or funded financial instruments, with the exception of measures of a clearly fiscal nature. This exception probably follows from the special legal basis contained in Article 192(2)(a) TFEU.[497] Article 10 necessitates a similar greening of tariffs and regulations for net-bound energy. Article 11 allows for government funds to subsidise energy efficiency, albeit without prejudice to Articles 107 and 108 TFEU. These funds should also target higher risk sectors and may not compete with commercially financed energy efficiency improvement measures. It is submitted that anything else would render these funds unacceptable under Article 107 TFEU anyhow.[498] On the basis of Article 12 the Member States must ensure the availability of energy audits. Final consumers have an important role to play in the directive, as they will ultimately have to increase energy efficiency. Article 13(1) of the directive envisages the introduction of meters that will adequately show the individual consumer's energy consumption. Moreover, when old meters are replaced such new meters must always be provided, unless this would not be cost-effective in relation to the long term energy savings. Moreover, energy bills should also include information that will enable the consumer to reduce energy consumption (Article 13(2) and (3)). Member States may decide to not apply Articles 6 and 13 for small energy distributors. The directive must be implemented before 17 May 2008.[499] In the meantime, the Commission has submitted a proposal for a new directive on energy efficiency that will require, *inter alia*, the establishment of binding energy saving targets for the Member States.[500]

Directive 2010/31 aims to increase the energy efficiency of buildings. It does so by providing for, *inter alia*, a framework for the calculation of the energy efficiency and by providing for minimum energy efficiency requirements. The minimum energy efficiency requirements are to be set by the Member States and may differentiate between various categories of buildings (Article 4). The Member States are then to take the necessary measures to ensure that new buildings will meet the minimum requirements (Article 6). For exist-

---

[497] Interestingly, Article 192(2) TFEU refers to measures of a *primarily* fiscal nature.

[498] See Chapter 7, section 7.3 and the Guidelines for State Aid for Environmental Protection according to which state aid is allowed only to correct market failures or if it will help to promote sustainable development.

[499] The reporting obligation should however be implemented before 17 May 2006.

[500] COM (2011) 370.

ing large buildings that undergo a major renovation, as defined in Article 2(1), the Member States must also take the necessary measures to ensure that the minimum requirements are met (Article 7). In both cases the economic feasibility of such energy saving measures must be taken into account. This shows the general trade-off between costs and environmental investments. However, with regard to investments in energy efficiency this is slightly more complicated in that such investments will lead to reduced energy consumption and thus lower operating costs. In this regard it is interesting to see how this directive respects the subsidiarity principle by allowing the Member States unlimited discretion in setting the minimum requirements. This may very well result in a distortion of the level playing field, as higher standards will often result in higher building costs. Here we see that the 2010 is more detailed than its predecessor because it contains rules on the calculation of the cost-optimal levels of minimum energy performance requirements (Article 5). Article 9 requires all new buildings to be nearly zero-energy buildings by 2021. Such buildings use almost no energy and whatever energy is used should be 'to a very significant extent' renewable energy (Article 2(2)). The directive further provides for rules on the inspection of large boilers and large air conditioning systems (Articles 14 and 15). Most interesting for consumers is probably the mandatory energy performance certificate that will have to be provided with the building when it is constructed, sold or rented out (Article 12(1)(a)).

The final flanking measure that is part of the Energy and Climate Package and deserves mention here is the Directive on geological storage of carbon dioxide or CCS Directive.[501] This directive contains the framework for the safe deployment of carbon capture and storage technology. This technology essentially consists of three phases: the capture phase where carbon dioxide is separated from other emissions and compressed. This is followed by the transportation phase and finally and most importantly, the permanent storage of the captured CO_2. All three phases are regulated by the directive. As regards capture, the directive requires all large combustion installations to investigate the possibility of carbon capture. If this turns out to be possible, the installation must be made capture ready (Article 33).[502] This means that an area of land that is about the size of a football field must be set aside. As regards capture and transport, the EIA Directive is amended so as to include the capture and transport infrastructure in the scope of the IEA Directive (Article 31).[503] The regime is most elaborate with regard to the actual storage of captured CO_2. Here we find a rather extensive framework for site selection and exploration (Articles 4 and 5) and storage permits (Articles 6-11). These provisions put the bar very high in

---

[501] Directive 2009/31, OJ 2009 L 140/114, commonly referred to as the Directive on carbon capture and storage (CCS). For an analysis see Roggenkamp & Woerdman (2009).

[502] Note that this provision actually amends the IPPC Directive. See on the identical provision in the IE Directive section 6.3 above.

[503] Above section 3.

terms of safety and are clearly meant to inspire public confidence in this new technology.[504] They even envisage the mandatory notification to the Commission of such storage permits, resulting in a review by the Commission (Article 10). Because the idea behind CCS is that the stored CO2 remains stored for a very long time (if not eternally), there are also provisions on post-closure obligations (Articles 17-20). Ensuring permanent storage of carbon dioxide is to a large extent to be achieved though the selection of the right storage site. This is regulated by Article 4(3) that requires a risk assessment[505] and Article 4(4) according to which storage permits may only be granted to those sites where there is no significant risk of leakage and no significant environmental or health risks exist. Finally, the Directive prohibits in-water storage of carbon dioxide (Article 2(4)) and third party access to transport and storage facilities (Article 21). The Directive should have been implemented before 25 June 2011. In connection with CCS and renewables, we should also refer to Article 10a(8) of the ETS Directive.[506] This provision sets aside 300 million allowances from the new entrants reserve for the subsidisation of CCS demonstration projects and innovative renewable energy projects.

Eventhough it is strictly speaking not part of the Energy and Climate Package, the Ecotaxation Directive[507] has been identified by the Commission as a potentially important flanking measure. With its proposal for an amendment of this Directive the Commission intends to ensure that the Ecotaxation Directive fits in seamlessly with the ETS Directive.[508] In view of the current plethora of exemptions and temporary derogations from the minimum ecotaxation prescribed by the directive, it is highly unlikely that the proposal, that will result in higher taxes on, *inter alia*, automotive fuels, will be accepted by the Council as it is.

14 Legislation on Noise

European legislation on noise can broadly be divided into two categories. In the first place there are directives harmonising national regulations on anything from motor mowers to vehicles and prescribing maximum permissible noise levels. In the second place there is more recent legislation dealing not so much with the sources of noise, but with the environmental effects of it. The first group of legislation stipulates that products which do not meet the standards may not be marketed. Although primarily focusing on the

---

[504] For an analysis to what extent the Member States could enact more stringent norms see Holwerda (2011).

[505] The framework for this assessment is set out in Annex I.

[506] Above section 13.1.

[507] Directive 2003/96, OJ 2003 L 283/51, later amended. See further Chapter 2, section 7.4 and Chapter 7, section 7.3

[508] COM (2011) 169 at 6.

functioning of the internal market, these directives are a fine example of the application of the prevention and the source principles.[509] There used to be different directives for various categories of products, but these have been replaced by Directive 2000/14 on noise emissions of equipment for use outdoors.[510] This directive may be regarded as implementing total harmonisation. In other words, products which meet the requirements of the directive in question may not be barred from markets for reasons of the noise they produce. There is furthermore legislation on noise emitted by household appliances,[511] motor vehicles[512] and on the protection of workers from the risks related to exposure to noise at work.[513] There are also directives on noise produced by aircraft. For example, Directive 80/51 on the limitation of noise emissions from subsonic aircraft[514] and Directive 89/629 for the limitation of noise emission from civil subsonic jet aeroplanes.[515] The latter directive requires the Member States to ensure that civil subsonic jet aircraft registered in their territories after 1 November 1990 are only used in their territory or in the territory of other Member States if they have been granted a noise certificate on the basis of certain noise emission standards.

An example of the second group of noise related legislation is Directive 2002/30 which contains rules and procedures for the introduction of noise-related restrictions at airports in the Member States.[516] It constitutes a shift from the old aircraft-based noise regulation described above to an approach where noise is dealt with on the basis of the airport and its environment. Based on Article 100(2) TFEU, this is a measure aimed at safeguarding the internal market and at the same time protecting people from the harmful effects of noise. It furthermore seeks to promote sustainable airport development. The directive adopts the so-called balanced approach of the ICAO,[517] according to which noise management requires assessment of the following four factors: reduction of airplane noise at source, land-use planning, noise abatement opera-

---

[509] Cf. Van Calster (1997) at 174 and McManus (2005).

[510] OJ 2000 L 162/1, later amended.

[511] Directive 86/594, OJ 1986 L 344/24, later amended and now repealed by Directive 2005/32, OJ 2005 L 191/29.

[512] Directive 70/157, OJ 1975 L 42/1, later amended.

[513] Directive 2003/10, OJ 2003 L 42/38, later amended.

[514] OJ 1980 L 18/26, repealed by Regulation 1592/2002, OJ 2002 L 240/1. See on this directive Case C-389/96 *Aher-Waggon GmbH* [1998] ECR I-4473, where the Court ruled that Article 34 TFEU does not preclude national legislation which makes the first registration in national territory of aircraft previously registered in another Member State conditional upon compliance with stricter noise standards than those laid down by Directive 80/51, while exempting from those standards aircraft which obtained registration in national territory before that directive was implemented.

[515] OJ 1989 L 363/27, later amended. See also Directive 92/14, OJ 1992 L 76/12, according to which Member States must ensure that aircrafts covered by Directive 89/629 are no longer used unless a noise certificate has been granted (Article 2).

[516] OJ 2002 L 85/40.

[517] International Civil Aviation Organisation, see recital 10 of the preamble.

tional procedures and operating restrictions[518] (Article 4(1) in connection with 2(g)). The directive also recognises that the balanced approach may not be sufficient to achieve effective and sustainable noise reduction (recital 11). It therefore allows for more stringent measures, such as more stringent noise standards and actions to take noisy aircraft out of service.[519] This takes the form of operating restrictions for noisy aircraft, i.e. a limitation of the use of these aircraft. Such operating restrictions must be the result of an environmental assessment (Article 5) and must be notified in advance. Moreover, the aircraft operator must have a right to appeal a decision containing the operating restrictions (Article 12). Article 6 allows for operating restrictions that may entail a restriction of up to 20% of aircraft movements for noisy aircraft. For city airports (Article 2(b) and Annex I) more stringent rules are allowed (Article 6(2)). There is an exemption for noisy aircraft registered in developing countries (Article 8) and an exemption for aircraft operations of an exceptional nature (Article 9), which is drafted in very vague terms. Article 7 restricts the retroactive application of the directive.[520] The directive repeals the so-called Hushkits Regulation, which dealt with the registration and operation of aircraft fitted with noise reduction systems ('hushkits').[521]

Just as Directive 2002/30 shifts the focus of legislation away from the regulation of sources to an assessment of the environmental effects of noise, Directive 2002/49 also adopts the environmental approach.[522] Directive 2002/49 can moreover be characterised as a framework directive, along the lines of the Water Framework Directive and the Framework Directive for Ambient Air Quality. The Noise Framework Directive aims to avoid, prevent or reduce the harmful effects, including annoyance, due to exposure to environmental noise (Article 1). To this end the directive envisages firstly the determination of exposure to noise by means of so-called noise mapping (Article 1(a) in connection with Articles 3(r) and 7). The results of this noise inventory (noise maps) and the effects of exposure to noise should be made available to the public (Article 1(b) in connection with Article 9). The directive further requires the adoption of action plans to prevent and reduce environmental noise where necessary and particularly where exposure levels can induce harmful effects on human health. Such action plans must moreover aim to preserve environmental noise quality where it is good (standstill; Article 1(c) in connection with Article 8). Article 1(2) indicates that the directive can also function as a basis for emissions-based European legislation for other sources than those already covered by Directive 2000/14. The directive applies only to environmental noise to which humans are exposed and excludes noise caused by the exposed person himself, noise from domestic

---

[518] See, on the concept of operating restrictions, Case C-120/10 *European Air Transport SA*, Judgment of 8 September 2011, paras. 22-34.

[519] These are referred to as marginally compliant aircraft, Article 2(c).

[520] See on this provision Case C-422/05 *Commission* v. *Belgium* [2007] ECR I-4749, paras. 40-49.

[521] Regulation 925/1999, OJ 1999 L 115/1.

[522] Directive 2002/49, OJ 2002 L 189/12, hereafter the Noise Framework Directive.

activities, created by neighbours, noise at work places,[523] noise inside transport means and noise from military activities (Article 2). Central to the directive is the concept of environmental noise, defined in Article 3(a) as unwanted or harmful outdoor sound created by human activities. Interestingly, this definition includes noise during concerts, as this will – depending on the noise levels – be harmful to human health, even if it is wanted, and is not created by that person himself. The result of this could be that noise levels may have to be mitigated at concerts. As may be recalled from the objectives, the first step in the directive is to determine exposure to noise by means of noise mapping. This involves four indicators: Lden (noise during day, evening and night), Lday (noise during day), Levening (noise during the evening) and Lnight (noise during the night). Lden, Lday and Levening indicate annoyance and Lnight indicates sleep disturbance. Using these indicators, the Member States have to produce strategic noise maps before 30 June 2007, which show the exposure to noise in the preceding calendar year (Article 7). Articles 5 and 6 contain the detailed rules for the use of these indicators and the assessment methods. These strategic noise maps will show the environmental noise in major agglomerations of more than 250,000 inhabitants and for all major roads which have more than 6 million vehicle passages per year, major railways with more than 60,000 train passages per year and major airports (more than 50,000 take-offs or landings per year). Such strategic noise maps must be updated at least every five years (Article 7(4)). On the basis of these strategic noise maps action plans must be drawn up. These plans focus on places near major roads, major railways and major airports and agglomerations. Such plans must also aim to protect quiet areas (Article 8(1)(b)). In this regard it may be noted that a quiet area may not necessarily be entirely quiet. From the context it may be inferred that the quiet area referred to in Article 8(1)(b) is actually a quiet area in an agglomeration. This means that quiet is defined on the basis of exposure to noise below a certain limit value (Article 3(l)), in contrast to the concept of a quiet area in open country (Article 3(m)). The directive explicitly states that the measures contained in the plans are at the discretion of the Member States, effectively ruling out the direct effect. However, the second obligation arising from Article 8(2)(b) could probably be construed as an enforceable right requiring measures to deal with excesses of the limit values. These limit values can be set by the Member States (Article 3(s)). The Member States are free to set these, but an extrapolation of the Court's jurisprudence on similar provisions in other directives, such as Article 4(2) of the EIA Directive will probably result in a limitation of this discretion in view of the environmental objectives of the Framework Noise Directive. The directive contains various provisions dealing with the information of the public (Article 9) and public consultation (Article 8(7)). There are furthermore provisions on reporting to the Commission and reporting by the Commission to the Council and the European Parliament. On the basis of the Commission reports, additional measures regarding specific sources may be contemplated (Article 11(2)(b)). The directive should have been implemented before 18 July 2004.

---

[523] For noise at work places see Directive 2000/13, see above in this section.

15 Legislation on Dangerous Substances

European legislation on dangerous substances underwent a complete overhaul in 2006 with the entry into force of the REACH package. REACH refers to the Registration, Evaluation, Authorisation and Restriction of Chemicals and the package consists of Regulation 1907/2006[524] and Directive 2006/121.[525] As a result of REACH, the old cornerstone of European policy on chemicals, Directive 76/548 on the classification, packaging and labelling of dangerous substances, has been amended and will be replaced by the Regulation on Classification, Labelling and Packaging of dangerous substances.[526] Moreover, several directives and regulations have been replaced or amended in order to create one uniform system for chemicals. Below, we will first analyse the REACH Regulation and then analyse the REACH Directive. Finally we will look at legislation concerning the export and import of chemicals and a specific category of chemicals: pesticides and biocides.

15.1 The REACH Regulation

At more than 800 pages in the Official Journal, the REACH Regulation is an impressive legislative feat.[527] It applies to all substances, which is given a very wide definition (Article 1 in connection with 3(1)). Radioactive substances, substances in customs control, waste and so-called non-isolated intermediates (intermediary chemicals that remain in the installation used for their creation (Article 3(15)(a)) are outside the scope of the REACH Regulation (Article 2(1) and (2)). Moreover, the regulation does not apply to the transport of substances and it applies without prejudice to the specialised regimes for certain substances, such as radioactive substances, medicinal products, chemicals for use in foodstuffs (Article 2(4), (5) and (6)).

Central to the REACH Regulation is the duty for producers and importers to register substances in a database managed by the European Chemicals Agency (ECA) that is established by the regulation (Title X). This registration requirement implements the principal duty laid down in Article 1(3) according to which the producers, importers and downstream users of substances are responsible for ensuring that substances will not adversely affect human health or the environment. Registration is required before a substance can be marketed (Article 5).[528] As a rule, registration is required for substances imported or produced in quantities exceeding one ton per year (Article 6) as well as for articles contain-

---

[524] OJ 2006 L 396/1, corrected text to be found in OJ 2007 L 136/3. Later amended. In Case C-558/07 S.P.C.M. [2009] ECR I-5789, the ECJ rejected a claim that the REACH Regulation was invalid because of violations of the principle of proportionality.

[525] OJ 2006 L 396/850.

[526] See section 15.2 below. Cf. in general on European chemicals legislation, Pallemaerts (2005).

[527] For a governance analysis of the REACH Regulation see Scott (2009).

[528] See also Article 128(1), which contains the free movement clause.

ing substances above a certain threshold (Article 7). However, the regulation contains a number of exceptions to this rule for polymers,[529] substances covered by specialised regimes and substances considered harmless (Listed in Annex IV). There is an exception for substances used in research and development (Article 9). Finally, there are transitional rules contained in Article 23. The rule is that the registration duty applies from 1 June 2008 onwards. Pursuant to Article 23, however, the entry into force of the registration requirement may be as late as 1 June 2018 depending on the quantities involved and the dangerousness of the substance. These transitional rules apply only to so-called phase-in substances, a term that is defined in Article 3(20) as basically encompassing substances marketed before 1 January 1995.[530] These transitional rules apply only to substances preregistered between 1 June 2008 and 1 December 2008 (Article 28).

The registration involves the submission of a technical dossier including formal details such as the name of the producer or importer and the identity of the substance but also, and most importantly, all physicochemical, toxicological and ecotoxicological information (Article 12). The exact detail and content of this information depends on the quantity of the substance imported or produced and is set out in Annex VII and VIII.

As the information contained in the technical dossier will often be expensive to gather, the regulation provides for various mechanisms to avoid duplication. Firstly, it envisages joint registration (Article 11). Secondly, substances subject to notification and approval as part of specialised regimes, such as plant protection products, are regarded as being registered (Article 15). Thirdly, Title III contains various rules on data sharing and the avoidance of animal tests.[531] On the basis of these provisions there is a duty to inquire prior to registration to see whether there are prior registrations. If this inquiry yields that tests on vertebrate animals have already been conducted less than 12 years ago, the regulation prohibits repetition of these tests (Article 26(3)). Furthermore, the regulation envisages a procedure whereby the ECA can require sharing of data subject to payment of a proportionate part of the costs involved in the generation of these data (Article 27). The information contained in the registration should be communicated through the supply chain, and notably downstream (i.e. to the users of the substances; Title IV).

---

[529] Article 6(3) requires registration of the monomer substances that react to make polymers. See on this concept Case C-558/07 *S.P.C.M.* [2009] ECR I-5789, paras. 18-38. See on this case Laffineur (2010).

[530] It also includes so-called existing substances listed in the European Inventory of Existing Commercial Substances EINECS.

[531] The testing methods themselves have been largely harmonised through the principles of so-called Good Laboratory Practices (GLP), as defined in Directive 2004/10 on the application of the principles of good laboratory practice (GLP) and the verification of their applications for tests on chemical substances (OJ 2004 L 50/44), Directive 2004/9 on the inspection and verification of GLP (OJ 2004 L 50/28), later amended and Commission Regulation 440/2008 on testing methods pursuant to the REACH Regulation, OJ 2008 L 142/1.

The second step in the REACH system relates to the evaluation of substances. This takes place on the basis of Title VI and can take two forms: dossier and substance evaluation. Dossier evaluation involves the ECA checking to see whether animal tests proposed in a registration are necessary (Article 40). The ECA may also check registrations in so as to ascertain conformity of the technical dossier with Articles 10, 12 and 13 of the REACH Regulation (Article 41). Substance evaluation takes place on the basis of Article 44 and further and involves the ECA and Member State authorities conducting tests themselves. The regulation contains a system for allocating specific evaluations to the various national authorities.

The third step concerns the authorisation of substances (Title VII). This aims to ensure the good functioning of the internal market while at the same time assuring that the risks from substances of very high concern are properly controlled (Article 55). Moreover, such substances are to be replaced by suitable alternative substances or technologies where this is economically and technically viable. Just as with the registration-phase, the manufacturers and importers must actually do the required research. These substances of very high concern are defined in Article 57(a)-(f) as substances that are carcinogenic, mutagenic, toxic for reproduction, (very) persistent, bioaccumulative and toxic or any other substance outside the previous categories for which there it scientific evidence of probably serious effects to human health or the environment, such as substances that have endocrine disrupting properties (so-called Annex XIV-substances). The last category opens up the Annex XIV list, in accordance with the precautionary principle.[532] Article 56(1) contains a general prohibition of marketing so-called Annex XIV-substances, subject to a number of exceptions. Firstly, the prohibition applies only after the sunset-date (Article 58(1)(c)(i)). This relates to the procedure whereby the ECA can decide to place a substance in the Annex XIV list. This procedure allows for the continued use of these substances upon application to the ECA (Article 58(1)(c)(ii)) until a decision concerning the authorisation is taken. Secondly, the prohibition does not apply where the use of the substance has been authorised (Article 56(1)(a) and (b)). Thirdly, the prohibition is declared inapplicable by Article 58(4) and (5) for a number of categories of substances.

Whereas it is the ECA that decides on placing a substance in the Annex XIV list, it is for the Commission to decide on the authorisations. From this division of responsibilities it could be inferred that it is for the ECA to protect human health and the environment in the light of the precautionary principle, whereas it is for the Commission to balance this with economic arguments and ensure the proper functioning of the internal market. The procedure for an authorisation decision is laid down in Article 60. According to Article 60(2) authorisations may only be granted if the risk to human health or the environment are adequately controlled. A further limit to the authorisation can be found

---

[532] For an analysis from the perspective of governance and the precautionary principle see Fleurke & Somsen (2011).

in Article 60(3) according to which certain substances may not be authorised (substances for which no safe threshold may be determined, and substances that have (very) persistent, bioaccumulative and toxic properties). This exception is, however, subject to yet another exception contained in Article 60(4) that allows for an authorisation if it is shown that the socio-economic benefits outweigh the risk to human health or the environment (the balancing test) and if there are no suitable alternative substances or technologies (the alternatives test). It is not entirely certain if it is for the Commission or the applicant to show that the socio-economic benefits outweigh the risks, as it is the Commission that takes the decision whereas Article 60(5(b) refers to the applicant as the person for whom the technical and economic feasibility of alternatives is to be taken into account. The latter provision also appears to further define the suitability-requirement in Article 60(4) as encompassing technical and economic consid-erations. The inclusion of economic considerations as part of the suitable alternatives test is wrong in our opinion as an economic appraisal is also part of ascertaining the socio-economic benefits, and the alternatives test cannot be seen as part of the balancing test.

The REACH Regulation allows for so-called restrictions (Title VIII) for substances. Such restrictions take the form of placing a substance in Annex XVII by a Commission decision following a proposal by a Member State, the ECA or the Commission itself. The procedure for such decisions is set out in Article 69-73. Restriction decisions are only allowed if there is an unacceptable risk to human health or the environment, which needs to be addressed on a European-wide basis. Such decisions shall take into account the socio-economic impact of the restriction, including the availability of alternatives (Article 68). In contrast to the authorisation decision (Article 60), socio-economic impacts appear to have a smaller role here and cannot outweigh the risks to human health and the environment. The REACH Regulation contains a special appli-cation of Article 114(4) TFEU in the form of Article 67(3), which allows the Member States to maintain in force any more stringent restrictions for Annex XVII substances subject only to the requirement that such restrictions have been notified according to the Treaty. A Commission decision is therefore not necessary.

Titles IX and X contain the rules for the establishment and working of the ECA including provisions on legal protection against decisions taken by the ECA. The following decisions may be appealed (Article 91(1)):
· Article 9 – Conditions for the use of substances in research and develop-ment;
· Article 20 – Decisions concerning the completeness of registration of substances;
· Article 27(6) – Decisions on the sharing of information from prior regis-trations;
· Article 30(2) & (3) – Decisions on the repetition of animal tests and shar-ing of costs involved;
· Article 51 – Decisions on dossier evaluation.

Such an appeal shall have a suspensive effect (Article 91(2)). The requirements for standing under Article 91 basically conform to those used under Article 263 TFEU. Only the addressee or those who are directly and individually concerned can appeal. Moreover such appeals must be brought within three months of the notification of the decision. Appeals on the basis of Article 91 will be decided by the Board of Appeal of the ECA (Article 93). Decisions of the Board of Appeal and all decisions of the ECA that cannot be appealed on the basis of Article 91 may be appealed before the Court of First Instance or the Court of Justice in accordance with Article 263 TFEU (Article 94(1)). Failure to act of the ECA may be the subject of proceedings pursuant to Article 265 TFEU. Concerning the above system of legal protection a number of comments are possible. Firstly, the regulation does not envisage Article 265 TFEU-proceedings against a failure to act on the part of the Board of Appeal. Secondly, it may be recalled that there is a two-month time limit for appeals pursuant to Article 263 TFEU, whereas Article 92 contains a three-month period in this regard. Finally, by allowing for appeals in accordance with Article 263 TFEU against ECA decisions not mentioned in Article 91 and Commission decisions pursuant to the REACH Regulation, the rules on standing, and particularly those dealing with individual concern, become relevant. From the perspective of the importers and manufacturers much depend on whether these decisions are taken on the basis of substances, or on the basis of applicants. The latter option will greatly increase the possibilities of a manufacturer or importer being individually concerned.[533]

Title XI contains the rules on the classification and labelling of substances. This title basically declares Directive 76/548, as amended by the REACH Directive,[534] applicable. Title XII deals with information and reporting. Article 118 declares Regulation 1049/2001 on access to information applicable to the ECA. However, paragraph 2 restricts the access to this information by declaring, *inter alia*, details on the full composition of a preparation and the precise use of a substance will normally undermine the protection of the commercial interests. This means that information relating to these aspects may be withheld. Interestingly, the word 'normally' in Article 118(2) appears to allow for exceptions to this general duty not to disclose the information. Title XIII and XIV deal with the competent authorities in the Member States and the enforcement of the REACH Regulation. Finally, Title XV contains the transitional and final provisions. Basically, the regulation entered into force on 1 June 2007 and it applies from 1 June 2008 onwards. Since it is based on Article 114 TFEU, the REACH Regulation contains a free movement clause (Article 128(1)). Paragraph 2, however, allows the Member States to maintain or enact national rules on the protection of workers, human health or the environment insofar as these rules are outside the scope of the regulation.[535] Article 129 contains the safeguard clause, allow-

---

[533] See further Cana (2004) at 107.

[534] See section 15.2 of this chapter.

[535] See, concerning Directive 76/769, Case C-473/98 *Kemikalieninspektionen* v. *Toolex Alpha* [2000] ECR I-5681, para. 30.

ing for Member State action where there is an urgent risk for human health or the environment. The REACH Regulation replaces the Marketing of Dangerous Substances Directive from 1 June 2009 onwards (Article 139).[536]

15.2   Directives on the Classification, Packaging and Labelling of Dangerous Substances and Preparations

Directive 76/548 was amended several times. The most important amendments are referred to as the sixth[537] and seventh amendment.[538] On 1 June 2008 it was amended by the REACH Directive 2006/121. The sixth amendment introduced a system of notification for new chemicals throughout the EU. The directive contained a different regime for existing substances, in other words substances which were already on the market before 18 September 1981.[539] The Commission was required to draw up an inventory of these substances, based on the information provided by the Member States.[540] With the REACH Directive, the distinction between new and existing substances has disappeared and as a result the rules on the notification of new substances have been repealed. The directive also contained provisions that applied equally to new and existing substances. For example, the Member States were not allowed, on grounds relating to notification, classification, packaging or labelling, to prohibit, restrict or impede the placing on the market of substances, old or new, which complied with the provisions of the directive.

Finally, the directive provided that Member States might provisionally prohibit the sale of a substance or subject it to special conditions in its territory where it constituted a hazard for man or the environment, even if it did comply with the provisions of the directive. The Member State in question was required to inform the Commission and the other Member States immediately, after which the Commission would consult the Member States and, within six weeks, give its view and take appropriate measures.[541] The directive provided a fine

---

[536] Directive 76/769 on the marketing and use of certain dangerous substances and preparations OJ 1976 L 262/201, amended many times since then.

[537] Directive 79/831, OJ 1979 L 259/10.

[538] Directive 92/32, OJ 1992 L 154/15.

[539] The collection, circulation and accessibility of information on 'existing' substances (substances included in the European Inventory of Existing Commercial Substances, EINECS) and the evaluation of the risks of these substances to man and the environment are the subject of Regulation 793/93 (repealed with effect from 1 June 2008, cf. Article 139 of the REACH Regulation), OJ 1993 L 84/1, on the evaluation and control of the risks of existing substances.

[540] This was published in OJ 1990 C 146.

[541] Case C-43/90 Commission v. Germany [1992] ECR I-1909. On the application of the safeguard clause in Article 23 the Court ruled that it is clear that when a measure is being notified, it is unnecessary to state in so many words that it is a provisional measure. Simple notification is sufficient.

example of total harmonisation.[542] The seventh amendment introduced substantial changes to the sixth amendment and represents a general tightening-up of European policy on dangerous substances. It contains amended provisions on the testing of substances (Article 3[543]) and the classification of substances according to categories such as 'dangerous for the environment', 'mutagenic', 'carcinogenic' (Article 4). Article 6 requires traders and importers to carry out an investigation of 'existing' dangerous substances, on the basis of which they are required to label and package the substances.

This directive is intended to achieve total harmonisation. Member States may not prohibit, restrict or impede the placing on the market of substances which comply with its requirements, on grounds relating to notification, classification, packaging or labelling within the meaning of the directive (Article 30). Only where a Member State, in the light of new information, has justifiable reasons to consider that a substance, which has been accepted as satisfying the requirements of the directive, nevertheless constitutes a danger for man or the environment, by reason of classification, packaging or labelling which is no longer appropriate, may it take temporary measures to address the situation (Article 31). The Commission must be informed of such action, and if it considers action to be necessary, this may lead to adaptation of the relevant European legislation. However, the directive does not harmonise the conditions under which dangerous substances may be *marketed* or *used,* which are still matters that fall within the purview of national legislation.[544]

In addition to Directive 67/548 on dangerous substances, the classification, packaging and labelling of dangerous preparations is harmonised by Directive 1999/45.[545] This directive works in much the same way as Directive 67/548 and the scope is defined primarily by the concept of 'preparation'. This is defined as 'mixtures or solutions composed of two or more substances', setting a clear boundary between the two directives.

Both directives will be repealed by Regulation 1272/2008 with effect from 1 June 2015.[546] The effect of this is to implement the Globally Harmonised System of Classification and Labelling of Chemicals (GHS) in the EU. To this end, the regulation essentially combines the GHS approach with existing EU law on the classification and labelling and the REACH Regulation.

---

[542] Case 278/85 *Commission* v. *Denmark* [1987] ECR 4069. See also Chapter 3 for a more exhaustive treatment of this case.

[543] Such tests shall be conducted in accordance with the REACH Regulation, Article 1(3) of the REACH Directive.

[544] Case C-473/98 *Kemikalieninspektionen* v. *Toolex Alpha* [2000] ECR I-5681, para. 29.

[545] OJ 1999 L 200/1, later amended.

[546] OJ 2008 L 353/1.

15.3   Legislation on Pesticides and Plant Protection Products

There are several European measures relating to the agricultural, internal market, human health and environmental aspects of the use of plant protection products and pesticides:
- · legislation on the marketing of plant protection and biocidal products;
- · legislation on maximum residue levels of pesticides;
- · legislation on the sustainable use of pesticides.

Apart from these specialised regimes, 'standard' EU law on the classification, labelling and packaging of chemicals applies to pesticides and plant protection products as well. As the above sections on the REACH-package have shown, this is generally complex legislation containing an intricate balance between environmental and health concerns subject to the precautionary principle and economic interests.

15.3.1   Legislation on the Marketing of Plant Protection Products and Biocides

Regulation 1107/2009 contains the rules on the placing on the market of plant protection products (insecticides, herbicides and fungicides).[547] It replaces two directives that has been amended several times and to increase legal certainty and consistency, the form of a regulation was chosen. Article 1 of the regulation defines the subject matter and objective and in doing so refers to the precautionary principle (Article 1(4)). The scope of the regulation is confined to plant protection products (Article 2(1)) as well as active substances, which includes mirco-organisms. Finally so-called safeners, synergists and co-formulants, which are basically substances that have little or no effectiveness of themselves but they are added to plant protection products to increase their effectiveness or safety. This adds up to a wide scope. Chapter II contains the rules for the approval of active substances, safeners, synergists and co-formulants. Between these four categories, the rules for active substances and safeners and synergists are the most elaborate and strict and the regime for co-formulants is the least strict. The approval criteria for active substances are listed in Article 4 of the regulation. Basically, these criteria ensure that the active substance, when used properly, shall not have any negative effects on human health, plants or plant products, the environment and it shall be sufficiently effective for improving plant production (Article 4(3)(a)-(e)). Approval of an active substance may be conditional (Article 6) and the approval procedure is set out in Articles 7-21 and basically involves an application with the authorities of one Member State (the rapporteur Member State). The rapporteur Member State will then prepare a report that will be made publicly available by the European Food Safety Authority who will also come to a conclusion on the approval

---

[547] OJ 2009 L 309/1. It repeals Directive 91/414, OJ 1991 L 230/1 and Directive 79/117, OJ 1979 L 33/36.

of the active substance. This conclusion will then lead to a review report and a draft regulation drawn up by the Commission and submitted to the Committee on the Food Chain and Animal Health (Article 13(1)). On the basis of the review report and other relevant factors as well as the precautionary principle, the approval regulation is then adopted (Article 13 (2)).[548] Such approval regulations will also have the effect of including the active substance on the EU list of approved active substances.[549] First approval may not exceed a period of ten years (Article 5) and it is for the producer of the active substance to then show as part of the renewal process that the substance is still considered safe in conformity with the criteria laid down in Article 4 (Articles 14-20). Finally, approval may always be reviewed, for example in the light of new scientific and technical knowledge indicating that the substance may compromise the objectives of the Water Framework Directive (Article 21). For low-risk substances, the approval period can be fifteen years. Article 25 declares the same procedure applicable to the approval of safeners and synergists, however without the derogation for low-risk substances. For co-formulants, no real procedure is established, but only the substantive criteria for acceptability are listed (Article 27). Unacceptable co-formulants will be put on the list in Annex III to the regulation. The effect of this regime is that plant protection products may not be marketed if they have not been authorised in accordance with the regulation (Article 28(1)), unless one of the derogations in Article 28(2) applies. This authorisation by the Member States takes place on the basis of Article 29. To ensure the integration of the internal market, Article 40 requires mutual recognition of the authorisations by the Member State authorities. This means that the holder of the authorisation will have to apply for authorisation in all other Member States where he intends to market the product. However, such authorisation should be based on mutual recognition of the earlier authorisation provided that this pertains to the same use of the product under comparable agricultural practices in the same zone.[550] Quite like the approval procedure, authorisations may also be reviewed and withdrawn. The regulation further contains procedures for low-risk plant protection products (Article 47), genetically modified organisms that work as plant protection products (Article 48)[551] and treated seeds (Article 49). Furthermore, the regulation contains a regime similar to that in the REACH Regulation concerning testing, data sharing and access to information, as well as provisions on the packaging, labelling and advertising of the products. These rules are similar to the old regime laid down in the two repealed directives.

---

[548] E.g. Commission Implementing Regulation 820/2011 Approving the active substance terbuthylazine, OJ 2011 L 209/18.

[549] This list can be found in Commission Implementing Regulation 540/2011, OJ 2011 L 153/1, later amended.

[550] These zones are defined in Annex I.

[551] Here the rules on the assessment of such organisms are declared applicable in addition to those in the regulation.

When discussing the marketing of plant protection products and pesticides, mention must also be made of Directive 98/8 concerning the placing of biocidal products on the market.[552] These are a group of pesticides used primarily by industry and in the home to combat harmful organisms.

The structure of Directive 98/8 is similar to that of Regulation 1107/2009, in particular the system of 'dual authorisation'.[553] On the one hand the directive provides for the establishment at European level of a positive list of active substances which may be used in biocidal products and on the other it contains rules on the authorisation and the placing on the market for use of biocidal products within the Member States. Like the regulation mutual recognition of authorisations is a key element (Article 4).[554]

Member States are required to ensure that a biocidal product shall not be placed on the market and used in their territory unless it has been authorised (Article 3(1)). However, the directive distinguishes a special category of 'low-risk biocidal products', for which a simpler procedure applies (Article 3(2)). Authorisations shall be granted for a maximum period of 10 years (Article 3(6)).

Article 5 provides that Member States shall authorize a biocidal product only if the active substances it includes are listed in Annex I or IA of the directive and it is established that the biocidal product is sufficiently effective, has no unacceptable effects on the target organisms, such as unacceptable resistance or cross-resistance or unnecessary suffering and pain for vertebrates, and has no unacceptable effects on human or animal health, or on surface water and groundwater, and has no unacceptable effect on the environment. Article 5(2) provides that a biocidal product classified as toxic, very toxic or as a category 1 or 2 carcinogen, or as a category 1 or 2 mutagen or classified as toxic for reproduction category 1 or 2, shall not be authorised for marketing to, or use by the general public.

During the period for which an authorisation has been granted, it may be reviewed at any time if there are indications that any of the conditions referred to in Article 5 are no longer satisfied (Article 6).

An authorisation shall be cancelled if:
  · the active substance is no longer included in Annex I or IA;[555]
  · the conditions for obtaining the authorisation are no longer satisfied;

---

[552] OJ 1998 L123/1, amended many times since then. The directive is based on Article 100a, now Article 114 TFEU, making it clear that its primary objective is the functioning of the Internal Market. Cf. Wilson (1998).

[553] Cf. Vogelezang-Stoute (2004) at 133.

[554] See Case C-433/02 *Schreiber* [2004] ECR I-7275, paras. 34-39 on the application of Article 4(1).

[555] See for the inclusion of an active substance in Annexes I, IA or IB, Articles 10 and 11 of the directive. See further Case C-433/02 *Schreiber* [2004] ECR I-7275 where the Court adopts a precautionary approach to substances and classifies blocks of Cedar wood as biocidal because the cedar oil in them repels insects. Note, however, that this was the result of the fact Annex IA and IB had not been adopted. At this moment several substances have been included in Annex I, see, most recently, Directive 2011/81, OJ 2011 L 243/16.

· it is discovered that false or misleading particulars were supplied concerning the facts on the basis of which the authorisation was granted (Article 7).

Application for authorisation shall be made by the person who will be responsible for the first placing on the market of a biocidal product in a particular Member State. Every applicant shall be required to have a permanent office within the EU (Article 8).

Article 10(5) is also interesting. It provides that an entry of an active substance in Annex I, IA or IB may be refused or removed if there is another active substance for the same product type which, in the light of scientific or technical knowledge, presents significantly less risk to health or to the environment. This is known as the 'substitution principle'.

The directive also contains provisions concerning the use of data held by competent authorities for other applicants (Article 12), cooperation in the use of data for second and subsequent applications for authorisation (Article 13), derogation from the requirements (Article 15), transitional measures (Article 16),[556] research and development (Article 17), information exchange (Article 18), confidentiality (Article 19) and the classification, packaging and labelling of biocidal products (Article 20[557]). The 'standard' safeguard clause can be found in Article 32.

15.3.2 Pesticide Residues

There are several directives pertaining to the setting of maximum residue levels (MRL) in agricultural products, such as fruit and vegetables,[558] cereals,[559] foodstuffs of animal origin,[560] and products of vegetable origin), and honey.[561] These directives have been repealed by Regulation 396/2005 because the directives were amended several times and a clarification was considered necessary.[562] The process of repeals depends on the adoption and

---

[556] See on the transitional rules: Case C-316/04 *Stichting Zuid-Hollandse Milieufederatie* [2005] ECR I-9759.

[557] The reference to Directive 88/379 must be read as a reference to Directive 99/45; see Article 21(3) of Directive 99/45, OJ 1999 L 200/1. Note that Directive 99/45 will be repealed by Regulation 1272/2008.

[558] Directive 76/895 relating to the fixing of maximum levels for pesticide residues in and on fruit and vegetables, OJ 1976 L 340/26, frequently amended.

[559] Directive 86/362 on the fixing of maximum levels for pesticide residues in and on cereals, OJ 1986 L 221/37, frequently amended.

[560] Directive 86/363 on the fixing of maximum levels for pesticide residues in and on foodstuffs of animal origin, OJ 1986 L 221/43, later amended.

[561] Directive 90/642 on the fixing of maximum levels for pesticide residues in and on certain products of plant origin, including fruit and vegetables, OJ 1990 L 350/71, frequently amended.

[562] Regulation 396/2005 on maximum residue levels (MRL Regulation), OJ 2006 L 70/1. See also Directive 2002/63 on sampling for the control of pesticide residues, OJ 2002 L 187/30.

publication of regulations establishing Annex I-IV pursuant to the MRL Regulation. At this moment Regulation 178/2006 establishing Annex I to the MRL Regulation has been adopted.[563] Annex II (setting MRLs), Annex III (setting temporary MRLs) and Annex IV (substances for which no MRL is considered necessary) have not been adopted yet. This means that only chapters I, IV and VI to X of the MRL Regulation apply with effect from 5 April 2005. The MRL Regulation is based on Articles 37 and 152(4)(b) EC[564] and aims to ensure a high level of consumer protection and harmonised provisions relating to pesticide residues. The MRL Regulation should be seen in the context of the General Food Law[565] and Regulation 1107/2009 on plant protection products.

Chapter I of the MRL Regulation contains the general provisions and determines the scope. The MRL Regulation applies to products of plant or animal origin, whether processed or not, covered by Annex I. It does not apply to products of animal or plant origin that are not intended for food or feed or to products treated before export to third countries (Article 2). Finally, the regulation applies without prejudice to the Biocides Directive[566] and a directive on undesirable substances in animal feed[567] and the regulation on residues of veterinary medicines.[568] Article 4(1) enables the Commission to adopt Annex I. It further envisages the adoption of Annex IV containing plant protection products for which no MRL needs to be set. To this date Annex IV has not been adopted. Chapter II, which does not apply yet, contains the procedure for application of an MRL. This procedure commences with an application to the Member State which is then forwarded to the European Food Safety Authority (EFSA)[569] and the Commission along with an evaluation by the Member State. The evaluation shall take place in accordance with the uniform principles adopted pursuant to Directive 91/414. The EFSA will then give a reasoned opinion on, in particular, the risks to consumers and animals (Article 10(1)) within a maximum to six months from the date of receipt of the application (Article 11). Article 12 contains the procedure for the assessment of existing MRLs by the EFSA. MRLs are set by means of a Commission regulation pursuant to Article 14(1). This regulation may result in the inclusion of a new or modified MRL in Annex II or the inclusion of a new or modified temporary MRL in Annex III (Article 15). The Commission may also reject the application for an MRL by means of a decision. Article 16 contains the procedure for setting temporary MRLs. When the (temporary) MRLs have been set in Annex II and III, Chapter III, which does not apply yet, contains the rules on the MRLs applicable to products of plant and

---

[563] Regulation 178/2006, OJ 2006 L 29/3.

[564] Currently Articles 43 and 169 TFEU.

[565] Regulation 178/2002, OJ 2002 L 31/1, as amended by Regulation 1642/2003, OJ 2003 L 245/4.

[566] See above, section 15.3.

[567] Directive 2002/32, OJ 2002 L 140/10.

[568] Regulation 2377/90, OJ 1990 L 224/1.

[569] The MRL Regulation refers to the authority as defined in Article 22 of Regulation 178/2002, OJ 2002 L 31/1.

animal origin. Article 18(1)(a) dictates that Annex I products must comply with
the MRLs set in Annex II and III. The default obligation is set out in Article
18(1)(b), according to which the residue may not exceed 0.01 mg/kg for Annex I
products for which no MRL is set or for active substances not listed in Annex IV.
Products that comply with the MRLs benefit from a free movement clause (Article 18(2)). Article 18(3) allows for exceeding the MRLs provided that there are
adequate controls to ensure that these products are not immediately consumed.
The provisions of Chapter III do not apply to products produced or imported into
the EU before the date of application of that chapter. Chapter IV requires the
Commission to incorporate the existing MRLs in Annex II (Article 21). MRLs set
pursuant to Regulation 1107/2009 should similarly be incorporated as temporary MRLs in Annex III (Article 22). The level at which these temporary MRLs
should be set is the lowest level that can be achieved in all Member States on the
basis of good agricultural practice (Article 25). The term good agricultural practice (GAP) is defined in Article 3(2)(a) as the nationally recommended, authorised or registered safe use of plant protection products under actual conditions.
This implies a correct application of Regulation 1107/2009. Chapter V, which
does not apply yet, contains rules on controls, reports and sanctions. It envisages national controls (Article 26) on the basis of a national control programmes
(Article 30) and a European control programme (Article 29). Interestingly,
Article 30(3) merely allows for internet publication of the names of the retailers,
traders or producers whose products exceeded the MRLs whereas recital 34 is
formulated in a more imperative manner. On the basis of the national reports
an Annual Report shall be drawn up by the EFSA (Article 32). Chapter VI allows
for emergency measures by the Commission or a Member State. Chapter VII
contains rules on support measures for harmonised MRLs. Such measures may
be fully subsidised by the EU (Article 37(1)). Chapter VIII deals with the coordination of applications for MRLs. Chapter IX contains the procedure for the adoption of the implementing legislation. Chapter X contains the final provisions.

15.3.3 Sustainable Use of Pesticides

Up to 2009 the EU essentially only regulated the beginning
and the end of plant protection products and pesticides, with the use of these
substances being largely unregulated. This gap was addressed in the Commission's 2006 thematic strategy on the sustainable use of pesticides and resulted
in the Framework Directive on the Sustainable Use of Pesticides.[570] Contrary to
the abovementioned rules, this is an environmental measure, based on Article
175 EC, currently Article 192 TFEU. As a result, it applies without prejudice to
other regulatory schemes concerning plant protection products and pesticides.
Moreover, the directive explicitly states that it does not preclude the Member
States from prohibiting or restricting the use of pesticides on grounds related
to the precautionary principle (Article 2(3)). Basically, the directive applies to

---

[570] Directive 2009/128, OJ 2009 L 309/71.

biocides and plant protection products as they are regulated by the instruments mentioned in section 15.3. Central to the directive is the duty on the part of the Member States to adopt National Action Plans with a view to reducing the risks of pesticide use for human health and the environment (Article 4). More practical are the provisions on the sales of pesticides. These essentially require that distributors have a minimum amount of trained persons who are certified (Article 6(1)). Very small distributors may be exempted from this requirement provided that they do not sell any – to put it simply – dangerous pesticides for non-professional users. Moreover, the directive requires pesticide application equipment to be checked with regard to compliance with the criteria in Annex II regularly. Until 2020 the maximum period between checks is five years, and after that it is reduced to three years (Article 8(1)). Moreover, all equipment is to be checked before 14 December 2016 and equipment that did not pass is not to be used after this date (Article 8(2)). There is, however, a possibility to derogate for low scale equipment (Article 8(3)). Further to the application of pesticides, the directive prohibits aerial spraying, subject to some rather restricted exceptions (Article 9). The directive requires the Member States to ensure that pesticide use is coordinated with the Water Framework Directive and that pesticide use in specific vulnerable areas is prohibited or regulated (Article 12). On a similar note, the Member States are to adopt rules on the handling and storage of pesticides and empty packaging (Article 13). The final provision worth mentioning concerns integrated pest management. On the basis of Article 14 the Member States must adopt an integrated pest management that reduces pesticide use and prioritising non-chemical products. The directive should be implemented before 14 December 2011.

15.4   Import and Export of Dangerous Chemicals

For some time now the dangers for man and the environment of the international trade in dangerous chemicals have been the subject of attention within the context of several international organisations, such as the OECD, UNEP and FAO. These organisations have established a procedure of 'prior informed consent' (PIC), which is intended to prevent substances being exported to third countries without the importing country having given its consent. On 11 September 1998 the Rotterdam Convention was signed by the EU.[571] The Rotterdam Convention is implemented by means of Regulation 304/2003.[572] In doing so, Regulation 304/2003 is actually more stringently protective than the Rotterdam Convention.[573]

---

[571] Approved by Decision 2003/106, OJ 2003 L 63/27. This decision has been annulled by the ECJ in Case C-94/03 *Commission* v. *Council* [2006] ECR I-1, because the wrong legal basis had been used.

[572] OJ 2003 L 63/1, later amended. Regulation 304/2003 repeals the old PIC Regulation 2455/92, OJ 1992 L 251/13. In Case C-178/03 *Commission* v. *Council and EP* [2006] ECR I-107, the ECJ has annulled Regulation 304/2003 because the wrong legal basis had been used. The effects of that regulation are maintained.

[573] Recital 4 of the Preamble to Regulation 304/2003.

The main provision in the regulation is a PIC procedure for the export of certain dangerous chemical substances (and preparations) from the EU to third countries. The regulation is more stringent in that it covers not only the substances in the Rotterdam Convention list[574] but also all substances subject to restrictions and bans within the EU.[575] In addition the regulation applies to the classification, packaging and labelling of all chemicals exported.

Article 6 declares a certain PIC procedure applicable to chemicals in the three parts of Annex I. Part 1 chemicals are subject to the export notification procedure laid down in Article 7. Part 2 chemicals fall under Article 7 and the PIC notification procedure in Article 10. Part 3 chemicals are subject to the PIC procedure. The level of detail and specific information to be submitted as part of the procedure also differs for the various parts of Annex I.

Briefly, the export notification procedure in Article 7 involves the following. When a chemical subject to notification is due to be exported from the EU to a third country *for the first time*, the exporter must provide the national authorities with certain information. The authorities must then check the completeness of the information in the light of Annex III and forward the information to the Commission who will then take the necessary measures to ensure that the country of destination receives notification of the intended export (Article 7(1)). The Commission compiles a database of all notifications (Article 7(1) third paragraph. No new notification is required for subsequent exports to a third country, unless there has been a major change to European legislation in respect of the substance in question or the composition of the preparation has been changed (Article 7(3)). The export notification procedure no longer applies when the PIC procedure applies and the importing country has decided to consent or not to consent in the import and this decision has been received by the Commission and forwarded to the Member States (Article 7(5)). However, the importing country may still require notification, in which case the export notification procedure will also still apply. Finally, the notification requirement may be waived by the importing country.

Article 10 contains a special PIC procedure for chemicals that are severely restricted or banned in the EU. The notification of exports of these chemicals must comply with Annex II (Article 10(2)).

Article 13(6) prohibits the export of chemicals in parts 2 or 3 of Annex I unless explicit consent has been received from the importing country. For part 3 chemicals such consent may also be in the form of a circular by the secretariat of the Rotterdam Convention (Article 16(3)(ii)). Article 14(2) categorically prohibits the export of the chemicals listed in Annex V.

Besides the PIC procedure, the regulation contains two further instruments for the protection of man and the environment outside the EU. Article 13(7) prohibits the export of chemicals later than six months before the expiry date. Moreover exporters are to ensure that the size of containers is optimised to as

---

[574] Article 2(1)(a) and Part 3 of Annex I.
[575] Article 2(1)(b) and Part 1 and 2.

to minimise the risk of the creation of obsolete stocks. This provision intends to prevent stockpiling of old chemicals in other countries. The second instrument relates to the classification, packaging and labelling of chemicals. Article 16 provides that dangerous chemicals which are intended for export are subject to the measures on packaging and labelling contained in the directives and the regulation.[576] As far as practicable the information on the label must be given in the language of the country of destination or of the area of intended use (Article 16(4)). Moreover, information on the storage conditions and shelf life should be relevant to the local conditions in the importing country (Article 13(8)).

In fact, Article 16 extends the application of the above directives to products intended for third countries. However, it is not clear whether Article 16 must be regarded as having the characteristics of a directive or a regulation. In other words, does it require transposition into national legislation, as the other provisions of the directives in question do, or is it in fact directly applicable? In the latter case exporters are required to act in conformity with its provisions, even without further implementing measures. The special labelling requirements in the regulation, such as Article 13(8) in our view support the conclusion that these rules have the characteristics of a Regulation. This would mean that they apply directly, even if the directives in question had not been implemented. From 2015 onwards, when the regulation replaces the directives, this will no longer be an issue.

16   Legislation on Genetically Modified Organisms

The European rules on genetically modified organisms and micro-organisms (GMOs and GMMs) are contained in two directives and thee regulations.
- Directive 2009/41 on the contained use;[577]
- Directive 2001/18 on the deliberate release;[578]
- Regulation 1829/2003 on genetically modified food and feed;[579]
- Regulation 1830/2003 on the traceability and labelling;[580]
- Regulation 1946/2003 on transboundary movements.[581]

These five instruments basically form a triptych, where Directive 2009/41 contains rules on the contained use, Directive 2001/18 and Regulation 1829/2003 and 1830/2003 deal with the deliberate release of GMOs and Regulation 1946/2003 is concerned with the transboundary movements of GMOs.

---

[576] See section 15.2 above.

[577] OJ 2009 L 125/75, repealing Directive 90/219, OJ 1990 L 117/1.

[578] OJ 2001 L 106/1, later amended. This directive repeals Directive 90/220, OJ 1990 L 117/15.

[579] OJ 2003 L 268/1, later amended.

[580] OJ 2003 L 268/24, later amended.

[581] OJ 2003 L 287/1.

GMMs are defined in the Contained Use Directive and the Deliberate Release Directive as micro-organisms in which the genetic material has been altered in a way that does not occur naturally (Article 2(b)). Annex I, Part A, contains an indicative list of genetic modification techniques, whereas Annex I, Part B, contains a number of techniques that will not result in genetic modification resulting in the organisms falling outside the scope of the directive. An important question in this regard is what qualifies as an 'organism' when genetically modified organisms produce pollen that in turn will also be genetically modified. In a case involving beekeepers whose honey contained traces of genetically modified pollen, the Court ruled that the question whether or not pollen, which are incapable of reproduction, can qualify as an organism depends on the possibility of the pollen 'transferring genetic material taking due account of the scientific data available and considering all forms of scientifically-established transfer of genetic material'.[582]

Another central concept is 'contained use' which is defined as any operation in which micro-organisms are genetically modified or in which GMOs are cultured, stored, etc. and for which specific containment measures are used to limit their contact with, and to provide a high level of safety for, the general population and the environment (Article 2(c)). Even where an organism would qualify as a genetically modified organism, Article 3(1) provides a derogation from the scope of the directive[583] for (a) organisms where the genetic modification is the result of the techniques listed in Annex II A and (b) so-called safe GMMs as listed in Annex II C.[584] This derogation is, however, without prejudice to Article 4(1) that contains a general duty for Member States to ensure that appropriate measures are taken to avoid adverse effects on human health or the environment. For all other GMMs the directive applies, including the general obligation laid down in Article 4(1). To meet this obligation, the user is required to carry out an assessment of the contained uses as regards the risks to human health and the environment that these contained uses may incur (Article 4(2)). This assessment shall result in the final classification of the contained uses in four classes. Class 1 consists of activities implying 'no or negligible' risk, Class 2 those implying 'low' risk, Class 3 'moderate' risk and Class 4 'high' risk. Each class corresponds with a given containment level. Where there is doubt as to which class is appropriate for the proposed contained use, the more stringent protective measures shall be applied unless sufficient evidence, in agreement with the competent authority, justifies the application of less stringent measures (Article 4(4)).

---

[582] Case C-442/09 *Bablok and others*, Judgment of 6 September 2011, para. 60-61. Note that even when the pollen themselves do not qualify as organisms, their presence in food and foodstuffs may still fall within the scope of the Regulation on Genetically Modified Food and Feed, see below in this section.

[583] Further derogations relate to the transport of GMMs (Article 3(2)) and the deliberate release (Article 3(3)), where other legislation applies.

[584] This distinction between safe GMMs and all other GMMs was introduced earlier by an amendment to Directive 90/219 by Directive 98/81, OJ 1998 L 330/13.

Article 5 provides that the user shall apply the general principles and the appropriate containment and other protective measures set out in the directive so as to keep workplace and environmental exposure to any GMMs to the lowest reasonably practicable level, and so that a high level of safety is ensured.

Depending on the class of contained use, various notification requirements apply. Under Article 6, when premises are to be used for contained uses *for the first time,* the user will be required to notify the competent authorities. However, once this has been done, subsequent Class 1 contained use may proceed without further notification (Article 7). Notification must be given of every Class 2 contained use, but if a previous notification has been given and any associated consent requirements have been satisfied, the Class 2 contained use may proceed immediately following the new notification (Article 8(2)). If no previous notification has been given, the Class 2 contained use may not proceed until 45 days after submission of the notification. Finally, a Class 3 or higher class of contained use may not proceed without the prior written consent of the competent authority (Article 9(1) and (2)). The competent authority is required to communicate its decision at the latest 45 days after submission of the new notification in cases where a previous notification has been submitted, or at the latest 90 days after submission of the notification, in other cases. Each specific notification requirement also specifies the information that is required to be given. Article 11(1) requires the user to notify the competent authority of new information or changes in the contained use which could have significant effects on the risks involved. Interestingly, the mandatory nature of this requirement to forward new information is not reflected in the authority's duty to act upon such information as it *may* require modification, suspension or termination of the contained use (Article 11(2)). It is submitted that in the light of the directive's objectives such new information must result in a reaction on the part of the authority that protects human health and the environment. Furthermore, the directive allows, but does not require, public consultations (Article 12), drawing up emergency plans and furnishing information on safety measures (Articles 13 to 15),[585] ensuring control and supervision by the authorities (Article 16), reporting ((Article 17) and the confidentiality of certain information (Article 18).[586] Here we see that certain information shall not be considered confidential (Article 18(2)).

The non-accidental release of genetically modified organisms is regulated by the Deliberate Release Directive 2001/18 which defines 'deliberate release' as any intentional introduction into the environment of a GMO, for example by placing it on the market, without such containment measures (Article 2(3)).

---

[585] See Case C-429/01 *Commission* v. *France* [2003] ECR I-14355, where the Court finds that the implementation of Article 14(a) requires a legal obligation to determine on a case by case basis whether a emergency action plan is necessary (paragraph 41). Moreover Article 14(b) dictates that such emergency plans must be made available as such, not as part of more general information published (paragraph 59).

[586] See Case C-429/01 *Commission* v. *France* [2003] ECR I-14355 paras. 74-88 on the implementation of Article 19(2) and (3).

From this definition and the definition of contained use, set out above in this paragraph, it is clear that Directive 90/219 is primarily concerned with the measures necessary to reduce the potential risks for man and the environment that can arise in working with GMMs, while Directive 2001/18 concerns the use of GMOs for research and development and commercial purposes. This is also reflected in the different legal basis. Whereas the Contained Use Directive is based on Article 130s EC (now Article 192 TFEU), Directive 200/18 has been adopted on the basis of Article 144 TFEU. Directive 2001/18 is not only concerned with the protection of human health and the environment, but also the removal of barriers to trade caused by disparities in national rules, are important aims.

The scope of Directive 2001/18 is defined by the term GMO, which is comparable to that employed by Directive 90/219, with the exception that humans are explicitly excluded (Article 2(2)). Moreover, Article 3(1) excludes certain categories of organisms (resulting from the techniques listed in Annex I B) and Article 2(2)(b) excludes certain techniques (listed in Annex IA, part 2) from the term genetic modification, and thus also from the scope of the directive.[587] Directive 2001/18 contains provisions on the deliberate release of GMOs for research and development purposes (Part B; Articles 5 to 11) and on the placing on the market of products containing GMOs (Part C; Articles 12 to 24). It imposes a general obligation on the Member States to ensure in accordance with the precautionary principle that all appropriate measures are taken to avoid adverse effects on human health and the environment (Article 4(1)).

As far as the deliberate release of GMOs for research and development purposes is concerned, a notification must be submitted to the competent authority, including a technical dossier with information on the dangers for human health or the environment (Article 6). The competent authority may either accept the notification, in which case the release may proceed, or indicate that the release does not fulfil the conditions of the directive and the notification is rejected (Article 6(5)(a) or (b)). Only after express consent is the release allowed, and then only in conformity with any conditions required in the consent (Article 6(8)). Article 7 allows for the introduction by means of a Commission decision of a simplified procedure for the release of GMOs with which sufficient experience has been gathered. Part B further contains rules on the consultation and information of the public (Article 9), reporting obligations (Article 10) and the exchange of information between the authorities and the Commission (Article 11).

Part C similarly envisages notification and consent for the placing on the market of products containing GMOs (Article 13). However, as the placing on the market has an effect on all the Member States, there is a procedure whereby the competent authority must forward the notification to the Commission and

---

[587] It may be noted that Annex I B is more restrictive compared to the corresponding Annex II, part A, of Directive 90/219.

the competent authorities of the other Member States. Furthermore, in comparison with Part B additional information must be submitted, including information on the effects on the ecosystems which may be affected by the use of the product and on the packaging and labelling of the product (Article 13(2)). The competent authority must then prepare an assessment report that contains an indication whether the decision is going to be negative (no consent for marketing) or positive (consent for marketing). In case of a negative assessment, the report will be sent to the notifier alone and the notification will be rejected in a reasoned decision (Article 14(2), first indent) in connection with Article 14(3(b) and Article 15(2)). Positive assessments must be forwarded to the Commission which shall forward it to the other competent authorities (Article 14(2), second indent). The other competent authorities and the Commission then have 60 days to raise reasoned objections. If no such objections are raised in the 60-day period, the competent authority shall give consent. In case of objections, the authorities and Commission have an extra 45 days (in total 105 from the date of notification) to resolve outstanding issues (Article 15(3)). If these issues are resolved, consent is given.[588] When the issues are not resolved Article 18 provides for a Commission decision within 120 days. If the Commission has taken a positive decision, the competent authority that received the original notification will give its written consent to the notification so that the product in question may be placed on the market (Article 18(2)). Consent decisions should comply with the requirements set out in Article 19(3) and may not be given for more than 10 years (Article 15(4)). Article 19(3)(e) requires the labelling of the product to clearly state that it contains genetically modified organisms. Once a product has received written consent, the principle of mutual recognition laid down in Article 19(1) applies. Moreover, the product benefits from a free movement clause (Article 22),[589] but the Member States may also use a safeguard clause (Article 23)[590]. It may then be used without further notification throughout the EU,

---

[588] See on the procedure (Article 13) in the old Directive 90/220, Case C-6/99 *Association Greenpeace France* v. *Ministère de l'Agriculture et de la Pêche* [2000] ECR I-1651. According to the Court this procedure is to be interpreted as meaning that, if, after an application for placing a GMO on the market has been forwarded to the Commission, no Member State has raised an objection, in accordance with Article 13(2) of that directive, or if the Commission has taken a favourable decision under paragraph (4) of that provision, the competent authority which forwarded the application, with a favourable opinion, to the Commission *must* issue the consent in writing, allowing the product to be placed on the market. However, irregularities at the national level might have an effect on the legality of the Commission's decision and subsequent decisions at national level implementing the Commission's decision.

[589] Note that a blanket ban on the use of genetically modified organisms violates this clause, see Case C-165/08 *Commission* v. *Poland* [2009] ECR I-6843.

[590] See, however, Joined Cases C-58/10 to C-68/10 *Monsanto and others*, Judgment of 8 September 2011, paras. 43-63, where the Court finds that a GMO authorised for planting under the old Deliberate Release Directive may be subject to the safeguard clause in that directive. In this case the safeguard clause in the Regulation on Genetically Modified Food and Feed can be used.

provided the specific conditions of use and the environments and/or geographical areas stipulated in these conditions are strictly adhered to. A list of all products receiving final written consent is published in the Official Journal (Article 24(2)).[591] The directive contains a procedure whereby lighter notification requirements may be adopted (Article 16) and a renewal procedure (Article 17). This procedure is basically comparable to that set out in Articles 14 and 18. Notable differences are the shorter time-limits and the fact that the consent maybe given for a longer period (Article 17(6)). Notification for a renewal of consent does not stand in the way of continued marketing in accordance with the conditions laid down in the original consent (Article 17(9)).

The free movement clause in the directive rules out more stringent measures. The directive does, however, contain a safeguard clause, by which Member States may provisionally restrict or prohibit the use or sale of such products where they nevertheless have justifiable reasons to consider that a product constitutes a risk to human health or the environment (Article 23).[592] The Commission must immediately be informed of such action and then has 60 days to take a decision on the matter. Member States may also invoke the procedure under Article 114(4) or (5) TFEU to maintain or introduce more stringent measures. In Decision 2003/653, the Commission rejected Austria's application for a derogation from Directive 2001/18 on the basis of Article 95(5).[593]

The directive further contains a requirement to produce reports (Article 31) and provisions on access to information and confidentiality (Article 25)[594] and labelling (Article 26). Article 26a is the result of Regulation 1829/2003 on genetically modified food and feed and requires the Member States to take the necessary measures to avoid the unintentional presence of GMOs in other products.[595]

Given the anxiety regarding the presence of genetically modified organisms in the foodchain, it should not come as a surprise that this matter is regulated at

---

[591] See for instance Commission Decision 98/292 concerning the placing on the market of genetically modified maize (*Zea mays L. line Bt-11*), OJ 1998 L 131/28. Commission Decision 2007/364 concerning the placing on the market of a carnation (*Dianthus caryophyllus L., line 123.2.38*) genetically modified for flower colour, OJ 2007 L 138/50.

[592] See Case C-6/99 *Association Greenpeace France* v. *Ministère de l'Agriculture et de la Pêche* [2000] ECR I-1651.

[593] OJ 2003 L 230/34. An appeal against this decision was rejected in Joined Cases T-366/03 and T-235/04 *Land Oberösterreich and Republic of Austria* v. *Commission* [2005] ECR II-4005. Upheld by the ECJ in Joined Cases C-439/05 P and C-454/05 P, [2007] ECR I-7141.

[594] See in this regard Case C-552/07 *Commune de Sausheim* v. *Pierre Azelvandre* [2009] ECR I-987, paras. 29-55, where the Court first indicates that the exactness with which the location of the release must be made public depends on the information submitted to the auhorities as part of the authorisation procedure. Moreover, the confidentiality regime in the directive is considered to be exhaustive harmonisation resulting in the impossibility to rely on considerations of public order and security to restrict access to the information concerning the location.

[595] Regulation 1829/2003, OJ 2003 L 268/1, Article 43(2).

EU level as well. The Regulation on Genetically Modified Food and Feed, Regulation 1829/2003, is quite similar to Directive 2001/18 in that it also seeks to protect the environment, human health, animal welfare and consumer interests whilst ensuring the effective functioning of the internal market (Article 1(a)).[596] It must be read in conjunction with sister Regulation 1830/2003 on the traceability and labelling of GMOs[597] and the General Food Law Regulation.[598] The Regulation on Genetically Modified Food and Feed applies to (a) GMOs for food use; (b) food containing or consisting of GMOs; (c) food produced from or containing ingredients produced from GMOs.[599]

Regulation 1829/2003 contains a chapter on genetically modified food (chapter II) and a chapter on genetically modified feed (chapter III). Genetically modified food and feed may not be placed on the market without an authorisation (Article 4(2)(food) and 16(2)(feed)). Such authorisation may only be granted if the applicant shows that the food or feed does not have adverse effects on human health, animal health or the environment, and mislead the consumer. Moreover, the food or feed must not differ from the food or feed it intends to replace to such an extent that this is nutritionally disadvantageous (Article 4(1) in connection with 4(1) and 16(3) in connection with 16(1)). The procedures for the authorisation of GM food and feed are comparable and similar to that laid down in Directive 2001/18. The procedure starts with an application for authorisation with the national competent authority. That competent authority will then inform the European Food Safety Authority (EFSA), which will in turn inform the other Member State's competent authorities and the Commission. The EFSA will then issue an opinion on the authorisation which may be positive or negative (Articles 6 and 18). The Commission will then decide on the authorisation (Articles 7 and 19). Interestingly, the regulation explicitly provides that such authorisation shall not lessen the general civil and criminal liability of any food operator in respect of the food concerned (Articles 7(7) and 19(7)), which effectively rules out a permit-defence. The regulation further contains a procedure for the renewal of existing authorisations on the basis of previous legislation (Articles 8 and 20) and renewals of authorisations granted on the basis of the regulation (Articles 11 and 23). Moreover there are provisions on the, supervision of the conditions imposed in the authorisation (Articles 9 and 21), the

---

[596] OJ 2003 L 268/1. We see that the Court refers to this objective of protecting human health when it construes a wide interpretation of central concepts of the regulation, Case C-442/09 *Bablok and others*, Judgment of 6 September 2011, paras. 82 and 100.

[597] OJ 2003 L 268/24.

[598] Regulation 178/2002, OJ 2002 L 31/1, later amended.

[599] Concerning item (c), the Court found that honey produced with genetically modified pollen comes under this category, Case C-442/09 *Bablok and others*, Judgment of 6 September 2011, para. 69-92. It should be taken into account that the presence of pollen was the unavoidable result of the production process and thus the unintentional, unadventitious or technically unavoidable nature of this presence was irrelevant. This does not mean, however, that the honey should be labelled as genetically modified in view of the threshold laid down in Article 12.

modification, suspension and revocation of authorisations (Articles 10 and 22). Finally, both chapters contain similar rules on labelling, which boil down to an obligation to clearly state that the food or feed contains or consists of genetically modified organisms (Articles 13 and 25). Such labelling is, however, not required if the presence of GMOs is below a certain threshold (0.9%) and this presence is adventitious or technically unavoidable (Articles 12(2) and 24(2)).[600] According to Articles 12(3) and 24(3) operators must be able to show that they have taken the necessary steps to ensure that the presence was adventitious. This implies that the authorisation should contain rules to minimise the chance of adventitious presence of GMOs (conditions or restrictions for use or handling; Article 7(5) in connection with Article 6(5)(e) and Article 19(5) in connection with Article 18(5)(e)). Chapter IV contains the common provisions on public access (Article 29) and confidentiality (Article 30). Concerning the latter it is interesting to see that it is much more comprehensive as regards the information that will always be public compared to Directive 2001/18.[601] This is odd given that Directive 2001/18 and Regulation 1829/2003 both concern the exposure of humans and the environment to GMOs. The provision on data protection (Article 31) is similarly interesting when compared to the REACH Regulation. It may be recalled that the REACH Regulation contains a procedure for the mandatory sharing of animal test results,[602] whereas Article 31 explicitly provides for the protection of the test data, which may also include results of animal tests. Furthermore, the safeguard procedure in the General Food Law Regulation is declared applicable (Article 34),[603] various regulations are repealed (Article 37) and a number of Regulations and Directives are amended.[604] Finally, the regulation contains information on the application of the Cartagena Protocol (Article 44) and transitional measures (Articles 46 and 47).

The third and final panel in the triptych is formed by Regulation 1946/2003 on the transboundary movements of GMOs.[605] This regulation implements the Cartagena Protocol on Biosafety[606] by regulating the transboundary movements of GMOs that may have adverse effects on the conservation and sustainable use of biological diversity, also taking into account human health (Article 1). The regulation applies without prejudice to Directive 2001/18. The regulation

---

[600] See, however, Article 47 for transitional rules in this regard.

[601] In fact the list in Article 25(4) of Directive 2001/18 is more like that in Article 19(3) of Directive 90/219 on the contained use.

[602] See above, section 15.1.

[603] See, on the procedural elements of this safeguard clause and the interpretation in the light of, *inter alia*, the precautionary principle Joined Cases C-58/10 to C-68/10 *Monsanto and others*, Judgment of 8 September 2011, paras. 64-74. Paragraphs 75-81 relate to the substantive aspects of the safeguard clause.

[604] Notably Directive 2001/18, see above in this section.

[605] OJ 2003 L 287/1.

[606] Article 1 and recital 3 of the preamble to Regulation 1946/2003. The Cartagena Protocol was concluded on behalf of the Community by Decision 2002/628, OJ 2002 L 201/48, See also Opinion 2/00 [2001] ECR I-9713.

distinguishes between exports (Chapter II) and unintentional transboundary movements (Chapter III) of GMOs. The former are subdivided into GMOs intended for deliberate release and GMOs intended for direct use as food, feed or for processing. GMOs intended for deliberate release are subject to a prior informed consent (PIC)-procedure, whereby express written consent of the importing country is required (Article 5(1)). The parties to the Cartagena Protocol may agree on a lighter procedure for categories of GMOs which would then be subject to an exception (Article 8). For GMOs intended for direct use as food, feed or for processing the PIC procedure in Article 10 applies. GMOs intended for contained use are not subject to the PIC procedure, provided that the transboundary movements comply with the national standards of the importing country (Article 11(1)). Article 12 lays down the rules for identification and documentation. Chapter III on unintentional transboundary movements is quite short. It only contains a general duty on the part of the Member States to take appropriate measures to prevent unintentional movements (Article 14(1) and a procedure for the information of the public and consultation of the affected or potentially affected Member States. Chapter IV contains the procedure for participation in the international information procedure set up under the Cartagena Protocol (Article 15) as well as provisions on confidentiality (Article 16). The latter rules are comparable to those under Directive 2001/18.

17   Legislation on Waste

European waste law has been described as 'strangely engaging'[607] and has even resulted in a former ECJ judge expressing his amazement at the judicial effort put into defining the concept of 'waste'.[608] Central to European waste law is the Waste Framework Directive.[609] It defines central concepts such as 'waste', contains a general duty to ensure waste is treated in an environmentally friendly fashion and provides for detailed measures concerning specific types of waste.[610] There are a number of directives that deal with specific waste streams and methods of treating waste, such as:

· packaging waste;
· waste electrical and electronic equipment;
· waste incineration;
· landfill of waste.

Finally, there is a regulation on shipments of waste. Below we will first examine the Waste Framework Directive. Then we will look at some of the directives deal-

---

[607] Lee (2000) at 213.

[608] Former judge Kapteyn, as cited by Tieman (2003) at 5.

[609] Directive 2008/98, OJ 2009 L 312/3.

[610] See, on the framework character, Case C-252/05 *Thames Water* [2007] ECR I-3883 para. 39. See on the general character of the directive: Joined Cases 372-374/85 *Traen* [1987] ECR 2141.

ing with specific waste streams and methods of waste treatment. Finally, we will look at the Waste Shipments Regulation.

17.1   The Waste Framework Directive

The concept of waste

Directive 2008/98, The Waste Framework Directive contains the general rules that apply to all categories of waste.[611] Central to this directive and the rest of European waste law is the concept of 'waste'. 'Waste' is defined as any substance or object which the holder discards or intends or is required to discard' (Article 3(1)). Article 2 excludes a number of categories from the scope of the directive, such as gaseous effluents emitted into the atmosphere (Article 2(1)(a)). This is particularly interesting in connection with the implementation of the Kyoto Protocol, where so-called carbon capture is contemplated. This means that carbon dioxide is filtered out, compressed and possibly sold or (permanently) stored underground, which would make it waste within the meaning of the directive.[612] Article 2(2) contains an exception for categories insofar as these are covered by other EU legislation.[613] The old directive defined waste in a similar manner however it also contained a reference in to a list contained in Annex I. This was not really helpful in determining what is waste and as such it has been scrapped. Annex I, for example, listed 16 specific categories of waste[614] and concluded with category Q16 referring to 'Any materials, substances or products which are not contained in the above mentioned categories.' A literal interpretation of Q16 would thus mean that all substances should be regarded as waste! This is obviously not what was intended. But what then is the exact meaning of 'waste'? The Court of Justice has addressed this point on numerous occasions,

---

[611] OJ 2008 L 312/3, it repeals Directive 2006/12, OJ 2006 L 114/9. This directive repealed Directive 75/442, OJ 1975 L 194/47 as amended by Directive 91/156, OJ 1991 L 78/32. Moreover, the directives on Waste Oils and Hazardous Waste are repealed and integrated in this directive. See for a discussion of the Commission's proposal: Pocklington (2006).

[612] Subject to the exception for non-waste by-products, see below in this section.

[613] The old directive only refers to other legislation, but the ECJ has made it clear in Case C-114/01 *AvestaPolarit Chrome* [2003] ECR I-8725, that it refers to Community (now EU) legislation and national legislation implementing the Framework Directive (paras. 44-53). This was confirmed in Cases C-416/02 *Commission v. Spain* [2005] ECR I-7487, para. 99 and C-121/03 *Commission v. Spain* [2005] ECR I-7569, para. 69. Case C-252/05 *Thames Water* [2007] ECR I-3883, paras. 33-34 adds to this the requirement that such legislation must contain precise obligations concerning waste management and offer a level of protection at least equivalent to that resulting from the Waste Framework Directive. It may be noted that these conditions were not codified in the directive.

[614] Q4, for example, relates to materials spilled including materials contaminated as a result of the mishap. See concerning the classification as waste of leaked hydrocarbons and the contaminated soil Case C-1/03 *Van der Walle* [2004] ECR I-7613. See also Case C-252/05 *Thames Water* [2007] ECR I-3883, on leaked sewage water as waste, paras. 28-29.

and much of this case law is still relevant today, if only to explain the Court's reasons for the interpretation of the concept of waste.[615]

In *Vessoso and Zanetti*, the competent Italian court, the Pretura di Asti, referred to the Court for a preliminary ruling on whether the concept of waste was to be understood as excluding substances and objects which are capable of economic reutilisation.[616] The Court held that it was clear from the preambles to the directive and from various of its provisions that a substance of which its holder disposes may constitute waste within the meaning of the directive even when it is capable of economic reutilisation.

The second part of the Pretura's question sought to ascertain whether the concept of waste presumes that a holder disposing of a substance or an object intends to exclude all economic reutilisation of the subject or object by others. The Court observed that the directive referred generally to any substance or object of which the holder disposes, and draws no distinction 'according to the intentions of the holder disposing thereof'. Moreover, the provision specified that waste also includes substances or objects which the holder 'is required to dispose of pursuant to the provisions of national law in force'. The essential aim of the directive, namely the protection of human health and the safeguarding of the environment, would have been jeopardized if the application of the directive was dependent on whether or not the holder intended to exclude all economic reutilisation by others of the substances or objects of which he disposes. The Court concluded that the concept of waste does not presume that the holder disposing of a substance or an object intends to exclude all economic reutilisation of the substance or object by others.[617]

In *Tombesi* the Court ruled that this interpretation is not affected by the amendments of Directive 91/156.[618] The system of supervision and control established by the directive is intended to cover all objects and substances discarded by their owners, even if they have a commercial value and are collected on a commercial basis for recycling, reclamation or re-use. The objectives of the directive still provide a guiding principle for its interpretation.[619]

---

[615] See for some Dutch case law Tieman (2003).

[616] Joined Cases C-206 and C-207/88 *Vessoso and Zanetti* [1990] ECR I-1461. Confirmed in Case C-422/92 *Commission* v. *Germany* [1995] ECR I-1097.

[617] To some extent this decision was confirmed in the *Walloon Waste* case where the Court decided that waste, whether or not capable of recycling, was covered by rules on the free movement of goods, Case C-2/90 *Commission* v. *Belgium* [1992] ECR I-4431.

[618] Joined Cases C-304/94, C-330/94, C-342/94 and C-224/95 *Tombesi a.o.* [1997] ECR I-3561, para. 48.

[619] Joined Cases C-418/97 and C-419/97 *ARCO Chemie Nederland* [2000] ECR I-4475, para. 37. See, however, on the precise nature of these objectives and how this relates to the Court's case law, Scotford (2007).

However, one major problem remains: it is still not clear what is the correct interpretation of 'to discard'. In *Inter-Environment* the Court acknowledged that that the scope of the term 'waste' turns on the meaning of the term 'discard'.[620] The Court observed:

> 'It is also clear from the provisions of Directive 75/442, as amended, in particular from Article 4, Articles 8 to 12 and Annexes IIA and IIB, that the term 'discard' covers both disposal and recovery of a substance or object. As the Advocate General has pointed out in paragraphs 58 to 61 of his Opinion, the list of categories of waste in Annex I to Directive 75/442, as amended, and the disposal and recovery operations listed in Annexes IIA and IIB to that directive demonstrate that the concept of waste does not in principle exclude any kind of residue, industrial by-product or other substance arising from production processes. This finding is further supported by the list of waste drawn up by the Commission in Decision 94/3[621].'

The reference to the disposal and recovery operations listed in Annexes IIA and IIB (now Annex I and II) seems to suggest that they are indicative in this respect.[622] However, the mere fact that something undergoes one of the treatments listed in the Annexes do not necessarily mean any substance treated accordingly has to regarded as waste being discarded, as the Court made perfectly clear in *ARCO Chemie*.[623] Nor is it decisive if substances, without any further significant processing, can be used as fuel under environmental sound conditions.[624] Although indicative, this does not necessarily exclude a substance of being waste.

---

[620] Case C-129/96 *Inter-Environnement Wallonie ASBL* v. *Waals Gewest* [1997] ECR I-7411. Confirmed in Joined Cases C-418/97 and C-419/97 *ARCO Chemie Nederland* [2000] ECR I-4475. Cf. also English High Court 9 November 1998 *Mayer Parry Recycling* v. *Environment Agency* [1999] Env. L.R. 489 in which Carnwath J stated that the term 'discard' encompasses not only the disposal of waste but also its consignment to a recovery operation.

[621] Footnote by the authors: as required by Article 7(1), the Commission has drawn up a list of wastes, the 'European Waste Catalogue' (EWC). This is however no means an exhaustive list. The current EWC is to be found in Decision 2000/532, OJ 2000 L 226/3, as amended by Decision 2001/537, OJ 2001 L 203/18. According to Case C-194/01 *Commission* v. *Austria* [2004] ECR I-4579, paras. 44-48) the EWC does not have to be literally transposed in national law.

[622] See on the so-called 'Euro Tombesi Bypass' Van Calster (2000) 165-169.

[623] Joined Cases C-418/97 and C-419/97 *ARCO Chemie Nederland* [2000] ECR I-4475, para. 49. See on the interpretation of some aspects of Annex II A, Joined Cases C-175/98 en C-177/98 *Lirussi and Bizzaro* [1999] ECR I-6881.

[624] Joined Cases C-418/97 and C-419/97 *ARCO Chemie Nederland* [2000] ECR I-4475, para. 72.

Particularly in connection with so-called by-products there has been considerable judicial activity,[625] that is now codified in the form of Article 5 of the Waste Framework Directive. According to this provision a substance resulting from a production process the primary aim of which is not the production of that substance of may not be waste, but rather a by-product if the following cumulative conditions are met:

a) further use of the substance or object is certain;
b) the substance or object can be used directly without any further processing other than normal industrial practice;
c) the substance or object is produced as an integral part of a production process; and
d) further use is lawful, i.e. the substance or object fulfils all relevant product, environmental and health protection requirements for the specific use and will not lead to overall adverse environmental or human health impacts.

This exception for by-products relates to the fact that the directive contains what has been called two layers of prevention that can be identified in the waste hierarchy (Article 4).[626] The first layer tries to prevent waste from being produced in the first place (Article 4(1)(a)). The second (regulatory) layer tries to prevent environmental damage from occurring once waste has been produced (Article 4(1) (b) and (c)). The first layer would thus result in a concept of waste that excludes by-products that can be used, so as to avoid the interference that results from the application of waste legislation. The second layer, however, would lead to a very wide concept of waste and thus a wide scope of waste legislation to ensure that such by-products do not harm the environment. This difficulty also ties in rather nicely with the rather thin line that is tread when distinguishing between the recovery (Annex II) of waste and normal use of a (secondary) raw material.[627]

As it essentially codifies existing case law, these cases may also be used to explain elements of this exception. Concerning, firstly, the rule that only products that are not the primary aim of the production process fall in this scope, we may refer to *Saetti*. This case concerned petroleum coke, which is one of the substances resulting from the refining of crude oil, that was used to fire a power plant. The Court held that since the production of the petroleum coke was the

---

[625] Case C-114/01 *AvestaPolarit Chrome* [2003] ECR I-8725. The lawfulness can also follow from national law, see Case C-121/03 *Commission v. Spain* [2005] ECR I-7569, where the ECJ refers to the Good Agricultural Practice laid down by the Spanish authorities. See also cases C-416/02 *Commission v. Spain* [2005] ECR I-7487 and C-121/03 *Commission v. Spain* [2005] ECR I-7569. These judgments have been analysed by the Commission in its interpretative communication on waste and by-products, COM (2007) 59 final.

[626] Scotford (2007) at 8.

[627] See the opinion of Advocate General Jacobs in Joined Cases C-304/94, C-330/94, C-342/94 and C-224/95 *Tombesi a.o.* [1997] ECR I-3561, para. 54.

result of a technical choice, it was not a production residue.[628] Moreover, even in the absence of a technical choice the Court classified the petroleum cokes as one of the many fuels intended to be produced in the refining process and thus excluded it from the definition of waste if its use a fuel is certain.

In *Palin Granit* and *AvestaPolarit*, the ECJ further refined the distinction between production residues (waste) and non-waste by-products. In *Palin Granit* the basic question was whether the irregularly shaped granite blocks that are produced when quarrying for large granite blocks were to be regarded as waste or by-products that the owner does not want to discard but simply stores for sale at a later time. Concerning the first criterion, certainty of further use, the Court held that the likelihood of certainty that a residue will be reused increases if there is a financial advantage in doing so.[629] It is uncertain whether this reasoning still applies to the current Waste Framework Directive, given that it does not appear to allow for varying degrees of certainty. Thus, if the reuse is not certain and will only occur after an indefinite period the leftover stone constitutes waste for the duration of that storage. The rationale behind this is that the directive also seeks to protect the environment from the nuisance arising from the storage of the leftover stone.[630] This exception for non-waste by-products does not apply to consumption residues, unless they are second-hand goods that will certainly be reused in a similar manner without prior processing.[631]

From *Palin Granit* it is clear that a substance may constitute waste until it is reused. That brings us to the end of the classification of a substance as waste. The Court has elucidated this point in *Mayer Parry*. This case concerned a scrap metal recycling company that basically sorts, cleans and shreds metal packaging waste and then sells it to steelmakers. Mayer Parry wanted to be officially recognised as reprocessor. This would require its process to be brought under the heading of recycling within the meaning of the Packaging Waste Directive.[632] The Court thus defined recycling as meaning that the reprocessing of packaging waste must enable new material or a new product possessing characteristics comparable to those of the material from which the waste was derived to be obtained.[633] According to the Court the recycling process was only completed when the steelmakers turned the scrap metal into new metal sheets that could be used in the packaging industry etc. Applied to the *Palin Granit* case this means the granite blocks would cease to be waste only when they would actually be used in, for example, dyke reinforcement works. The reasoning in *Mayer*

---

[628] Order in Case C-235/02 *Saetti* [2004] ECR I-1005, para. 45.

[629] Case C-9/00 *Palin Granit* [2002] ECR I-3533, para. 37.

[630] Case C-9/00 *Palin Granit* [2002] ECR I-3533, paras. 36-39. See also C-114/01 *AvestaPolarit Chrome* [2003] ECR I-8725, paras. 36-38.

[631] Case C-457/02 *Niselli* [2004] ECR I-10853, paras. 48-49.

[632] These findings also hold for the Waste Framework Directive, Case C-444/00 *Mayer Parry* [2003] ECR I-6163, para. 93.

[633] Case C-444/00 *Mayer Parry* [2003] ECR I-6163, para. 73.

Parry has been codified in the form of Article 6 of the Waste Framework Directive. This holds that certain waste shall cease to be waste when it has undergone a recovery, including recycling, operation and complies with specific criteria to be developed in accordance with the following conditions:

a) the substance or object is commonly used for specific purposes;
b) a market or demand exists for such a substance or object;
c) the substance or object fulfils the technical requirements for the specific purposes and meets the existing legislation and standards applicable to products; and
d) the use of the substance or object will not lead to overall adverse environmental or human health impacts.

By and large, the criteria for the end of waste status and by-product exception are similar. Both essentially require that the resulting object is fit for further use and that such use will occur. An important difference between Article 5 and Article 6 is that the latter appears to be an instruction for the EU and national[634] legislator, rather than a directly effective provision. It has resulted in a regulation holding the criteria for the end of waste status for metal scrap.[635] Whatever the correct interpretation of the concept of waste may be, it should be noted that, as the Waste Framework Directive is based on Article 175 EC, now Article 192 TFEU, it does not prevent Member States from defining another interpretation meaning of waste, provided that this results in a more stringent environmental protection. The above section has shown that it is uncertain whether a higher level of environmental protection would actually necessitate a wider or rather more restricted concept!

Obligations for the Member States

Article 4, as was already mentioned, contains the so-called waste hierarchy and requires Member States to take appropriate measures to encourage:
· the prevention of waste production;
· preparation for re-use;
· recycling;
· other means of recovery, such as energy recovery and finally disposal.[636]

The waste hierarchy makes waste prevention the first objective, followed by recovery of waste. Disposal of waste should be the last option. However, Article 4(2) explains that for certain waste streams a departure from the hierarchy may deliver better overall environmental outcomes.

---

[634] See Article 6(4).

[635] Regulation 333/2011, OJ 2011 L 94/2.

[636] The *Balsamo* case made clear that a provision like Article 3 of the old directive does not stand in the way of a municipal prohibition of the sale of non-biodegradable plastic bags; Case 380/87 *Balsamo* [1989] ECR 2491.

The distinction between recovery and disposal of waste has important consequences for the regime applicable to shipments of waste. Moreover, both categories are mutually exclusive.[637] Furthermore, the distinction between recovery and disposal is fraught with definitional difficulties. In *ASA*, the Court stated that the essential characteristic of a waste recovery operation is that its principal objective is that the waste serves a useful purpose in replacing other materials which would have had to be used for that purpose, thereby conserving natural resources.[638] Prior treatment before the waste is put to its useful purpose is not required for the classification as recovery, as is the possibility to reclaim or subsequently reuse the waste. In a later case the Court applied this rule to the distinction between incineration and use as fuel. The Court held that the combustion of waste constitutes a recovery operation where its principal objective is that the waste can fulfil a useful function as a means of generating energy, replacing the use of a source of primary energy which would have had to have been used to fulfil that function.[639] This has now been codified in Annex II, where the asterisk for item R1 basically contains an energy generation or energy efficiency criterion.[640] Waste co-incinerators will thus only qualify as recovery operations only if they meet the energy efficiency criterion. A waste co-incinerator that fails to meet the criterion will be placed on the equal footing with landfilling, which is cheaper but environmentally less advantageous.[641]

Articles 8-12 require the Member States to basically put the waste hierarchy into effect. To this end they may enact so-called extended producer responsibility schemes (Article 8). Such schemes intend to make producers of products responsible for the waste their products become when they have reached the end of the lifecycle. The idea is that these producers then have an incentive to minimise the waste generated and – if waste is generated – to reduce the costs of treating the waste. The idea of producer responsibility can be seen in the Ecodesign Directive[642] as well as various directives concerning certain waste streams.[643] Similar, though at times less elaborate, provisions exist for re-use, recovery and disposal. Article 11(2) merits mention here, because it contains

---

[637] Case C-6/00 *ASA* [2002] ECR I-1961, paras. 62-63.

[638] Case C-6/00 *ASA* [2002] ECR I-1961, para. 69, confirmed in Joined Cases C-307/00 to C-311/00 *Oliehandel Koeweit* [2003] ECR I-1821, para. 87.

[639] Case C-228/00 *Commission v. Germany* [2003] ECR I-1439, para. 46. As a result the calorific value of waste was abandoned. Instead the classification turns on the following three criteria: energy generation, combustion should create more energy than is consumed (energy surplus) that should effectively be used and the greater part of the waste must be consumed and the greater part of the energy used.

[640] This is also referred to as the R1 formula: see the Commission Guidance in this respect available from: http://ec.europa.eu/environment/waste/framework/pdf/guidance.pdf (last visited 7 October 2011).

[641] See in this connection section 17.2 below on the Packaging Waste Directive and section 17.8 on the Landfill Directive.

[642] See above, section 8.3.

[643] See below, section 17.

recycling and re-use targets for certain waste streams. Member State policy in this regard is governed by the overarching principles of Article 13. This provision requires Member States to ensure that waste is recovered or disposed of without endangering human health and without using processes or methods which could harm the environment (water, air, soil, plants and animals) or causing a nuisance through odours or noise or adversely affecting the countryside or places of special interest.[644] The abandonment, dumping or uncontrolled disposal of waste must be prohibited. Article 13 is however not directly effective.[645] In the light of the *Lombardia* case it was not easy to see what status, if any, the objectives of Article 13 might have.[646] However, some clarification on this point has been given by the Court in the Case C-387/97 and the *San Rocco* case.[647] In Case C-387/97 the Court ruled that the obligations flowing from Article 13 were 'independent' of the more specific obligations contained in the directive. And in *San Rocco* the Court ruled that whether Article 13 of the directive imposes obligations on Member States must be separated from the question of whether the provisions have direct effect and may be relied upon directly by individuals as against the State. The Court went on by stating that whilst Article 13 does not specify the actual content of the measures which must be taken in order to ensure that waste is disposed of without endangering human health and without harming the environment, it is nonetheless true that it is binding on the Member States as to the objective to be achieved, whilst leaving to the Member States a margin of discretion in assessing the need for such measures. If a situation is not in conformity with the objectives laid down in Article 13 and if that situation persists and leads in particular to a significant deterioration in the environment over a protracted period without any action being taken by the competent authorities, it may be an indication that the Member States have exceeded the discretion conferred on them by that provision. Although Article 13 is not directly effective it imposes certain legal obligations on the Member States anyway.

Of great importance are the self-sufficiency and proximity principles enshrined in Article 16. Member States are required to establish an integrated and adequate network of disposal installations and installations for the recovery

---

[644] Cf. on the question of applicability of the predecessor of this provision (Article 4 of the old directive) and temporary storage of waste, Joined Cases C-175/98 and C-177/98 *Lirussi and Bizarro* [1999] ECR I-6881, para. 54.

[645] Case C-236/92 *Comitato di coordinamento per la difesa della Cava* v. *Regione Lombardia* [1994] ECR I-485.

[646] Cf. English Court of Appeal 5 May 1998 *Regina* v. *Bolton Metropolitan Council*, ex parte *Kirkman* [1998] *Journal of Planning and Environment Law* 787.

[647] Case C-387/97 *Commission* v. *Greece* [2000] ECR I-5047 and Case C-365/97 *Commission* v. *Italy* [1999] ECR I-7773 *(San Rocco)*. See further Case C-135/05 *Commission* v. *Italy* [2007] ECR I-3475; Case C-494/01 *Commission* v. *Ireland* [2005] ECR I-3331, in connection with a general and persistent infringement and Case C-297/08 *Commission* v. *Italy* [2010] ECR I-1749 *(Campania)*. These cases concern the predecessor of Article 13, Article 4 of the old directive.

of household waste.[648] The network must enable the EU as a whole to become self-sufficient in waste disposal and the Member States to move towards that aim individually (Article 16(2)). The network must also enable waste to be disposed of in one of the nearest appropriate installations (Article 16(3)). The text of Article 5 does not indicate precisely how the two principles should operate together. It may be noted in this connection that Article 16 apparently implies a minor contradiction. Article 16(2) requires Member States to move towards self-sufficiency on a national basis, whereas in Article 16(3) emphasis is on the proximity principle. Where the nearest waste disposal installations are situated in another country, the two principles clash. This is more prominent when we look at the second paragraph of Article 16(1). This allows Member States to restrict the import of waste destined for recovery in a co-incineration plant where the import of such waste would mean that the nationally produced waste must be disposed of or treated in a manner that does not comply with the national waste management plan. In view of the fact that waste qualifies as a good within the meaning of Article 34 TFEU, this EU-mandated import restriction is problematic.[649] In response to questions in the European Parliament, the Commission has observed, concerning the version of this provision in the old directive, that the proximity principle should not be applied too strictly or absolutely. It must be interpreted flexibly, taking account of geographical circumstances and the need for specialised installations for certain types of waste. The Commission expressly acknowledged that specific shipments of waste may not be in conformity with the principle of proximity.[650] In the *Dusseldorp* case the Court ruled that the principles of self-sufficiency and proximity could not be applied to waste for recovery.[651] And in its Resolution of 7 May 1990 on waste policy[652] the Council specified that the objective of self-sufficiency in waste disposal does not apply to recycling. This appears to have been set aside with the new Waste Framework Directive. The bottom line is that self-sufficiency at national level sits in rather uneasily with European integration.

The Waste Framework Directive also makes the Member States responsible for the environmentally sound management of hazardous waste (Article 17),[653] waste oils (Article 21) and bio-waste (Article 22).

---

[648] See on this provision Joined Cases C-53/02 and C-217/02 *Commune de Braine-le-Château a.o.* [2004] ECR I-3251; Case C-494/01 *Commission v. Ireland* [2005] ECR I-3331, paras. 149-158 and Case C-297/08 *Commission v. Italy* [2010] ECR I-1749 (*Campania*), paras. 68-71.

[649] Note further that this is in derogation to the Waste Shipments Regulation, see below section 17.7.

[650] OJ 1994 C 32/8; cf. also OJ 1993 C 6/37-38.

[651] Case C-203/96 *Dusseldorp* [1998] ECR I-4075, para. 30.

[652] OJ 1990 C 122/2.

[653] Note that there are extra provisions concerning hazardous waste, for example prohibiting the mixing of hazardous waste

Article 28 requires Member States to draw up waste management plans.[654] Legislation or specific measures amounting only to a series of ad hoc normative interventions that are incapable of constituting an organised and coordinated system for the disposal of waste cannot be regarded as plans under the directive.[655] Article 29 requires the Member States to enact similar plans for waste prevention. Of course the Member States themselves will not perform the actual collection and treatment of waste. This is done by (private) companies subject to a permitting scheme.

Undertakings which carry out waste treatment (defined in Article 3(14)) operations must obtain a permit from the competent authority (Articles 23(1)).[656] Exemptions may be granted in certain cases (Article 24) and subject to conditions,[657] for example for undertakings which carry out their own waste disposal at the place of production (Article 25).

The directive further contains provisions on reporting to the Commission (Article 33), periodic inspections (Article 34),[658] record-keeping by undertakings (Article 35) and on the cost of disposing of waste (Article 14). The latter provides that, in accordance with the polluter pays principle, the cost of waste treatment must be borne by:[659]

· the original waste producer or
· by the current or previous waste holders.

Together with the provision on extended producer responsibility and Article 15 on responsibility for waste management this provision sheds some light on the interesting question concerning the division of responsibilities for waste management (including the prevention of waste). Here we see a close cooperation between the market and the public authorities, whereby notably prevention and the lifecycle analysis presuppose private involvement. The polluter pays principle provides a potentially powerful tool to influence private decision-making in this regard, as pricing waste production will give the holder of the waste an incentive to minimise waste production and the associated costs. However, for certain categories of waste, establishing a direct link between the waste producer/holder and the amount of waste produced by them may be very

---

[654] See on Article 7 (in connection with Article 9) of the old directive Joined Cases C-53/02 and C-217/02 *Commune de Braine-le-Château a.o.* [2004] ECR I-3251.

[655] Case C-387/97 *Commission v. Greece* [2000] ECR I-5047, para. 76.

[656] See on these provisions in the old directive Case C-494/01 *Commission v. Ireland* [2005] ECR I-3331, where the Court also links the failure to actually apply and enforce the permit requirement (Articles 9 and 10 of the old directive, see para. 118) to an infringement of Article 4 of the old directive (paras. 169-176).

[657] See on the requirement to fix maximum thresholds Case C-103/02 *Commission v. Italy* [2004] ECR I-9127, paras. 26-35.

[658] See on these provisions Case C-494/01 *Commission v. Ireland* [2005] ECR I-3331, paras. 190-192.

[659] See for an interpretation Case C-188/07 *Commune de Mesquer* [2008] ECR I-4501, para. 71.

difficult if not impossible. For this reason, the Court has interpreted Article 14 as not precluding a waste tax or charge that varies depending on the estimated quantity of waste produced and is not related to the volume of waste actually produced, provided that the tax is not disproportionate to the amount of waste actually produced.[660] It is submitted that this is a rather 'defensive' interpretation of the polluter pays principle that appears to be primarily intended to protect polluters from costs from increasing beyond what can be attributed to waste management. It says little, if anything at all, about the incentivising nature of the polluter pays principle.

Hazardous waste

Directive 91/689 specifically addressed *hazardous* waste.[661] At this moment, however, the provisions concerning hazardous waste have been integrated in the Waste Framework Directive. The directive applies to all wastes which have one or more of a number of properties ('explosive', 'carcinogenic', 'mutagenic' etc.) listed in Annex III to the directive (Article 3(2)).[662] This essentially codifies the judgment in the *Fornasar* case where the Court ruled that that the decisive criterion, as regards the definition of 'hazardous waste, is whether the waste displays one or more of the properties listed in Annex III to the directive.[663] As a result the list of hazardous wastes is not fully harmonising, which is now also acknowledged in Article 7(2) of the Waste Framework Directive.[664]

The directive contains numerous additional, more stringent provisions aimed specifically at hazardous waste. For example:

· the derogation from the permit requirement does not apply to hazardous waste (Article 24(a));
· stricter requirements apply to the preservation of records (Article 35(2));
· it requires the proper packaging and labelling of hazardous waste (Article 19).

Finally, the Waste Oils Directive has also been integrated into the new Waste Framework Directive. Because of the environmental hazards involved in the disposal of waste oils, the Council adopted specific rules on the subject in Directive 75/439.[665] At this moment the rules concerning waste oils are contained in

---

[660] Case C-254/08 *Futura Immobiliare srl Hotel Futura* [2009] ECR I-6995.

[661] OJ 1991 L 377/20, as amended by Directive 94/31, OJ 1994 L 168/28. Repealed with effect from 12 December 2010.

[662] Council Decision 94/904 establishing a list of hazardous waste pursuant to Article 4(1) of Council Directive 91/689 on hazardous waste, OJ 1994 L 356/14. Cf. de Sadeleer & Sambon (1997). Decision 94/904 has now been replaced by Decision 2000/532, OJ 2000 L 226/3, as amended by Decision 2001/537, OJ 2001 L 203/18.

[663] Case C-318/98 *Fornasar* [2000] ECR I-4785, para. 56.

[664] The hazardous waste list does not prevent the Member States from classifying as hazardous waste other than that featuring on the list, Case C-318/98 *Fornasar* [2000] ECR I-4785, para. 51.

[665] OJ 1975 L 194/31, as amended by Directive 2000/76, OJ 2000 L 332/91 and repealed from 12 December 2010.

Article 21 of the Waste Framework Directive. This requires the Member States to take the necessary measures to ensure that waste oils are collected separately and not mixed, insofar this is economically and technically feasible, where such mixing would impede treatment. As regards treatment, the directive expresses an indirect preference for the processing of waste oils by regeneration rather than by combustion (Article 21(3)).[666] The Court has repeatedly held that this priority for regeneration is to be taken seriously. Studies undertaken to examine the feasibility of such regeneration are allowed, provided that they lead to tangible steps.[667] Moreover, problems envisaged with the economic viability of the regeneration do not justify a departure from the priority for regeneration as such problems could be overcome by the Member States objection against shipments of waste oils (Article 21(3)).[668]

17.2   Packaging and Waste Packaging

Prevention is the important theme of Directive 94/62 on packaging and packaging waste.[669] This directive aims to harmonise national measures concerning the management of packaging and packaging waste in order, on the one hand, to prevent any impact thereof on the environment and, on the other hand, to ensure the functioning of the internal market and to avoid obstacles to trade and distortion and restriction of competition within the EU. In the light of this clearly dual objective,[670] the fact that the Council based the directive solely on Article 100a EEC (now Article 114 TFEU) seems slightly odd. In view of the judgment in the *TiO2* case, it would have been more logical for it to have been based both on Article 100a (now Article 114 TFEU) and on Article 130s (now Article 193 TFEU).[671] The first priority of the directive is the prevention of the production of packaging waste (Article 1(2)). Reusing packaging, recycling and other forms of recovering packaging waste and, hence, reducing the final disposal of such waste are regarded as additional fundamental principles.[672]

The directive covers all packaging placed on the market in the EU and all packaging waste, whether it is used or released at industrial, commercial, office, shop, service, household or any other level, regardless of the material used (Article 2(1)). In addition to the general obligation contained in Article 4, requiring the Member States to take the necessary preventive measures, the directive lays down a number of more concrete requirements. On the subject of recovery

---

[666] See on Member States obligations to take measures necessary to give priority to the processing of waste oils by regeneration, Case C-102/97 *Commission v. Germany* [1999] ECR I-5051.

[667] Case C-424/02 *Commission v UK* [2004] ECR I-7249, para. 25.

[668] Case C-92/03 *Commission v. Portugal* [2005] ECR I-867, paras. 33-36. See section 17.7 below on the shipments of waste. See further on the preference for regeneration and the impact on the free movement of goods: Case 240/83 *ADBHU* [1985] ECR 531 and Case 172/82 *Inter-Huiles* [1983] ECR 555.

[669] OJ 1994 L 365, later amended.

[670] Cf. Case C-463/01 *Commission v. Germany* [2004] ECR I-11705, para. 37.

[671] See Chapter 2, section 4.

[672] See on the legal importance of a such hierarchy of principles Van Calster (2000) at 196-197.

and recycling,[673] it provides that, no later 31 December 2008, a minimum of 60% as a maximum by weight of the packaging waste must be recovered or incinerated with energy recovery[674] and that between 55% as a minimum and 80% as a maximum by weight of the totality of packaging materials contained in packaging waste must be recycled with specific minimum recycling targets set for individual packaging waste streams. ((Article 6(1)(e)). Member States which have, or will, set programmes going beyond the targets are permitted to pursue those targets on the condition that these measures avoid distortions of the internal market and do not hinder compliance by other Member States with the directive (Article 6(10)). This provision also contains a notification require-ment similar to that in Article 114(4-5) TFEU. Member States are required to inform the Commission of measures going beyond the targets of the direc-tive. The Commission must confirm these measures, after having verified, in cooperation with the Member States, that they are consistent with the conditions just mentioned and do not constitute an arbitrary means of discrimination or a disguised restriction on trade between Member States.[675]

Furthermore, the directive requires Member States to take the necessary measures to ensure that systems are set up to provide for:

- the return and/or collection of used packaging and/or packaging waste from the consumer;
- the reuse or recovery of packaging and/or packaging waste collected (Arti-cle 7).[676]

Such systems may take the form of agreements between industry and the Member State authorities, as the directive explicitly envisages implementation by means of such agreements (Article 22(3a)). This means that the competition rules may apply[677] as well as the provisions on the free movement of goods.[678] According to Article 9 Member States must ensure that packaging may be placed on the market only if it complies with all essential requirements defined by the directive. Article 11 contains some specific provisions on concentration levels of heavy materials (lead, cadmium, mercury and hexavalent chromium) present in packaging. Member States must not impede the placing on the market of packaging which satisfies the provisions of the directive (Article 18).

---

[673] The Court has held that there is no hierarchy between these two, Case C-463/01 *Commission* v. *Germany* [2004] ECR I-11705, para. 40.

[674] The reference to incineration with energy recovery as a means to achieve the recovery targets has been included by Directive 2004/12, OJ 2004 L 47/26, as a response to the Court's strict interpretation of recovery, see section 17.1.

[675] See for an application of Article 6(6), the predecessor of Article 6(10), Commission Decision 99/42, OJ 1999 L 14/24 and Decision 2003/82, OJ 2003 L 31/32.

[676] See on the conditions for systems set up pursuant to Article 7, Case C-309/02 *Radlberger* [2004] ECR I-11763, paras. 39-50.

[677] See, e.g. Case T-419/03 *Altstoff Recycling Austria*, Judgment of 22 March 2011.

[678] Case C-463/01 *Commission* v. *Germany* [2004] ECR I-11705, paras. 44-52, see further Chapter 6.

Finally, the directive contains provisions on the marking of packaging (Article 8), on information (Articles 12 and 13), management plans (Article 14) and economic instruments (Article 15).

17.3   End of Life Vehicles

Directive 2000/53 implements the principle of producer responsibility for so-called end of life vehicles.[679] This term broadly refers to automobiles that have become waste (Article 2(2)). Central to the directive is the duty for the Member States to ensure that importers and manufacturers of vehicles are responsible for the collection and reuse and recovery of end of life vehicles. This producer responsibility will also have a preventive effect in that the producers will thus have an incentive to minimise the costs of reuse and recovery by improving the recyclability of their vehicles. Article 4(1)(b) requires an integration of these environmental considerations in the design stage of production. The prevention aspect of the directive further translates into a restriction on the use of certain substances such as heavy metals and a duty on the Member States to encourage the use of recycled materials.

The actual producer responsibility attaches to the collection and reuse and recovery of end of life vehicles. To make the collection system as consumer friendly as possible there is a duty to take back end of life vehicles at least free of charge (Article 5(4), first subparagraph), provided the vehicle is still intact (Article 5(4), third subparagraph). Setting up and financing this system is the responsibility of the economic operators (Article 5(1), first indent, and Article 5(4) second subparagraph). The treatment of the vehicles thus collected is subject to the rules in Article 6. Once collected, the vehicles and their parts should as a priority be reused, then recovered or recycled (Article 7(1)). Moreover, the economic operators must attain certain reuse and recovery rates for end of life vehicles (Article 7(2)). The directive further contains provisions on the coding of parts in order to facilitate their reuse and recovery (Article 8) and envisages European legislation on the recyclability and reusability of vehicle parts (Article 7(4) and (5)). Implementation of the directive can take place through agreements between the Member States and the economic operators (Article 10(3). The duty to set up a collection system applies only to vehicles marketed after 1 July 2002 and, from 1 January 2007 onwards, to vehicles marketed before 1 July 2002 (Article 12(2)). However, the Member States may opt for an early implementation (Article 12(3)).

17.4   Waste Electrical and Electronic Equipment

The producer responsibility principle has similarly been implemented for electrical and electronic equipment. Although they started out as one proposal, there are now two relevant directives. Directive 2011/65 contains

---

[679] OJ 2000 L 269/34, later amended.

rules on the restriction of certain hazardous substances (ROHS).[680] The ROHS Directive is based on Article 114 TFEU and contains predominantly product-related rules according to which from 21 July 2011, new electrical and electronic equipment put on the market does not contain any of the substances listed in Annex II (Article 4(1)). This basic rule is however subject to exceptions for products mentioned in Article 4(3)-(5) and the products and applications listed in Annexes III and IV.

Directive 2002/96 contains the actual producer responsibility scheme and is often referred to as the waste electrical and electronic equipment (WEEE) Directive.[681] Like the End of Life Vehicles Directive, the WEEE Directive contains a general duty for the Member States to encourage ecodesign (Article 4). The producer responsibility attaches to the separate collection. The Member States are responsible for ensuring that WEEE is collected separate from other waste streams (Article 5(1). For WEEE from private households, however, there is an additional duty to ensure that such waste may be returned at least free of charge (Article 5(2)(a)). One very consumer friendly method of collecting WEEE is the so-called old-for-new obligation laid down in Article 5(2(b), according to which the distributor is required to take back at least free of charge the old appliance whenever a new similar appliance is sold. This old-for-new obligation applies irrespective of the brand and may only be disapplied when the old appliance is incomplete or contaminated with other waste (Article 5(2), last paragraph). The WEEE thus collected should be treated in accordance with the rules laid down in Article 6. Article 7 requires the Member States to ensure that the producers and importers of electrical and electronic equipment set up a system that will guarantee specified minimum levels of reuse, recycling and recovery of the WEEE. As a basic rule, the costs for the collection and treatment of WEEE are to be borne by the importers and producers of the appliances (Articles 8 and 9). They may choose to do so individually or collectively.[682] As a result of the old-for-new obligation and the relatively long lifespan of electrical equipment, the WEEE initially collected will be so-called historical waste, i.e. equipment put on the market before 13 August 2005.[683] Moreover, part of the historical waste will be orphaned waste, i.e. equipment marketed by a manufacturer or importer that may have ceased to be active on the market. For WEEE from private households the financial burden arising from this should be overcome by the obligation for the producers and importers to join a collective system to which all importers and producers contribute proportionately (Article 8(3)). In addition, the directive allows the producers and importers to show these costs separately during

---

[680] OJ 2011 L 174/88. It repeals Directive 2002/95, OJ 2002 L 37/19.

[681] OJ 2002 L 37/24, amended later.

[682] Collectively accepting a producer responsibility may result in the applicability of Article 101 or 102 TFEU. See Chapter 7, sections 3 and 4 in particular.

[683] One year after the deadline for implementing the directive; Article 17(1).

a transitional period that lasted until 13 February 2011.[684] After the transitional period it is no longer allowed to separately show the costs of collection and treatment (Article 8(2), third subparagraph). For non-private household historical WEEE there are special financial provisions that allow for some of these costs to be borne by the non-private household. Given that the distinction between private households and other users is financially so important, it is surprising to see that the definition of what constitutes a private household is anything but clear. Article 3(k) includes commercial, industrial, institutional and other sources which produce WEEE that is, because of its nature and quantity, similar to that from private households. This allows for Member States to include SMEs and schools in the definition of a private household and thereby free them from all costs arising from the separate collection and treatment of WEEE. Articles 10 and 11 contain provisions on the information to be supplied to the consumer and treatment facilities. Finally, the directive contains provisions dealing with reporting, comitology and implementation. The WEEE Directive also allows for implementation by means of an agreement between the sector concerned and the Member State (Article 17(3)).

17.5   Waste Batteries and Accumulators

Batteries and accumulators often contain dangerous substances such as heavy metals. The European legislature therefore considered it necessary to have product rules and rules concerning their separate collection and safe treatment once these batteries become waste. Directive 2006/66 contains these rules and is based on Article 95 as well as 175 EC (Currently Article 114 and 193 TFEU).[685] This directive replaces, with effect from 26 September 2006 the old Batteries Directive.[686] The product related rules consist of a ban for batteries and accumulators containing mercury and cadmium above a certain threshold (Article 4(1)(a) and (b)). However, both bans are subject to exceptions. For mercury, the threshold for the ban increases from 0.0005% to 2% for so-called button cells (Article 4(2)) and for cadmium the prohibition is declared inapplicable for batteries intended for use in emergency and alarm systems, medical equipment and cordless power tools (Article 4(3)).[687] Article 6 contains the free movement clause for batteries meeting the requirements of the directive and corresponding duty the restrict the marketing of all other batteries. The final part of the product rules is contained in Article 21 and deals with the labelling of batteries and accumulators.

---

[684] Eight years after the date of entry into force of the WEEE Directive. For a specific category the transitional period is ten years.

[685] OJ 2006 L 266/1, corrected in OJ 2006 L 311/58. Hereafter we will only refer to batteries when accumulators are also included.

[686] Directive 91/157, OJ 1991 L 78/38.

[687] A Commission report on the continuation of this exemption can be found in COM (2010) 698.

The rules on separate collection and safe treatment take the form of a mitigated producer responsibility, in that the Member States have an independent
obligation to set up a collection infrastructure in addition to the collection to be
undertaken by the producers. In this regard a distinction is made between portable batteries on the one hand and industrial and automotive batteries on the
other (recital 8 of the preamble). A portable battery is defined as a sealed battery
that can be hand-carried and is not an automotive or industrial battery (Article 3(3)). Automotive batteries are those used for starting, lighting or ignition
in cars (Article 3(5)) and industrial batteries are those designed exclusively for
industrial or professional uses (Article 3(6)).[688] The general framework for the
collection is laid down in Article 8(1) and requires the collection to be end-user
friendly. For portable batteries this means that distributors that supply such
batteries are required to take back waste batteries for free (Article 8(1)(b) and
(c)). For industrial and automotive batteries a similar duty to take back waste
batteries applies (Article 8(3)), albeit without the stipulation that such collection
must take place without any costs to the end-user. Only for automotive batteries from private non-commercial vehicles it there a duty take them back for free
(Article 8(4), last sentence). Article 16 requires the Member States to ensure that
producers pay the separate collection, treatment and recycling.[689] Such costs
shall not be shown separately to end-users (Article 16(4)). Interestingly, there is
no transitional regime for batteries (Article 16(6)), whereas the WEEE and End
of Life Vehicles Directives do provide for a such rules in view of historical waste.
Finally, it worth mentioning that in accordance with Article 18 Member States
may exempt small producers from the financial obligations. Such exemptions
have to be approved by the Commission (Article 18(2) and (3)), which appears
very sensible in view of the obvious effects that such exemptions may have on
the internal market and given that the definition of a small firm is gnomic at
best and leaves the Member States considerable room for discretion.

Article 9 provides for the introduction of differentiated taxes by the Member
States to promote environmental improvements concerning batteries. Such measures must be notified to the Commission. Articles 10 and 12 contain targets
for the collection and treatment and recycling of waste batteries. Concerning
the treatment and recycling, the distinction between portable and industrial
and automotive batteries is again relevant as the first subparagraph of Article
12(1) allows for the disposal in landfills or in underground storage of portable
batteries that contain lead, mercury or cadmium. This disposal – as opposed to
recycling – is allowed when no viable end market is available or if this method
of phasing out of heavy metals is shown to be preferable over recycling. In
determining whether or not disposal is preferable economic, environmental
and social impacts have to be taken into account. For industrial and automotive batteries this method of disposal is not allowed (Article 14). In any case

---

[688] Recitals 9 and 10 of the preamble contain indicative lists of these categories.

[689] Article 16(2) requires the Member States to ensure that double charging is avoided because the producers will already have to bear these costs on the basis of the WEEE and End of Life Vehicles Directives.

the recycling efficiencies contained in Article 12(4) in connection with Annex II, part B will have to be achieved.[690] Article 11 requires the Member States to ensure manufactures design products in a way that will facilitate the removal of waste batteries. This is particularly relevant in connection with the WEEE[691] and the End of Life Vehicles Directives. Article 20 contains rules on information for end-users, Articles 22 to 25 contain the standard provisions on reporting, comitology and penalties. Finally, Articles 26 and 27 contain the rules for the implementation, which could also involve the use of agreements between the Member State and the economic operators concerned.

17.6   Mining Waste

In response to several high profile accidents with mining waste, the EU has adopted a Mining Waste Directive.[692] Based on the environmental legal basis, the directive aims to prevent and reduce the effects on the environment and human health brought on as a result of the management of mining waste. This is rather more accurately defined by Article 2(1) as waste resulting from the prospecting, extraction, treatment and storage of mineral resources and the working of quarries or, in short, extractive waste. However, Article 2(2) defines an exception to the scope for, *inter alia*, waste generated in offshore extractive activities. Moreover, certain other forms of extractive waste are subject to a lighter regime (Article 2(3)). The effect of the inclusion of mining waste in the scope of this directive is that the Landfill Directive[693] does not apply (Article 2(4)). The directive contains a duty of care very similar to that in the Waste Framework Directive (Article 4).[694] This general duty of care is to be implemented through the waste management plan, part of which is the major-accident prevention policy, that is to be drawn up by the operator (Articles 5 and 6). Such a waste management plan is a precondition for the environmental permit that is required for all waste facilities. This encompasses all areas designated for the accumulation or deposit of extractive waste, whether in a solid or liquid state or in solution or suspension. Whether or not such a deposit will also qualify as a waste facility depends on the type of extractive waste[695] and the duration of storage. Category A waste facilities and facilities for waste characterised as hazardous in the waste management plan will be waste facilities irrespective of the duration.[696] Facilities for hazardous waste generated unexpectedly will only

---

[690]See Article 15(2) on the proof needed to take into account recycling operations that take place after export to non-member state countries.

[691] See also Article 12(3).

[692] Directive 2006/21, OJ 2006 L 102/15.

[693] See below section 17.8.

[694]Cf. Article 13 of the Waste Framework Directive, section 17.1 above.

[695] Further rules for the classification of waste can be found in Decision 2009/360, OJ 2009 L 110/48.

[696]The criteria for this classification are set out in Annex III. See further Decision 2009/337, OJ 2009 L 102/7.

require a permit for a duration in excess of six months. This period is extended to more than one year for facilities for non-hazardous non-inert waste and finally the storage of unpolluted soil, non-hazardous prospecting waste, waste resulting from the extraction, treatment and storage of peat and inert waste[697] will only qualify as a waste facility if it is stored for more than three years (Article 3(15)). Finally, the directive contains provisions on public consutlation (Article 8), transboundary aspects (Article 16) and the relation with the Water Framework Directive (Article 13), post-closure procedures (Article 12) and the financial guarantee that must be required by the Member States (Article 14).[698] This is particularly interesting as it is closely related to the environmental liability for such operations.[699]

17.7   Legislation on Transfrontier Shipments of Waste

General remarks

Regulation 259/93, replacing Directive 84/631[700], on the supervision and control of shipments of waste within, into and out of the EC[701] – the 'old' Basel Regulation – has applied since 6 May 1994. With effect from 12 July 2007 it has been replaced with Regulation 1013/2006, hereafter referred to as the Basel Regulation.[702] The regulation is an extremely complicated piece of legislation. One of the reasons for this is that it serves to implement not only the EU's own objectives in the waste sector, but also several of its international law obligations. In this connection it should be noted that the EU is itself a party to the 1989 Basel Convention on the Control of Transboundary Movements of Hazardous Waste and their Disposal,[703] in addition to the Member States. Moreover, Article 39 of the Lomé IV Convention[704] contains provisions on waste and the EU has approved the decision of the OECD Council on the control of transfrontier movements of wastes destined for recovery operations.[705] Finally, the conclusion of the EEA Convention[706] and the changing position of the EFTA

---

[697] The term 'inert waste' has been clarified through Decision 2009/359, OJ 2009 L 110/46.

[698] Further rules have been set by Decision 2009/335, OJ 2009 L 101/25.

[699] The waste facilities are included in the Environmental Liability Directive, see above this chapter, section 9, by virtue of Article 15 of the Mining Waste Directive.

[700] OJ 1984 L 326/31, later amended.

[701] OJ 1993 L 30/1, later amended. The regulation is correctly based on Article 130s EC (now Article 192 TFEU); Case C-187/93 *EP v. Council* [1994] ECR I-2857. See also Chapter 1. In addition, several French importers of waste have had their cases declared inadmissible by the Court, Case C-209/94 P *Buralux v. Council* [1996] ECR I-615.

[702] OJ 2006 L 190/1, later amended, see Article 61(1) concerning the repeal of the old Basel Regulation.

[703] OJ 1993 L 39/23.

[704] OJ 1991 L 229.

[705] Recital 5 of the preamble to the Basel Regulation. Notice that this decision has been revised by Decision C(2001) 107 final.

[706] OJ 1994 L 1.

States in the light of this also influenced the content of the regulation. In view of this complex background, only the main contours of the regulation will be given here.

The Basel Regulation distinguishes between shipments of waste between the Member States and shipments into and out of the EU, i.e. to and from third countries. Concerning the latter a further distinction is made between EFTA countries, OECD Decision-countries and non-OECD Decision countries. A second important distinction relates to the recovery or disposal that the waste will subjected to following the shipment.[707] Basically, this means that shipments destined for recovery benefit from less restrictions compared to shipments destined for disposal.[708] Finally, it is important to notice that there are categories (lists) of waste to which different regimes apply. Compared to the 'old' Basel Regulation things have become a bit less complex given that the number of lists has been reduced from three to two, as have the number of procedures. The old Basel Regulation had three lists, the so-called green, amber and red list. Generally speaking the categorisation as green, amber or red list waste corresponded with increasing danger to human health and the environment and thus more stringent procedures and rules for shipments. The current Basel Regulation only distinguishes between a green list (Annex III) and an amber list (Annex IV). In addition, there is a list of wastes where the export is prohibited (Annex V). Shipments of green list waste are subject to a general information requirement, whereas shipments of amber list waste are subject to a prior informed consent procedure.

Shipments of waste between Member States

Title II (Articles 3 to 32) concern shipments of waste between Member States. These are subject to a prior notification and consent (PIC) procedure or a general information requirement. The applicability of the two procedures is set out in Article 3 according to which the PIC procedure applies to all shipments of waste destined for disposal (Article 3(1)(a)), shipments of mixed municipal waste (Article 3(5)) and in case of shipments destined for recovery (Article 3(1)(b)):[709]

· wastes listed in Annex IV[710] and IVA;
· wastes not classified under a single entry in Annex III, IIIB, IV or IVA;
· mixtures of wastes[711] not classified under a single entry in Annex III, IIIB, IV or IVA.

---

[707] See this chapter, section 17.1 on the definition of recovery and disposal.

[708] Case C-203/96 *Dusseldorp* [1998] ECR I-4075, para. 33.

[709] Note that incoming shipments destined for recovery may also be restricted, by derogation from the Basel Regulation, on the basis of Article 16(1) of the Waste Framework Directive.

[710] This includes wastes listed in Annexes II and VIII to the Basel Convention.

[711] See on the classification of mixtures of wastes under the old Basel Regulation Case C-259/05 *Omni Metal Service* [2007] ECR I-4945 and Case C-192/96 *Beside and Besselsen* [1998] ECR I-4029.

The general information requirement applies to all shipments in excess of 20 kilograms of waste
- · listed in Annex III or IIIB;
- · that are mixtures not classified under a single entry in Annex III of two or more wastes listed in that Annex provided that the mixing does not impair the environmentally sound recovery and that the mixture is listed in Annex IIIA.

The PIC procedure is set out in Article 4, which deals with the prior notification,[712] and Article 9, which contains the provisions on the consent required of the authorities of dispatch, transit and destination. The notification is to be submitted to the authority of dispatch (Article 4), which will check it for completeness (Article 4(2))[713] and then forward the notification to the authority of destination.[714]

According to Article 9(1) the authorities of dispatch, destination and – if relevant – transit have 30 days to consent to the shipment (with or without conditions (Article 9(1)(a) or (b)) or to raise objections. Tacit consent will be assumed if no objection is raised within this 30-day period.

Article 11 contains the grounds for objections against shipments of waste destined for disposal whereas Article 12 lists the grounds for objections against shipments destined for recovery. Both provisions have the following grounds in common:[715]
- · the planned shipment, disposal or recovery would be contrary to national legislation on environmental protection, public order or public health concerning actions taking place in the objecting country (Article 11(1)(b) and 12(1)(b));
- · the notifier or consignee has previous convictions for violations of environmental law (Article 11(1)(c) and 12(1)(d));
- · the notifier or treatment facility has repeatedly failed to comply with Arti-

---

[712] See, on the person who is the notifier under the old Basel Regulation Case C-215/04 *Pedersen* [2006] ECR I-1465. This case turned on Article 2(1)(g) of the Old Basel Regulation according to which a licensed waste collector may exceptionally be considered the notifier. Article 2(15) of the current Basel Regulation no longer requires this exceptional nature.

[713] From Case C-6/00 *ASA* [2002] ECR I-1961, para. 48, it may be inferred that this check may not result in the authority's *ex officio* reclassification of the objective of the shipment from recovery to disposal. The authority can, however, raise objections against a shipment. In *ASA* the Court held that this should take place on the basis of the classification error, the current Basel Regulation provides for an objection to the shipment in Article 12(1)(h). See further Case C-472/02 *Siomab* [2004] ECR I-9971, paras. 27 and 28.

[714] The authority of destination will, if necessary, forward the notification to the authority of transit, Article 7(1).

[715] The Member State of transit may only raise the objections under Article 11(1)(b), (c), (d) and (f), Article 11(2) and Article 12(1)(b), (d), (e) and (f), Article 12(2).

cle 15 (on interim recovery and disposal operations) and 16 (on conditions following consent; Article 11(1)(d) and 12(1)(e));
- the planned shipment conflicts with international obligations for the Member States or the EU (Article 11(1)(f) and 12(1)(f));
- the treatment will take place in an IPPC-installation[716] that does not apply the best available techniques (Article 11(1)(h) and 12(1)(i));
- the treatment is not in accordance with binding European environmental protection standards relating to the disposal or recovery (Article 11(1)(j) and 12(1)(j)).

As was mentioned above, shipments destined for disposal are subject to a stricter regime than shipments destined for recovery. For one, all shipments of mixed municipal waste destined for disposal may be objected to (Article 11(1) (i)). Moreover, the implementation of the principles of proximity, priority for recovery and self-sufficiency may result in systematic objections to all shipments of waste intended for disposal (Article 11(1)(a)). Article 11(1)(g) allows for a similar restriction of shipments of waste. This brings us back to the difficulties already identified above in connection with the principle of self-sufficiency and proximity.[717] Taken together these principles have resulted in the Member States setting up waste management structures on a primarily (if not purely) national basis. Moreover, in order to ensure the profitability of the disposal installations that make up such structures, exports of waste will often be minimised as this guarantees optimal use of these facilities.[718] We have already noted that the proximity principle may actually plead for an export of waste if the treatment installation in another Member State is closer than the national installation. Furthermore, a closer reading of the principle of self-sufficiency reveals that it is about self-sufficiency at European and national levels. The Basel Regulation and the Waste Framework Directive are therefore ambiguous with regard to the legality of such predominantly national waste management structures. The requirement in the heading of Article 11(1) that objections must be in accordance with the Treaty, and thus the provisions on the free movement of goods, has not proven helpful in solving this problem either.[719] Finally, Member States may exercise their right pursuant to the Basel Convention to restrict the import of hazardous waste (Article 11(1)(e)).

Shipments of waste destined for recovery may meet with the following objections:
- the planned shipment or recovery is not in accordance with the Waste

---

[716] See section 5 above.

[717] This chapter, section 17.1.

[718] See, for example, Case C-203/96 *Dusseldorp* [1998] ECR I-4075 and Case C-209/98 *Sydhavnens* [2000] ECR I-3743, where the Member States invoked reasons relating to the profitability of waste treatment installations to justify (possible) restrictions of the export of waste.

[719] See Case C-324/99 *DaimlerChrysler* [2001] ECR I-9897.

Framework Directive (Article 12(1)(a));[720]
· the planned shipment or recovery is not in accordance with the national standards of the country of dispatch (Article 12(1)(c));
· the ratio of the recoverable and nonrecoverable waste, the estimated value of the materials to be finally recovered or the cost of the recovery and the cost of the disposal of the nonrecoverable fraction do not justify the recovery under economic and environmental considerations (Article 12(1)(g));[721]
· the waste is shipped for disposal instead of recovery (Article 12(1)(h));
· the waste will not be treated in accordance with waste management plans drawn up in order to meet binding European recycling or recovery targets.[722]

The objection listed in Article 12(1)(c) is particularly interesting as it could allow the Member States the possibility to systematically restrict shipments of waste destined for recovery in a manner similar to the way shipments for disposal may be restricted. By setting higher national recovery standards, a Member State could simply block the export of waste destined for recovery. The fact that Article 12(1)(c) requires such objections to respect the need to ensure the proper functioning of the internal market will not resolve this problem as setting higher standards for recovery operations that take place on the territory of a Member State will fall outside the scope of the free movement provisions (as a wholly internal situation). Moreover, European standards on recovery will invariably constitute minimum harmonisation in view of Article 176 EC. In this regard, the exceptions listed in (i) and (ii) are probably more effective. Under (i), a Member State may not object against a shipment if the recovery in another Member State conforms to a European minimum standard. Moreover, if the recovery in the other Member State takes place under conditions that are 'broadly equivalent' to those in the state of dispatch the objection cannot be raised either (ii). Whatever more stringent national recovery standards exist, they must have been notified (iii).[723] Article 12(1)(c) is furthermore interesting in connection with Article 12(1)(a). The latter provision closely follows Article 7(4)(a), first indent, of the old Basel Regulation which has been interpreted by the Court as allowing the Member State of dispatch, in assessing the effects on health and the environment of the recovery envisaged at the destination, provided it complies with the principle of proportionality, to rely on the criteria

---

[720] See, concerning Article 7(4)(a), first indent, of the old Basel Regulation, Case C-227/02 *EU Wood Trading* [2004] ECR I-11957, where the fact that treatment abroad does not meet the environmental standards of the country of dispatch could be raised as an objection to the shipment. This ground for objection is now included in Article 12(1)(c).

[721] See, concerning the identical Article 7(4)(a), fifth indent, of the old Basel Regulation, Case C-113/02 *Commission v. Netherlands* [2004] ECR I-9707, paras. 17-25.

[722] See sections 17.2 to 17.5 above concerning such targets with regard to batteries, WEEE and packaging waste.

[723] See section 2.1 above concerning the Notification Directive.

to which, in order to avoid such effects, the recovery of waste is subject in the State of dispatch, even where those criteria are stricter than those in force in the State of destination.[724] It appears that the Court thus allows the Member States more leeway under Article 12(1)(a), particularly in view of the fact that the Court also held that the mere fact that national legislation is more stringent does not necessarily mean that it is disproportionate.[725]

To reduce the administrative burden arising from the PIC procedure, the possibility of general notifications for more than one shipment is envisaged (Article 13) as well as the possibility of preconsenting to certain recovery facilities (Article 14).

The general information procedure applies to the categories of waste listed in Article 3(2) and (4) and is set out in Article 178. Basically, this procedure requires certain information to accompany the shipment. No prior consent is required. The general requirements applying to all shipments of waste are set out in Articles 19-21 and include a prohibition of mixing waste and a duty to keep information for at least three years after the shipment. Articles 22-25 relate to the duty to take back waste when the shipment or treatment cannot be completed. In this case costs for the take-back shall primarily be borne by the notifier (Article 23(1)(a)).[726] For illegal shipments (Article 2(35))[727] a similar framework applies (Articles 24 and 25). As far as these costs are concerned, the Basel Regulation lays down an obligation to secure a financial guarantee or insurance (Article 6). Chapter 5 contain general administrative rules. Chapter 6 contains specialised rules on shipments within the EU with transit via third countries.

The rules on the shipment of waste do not apply to shipments within a Member State (Article 2(34)). Here the regulation requires only that the Member States establish an appropriate system for the supervision and control of such shipments and that the system takes account of the need for coherence with the European system established by the regulation (Article 33(1)). This allows Member States the necessary freedom to arrange matters as they see fit within their own jurisdiction.

Exports of waste out of the EU

As far as exports of waste are concerned, the regulation distinguishes between EFTA countries and non-EFTA countries and between OECD and

---

[724] Case C-227/02 *EU Wood Trading* [2004] ECR I-11957, paras. 44-54.

[725] Case C-227/02 *EU Wood Trading* [2004] ECR I-11957, para. 51.

[726] See Case C-389/00 *Commission* v. *Germany* [2003] ECR I-2001, where the Court finds a mandatory contribution to a solidarity fund to constitute a charge of equivalent effect prohibited under Articles 23 and 25 EC, now Articles 28 and 30 TFEU.

[727] Cf. Case C-192/96 *Beside* [1998] ECR I-4029, where the Court ruled 'that the Member State of destination may not unilaterally return waste to the Member State of dispatch without prior notification to the latter; the Member State of dispatch may not oppose its return where the Member State of destination produces a duly motivated request to that effect.'

non-OECD countries. Furthermore the two lists and the distinction between recovery and disposal are relevant.

The basic rule is a prohibition of all exports for disposal (Article 34(1)), with an exception for EFTA countries that are also a party to the Basel Convention (Article 34(2)). In case of such exports to EFTA countries Article 35 declares the regime for shipments within the EU applicable, albeit subject to a few procedural changes (set out in Article 35(2) and (3)).

In the following cases exports for recovery to non-OECD decision countries are also prohibited (Article 36(1)):

· hazardous waste (Annex V), including mixtures with non-hazardous wastes;

· waste where the country of dispatch has reasons to believe that they will not be managed in an environmentally sound manner (the rules for establishing this are set out in Article 49).

The procedures for exporting waste listed in Annex III or IIIA, green list waste) is laid down in Article 37 and also involves a procedure whereby the Commission requests from the non-OECD country a decision according to which the import will be prohibited, subject to the PIC procedure set out in Article 35 or subject to the general information requirement (Article 18). A list with these decisions is included in a Commission regulation (Article 37(2)).[728]

For exports of green and amber list waste OECD decision countries the provisions for shipments of waste within the EU apply (Article 38(1)), again subject to the changes and additions listed in Article 38(2), (3) and (5). This means that the PIC procedure and the general information requirement are applicable with the scope of the PIC procedure being slightly widened.[729] Finally, exports of waste to the Antarctic are prohibited (Article 39), as are exports for disposal in overseas countries (Article 40(1)).

Imports of waste into the EU

In principle all imports into the EU of waste for disposal are prohibited (Article 41(1)). Exceptions apply to the countries which are parties to the Basel Convention, countries with which the EC and its Member States have concluded agreements and countries subject to war or crisis. Again the regime for intra-EU shipments is declared applicable (Article 42) subject to procedural changes and additions.

Imports of waste destined for recovery are subject to a comparable regime with the exception that such imports will also be allowed from OECD decision countries (Article 43(1)). The same procedure also applies to non-OECD decision countries which are party to the Basel Convention (Article 45). Imports of waste

---

[728] Currently Regulation 801/2007, OJ 2007 L 179/6, repealing Regulation 1547/1999.

[729] For example shipments of waste listed in Annex IIIA and IIIB are subject to the PIC procedure whereas they are subject to the general information requirement as far as intra-Union shipments are concerned (Article 38(2)(a) and (b)), this paragraph appears to be erroneously numbered as 1).

from overseas countries for recovery are subject to the regime applicable to intra-EU shipments.

Transit and other provisions

The Basel Regulation also contains specific provisions on the transit of waste through the EU for disposal and recovery outside the EU (Articles 47 and 48). Finally, it contains several general provisions dealing with matters such as the general duty on the part of all the parties involved in a shipment to take all steps to ensure that the environment is protected (Article 49), enforcement (Article 50), reporting and other procedural and organisational issues surrounding the application of the regulation (Articles 51-56). Finally, the regulation repeals the old Basel Regulation with effect from 1 July 2007, albeit subject to transitional rules contained in Article 62. Moreover the regulation envisages transitional rules for certain Member States (Poland, Slovakia, Bulgaria and Romania, Article 63).

17.8   Landfill of Waste

Very broadly formulated environmental objectives can be found in the Landfill Directive, Directive 1999/31.[730] According to Article 1 the directive's overall objective is 'to prevent or reduce as far as possible negative effects on the environment, in particular the pollution of surface water, groundwater, soil and air, and on the global environment, including the greenhouse effect, as well as any resulting risk to human health, from landfilling of waste, during the whole life-cycle of the landfill.'

Each landfill shall be classified in one of the following classes:
- landfill for hazardous waste;
- landfill for non-hazardous waste;
- landfill for inert waste.

Member States must take measures to ensure that only waste that has been subject to treatment is landfilled. This provision may not apply to inert waste for which treatment is not technically feasible, nor to any other waste for which such treatment does not contribute to the objectives of the directive, by reducing the quantity of the waste or the hazards to human health or the environment (Article 6(a)). Only hazardous waste that fulfils the criteria set out in Annex II of the directive may be assigned to a hazardous landfill (Article 6(b)).

Article 6 (c) provides that landfill for non-hazardous waste may be used for:
- municipal waste;
- non-hazardous waste of any other origin, which fulfil certain criteria set out in Annex II of the directive;
- stable, non-reactive hazardous wastes (e.g. solidified, vitrified), with leaching behaviour equivalent to those of the non-hazardous mentioned above.

---

[730] OJ 1999 L 182/1, later amended.

However, these hazardous wastes shall not be deposited in cells destined for biodegradable non-hazardous waste.

Inert waste landfill sites shall be used only for inert waste (Article 6(d)). Annex I lists general requirements for all classes of landfills.

The following wastes may not be accepted in landfills, for example, liquid waste, waste which is explosive, corrosive, oxidising, highly flammable or flammable, hospital and other clinical wastes, whole used tyres or any other type of waste which does not fulfil the acceptance criteria set out in Annex II (Article 5(3)). The dilution of mixture of waste solely in order to meet the waste acceptance criteria is prohibited (Article 5(4)).

In Articles 7-9 the directive introduces a specific permit procedure for all classes of landfill in accordance with the general licensing requirements already set out in the Waste Framework Directive and the general requirements of the IPPC Directive and the Industrial Emissions Directive.[731]

Members States are required to take measures to ensure the competent authority does not issue a landfill permit unless it is satisfied that the landfill project complies with all the relevant requirements of the directive, the management of the landfill will be in the hands of a natural person who is technically competent to manage the site and that professional and technical development and training of landfill operators and staff are provided. They must also ensure that measures are taken to prevent accidents and limit their consequences. Furthermore, they must ensure that adequate provisions, by way of a financial security or any other equivalent have been made by the applicant prior to the commencement of disposal operations to ensure that the obligations (including after-care provisions) arising under the permit issued are discharged and that the closure procedures required by Article 13 are followed. Prior to the commencement of disposal operations, the competent authority is required to inspect the site in order to ensure that it complies with the relevant conditions of the permit. However, this will not reduce in any way the responsibility of the operator under the conditions of the permit.

An interesting reference to the polluter pays principle can be found in Article 10 of the directive.[732] All of the costs involved in the setting up and operation of a landfill site, including the cost of the financial security, and the estimated

---

[731] Landfills receiving more than 10 tonnes per day or with a total capacity exceeding 25,000 tonnes, excluding landfills of inert waste are subject to the provisions of the IPPC Directive (Annex I sub 5.2 of the directive) and the Industrial Emissions Directive (Annex I , point 5.4). In respect of the technical characteristics of landfills, Directive 99/31 contains, for those landfills to which the IPPC Directive / Industrial Emissions Directive is applicable, the relevant technical requirements in order to elaborate in concrete terms the general requirements of that directive. The relevant requirements of those directivea shall be deemed to be fulfilled if the requirements of Directive 99/31 are complied with; Article 1(1) Directive 99/31.

[732] See on the interpretation of this provision Case C-172/08 *Pontina Ambiente* [2010] ECR I-1175, paras. 32-41.

costs of the closure and after-care of the site for a period of at least 30 years must be covered by the price to be charged by the operator for the disposal of any type of waste in that site. This to ensure that the polluter does indeed pay!

The provisions of Article 13 on closure and after-care are important, because landfills can pose a threat to the environment not only in the short but also in the long term. More particularly, measures must be taken against the pollution of groundwater by leachate infiltration into the soil.

A landfill may only be considered definitely closed after the competent authority has carried out a final on-site inspection, has assessed all the reports submitted by the operator and has communicated to the operator its approval for the closure. This shall not in any way reduce the responsibility of the operator under the conditions of the permit (Article 13(b)). After a landfill has been definitely closed, the operator remains responsible for its maintenance, monitoring and control in the after-care phase for as long as may be required by the competent authority. The operator is required to notify the competent authority of any significant adverse environmental effects revealed by the control procedures and must follow the decision of the competent authority on the nature and timing of the corrective measures to be taken (Article 13(c)). For as long as the competent authority considers that a landfill is likely to cause a hazard to the environment and without prejudice to any European or national legislation as regards liability of the waste holder, the operator of the site shall be responsible for monitoring and analysing landfill gas and leachate from the site and the groundwater regime in the vicinity of the site (Article 13(d)).

The directive also aims to achieve a reduction of the amount of biodegradable waste going to landfills (Article 5). National strategies have to be set up, which must ensure that not later than 15 years after the date laid down for transposition, biodegradable municipal waste going to landfills must be reduced to 35% of the total amount (by weight) of biodegradable municipal waste produced in 1995.[733]

Furthermore, the directive lays down detailed rules on waste acceptance procedures (Article 11) and control and monitoring procedures in the operational phase (Article 12).[734] It contains a detailed time-table to ensure that existing landfills will meet the requirements of the directive as soon as possible and within eight years after the transposition deadline at the latest (Article 14).

17.9   Other European Legislation on Waste

One of the few European rules dealing specifically with protection of the soil is contained in Directive 86/278 concerning the use of sewage sludge in agriculture.[735] The core of the directive is a prohibition of the use of

---

[733] See on national strategies that are more stringent Case C-6/03 *Eiterköpfe* [2005] ECR I-2753.

[734] Decision 2003/33 contains the criteria and procedures for the acceptance of waste at landfills, OJ 2003 L 11/27.

[735] OJ 1986 L 181/6, as amended by Regulation 807/2003, OJ 2003 L 122/36.

sludge where the concentration of certain heavy metals exceeds the limit values laid down in the directive.

Finally, the Commission has issued a Green Paper on ship dismantling[736] which is interesting in connection with a Commission communication on abandoned offshore oil and gas installations.[737] In both cases the Commission essentially advocates international action to address the problems involved. In both cases the European Parliament has adopted a resolution, but nothing further has come from this. As part of its Thematic Strategy on Waste, the inclusion of more waste streams is advocated by the Commission.[738]

18 Legislation Concerning Nuclear Safety

18.1 The Euratom Directive on Basic Safety Standards

Member States are required to have implemented Directive 96/29/Euratom laying down basic safety standards for the protection of the health of workers and the general public against the dangers arising from ionizing radiation before 13 May 2000.[739] By that date the directive replaces the 'old' Euratom directives laying down basic standards of radiation protection.[740]

The new directive applies to all practices which involve a risk from ionizing radiation emanating from an *artificial* source or from a *natural* radiation source in cases where natural radionuclides are or have been processed in view of their radioactive, fissile or fertile properties. It also applies to other work activities which involve the presence of natural radiation sources and lead to a significant increase in the exposure of workers or members of the public which cannot be disregarded from the radiation protection point of view and to any intervention in cases of radiological emergencies or in cases of lasting exposure resulting from the after-effects of a radiological emergency. The directive does not apply to exposure to radon in dwellings or to the natural level of radiation, i.e. to radionuclides contained in the human body, to cosmic radiation prevailing at ground level or to above ground exposure to radionuclides present in the undisturbed earth's crust (Article 2(4)).

Practices covered by the directive must be reported or be made subject to a prior authorisation (Articles 3 and 4).

Member States shall ensure that all new classes or types of practice resulting in exposure to ionizing radiation are justified in advance of being first adopted or first approved by their economic, social or other benefits in relation to the health detriment they may cause (Article 6(1)). Existing classes or types of prac-

---

[736] COM (2007) 269 final.

[737] COM (98) 49 final.

[738] See for the Thematic Strategy COM (2005) 666. A progress report can be found in COM (2011) 13.

[739] OJ 1996 L 159/1, corrected in OJ 1996 L 314/20.

[740] OJ 1980 L 246/1, later amended.

tice may be reviewed as to justification whenever new and important evidence about their efficacy or consequences is acquired. In addition each Member State shall ensure that:

· in the context of optimisation all exposures shall be kept as low as reasonably achievable, economic and social factors being taken into account (the 'ALARA' principle);
· the applicable dose limits are not exceeded.

The directive contains several dose limits.[741] For example in Article 9, which lays down a limit on the effective dose for exposed workers of 100 millisieverts in a consecutive five-year period, subject to a maximum effective dose of 50 mSv in any single year.

In addition, the directive contains provisions on, for example, operational protection of exposed workers, apprentices and students, including medical surveillance (Articles 17 to 39), rules on significant increase in exposure due to natural radiation sources (Articles 40 to 42), provisions on the implementation of radiation protection for the population in normal circumstances (Articles 43 to 47) and measures to be taken in the case of radiological emergencies[742] (Articles 48 to 53). In cases of transboundary effects there is a duty to cooperate with other affected Member States and non-Member States alike (Article 50(4)).

18.2   The Regulations on Radioactive Foodstuffs

Following the nuclear accident at Chernobyl on 26 April 1986, the European legislature adopted two measures designed to prevent the marketing of contaminated agricultural products in the EU. Regulation 3955/87 concerned imports of contaminated agricultural products from third countries,[743]

---

[741] In Case C-376/90, the Court decided that the limit doses laid down in the 'old' directive must be regarded as a form of minimum harmonisation and that Member States are entitled to set stricter limit doses; Case C-376/90 *Commission* v. *Belgium* [1992] ECR I-6153. This case law is undoubtedly still valid with respect to Directive 96/29. See also Chapter 3.

[742] See also Directive 89/618 on informing the general public about health protection measures to be applied and steps to be taken in the event of a radiological emergency, OJ 1989 L 357/31. Under this directive, Member States must ensure that the population likely to be affected in the event of a radiological emergency is given certain information. The information must be permanently available to the public. In the event of a radiological emergency, Member States are required to ensure that the population is informed without delay of the facts of the emergency, of the steps to be taken, and of the health protection measures applicable to the specific case. The directive also provides for the information of persons who might be involved in the organisation of emergency assistance in the event of a radiological emergency. Note that this directive and all other Euratom-provisions do not apply to military use of nuclear energy, Case C-65/04 *Commission* v. *UK* [2006] ECR I-2239.

[743] OJ 1987 L 371/14. Case C-62/88 *EP* v. *Council* [1990] ECR I-1527. In this case the Court held that the fixing of maximum permitted levels of radioactive contamination for agricultural products falls within the scope of commercial policy powers under Article 207 TFEU. See also Chapter 2.

while Regulation 3954/87 concerned the placing on the market of contaminated agricultural products within the EU.[744] The regulations both prohibit the release for free circulation or placing on the market of agricultural products which exceed the maximum permitted levels of radioactive contamination laid down in the regulations.

As Regulation 3955/87 applied only until 31 March 1991, it was replaced in 1990 by Regulation 737/90[745] and, more recently, the latter was replaced by Regulation 733/2008.[746] The essence of the new regulation, making the release for free circulation of products subject to their meeting fixed maximum levels, is the same as in Regulation 3955/87. Following the nuclear accident at Fukushima the EU adopted several regulations on the basis of the General Food Law Regulation.[747]

18.3   Management of Radioactive Waste

Radioactive waste is one of the most significant environmental problems associated with nuclear technology. To ensure that it is managed safely throughout the European Union, Directive 2011/70 establishing an EU framework for the responsible and safe management of spent fuel and radioactive waste has been adopted.[748] It applies without prejudice to the basic standards directive and supplements the basic standards laid down in Article 30 Euratom. As regards the scope, the directive does not apply to radioactive mining waste, which is covered by the Mining Waste Directive.[749] The central obligation rests upon the Member States who are required to adopt a national framework comprising a regulatory and organisational network (Article 5) as well as establish a competent authority (Article 6) concerning radioactive waste. These are then to ensure sites where radioactive waste is managed are subject to a licensing scheme. Moreover, the Member States shall ensure that responsibility for radioactive waste is assigned to the license holder and cannot be delegated (Article 7). The most interesting provision in this directive concerns the financial resources, as the long-term management required for radioactive waste often involves very

---

[744] OJ 1987 L 371/11. Case C-70/88 *EP* v. *Council* [1991] ECR I-4529. See further the discussion of the case in Chapter 2. In this case the Court held that the purpose of the prohibition on trading in products that had been contaminated with radioactivity was to protect the public health. The regulation was therefore correctly based on Article 31 of the Euratom Treaty.

[745] OJ 1990 L 82/1, as being amended by Regulation 806/2003, OJ 2003 L 122/1. See also Commission Regulation 1635/2006 laying down detailed rules for the application of Regulation 737/90, OJ 2006 L 306/3.

[746] OJ 2008 L 201/1.

[747] Regulation 178/2002, see above section 15.3. Most recently Commission Implementing Regulation 961/2011 was adopted concerning this accident, OJ 2011 L 252/10.

[748] OJ 2011 L 199/48.

[749] See above section 17.6.

significant sums. Here Article 9 requires the Member States to ensure that the national framework requires that adequate financial resources be available especially for the management of spent fuel and radioactive waste. Whether the nuclear industry is actually going to have to pay for this is left open in the directive, as it only indicates that the Member States shall take 'due account' of the responsibility of spent fuel and radioactive waste generators. Furthermore, the Member States are to adopt national programmes (Article 11) and report to the Commission (Article 14). The directive provides for a special transparency regime (Article 10). Finally, the directive must be transposed before 23 August 2013. Part of the management of radioactive waste may well be its transport.

In view of the fact that the Basel Regulation does not cover shipments of radioactive waste,[750] specific legislation was needed to cover such shipments. This was provided by Directive 92/3.[751] With effect from 25 December 2008, Directive 92/3 was replaced by Directive 2006/117/Euratom.[752] This repeal was necessitated by the need to clarify and streamline the procedures and the need to ensure consistency with other provisions of European law[753] and international obligations.[754] Directive 2006/117 maintains the distinction between intra-EU shipments and extra-EU shipments and, albeit in slightly simplified form, the PIC procedure for intra-EU shipments (Articles 6 and 9). Importantly, spent nuclear fuel intended for reprocessing is now also included in the scope of the directive (Article 1(2)).[755] Another important change relates to the inclusion of grounds for a refusal of consent (Article 6(3)). Member States of transit may refuse consent if they consider the transport to be contrary to international, European or national legislation on such transports (Article 6(3(a)), whereas Member States of destination may additionally invoke relevant legislation on the management of radioactive waste or spent fuel (Article 6(3)(b)). Interestingly, this leaves open the question of whether the legislation relied on by the Member State of destination on the management must originate from the international, European or national level. Similar to Directive 92/3, any conditions attached to the consent may not be more stringent than those laid down for similar ship- ments within that Member State. It is submitted that this basic non-discrimina- tion rule should not only apply to the conditions attached to consents, but also to the decision whether or not to grant consent. It may furthermore be inferred from this that such consent may be withheld on the basis of national legislation on the management of nuclear waste or spent fuel, provided that this is non-

---

[750] See Article 1(3)(c) of Regulation 1013/2006, see above, section 17.7.

[751] OJ 1992 L 35/24. Cf. also Council Resolution on radioactive-waste management, OJ 1994 C 379/1.

[752] OJ 2006 L 337/21.

[753] Such as Directive 2003/122/Euratom on high-activity sealed radioactive sources, OJ 2003 L 346/57.

[754] See Decision 2005/84/Euratom, OJ 2005 L 30/10 approving the accession of the European Atomic Energy Community to the 'Joint Convention on the Safety of Spent Fuel Management and on the Safety of Radioactive Waste Management'.

[755] See also recital 6 of the preamble.

discriminatory, irrespective of whether or not such national legislation is more stringent than international or European legislation.[756]

19   Legislation on the Conservation of Nature[757]

Although the legal competence in the field of nature conservation was initially doubted by many (in view of the lack of any relevance to market integration), a large number of measures have been adopted since 1979 ranging from Directive 99/22 relating to the keeping of wild animals in zoos[758] via the Protocol on Protection and Welfare of Animals[759] to Regulation 2158/92 on protection of the Community's forests against fire.[760] European legislation on the conservation of nature is to some extent designed to fulfil obligations resulting from international treaties concluded by the EU, like the 1979 Berne Convention on the Conservation of European Wildlife and Natural Habitats,[761] the 1979 Bonn Convention on the Conservation of Migratory Species of Wild Animals[762], the 1992 Convention on Biological Diversity[763] and the Agreement on the International Dolphin Conservation Programme.[764]

Under the present Treaties the objectives set out in Article 191 TFEU must be regarded as more than sufficient to enable further measures to protect wildlife, flora and fauna. In addition to wildlife, the Treaties now also acknowledge the importance of animal welfare in general in the form of Article 13 TFEU. Nevertheless, these areas above all are likely to feel the impact of the subsidiarity principle, particularly where there is no question of the protection of threatened or transboundary nature values.

19.1   The Wild Birds Directive

The general scope of the directive
Directive 79/409 contained the general rules on the conservation of wild birds.[765] With effect from 14 February 2010 it was repealed by the codifying Directive 2009/147. According to Article 1, the directive relates to the

---

[756] See, in connection with a similar problem in the context of shipments of other waste, section 17.7 of this chapter.

[757] Cf. in general on the subject De Sadeleer (2005A).

[758] OJ 1999 L 94/24.

[759] Attached to the 'Amsterdam Treaty'.

[760] OJ 1992 L 217/3, as amended by Regulation 308/97, OJ 1997 L 51/11.

[761] OJ 1982 L 38/3.

[762] OJ 1982 L 210/11.

[763] OJ 1993 L 309/1. Cf. also the Cartagena Protocol on Biosafety, adopted by the EU on 29 January 2000 and Commission Communication on a European Community Biodiversity Strategy, COM (98) 42.

[764] Council Decision 1999/337, OJ 1999 L 132/1.

[765] OJ 1979 L 103/1, as amended by Directive 2006/105, OJ 2006 L 363/368.

conservation of all species of naturally occurring birds in the wild state[766] *in the European territory of the Member States.*[767] From the case law of the Court it is clear that it is not sufficient, when a Member State is implementing the directive, for it to confine itself to those species found in its territory.[768] After all, species occurring elsewhere may be transported to that Member State, or kept there or sold, alive or dead. By including in national legislation only those species occurring in their own territory, Member States would fail to provide the protection required by the directive. The case law shows that Member States not only have a responsibility to protect species occurring in their own territory, but that their responsibility extends to the whole territory of the EU. This is borne out by the Court's regular confirmation that the effective protection of birds is typically a transfrontier environment problem entailing common responsibilities for the Member States.[769]

The directive covers the protection, management and control of these species and lays down rules for their exploitation. The third recital of the preamble expresses the underlying consideration that effective bird protection is typically a transfrontier environmental problem entailing common responsibilities for the Member States. As was noted in Chapter 4, the Court has taken this to imply a stricter requirement than usual in its assessment of the implementation of the directive by the Member States.

Article 2 of the directive contains a general obligation for the Member States. They are required to take the requisite measures to maintain the population of the species in question at a level which corresponds in particular to ecological, scientific and cultural requirements, while taking account of economic and recreational requirements. The question that has arisen in respect of Article 2, in particular from the fact that it indicates that bird protection has to be balanced against other interests, is whether that provision constitutes an independent derogation from the general requirements of the directive. The Court has consistently stated that it does not.[770]

In order to achieve effective protection, the directive contains measures to protect the habitats and to limit the hunting of, and trading in, bird species. As

---

[766]The directive is not applicable to specimens of birds born and reared in captivity, Case C-149/94 *Vergy* [1996] ECR I-299. Therefore Member States remain competent to regulate trade in those specimens, subject of course to Articles 34-36 TFEU.

[767] Although the Court held in Case C-202/94 *Van der Feesten* [1996] ECR I-355, para. 18, that the directive also applies to bird subspecies which occur naturally in the wild only outside the European territory of the Member States if the species to which they belong or other subspecies of that species occur naturally in the wild within the territory in question.

[768] For example, Case 247/85 *Commission* v. *Belgium* [1987] ECR 3029 and Case C-149/94 *Vergy* [1996] ECR I-299.

[769] Case 262/85 *Commission* v. *Italy* [1987] ECR 3073.

[770] Case 247/85 *Commission* v. *Belgium* [1987] ECR 3029; Case C-435/92 *Association pour la protection des animaux sauvages* [1994] ECR I-67; Case C-44/95 *Royal Society for the Protection of Birds* [1996] ECR I-3805.

far as the former is concerned, Article 3 provides that Member States must take the requisite measures to preserve, maintain or re-establish a sufficient diversity and area of habitats for all the species of birds covered by the directive. The following measures are specifically mentioned:
· creation of protected areas;
· upkeep and management in accordance with the ecological needs of habitats inside and outside the protected zones;
· re-establishment of destroyed biotopes;
· creation of biotopes.

Special conservation measures

Special conservation measures must be taken for a number of species mentioned in Annex I of the directive (Article 4(1)).[771] Member States are required to classify in particular the most suitable territories in number and size as special protection areas for the conservation of these species. This requirement led to the additional requirement that Member States should take appropriate steps to avoid pollution or deterioration of habitats or any disturbances affecting the birds in these protection areas (Article 4(4)). Moreover it also had some measure of external effect: by virtue of the same provision, Member States are expressly required to strive to avoid pollution or deterioration of habitats outside these protection areas. However, Article 7 of the Habitats Directive provides that any obligations arising under Article 4(4) of the Wild Birds Directive shall be replaced by Article 6(2), (3) and (4) of the Habitats Directive from the date of its implementation. As will appear in the discussion of the Habitats Directive below, the possibilities of derogating from the legal consequences of classifying a special protection area under the Habitats Directive are far wider than under the Wild Birds Directive. In fact, the latter directive contains no express grounds allowing derogation. In the *Leybucht* case the Member States' obligations to classify special protection areas were at issue.[772] The Court acted on the principle that Member States do have a certain discretion in deciding whether or not to designate a given area as a special protection area for birds. However, in the *Marismas de Santoña* case, it transpired that this discretion may be very limited in any particular case, if it exists at all.[773] In that case the area in question was held to constitute one of the most important ecosystems of the Iberian peninsula, where various migratory birds and species threatened with extinction exist. The Court decided that this area should have been classified a special protection area. Further clarification on the margin of discretion avai-

---

[771] See on the interpretation of Article 4(1), Case C-535/07 *Commission v. Austria*, Judgment of 14 October 2010, paras. 56-66.

[772] Case C-57/89 *Commission v. Germany* [1991] ECR I-883.

[773] Case C-355/90 *Commission v. Spain* [1993] ECR I-4221. Cf. also Case C-166/97 *Commission v. France* [1999] ECR I-623, with respect to the French failure to classify a sufficiently large special protection area in the Seine estuary and Case C-96/98 *Commission v. France* [1999] ECR I-8531, with respect to the failure to classify a sufficiently large special protection area in the Poitevin Marsh.

lable to the Member States was given by the Court in Case C-3/96. The Court made it perfectly clear,[774]

> 'that the Member States' margin of discretion in choosing the most suitable territories for classification as SPAs does not concern the appropriateness of classifying as SPAs the territories which appear the most suitable according to ornithological criteria, but only the application of those criteria for identifying the most suitable territories for conservation of the species listed in Annex I to the Directive.'

In this context it is important to note the relevance of IBA 89 (Inventory of Important Bird Areas in the European Community). In para. 70 of the above mentioned case the Court attributed a *de facto* binding effect to the IBA 89, albeit that the Member States may produce evidence to the contrary. In view of the fact that the Netherlands had failed to do this, the Court applied the IBA 89 as a criterion by which to judge whether the Netherlands had fulfilled its classification obligations under Article 4(1) of the Wild Birds Directive.[775]

This case law must necessarily also affect Member States' freedom to declassify SPAs. As long as the areas fulfil the conditions of Article 4(1), declassification, for instance through a reduction in size, does not seem possible, unless Article 6(2-4) of the Habitats Directive can be applied. Of course, for a complaint of infringement of the directive by reason of the declassification to be upheld, it is necessary, in any event, for the area in question to have been part of a classified SPA, or an area that should have been so classified.[776]

Once an area has been classified as a protection area, or if it should have been, as in the *Marismas de Santoña* case, the obligations to avoid pollution laid down in Article 6(2) of the Habitats Directive apply.[777] Most importantly it requires Member States to take appropriate steps to avoid, *inter alia*, deterioration of habitats in the SPAs classified pursuant to Article 4(1).[778]

In the *Leybucht* case the Court held that Member States are not free to derogate at will from these obligations. They do not have the same discretion under Article 4(4) as they do in choosing which areas to classify. Derogation can be

---

[774] Case C-3/96 *Commission* v. *Netherlands* [1998] ECR I-3031, para. 61.

[775] See Case C-235/04 *Commission* v. *Spain* [2007] ECR I-5415, para. 23-40, where the Court attributes a similar binding effect to the IBA 98, which is an updated version of the IBA 89.

[776] Cf. Case C-96/98 *Commission* v. *France* [1999] ECR I-8531, paras. 48-56. Simply the rectification of an error in the classification of an SPA does not constitute a declassification.

[777] Cf. also Case C-166/97 *Commission* v. *France* [1999] ECR I-623, para. 48 and Case C-96/98 *Commission* v. *France* [1999] ECR I-8531, para. 41.

[778] In both its original version and as amended by the Habitats Directive, Case C-96/98 *Commission* v. *France* [1999] ECR I-8531, para. 35. In this case the drying out of wetlands, marine-farming construction and embankment works, thereby disturbing bird life, and the falling of the average population of wintering ducks were accepted as evidence that France failed to take appropriate measures to avoid deterioration of the areas concerned.

justified only on exceptional grounds, grounds which correspond to a general interest which is superior to the general interest represented by the ecological objective of the directive. The Court stressed that the economical and recreational interests referred to in Article 2 cannot be considered such interests. Nor did the Court regard fishing interests as a sufficiently serious reason. On the other hand, it did regard 'the danger of flooding' and 'the protection of the coast' as constituting sufficiently serious reasons to justify measures which would adversely affect the ecology of the special protection areas, as long as the measures contemplated were confined to a strict minimum and the disturbance arising from the construction work itself did not exceed what was necessary to carry it out.

On the subject of interests which would not be regarded as sufficiently serious to justify such measures, it appeared in the *Leybucht* case that measures which would adversely affect a special protection area were possible, under certain circumstances. There the measures in question would have resulted in the formation of new areas of considerable ecological importance. Such 'offsetting ecological benefits' might justify measures which Article 4(4) would otherwise not allow. This strict approach to Article 4(4) by the Court in the *Leybucht* case was largely confirmed in the *Marismas de Santoña* case.

Whether these judgments are still relevant is extremely doubtful, in view of the fact that, since the expiry of the period for implementation of the Habitats Directive, Article 4(4) of the Wild Birds Directive has been replaced by the derogations in the Habitats Directive.[779] However, in its first judgment since then, in the *Lappel Bank* case, the Court seems to want to maintain a strict approach as far as possible.[780] It confirmed that Article 6(4) of the Habitats Directive only affects measures encroaching upon Special Protection Areas already designated as such. Consequently, under the Habitats Directive, SPAs must be designated only on the basis of the – above all ornithological – criteria of Article 4 of the Birds Directive.

Restrictions on hunting and trading

To restrict the hunting of, and trading in, protected species of birds the directive contains three basic provisions. First, it prohibits the deliberate[781] killing or capture of birds, the deliberate destruction of, or damage to, their nests and eggs or removal of their nests (Articles 5 and 6(1)).

---

[779] As will appear below, these are much wider than those formulated in the *Leybucht* case. In this respect the Habitats Directive must clearly be regarded as a retrograde step for conservation law.

[780] Case C-44/95 *Royal Society for the Protection of Birds* [1996] ECR I-3805. Confirmed in Case C-209/04 *Commission v. Austria* [2006] ECR I-2755, para. 40. See for national case law applying this doctrine: German *Bundesverwaltungsgericht* 19 May 1998, *NVwZ* 1998, 961 on the planning of the track of the Ostseeautobahn.

[781] Cf. on this Case 412/85 *Commission v. Germany* [1987] ECR 3503. See for an interpretation of 'deliberate' in Article 12 Habitats Directive the English High Court, Queen's Bench Division (Maurice Kay J) 5 November 1999 *Regina v. Secretary of State for Trade and Industry, ex parte Greenpeace* [2000] Env. L.R. 221.

Second, it provides for derogations from these general prohibitions in respect of the species referred to in the Annexes. Thus, the sale of species mentioned in Annex III and the hunting of species mentioned in Annex II may be allowed, provided certain conditions and restrictions are observed (Article 6(2) to 6(4) and Article 7). This means that the general prohibitions remain in force for the species not mentioned in the Annexes, or if the conditions and restrictions are not observed. For instance, Article 7(4) provides that Member States must ensure that species to which hunting laws apply are not hunted during the rearing season or during the various stages of reproduction (nor, in the case of migratory species, during their return to their rearing grounds). The Court requires the Member States to lay down that period with particular care:

> 'Protection against hunting activities cannot be confined to the majority of the birds of a given species, as determined by average reproductive cycles and migratory movements. It would be incompatible with the objectives of the directive if, in situations characterized by prolonged dependence of the fledglings of the parents and early migration, part of the population of a given species should fall outside the protection laid down.'[782]

A method by which the closing date for hunting was fixed by reference to the period during which migratory activity was at its peak was considered incompatible with Article 7(4).[783] The same applied to those methods which take into account the moment at which a certain percentage of birds have started to migrate, or those which consist in ascertaining the average date of the commencement of pre-mating migration. More generally the Court reached the following conclusion:

> 'Methods whose object or effect is to allow a certain percentage of the birds of a species to escape such protection do not comply with that provision.'

A second important question in this judgment was whether the national authorities are empowered by the directive to fix staggered closing dates for hunting which vary according to the species concerned. In principle this is not acceptable, the Court held, unless the Member State concerned can produce scientific evidence that staggering the closing dates does not impede the complete protection of the species of bird in question. As to whether the directive permits the closing of hunting to be fixed at different dates in different parts of the territory of a Member State, the Court noted that this was in itself compatible with the directive. Here, too, the only requirement is that the complete protection of migratory birds is guaranteed.

---

[782] Case C-157/89 *Commission v. Italy* [1991] ECR I-57.

[783] Case C-435/92 *Association pour la protection des animaux sauvages* v. *Préfet de Maine-et-Loire en Préfet de la Loire-Atlantique* [1994] ECR I-67.

And third, under Article 9, Member States may derogate from the general prohibitions and the provisions on hunting and trading, if three conditions are met:[784]

- there must be no other satisfactory solution;[785]
- the derogation must be for one of the reasons listed, exhaustively, in Article 9(1)(a) (*inter alia*, to prevent serious damage[786] to crops, livestock, forests, fisheries and water);
- it must specify the details laid down in Article 9(2), designed to ensure the derogations are kept to what is strictly necessary and to enable control by the Commission. Thus the derogations must, for example, specify the species which are subject to the derogations, the means authorised for capture, and the controls which will be carried out.

The Court has devoted particular attention to the transposition of these derogations (they constitute an exhaustive list) provided for in Article 9 into national law.[787] It requires that the essential elements of Article 9 are transposed completely, clearly and unequivocally into the national rules.[788] This is necessary to ensure that the derogations are applied in a strictly controlled and selective manner. Although the provisions of Article 9 allow a fair degree of derogation from the general protective rules, they must nevertheless be applied precisely and specifically, in order to meet clearly defined conditions and specific situations.

Other provisions

The directive also contains provisions on research (Article 10), prevention of damage to local flora and fauna by the introduction of exotic species of bird (Article 11), reports (Article 12) and a standstill requirement (Article 13).

Article 14 allows Member States to take stricter protective measures than provided for under the directive. This was what was at issue in the *Red Grouse* case.[789] The case concerned the question whether a Dutch prohibition on the importation of red grouse was justified by the directive, in particular given the fact that red grouse do not normally occur in the Netherlands. Red grouse

---

[784] Cf. on the interpretation of Article 9, Case C-10/96 *Ligue Royale Belge pour la Protection des Oiseaux and Société d'Études Ornithologiques AVES* v. *Région Wallonne* [1996] ECR I-6775; Case C-344/03 *Commission* v. *Finland* [2005] ECR I-11033 and Case C-60/05 *WWF Italia* [2006] ECR I-5083.

[785] See on the interpretation of this concept Case C-76/08 *Commission* v. *Malta* [2009] ECR I-8213, paras. 46-68. Note that the matter at hand in this case, sping hunting of quails and turtle doves, has also been subject of an application for interim measures in Case C-76/08 R *Commission* v. *Malta* [2008] ECR I-64.

[786] Cf. the questionable judgment of the Scottish Court of Session *the petition of the RSPB and the Wildfowl and Wetlands Trust* v. *Secretary of State for Scotland* [2000] Env. L.R. 168.

[787] Case 236/85 *Commission* v. *Netherlands* [1987] ECR 3989.

[788] Case 262/85 *Commission* v. *Italy* [1987] ECR 3073 and Case C-118/94 *Associazione Italiana per il WWF a.o.* v. *Regione Veneto* [1996] ECR I-1223.

[789] Case C-169/89 *Gourmetterie v.d. Burg* [1990] ECR I-2143.

is one of the species named in Annex III/1 of the directive, which means that certain marketing activities are allowed, provided the birds have been legally killed or captured or otherwise legally acquired. That the birds in question had been legally killed was not disputed. The Dutch Government invoked Article 14, which allows the Member States to adopt stricter protective measures, to justify the prohibition. According to the Court, the power to take stricter protective measures in regards of birds named in Annex III/1 is the exclusive prerogative of the Member States where they normally occur. Apparently there can thus be no question of a common responsibility for those species which are neither threatened with extinction nor migratory!

19.2   The Habitats Directive

Like the Wild Birds Directive, Directive 92/43 on the conservation of natural habitats and of wild fauna and flora[790] – the Habitats Directive – provides on the one hand for measures to protect conservation areas (Articles 3 to 11), and on the other for measures to protect species (Articles 12 to 16). It can be argued that the directive is not only applicable on the territory of the Member States, but on all areas under their jurisdiction, including the Continental Shelf and/or any Economic and Exclusive Zone.[791]

Among the measures designed to protect conservation areas, the key measure is the designation of special areas of conservation (SAC), with a view to setting up a coherent European ecological network of such areas under the title Natura 2000 (Article 3(1)). This network is to include the special protection areas classified by the Member States under the Wild Birds Directive. Annex I lists the various types of natural habitat of Community interest which require conservation, while Annex II lists the species of animals and plants whose habitats require protection. The lists designate certain habitat types and species as priority types and species.

SACs are designated according to a procedure laid down in the directive. The Member States must propose a list indicating which natural habitat types and which species occur in their territory that are eligible for protection. In this phase of the procedure only conservation related arguments are allowed and non-inclusion of a site on economic, cultural and social grounds is not allowed.[792] A distinction must be made between priority habitats and species and those which do not have priority. On the basis of these national lists, the Commission is required to establish a list of sites of Community importance (Article 4(2)).[793] Where the Commission finds that a national list fails

---

[790] OJ 1992 L 206/7, later amended.

[791] Case C-6/04 *Commission* v. *UK* [2005] ECR I-9017, para. 119. See also English High Court, Queen's Bench Division (Maurice Kay J) 5 November 1999 *Regina* v. *Secretary of State for Trade and Industry*, ex parte *Greenpeace* [2000] Env. L.R. 221.

[792] Case C-226/08 *Stadt Papenburg* [2010] ECR I-131, paras. 27-33.

[793] See, e.g. Commission Decision 2011/84, OJ 2011 L 40/1. OJ 2011 L 33 and L 40 contain similar lists.

to mention a site, a bilateral consultation procedure must be initiated (Article 5(1)). If the dispute remains unresolved, the Council, acting on a proposal from the Commission, may decide to place the site on the list. This decision must, incidentally, be taken unanimously, so that the Member State in question can prevent the site being regarded as a site of Community importance against its will. When a site has been adopted as a 'Site of Community Importance' (SCI), the Member State concerned must designate it as a special area of conservation as soon as possible and within six years at most (Article 4(4)). The entire procedure can thus take up to 12 years! The actual designation of a site as a special area of conservation by a Member State is of only limited importance. This is because the legal consequences of designation take effect as soon as the site is placed on the list by the Commission (Article 4(5)).[794] Furthermore, the Court made clear that although the protective measures of Article 6(2-4) are required only as regards sites which are on the list of sites selected as sites of Community importance adopted by the Commission, this does not mean that the Member States are not to protect sites as soon as they propose them as sites eligible for identification as sites of Community importance on the national list transmitted to the Commission. In that case the Member States are required 'to take protective measures appropriate for the purpose of safeguarding that ecological interest'.[795]

Article 6 sets out the legal consequences of designation as a special area of conservation.[796] In the first place, Member States must establish the necessary conservation measures involving, if need be, appropriate management plans (Article 6(1)). They must also take steps to avoid the deterioration of habitats in the special areas of conservation and to avoid disturbance of the species for which the areas have been designated (Article 6(2)).[797] The Dutch *Raad van State*, applying the *Kraaijeveld* doctrine, argued in the *Buitengebied Texel* case that Article 6(2) of the Habitats Directive has direct effect.[798]

Article 6(3) provides that the competent authorities must agree to any plan or project likely to have a significant effect on the site only after having ascertained that it will not adversely affect the integrity of the site concerned.[799] Only after

---

[794] Except for the provisions of Article 6(1) which apply only when a SCI has been designated as a SAC.

[795] Case C-117/03 *Dragaggi a.o.* [2005] ECR I-167, paras. 25-29. Cf. also Case C-244/05 *Bund Naturschutz in Bayern a.o.* [2006] ECR I-8445.

[796] Cf. in general the Commission's interpretation guide for Article 6 of the Habitats Directive: Managing Natura 2000 sites; the provisions of Article 6 of the 'Habitats' Directive 92/43/EEC, Brussels, April 2000.

[797] See, on the relation between Article 6(2) and 6(4), Case C-127/02 *Waddenvereniging and Vogelbeschermingsvereniging* [2004] ECR I-7405 (*Waddenzee*), paras. 91-96. Cf. on Article 6(2) also Case C-241/08 *Commission v. France*, Judgment of 4 March 2010.

[798] Dutch *Raad van State* 31 March 2000 *Buitengebied Texel* [2000] AB 303. See on the possible direct effect of Article 6 with respect to areas not formally designated as a SAC, Chapter 5, section 2.1.

[799] In Case C-127/02 *Waddenvereniging and Vogelbeschermingsvereniging* [2004] ECR I-7405 (*Waddenzee*), para. 38, the Court held that Article 6(2) and 6(3) cannot apply concomitantly. However, the Court does not rule out a safety net-role for Article 6(2); see para. 37. For an application of this safety net role, see

such an assessment has been carried out and after the opinion of the general public has been obtained may the competent national authorities agree to the plan or project.[800]

This provision is worded in such a way so as to imply that it also applies to projects and plans outside the protected area but having effects within it. In the same way as was true of the Wild Birds Directive, the protective measures appear to have some degree of external effect. Moreover, this provision involves a two-stage assessment of the environmental impact. If it cannot be excluded, on the basis of objective information, that the plan or project will have a significant effect on that site, either individually or in combination with other plans or projects, a second in-depth assessment is required.[801] Concerning the plans and projects that would require such an assessment, the Court has adopted a wide interpretation that also includes periodically recurring projects (such as dredging a river) where the project was approved before the entry into force of the directive.[802] This interpretation is grounded in the directive's conservation objectives.[803]

The scene for this first assessment is set in the light of the precautionary principle and the high level of protection.[804] In the *Waddenzee* case the Court held that this in-depth assessment in accordance with Article 6(3):

'provides for an assessment procedure intended to ensure, by means of a prior examination, that a plan or project which is not directly connected with or necessary to the management of the site concerned but likely to have a significant effect on it is authorised only to the extent that it will not adversely affect the integrity of that site'.[805]

As regards the assessment that should take place, the Court has put the bar quite high indeed.[806] Pursuant to the precautionary principle, national authori-

---

Case C-304/05 *Commission v. Italy* [2007] ECR I-7495, where the Court held that on the one hand Articles 6(3) and 6(4) and on the other hand Article 6(2) were infringed (paras. 91-96).

[800] Cf. Case C-256/98 *Commission v. France* [2000] ECR I-2487.

[801] Case C-127/02 *Waddenvereniging and Vogelbeschermingsvereniging* [2004] ECR I-7405 (*Waddenzee*), para. 45.

[802] Case C-226/08 *Stadt Papenburg* [2010] ECR I-131, paras. 39-42.

[803] Case C-226/08 *Stadt Papenburg* [2010] ECR I-131, para. 43.

[804] Case C-127/02 *Waddenvereniging and Vogelbeschermingsvereniging* [2004] ECR I-7405 (*Waddenzee*), para. 44.

[805] Case C-127/02 *Waddenvereniging and Vogelbeschermingsvereniging* [2004] ECR I-7405 (*Waddenzee*), para. 34. Confirmed in Case C-239/04 *Commission v. Portugal* [2006] ECR I-10183 (*Castro Verde*), para. 19 and Case C-304/05 *Commission v. Italy*, [2007] ECR I-7495, para. 56.

[806] The original proposal basically required an EIA, this was replaced with the requirement that an assessment take place. In Case C-127/02 *Waddenvereniging and Vogelbeschermingsvereniging* [2004] ECR I-7405 (*Waddenzee*), para. 42 the Court equates this terminology with that of the EIA Directive thereby suggesting that an EIA may be the appropriate assessment. It may be noted that the EIA Directive does not

ties must be *certain* that no negative effects will occur. Concerning the level of certainty the Court has held that 'no reasonable scientific doubt may remain' and that the authorities have to rely on the best scientific knowledge in the field.[807] Importantly, the Court has held that Article 6(3) may be relied upon in a national court.[808]

The requirement of Article 6(3), that any plan or project likely to have a significant effect on a site may be carried out only after 'appropriate assessment' of the implications for the site in view of the site's conservation objectives, deserves special attention. Only after such an assessment has been carried out and after the opinion of the general public has been obtained may the competent national authorities agree to the plan or project.[809] However, in view of the fact that the Habitats Directive has been adopted on the basis of Article 192 TFEU, stricter measures are allowed. This could also amount to a prohibition of activities that could endanger wildlife in the habitat. As a result, an Italian ban on the construction of large wind turbines not intended for self-consumption in a conservation area and a 200-metre buffer zone around the habitat, was compatible with the Habitats Directive.[810]

The only derogations from the requirements of Article 6(2-3) are those in Article 6(4).[811] Recourse to Article 6(4) is only possible after an assessment that complies with the framework laid down in Article 6(3).[812] If there are imperative reasons of overriding public interest[813], including those of a social or economic nature, a plan or project may nevertheless be carried out in spite of a negative assessment of the implications for the site. In that case the Member State is required to take all compensatory measures necessary to ensure that the overall coherence of Natura 2000 is protected.[814] According to the Commission the compensation can consist of:

---

necessarily apply to projects by virtue of their location in a protected area, see preamble Directive 97/11 OJ 1997 L 73/5.

[807] For example Case C-304/05 *Commission* v. *Italy* [2007] ECR I-7495, para. 59. This case also provides a fine example of how the Court will examine whether or not an assessment complies with these requirements, see paras. 60-70.

[808] Case C-127/02 *Waddenvereniging and Vogelbeschermingsvereniging* [2004] ECR I-7405 (*Waddenzee*), para. 69.

[809] Cf. Case C-256/98 *Commission* v. *France* [2000] ECR I-2487.

[810] Case C-2/10 *Azienda Agro-Zootecnica Franchini*, Judgment of 21 July 2011, paras. 44-58.

[811] To determine the temporal scope of this provision the Court has adopted an approach that is similar to that developed for the EIA Directive (section 3 above), see Case C-209/04 *Commission* v. *Austria* [2006] ECR I-2755, paras. 57, 58.

[812] Case C-304/05 *Commission* v. *Italy* [2007] ECR I-7495, para. 83.

[813] The concept of 'imperative reasons of overriding public interest' is not defined in the directive. The Dutch *Raad van State* argued that large-scale house-building plans near Amsterdam could be considered as falling within the concept; Dutch *Raad van State* 11 January 2000 *IJmeer building* [2000] *NJB* 463 nr. 9.

[814] Cf. the *Leybucht* case, Case C-57/89 *Commission* v. *Germany* [1991] ECR I-883, though the 'offsetting ecological benefits' there were actually at the same site.

· recreating a habitat on a new or enlarged site, to be incorporated into
  Natura 2000;
· improving a habitat on part of the site or on another Natura 2000 site,
  proportional to the loss due to the project;
· in exceptional cases, proposing a new site under the Habitats Directive.[815]

However, where the site hosts a priority habitat or species, the derogations
allowed are more limited. The second paragraph of Article 6(4) provides that the
only considerations which may be raised are those relating to human health or
public safety, or to beneficial consequences of primary importance for the environment. However, 'other imperative reasons of overriding public interest' may
also justify derogation, though only after the Commission has given its opinion.

These 'overriding interests' clearly allow Member States more discretion to
derogate from the obligations resulting from designation as a special protection area than was allowed by the Court in the *Leybucht* case. There, economic
reasons were expressly excluded. As Article 6(2), (3) and (4) of the Habitats
Directive expressly replaces any obligations arising under Article 4(4) of the
Wild Birds Directive (Article 7), the Council clearly intended to deflect of the
Court's case law under the Wild Birds Directive it was not happy with.

It is not clear what the legal consequences are if no compensatory measures
can be taken which are capable of protecting the coherence of Natura 2000. The
wording of Article 4, and the objective of the directive, suggest that the project
could not in that case be carried through.

The Habitats Directive also prohibits the deliberate[816] capture or killing of
animal species needing strict protection (listed in Annex IV), the deliberate
disturbance of these species, the deliberate destruction or taking of eggs from
the wild, or the deterioration or destruction of breeding sites or resting places
(Article 12(1)). In principle, the keeping of, or trading in, these species is prohibited (Article 12(2)).

Article 13 provides for the protection of the plant species listed in Annex IV,
requiring the prohibition of the deliberate picking, collecting, cutting, uproot-
ing or destruction of such plants in their natural range in the wild (Article 13(1)).
Keeping or trading in these species is also, in principle, prohibited.

A slightly less stringent regime applies to animal and plant species listed in
Annex V. Taking them in the wild and exploiting them is not necessarily prohibited, but may be made subject to certain control measures. The most important
restriction is the prohibition of indiscriminate means capable of causing local
disappearance of, or serious disturbance to, populations of such species (Article
15(a)).

---

[815] See the Commission's interpretation guide for Article 6 of the Habitats Directive: Managing Natura
2000 sites; the provisions of Article 6 of the 'Habitats' Directive 92/43/EEC, Brussels, April 2000 at 41.

[816] Cf. on the notion of 'deliberate' Case C-221/04 *Commission* v. *Spain* [2006] ECR I-4515, para. 71, and, in
relation to Article 22 Habitats Directive, Case C-249/07 *Commission* v. *Netherlands* [2008] ECR I-174. Cf.
also English High Court, Queen's Bench Division (Maurice Kay J) 5 November 1999 *Regina* v. *Secretary
of State for Trade and Industry*, ex parte *Greenpeace* [2000] Env. L.R. 221.

The derogations mentioned in Article 16 are clearly more extensive than those in the Wild Birds Directive. Derogation is allowed, among other things:

- in the interest of protecting wild fauna and flora and conserving natural habitats;
- to prevent[817] serious damage, in particular to crops, livestock, forests, fisheries and water and other types of property;
- in the interests of public health and public safety, or for other imperative reasons of overriding public interest, including those of a social or economic nature and beneficial consequences of primary importance for the environment;
- for the purpose of research and education, of repopulating and reintroducing these species and for the breeding operations necessary for these purposes, including the artificial propagation of plants.

Unlike the derogations allowed in the context of the special protection areas, the ones allowed for the protection of species are not stated to be applicable *mutatis mutandis* to the Wild Birds Directive. It must therefore be assumed that, within the scope of the Wild Birds Directive, derogations are possible only from the prohibitions on capture and marketing referred to in Article 9 of that directive.

19.3   The CITES Regulation

On 3 March 1973, the Convention on international trade in endangered species of wild fauna and flora, or CITES, was opened for signature in Washington. The Convention was intended to protect endangered species of wild fauna and flora by regulating international trade in these species. The EC is not as such a party to the Convention, which does not allow for accession by international organisations. The Convention is applied unilaterally by the EU, first through Regulation 3626/82[818] and now by Regulation 338/97 on the protection of species of wild fauna and flora by regulating trade therein.[819] The Court has consistently held that the CITES Regulation is to be interpreted in the light of the CITES Convention.[820]

The regulation sets out four different protection regimes. Annex A corresponds to Appendix I of CITES; Annex B to Appendix II; Annex C to Appendix III, while Annex D contains species which are not listed in one of the CITES Appendices. In this respect the regulation actually has a wider scope than CITES.

---

[817] Cf. on the issuing of hunting permits on a *preventive* basis Case C-342/05 *Commission v. Finland* [2006] ECR I-4713.

[818] OJ 1982 L 384/1, amended many times since then.

[819] OJ 1997 L 61/1, later amended. Implemented by Regulation 865/2006, OJ 2006 L 166/1.

[820] Case C-510/99 *Tridon* [2001] ECR I-7777, para. 25 and Case C-154/02 *Nilsson* [2003] ECR I-12733, para. 39.

The import into the EU of Annex A and B species is subject to completion of the necessary checks and the prior presentation, at the border customs office at the point of introduction, of an import *permit* issued by a management authority of the Member State of destination (Article 4(1) and(2)). The import of Annex C and D species is only subject to completion of the necessary checks and the prior presentation, at the border customs office at the point of introduction, of an import *notification* (Article 4(3) and (4)).

The import permit for Annex A and B species may only be issued when the following conditions have been met (Article 4):

- the competent scientific authority has advised that the introduction into the EU would not have a harmful effect on the conservation status of the species or on the extent of the territory occupied by the relevant population of the species;[821]
- the applicant provides documentary evidence (an export permit or a re-export certificate) that the specimens have been obtained in accordance with the legislation on the protection of the species concerned;
- the competent scientific authority is satisfied that the intended accommodation for a live specimen at the place of destination is adequately equipped to conserve and care for it properly;
- the management authority is satisfied that the specimen is not to be used for primarily commercial purposes;
- the management authority is satisfied that there are no other factors relating to the conservation of the species which militate against issuance of the import permit;
- in the case of introduction from the sea, the management authority is satisfied that any live specimen will be so prepared and shipped as to minimize the risk of injury, damage to health or cruel treatment.

Any permit or certificate issued under the regulation may stipulate conditions and requirements to ensure compliance with its provisions (Article 11(3)).

Permits and certificates issued by the competent authorities of the Member States are valid throughout the EU (Article 11(1)). This does however limit their power to adopt or maintain stricter measures.[822] Member States are required to recognize the rejection of applications by the competent authorities of the other Member States, where such rejection is based on the provisions of the regulation. However, this need not apply where the circumstances have significantly changed or where new evidence to support an application has become available

---

[821] Cf. Case C-182/89 *Commission* v. *France* [1990] ECR I-4337. In that case, under Regulation 3626/82, the French Government contended that the only decisive factor as regards the granting of import permits was the favourable opinion of the national scientific authority in the importing country, which had been obtained in this case. This argument was rejected by the Court. This case law seems still to be valid under the new regulation.

[822] Cf. the much more elaborate provision of Article 15 of the 'old' CITES Regulation 3626/82.

(Article 6(4)). The *export or re-export* of Annex A, B and C species also requires a permit, which may be issued only when certain conditions have been met (Article 5). It should be noted that the regulation only applies to trade with third countries and does not affect the free movement of goods within the EU. Finally, the regulation also provides for derogations (Article 7), provisions relating to the control of commercial activities (Article 8),[823] movement of live specimens (Article 9), monitoring of compliance and investigation of infringements (Article 14), and sanctions (Article 16).

19.4 The Seal Pups Directive and Seal Products Regulation

Directive 83/129, concerning the importation into Member States of skins of certain seal cubs and products derived therefrom,[824] aims to protect seal cubs living outside the territory of the EU. Under the directive, Member States were required to ensure that the products listed in an Annex were not commercially imported into their territories. The directive was originally to apply from 1 October 1983 to 1 October 1985, but its duration was extended to 1 October 1989 and in 1989 the Council agreed to extend its application indefinitely.[825] The trade in seal products has been largely prohibited by means of Regulation 1007/2009.[826] According to this regulation only the marketing of products made from traditionally hunted seals by Inuit and other indigenous people is allowed (Article 3). An exception to this ban is made for seal products where the hunt was conducted solely for the sustainable management of marine resources and for the occasional import of seal products exclusively for the personal use of travellers and their families (Article 3(2)).[827] Seal products that comply with the regulation profit from a free movement clause (Article 4).

19.5 The Whales Regulation

Regulation 348/81 on common rules for imports of whales or other cetacean products[828] is intended for the conservation of the cetacean species. This calls for measures which will restrict international trade. According to the preamble, these should be European-level measures and should at the same time respect the EU's international obligations.

---

[823] See, on the interpretation of this provision, Case C-510/99 *Tridon* [2001] ECR I-7777 and Case C-154/02, *Nilsson* [2003] ECR I-12733.

[824] OJ 1983 L 91/30.

[825] Directive 89/370, OJ 1989 L 163/37.

[826] OJ 2009 L 286/36. Cf. also Case T-18/10 *Inuit Tapiriit Kanatami a.o.*, Judgment of 6 September 2011.

[827] The implementing rules in this regard have been set by Commission Regulation 737/2010, OJ 2010 L 216/1.

[828] OJ 1981 L 39/1, later amended.

The primary operational part of the regulation is contained in Article 1.
From 1 January 1982 the introduction into the EU of the products listed in
the Annex is subject to the production of an import licence. However, no such
licence will be issued in respect of products to be used for commercial purposes.

19.6   The Leghold Trap Regulation

Regulation 3254/91 is intended to abolish the use of leghold
traps to catch and kill certain species of animal.[829] Leghold traps are devices
designed to restrain or capture an animal by means of jaws which close tightly
upon one or more of the animal's limbs, thereby preventing withdrawal of the
limb or limbs from the trap. The animals thus trapped and killed are used to
make furs. This inhuman manner of trapping animals must have been prohibited by 1 January 1995 at the latest (Article 2). In addition the regulation
prohibits the introduction into the EU of the pelts of the animal species listed in
Annex I, unless the Commission has determined that, in the country where the
pelts originate:
- there are adequate administrative or legislative provisions in force to
  prohibit the use of the leghold trap or
- the trapping methods used meet internationally agreed humane trapping
  standards.

Annex I names the following species, among others: the beaver, otter, wolf,
sable, badger, marten, ermine, and even the musk rat.

Implementation of this controversial[830] regulation has been dogged by difficulties.[831] These were largely due to conflicts with the principal fur-exporting
countries, in particular Canada, the United States and Russia.[832] Ultimately,
in early 1988, the Council approved a Decision concerning the conclusion of
an Agreement on international humane trapping standards between the EC,
Canada and the Russian Federation.[833] The Leghold Trap Regulation is implemented in the EU by Commission Regulation 35/97.[834] A proposal to amend the
Leghold Trap Regulation was withdrawn.[835]

---

[829] OJ 1991 L 308/1.

[830] Cf. Case T-228/95 R *S. Lehrfreund Ltd.* v. *Council* [1996] ECR II-111.

[831] See Commission Regulation 1771/94, OJ L 1994 184/3.

[832] Cf. Harrems (1998).

[833] Decision 98/142/EG concerning the conclusion of an Agreement on international humane trapping
standards between the European Community, Canada and the Russian Federation and of an Agreed
Minute between Canada and the European Community concerning the signing of the said Agreement,
OJ 1998 L42/40.

[834] OJ 1997 L 8/2.

[835] COM (1995) 737, see OJ 1999 C 235/7.

BACKES & VERSCHUUREN (1998)

C.W. Backes and J. Verschuuren, 'The Precautionary Principle in International, European and Dutch Wildlife Law' [1998] *Colorado Journal of International Environmental Law and Policy* 43-70.

BACKES ET AL. (2005)

C.W. Backes, T. van Niewerburgh and R.B.A. Koelemeijer, 'Transformation of the first Daughter Directive on air quality in several EU Member States and its application in practice' [2005] *EELR* 157-164.

BARNARD (2010)

C. Barnard, *The Substantive Law of the EU. The Four Freedoms* (Oxford 2010).

BALLESTEROS (2009)

Marta Ballesteros, 'EU Enforcement Policy of Community Environmental law as presented in the Commission Communication on implementing European Community Environmental law', *elni Review* 2009/2, 54-62.

BÄR & KRAEMER (1998)

S. Bär and R.A. Kraemer, 'European Environmental Policy after Amsterdam' [1998] *JEL* 315-330.

BENSON & JORDAN (2008)

D. Benson and A. Jordan, 'A Grand Bargain or an "Incomplete Contract"? European Union Environmental Policy after the Lisbon Treaty' [(2008] *EEELR* 280-290.

BETLEM (2005)

G. Betlem, 'Environmental Liability and Private Enforcement – Lessons from the European Court of Justice and European Mining Laws' [2005] 4 *YEEL* 117-148

BLEEKER (2009)

A. Bleeker, 'Does the Polluter Pay? The Polluter-Pays Principle in the Case Law of the European Court of Justice' [2009] *EEELR* 289-306.

BLOMBERG (2008)

A.B. Blomberg, 'European Influence on National Environmental Law Enforcement: Towards an Integrated Approach' [2008/2] *REALaw* 39-81.

BOHNE & DIETZE (2004)

E. Bohne and D. Dietze, 'Pollution Prevention and Control in Europe Revisted' [2004] *EELR* 198-217.

BONGAERTS (1999)

J. Bongaerts, 'Carbon Dioxide Emissions and Cars: An Environmental Agreement at EU level' [1999] *EELR* 101-104.

BUGGE & VOIGT (2008)

H.C. Bugge, C. Voigt (eds.), *Sustainable Development in International & National Law* (Groningen 2008).

CADDELL (2010)

R. Caddell, 'Caught in the Net: Driftnet Fishing Restrictions and the European Court of Justice' [2010] *JEL* 301-314.

VAN CALSTER (1997)

G. van Calster, 'EC Noise Legislation and Policy' [1997] *EELR* 174-181.

VAN CALSTER (2000)

G. van Calster, 'The Legal Framework for the Regulation of Waste in the European Community' [2000] 1 *YEEL* 161-224.

VAN CALSTER & DEKETELAERE (1998)

G. van Calster and K. Deketelaere, 'Amsterdam, the Intergovernmental Conference and Greening the EU Treaty' [1998] *EELR* 13-25.

CANA (2004)

R. Cana, 'Registration, Evaluation, Authorisations and Restrictions of Chemicals: An Analysis' [2004] *EELR* 99-109.

COFFEY & FERGUSSON (1997)

C. Coffey and M. Fergusson, 'European Community Funding for Sustainable Development: the Role of the Cohesion Fund' [1997] *RECIEL* 77-85.

COMTE & KRÄMER (2004)

F. Comte & L. Krämer (eds), *Environmental Crime in Europe; Rules of Sanctions* (Groningen 2004).

DAVIES (2004)

P.G.G. Davies, *European Union Environmental Law; An Introduction to Key Selected Issues* (Aldershot 2004).

DHONDT (2005)

N. Dhondt, 'Integration of Environmental Protection into the EC Energy Policy' [2005] 4 *YEEL* 247-302.

DOPPELHAMMER (2000)

M. Doppelhammer, 'More Difficult than Finding the Way Round Chinatown? – The IPPC Directive and its Implementation' [2000] *EELR* 199-206, 246-252.

EBBESON (2011)

J. Ebbeson, 'Access to Justice at the National Level. Impact of the Aarhus Convention and European Union Law' in: M. Pallemaerts (ed.), *The Aarhus Convention at Ten. Interactions and Tensions between Conventional International Law and EU Environmental Law* (Groningen 2011).

EVANS (1999)

A. Evans, *The EU Structural Funds* (Oxford 1999).

FAURE (1998)

M. Faure, 'Harmonisation of Environmental Law and Market Integration: Harmonising for the Wrong Reasons?' [1998] *EELR* 169-175.

FAURE (2010)

M.G. Faure, 'Effective, Proportional and Dissuasive Penalties innthe Implementation of the Environmental Crime and Ship-source Pollution Directives: Questions and Challenges' [2010] *EEELR* 256-278.

FLEURKE (2008)

Floor M. Fleurke, 'What Use for Article 95(5) EC? An Analysis of Land Oberösterreich and Republic of Austria v Commission' [2008] *JEL* 267-278.

FLEURKE & SOMSEN (2011)

F. Fleurke, H. Somsen, 'Precautionary regulation of chemical risk: How REACH confronts the regulatory challenges of scale, uncertainty, complexity and innovation' [2011] *CMLRev.* 357-393.

FRENCH (1998)

D. French, '1997 Kyoto Protocol to the 1992 UN framework Convention on Climate Change' [1998] *JEL* 227-239.

DE GRAAF & JANS (2007)

K.J. de Graaf, J.H. Jans 'Liability of Public Authorities in Cases of Non-enforcement of Environmental Standards', in: [2007] *Pace Environmental Law Review* 377-398.

GRIMEAUD (2001)

D. Grimeaud, 'Reforming EU Water Law: Towards Sustainability' [2001] *EELR* 41-51.

EVANS (1999)

A. Evans, *The EU Structural Funds* (Oxford: Oxford University Press 1999).

HANNEQUART (1993)

J.P. Hannequart, *Het Europees recht inzake afvalstoffen* (Brussel 1993).

HARREMS (1998)

N. Harrems, 'The Leghold Trap Regulation and Potential Pitfalls During the Dutch Presidency of the EU' [1998] *EELR* 7-12.

HARRYVAN & JANS (2010)

G.J. Harryvan & J.H. Jans, 'Internal Review of EU Environmental Measures. It's True: Baron van Munchausen Doesn't Exist! Some Remarks on the Application of the So-Called Aarhus Regulation' [2010/2] *REALaw*, 51-63.

HEDEMANN-ROBINSON (2007)

M. Hedemann-Robinson, *Enforcement of European Union Environmental Law* (London and New York 2007).

HEDEMANN-ROBINSON (2010)

M. Hedemann-Robinson, 'Enforcement of EU Environmental Law and the Role of Interim Relief Measures' [2010] *EEELR* 204-229.

HEYVAERT (2006)

V. Heyvaert, 'Guidance without constraint: assessing the impact of the precautionary principle on the European Community's chemicals policy' [2006] 6 *YEEL* 27-60.

HILSON (2005)

C. Hilson, 'The Role of Discretion in EC Law on Non-Contractual Liability' [2005] *CMLRev.* 677-695.

HOLDER (1996)

J. Holder, 'Case law analysis. A dead end for direct effect?: prospects for enforcement of European Community environmental law by individuals. Comitato di Coordinamento per la Difesa della Cava and Others v Regione Lombardia and Others' [1996] *JEL* 313-335.

HOLDER (2004)

J. Holder, *Environmental Assessment* (Oxford 2004).

HOWARTH (2009)

W. Howarth, 'Aspirations and Realities under the Water Framework Directive: Proceduralisation, Participation and Practicalities' [2009] *JEL* 391-417.

JACK (2011)

B. Jack, 'Enforcing Member State Compliance with EU Environmental Law: A Critical Evaluation of the Use of Financial Penalties' [2011] *JEL* 73-95.

JANS (2006)

J.H. Jans, 'Did Baron von Munchausen ever visit Århus? Some Critical Remarks on the Proposal For A Regulation on the Application of the Provisions of the Aarhus Convention to EC Institutions and Bodies' in: R. Macrory (ed.), *Reflections on 30 Years of EU Environmental Law; A High Level of Protection?* (Groningen 2005) 475-490.

JANS (2007)

J.H. Jans, 'Minimum Harmonisation and the Role of the Principle of Proportionality' in: *Umweltrecht und Umweltwissenschaft; Festschrift für Eckard Rehbinder*, Martin Führ, Rainer Wahl & Peter von Wilmowsky (Herausgeber) (Berlin 2007) 705-717.

JANS (2008)

J.H. Jans, 'Environmental Spill-Overs from the European Court of Justice' [2008] *Fordham Int'l LJ* 1360.

JANS (2010)

J.H. Jans, 'Stop the Integration Principle?' [2010] *Fordham International Law Journal*, 1533-1547.

JANS (2011)

J.H. Jans, 'Who is the referee? Access to Justice in a Globalised Legal Order. A Case Analysis of ECJ Judgment C-240/09 Lesoochranárske zoskupenie of 8 March 2011' [2011/1] *REALaw*.

JANS ET AL. (2007)

J.H. Jans, R. de Lange, S. Prechal and R.J.G.M. Widdershoven, *Europeanisation of Public Law* (Groningen 2007).

JANS & DE JONG (2002)

J.H. Jans and M. de Jong, 'Somewhere between Direct Effect and Rewe/Comet; some remarks on Dutch public law, procedural defects and the EIA Directive' in: K.H. Ladeur (ed.) *The Europeanisation of Administrative Law: Transforming National Decision-Making Procedures* (Aldershot 2002) 68-93.

JANS & SQUINTANI (2009)

J.H. Jans & L. Squintani, '"Gold plating" of European Environmental Measures?' (with A. Aragão, R. Macrory and B.W. Wegener) [2009] *JEEPL* 417-435.

JENDROSKA (2005)

J. Jendroska, 'Public Information and Participation in EC Environmental Law; Origins, Milestones and Trends' in: R. Macrory (ed.), *Reflections on 30 Years of EU Environmental Law; A High Level of Protection?* (Groningen 2005) 63-84.

JONES & SUFRIN (2010)

B. Jones and A. Sufrin, *EU Competition Law* (Oxford 2010).

KEESSEN ET AL. (2010)

A.M. Keessen, J.J.H. van Kempen, M. van Rijswick, J. Robbe, and C.W. Backes, 'European River Basin Districts: Are They Swimming in the Same Implementation Pool?' [2010] *JEL* 197-221.

KINGSTON (2009)

S. Kingston, *The Role of Environmental Protection in EC Competition Law and Policy* (PhD Leiden) available from: https://openaccess.leidenuniv.nl/bitstream/1887/13497/1/Suzanne+Kingston+PhD+Thesis.pdf.

KINGSTON (2010)

S. Kingston, 'Integrating Environmental Protection and EU Competition Law: Why Competition Isn't Special' [2010] *European Law Journal*, 780-805.

KOCH & ZIEHM (2005)

H.-J. Koch & C. Ziehm, 'Marine Safety and Protection of the Marine Environment' in: R. Macrory (ed.), *Reflections on 30 Years of EU Environmental Law; A High Level of Protection?* (Groningen 2005) 309-324.

KRÄMER (2007)

L. Krämer, *EC Environmental Law* (London 2007).

KRÄMER (2003A)

L. Krämer, 'Vertraulichkeit und Öffentlichkeit Europäisches Vorverfahren und Zugang zu Informationen', in: L. Krämer (ed.), *Recht und Um-Welt; Essays in Honour of Prof. Dr. Gerd Winter* (Groningen 2003) 153-170.

KRÄMER (2009)

> L. Krämer, 'The European Commission's Opinions under Article 6(4) of the Habitats Directive' [2009] *JEL* 59-85.

KRÄMER (2009A)

> L. Krämer, 'The environmental complaint in EU law' [2009] *JEEPL* 13-35.

KUIK & OOSTERHUIS (2008)

> O. Kuik and F. Oosterhuis, 'Economic Impacts of the EU ETS: Preliminary Evidence' in: M. Faure and M. Peeters (eds.), *Climate Change and European Emissions Trading* (Cheltenham 2008).

LAFFINEUR (2010)

> J.-L. Laffineur, 'First ECJ Ruling on REACH: Chossing Registration over Exemption', 22 *JEL* 135.

LANGE (2008)

> B. Lange, *Implementing EU Pollution Control: Law and Integration* (Cambridge 2008).

LAVRANOS (2009)

> N. Lavranos, 'The Epilogue in the MOX Plant Dispute: An End Without Findings' [2009] *EEELR* 180-184.

LEE (2005)

> M. Lee, *EU Environmental Law: Challenges, Change and Decision-Making* (Oxford 2005).

LEE (2008)

> M. Lee, *EU Regulation of GMOs: Law, Decision-making and New Technology* (Cheltenham 2008).

DE LEEUW & PRECHAL (2007)

> M.E. de Leeuw, A. Prechal, 'Dimensions of Transparency: The Building Blocks for a New Legal Principle?' [2007] *REALaw* 51-62.

LENAERTS (1993)

> K. Lenaerts, 'The Principle of Subsidiarity and the Environment in the European Union: Keeping the Balance of Federalism' [1993] *Fordham International Law Journal* Volume 17, Issue 4, 846-895.

LUDWIG & O'GORMAN (2008)

> R. Ludwig & R. O'Gorman, 'A Cock and Bull Story?—Problems with the Protection of Animal Welfare in EU Law and Some Proposed Solutions' [2008] *JEL* 363-390.

MACRORY (2004)

> R. Macrory (ed.), *Principles of European Environmental Law* (Groningen 2004).

MACRORY (2005)

> R. Macrory (ed.), *Reflections on 30 Years of EU Environmental Law; A High Level of Protection?* (Groningen 2005).

MACRORY (2005A)

R. Macrory, 'The Enforcement of EU Environmental Law; Some Proposals for Reform', in: R. Macrory (ed.), *Reflections on 30 Years of EU Environmental Law; A High Level of Protection?* (Groningen 2005) 385-395.

MAHMOUDI (2005)

S. Mahmoudi, 'Integration of Environmental Considerations into Transport', in: R. Macrory (ed.), *Reflections on 30 Years of EU Environmental Law; A High Level of Protection?* (Groningen 2005) 185-196.

MARÍN DURÁN & MORGERA (2006)

G. Marín Durán & E. Morgera, 'Towards Environmental Integration in EC External Relations? A Comparative Analysis of Selected Association Agreements' [2006] 6 *YEEL* 179-210.

MARKOWSKI (2010)

M. Markowski, *The International Law of EEZ Fisheries. Principles and Implementation* (Groningen 2010).

MARKUS (2009

T. Markus, *European Fisheries Law. From Promotion to Management* (Groningen 2009).

MARR & SCHWEMER (2003)

S. Marr and A. Schwemer, 'The Precautionary Principle in German Environmental Law' [2003] 3 *YEEL* 125-148.

MARSDEN & DE MULDER (2005)

S. Marsden and J. de Mulder, 'Strategic Environmental Asssessment and Sustainability in Europe – How Bright is the Future?' [2005] *RECIEL* 50-62.

MCMANUS (2005)

F. McManus, 'European Noise Law' in: R. Macrory (ed.), *Reflections on 30 Years of EU Environmental Law; A High Level of Protection?* (Groningen 2005) 373-382.

MONTI (2008)

G. Monti, *EC Competition Law* (Cambridge 2008).

MONTINI (2005)

M. Montini, 'International Trade and Environmental Protection; The Treatment of National Measures Introducing Trade Restrictions on Environmental Grounds under WTO Law', in: R. Macrory (ed.), *Reflections on 30 Years of EU Environmental Law; A High Level of Protection?* (Groningen 2005) 531-552.

MONTINI (2009)

M. Montini, 'EC External Relations On Environmental Law', in: Joanne Scott (ed.), *Environmental Protection. European Law and Governance* (Oxford 2009) 127-170.

MOSSOUX (2010)

Y. Mossoux, 'Causation in the Polluter Pays Principle' [2010] *EEELR* 279-294.

MORENO (2005)

A-M. Moreno, 'Environmental Impact Assessment in EC Law; A Critical Appraisal' in:, R. Macrory (ed.), *Reflections on 30 Years of EU Environmental Law; A High Level of Protection?* (Groningen 2005) 43-60.

MORTELMANS (2002)

K.J.M. Mortelmans, 'The Relationship Between the Treaty Rules and Community Measures for the Establishment and Functioning of the Internal Market – Towards a Concordance Rule' [2002] *CMLRev.* 1303-1346.

NIEDZWICKI (2007)

Matthias Niedzwicki, *Präklusionsvorschriften des öffentlichen Rechts im Spannungsfeld zwischen Verfahrensbeschleunigung, Einzelfallgerechtigkeit und Rechtsstaatlichkeit* (Berlin 2007).

NOTARO (2000)

N. Notaro, 'European Community Waste Movements: the Copenhagen Waste Case' [2000] *EELR* 304-312.

OLIVER (1999)

P. Oliver, 'Some Further Reflections on the Scope of Articles 28-30' [1999] *CMLRev.* 783-806.

OLIVER (2010)

P. Oliver, 'Of Trailers and Jet Skis: Is the Case Law on Article 34 TFEU Hurtling in a New Direction?' [2010] *Fordham International Law Journal* 1423-1471.

PAGH (2005)

P. Pagh, 'The Battle on Environmental Policy Competences; Challenging the Stricter Approach: Stricter Might Lead to Weaker Protection', in: R. Macrory (ed.), *Reflections on 30 Years of EU Environmental Law; A High Level of Protection?* (Groningen 2005) 3-16.

PALLEMAERTS (2005)

M. Pallemaerts, 'EC Chemicals Legislation: A Horizontal Perspective' in: R. Macrory (ed.), *Reflections on 30 Years of EU Environmental Law; A High Level of Protection?* (Groningen 2005) 199-230.

PALLEMAERTS (2011)

M. Pallemaerts (ed.), *The Aarhus Convention at Ten. Interactions and Tensions between Conventional International Law and EU Environmental Law* (Groningen 2011).

PALLEMAERTS (2011A)

M. Pallemaerts, 'Access to Environmental Justice at EU Level. Has the 'Aarhus Regulation' Improved the Situation? in: M. Pallemaerts (ed.), *The Aarhus Convention at Ten. Interactions and Tensions between Conventional International Law and EU Environmental Law* (Groningen 2011).

PEETERS & DEKETELAERE (2006)

M. Peeters, K. Deketelaere (eds.), *EU Climate Change Policy; The Challenge of New Regulatory Initiatives* (Cheltenham 2006).

PEREIRA (2008)

R. Pereira, 'On the Legality of the Ship–Source Pollution 2005/35/EC Directive – The Intertanko Case and Selected Others' [2008] *EEELR* 372-383.

PRECHAL (2005)

S. Prechal, *Directives in European Community Law* (Oxford 2005).

PRECHAL & HANCHER (2002)

S. Prechal and L. Hancher, 'Individual Environmental Rights: Conceptual Pollution in EU Environmental Law' [2002] 2 *YEEL* 89 *et seq.*

POCKLINGTON (2006)

D. Pocklington, 'The Significance of the Proposed Changes to the Waste Framework Directive' [2006] *EELR* 75-87.

PONS (2001)

J.F. Pons, *European Competition Policy for the Recycling Markets*, speech delivered at the Pro Europe International Congres 2001, to be found on http://ec.europa.eu/comm/competition/speeches/text/sp2001_015_en.pdf.

REICHL (2010)

Jane Reichel, 'Judicial Control in a Globalised Legal Order – A One Way Track?' [2010/2] *REALaw* 69-87.

REVESZ (2000)

R.L. Revesz, 'Environmental Regulation in Federal Systems' [2000] 1 *YEEL* 1-35.

RODI (2006)

M. Rodi, 'Motorway Tolls and Sustainable Transport Policy' [2006] 6 *YEEL* 1-26.

ROLLER (2005)

G. Roller, 'Liability' in: R. Macrory (ed.), *Reflections on 30 Years of EU Environmental Law; A High Level of Protection?* (Groningen 2005) 129-140.

DE SADELEER (2005)

N. de Sadeleer, *Environmental Principles: From Political Slogans to Legal Rules* (Oxford 2005).

DE SADELEER (2005A)

N. de Sadeleer, 'EC Law and Biodiversity' in: R. Macrory (ed.), *Reflections on 30 Years of EU Environmental Law; A High Level of Protection?* (Groningen 2005) 351-370.

DE SADELEER (2006)

N. de Sadeleer, 'The Precautionary Principle in EC Health and Environmental Law' [2006] *European Law Journal* 139-172.

DE SADELEER (2009)

N. de Sadeleer, 'Liability for Oil Pollution Damage versus Liability for Waste Management: The Polluter Pays Principle at the Rescue of the Victims: Case C-188/07, Commune de Mesquer v Total France SA [2008] 3 CMLR 16, [2009] Env LR 9' [2009] *JEL* 299-307.

DE SADELEER ET AL. (2005)

Nicolas de Sadeleer, Gerhard Roller & Miriam Dross (eds.), *Access to Justice in Environmental Matters and the Role of NGOs; Empirical Findings and Legal Appraisal* (Groningen 2005).

SCHWERDTFEGER (2007)

A. Schwerdtfeger, 'Schutznormtheorie and Aarhus Convention – Consequences for German Law' [2007] *Journal of European Environmental and Planning Law* 270-277.

SCOTFORD (2007)

E. Scotford, 'Trash or Treasure: Policy Tensions in EC Waste Regulation' [2007] *JEL* 1-22.

SCOTT (2000)

J. Scott, 'Flexibility in the Implementation of EC Environmental Law' [2000] 1 *YEEL* 37-60.

SCOTT (2009)

J. Scott, 'REACH: Combining Harmonization and Dynamism in the Regulation of Chemicals' in: J. Scott, (ed.), *Environmental Protection* (Oxford 2009).

SCHRAUWEN (2006)

Case note penalty payments; Annette Schrauwen [2006] *JEL* 289-299.

SCHWENSFEIER (2009)

Hans Roland Schwensfeier, *Individuals' Access to Justice Under Community Law* (diss. Groningen University 2009).

SEINEN (2005)

A.T. Seinen, 'Staatssteun voor milieubescherming: uitzonderingen op het verbod' [2005] *M&R* 66-71.

SEVENSTER (2000)

H.G. Sevenster, 'The Environmental Guarantee After Amsterdam: Does the Emperor Have New Clothes?' [2000] 1 *YEEL* 291-310.

SHEATE (2003)

W.R. Sheate, 'The EC Directive on Strategic Environmental
Assessment: A Much-Needed Boost for Environmental Integration'
[2003] *EELR* 331-347.

SOLTÉSZ & SCHATZ (2009)

U. Soltész & F. Schatz, 'State Aid for Environmental Protection—The
Commission's new Guidelines and the new General Block Exemption
Regulation' [2009] *Journal for European Environmental & Planning Law*
141-170.

SOMSEN (2003)

H. Somsen, 'Current Issues of Implementation, Compliance and
Enforcement of EC Environmental Law; A Critical Analysis', in: L.
Krämer (ed.), *Recht und Um-Welt; Essays in Honour of Prof. Dr. Gerd
Winter* (Groningen 2003) 415-428.

STRECK & FREESTONE (2005)

C. Streck and D. Freestone, 'The EU and Climate Change' in: R.
Macrory (ed.), *Reflections on 30 Years of EU Environmental Law; A High
Level of Protection?* (Groningen 2005) 87-106.

TEMMINK (2000)

H. Temmink, 'From Danish Bottles to Danish Bees: The Dynamics of
Free Movement of Goods and Environmental Protection – a Case Law
Analysis' [2000] 1 *YEEL* 61-102.

THOMAS (2008)

H. Thomas, 'Declassification of Protected Areas under the Habitats
and the Wild Birds Directive' [2008] *EEELR* 3-11.

TIEMAN (2003)

J.R.C. Tieman, *Naar een nuttige toepassing van het begrip afvalstof : over
de betekenis en toepassing van kernbegrippen van internationaal, Europees
en Nederlands afvalstoffenrecht* (Deventer 2003).

TIMMERMANS (2006)

C.W.A. Timmermans, 'Creative Homogeneity' in: M. Johansson, N.
Wahl, U. Bernitz (eds.), *Liber Amicorum In Honour Of Sven Norberg; A
European For All Seasons* (Brussel 2006) 471-484.

TOLSMA ET AL. (2009)

H.D. Tolsma, K.J. de Graaf and J.H. Jans, The Rise and Fall of Access
to Justice in the Netherlands [2009] *JEL* 309-321.

TOWNLEY (2009)

C. Townley, *Article 81 EC and Public Policy* (Oxford 2009).

TROUWBORST (2006)

A. Trouwborst, *Precautionary Rights and Duties of States* (Leiden/
Boston 2006).

VANDEKERCKHOVE (1994)

K. Vandekerckhove, 'The Polluter Pays Principle in the European
Community' [1993] *YEL* 201-262.

VANDAMME (2005)

T.A.J.A. Vandamme, *The Invalid Directive; The Legal Authority of a Union Act Requiring Domestic Law Making* (Groningen 2005).

VAN RIJSWICK (2003)

H.F.M.W. van Rijswick, *The Water Framework Directive; Implementation into German and Dutch Law* (Utrecht 2003).

VAN RIJSWICK & VOGELEZANG-STOUTE (2008)

H.F.M.W. Van Rijswick and E.M. Vogelezang-Stoute, 'The Influence of Environmental Quality Standards and the River Basin Approach taken in the Water Framework Directive on the Authorisation of Plant Protection Products' [2008] *EEELR* 78-89.

VEDDER (2002)

H.H.B. Vedder, *Competition Law, Environmental Policy and Producer Resposibility* (Groningen 2002).

VEDDER (2003)

H.H.B. Vedder, *Competition Law and Environmental Protection in Europe – Towards Sustainability?* (Groningen 2003).

VEDDER (2009)

H.H.B. Vedder, 'Of Jurisdiction and Justification. Why Competition is Good for 'Non-Economic' Goals, But May Need to be Restricted' [2009] *The Competition Law Review* 51-75.

VEDDER (2010)

H.H.B. Vedder, 'The Treaty of Lisbon and European Environmental Law and Policy' [2010] *JEL* 285-299.

VEDDER (2011A)

H.H.B. Vedder, 'Diplomacy by Directive' in: M. Evans & P. Koutrakos (eds.), *Beyond the Established Legal Borders* (Oxford 2011) 105-122.

VEDDER (2011B)

H.H.B. Vedder, 'The Climate Challenge to Competition' in: M.M. Roggenkamp & U. Hammer (eds.) *European Energy Law Report VII* (Antwerp 2011).

VERANNEMAN (2008)

Barbara Veranneman, 'Environmental Services, Permits and the "Bolkestein Directive"' [2008] *EEELR* 156-164.

VERHOEVEN (2011)

Maartje Verhoeven, *The Costanzo Obligation. The obligations of national administrative authorities in the case of incompatibility between national law and European law* (Mortsel 2011).

VERSCHUUREN (2000)

J. Verschuuren, 'EC Environmental Law and Self-Regulation in the Member States: in Search of a Legislative Framework' [2000] 1 *YEEL* 103-121.

VERSCHUUREN (2005)

J. Verschuuren, 'Shellfish for Fishermen or for Birds? Article 6
Habitats Directive and the Precautionary Principle 17' [2005] *JEL*
265-283.

VOGELEZANG-STOUTE (1999)

E.M. Vogelezang-Stoute, 'European Community Legislation on the
Marketing and Use of Pesticides' [1999] *RECIEL* 144-151.

VOGELEZANG-STOUTE (2004)

E.M. Vogelezang-Stoute, *Bestrijdingsmiddelenrecht* (Deventer 2004).

WARD (2000)

A. Ward, 'Judicial Review of Environmental Misconduct in the
European Community: Problems, Prospects and Strategies' [2000] 1
YEEL 137-159.

WEISHAAR 2009

S. Weishaar, *Towards Auctioning: The Transformation of the European
Greenhouse Gas Emissions Trading System* (Austin 2009).

WENNERÅS (2004)

P. Wennerås, 'State Liability for Decisions of Courts of Last Instance in
Environmental Cases' [2004] *JEL* 329-340.

WENNERÅS (2006)

P. Wennerås, 'A New Dawn for Commission under Articles 226 and
228 EC: General and Persistent (GAP) Infringements, Lump Sums
and Penalty Payments' [2006] *CMLRev.* 31-62.

WENNERÅS (2007)

P. Wennerås, *The Enforcement of EC Environmental Law* (Oxford 2007).

WENNERÅS (2008)

P. Wennerås, 'Towards an ever greener Union? Competence in the
field of the environment and beyond' [2008] *CMLRev.* 1645-1685.

WILKINSON (2008)

D. Wilkinson, D. Benson and A. Jordan, 'Green Budgeting', in: A.
Jordan and A. Lenschow (eds), *Innovation in Environmental Policy?
Integrating the Environment for Sustainability* (Cheltenham 2008) 81.

WILLIAMS (2005)

R. Williams, 'Community Development Cooperation Law, Sustainable
Development and the Convention on Europe: From Dislocation to
Consistency?' [2005] 4 *YEEL* 303-375.

WIERS (2002)

J. Wiers, *Trade and Environment in the EC and the WTO; A Legal
Analysis* (Groningen 2002).

WILSON (1998)

G. Wilson, 'The Biocidal Products Directive' [1998] *EELR* 204-206.

WINTER (1996)

G. Winter, 'Subsidiarität und Deregulierung im Gemeinschaftsrecht'
[1996] *EuR* 247-269.

WINTER (1998)

G. Winter, 'Die Sperrwirkung von Gemeinschaftssekundärrecht für einzelstaatliche Regelungen des Binnenmarkts mit besonderer Berücksichtigung von Art. 130t EGV' [1998] *DöV* 377-381.

WINTER (1999)

G. Winter, 'Individualrechtsschutz im deutschen Umweltrecht unter dem Einfluß des Gemeinschaftsrechts' [1999] *NVwZ* 467-475.

WINTER (2000)

G. Winter, 'Die Steuerung grenzüberschreitender Abfallströme' [2000] *DVBl.* 657-669.

WINTER (2004)

G. Winter, 'The Legal Nature of Environmental Principles in International, EC and German Law', in: R. Macrory (ed.) *Principles of European Environmental Law* (Groningen 2004) 10-28.

WINTER (2005)

G. Winter, 'Matching Tasks and Competences in the EC Multi-level Environmental Administration', in: R. Macrory (ed.), *Reflections on 30 Years of EU Environmental Law; A High Level of Protection?* (Groningen 2005) 399-414.

WINTER ET AL. (2008)

G. Winter, J.H. Jans, R. Macrory and L. Krämer, 'Weighing up the EC Environmental Liability Directive' [2008] *JEL* 163-191.

WHISH (2008)

R. Whish, *Competition Law* (London 2008).

WOERDMAN, CLÒ & ARCURI (2008)

E. Woerdman, S. Clò, and A. Arcuri, 'European Emissions Trading and the Polluter –Pays Principle: Assessing Grandfathering and Over-Allocation' in: M. Faure and M. Peeters (eds.), *Climate Change and European Emissions Trading* (Cheltenham 2008).

Table of Cases

Index